Writer's Guide and Index to English

WRITER'S GUIDE

AND INDEX

TO ENGLISH

BY **PORTER G. PERRIN**, COLGATE UNIVERSITY

SCOTT, FORESMAN AND COMPANY

CHICAGO   ATLANTA   DALLAS   NEW YORK

Preface

THIS *Writer's Guide and Index to English* presents a description of current American usage and style in a background of the activity of writing. Its topics range from commas and hyphens to the complex process of writing. It treats particular questions of punctuation, spelling, words, grammar, sentence and paragraph movement, and more general principles of language development. The aim is to give enough information about our living and lively language to help a student answer questions about what he should say or write as an educated person.

The standard of usage the book recommends is good Informal English, the English of more or less educated and socially established people as they carry on their everyday work and as they take their part in public affairs. The less widely used Formal English is also described, and academic usage, as in research papers. But since few students are to become academic persons, the style recommended is more widely applicable, more democratic, more variously adaptable to actual speaking and writing.

To encourage this style, the book does not rely on rules—explicit prohibitions and commands, though it has plenty of specific suggestions—so much as on cultivating an attitude toward language. The core of this approach is *understanding why one word or construction is better than another and in what circumstances it is better*. It suggests a principle—appropriateness—and indicates how by considering the appropriateness of his language a person can decide for himself what to say or write in a given spot. In this way he takes the responsibility for his own expression and for his growth in the natural, confident, effective speaking and writing which constitute Good English.

The chief difference between this *Writer's Guide and Index to English* and the earlier *Index to English* is in the arrangement. The topics which teachers are most likely to want to assign for specific class discussion are in the thirteen preliminary chapters. Each of these chapters is supplied with exercises. More specific points which would generally be used only for reference are in alphabetical articles in Part Two.

The arrangement is still flexible, for the chapters are sufficiently independent so that a course can be begun with the topics the students need most or that the teacher prefers. Obviously Chapters 1 and 2 (Varieties of English and Good English) are fundamental to a profitable use of the material on style and usage, since they define the goal toward which to work. They should be taken early, as a background for later work, perhaps read rapidly, and later studied in more detail. They also make a break with earlier teaching and so help raise the work in a composition course to a distinctly college level.

Chapter 12, The Writing Process, is basic for the work of composition, and would naturally be taken before themes of any length were assigned. The chapters on Paragraphs (3 and 4), Sentences (5 and 6), and Words (7 and 8) can be taken as those subjects are to be emphasized. Chapters 6 and 8 are on style and could be postponed to a later part of the course. Chapters 9 ("Minimum Essentials"), 10 (Spelling), and 11 (Punctuation) could be used early as the basis for a review of mechanical matters, or made the basis for intensive drill if a class needs it, or with a well-prepared class they could be omitted. Chapter 13, The Research Paper, obviously comes at the point at which that assignment is made.

The alphabetical articles in Part Two, or the "Index," are primarily for individual reference (or browsing), for assignment to particular students who need certain points, or for reference by the student at the time of writing or revising his papers. The "Index" also contains some seventy-five specific correction entries, reached through the abbreviations listed inside the back cover and identified in the book by special marginal abbreviations. Besides the topics they refer to, scores of common lapses from Good English can be marked by putting a ring around the word in question, to show that the "Index" has a specific entry on it. In this way the abstractness of numbers is avoided and both teacher and student can think in terms of the subject itself.

Since the *Writer's Guide and Index to English* is based largely on recent linguistic scholarship, it is greatly indebted to linguists of the last generation or two. The books most referred to in compiling it are listed in the Bibliography on pages xi-xii. Some more specific sources are noted in particular articles. The most useful book appearing since the first edition is C. C. Fries, *American English Grammar*, which is frequently referred to and to which I should like to acknowledge a special debt.

Many specific suggestions have come in the course of a pleasant correspondence set in motion by the first edition. I am grateful for many bits of useful advice. The largest number came from Professors James B. McMillan, Fred A. Dudley, and Arthur H. Nethercot. The revision throughout owes much to Mr. Harrison Platt.

Authors and publishers have generously given permission to use the many illustrative quotations. Their aid is gratefully recognized in the list of Acknowledgments on page 789.

I hope that the book will encourage a fruitful study of the resources of our language and lead to lively and purposeful writing and prove itself a convenience to teachers and a help to students.

P. G. P.

Contents

Contents

Bibliography

THE FOLLOWING WORKS have been the most useful in gathering the material for this book. They are frequently referred to (usually by author's name only) in the chapters and in particular articles of Part Two, the *Index*.

Aiken, Janet R., *Commonsense Grammar*, New York, 1936. An informal presentation of functional grammar

American Speech, a periodical, founded in 1925, containing much direct observation of current American usage, especially vocabularies of particular regions and vocations

Ballard, Philip B., *Thought and Language*, London, 1934. A penetrating and readable discussion of many ordinary problems in language

Baugh, Albert C., *A History of the English Language*, New York, 1935. A substantial and readable history of the language

Bloomfield, Leonard, *Language*, New York, 1933. Especially useful for dialects and language change and for general principles of language study

Curme, George O., *Syntax*, Boston, 1931, and *Parts of Speech and Accidence*, Boston, 1935. A very full and probably the most accurate grammar of modern English

Dobrée, Bonamy, *English Prose Style*, Oxford, 1934. The most illuminating discussion of contemporary prose

Fowler, H. W., *A Dictionary of Modern English Usage*, Oxford, 1926. A full and readable commentary on debatable points in modern English, especially British, usage

Fries, C. C., *American English Grammar*, New York, 1940. A number of points of grammar, discussed with special references to differences between levels of usage

Gardiner, Alan H., *The Theory of Speech and Language*, Oxford, 1932. Gives special attention to the communication of meaning

Goldberg, Isaac, *The Wonder of Words*, New York, 1938. Readable chapters on current linguistic problems

Hall, J. Lesslie, *English Usage*, Chicago, 1917. Discusses historically 141 locutions on which usage is divided or questioned

Hayakawa, S. I., *Language in Action*, New York, 1941. A readable introduction to semantics

Jespersen, Otto, *Essentials of English Grammar*, New York, 1933. An abridgment of Jespersen's four volume *Modern English Grammar*, which was one of the first attempts at a description of English in the light of modern language study

Kennedy, Arthur G., *Current English*, Boston, 1935. Contains a great deal of general linguistic information focused on current English. The book has a very full bibliography which makes possible further study of almost any language problem

Kenyon, John S., *American Pronunciation*, 6th ed.; Ann Arbor, 1935. A full discussion of pronunciation in the United States

Krapp, George P., *The Knowledge of English*, New York, 1927. A book that bridges the gap usually left between grammar and style

Leonard, Sterling A., *Current English Usage*, Chicago, 1932. A compilation of judgments by writers and linguists on various debated questions of English usage

McKnight, George H., *English Words and Their Backgrounds*, New York, 1923. A study of the English vocabulary and its evolution

Oxford English Dictionary. The great storehouse of information on the meaning and history of English words

Pooley, Robert C., *Grammar and Usage in Textbooks on English*, Madison, 1933. A critical examination of the usage recommended in a number of textbooks

Rickert, Edith, *New Methods for the Study of Literature*, Chicago, 1927. Suggestions for detailed study of qualities of style

Robertson, Stuart, *The Development of Modern English*, New York, 1934. Gives more attention to the background of debatable points in current usage than most histories do

Standard Dictionary, Unabridged and College sizes, 1936—

The University of Chicago Press, *A Manual of Style*, 10th ed.; Chicago, 1937. The stylebook of a distinguished publishing organization

Webster's Dictionary, Second Edition of the New International (1934), Fifth Edition of the Collegiate size (1936)

More specific works are cited in the various articles to which they are appropriate.

PART ONE

WRITER'S GUIDE

Varieties of English

WE BEGAN TO LEARN our language by imitating what our
parents and others around us said and very soon picked up enough
words to make our wants known and then to talk with others.
When we got beyond the stage of wailing and grabbing, our
parents were so pleased to have us talk that they accepted some
of our own infantile contributions to the English vocabulary. In
one family milk was *nuck,* a hammer an *agboo,* an elephant an
umpydump, a screwdriver a *toodle-oodle-da.* We used our own
forms of words and syntax of our own: One youngster, struggling with our irregular verbs, said "Mother did gave me a lot of
pants. She shouldn't have gaven me so much pants this summer." For a while the grown-ups thought this sort of language
was cute and perhaps they even went so far as to use it themselves when talking to us. But by the time we were four or five,
they began to laugh at our childish sounds, childish words, and
childish constructions and in other ways gave us to understand
that they expected us to talk about as they talked. So far as we
could talk that way, we did.

Starred items in the margins of these pages or in the text itself refer to
articles in the alphabetical part of the book or to pages in the preliminary
chapters that discuss the subject in more detail.

* Grammar
* Chapter 9,
p. 250

In school we added to the skill in using the language that we had picked up at home by learning to read and to write. We studied "grammar," which told us that "It is I" and other expressions were correct and "It is me" and a lot more were not, usually without telling why. Most of us did our lessons, as lessons, and though we tried to follow this grammar while in the schoolroom, outside we talked about the same way we always had. But some of us began to realize that English, which we supposed we just talked naturally, was a pretty complex matter and that opinions about it differed, sometimes violently.

1. The realistic study of Good English

Those of us who reach college and feel that we are almost ready to take our places in public affairs realize, whether we pay any special attention to our English or not, that sometimes a good deal depends on our speech or writing. Part of the impression we make on others certainly does, and even more important things depend on it, like social position or jobs. Most of the time of course we are unconscious of our words and constructions, unless some expression puzzles us or attracts special attention. When meeting new people, or people from a different social circle, or when we have to "give a talk" or write something that will be printed or an important letter, perhaps when applying for a job, we may become acutely conscious of *how* we are speaking or writing.

To meet these various calls on our powers of expression with ease and confidence, we need a practical, realistic knowledge of the possibilities of English usage, of what successful speakers and writers do with words. We need also an understanding of how to choose the most effective forms of expression for ourselves, and sufficient practice so that the sort of English we wish to use comes to us easily and naturally. We can gain such habits of expression not by memorizing rules and trying to apply them but by reading and listening to good writers and speakers and occasionally pausing to examine how they gain their effects. To do this some general knowledge of how language works is necessary.

The first step to forming such habits is knowing the varieties of English that are in actual use. Our language, like every widely used language, is not one single group of words and constructions, everywhere the same, but a variety of such groups that have much in common but are still far from uniform. A *mature use of English means speaking or writing the sort of*

2

English that is appropriate to the situation in which we find ourselves, for "English" is not just good; it is good under certain conditions. *Chapter 2, p. 35

The three principal sources of variations in English are time, place, and situation, and in each of these three categories there are usually some differences between the spoken, or *colloquial*, and the *written* language. To begin the discussion of Good English, we shall look realistically at these three sources of variation. It is important now for you to understand this approach, which will be new to most of you, and the general principles, without worrying too much about particulars. A later review of this chapter, after Chapter 2 (which supplements it and brings its points closer to your usage) and some of the later chapters (such as 5 and 6 on Sentences) will make you more at home with this approach to Good English. *Colloquial and written English

2. Variations due to time

It is natural that language used by millions of people over centuries should change, slowly and perhaps imperceptibly. We know from reading older literature that our language has changed a good deal in the centuries that it has been spoken and written. A play by Shakespeare needs a good many notes to tell us what the words meant to the people who heard them over three hundred years ago. If we go back far enough, English seems like a foreign language, though we recognize the ancestors of some of our current words.[1] Language changes as naturally as other customs do—in clothes, food, literary fashions. *Change in language *English language

The forms and meanings of words, pronunciations, and grammatical constructions can be classified in four groups according to their standing in time:

Obsolete: Once current but no longer in use
Archaic: Disappearing from use; used occasionally or under certain circumstances
Current: The great body of English that can be used without attracting attention as being either new or old
New: Newly coined words; new meanings of old words; fresh slang; recent borrowings from other languages; revivals of old words; new idioms

---

[1] For further discussion, see histories of the English language, especially Baugh, and Robertson; Otto Jespersen, *Growth and Structure of the English Language* (various editions); Kennedy, § 13; McKnight, Chapter 27; *Oxford English Dictionary*. (Full titles for works mentioned by author only will be found in the Bibliography of this book, pages ix-x.)

Obviously these groups are relative—it is hard to draw a definite line between obsolete and archaic, or to tell when a word or construction is sufficiently uncommon to be called archaic, or to say when a new locution should be regarded as a reputable member of the language. But about the great majority of words, the current words, there can be no question.

2a. Obsolete expressions. Turns of expression that have completely disappeared from use offer little trouble. There is little temptation to refer to a *bottle* of hay, or to use *can* in the sense of "know," or *kind* for "family" or "blood-relationship." Dictionaries contain many obsolete words to help us read older literature or enter into the life of past times. But since Webster's *Dictionary* marks "Obsolete" only words for which no evidence of use since 1660 could be found, obviously it includes many practically if not actually obsolete words that are marked "Archaic."

2b. Archaic English. Words are disappearing from use continually, in part because of changes in living that make them no longer necessary—as people no longer travel by the method that used to be known as *ride and tie*, or have *antimacassars* on the backs of chairs; men no longer wear *ruffs* or even *dusters*, or eat *flummery*, and so on. Fashion or taste drives out some words or some senses of words, as *betrothed* has given way to *fiancee*, *jape* to *joke*, *admire* is no longer used in the sense of "wonder," and some words become less expressive as they lose their suggestiveness, like *parti-colored*. Constructions change as well as words, as in the use of infinitives and participles and the subjunctive mood. Changes in pronunciations sometimes affect phrases, as the pronunciation of the *h*-sound in *historical* leads to the use of *a historical* instead of *an historical*.

Archaic language survives in certain situations, conspicuously in church services which still employ *thou*, and in many words from the Bible and the Book of Common Prayer. Some words have been associated with a certain tradition of poetry, but recent poets of importance have been able to express themselves in the current language (or have even experimented beyond the typical current vocabulary). Beginners in verse need to be warned against *yesteryear*, *olden*, *e'en*, *wight*, and other archaic words which often stamp their work as immature.

A few archaic or even obsolete words survive in set phrases, such as "much *ado*," "in good *stead*," and many are preserved in uneducated speech after they have disappeared from more reputable English. A good many words replaced by genteel

*fiancé

*Infinitives
*Participles
*Subjunctives

*a, an

*Experiment
in English

4

expressions in polite speech survive in uneducated English, and many used only in a definite locality are archaic (*unbeknownst, cheapen* in the sense of "bargain for"). In old stories, especially in fairy tales and in children's stories, archaic words and constructions are found, sometimes puzzling the youngsters: "Goldilocks was now *in high glee,* and *thought to* enjoy herself by eating up all the porridge in the little bowl." These are gradually being modernized.

In conspicuously formal style many older locutions are found —*twain, deem, therein, wherein, whereupon, whosoever, methinks,* and so on. By no means all of these are labeled "Archaic" or "Rare" in dictionaries, though they have passed out of the main current of English.

Archaic words are still thought by some to be an easy form of humor—so that writers for college comics and some others fall back on *quoth* and *wight* and *steed.* This is part of the elephantine levity that leads to pompous and boring writing, and fortunately the style is disappearing.

In college writing there are few excuses for archaisms, except occasionally to preserve the flavor of a past time, as in a historical paper. English majors especially need to remember that, though their reading may be in the sixteenth or the nineteenth centuries, they are speaking and writing for the twentieth. The archaic style of their reading may pass over into their writing if they do not keep in close touch with current literature.

2c. Current English. Whether or not words and constructions are current rarely raises any question. They are the expressions we hear around us daily, that we find in reading magazines and recent books. This observation is a safer guide to which words are current than are dictionaries, because a great many words that they do not label "Archaic" or "Rare" really are used very seldom in writing, and almost never in conversation. Words, constructions, and "style" change somewhat even from generation to generation. The last forty years has seen the addition of many words, the dropping of many from general use, and a tendency toward more concise idioms and constructions, as compared with nineteenth-century style. This *Guide and Index* describes our current language. It can help develop your observation of the actually usable body of English and perhaps help increase your sensitiveness to what is best in contemporary usage. *When you write naturally, from your observation, you usually write current English, and you should aim for no other kind.* In the 1940s write for the 1940s.

5

2d. New words and constructions. People used to shy away from new words until they had "proved themselves a permanent part of the language." Dictionary editors watch new words in books and magazines and include them if they continue to be used. But users of the language need not be so hesitant. The use of a word should depend on its fitness rather than on passing a probationary period, and acceptance by a dictionary should be a result of use. Obviously the name of a new invention or of a new social situation is needed immediately and should be freely used, though there may be a question of its exact form, as in *airplane—aeroplane*. There need be no hesitation about such words as *televise, blitzkrieg, draftee, sit-down strike, candid camera, newscast*. Such words come from a need to name something. But it is wise to hesitate before adopting new words for things that have already been named. This is especially true of the large number of abstract words that higher education and specialization in occupations seem to be substituting for common activities and situations, such as *recreational facilities, urban area*.

New words make their way rather slowly into more formal literary usage. *But most writers today take a new word whenever it fits their meaning and is appropriate to their type of writing and will not trouble their readers.* Occasionally they may even coin a word to serve their purposes. A number of the articles in this *Guide and Index* treat specific points from the frontiers of usage, especially in the written language.

3. Variations due to place: dialects and localisms

In describing variations of language due to time it is easiest to draw illustrations from written words; in variations due to place, since we can observe them in the speech of people we meet, we can observe pronunciation and idioms as well as written forms.

No language is spoken exactly the same way in all parts of the country or in the various countries in which it is used. We can easily spot an Englishman because some of his sounds and some of his words and constructions are different from those that we are used to in the United States. We can also tell very often what part of our country a person comes from by listening to him talk, or at least we can be sure that he comes from some other region than our own. These differences in words, sounds, stress, phrasing, and grammatical habits that are characteristic of fairly definite regions are called *dialects*, or more accurately a dialect is speech that does not attract attention to itself

*airplane
*vitamin

*Big words,
p. 220
*Scientific
and technical writing

*Origin of
words, § 2a

*American
and British
usage

among the residents of a region. Every one of us speaks a dialect, or several dialects. *A pronunciation, a word or meaning of a word, or an idiom that from natural and usually traceable historical reasons is current in one region and not in others is called a provincialism or a localism.*[1]

Dialects exist because of the separation of groups of speakers. They are not peculiar to backward regions, for the "Oxford accent" forms a minor dialect and the people of Boston and of New York speak differently from their neighbors. Nor do they depend upon education or social standing. An educated, as well as an uneducated, westerner will speak somewhat differently from a southerner or New Englander of a similar degree and quality of education. A dialect may show traits from foreign languages spoken by large numbers of people in the region, as in sections of Pennsylvania or in the Scandinavian sections of the Middle West. It may show traits of a neighboring language or of earlier settlement, like the Spanish elements in the English of the Southwest or the French in New Orleans or the Dutch in New York and the Hudson valley.

3a. Dialects in the United States. There are recognizable dialects in the United States, but we should realize at the outset that they show fewer differences than would be expected in a country of such size, many fewer than are shown by the dialects in the much smaller England. The relative freedom of movement of the American people, transportation facilities that have prevented even the Rocky Mountains from marking a linguistic boundary, the educational system, the circulation of the national magazines and of books, and more recently the radio—all keep people who are thousands of miles apart speaking substantially the same language.

Three major American dialects are recognized: *New England* (including a strip of eastern New York), *Southern* (south of Pennsylvania and the Ohio River, extending west of the Mississippi, into Texas), and *Western*, the most extensive of the three, sometimes called *General American*. Minor dialects exist within these three main dialects, as in the Ozarks, or in New York City, but the differences between the speech of California

---

[1] Baugh, Chapter 11, especially § 250; *Dictionary of American English*; Otto Jespersen, *Mankind, Nation and Individual from a Linguistic Point of View* (Oslo, 1925); G. P. Krapp, *The English Language in America* (New York, 1925), pp. 225-73; *Linguistic Atlas of the United States and Canada* (in progress). Many articles in the magazine *American Speech* record facts of various American dialects.

and Illinois are less than the differences between either of these and, say, Virginia or Massachusetts. As a result of the work being done on *The Linguistic Atlas of the United States and Canada,* the boundaries of these dialects are being more exactly drawn. Professor Kenyon estimated (*American Pronunciation,* p. 14) that approximately 11,000,000 people spoke the New England dialect, 26,000,000 the Southern, and 90,000,000 the Western.

DIALECTS IN THE UNITED STATES

A professional student of the English language will observe many differences in pronunciation, words, and idioms between these regions, but some are obvious enough to be sensed by anyone. Some New Englanders will use a broad *a* (äsk, gräss, päst) where most Americans have short *a*; they will usually slight *r* (bän for *barn*), though before a word beginning with a vowel they may sound an *r* where there is none in the spelling (idea*r* of). A Westerner will have a distinct, perhaps even a rolled, *r* and will usually say ä in words spelled with short *o*: pänd—*pond,* hät—*hot,* and so on. A Southerner will usually omit his final *r* (as in *suh,* the popular spelling of *sir,* and in words like *door*— dō, or dō'ə). His long *i* has an ä quality as in the popular spelling A*h* for *I.* East Side New York has its distinctive sounds as in *goil* [*girl*]. And so on. Besides these typical vowel sounds, the regions have their characteristic stress and speech rhythm, from rapid to drawling delivery.

In vocabulary, different words will be found for many common objects. Which of the following is used in your locality? Or is some other word used?

8

bag—sack—poke
piazza—porch—stoop—veranda
griddle lifter—lid lifter—stove handle—stove hook—stove lifter
doughnut—fried cake—cruller
gumshoe—overshoe—rubber
sour milk—clabber—clabbered milk—loppered milk
see saw—teeter totter—teeter board

The accompanying map shows several words that are used within the relatively small limits of New England for the common earthworm: *angleworm, angledog, easworm* (for *eastworm*), *fish worm*. In other regions it is known by some of these names and by others as well.

DIALECT CHART FOR "EARTHWORM"

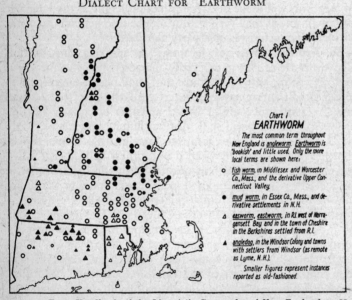

Chart I
EARTHWORM

The most common term throughout New England is *angleworm*. *Earthworm* is 'bookish' and little used. Only the more local terms are shown here:

○ *fish worm*, in Middlesex and Worcester Co., Mass., and the derivative Upper Connecticut Valley.

● *mud worm*, in Essex Co., Mass., and derivative settlements in N.H.

△ *easworm, eastworm*, in R.I. west of Narragansett Bay and in the town of Cheshire in the Berkshires settled from R.I.

▲ *angledog*, in the Windsor Colony and towns with settlers from Windsor (as remote as Lyme, N.H.).

Smaller figures represent instances reported as old-fashioned.

From *Handbook of the Linguistic Geography of New England*, p. 38

Besides these varying names for common objects, each region has special words for local features of the landscape or for occupations that are more or less local: *coulee, hogback, sierra, mesa; mesquite, loco (weed), piñon, shang (ginseng); mule skinner, vara* (a surveyor's measure in the Southwest), *rodeo, fattening* (food for hogs).

Besides pronunciations and special words, there are a good many local idioms, like the Southern "I would *like for* you to do it." Conspicuous are those that show the influence of for-

9

eign languages, like "I'm going to catch me some supper" and those of Pennsylvania German-English: He is going away, not? The potatoes are all. Never mind, it don't make [doesn't work]. The paper wants rain tomorrow.

Increased travel, education, and reading are probably reducing the localisms of the United States as the dialects of England are being pressed out of existence. Words peculiar to a local terrain or to local occupations will probably survive, since they fill a real need and usually have no equivalents in other dialects. The vogue of plays and stories with strong local flavor and of radio programs that grow out of homely New England, Southern, or Western backgrounds is familiarizing all parts of the country with a great deal of local usage. It may be that this public use of localisms will make one region more tolerant of the language of others, and it may very well introduce into general use words formerly characteristic of a particular locality.

3b. Appropriateness of localisms in speaking and writing.

*Exercise 9, p. 32

Localisms are of course especially characteristic of conversation and of writing between friends, and they play a larger part in uneducated than in educated usage. Still, the speech of a Westerner, a Southerner, and a New Englander of equal education and social standing will show distinct differences. People's attitudes toward the use of localisms vary greatly. Some believe that localisms should be weeded out; others believe that a person should retain as much as possible of the flavor of his native speech. It is a problem each person will have to settle for himself, on the basis of appropriateness and effectiveness.

In formal English, localisms are avoided. The pronunciation of most formal speakers tends to approximate Eastern (or southern British) usage or some sort of stage English. Their words characteristically come from the general, especially the more elevated, segment of the English vocabulary. In formal written English distinctive localisms would have about the standing of colloquialisms or perhaps even of slang and would be used only for special effects, and usually apologized for by being placed in quotation marks.

In more casual informal English, of course, localisms have more place. An educated person will tend to shed the more conspicuous local pronunciations of his youth and he may have little occasion to use purely local words. But conscious effort to change his speech to a different pattern will often result in an unhappy combination of elements from both. Natural, gradual, unconscious change is best.

Localisms are necessary to narrative, both in histories and in stories and plays. Consider this meal from a novel of Florida:

> There were poke-greens with bits of white bacon buried in them; sand-buggers made of potato and onion and the cooter he had found crawling yesterday; sour orange biscuits and at his mother's elbow the sweet potato pone. He was torn between his desire for more biscuits and another sand-bugger and the knowledge, born of painful experience, that if he ate them, he would suddenly have no room for pone. The choice was plain.—MARJORIE KINNAN RAWLINGS, *The Yearling*, p. 12

Localisms often bring a fresh, personal note into discussions of ideas. Obviously in speaking or writing for a definite audience, local terms are appropriate if they are used naturally.

In college writing the same test of fitness applies. Many young people first become conscious of their native speech when they go away to school or college. They should study their speech if it attracts attention, but they should not abandon it just because classmates remark about it. They should try to find what in it is appropriate and effective and what seems so conspicuous that it defeats easy communication. But we should hate to see everyone's speech smoothed to the colorless, placeless tones of a chain radio announcer. *Localisms are usually out of place in strictly academic writing, term papers, and so on, but in more personal papers, as in a composition course, they may help give a pleasing personal note.* Their expressiveness and appropriateness will be sufficient reasons for their use.

4. Variations due to situation: levels of usage

Many words of similar meaning that are in current use and that are not affected by difference of place cannot be used interchangeably in all situations. Consider these groups:

*Exercise 5, pp. 30-31

> indigent, impecunious, in want, penniless, poverty-stricken, poor, hard up, broke, flat
> spent, fatigued, weary, exhausted, tired, worn-out, played out, used up, dog tired, all in, pooped
> lunatic, demented, mad, insane, crazy, out of his mind, bughouse, nutty
> stripling, youth, lad, boy, youngster, kid, punk

*Connotation, p. 189

Similarly, there are many idioms and constructions carrying the same idea but suggesting different sorts of speech:

> dare not, daren't, do not dare, don't dare, dassent
> were it not for, if it were not for, if it was not for, if it wasn't for, if it want for

11

Probably most of us would not use *indigent, spent, stripling*—they suggest old-fashioned or rather pedantic usage. We would all use *poor, tired, crazy* and some of the other words. And we would probably all use *broke, all in, nutty* under some circumstances, as when we were in casual company, but perhaps not when we were talking to others, perhaps not to our parents or teachers or to someone on whom we wanted to make "a good impression." These differences are due not to the meaning of the words but to the circumstances in which they have been generally used and which they suggest. *That is, usage differs according to the education, occupation, social standing of people; and words and constructions suggest and carry with them traces of the way in which they are habitually used.*

There is no universally accepted system of naming these different levels of usage, but considerable progress has been made in describing various types of English.[1] In this book three principal levels are presented, *Formal* English, *Informal* English, and *Vulgate* English, and subordinate levels like *Shoptalk, Familiar* English, *Newspaper* English, and others shown in the table opposite.

This presentation of English tends to emphasize the differences between levels of usage. They exist, and Good English to a large degree depends on knowing which of various possible words or forms should be used in a particular speech or piece of writing, as we shall see in the next chapter. But we should not forget that many traits are common to all levels: the names of things (*apples, tree, paint* . . .) and of acts (*dance, buy, drive* . . .) and thousands of other words; in general the forms of words, the plural of nouns in -*s*, the present indicative singular of verbs in -*s*, the forms of the pronouns, though these show some variety; the word order in phrases and sentences; and so on. Any speaker or writer can draw on this common stock of English. At the same time he should be master of the traits of some of the various levels of English. Taking notes of locutions on the different levels is one way to learn the traits.

4a. Informal English. Of the three main levels, Informal English is the most generally met with in the ordinary life of people of good social standing, who are more or less concerned

---

[1] Bloomfield, p. 52; *Current English Usage;* Fries treats current American usage according to levels in *American English Grammar;* Kennedy, § 7; Kenyon; G. P. Krapp, *A Comprehensive Guide to Good English* (Chicago, 1927), pp. xii-xix; Sterling A. Leonard and H. Y. Moffett, "Current Definitions of Levels in English Usage," *The English Journal,* 1927, xvi, 345-59.

LEVELS OF ENGLISH USAGE

PRINCIPAL LEVELS	SUBORDINATE LEVELS	CHARACTERISTIC USES
		Chiefly spoken
VULGATE— Not much touched by school instruction	(Includes many localisms)	Conversation of the mass of people
		Some comic strips; radio programs
		Conversation in plays, stories
		Spoken and written
	Shoptalk	Talk in factories, garages, shops, offices — in all sorts of work
	Slang	Familiar and light conversation; humorous, sporty writing
INFORMAL— Writing and speaking of educated people of some social standing	Familiar English	Talk and letters between intimates; diaries; some light writing
	(Typical informal English)	Talks to general audiences
		Magazine articles and books on subjects of general interest
		Most plays and novels and short stories; a good deal of poetry
	Newspaper English	News stories, features, editorials
	Business English	Business letters, circulars; advertising
		More often written than spoken
FORMAL— Writing and speaking of educated people for restricted groups		Addresses and lectures to restricted audiences
		Literature of limited circulation: essays, much poetry, some fiction
	Academic writing	Textbooks, reference works, dissertations
	Scientific and technical writing	Books and articles dealing with special subjects for professional audiences

with public affairs. *It is the typical language of an educated person going about his everyday business. It lies between the uncultivated vulgate on one side and the more restricted formal level on the other.*[1] It is used not only for personal affairs but for most public affairs—of business and politics, for example, except in strictly legal matters—for most newspaper and magazine articles, for the bulk of fiction and drama, for a great deal of poetry. In the last generation or so it has come to dominate English writing, partly in reaction against the more elaborate style of the nineteenth century. It has a long and honorable tradition. Informal usage is characteristic of the pamphleteers and popular storytellers of Elizabethan literature; of the plainer portions of the English Bible, especially of the direct narratives in the New Testament; of the works of such writers as Defoe and Fielding and to a large degree of Swift.

Formal English is passed on chiefly through reading and pulpit and platform speaking and so represents in many respects the usage of the preceding generation of educated writers; informal English lies closer to current speech. It is not speech exactly reproduced, especially since the written vocabulary is larger than the spoken, but its movement is largely colloquial, the movement of spoken English refined, tidied up, shorn of its looseness. Whenever they are exact enough to convey the intended meaning, colloquial words are used; they are likely to be concrete, close to experience, and familiar to a large number of readers. The sentences are likely to be short and simple, direct in movement, as contrasted with the more elaborate sentences of formal English. The allusions are more to people, places, objects, things done than to literature or history. The dangers of informal style are flatness and inexactness; its strength lies in clearness and readability.

Here is the opening paragraph of Miss Willa Cather's novel *O Pioneers!*

> One January day, thirty years ago, the little town of Hanover, anchored on a windy Nebraska tableland, was trying not to be blown away. A mist of fine snowflakes was curling and eddying about the cluster of low drab buildings huddled on the gray prairie, under a gray sky. The dwelling-houses were set about haphazard on the tough prairie sod; some of them looked as if they had been moved in overnight, and others as if they were straying off by themselves, headed straight for the open plain.

[1] Ballard, Chapter 10, "Toward Simplicity"; Dobrée, Part 4, "The New Way of Writing."

Margin notes:

*Business English

*Legal language

*Colloquial and written English

*Exercise 4, p. 30

*Sentence weight, p. 151

*Allusion, p. 241

None of them had an appearance of permanence, and the howling wind blew under them as well as over them. The main street was a deeply rutted road, now frozen hard, which ran from the squat red railway station and the grain "elevator" at the north end of the town to the lumber yard and the horse pond at the south end. On either side of this road straggled two uneven rows of wooden buildings; the general merchandise stores, the two banks, the drug store, the feed store, the saloon, a post-office. The board sidewalks were gray with trampled snow, but at two o'clock in the afternoon the shopkeepers, having come back from dinner, were keeping well behind their frosty windows. The children were all in school, and there was nobody abroad in the streets but a few rough-looking countrymen in coarse overcoats, with their long caps pulled down to their noses. Some of them had brought their wives to town, and now and then a red or a plaid shawl flashed out of one store into the shelter of another. At the hitch-bars along the streets a few heavy work-horses, harnessed to farm wagons, shivered under their blankets. About the station everything was quiet, for there would not be another train in until night.—WILLA CATHER, *O Pioneers!* pp. 3-4

None of us could keep his eyes quite so firmly fixed on a street in describing it to a friend: We would probably take several sentences to say "The main street was a deeply rutted road, now frozen hard, which ran from the squat red railway station to the grain 'elevator' at the north end of the town to the lumber yard and the horse pond at the south end"; and perhaps most of us would not say "eddying" or "abroad in the streets." But the general tone is of the natural speech of educated people, conversation refined. Many of the phrases sound like conversation: "moved in overnight," "headed straight for the open plain," and "there would not be another train in until night." Through this direct and simple informal writing we come to see the village of Hanover—and to have a feeling of confidence in the writer who stands behind the words.

In the following paragraph from a short story there are no words or phrases, except perhaps *nevertheless* and *leaps into proportion*, that would not be freely used in ordinary speech, but it conveys an unmistakable atmosphere of suppressed emotion.

The man who expected to be shot lay with his eyes open, staring at the upper left-hand corner of his cell. He was fairly well over his last beating, and they might come for him any time now. There was a yellow stain in the cell corner near the ceiling; he had liked it at first, then disliked it; now he was coming back to liking it again.

He could see it more clearly with his glasses on, but he only put on his glasses for special occasions now—the first thing in the morning, and when they brought the food in, and for interviews with the General. The lenses of the glasses had been cracked in a beating some months before, and it strained his eyes to wear them too long. Fortunately, in his present life he had very few occasions demanding clear vision. But, nevertheless, the accident to his glasses worried him, as it worries all near-sighted people. You put your glasses on the first thing in the morning and the world leaps into proportion; if it does not do so, something is wrong with the world.—STEPHEN VINCENT BENÉT, "The Blood of the Martyrs," *Thirteen O'Clock*, p. 23

Informal English is especially appropriate to personal narrative, since most people are informal except on special occasions. In fact, formal English often suggests pretentiousness or lack of sincerity. In this passage from *Life With Father*, the sentences outside the dialog have a conversational movement, and some of the phrases (*pretty things, She didn't like it a bit, his blood pressure and everything*) are definitely colloquial. Even contractions are used, to carry out the natural rhythm.

Mother used to go to the cemetery in Woodlawn with her arms full of flowers, and lay the pretty things by some headstone, as a sign of remembrance. After a while she bought a cast-iron chair and left it out there, inside the square family plot, so that when it took her a long time to arrange her flowers she could sit down and rest. This was a convenience, but unluckily it was also a worry, because absent-minded visitors to neighboring graves began to borrow that chair. They dragged it off across the grass to sit and grieve in, and forgot to return it. Mother then had to hunt around for it and drag it back, which made her feel cross, and thus spoiled the mood she had come out in. She didn't like it a bit.

One Sunday when she herself was past seventy, and when Father in spite of his blood pressure and everything was nearly eighty, she asked him if he wouldn't like to drive out with her to Woodlawn. She hadn't any flowers to take, but she had happened to think of that chair, though she didn't say so to Father. She merely said that it was a beautiful day and it would do him good to go out.

Father refused. Positively. He winked robustly at me and said to Mother, "I'll be going out there soon enough, damn it."

Mother said that he ought to come because one of the headstones had settled and she wanted him to tell her whether he didn't think it needed attention.

Father asked whose headstone it was, and when Mother told him, he said: "I don't care how much it's settled. I don't want to be buried with any of that infernal crowd anyhow."

Mother of course knew how he felt about some of the family, but she said that he wouldn't mind such things when it was all over.

Father said yes he would. He became so incensed, thinking of it, that he declared he was going to buy a new plot in the cemetery, a plot all for himself. "And I'll buy one on a corner," he added triumphantly, "where I can get out!"

Mother looked at him startled but admiring, and whispered to me, "I almost believe he could do it."—CLARENCE DAY, *Life With Father*, pp. 257-58

In presenting information and discussing ideas, formal English is often used, because the material is likely to be intended for a rather restricted group of readers. *But more and more, information and ideas are being presented in a style which is basically informal.* Certain precise or technical words not in the usual colloquial vocabulary are necessary (as *shaman, ethos, possession* in the selection that follows from a book on ethnology), but the pattern of sentences and the more general part of the writer's vocabulary may be informal and so increase the readability and often the impressiveness of the book or article.

A chief of the Digger Indians, as the Californians call them, talked to me a great deal about the ways of his people in the old days. He was a Christian and a leader among his people in the planting of peaches and apricots on irrigated land, but when he talked of the shamans who had transformed themselves into bears before his eyes in the bear dance, his hands trembled, and his voice broke with excitement. It was an incomparable thing, the power his people had had in the old days. He liked best to talk of the desert foods they had eaten. He brought each uprooted plant lovingly and with an unfailing sense of its importance. In those days his people had eaten "the health of the desert," he said, and knew nothing of the insides of tin cans and the things for sale at butcher shops. It was such innovations that had degraded them in these latter days.

One day, without transition, Ramon broke in upon his descriptions of grinding mesquite and preparing acorn soup. "In the beginning," he said, "God gave to every people a cup, a cup of clay, and from this cup they drank their life." I do not know whether the figure occurred in some traditional ritual of his people that I never found, or whether it was his own imagery. It is hard to imagine that he had heard it from whites he had known at Banning; they were not given to discussing the ethos of different peoples. At any rate, in the mind of this humble Indian the figure of speech was clear and full of meaning. "They all dipped in the water," he continued, "but their cups were different. Our cup is broken now. It has passed away."

Our cup is broken. Those things that had given significance to the life of his people, the domestic rituals of eating, the obligations of the economic system, the succession of ceremonials in the villages, possession in the bear dance, their standards of right and wrong—these were gone and with them the shape and meaning of their life. The old man was still vigorous and a leader in relationships with the whites. He did not mean that there was any question of the extinction of his people. But he had in mind the loss of something that had value equal to that of life itself, the whole fabric of his people's standards and beliefs. There were other cups of living left, and they held perhaps the same water, but the loss was irreparable. It was no matter of tinkering with an addition here, lopping off something there. The modelling had been fundamental, it was somehow all of a piece. It had been their own.—RUTH BENEDICT, *Patterns of Culture*, pp. 21-22

Besides the serious uses of informal English, there is of course its lighter vein, a sort of informal informality. This shows usually a wider range of language in both words and constructions, from appropriate slang and actual colloquial to nearly formal usage, and moves with enough force to fuse these varied elements into one pattern of expression. It is especially useful for brief comments, which, like the one that follows, may be serious enough, but which at the moment the writer is treating in a far from earnest tone.

One scientist has an idea that it might be fun to dig a hole down into the earth deeper than anybody has ever gone before, and poke around down there. He says there's some swell gas in the earth's core and we ought to let it out because it would be such a great supply of power. Well, pardon us, but we have a counter-plan calling for the formation of a non-power-loving organization called the Society for Letting Well Enough Alone. The S.L.W.E.A. would be founded on the notion that Science is a busybody, and that some day, thanks to Science, we'll hear a loud noise, see a stream of yellow flame in the sky, and zippo, there won't be any more earth, any more sky, any more science, or any more coconut oil. Hereafter, any scientist who wants to try an experiment involving the whole earth is going to have to get permission from the S.L.W.E.A. That goes for side trips into the stratosphere, chemical twiddling of all sorts, and boring holes into the center of the works. The earth is the property of all of us; scientists have got to quit claiming her as their oyster. The earth, just as she stands, has a lot of qualities which we cherish: we like the climate, we like the food, and we like the view from the porch. Nobody is going to let the gas out of her, if we can prevent it. If scientists have to let the gas out of some-thing, let 'em buy a nickel balloon.—*The New Yorker*, June 30, 1934

The advantages of informal English are obvious. It is appro-priate to most subjects, and it reaches a wide reading public, since it can appeal to general readers as well as to those who may also belong in the restricted group to which formal Eng-lish is customarily directed. Above all, it is appropriate to most writers, since it allows them to write with a good deal of natural-ness, to base their writing on their speech instead of on a less familiar idiom. It is the necessary English for everyday writing, and equally effective for literature. George Herbert Palmer said of English literature, "Its bookish times are its decadent times, its talking times its glory" (*Self-Cultivation in English*, p. 10).

A variety of informal language that is of less general use is Familiar English. When we write for our own convenience or amusement, and when we talk or write to members of our family and intimate friends, we use English more casually than when addressing strangers or people with whom we are only slightly acquainted. *This Familiar English is not slipshod but simply more free than the English we use in our public appearances.* Its basis is our natural speech, and the colloquial traits are carried over into writing such as letters or diaries. Contrac-tions, abbreviations, clipped words, nicknames, and shortened constructions are characteristic of familiar English. Localisms, shoptalk, slang, various sorts of play with words (like *tantru-mental*) are likely to appear in familiar writing.

Although a few words, like *boyfriend and girlfriend*, are characteristic of familiar English, for the most part such Eng-lish is not so much a separate kind as an adaptation of various characteristics of other levels, especially of the informal collo-quial. Since the reader is well known, the writer can meet him naturally, and since usually writer and reader have a good deal in common, much can be taken for granted, both in material, allusion to common experiences, and in the special connotation of words. A word may set a group of friends to laughing in a way quite mystifying to a stranger, just because it has some special association for them in their common experience.

Since familiar English is chiefly for communication between people intimately acquainted, it rarely finds its way into print. Even most published letters are in informal rather than familiar English, and often the more familiar parts have been cut out by editors. There is no excuse for carelessness in writing our friends, but we should make every possible use of the small bits of language we hold in common, and draw freely upon our individual stock of words and constructions—to make the communication on paper come as close as possible to what we would say to them in conversation. In what we write for unknown readers we shall have to be somewhat more impersonal and go further toward meeting their expectations.

4b. Vulgate English. From the point of view of an educated person, the everyday speech of many, probably of most, English speaking peoples bristles with "vulgar" words and forms and with "bad grammar." This level of speech we are calling *vulgate English*, the name popularized by H. L. Mencken in *The American Language* and given in *Webster's International Dictionary* as the third sense of *vulgate*, "Vulgar speech or language."[1]

This speech level is a very real and very important part of the English language. It is not made up of lapses from any brand of reputable or standard English; it is the soil out of which much reputable English has grown. It works very well in carrying on the private affairs of millions of people and is consequently worthy of study and of respect. That it is not used in carrying on public affairs—not used in business, government, or literature—is due to social rather than to linguistic causes. Nor is it ordinarily printed, since, for various historical and social reasons, the printable language is a selection of words, forms, and constructions now considered appropriate to public affairs.

Vulgate English is in many respects different from formal and informal English, most conspicuously so perhaps in the use of pronouns and verb forms and in the free use of localisms. Many of its words are much older as far as English is concerned than the more genteel words that have replaced them in "society": *stink* (instead of *stench* or some even less vigorous noun), and the like. Many of the forms and constructions are hundreds of years old and have a continuous history back to a time when they were reputable: Chaucer could use a double negative occasionally; *ant* (*are not*) and *you was* were reputable in the eighteenth century; "dropping the *g*" in words ending in *-ing* is a continuation of an original participial ending. Many other features of vulgate English are equally natural developments of the language that by some accident of dialect or other circumstance did not become adopted in more formal English.

*Bad grammar

*Foundations of Good English, p. 37

*Double negative

*G, § 5

---

[1] Leonard Bloomfield, "Literate and Illiterate Speech," *American Speech*, 1927, ii, 432-39; Fries; H. L. Mencken, *The American Language* (4th ed., New York, 1936).

20

Vulgate English is of course primarily spoken. Its forms (like *dassent, scairt, he don't* . . .) are not particularly conspicuous when we hear them spoken rapidly and with appropriate, not exaggerated, emphasis. It appears in many radio programs, in plays, and in the conversation of stories. It is used in many comic strips—often intensified, for genuine speakers of vulgate would not use so many double negatives, for instance, as some comic-strip characters are made to. Occasionally a vulgate proverb or formula is drawn on in informal writing:

> Them's hard words, Mr. Hutchins. They won't appeal to the fathers of two-hundred-pound, six-foot-two halfbacks.—JOHN R. TUNIS, "Who Should Go to College?" *Ladies' Home Journal*, Sept. 1938

Vincent McHugh's *Caleb Catlum's America* is a tour de force in that it is a complete book written in this level. Except for *shut* at the end of the first paragraph, which should probably be *shet*, this is convincing (correct) vulgate:

> Barney showed up two-three days later, red-eyed from carousing, with big patches bit out of his hide. I put him to work helping me round up my outfit from the North and by the end of the week we settled our passage in a keelboat bound upriver to St. Louis. We didn't pass no words about Felice. We was both mighty pleased to be shut of all them women.
>
> One morning two-three days upriver we tied up at the bank by a little shanty-town named Luna, Arkansas. Keelboat captain was taking on water and supplies. I left Barney on deck sleeping sprawled out in the sun and went moseying on off by myself to stretch the kinks out of my legs.
>
> I meandered out past the town till I come to a patch of woodland. Sun was shining hot and still and I hear the noise of a bucksaw in a little clearing further on. Mighty pleasant sound she made, all mixed in 'mongst the bird-calls. I calculated I'd stroll out that way and show them boys the tricks of handling a blade.
>
> Pretty soon I could make out something kind of sticking up top and when I come closer to it I see I was looking at what must be pretty near the biggest Negro in the world. Even Pop couldn't give him moren'n an inch or two. He was standing there quiet in the middle of the clearing, looking down easy and smiling, whilst these two white Crackers with a bucksaw cut his leg off 'bout halfway to the knee.
>
> They was mighty near through it when I come up to them.
>
> "What's the trouble, boys?" I says. "Anything calls for a doctor I'll be glad to help out. Got some reputation in that line myself."

21

Crackers didn't take no notice at first, sawing away like they was in a dream. Then they let go the handles, slow-like, and stretched out on the ground, turning their chaws of tobacco over and spitting 'fore they spoke.

"Naw," one of 'em says. "We're jest aimin' to cut this feller up fer firewood. Plumb tired out a'ready. Pow'ful slow work, ain't it, Fred?"—VINCENT McHUGH, *Caleb Catlum's America*, p. 146

Schools carry on their work in the language of the upper social classes, usually in formal English. Students who go into the professions, into many branches of business, and into most white-collar jobs continue to use more or less consistently the more formal language. Those who go into manual labor and the less well paid and less socially elevated jobs return to the use of vulgate English—naturally and necessarily. But the increased number of white-collar jobs and the greater number of contacts between white-collar and other workers is reducing somewhat the currency of vulgate English, or at least is producing a more or less unhappy mixture of vulgate and "educated" sounds and forms.

In the lower schools where the pupils are likely to be in daily contact with vulgate speech, it forms a serious problem for teachers. At the college level it is seldom a problem, though an occasional vulgate idiom slips into writing. The speech of many college students is more crude than their supposed social standing would warrant, a poor background for their writing.

The objection to this level of speech should be clear. It is not that its grammar is "bad," but that *vulgate words and constructions are not appropriate to the readers college students and college graduates are trying to reach or to the subjects they are handling.* Complex ideas and dignified subjects cannot be discussed adequately in the relatively limited vocabulary of

*Conversation

vulgate English. Vulgate is necessary in writing conversation of many characters in stories, or at least it should be approximated, and it should be used occasionally to give a note of realism to portraits of real people who naturally speak it or in accounts of their acts. But any other use of it must be judged by fitness. *When a locution in this book is marked "vulgate," it should not be used except for good reason. Expressions marked "colloquial" and "vulgate" are sometimes used in the conversation of educated people but rarely in their writing.*

Two types of vulgate speech are not confined to the uneducated and are used to a greater or less extent by people of all classes. They are often represented in good informal speech and sometimes in writing and so deserve specal comment here.

1) SLANG. It is hard to draw a line between slang and colloquial or informal English. The central trait of slang comes from the motive for its use, which is usually a desire for novelty or for vivid emphasis.[1] Other levels of the language have ways of expressing the ideas of slang words, but their tone is quieter, more conventional. Young people like novelty, and so do fashionable and sporty grown-ups. Slang is especially common in talking about sports and all sorts of amusements and for all kinds of everyday activities—eating, drinking, use of money, traveling, and relations between people. For racy discussion ordinary English words do not seem colorful enough for some sprightly spirits and they adapt words to suit their moods—and others take up their inventions.

Slang words are made by natural linguistic processes. The slang quality may lie in the stress of a word: *positive'ly*, that was *some'* party. The slang expression may be a fashionably overused expression, without any essential change of meaning: *so what*, or *what have' you*. Slang abounds with clipped words: *bunk, razz, goo*; and with compounds and other derivatives of ordinary words: *screwball, sourpuss, tough break, ritzy, cockeyed*. Many slang words are borrowed from shoptalk, especially from the shoptalk of sports, of criminal activities, and of popular lines of work like movie production, and used in more general situations: *punk, scram, close-up* (*klōs' up'*), *behind the eight ball*. And a great many are figurative uses of words from the general vocabulary: *a mean swing, lousy, a good egg, a five-minute egg, drugstore cowboy, pain in the neck, a bird, a peach*. To *park* a car is general English; to *park* a hat or a piece of gum is slang.

Many slang words have short lives—*skiddoo, twenty-three, vamoose, beat it, scram* have succeeded each other within a generation. Words for being drunk, for girls, and words of approval (*tops, a wow*) and disapproval (*wet, screwy*) change almost from year to year. Many slang words prove more permanently useful and become part of the general colloquial and familiar vocabulary (*date, boyfriend, shebang*), and others become current in informal English (*highbrow, lowbrow, close-*

Origin of words

---

[1] Lester V. Berry and M. V. Van den Bark, *The American Thesaurus of Slang* (New York, 1942); J. S. Farmer and W. E. Henley, *Dictionary of Slang and Colloquial English* (New York, 1929); Eric Partridge, *A Dictionary of Slang and Colloquial English* (London, 1933). Most books dealing with language or with English have sections on slang.

up). In this way slang contributes words to the general English vocabulary. Dictionaries tend to be conservative in their treatment of such words and mark as "Slang" many that are actually regular colloquial words, in general informal use.

Slang belongs primarily to familiar and rather flashy speech, to which it can give a note of freshness. This freshness wears off after some hundreds of repetitions so that the prime virtue of the words is lost. In writing, slang is less often appropriate, partly because of triteness and partly because many of the words name general impressions instead of specific ones, so that they rank with *nice* and *good*. *Slang is generally out of place in formal writing* (as in "The Jews have experienced many *tough breaks* since the War"), and if used for some special purpose would ordinarily be put in quotation marks. *In informal writing, slang is often appropriate, as in discussions of sports, of campus affairs, and light subjects*, though even with such subjects appropriateness to the expected readers should be considered. If slang expressions are appropriate, they should be used without apology (that is, without quotation marks), and if they are not appropriate, they should not be used. The chief objections to them, aside from their flashiness, are to their overuse and to their use in place of more exact expressions. Chiefly they are valued for their lively connotation.

* **Counter words**

2) SHOPTALK. *Shoptalk* is the offhand talk of people in various occupations, from medicine and law to ditchdigging and panhandling.[1] It varies of course with the social class and personal taste of its users, from the talk of a garage hand, to that of an automotive engineer, or a professor of physics. Many of its words are the necessary names for materials and processes and tools and other objects and people—for everything that is commonly referred to in a line of work—like *em, en, pica, pi, spreaders, platen, rule, chase,* and so on from a printing shop. Workmen need names for thousands of things the laymen don't know exist. These words would be regarded as a part of the general informal vocabulary of English if they were needed outside the vocation. Shoptalk may often include formal technical and scientific words, as in the conversation of internes and nurses, but it is set off from formal technical and professional writing by the colloquial (and often vulgate) tone and by the presence of the slang of the field, which would not be found at the formal level.

[1] *American Speech* has many articles dealing with the vocabularies of particular occupations.

Shoptalk uses all the freedom of slang in forming words and putting them together, making a vigorous and figurative vocabulary, often shocking to polite ears. A *mike* may be a microphone in a radio studio, a microscope in a laboratory, a micrometer in a shop; *hypo* is a fixing bath to a photographer, or a hypodermic injection in medical context; *soup* is the name of a pourable mixture in scores of manufacturing processes. Racing has *place, show, on the nose, tipster, bookie*; unlisted securities are *cats and dogs*; football men have *skull practice*; a student pilot must *dual* for many hours before he is allowed to *solo*; a *gagman* makes up the comedian's lines; the announcer's advertising speech is a *plug*; and so on.

Shoptalk is appropriate and necessary in informal speaking or writing about the particular occupation in which it is used. It is usually out of place in formal writing. Much of it is useful when borrowed for use about other subjects, like *fade-out* (from the movies), and may become general slang, like *juice* (electricity) and *third degree*. The suggestion of different shop vocabularies varies, as the suggestion of business terms (*contact, **proposition, in the red*) is unpleasant to many people not in business, but the words from sailing (*aft, amidships*) seem romantic and have more general appeal. Shoptalk constitutes one of the liveliest parts of the vocabulary and is contributing more and more to the general vocabulary of the language.

4c. Formal English. Formal English bears the relation to informal English that formal dress or a uniform does to the clothes worn at everyday work in office or store and at informal social gatherings. It is one of the major levels of usage, characteristic of many speakers and writers whose interests or work have involved a good deal of reading. A person's conversation may be formal, though usually it would be less so than his writing, for the background of this level is written literature. Formal English is usually found in books and articles of mature interest, intended for circulation among a rather restricted group, among teachers, ministers, doctors, lawyers, and others of specialized intellectual interests. The appeal of formal usage is in two quite different directions. One is impersonal, as in academic and scientific writing—textbooks, dissertations, reports of experiments and other practical sorts, like legal papers; the other is more personal, as in literature—literary essays, a good deal of poetry and poetic drama, and the less popular fiction. These two types of formal writing make quite different appeals, but the traits of their language have a good deal in common.

* Academic writing
* The Research Paper, p. 319
* Scientific and technical writing
* Legal language
* Heightened style

25

The most conspicuous trait of formal English is its vocabulary, the use of words that belong to the written rather than to the commonly spoken language. Such words are likely to be used little in colloquial English, to be associated with the literary, or scholarly, tradition (*nonchalant, invidious, congenial, habitable . . .*). They are also likely to be more exact in meaning, especially those in scientific writing, than words whose edges have been worn by everyday use. For people familiar with them they often carry a great deal of suggestiveness (*ceremonial, eternity, dogma, fated . . .*) and often have some charm of sound or rhythm (*quintessence, immemorial, memorable . . .*).

*Long and short constructions, p. 163

*Aggregating sentences, p. 152

*Parallelism and balance, p. 159
*Triads
*Allusion, p. 241

In formal English the constructions are usually filled out: relative pronouns are not omitted, prepositions and conjunctions are repeated in parallel constructions, and so on. Short cuts characteristic of colloquial and informal English are not taken. Sentences are likely to be of the aggregating type, somewhat longer than in informal writing, binding more ideas together. They are usually more elaborately constructed, with parallel and balanced clauses, and are frequently periodic, that is, the complete meaning is suspended till the end. Items are often put in series of three. Modifiers, as in this sentence, often interrupt the usual word order. Allusions to literature and to events of the past are more common than allusions to current affairs.

This does not mean that formal writing is weak or dull, though its dangers lie in that direction, but that, from the nature of its language, its appeal is necessarily somewhat limited. Unless the average reader is considerably interested in the subject, he is likely to turn aside. But the special audience which is aimed at will not only follow the material but, if it is really well handled, appreciate the style as well.

Many examples of formal or rather formal writing are scattered through this book. Here three are given to emphasize the traits that have just been mentioned. In the first, from a novel, there are a few definitely formal words (*bejewelled, symposium*), a few formal idioms (*after the manner of, that longed always, there would ensue*), a literary use of adjectives (*dry regret, wise sad anecdotes*). There are several triads, many words with literary associations, and a conspicuous use of parallelism, balance, and climax.

Generally the reunion had been several hours under way before Camila was able to join them after her performance at the theatre. She would arrive towards one o'clock, radiant and bejewelled and very tired. The four men received her as they would a great queen. For an hour or so she would carry the conversation, but gradually reclining more and more against Don Andrés' shoulder she would follow the talk as it flitted from one humorous lined face to the other. All night they talked, secretly comforting their hearts that longed always for Spain and telling themselves that such a symposium was after the manner of the high Spanish soul. They talked about ghosts and second-sight, and about the earth before man appeared upon it and about the possibility of the planets striking against one another; about whether the soul can be seen, like a dove, fluttering away at the moment of death; they wondered whether at the second coming of Christ to Jerusalem, Peru would be long in receiving the news. They talked until the sun rose, about wars and kings, about poets and scholars, and about strange countries. Each one poured into the conversation his store of wise sad anecdotes and his dry regret about the race of men. The flood of golden light struck across the Andes and entering the great window fell upon the piles of fruit, the stained brocade upon the table, and the sweet thoughtful forehead of the Perichole as she lay sleeping against the sleeve of her protector. There would ensue a long pause, no one wishing to make the first move to go, and the glances of them all would rest upon this strange beautiful bird who lived among them.—Thornton Wilder, *The Bridge of San Luis Rey,* pp. 179-80

In the next paragraph, from Mr. Santayana's famous analogy of the spirit of Englishmen and of skylarks, are several of the same traits. Every word counts, and many are of such exact and compressed meaning that they demand considerable thought (*spontaneity in them has its ebb-flow in mockery*). There is distinctive effect from sound and rhythm (*the quintessence of many a sunlit morning*). The phrase *tight little selves* crystallizes a complex idea, and the final sentence is an aphorism of wide application.

How many an English spirit, too modest to be heard here, has now committed its secret to that same heaven! Caught by the impulse of the hour, they rose like larks in the morning, cheerily, rashly, to meet the unforeseen, fatal, congenial adventure, the goal not seen, the air not measured, but the firm heart steady through the fog or blinding fire, making the best of what came, trembling but ready for what might come, with a simple courage which was half joy in living and half willingness to die. Their first flight was often their last. What fell to earth was only a poor dead body, one of a million; what remained above perhaps nothing to speak of, some boyish sally or wistful fancy, less than the song of a lark for God to treasure up in his omniscience and eternity. Yet these common brave fools knew as well as the lark the thing that they could do, and did it; and of other gifts and other adventures they were not envious. Boys and free men are always a little inclined to flout what is not the goal of their present desires, or is beyond their present scope; spontaneity in them has its ebb-flow in mockery. Their tight little selves are too vigorous and too clearly determined to brood much upon distant things; but they are true to their own nature, they know and love the sources of their own strength. Like the larks, those English boys had drunk here the quintessence of many a sunlit morning; they had rambled through these same fields, fringed with hedges and peeping copse and downs purple with heather; these paths and streams had enticed them often; they had been vaguely happy in these quiet, habitable places. It was enough for them to live, as for nature to revolve; and fate, draining in one draught the modest cup of their spirit, spared them the weary dilution and waste of it in the world. The length of things is vanity, only their height is joy.—GEORGE SANTAYANA, "At Heaven's Gate," *Soliloquies in England and Later Soliloquies*, pp. 115-16

The third paragraph shows a full and careful development of an idea, presupposing an active interest in both past and present. Its style is somewhat academic, but more graceful than most academic prose. (Note the rhythm of the last sentence.)

And now, in our day, the first act in the social revolution, accompanied and sustained by the communist faith, has just been staged in Russia. Between the Russian and the French revolutions, as between the democratic and the communist faiths, there are no doubt many points of difference; but what concerns us is that the differences, in the long view, are probably superficial, while the similarities are fundamental. If we, the beneficiaries of the French Revolution, fail to note the similarities, it is because we are easily deceived by a slight difference in nomenclature (for "people" read "proletariat," for "aristocrats" read "*bourgeoisie*," for "kings" read "capitalistic government"); and we are more than willing to be deceived because we, the beneficiaries of the French Revolution, would be the dispossessed of the Russian Revolution should it be successful throughout the western world. Like Diderot's Rameau, we are disposed, naturally enough, to think, "The devil take the best of possible worlds if I am not a part of it." But whatever we think, the plain fact is that the Russian Revolution which menaces us, like the French Revolution which destroyed the possessing classes of the *Old Régime* that we might succeed them, is being carried through in behalf of the dispossessed classes. It aims at nothing less than the establishment of liberty and equality ("true liberty and equality", this time, of course) in place of tyranny and exploitation. For the accomplishment of this object it employs, deliberately, as a temporary but necessary measure, a dictatorship of the faithful similar to that which functioned in '93. And the Bolsheviks who control the Council of Commissars, like the Jacobins who controlled the Committee of Safety, regard themselves as the fated instruments of a process which will inevitably, in the long run, break down the factitious division between nations by uniting all the oppressed against all oppressors. "If cabinets unite kings against the people," exclaimed Isnard in 1792, "we will unite peoples against kings." Similarly, the Bolshevik leaders, following Karl Marx, call upon the "proletarians of all countries" to unite against all *bourgeois*-capitalist governments. The Russian is most of all like the French Revolution in this, that its leaders, having received the tablets of eternal law, regard the "revolution" not merely as an instrument of political and social reform but much more as the realization of a philosophy of life which being universally valid because it is in harmony with science and history must prevail. For this reason the Russian Revolution like the French Revolution has its dogmas, its ceremonial, its saints. Its dogmas are the theories of Marx interpreted by Lenin. The days which it celebrates are the great days of the Revolution. Its saints are the heroes and martyrs of the communist faith. In the homes of the faithful the portrait of Lenin replaces the sacred icons of the old religion, and every day the humble builders of a new order make pilgrimages to holy places.—CARL L. BECKER, *The Heavenly City of the Eighteenth-Century Philosophers*, p. 163

The usefulness of formal English, as of other levels of English, depends upon appropriateness—appropriateness to the writer, to the subject, and to the reader. Students often write more formally than their subjects require, but they need to remember that formal English is characteristic of much mature writing and that as educated people they should be able to understand and to appreciate its qualities.

Especially those who are going into the professions of law, ministry, medicine, teaching, and science and those who are going to play a part in public affairs as editors, publicists, or as intelligent and influential citizens need to be able to write with sufficient dignity to reach their colleagues. To many readers one of the factors in their enjoyment of a work of literature is the contrast between its formal expression and their own everyday informality. This enjoyment can be abused by writers, and often is, but it is one motive for a student's development in range of expression so that he can at different times appeal to various groups of readers.

29

Exercises

These exercises are to give you practice in observing and describing the varieties of English with which you naturally come in contact.

1. Answer these questions with reference to their bearing on your present use of English:

   1. Where did you grow up?

   2. What places have you lived in long enough to have some impression of the language used in them? When were you there?

   3. Are you conscious of any specific influences on your speaking or writing—particular people, teachers, textbooks, English courses, work. . . ?

   4. With what social levels are you most familiar? What are the typical occupations of adults in the group with which you are most familiar? What is the typical educational level?

   5. What foreign languages, ancient or modern, do you know something of (and about how much)?

   6. What kind of books and what writers do you read from preference? What periodicals? Give a fairly full list.

   7. What kinds of books and periodicals were readily available in your home?

   8. Do you regularly read a newspaper? What sections (including comic strips)?

2. Characterize your typical speech and your typical writing in terms of regional English and in terms of levels of usage. If your speech deviates from general English, give examples of words, pronunciations, and constructions which you habitually use.

3. Keep a speech notebook and write down characteristic campus slang, phrases, pronunciations. After a period of recording, write a paper or prepare your material for class discussion on the student speech at your college. A method of recording usage is illustrated on page 592. For suggestions both on organizing the paper and on the earlier recording, read some of the vocabulary articles in *American Speech*.

4. Read *Colloquial and written English and be ready to discuss the relation between your speech and your writing and also those of your friends. Be honest.

5. Arrange the following words in groups according to your judgment of the level of usage in which they are characteristically used. Refer to a dictionary if necessary. (Study table showing levels of usage on page 13.)

*Pages
14-19

30

abrasion	hellion	spheroid
altercation	hombre	stand-in (noun)
bail out	home	swizzle stick
breakdown (noun)	huffy	tergiversation
cinema	invertebrate	thrice
cultus	jalopy	toggle joint
dandle-board	k.o.	tort
dicker (verb)	pelt (noun)	utopian
esoteric	plunk	vernal
esurient	quest	victuals
gotta	rainfall	warlock
grout	ritzy	watt-hour
gumshoe	side meat	write-up (noun)

6. Classify the following words as formal or informal. List an appropriate synonym for each word in the *other* level.

autumnal	dive (noun)	coöp
bovine	mangy	oleaginous
sleeping sickness	pay	gnarled
polyomyelitis	ad lib	tycoon
demented	onus	upstage
job	often	unicameral

7. You might say any of the following in talking. How would you write the equivalent idea more formally? *Pages 11-14

1. Who do you want to speak to?
2. That was what he'd been trying to think of.
3. Come any time you like.
4. He likes to run with the ball, and he got plenty of it in the pony backfield.
5. Engraving is when the letters are raised up so that you can feel them with your finger.
6. If you get a kick out of horseback riding, get on one of ours.
7. Hold on tight when we hit the curve.
8. I saw the headline in a paper a man had across the aisle.
9. It's exactly that I'm complaining about.
10. "By gosh," the coach chuckled, "it's him again."

8. Classify the following constructions as formal or informal, and list an equivalent construction in the *other* level.

1. Were I in your position, I should be uncertain how to proceed.
2. Who are you looking for?
3. Let it not be thought that heroism has withered with the generations.

31

4. This was the lock the key was made for.

5. As in foreign, so in domestic reputation, the artist maintains the greatest and most slavish following by remaining always somewhat the alien, a being ever remote and unknowable.

*Pages 10-11

9. Listen to one or more radio programs wholly or partly in dialect: Bob Burns, Amos and Andy, Lum and Abner. Note words, idioms, pronunciations. Do the accent and dialect sound genuine? Does dialect add effectiveness to the program? Make similar notes on a magazine story or novel using dialect.

10. Make up a list of special *war words* and classify them as technical, shoptalk, informal, etc.

11. Study the following articles and be prepared to discuss the positions these words hold in our language.

*depot	*height—heighth
*drunk	*inside (of)
*due to	*let (leave)
*either (pronunciation)	*no account
*enthuse	*pants
*faze	*plenty
*try and—try to	*show up

12. Analyze the language in each of the following selections. Comment in detail on the use of words: obsolete, archaic, or current; localisms, dialect, foreign words, or standard American; formal, informal, or vulgate. Notice also the length and movement of the sentences. Your analysis should incidentally fix the level and time of each passage, but merely a correct classification of the passage is not a satisfactory answer.

1. We shall all agree that the fundamental aspect of the novel is its story-telling aspect, but we shall voice our assent in different tones, and it is on the precise tone of voice we employ now that our subsequent conclusions will depend.

Let us listen to three voices. If you ask one type of man, "What does a novel do?" he will reply placidly: "Well—I don't know—it seems a funny sort of question to ask—a novel's a novel—well, I don't know—I suppose it kind of tells a story, so to speak." He is quite good-tempered and vague, and probably driving a motor-bus at the same time and paying no more attention to literature than it merits. Another man, whom I visualize as on a golf-course, will be aggressive and brisk. He will reply: "What does a novel do? Why, tell a story of course, and I've no use for it if it didn't. I like a story. Very bad taste on my part, no doubt, but I like a story. You can take your art, you can take your literature, you can take your music, but give me a good story. And I like a story to be a story, mind, and my wife's the same." And a third man he says in a sort of drooping regretful voice, "Yes—oh, dear, yes—the novel tells a story." I respect and admire the first speaker. I detest and fear the second. And the third is myself. Yes, oh, dear, yes—the novel tells a story. That is the fundamental aspect without which it could not exist. That is the highest factor common to all novels, and I wish that it was not so, that it could be something different—melody, or perception of the truth, not this low atavistic form.—E. M. FORSTER, *Aspects of the Novel*, pp. 44-45

2. A fellow that knows every inch of Europe was telling me there ain't a what you might call really comfortable train in the whole length and breadth of the Old Country.—SINCLAIR LEWIS, *The Man Who Knew Coolidge*

3. The rubberlegger has made his appearance in Hollywood and he ain't Leon Errol. He's suspiciously like the same guy who was selling phoney perfume smuggled in from Tia Juana. His racket is equally as gyppy and Hollywood as usual has fallen. In fact several smart lads at the studio and around the Hollywood-Vine sector have been taken. They'd like to squawk, but who'll listen?

The pitch is simple. From a corner of his mouth, the peddler advises the boys that he has a hot tire. It's brand new. The paper wrapping is still around it. Serial numbers and everything are right there. You can see them yourself. Pal of his, truck driver for a big store, grabbed it. All you have to do is run a file over the serial number. That's to protect his pal. The price? The pal has a sick wife. He'll let it go cheap. Can you see the tire? Sure. He'll have it out to your house tonight. Cash, though. No checks. Simple?

Night arrives and so does the guy with the tire. It looks like the McCoy. Wrapped in the original paper wrapping and everything. He'll tear off some of the wrapping just to prove what a bargain he is giving you. He just happens to tear off about seven inches of paper right where the brand and serial number is. That's luck. That also clinches the sale. Here's the dough and the sucker promises to file off the serial number pronto. The deal is made and off goes the Kind-Friend-in-the-Great-Emergency.

Mr. Beat-the-Rubber-Shortage hustles back to the garage to better examine his smart buy. He tears off the remainder of the wrapper and with it gets a belly drop. There's about a 10-inch section of new rubber, serial and brand included. The rest of the tire is a broken down affair rescued from some tire dump.

About a dozen sharp lads have been taken, but they ain't talkin'. Who's going to listen?—*Variety*, February 11, 1942

4. Following the above instructions, comment on the paragraph by Carl L. Becker, page 28.

5. Analyze the selection by Vincent McHugh, p. 21.

13. Discuss the levels of usage (both in words and in constructions) shown in some illustrative paragraphs in this book. For example, look at the selections from Aldous Huxley, page 102, Otis Ferguson, pages 156 and 232, Peter Fleming, page 107, Stephen Vincent Benét, page 15, P. G. Wodehouse, page 512.

*Pages 3-5

14. The following passage was written in the fourteenth century. Pick out words now obsolete, words rarely used now, and words still in common use. Notice differences in spelling. Pick out phrases in which word order is conspicuously different from the modern order. Comment on the form and construction of each of the following: to blessen (line 1), him (line 1), him (line 3), falle (line 4), how that (line 6), and goddes (line 7).

> This carpenter to blessen him bigan
> And seyde, "help us, seinte Frideswyde!
> A man woot litel what him shal bityde.
> This man is falle, with his astromye,
> In som woodnesse or in some agonye;
> I thoghte ay wel how that it sholde be!
> Men sholde nat knowe of goddes privetee."

15. Copy from a book or magazine, giving full reference to its source, a good paragraph showing formal usage; one showing informal usage. In the margin comment briefly on any distinctive words or constructions in them and then write a brief comparison of the usage in the two paragraphs.

16. Read the article *Foreign Words in English. Add some recent borrowings to the list from newspapers, magazines, or recent books.

17. Read *American and British Usage. To what extent are American and British different languages? Check your opinion against your experience in reading modern British books and in hearing British movies and radio speeches.

CHAPTER 2

Good English

To a student of language, all varieties of English are equally a part of the language, and one is to be observed and studied as much as another. But to a user of English, as some of the comments in Chapter 1 suggest, the varieties are by no means equal. They differ in the impression they make on people and in the sort of ideas they can communicate.

Every educated person naturally wants to speak and write what may be called "good English," just as he wants to "make a good personal appearance" and to "be intelligent." But the great range and variety of the English language raises numerous questions as to which of two or more words or expressions is preferable. Realizing that there are differences in usage makes a realistic and sensible approach to Good English easy, for then it becomes a matter of selection, of choosing the expression that is best for a speaker's or writer's specific purpose. *English is not just good; it is good in a particular place.*

1. Language as conduct

We can begin by looking at language as a part of conduct. It is much like the problems which face us in almost everything we do that comes under the eyes of others, in our manners, in

35

the jokes we tell, in our food, in our living quarters, in our political ideas. In dress, to make the most convenient parallel, we gradually develop something we call taste or judgment, in part by imitating others, consciously or unconsciously, in part by consulting people who are supposed to know what is good form, in part by following our own preferences in design and color and fabric.

Dress varies according to the taste of the individual; it varies among classes of people and with their occupations and activities. Overalls are appropriate and necessary for a good deal of work. Sports clothes that would be out of place in an office or a classroom are quite in order on a tennis court, at a beach, or on a hike. For formal occasions dress is definitely prescribed —at least for men, and women have definite conventions to meet. But usually our dress lies between the extremes of work or sport and full dress. It is comfortable; it reflects something of the taste of the person who chose it; it is in good taste without attracting attention; it is appropriate to going about our personal affairs, to work in stores and offices, to college classes, to informal social affairs. The attractive possibilities of everyday costume offer much opportunity for individual choice and judgment. A person needs to have and to be able to wear several kinds of clothes, and he needs to know for what occasion each is appropriate.

In language as in dress there are general expectations, conventions to be taken into account in speaking and writing, but there is also great leeway for personal choice. Anyone who is going to take his place in affairs needs to know the resources of the various sorts of English and when they can be profitably drawn on. On questions of English usage, books are often consulted—more often than on questions of manners, for there are many more books that can answer questions about language, especially dictionaries and handbooks. We can ask people who write well, and we can ask teachers who have made the study of our language part of their professional training. And we can always be watching what effective writers do, how the language is handled in the better books and magazines. This observation is especially important, because, as in dress and in manners, more or less conscious imitation of those we like and approve of will bulk very large in forming our own habits. *Very few will ever write with real ease unless they listen and read a good deal and so unconsciously absorb the ways of their language by direct experience with it as it is actually used.*

2. Foundations of Good English

There are, luckily, principles to help develop judgment in the use of good English and to guide in forming habits of effective speaking and writing.[1] Because we do not have a series of rules and prohibitions does not mean that "anything goes" or that there are not fairly definite goals toward which we constantly move.

*Fundamentals

2a. Limits of Good English set by the purpose of communication. The principal aim of speaking and writing is *appropriate communication*, the ability to convey our thoughts, wishes, and feelings to others so that they can see what we mean.

Of course anyone may talk to himself or write for his own amusement or relief, and then his usage would be his own affair. And a writer may experiment as much as he wishes, as James Joyce and Gertrude Stein and others have done, creating for themselves a limited audience or cult that is willing to study out their meaning in spite of handicaps. But there is no use giving suggestions or directions for such individualism. *The ordinary and principal function of language is direct communication, making someone understand or feel something that we want him to, or getting him to do something that we want him to.*

*Experiment in English

This fundamental purpose in speaking and writing prevents usage, complicated as it is, from falling into chaos and so sets the broad limits of Good English. We use words in the meanings they have acquired from their past use, and we try to make our statements in comprehensible patterns. The language itself, says Professor Jespersen, "has developed through an infinite number of solutions of such problems of communication as arise every instant of our daily life." Professor Fries defines the basis of Good English this way:

> From this point of view language is a means to an end, and that end is specifically to grasp, to possess, to communicate experience. Accordingly, that is good language, good English, which, on the one hand, most fully realizes one's own impressions, and, on the other, is most completely adapted to the purposes of any particular communication.—C. C. FRIES, *What Is Good English?* p. 120

[1] Ballard, Chapters 9, 10, 11; C. C. Fries, *American English Grammar,* Chapter 1 (an unusually good statement); C. C. Fries, *Teaching of the English Language* (New York, 1927), pp. 102-21; Otto Jespersen, *Mankind, Nation and Individual from a Linguistic Point of View* (Oslo, 1925), Chapter 5; Krapp, Chapter 13, The Morals of Good English, and Chapter 5, A Touchstone for English; Pooley, Chapter 7.

So far as the language used furthers the writer's intended effect, it is good; so far as it fails to further that effect, it is bad, no matter how "correct" it may be.

2b. Further limits of Good English set by social attitudes. A person can make his meaning clear—at least if he doesn't try to convey too complex matters—in any variety of English, but, in any variety of English, he cannot meet on an equal footing all levels of society. For various historical and social reasons Vulgate is frowned on in many quarters, though it works well enough in others. What we have called Informal and Formal English is one of the principal requirements for admission to the "upper" social classes, along with income, living quarters, dress, and manners. A person of sufficient intelligence and experience may be laughed at or snubbed because his speech is not quite what is expected in a social circle in which he wishes to move.

Furthermore, Informal and Formal English, as pointed out earlier, is the language of business, politics, science, and literature, of public affairs in general. From this use it deserves perhaps to be called "standard English," as Professor Fries defines it:

> On the whole, however, if we ignore the special differences that separate the speech of New England, the South, and the Middle West, we do have in the United States a set of language habits, broadly conceived, in which the major matters of the political, social, economic, educational, religious life of this country are carried on. To these language habits is attached a certain social prestige, for the use of them suggests that one has constant relations with those who are responsible for the important affairs of our communities. It is this set of language habits, derived originally from an older London English, but differentiated from it somewhat by its independent development in this country, which is the "standard" English of the United States. Enough has been said to enforce the point that it is "standard" not because it is any more correct or more beautiful or more capable than other varieties of English; it is "standard" solely because it is the particular type of English which is used in the conduct of the important affairs of our people. It is also the type of English used by the *socially acceptable* of most of our communities and insofar as that is true it has become a social or class dialect in the United States.—C. C. FRIES, *American English Grammar*, p. 13

The attention given to eliminating Vulgate expressions and encouraging the Formal and Informal levels of usage in schools and colleges is simply to help young people prepare themselves to take their part in public affairs, to speak and write for people who are more or less educated without attracting unfavorable attention and perhaps even with positive effectiveness. Much college writing must be regarded as practice for after-college writing.

At the lowest level this social pressure means conforming to the conventional grammar of those who carry on public affairs, especially as it appears in books and periodicals. Even if they have not been in the habit of using this sort of language at home, before they reach college, students have had several years of school instruction in the words and forms and constructions expected in "standard English." The instruction may vary among schools, and some of it may be antiquated, but no college student can truthfully say that he hasn't been exposed to it. If he doesn't write complete sentences, if he doesn't make his pronouns match their antecedents, and if he allows *Chapter 9, p. 250 other elementary lapses from the language of educated people, he should realize that the fault is principally his. He should take the responsibility for overcoming this handicap—not rely on a teacher to take it for him—so that he can enter the more or less educated class without attracting unpleasant attention to his speaking and writing. If he already has mastered these "minimum essentials," he can go on to the more interesting and more important problems of using reputable English.

Even limited to the Formal and Informal levels, English offers considerable variety and plenty of opportunities for choice. Since Good English is English that fits best the definite intention of a person to communicate something to a certain person or group, the answer to most questions of usage can be found by considering the appropriateness of the word or expression to the immediate purpose it is to serve. *This appropriateness is threefold: to the subject matter and the situation, to the expected readers or listeners, and to the speaker or writer himself.*

3. Appropriateness to the subject and situation

The subject that is being presented and the situation in which it is being presented very largely determine *the tone* of the usage and style to be used.[1] This tone depends chiefly on the level of usage and on the personal or impersonal quality of the style.

---

[1] Dobrée has chapters on the typical style of history, law, criticism, and other particular subjects.

3a. Choice of level of usage. In chapter 1 we noted a number of the typical uses of the various levels of usage, Formal, Informal, and Vulgate. Good judgment in choice of the appropriate levels is one of the signs of a practiced and mature writer.

*Levels of usage, p. 11

1) IN GENERAL SPEAKING AND WRITING. Slang may fit in a letter or in a popular newspaper column; it is out of place in discussing a serious or elevated subject. A talk to a general audience would usually be informal. Most fiction is informal. Writing by and for people in the professions (teachers, doctors, lawyers, various scientific and scholarly workers) is ordinarily formal. Textbooks have been dominantly formal, though now that they are being written more with the student readers in mind, they are somewhat less so. The language of a church service and of religious and philosophical discussion is formal, though some revivalists and others capitalize on obvious contrast with the usual tone. A popular political talk is usually full of words that appeal to feeling and perhaps to prejudice and may show an elaborate "oratorical" style of sentence that has been abandoned in most situations.

*Academic writing

*Scientific and technical writing

Most periodicals are edited in a pretty definite level of usage, although an article for a magazine of general circulation would usually be informal. *Time* is noted for its informality, its racy (and sometimes jumpy) experimental style; *Harper's* is more formal, the *Atlantic Monthly* more formal still, and certain magazines of definitely limited circulation, such as the *Yale Review* and scientific and professional journals, are conspicuously formal. Their usage varies in small mechanical matters like punctuation and spelling; it differs in the words used and in the length and complexity of sentences.

*Exercises 2 and 3. p. 59

Obviously a person needs to know the style that is typically used in the sort of speaking or writing that he is to do. He shouldn't try to write for a magazine he has never read, or try to write a technical report without having seen one, or try any type of speaking or writing with which he is unfamiliar. If he is faced with such a task, he should try in every way to find what is typically done—and follow that as a general suggestion unless he has good reason for some other usage.

2) IN A COMPOSITION COURSE. Students in a composition course face a slightly different problem from that of a writer for publication, since most of their writing is primarily for practice. The language of both the teacher and the students in a college classroom is naturally somewhat more formal than the

language of either is outside. The level of usage expected in themes will generally be defined by the instructor, in line with the practices and purposes of the institution. Usually the tone, as well as the method of work and the type of content, will be illustrated by readings, which can set an example for the usage expected. Unless the nature of an assignment specifically calls for formal style, as in a research or term paper, the usual goal in a composition course is good informal English, because it is the most generally useful type of English.

*Chapter 13, p. 319

For students (and for all other writers, too, for that matter), the chief consequence of paying attention to appropriateness to subject is the resolve *to treat simple subjects simply*, or, in terms of our levels of usage, to treat them informally. Most subjects are relatively simple, or at least the writer is going to give only a simplified version of them. Their interest and their importance are quite lost when the language is too formal. Amateur writers are often not content to be themselves but assume a dialect that is really foreign to them, too formal to be appropriate to them or to their subjects. A boy with a few shrewd remarks to make on modern suicides began this way:

> Through the ages, people have been accustomed to making a premature departure from this "vale of tears" by manifold means. Some favored hanging or a certain type of strangulation; others have been partial to poison, gunshot, or any of a variety of other methods.
>
> However, during recent years a radical change has occurred in the gentle art of self-elimination. This has been due in a large part to the advent of tall buildings. They are seemingly attracted by a strange fascination for the height in combination with a desire to put a spectacular end to their relations with this world.

He might seriously believe that this was better than saying in some simple way that hanging, poison, and shooting had given way to jumping off tall buildings, and then going directly into his subject. He might even object to being told that his sentences were bad English, worse perhaps than if they had contained actual vulgate expressions. The errors could be quite easily corrected, but these inflated and pompous paragraphs must be completely rewritten to be acceptable.

Perhaps the influence of teachers led a student to write:

> No more did I have to answer the demands of motorists, nor come home tired, dirty, and filled with pent-up emotions which I dared not loose during the day.

41

He will soon see that such formal idioms as *no more did I have to answer* (perhaps for "I no longer had to answer" or "Now I didn't have to wait on cranky motorists") and *which I dared not loose* are too formal for a normal young person's account of a summer working in a gas station.

Teachers and students will not always agree in their judgment of particular passages, though they will agree on a surprising number of them. But once students understand the principle of appropriateness they will never return to such unnecessary pomposity. It will be as natural to write informally about a personal experience as it is to talk informally about it. They will soon come to appreciate the simple appropriateness of this account of an interview with a dean:

> "I guess you're next, son," he said, motioning me into his office. Walking to a chair he had pointed out beside his desk, I sat down. "Well," he said, leaning way back in his swivel chair with his hands folded across his waist, "what seems to be your trouble?" "The trouble, sir, is that I have a couple of Fs as you already know." He didn't smile so I'm sorry I said that. Pulling out my deficiency report from a pile on his desk he read it with frowning eye-brows. Looking up at me he said, "How much studying have you been doing?" "Practically none, sir," I said in a weak cracking voice. Laying down the report he started in on a long speech on studying. He looked me straight in the eye and I tried to glare back at him but couldn't. I shook my head every once in a while and said "That's right," to show him that I was listening. He went on to explain how I should make out a time schedule and stick to it, how I should write out notes on little cards and carry them around with me so that I could review them at spare moments, outline this and outline that. Go to your professors and ask them for suggestions—they'll tell you how and what to study, get your tutor to help you. After he had finished, he got up, slapped me on the back and said, "So, son, get down to work and you'll pull through all right." "Thank you, sir, and good-day," I said as I rushed out of the office. Back to my room I slowly plodded, hands shoved deep in my pockets, chin on my chest, feeling very guilty indeed. Slumping into my chair I lit my pipe and began to think. "Gotta get down to work," I thought. "Guess I'll start—next week."

In a composition course, and out of one, keep a complex, formal style for complex and elevated subjects; write naturally and informally of ordinary matters. If you are conscious of the tone and level that is appropriate for the piece of writing you are doing, this is relatively easy. You can settle most problems of appropriateness to subject and situation for yourself simply by considering what the usual tone is in such articles.

3b. Choice between personal and impersonal styles. Some-what related to the level of usage is the degree to which a speaker or writer includes himself in his communication. This is more than the presence of *I*, for a personal style, at least in these days, tends to be informal and to include more individual traits of language, and an impersonal style tends to be more formal.

Obviously conversation among friends, accounts of personal experience, and "personal essays" involve the speaker or writer directly, and any attempt to avoid using *I* or to take out turns of expression with personal associations will make the style distant and too formal. This sentence shows the effects of being impersonal in an obviously personal matter:

> After a summer spent laboring quite industriously in a teeming metropolis, my return to college was looked forward to with greatest expectations.

Much of the production of writers who have a regular following of readers, such as newspaper columnists and regular reviewers of books, plays, and movies, will be distinctly personal. Conceited people will overuse *I*, but anyone with only an average concern for himself needn't worry, even when he is talking about himself.

*I (pronoun), § 2

The types of writing that are usually impersonal include editorials, most serious discussions of situations and of ideas, and all sorts of academic and professional writing, compilations of facts, term papers, dissertations. Students usually do rather well in personal writing but need practice in impersonal phrasing. It seems easier to begin a research paper on cancer with a personal note:

> I have chosen cancer for my subject because I have decided to make medicine my life's work, and because cancer is one of the most dreadful and baffling diseases known to the medical profession. Several of my family have died of cancer and I didn't know whether it was hereditary, so I decided, to find out. A positive cure has not been found as yet, nor has a positive cause . . .

In an impersonal paper, points such as those in the first two sentences in this example, if they are to be given at all, should be in a prefatory note. The paper should begin with some striking and important fact about the subject itself. The reader

43

knows that the writer has gathered the material and selected
what suits his purpose (as, for example, in this book). That can
be taken for granted, and if the statements are reasonable, if
they do not outrun the evidence, no objections will be raised.

Some conventional devices are handy in impersonal writing,
like the "editorial we," "the writer believes," "in the opinion of
the writer." These should not be used when a more personal
expression would be appropriate, but if they cannot be easily
avoided they are better than passive constructions or the colorless *one*, or subterfuges like "many believe," "it seems." The
following paragraphs give the writer's conclusions from a study
of the spelling bee in a typical formal and impersonal fashion.
(Footnotes giving evidence for facts are omitted here.)

> In the first half of the nineteenth century, spelling bees de-
> veloped naturally to meet an educational need felt by the popu-
> lace, and they may be counted as a genuine folk institution.
> The community participated without social barriers, in a fashion
> typical of democratic American social conditions. The revivals
> in recent years have often had an artificial, nostalgic quality, as
> when Webster's "Blue-Backed Speller" is selected as the au-
> thority and the caller of words is referred to as the "school-
> master." From the educational point of view, the bees have had
> severe critics and few defenders. Nevertheless, they are signifi-
> cant not only socially but linguistically. They take rank among
> the conservative influences in American speech. They are a factor
> that helps to account for the prevalence of spelling pronuncia-
> tions in the United States and for a central body of speech that
> does not yield to passing fashions. Spelling bees have been not
> only a mechanism of adjustment to the heavy burden of arbitrary
> English spelling, but also a determination of the course taken
> by the language.—ALLEN WALKER READ, "The Spelling Bee,"
> *PMLA*, June 1941, pp. 511-12

3c. Consistency in tone. It is obvious that the tone of a
passage should be consistent unless the writer has special reason

*Exercise 8,
pp. 51-52

for departing from it. The lines between the levels of usage
cannot be drawn precisely, but a conspicuous lapse from formal
to informal or the other way around should be avoided.

> FORMAL TO INFORMAL: If our Concert and Lecture program this
> year is not superior to that of any college in the country, *I'll
> eat every freshman lid on the campus.*
> INFORMAL TO FORMAL: *I could not help but marvel* at the speed
> with which the workmen assembled the parts.

A characteristic of the more vigorous styles is a wide range
of usage, in both words and constructions. H. L. Mencken and

Otis Ferguson often fuse slang and colloquialisms with formal and even distinctly bookish words. The expressions are unified by the vigor and naturalness with which they are brought together, and are not lapses from appropriateness. *Consistency is not so important as the fundamental appropriateness, but in general, informal writing should be kept informal, and personal too, if it is personal; and formal writing should be kept formal, and impersonal if it is impersonal.*

4. Appropriateness to reader or listener

If you are trying to reach a particular type of reader, you will adjust both your subject matter and your expression to him. To reach him, really to get your points across, you have to be more than merely intelligible; you have to meet him more or less on his own ground. You already do this automatically in your letters, writing in somewhat different ways to different persons. You no doubt adjust your expression somewhat to the expectation of different teachers. Certainly in many other situations you pay some attention to the language you believe is expected of you, as you do to the dress and conduct you believe are expected of you in meeting certain people. *Exercise 6, p. 51

Certain types of writing are in theory completely adjusted to their readers, notably newspaper writing and advertising. Although we realize that both often fail, either from cheapness or from dullness and unintended formality, in a general way they satisfy their ends. An advertisement for an expensive car is not written in the same style as one for a cheaper make, and the same product is presented differently in magazines of different appeal, especially if the appeals are to different income groups.

Trying to write without knowing who will read your words is discouraging. That is one reason why themes are sometimes difficult to write and why it is better for a student to try to visualize some particular audience, to direct his paper to some magazine, or, more commonly, to write for the class of which he is a member. Doing this will help him select material that will interest and inform them or at least will appeal to a certain part of the group, and it will help him judge what words and what kinds of sentences are appropriate. Remember that you are not writing for everyone anyway, but for a selected audience. Novels are for readers of differing tastes, and even the audiences of best sellers like *Gone With the Wind* and *Northwest Passage* and *The Keys of the Kingdom* are not identical.

45

For practice work in which you can choose your level of style, a firm informal style is probably best, for many people prefer it and anyone can be reached through it.

Specifically, considering the reader or listener leads to language that is clear, correct, and lively.

4a. Clearness. Since your aim is to convey some fact or opinion or fancy or feeling to a person or a group, appropriateness to a reader means clear expression. This means first, clear, exact words, and for the most part words that lie within the knowledge of the person you are addressing. If the subject requires words that you expect he may not understand, their meaning will usually be clear from the way they are used, or you can throw in a tactful explanation, or in extreme instances resort to formal definition or even a glossary. Words whose suggestion may be unpleasant to a reader should be avoided, as a matter of tact: *contact, proposition* in situations outside business, slang in formal contexts, and so on. Keeping in mind what courtesy demands will settle many questions.

contact

Readers of more education or at least of more experience in reading can take more elaborate sentences than those who read little or who will read hurriedly. But anyone will be pleased with direct, straightforward sentences.

Sentence weight, p. 151

4b. Correctness. A large part of this adaptation to a reader, especially for a beginner, is avoidance of errors and of other matters that might offend. People tend to judge us by superficial traits, in language as in other matters. Spelling, for example, bulks larger in most people's judgment of writing than it reasonably should. "Everyone," *The New Yorker* once remarked, "is at heart a proofreader." Certainly many people take delight in finding what are (or what they consider are) errors in language, especially in the writing or speech of those supposed to be educated or of anyone who is soliciting their favor. Again courtesy demands that a writer do his best in anything he is submitting to another, and small slips show carelessness that is a sign of discourtesy. Soiled manuscript, many interlineations, confusion of common forms like *its* and *it's*, *they're* and *their*, *affect* and *effect*, misspelling common words (*similiar* for *similar*) are ordinarily careless. They show that the writer just isn't bothering, that he is not doing as well as he easily could, and they are really an insult to his reader. A teacher has sympathy for honest confusion and for real lack of knowledge, but he will seldom bother to read beyond a few lines of a manuscript that is conspicuously careless. The real reason for

Chapter 10, p. 267

mastering the "minimum essentials" of English forms is to meet the expectations of educated readers.

4c. Interest. There is so much unavoidable dullness in the world that any reader (and perhaps especially any theme reader) will appreciate some liveliness in writing, in the expression as well as in the material. Striving for novelty is dangerous and its results often offensive. But frequently students in their teens hide behind a flat sort of language, squeeze all the life out of their writing until it sounds as though it was written by someone three times their age (and asleep at that). The words do not need to be sensational but just those that might be used in a reasonably active conversation. The sentences should not be formless or allowed to drag but should suggest an alert interest. Reference to things people do and say, plenty of lively detail to demonstrate ideas fully and to keep up interest, all help. A plan that gains attention at once and carries on the subject by natural stages is merely an extension of the smaller considerations for a reader.

*Originality, § 2

*Allusion, p. 241
*Chapter 4, p. 81

Some professional writers have set themselves this rule: "Don't write anything you couldn't read yourself." This means that you will choose your best available material, write it as interestingly and as carefully as you can, make it as genuinely readable as you can. If you promise yourself that you will not turn in a paper that you couldn't read yourself with interest and perhaps profit, you will be taking the responsibility for your work, doing composition of actual college grade—and you will be permanently improving your control of expression, laying a sure foundation for continued growth in Good English.

In general, satisfy your reader's expectations insofar as you believe they are worthy of respect. Only one warning is needed: *Don't aim at your reader's worst, compromising yourself and insulting him. Visualize him in his better moments and write for him as he is then.*

5. Appropriateness to speaker or writer

In the reader-writer or speaker-listener relationship, the writer or speaker actually dominates. He makes the choices; his judgment or unconscious sense of fitness finally controls.

The speech-usage of each one of us is constantly swinging backwards and forwards between the demands of society, and an individual expression of his momentary needs. . . . The more commonplace a person is, the more will his language bear the stamp of the community in which he lives: the more unique his nature, the more peculiarly his own will be the colouring of his language.—OTTO JESPERSEN, *Mankind, Nation and Individual from a Linguistic Point of View*, pp. 131, 204

This means that a person's language in the long run represents his personality, and it also suggests that the individual is finally responsible for the language he uses. To take this responsibility he first needs to make every effort to inform himself of the possibilities of English, by observing what is actually spoken and written, by using dictionaries and other reference works, by consulting people who have studied English as a language. Then he can apply this information in his own work according to his best judgment. There is nothing mysterious about the matter; it is just a natural process of learning and applying what is learned.

The most important step in the early stages of considering how to improve your language habits is to watch your own speech and your own writing to see what their good qualities are and what shortcomings they may have. Is your vocabulary large enough? Can you pronounce with confidence the words you need in conversation? Do you have trouble with any of the mechanics of writing—spelling, pronunciation, sentences? Does your language tend to be formal or is it predominantly informal? Do you rely much on slang or on common, threadbare words, or lapse into vulgate expressions? When you talk or write to someone older than yourself, or when you write a paper for a college course, do you choose the best part of your natural language or do you assume an entirely different sort of English?

And finally, *is the language you use consistent with the rest of your conduct?* Does your language in conversation represent your better self, or do you on occasion speak beneath yourself, or on others affect a more pretentious speech than is natural to you? If you are a rather casual person, informal in dress and manner, we should expect your English also to be informal; if you are conventional in dress and manner, we should expect your English to be rather formal. It is necessary for you also to realize the direction in which you are moving, for young people, especially in college, are changing, becoming more flexible in their ideas and manners or becoming more positive and conventional, or making some other change. Their language should be moving similarly. In a student's first papers in a composition course he should write as naturally as he can, so that both he and his teacher can see the present state of his language and so that they can decide together on the direction his growth should take to be appropriate to the rest of his conduct. Such growth will be in the direction of increasing sincerity.

This sincerity in usage and style is one of the conspicuous traits of the better contemporary writing. The English that we find in print is the English the writer would use in talking with his friends, tightened up a little and shorn of the irregularities that usually creep into talk, but still fundamentally informal. He does not appear at a distance, on a platform delivering an oration at us, but seems rather to be talking with us. We can come close to his mind as it actually works. In discussing "The New Way of Writing," Mr. Bonamy Dobrée, an English critic, says: "One would like to think that all of us will come to the stage of refusing to write what we would not, indeed could not, say, though that, of course, is not to limit our writing to what we actually do say" (*Modern Prose Style*, p. 229).

As a result of this approach to Good English you should have confidence in writing. The greatest handicap in writing is fear—fear of pencil and paper, fear of making a mistake, fear of offending the reader's (teacher's) taste. The opposite attitude, cockiness, is a nuisance and equally prevents good writing, but not so many students suffer from that as from inhibitions about writing. Psychologists can't tell us much about the mental activity involved in thinking or writing, but some of them believe that the fundamental condition for speaking or writing is a positive feeling of readiness—which amounts really to a sort of faith that when we open our mouths or sit down to our typewriters something appropriate to the occasion will come. A wide knowledge of the possibilities of current English, backed up by sufficient practice in writing for definite readers, should increase your confidence. Only with some such courage can you write at your best and give that extra something that places your writing above bare competency, that makes it really good English.

It is obvious that the three sorts of appropriateness here suggested for arriving at good English will not always be in harmony. When they conflict, the solution will have to come through the writer's judgment. The subject may seem to demand words that are not appropriate to the reader. The writer's ingenuity can usually solve such a problem, either by finding simpler words or by explaining the necessary but unfamiliar ones. The reader's expectation and the writer's natural manner of expression may be different. Such a conflict can be solved only by the writer—deciding how essential to his purpose his own turns of expression are, whether he can gracefully yield to the reader's expectation or whether his usage is so necessary to his sense of his subject that compromise is impossible. In the long run the writer's sense of fitness, his pride in his work, a craftsman's pride, will resolve most such conflicts.

Good English, then, is not primarily a matter of rules but of judgment. *A speaker or writer is not struggling up under a series of prohibitions but is trying to discover among the magnificent resources of modern English what best suits his purposes.* His desire to communicate something to another is fundamental; it sets the limits beyond which he will not ordinarily go. This general limitation is made more specific by considering whether the level of usage and the particular expressions are appropriate to the subject and the situation, to the expected readers, and finally and most important to the writer himself.

Exercises

These assignments give continued practice in observation of usage and style and an opportunity to begin judging their appropriateness.

1. Prepare a statement of the different levels of English you use and under what circumstances you use each. (*a*) In which level or levels do you feel you are most successful? When you are forced to use other levels, is the necessary shift considerable and difficult for you? (*b*) Is your characteristic level appropriate to your personality and temperament? (*c*) What comments and criticisms have been made on your past compositions?

*Pages 40, 45-47

2. Study a group of at least five magazines. From the general appearance, material (including illustrations), style, and vocabulary, try to determine what audience each magazine is aimed at. Consider the sex, the education, the economic level, and technical or non-technical interest of the readers. Make a similar study of the advertising. Does it confirm your first analysis?

*Pages 39-40

3. Describe the typical level of usage of each of the following magazines. What is its tone? Are level and tone appropriate to its material?

Time Magazine	*The Saturday Evening Post*
The New Yorker	*Collier's* or *Liberty*
The Atlantic Monthly	*The Nation* or *The New Republic*

The Journal of Experimental Zoology or
any scientific journal

4. Record constructions or expressions that you hear or read which raise questions of usage. Put each on a slip of paper or card as explained in *Linguistics §2. See if you can find them entered in dictionaries or other reference books. Try to make up your own mind as to their status in the language. Record short spellings that strike you: *technic, catalog, thru, TNT;* compounding and hyphening: *redhead, standin* (or *stand-in*), *socialite, cinemactor;* technical or shoptalk words recently come into use: *ack-ack, dive-bomb, blitz;* figurative or slang expressions with some currency: *in the doghouse, take a raincheck, behind the eight ball, headache.* *Blend

5. Find and copy a passage of 400-600 words which you would like to have your writing resemble. Comment on its use of words, its sentence length and sentence movement, its level of language, and any other qualities which strike you. Do not regard this as a chore. One good way to improve your writing is to copy writing you like and also to read it aloud.

6. On your next paper put a concise but definite statement of the audience it is intended for. Discuss the usage and style you employ in the paper under the heads of the three sorts of appropriateness. Your instructor, in correcting your paper, will take into account two points: the soundness of your purpose and the extent to which you have carried it out. *Pages 39-44

7. Prepare for classroom discussion, or writing, one or two of the following topics. Be sure to have in mind definite passages, situations, or whatever you need to make your discussion concrete and actually related to your writing problems.

1. The role (or relative roles) of reading, listening, speaking, and writing in the development of good English.

2. Your usual reading in newspapers, books, and magazines, and its effect on your own usage.

3. Should a person with some education ever speak Vulgate? When? Should an uneducated person ever try to speak or write Formal English? When?

4. What does *The New Yorker* mean and what sort of writing did it have in mind in the following statement: "English usage is sometimes more than mere taste, judgment, and education—sometimes it's sheer luck, like getting across the street."

5. What writing do you expect to do in college and after college? What then are your special needs?

8. Read carefully the following passages. Rewrite them and improve them. In each passage what basic flaws did you find

*Pages 39-42,
44-45
and remove when you rewrote? Would you say that bad English is something besides "mistakes" in spelling or grammar?

1. Every year when the Spring season rolls around it is indeed a welcome sight to see once more the emerging of track aspirants from their winter hideouts.

2. Many people read a book of fiction just for the sheer enjoyment gotten from it instead of any educational value. When a book is assigned for classwork, it is usually read with an attitude much apart from reading it of one's own volition. When a book is not picked apart to see what the author has tried to put across from a certain idea, more enjoyment is gotten from it.

3. Each Fall the college musters forth from its ranks about sixty would-be musicians desirous of a place in the University Band. There are different purposes in the minds of these men. Some enter the band for the academic credit that is given, others for the trips to various football games, and still others join because of the musical training that they will receive. I agree that all these reasons are sound, but I do believe that the organization itself needs consideration.

4. Last fall when the class of 1945 entered the hundreds of colleges and universities throughout the country, they left behind them an even larger tribe of high-school graduates of the class of 1940. A great many of these found jobs and settled down to average life, but another great group of them were unable to find work of any description, could not afford to go to college, and, as a result, have rapidly begun to learn what is perhaps the second oldest profession, that of loafing.

9. From your reading, especially from your textbooks, bring in passages that you found hard to understand. Try to decide whether the difficulty was due to the language used, to the complexity or unfamiliarity of the ideas, or to some other factor (not overlooking your own possible lack of effort).

10. Read the articles listed in the headnote to the alphabetical articles on page 349 and some others of your own choosing to see how the principles of Good English can be applied to particular problems of usage.

CHAPTER 3

The Forms and Uses of Paragraphs

1. **The purpose of paragraphs**
   a. To group statements   b. To separate statements   c. Visual marks of paragraphs

2. **Length of paragraphs**

3. **Writing paragraphs**
   a. Planning paragraphs   b. Topic sentences   c. Paragraphs in the first draft   d. Revising paragraphs

4. **Connection between statements** [in a paragraph]

5. **Transition between paragraphs**

6. **Beginning paragraphs**

7. **Concluding paragraphs**
   a. Unemphatic conclusions   b. Typical endings   c. Style

PARAGRAPHS HAVE TWO principal uses, holding together statements that are closely related and keeping apart statements that belong to somewhat different parts of a subject.[1]

1. The purpose of paragraphs

1a. To group statements. A paragraph is a group of related statements that a writer regards as a unit in the development of his subject. To the eye it appears as a unit because of the indention of its first word, because of its usually incomplete last line, and perhaps because of spacing. More essentially a paragraph appears to the mind as a unit because of the relation that exists and that is shown to exist between the statements it contains. These related statements represent a stage in the flow of the writer's thought, for his thought is continuous, even though it may not be consecutive in a logical sense. By the mechanical device of indention and by the inner connection between his statements, he indicates small stages in his material to help his reader see the movement of his thought as nearly as possible as he sees it. A paragraph is consequently a punctuation mark indi-

---

[1] E. H. Lewis, *The History of the English Paragraph* (Chicago, 1894). All rhetorics and handbooks have discussions of paragraphs.

cating a unit larger than a sentence and smaller than a whole article or chapter. It is a sign that the writer's natural, rapid, more or less helter-skelter "thought" has been prepared, arranged, organized, *edited* for a reader.

Though the preceding paragraph is not a model, it can illustrate the typical qualities of this unit of writing. Having decided to begin this chapter with a definition of *paragraph*, I tried to work into one direct and connected statement some account of what seemed to me the two most important features, the visual spacing and the internal connection of idea, both of which will be elaborated more fully. That is, the origin of the paragraph was in a group of related ideas that were to be presented to a reader. The group of statements that resulted (in a third rewriting) deserves to be called a paragraph not because it is a series of sentences set end to end. Rather it is a paragraph because here is a series of statements each of which contributes something to elaborating the subject announced in the first sentence, *A paragraph is a group of related statements that a writer regards as a unit in the development of his subject*. The individual sentences not only contribute to the general idea, but they are related to each other. A reader can pass from one to the next without a break in his thought. In fact, though the sentences might make some sense, if he began to read after the first one, he would not get their complete meaning. In *To the eye it appears as a unit . . .* the *it* refers back to *paragraph* in the preceding sentence; *More essentially* at the beginning of the third sentence implies that something pertinent has already been said; *These related statements* summarizes or echoes *the relation that exists and that is shown to exist between the statements it contains; he* in the next sentence refers to the writer mentioned; in *A paragraph is consequently a punctuation mark* the *consequently* shows the relation of the statement to the ones preceding. Such marks of continuity of idea show that the statements do not stand now in the haphazard way they had been "thought," actually with interruptions from my pretty active family, not to mention the more or less irrelevant ideas that were shooting around in my head. They also make the statements more concise and more accurate and more consciously directed than I would talk the same ideas before a class. Obviously a block of "more or less helter-skelter 'thought' has been prepared, arranged, organized, edited for a reader." There are other kinds of paragraphs, certainly more graceful and appealing ones, for this opening of the chapter is more formal

54

than paragraphs need to be, but any paragraph would show these qualities of consecutive thought movement to some degree.

1b. To separate statements. Looking at a single paragraph, this continuity of material is its most important feature; it is a handful of related statements. Considering a series of paragraphs, the obvious fact is that though each one relates to the subject of the paper, each develops a little different phase of it. That is, paragraphs separate as well as join. The indention is a sign to a reader that the thought is going to shift slightly, and he adjusts his attention automatically. (Can you imagine trying to read this chapter not divided into paragraphs?) Paragraphing also helps the writer separate his material into units that can be grasped easily and that will let him place emphasis where he wants it.

Where divisions should come is a matter of judgment. If the statements cannot be easily joined to what has gone before, probably a new paragraph is called for. To a considerable degree paragraphs follow rather definite patterns of length, as will be described in § 2; they are shorter if the matter is to be read rapidly, as in periodicals, and longer in books intended for slower and more careful reading. But the best guide is the writer's sense of the units of his material, the topics or stages that would be indicated in a very detailed outline. His purpose is to make the reader follow his thought, see it in the stages in which he sees it.

1c. Visual marks of paragraphs. The specific conventions of spacing for paragraphs can be quickly stated. In print a paragraph is indented by one em (that is, by a unit as wide as the type is high). In longhand manuscript the indention should be *Type enough to be clearly seen, about an inch in typical handwriting, perhaps a little less for smaller than average writing. In type- *Exercise 8, script a paragraph is indented from five to eight spaces. A stop pp. 79-80 on the tabulator bar can be set so that it will make uniform indentions with one pressure of the tabulator key when the carriage is pulled back to the left margin. In some business letters or mimeographed matter which is written single spaced, a block form is used in which the paragraph is not indented and the only sign is the line left between paragraphs. This form is not used for general manuscript.

Some students make their copy confusing by indenting the first line of each page, even when it is not the beginning of a paragraph, or by leaving part of the last line on a page blank so that it looks like the end of a paragraph. If you have formed

*Exercises 1
and 4, p. 74

either of these habits, you should break it. If you want to indicate the beginning of a paragraph in copy that you have written solid, put the paragraph symbol in the left margin and draw an angle before the first word of the new paragraph, like this:

```
   If you have formed either of these habits you
₱  should break it. |If you want to indicate the
   beginning of a paragraph in copy that you have
   written solid, put the paragraph symbol in the
```

If you want to indicate that copy you have written as two paragraphs should be joined as one, write *no₱* in the left margin and draw a line from the end of the preceding to the beginning of the following paragraph.

This simple visual device of paragraphing supports the more essential and more complex devices for showing the relation between ideas, described in § 5, page 65, in helping the reader see the stages in what you have to say. Looking at a paragraph as a whole, he finds a specific group of closely related statements that he can grasp as a unit. *Satisfying paragraphs are a sign that a writer has thought over his material and prepared it for a reader, but their real use is to help the reader get at the writer's meaning easily and definitely.*

2. Length of paragraphs

*Letters

Except in letters and other personal sorts of writing, the physical features of paragraphs are determined by the practices of periodical and book editors. Because of the usually simple narratives of news stories and the narrow columns, which make long unbroken stretches of type forbidding, and because they are intended for hasty reading, paragraphs in newspapers run distinctly short, the great majority of them being under 75 words, 20 to 50 words being typical. Paragraphs in magazines of restricted circulation approach book paragraphs in length, but in fairly popular magazines the paragraphs would rarely be 200 words long and typically run from 100 to 150 words. Books show great variety, but as a rule paragraphs of less than 125 words would be short and paragraphs of over 250 rather long except in books intended for a special audience. Fiction shows considerable variety in paragraph length, approximating periodical rather than book length. In any given article, of course, the paragraphs will vary considerably. It is obvious that subordinate points will be of differing importance, some deserving fuller and others shorter treatment.

Here are some figures from typical pieces of writing that illustrate characteristic paragraph lengths in factual writing. The first two are from news stories, the next two from magazine articles, and the remaining from books. They are based on a count of 16 consecutive paragraphs, except the Santayana essay, which contains only eight.

LENGTH OF PARAGRAPHS IN ORDER	LONGEST	SHORTEST	AVERAGE
Two news stories:			
93, 29, 75, 57, 23, 43, 40, 51, 26, 22, 43, 18, 18, 29, 24, 20	93	18	38
30, 38, 18, 53, 50, 29, 57, 56, 55, 71, 44, 30, 49, 23, 23, 36	71	18	41
Article in the *Atlantic Monthly*:			
66, 96, 113, 65, 85, 101, 83, 85, 86, 112, 69, 100, 100, 90, 136, 141	141	65	95
A *New Yorker* profile:			
192, 111, 99, 163, 13, 306, 137, 174, 110, 16, 274, 232, 245, 208, 95, 11	306	11	149
Carl Carmer, *Listen for a Lonesome Drum*:			
63, 55, 148, 173, 173, 58, 111, 87, 54, 71, 143, 167, 332, 163, 172, 40	332	40	126
Margaret Leach, *Reveille in Washington*:			
136, 211, 53, 118, 207, 135, 216, 83, 182, 129, 109, 302, 171, 55, 143, 100	302	53	147
From this chapter of *Writer's Guide and Index to English*:			
25, 190, 439, 117, 119, 146, 98, 41, 96, 180, 154, 199, 97, 110, 119, 63	439	25	137
George Santayana, "Skylarks":			
290, 180, 294, 333, 435, 159, 513, 438	513	159	330

There are some standard exceptions to these conventions of paragraphing. Each speech in a dialog is set off in a separate paragraph. Occasionally, in complex subject matter, a single sentence that shows the transition in thought between two paragraphs or sections will stand as a separate paragraph, and sometimes an important or emphatic sentence will deserve a paragraph by itself. In advertising and a good deal of busi-

*Conversation

ness writing, single sentences are indented as paragraphs for display purposes, the real paragraphs then being indicated by extra spacing between groups of these sentences. Editorials in some of the more popular papers are printed in this way, with gain in legibility as compared with the forbidding editorial pages of the more conservative papers, but writers usually find it harder to show relationship between their ideas in this form. It is more appropriate for short, suggestive statements than for presenting a "chain of reasoning."

All this discussion of length does not mean that a writer should stop to count the words in his paragraphs, as he writes or afterwards, but he should be able to visualize the length of his paragraphs as they would stand in typical magazine and book form. Most writers get about 200 words of longhand on a page and about 300 in double-spaced typing. It is obvious that *a writer should look closely at any page of his manuscript that shows more than two paragraph breaks*—not that they are necessarily wrong, but he should be sure that they represent actual stages of his material, that they are appropriate to the subject, to the reader, and to his own view of the subject. Conspicuously short paragraphs are likely to be symptoms that he is not developing his material sufficiently, is not putting in enough details, is not building enough small ideas together, or else that he is dividing his subject into too small units to guide his reader to an understanding of the relationships between points. As a rule paragraphs are shorter when the material is descriptive, made up chiefly of small details, or when it is narrative.

Similarly, *he should look closely at paragraphs that run over a manuscript page, to see if they are actually unified or if perhaps they shouldn't be broken up for emphasis or for the reader's convenience.* Paragraphs are likely to be longer than average when the thought is consecutive, emphasizing relationship between facts or ideas. In works of criticism, in philosophy and science, the paragraphs are rightly longer than in pictures of the life around us. Length is a symptom of other qualities of paragraphs, and is to be considered in the light of subject matter and purpose.

3. Writing paragraphs

3a. Planning paragraphs. After a writer has thought for a while about some material he proposes to communicate to a reader, it begins to take shape. As soon as he sees the general plan by which he will present it, he can see it as a series of small topics to be discussed. The topics may be noted in a formal or informal outline, or carried in his head. At the moment of writing this paragraph, I see this section in terms of its material as follows:

3. Writing paragraphs

1) Plan and paragraphing. Topic sentences
2) Writing first draft
3) Revising paragraphs—Asking questions
4) Common faults: (In form of questions)
   New or irrelevant or trivial points at end
   Thought turns a corner (connection non-existent)
   Lack of obvious connection (material actually
      related but the relationship not shown)
   Faulty emphasis

At present I expect the first topic will be worth one paragraph with another specifically on topic sentences; "Writing the first draft" will probably be two or three paragraphs, though I shouldn't be surprised if it developed into more. The final appearance of 3 and 4 will depend on how many of the possible illustrations in my file I put in. (The paragraphs may increase in number as the material expands on further thought.) I should expect a paragraph on the general purpose and method of revising, and one or more on each of the faults listed, and possibly a paragraph rounding out the topic or leading to section 4.

The point is that as a writer's material falls in line and he begins to see the scale of treatment, the paragraphs are forming in his mind—the place for them to form. The paragraphs do not necessarily match the headings of his outline, if he has one, a paragraph to a heading. Several subheads might be carried in a single paragraph (if the outline was very detailed). On the other hand, a single heading, because of the bulk of the discussion, might be treated in several paragraphs. But the paragraphs will *correspond* to the outline. *The more sure you are of the plan of your paper, the simpler it will be to shape the actual expression into paragraphs.*

(I had originally thought that the material of the foregoing two paragraphs would be in one, but it grew too long and so I broke it at a natural turn, *The point is*. . . . This gives better emphasis and is more convenient to read. Also I feel by now that "Topic sentences" deserves a special heading as well as a separate paragraph or two. The material is growing.)

3b. Topic sentences. A writer can often crystallize his material into paragraphs by means of a *topic sentence*, that is, a sentence that states the topic of the paragraph and perhaps summarizes

*Exercise 2, p. 74

some of its content. (The foregoing is the topic sentence of this paragraph.) A topic sentence is likely to state in general terms what is developed in specific detail in the rest of the paragraph. Sometimes it helps to write this sentence consciously, put it first, and then develop its idea. If you are having trouble focusing your material, this will help make it definite. Quite often a writer is not conscious of his topic sentences, but if his mind is working accurately the reader will usually find one. It is by no means always the first sentence, for a paragraph may build up to the statement of its topic rather than be suspended from it, and sometimes the idea is summarized somewhere in the middle. Topic sentences help readers get the gist of paragraphs; often they are the ones you underline in studying.

If the topic sentence stands first, it has usually a come-on note, leading the reader to expect further development. When Professor Schlichter begins a paragraph "A fourth way in which our economic order creates friction between workers and business owners is by its selling and advertising activities," we expect details of these selling activities and their bearing on unrest. When Lincoln Steffens starts a paragraph "One of the wrongs suffered by boys is that of being loved before loving," we expect a discussion of the idea or specific instances. In the following paragraph the topic sentence stands last, giving the significance of the illustrations that have preceded.

> Large automobile companies, in elaborate advertisements, present their skilled mechanics as "craftsmen," making a title of the term. A certain absurdity, yet almost a pathetic intensity, of this tendency is revealed in the yearning for the myth of individual handicraft betrayed by such phrases as "Tomato Soup . . . . by Campbell." General Motors still clings to the lost carriage maker in the insignia and motto, "Body by Fisher." *Personal* names for *mass* products are at a premium. There is commercial value in "Fanny Farmer" candies, or "Mrs. Wagner's Pie." A sense of the public psychology is revealed in these oblique apologies by manufacturers for the industrial standardization of their products. This is not to imply that there are not many commodities which industry produces with better results than could the individual. But it's worth noting that when the sewing machine was first invented especially high prices were charged for clothing made on it. "Untouched by human hands" was once the miraculous advertising appeal for other milled or machined commodities. *Yet today, the label "hand made" is worth an illogical amount in the retail value of many products.*
> —Scott Graham Williamson, *The American Craftsman*, p. 9

3c. Paragraphs in the first draft. People's habits of writing differ so that it is hardly safe to generalize on what they do in the actual process of composition. But it seems safe to say that if they have thought over their subject matter they will write several sentences without stopping (much), and that it would be well if they could get the habit of writing at least a whole paragraph at a time. Certainly you shouldn't let your attention wander after a statement that is intended to lead into another statement. Try to write a full paragraph before you let your attention shift to something else, or before you go to look for more material, or before you get up to walk around the room or chat with your roommate. Of course efficiency demands that you keep your attention fixed as much as possible on your writing, but if you do pause, try to pause between paragraphs or between the larger stages of your paper. *Make the writing of a paragraph continuous, so that it can keep as close as possible to your actual thinking.*

*Writing the first draft, p. 298

In general make your first drafts as full as you can. One of the fundamental knacks in writing is packing in details, using particular facts and particular pictures as contrasted with general statements. The details may be few but striking and representative, or they may be numerous, carrying force in part by their number. Vague statement and lack of detail is usually an element in unsuccessful writing. Instead of reading "The hat had a peculiar feather," the reader wants specific details so that he can see in what way the feather was "peculiar"; instead of "The people in the bleachers were of all shapes and sizes" he needs three or four details that would give a glimpse of the people—and at the same time let him feel that the writer had really seen the crowd he was talking about.

Successful detail does not have to be unusual but simply accurate enough to let the reader see and believe:

> His light blue eyes are watery, and deep wrinkles show in the corners as if they were used to squinting into the sunlight. His long narrow nose has a twist, as if it had had some exciting contacts and had lost to its opponents. His cheeks are thin and the skin is stretched tight over a determined jaw. His neck is encircled by a once brilliant black neckerchief which has now turned a powdery gray from the dust kicked up by the pushing cattle.

Most students (and other writers) who have trouble meeting the expected length of assigned papers would find their work easier if they would get the habit of developing details, first by seeing more small facts and bits of picture that their subject needs, and second by putting these details down on paper. Their manuscripts then would not only say more and be more convincing, but they would be much more interesting. Writing which is alive with concrete detail is also easier and more satisfying, because it has not been padded out with irrelevant matter but built by proper means. *It is much easier to draw a line through details that in revision seem unnecessary or out of place than it is to open up a paragraph and put more matter in.* Consequently put in too much rather than too little in the first draft and let the individual paragraphs grow to full size.

Since the first draft shows you for the first time your ideas definitely expressed in words, you will expect to rework it. *Make this revision easy by giving the first draft plenty of space on the paper.* Don't crowd the copy to the margins or let the lines stand so close together that you can't write new words between them. Some writers put only one paragraph on a page or use only the upper half of the sheet in the first writing, so that they have plenty of room for additions and alterations of all sorts. Work out some scheme of physical arrangement on paper so that your writing can be carried on with as little inconvenience as possible.

3d. Revising paragraphs. How much revision your paragraphs need depends of course on how well they appear in the first writing. The purpose of revision is to remove the faults and increase the virtues of the first draft, and in particular to examine so far as a writer ever can the fitness of his presentation for his intended readers. In paragraphs the good old principles of *unity* (singleness of idea or of impression), *coherence* (continuity, relation between statements), and *emphasis* (exactness with which the writer's view is interpreted for the reader) are useful checks.

*Exercise 3, p. 74

*Exercise 7, p. 77

To check for these matters in revision of paragraphs, it may be most convenient to ask yourself these questions:

1. Does each paragraph develop a single topic or a single stage of a topic?

One of the danger spots is at the end of the paragraph because we are likely to have afterthoughts and tack on a minor or somewhat unrelated statement. Often this statement can be thrown away, or put with the following paragraph, or tucked in inconspicuously at an earlier point in the same paragraph. Sometimes two really unrelated matters are put together, though more often the fault is neglecting to show the connection that actually exists between the statements. If the subject actually changes, turns a sharp corner within a paragraph, the paragraph should be divided at that point or it should be broken up and the material reorganized.

2. *Are any paragraphs conspicuously over- or underdeveloped?* This is partly a matter of physical length, as was described in § 2. More important, it is a matter of content. Are there too many details or illustrations or repetitions of idea? Readers who are unfamiliar with the subject or are hostile to it, or who are supposed to think slowly, need more elaboration; those more or less informed and sympathetic need less elaboration, unless it is used to arouse immediate interest. Usually amateur writers put in too few details rather than too many.

3. *Do the paragraphs end strongly and on the point that I want my readers to get especially?* This emphasis is not so important for accounts of personal experience, and perhaps not for other narrative, as it is for developing a line of reasoning. You want to be sure that your emphasis is to be clear to the reader, and the beginnings and ends of your paragraphs offer the emphatic position.

4. *Are the statements within a paragraph so related that my readers can follow naturally from one to the next?* Will the relation that is clear to me be clear to them? This continuity is the crux of writing good paragraphs and is elaborated in the next section.

4. Connection between statements in a paragraph

A writer's purpose in each paragraph is to advance his subject, to leave his reader more informed or interested at the end than he was at the beginning. Whether or not even a meaningful paragraph makes its full point depends largely on the movement given the subject matter, on the way the reader is led from one statement to the next. It is not enough that the relation between the statements is obvious to the writer; *it should be obvious also to the reader for whom it is intended.* To make sure of this the writer usually needs only to check his paragraphs in revision, taking a reader's point of view so far as he can. If it is difficult to pass from one statement to the next, the reader is thrown off the track. If the statements can be firmly tied together, they will probably compose a satisfactory paragraph and embody a consistent chain of thought. The connection must first exist in the ideas and then be shown.

The second sentence of the following paragraph does not follow from the first; it seems to make a new start. The whole paragraph needs to be rewritten from a definite point of view (either of the player trying to find a good polo pony or of the attempts that have been made to furnish good ponies) and the relation between the statements made clear:

> For many years men have been breeding, raising and schooling different types and breeds of horses in an effort to produce the ideal polo mount. When a player wishes to purchase a high-type pony, he looks for four things—quickness, speed, stamina, and ability to stop easily. A combination of these four essentials is difficult to find in one animal. Several have two or three of the qualifications, but very seldom do you find a pony with all four.

*Exercise 5, p. 74

Fortunately the means of showing the connection between statements are natural and simple. The common ones are:

1. Continuing the same subject from sentence to sentence in the same words, in synonyms, or by means of pronouns
2. Some words of the first sentence, perhaps the object, used as the subject of the second or at the beginning of the second
3. A pronoun referring to a word in the preceding sentence
4. A thought relationship (cause or effect, reason, illustration . . .) shown directly by a conjunction or adverb (*however, but, and* . . .) or only suggested
5. Parallel structure of the sentences

These are the verbal signs of the continuity of the subject matter, of the paragraph movement.

The following paragraph shows the most common of these signs of continuity.

(1) Critics have not been lacking, *of course*, who pointed out what a hash democracy was making of its pretensions to government. (2) *These critics* have seen that the important decisions were taken by individuals, and that public opinion was uninformed, irrelevant and meddlesome. (3) *They* have usually concluded that there was a congenital difference between the masterful few and the ignorant many. (4) *They* are the victims of a superficial analysis of the evils they see so clearly. (5) The *fundamental difference* which matters is that between insiders and outsiders. (6) *Their* relations to a problem are radically

Suggests continuation from a preceding paragraph

Subject of 1 repeated

Pronoun, referring to *critics*, subject of 1 and 2

Pronoun, as in 3 *Fundamental* contrasts with *superficial* of 4; *difference* repeated from 3 Pronoun *Their* refers to *insiders and outsiders* different. (7) Only the *insider* can make decisions, not because he is inherently a better man but because he is so placed that he can understand and can act. (8) The *outsider* is necessarily ignorant, usually irrelevant and often meddlesome, because he is trying to navigate the ship from dry land. (9) *That* is why excellent automobile manufacturers, literary critics and scientists often talk such nonsense about politics. (10) *Their* congenital excellence, if it exists, reveals itself only in their own activity. (11) The *aristocratic theorists* work from the fallacy of supposing that a sufficiently *excellent* square peg will also fit a round hole. (12) In short, like the democratic theorists, *they* miss the essence of the matter, which is, that competence exists only in relation to function; that men are not good, but good for something; that men cannot be educated, but only educated for something. — WALTER LIPPMANN, *The Phantom Public*, pp. 149-50

Insider repeated

Outsider repeated from 5, contrasting with *insider* in 7

Pronoun *That*, summarizing idea of 8

Pronoun *Their*, referring to the various nouns of 9

Echoes *critics* of first sentences; *excellent* echoes *excellence* of 10

Pronoun *they*, referring to *theorists* of 11

A firm, emphatic final sentence, topic sentence and goal of the preceding statements

5. Transitions between paragraphs

This continuity of ideas needs also to be shown from one paragraph to another. The connection between the parts of the subject, the words that lead the reader from one thought to another, are called *transitions*.

One of the most common weaknesses of amateur writing is beginning a later paragraph as though nothing had been said already, instead of building on what has gone before. The two following paragraphs could have been linked by some expression like "The principal advantage of the prep school is that every student gets individual attention."

I think that a preparatory school education is better than a high school education. During the last four years I went to prep school. Many times my friends would tell me that it was just a waste of time. They'd say, "Gosh! but you're missing a lot of fun" or "Don't be a sucker and spend the best four years of your life in prep school."

Individual attention is the main objective of prep schools. Classes are limited to ten or twenty students. We never had to study in a room where another class was reciting. The work is not entirely left to the pupil, as regular study halls are held. If one is low in a subject the prof will find time to tutor him. Tests are corrected and recorrected until every mistake is cleared. Most fellows coming to college from a prep school know how to study. This does not mean that they are smarter than anyone else but that they have been taught to budget their time.

There are two parts to indicating transitions: one is connecting with the topic of the whole paper, the other connecting with the topic of the preceding paragraph. If it can be done naturally, it is emphatic to name or allude to the topic of the article, or at least of a subdivision of the article, in the first sentence of each paragraph. In a run of six paragraphs dealing with the city of Buffalo in Carl Carmer's *Listen for a Lonesome Drum,* the city is named near the beginning of each:

> Buffalo is a place of contrasts—of big and distinctly different communities bound together into a huge blustery city beside the tossing waters of Erie, stormiest of the Great Lakes. . . .
>
> And the people in those depths are equally indifferent to the Lake Shore. To thousands of its people Buffalo means the golden glow and desperate drudgery of a steel furnace, the stuffy interior of a flour mill, . . .
>
> The casual wanderer through Buffalo's residential streets will not walk far without coming upon a corner redolent with the smell of beer and sauerkraut, cheese and apple dumplings. . . .
>
> Last and most powerful of the groups that make up Buffalo are the rich old families living in heavy elegance behind the respectable excesses of the scroll saw. . . .
>
> The four chief streams of Buffalo's population become aware of each other only at City Hall and in the downtown business section. . . .
>
> The Irish, the Germans, and the rich old families have kept Buffalo on the conservative side politically through most of its later history. . . . —CARL CARMER, *Listen for a Lonesome Drum,* pp. 36-46

And of ten paragraphs by Mr. Carmer on the city of Rochester, all but one name Rochester in the first sentence.

The connection with the paragraph immediately preceding is easier and perhaps more important. The purpose is to show the reader that the subject is being continued. When paragraphs are short, the signs of continuity may not differ essentially from those used between sentences. There are transitional words and phrases like *this* or *that* or other words that refer directly to a word or idea at the end of the preceding paragraph and transitional expressions like *on the contrary, another reason, in the second place, besides this,* and other indications of thought relationship. Such genuine connectives are more essential than the flabby *then too* or mechanical expressions like *Now let us turn to* . . . or *It is interesting to note* . . ., which are symptoms that the writer has not sensed the actual relationship between the points he is making.

Often it is enough to carry over an essential word or two or an idea in different words from the end of the preceding paragraph, as in the paragraphs by Professor Laski on page 356 of this *Guide and Index.*

> . . . In the great society, we could not for a day preserve its scale of living unless there were countless men and women applying their knowledge to the solution of these problems.
>
> But *the fundamental issues of society* are not the kind of problem *the expert* is accustomed to handle. . . .

A little attention to transitions in revision of a paper will make it easier for a reader to follow the line of thought.

6. Beginning paragraphs

The first few sentences of a paper have a double function: they must get the subject under way, or at least get definitely started toward it, and they should interest the reader enough to make him want to read on.

Regard for the reader is particularly important in beginnings. Amateur writers are often tempted to begin with their largest generalization, or to concoct an elaborate "introduction," or to begin routinely "In this paper I am going to show," or even to open with an apology. Of course while writing the first draft the important thing usually is just to get started, and it is unwise to wait until a perfect beginning arrives. A formalized opening will let the writer get under way, but he should realize that one of the chief points of revision is to look at his first sentences to see if they really meet the reader. It is the experience of many writers that their beginning paragraphs are their worst and should be simply discarded and the paper begun, as it often can be, with the second or third paragraph, or sometimes that a new opening must be written.

The reader's attention can be picked up by putting first the part of the subject that is nearest his concern or by beginning with details that have definite human interest. Perhaps the writer can dramatize some fact by putting it in action, having people say or do something. In the more routine sorts of writing, as in reference articles or scientific and scholarly articles, the writer may begin with an exposition of background or with a set quotation or with some general statement:

> The psychiatrist's interest in matters of child training and child rearing has come to equal the interest of the professional educator in these matters as an inevitable consequence of more available knowledge concerning the causes of the various disorders of personality.

That may be a good beginning for an audience that is interested in the subject, familiar with its vocabulary, and disposed to listen or read—though they too would probably not object to something more interesting. But such a remote beginning would never win the attention of a more general or more critical group. For these readers some specific details, an anecdote, an opinion dramatized—anything with human interest—would be more appropriate.

Of the ten informational articles in one number of *The Atlantic Monthly* all but two begin with some such dramatic presentation of their subject. One of the two formal openings is in an article on rackets, a subject that is so interesting to most readers that the author could risk such an abstract opening as this:

> A racket is a specific social phenomenon. It is a form of parasitism, for the racketeer does not produce goods or services; rather, he exacts a tribute from those who do provide goods and services; he lives upon both the employer and the employee by intimidation. He permits them to pursue their normal economic functions on condition that they recognize his right to levy upon them.—GEORGE E. SOKOLSKY, "Rackets and Labor"

An article on the labor policy of the United States, a subject which is equally complex but less sensational than racketeering, is begun with a bit of drama:

> A troubled employer recently came to my office holding a copy of the National Labor Relations Act before him. He insisted upon reading aloud, in mocking tones, those first words of the Act which state its objective as being 'to diminish the cause of labor disputes burdening or obstructing interstate and foreign commerce.' The grievance of this employer was that the Act, and the way it is administered, have not minimized labor disputes, but have caused them. His sincerity could not be questioned when he placed squarely upon the new labor policy full responsibility for the strikes and dissension that had come to his own plant.—GEORGE W. TAYLOR, "Toward a National Labor Policy"

There is a striking contrast in the beginnings of two articles about people. Both begin by mentioning specific qualities, but one, about Negroes, names the qualities without describing the people who possess them, in a way most people would find lifeless and dull:

> There is a quality in the Negro that has been rarely noticed, and perhaps never adequately described. I mean his psychic power, the beauty of his recognition of mystery, and the dark poesy of his sayings.—ARCHIBALD RUTLEDGE, "Insight"

The other, a portrait of Eduard Beneš, begins by emphasizing the fundamental traits of his character, but the man is described at the same time so that the qualities seem to belong clearly to a living person:

> Small, clean-shaven, and with a melancholy bitterness about his tightly shut mouth, President Beneš is a simple man, but distinguished in his simplicity. His grave, well-cut features are dominated by intense and highly intelligent eyes. You feel at once that here is a man who has fought and won many battles. His self-possession has the unmistakable evidence of will power and intelligence. He is a self-made man in the best sense of the word.—CARL JOACHIM FRIEDRICH, "Eduard Beneš"

Such a subject as streamlined trains naturally leads to drama—though many an amateur writer would have begun with something about the history or the principles of streamlining or with a general fact about its beginning:

> The rain chased itself straight down the shatterproof plate-glass window of the streamlined train. The Chicago passengers and porters with the luggage hurried along the red carpet under the canopies to each car entrance. A half minute to eight. 'All aboard!' Along the smooth steel length of the train the steps folded up as the doors were shut—except for the observation car, where the conductor stood to see that everything was in the clear before pushing the signal button to the engineer's gong. Eight o'clock! The last door shut, its steps folded, the train slid out.—WILLIAM C. ROGERS, "Open 'er Up!"

The other articles in this issue of the *Atlantic* also begin definitely and concretely:

> When the young husband and wife, Prince Albert and Queen Victoria, began to consider the education and upbringing of their family, the memories of their own early years were much in their minds. . . . —E. F. BENSON, "Daughters of Queen Victoria"

69

The settlement of outstanding issues between London and Dublin is a good deed shining in a naughty world. For this achievement, announced on Tuesday, April 26, the Governments of Mr. Neville Chamberlain and Mr. De Valera deserve equal credit.—W. HORSFALL CARTER, "Salute to Ireland," *The Atlantic Monthly*, September, 1938

The openings of these articles suggest that it is possible and effective to begin directly with some part of the material that is to be presented and that instead of leading up to the subject it should be started at once, and started as interestingly as possible. The reader who finds himself in the very first sentence in a definite time and place very often will be led to read on. Taking thought for a possible reader in beginning to write is as important when writing a theme as when writing an article, and paying attention to the opening sentences will help remove the impression that so many themes have of being written in a void.

7. Concluding paragraphs

The last paragraph of a paper, like the beginning paragraph, has a double function: It rounds out the subject that has been discussed, and besides this it represents a final emphasis. If it is rightly done it will leave the reader with exactly the impression the writer wishes him to carry away. It should also sound like a last paragraph, that is, by its subject matter and its style it should satisfy a reader's sense of ending. The style should be distinctive to leave a good impression.

There are no rules for making a satisfying conclusion, but some typical problems and practices follow:

7a. Unemphatic conclusions. There are two types of ending that are usually unsatisfactory: (1) A concluding paragraph made up of *minor details* or references to other matters that could be discussed but are not discussed in this particular paper is usually unemphatic. It sends the reader's mind off in other directions instead of concentrating it on what has been said. It is true that every subject suggests others and is in some way related to others, and sometimes this relation should be indicated. But if it is, or if incidental matters are referred to, they should be thrown in earlier in the paper, not allowed to blur the final emphasis. (2) An *apology* as a conclusion also weakens the effect. Often a writer feels quite properly that his subject needs a better treatment than he can give it; sometimes he needs to explain why the treatment is limited in some way. But the place for such qualifications is early in the paper (though not at the beginning, because there it would make a weak start). If such explanations are made early and briefly, the ending can then represent the best the writer is capable of and form a vigorous conclusion.

7b. Typical endings. (1) SUMMARY. A mechanical summary of what has been said is rarely needed in a short paper, and such bald statements as "In this paper I have shown that . . ." are inappropriate to an informal, readable paper. If the material has been very complex or in some way difficult to follow, a summary is sometimes necessary. A summary is more in keeping with a paper that has been formally presented, especially if the stages by which the ideas have been presented have not been closely related. Even a summary should end with the particular emphasis the writer intends.

This last paragraph from an article "Architecture and Geography" enumerates three types of architecture previously discussed and then ends strongly on a restatement of the idea that the writer himself has been especially interested in:

> So at present we seem to have three architectures—the "monumental," a cosmopolitan art based upon scholarship; the "period," based upon a sentimental love of the romantic past; and the "modern," based upon a carefully unsentimental practicality. At present all alike agree to ignore locality. Classic colonnades, Tudor half-timber manors, François premier chateâux, and concrete boxes spring up from Montreal to New Orleans regardless of differences of climate and tradition. History is bad to copy from, but it is accumulated experience. It tells us that every good architecture has been local—the product of local needs, local materials, and local climate. Our present age is not so widely different from other ages as some would like to imagine. A few telephones and aeroplanes are not going to change human nature, and for us, as for our forefathers, our locality will remain the moulding feature of our lives and of our architecture.—RAMSAY TRAQUAIR, *The Atlantic Monthly*, Aug. 1938

2) SUGGESTION OF ACTION. If the article has been a criticism of some thing or situation and is especially intended to lead to some action by the reader, the last paragraph should suggest what the action is and in so far as possible how it is to be carried out. "Something ought to be done about it" is too weak to be worth saying.

Often the effect aimed for is in thought rather than in action. For this, questions are often useful, but they should be genuine questions that suggest an answer, like "What will be the result of this move?" or "Will this be done?" The questions in the selection below suggest a definite line of thought:

If Mr. Hull wants the American public to follow him in his realism, he cannot object when they ask suspiciously:

Does the British Foreign Office determine American policy in European affairs, so that we too are now committed to a "realistic" attitude toward the treaty-violating states?

To what extent are the army generals and the navy admirals, with their intimate ties to the munitions industry, coaxing the State Department to encourage the export of our military products and manufacturing designs?—MELVIN M. FAGEN, "We Built the German Air Force," *The New Republic*, Nov. 23, 1938

3) ROUNDING OUT THE IDEA. In planning a paper a writer usually puts as his last topic the most important or most revealing of his various points. If this last topic has been rightly chosen, a direct statement of it will make a satisfying ending. Articles that are primarily series of facts or incidents can be concluded by a distinctive incident. This concludes an informal account of hockey as a sport:

Not all the spirit is taken out in "fierce fun" of this sort. The game is spotted with almost legendary feats of play in emergencies. Perhaps the most famous of these occurred during the Stanley Cup series of 1928. This is a three-out-of-five-game play-off between the leaders at a season's close—the world series of hockey. The New York Rangers had lost the first game and were battling to save the second. Suddenly, in the opening period, their goalie was struck down by a puck over the eye. He couldn't continue. Good goalies are so rare no team can afford to carry spares. There was a long delay. The Rangers, apparently, were through.

Then a gray-haired man appeared on the ice with the huge goal pads and gloves on. The galleries were silent a moment, then burst into spontaneous applause at the gallant gesture. Les Patrick, out of the game since 1921 and even in his playing days not a goalie, was skating into the Ranger nets. He was the Rangers' manager. But he was going in. The crowd applauded the spirit and sat back to await the massacre. It never came. Playing with a cold frenzy, Patrick turned back the attack of one of the greatest teams in the game and the Rangers won 2 to 1. For the third game they got another goalie and went on to win the series. That stand of the gray-haired Patrick is one of the game's legends now.—ROBERT F. KELLEY, "For a Fierce Game, There's Hockey," *The New York Times Magazine*, Feb. 27, 1938

The writer of this conclusion of a book states in a more formal style the idea that he wishes the reader to carry away and carefully focuses attention on what are to him the two most important words—"courage and magnanimity":

> Before the vast magnitude of the tasks ahead, man's spirit has for the moment faltered and his vision contracted. The public mood is apprehensive where it should be bold, and defensive where broad and generous policy is most required. Everywhere men fly to new tariffs and restrictions, to nationalist policies, domestic currencies, parochial purchasing and personal hoarding—like frightened rabbits each scurrying to his own burrow. Surely it is for the moment only. Which country of us has not, but a few years since, shown the resources we now require of courage, of personal devotion, of industrial and financial leadership, of public direction, in a need no greater and in a cause less worthy? We are, if we could but grapple with our fate, the most fortunate of the generations of men. In a single lifetime science has given us more power over nature, and extended further the range of vision of the exploring mind, than in all recorded history. Now, and now only, our material resources, technical knowledge, and industrial skill, are enough to afford to every man of the world's teeming population physical comfort, adequate leisure, and access to everything in our rich heritage of civilization that he has the personal quality to enjoy. We need but the regulative wisdom to control our specialized activities and the thrusting energy of sectional and selfish interests. To face the troubles that beset us, this apprehensive and defensive world needs now above all the qualities it seems for the moment to have abandoned—courage and magnanimity.—Sir Arthur Salter, *Recovery—The Second Effort*, p. 347

This conclusion of a comment on political attitudes is informal but comes to a definite and emphatic last statement that represents the writer's main point:

> It is no fun to be a political anemic. We believe in technocratic doctrine—feel that it is sound and that steps will have to be taken. We deplore a system which tends to elevate a few persons and degrade many. Yet, so fickle is the human animal, we find ourselves deriving an unwonted pleasure from signs of better times; that's how we know we are useless to reform movements. A reformer of any stamina hates recovery—he is happiest during a depression, knowing that only when great numbers of people are miserable is there any possibility of Change. We know it, too; but when we walk out in the cool of the afternoon and see shopkeepers sprucing up and stores looking busy and people sitting in cafés and having a good time, believe us it takes all our strength not to feel good about it, for we have

very little capacity for sustained dismality. We're not defending our temperament, merely pointing out a paradox: that Utopia's best friends are its worst enemies.—"Utopia's Friends," *The New Yorker*, May 25, 1935

7c. Style. The style of the final paragraph, as these examples have shown, is of special importance because it contributes conspicuously to the tone, whether it is a tone of humor, simple directness, encouragement, impressiveness, or some other. This means that the last paragraph should be especially scrutinized in revision to take out empty phrases, false phrases, and anything that might detract from the intended effect. It means also that the phrasing may need to be intensified slightly, that the words should be meaningful and, when possible, suggestive. In short, the ending should be as well expressed as you can make it, and the last sentence, the last phrase, should if possible be both exact and happy.

Exercises

The exercises of Chapter 3 are to emphasize the form of paragraphs, especially the continuity of thought.

1. Find in a book or magazine (not in a story) a good paragraph from 200 to 400 words long, discussing an idea. Copy it either in longhand or on the typewriter, as you ordinarily write your themes. Count the number of words and observe the space it requires in the form you use in writing your own papers.

*Pages 59-60   2. Pick out the topic sentence in the paragraph copied. Trace the thought connection through the paragraph, picking out words and phrases which show the relation of the individual sentences to each other or which indicate steps in the movement of the thought, as in §4.

*Pages 62-63   3. Are important ideas in the paragraph given strong emphasis? Does the paragraph end strongly? Does it introduce any new idea at the end? Write a general comment on the paragraph as a whole.

*Pages 56-58   4. Make a word-count of the paragraphs in one of your recent papers and consider their length in the light of §2 (Length of Paragraphs) in this chapter. If you find them conspicuously longer or shorter than typical paragraphs, look at them to see if they are appropriate to the material. If not, make notes of what you can do to bring them in line with typical paragraphs.

*Pages 63-65   5. In each of the following paragraphs find the topic sentence. Trace the movement of the writer's thought, dividing it where you can into steps. Pick out specific words or phrases which indicate successive steps, changes of direction, or the relation of ideas. What is the relation of the last sentence in each paragraph to the topic sentence and to the whole paragraph?

1. A fourth way in which our economic order creates friction between workers and business owners is by its selling and advertising activities. It is one of the strangest phenomena of modern industry that business men, who least of all desire unrest, should spend millions upon millions each year in creating it. In comparison with the expenditures of business organizations for the purpose of making people dissatisfied, those of the I. W. W. and other fomenters of discontent are small indeed. Nevertheless, the deliberate and systematic stimulation of dissatisfaction by industrial establishments appears to be an inherent characteristic of free capitalistic enterprise. It is inevitable that business houses should seek to extend their sales. To do this, they endeavor to make people desire things which they do not possess, to render them dissatisfied with their lot, to get them to aspire to a higher—or at least a more expensive—standard of living. Influenced by salesmen and advertising experts and emulative consumption—which in turn is skilfully stimulated by business enterprises—the wage earner's wants increase more rapidly than his earnings. What is more natural than that, feeling intensely the need for greater income, he should regard his income as unfairly low? As long as business spends huge sums on carefully planned efforts to make people discontented, individual enterprises must expect relations with their workers to be strained.—SUMNER H. SCHLICHTER, "The Organization and Control of Economic Activity," *The Trend of Economics*, edited by R. G. TUGWELL, p. 350

2. The defects of the present content and outlook of humanistic education as a preparation for leadership in a democratic society may all be summed up in the single statement that knowledge is encouraged as a means to more knowledge instead of being a means to action. The only part of the educational curriculum which makes demands on *ability to do* in contradistinction to *facility of expression* is experimental science. So individuals with conspicuous executive capacity, *i.e.*, ability to do as opposed to ability to dispute, are attracted to the natural sciences. Since neither natural science nor any form of manual craftsmanship are obligatory, nothing is done to develop general competence in those who elect a course of social studies because they lack constructive aptitude. The machinery of educational selection therefore operates to recruit the nation's statesmen from those who can talk glibly, write elegantly and argue forcibly without the capacity to act competently. When the need for

75

action is urgent, they can only continue to talk glibly, write elegantly and argue forcibly. If democracy can produce only leaders who can talk it is doomed, and we can only hope to preserve it by a policy of educational selection which favors competence more than fluency.—LANCELOT T. HOGBEN, *Retreat from Reason*, p. 11

3. We are inclined to look upon ourselves as the products of a growth from within, upon the unfolding of our personality as something that would have been the same upon Crusoe's manless island as it has been in the particular social environment of which we are a part. No belief could be more erroneous. The ideas that guide our lives and make us what we are have all been thrust upon us from without. Whether our outlook and attitudes, our manners and beliefs and prejudices shall be those of Australian aborigines, of ancient Romans or of twentieth century Americans depends not on ourselves but on the social environment into which we happen to have been born. Had there been no social environment, had we been shut off from earliest infancy from all human intercourse, we would have had neither outlook and manners, nor beliefs and prejudices, but would instead have been just a part of the animal creation around us, set off solely by the greater cunning of our brain. It is through society that we became what we are; through society that we became human.—JOHN A. UDMARK, *The Road We Have Covered*, p. 43

4. Many a night at the ringside I have heard laymen sitting in the forward rows explain to their ladies that the punishment which wrestlers inflict on one another really does not hurt them as they are used to it and cannot feel, anyway. This is of a piece with the assumption that the fishworm cannot feel. I am not sure that it is true. The fishworm wiggles and squirms when it is put upon the hook and the wrestler trumpets terribly and wooshes and writhes when it is being twisted in the ring. This may only mean that some vague intuition, such as turtles possess, is telling the wrestler not to go over on its back. Yet the wrestler is so amenable to training that it is comparatively easy to teach it to recognize a signal and, in violation of a strong natural instinct, to roll over on its back momentarily after thirty or forty minutes of wrestling, while the referee gives its adversary a slap on the shoulder signifying that it has won the contest.—WESTBROOK PEGLER, "Are Wrestlers People?" *The Bedside Esquire*, (1940), pp. 515-16

5. Here it was as if the pulse of life in plant and beast and man had slowed almost to immobility, taking its beat from the land itself, which had all eternity in which to change. Here life was marooned, and Time, like a slowly turning wheel, was

only night and day, night and day, summer and winter, birth and death, the ebb and swell of tides. Nothing showed for the passing of the ages but a minutely changing coastline, an infinitesimal wearing away of mountains, a barely discernible lifting of coral reefs. Still the ancient grass tree thrust its tall spear towards the sky; still the platypus laid its eggs and suckled its young as it had done in primeval times; and still through the high tops of the gum trees the blue thread of smoke from the black man's fire wavered into the uncorrupted air.—ELEANOR DARK, *The Timeless Land*, p. 9

6. Stories of unrest and food shortage coming out of Italy may be officially inspired and intended to deceive, but they need not be without a solid kernel of fact. Spring is the time of unrest, as men and women have known since the beginning of time. Spring brings the high peak in food shortage, as we have seen in our own times. It is simply the case that May 1 is seven or eight months since the last harvest and that the cupboard has been scraped bare.

Spring is also the beginning of the second planting season, and one of the commonest tragedies in the annals of the race is a starving agricultural population facing the bitter choice of eating its seed corn or putting it into the ground. Spring is the season for famine as well as for military offensives.—"Topics of the Times," *The New York Times*, May 2, 1942

6. In the same way study some of the paragraphs used as examples in this book, such as those on pages 108-113.

7. Each of the following paragraphs or groups of paragraphs is unsatisfactory in one or more ways: interrupted movement, change of direction, weak ending, lack of emphasis on important points, or even failure to group separate ideas together (over-paragraphing). Be ready to discuss in class the flaws in the organization of each paragraph. If possible, reorganize the material and rewrite each paragraph effectively. If it is not possible to build a good paragraph out of the material offered, or most of it, write a paragraph of your own explaining why it is impossible and suggesting changes of material. *Pages 62-63

1. Now, with the realization that there is a need for conservation and with increased protection, birds are increasing in numbers. Many states rear and restock game birds to prevent extinction. Animals killed for fur are now trying to be saved in all countries. The years 1919-21 brought about the sale of over one hundred million skins which were unfit to sell. Among these there were fourteen million muskrats, twenty-four million moles, and thirteen million opossums. It is easy to see why fur-bearers are getting scarce. Even during the time of depression nearly

five hundred thousand skins valued at nearly two and a quarter million dollars were shipped from Alaska. Many furs are worn in the summer time, which is quite useless. Women should remember that wool makes good clothes which are for winter use and does not require the death of its producer.

2. The average freshman upon entering college is faced with many personal adjustments. Probably for the first time in his life he finds that he has responsibilities. I know that I, for one, had to make these adjustments and face these responsibilities. Also I think that a large number of the upper class students have to face the problem, to a lesser extent, of organizing themselves again for the new college year.

My personal feeling about this change is the ease with which it is accomplished.

After three months of golf, sleeping, traveling and complete freedom I find it practically no hardship whatsoever to step back into the simple routine of college life. I no longer have that restless feeling that accompanies aimless living. I have found in these first few days that it is just this simple routine that I missed so much during the vacation.

Eating and sleeping somewhat regularly as compared with summer living is certainly a happy and healthful adjustment.

Classes and outside preparation do have their disadvantages but the satisfaction of getting something accomplished and the prospect of a few extra qualifications is ample reward.

Looking now into the future is also equally pleasant as it was this summer. Overlooking classes, a golf game next Sunday afternoon is more anxiously awaited than an ordinary golf game. In the same way that date at Skidmore will be worth two at home, and an occasional bull-session with friends in somebody's room can't be topped.

3. Safety is one of the biggest community projects under way at the present time. Education has taken upon itself to teach the youth of America to be careful and, in some cities, how to handle cars. Town meetings bring in speakers to talk on the subject and cultivate the true meaning of care on the highway. Safety posters are tacked to every other tree in town with the captions "Drive Carefully," "Not Over 50," "Obey Traffic Signals," and so on. One week a year is set aside as Safety Week, and drives are put on by the schools and town officials to create safety in the home and on the street. In the other 51 weeks we make up for the damage we didn't do during that "sacred" week. Automobile manufacturers come out with new safety devices and convince the public they are put on the car for the safety of the passengers. Yet they make cars that will travel 65, 75, and 80 miles an hour. With all these safety precautions there still

remains the fact that over 40,000 lives are snuffed out each year through automobile accidents, and the injured figure climbs up into the millions.

4. I know how powerful this rhythm can be for I played drums in many swing bands until two years ago. I've seen hundreds make fools of themselves—unashamed. They know what they're doing and they love it. Why is it possible for Benny Goodman's band to make $1,250,000 for playing at a theater in New York City for one week if the public doesn't love it? But our question is—why is there so much appeal in this type of music for the younger generation? They are the children of the parents who condemn them and the music. There must be something wrong someplace. which makes these children go seemingly insane every time someone beats a drum. Maybe the emotions of these people are so restricted that they will readily accept anything that will offer them a channel for release. But *it is* going too far, and *that* is my point. It is playing a too important part in the lives of the young people. This of course is not true for everyone—for what is—but it is true for the great majority.

8. The following passage was published in eight paragraphs. Study it to see where you think there should be paragraph breaks and be prepared to give your reasons. You may have more or less than eight. *Pages 55-56

As I walked out of the building two women ran up to me. "Oh, Mrs. Lindbergh," said one, "the women of America are so anxious to know about your clothes." "And I," said the other, "want to write a little article about your housekeeping in the ship. Where do you put the lunch boxes?" I felt depressed, as I generally do when women reporters ask me conventionally feminine questions. I feel as they must feel when they are given those questions to ask. I feel slightly insulted. Over in the corner my husband is being asked vital masculine questions, clean-cut steely technicalities or broad abstractions. But I am asked about clothes and lunch boxes. . . . I turned to look at the plane. Perched on top of the big pontoons, it seemed small and dainty. They were rolling it down the pier. I thought of all the emergency equipment for North and South, land and water, all parts of the world, packed into that little space. I thought of the two of us, ready to go in it anywhere, and I had a sense of our self-contained insularity. Islands feel like this, I am sure, and walled cities, and sometimes men. It was ready now; we could get in. "No, thank you, I don't need a ladder to climb up." A mechanic was just clambering out of my cockpit. I had a moment to wait and watch the crowd. A radio announcer was speaking into his microphone. "Mrs. Lindbergh," he started smoothly, with a glance at me, "is wearing a leather flying helmet and leather coat, and high leather flying boots." "Why!" I thought blankly, looking down at a costume which did not correspond at all to his description. What nonsense! It was much too hot to wear leather. The sun beat down on my bare head and sticky cotton blouse; the hot planks of the pier burned through my thin rubber sneakers. What made him say that, I wondered. Oh, of course, it isn't the conventional flying costume. They have to say that I am dressed in leather. I see, you needn't bother to tell me again, I thought, looking at the announcer. I know, "The Great Radio Public must not be disappointed!" The spray sluiced over the windshield as we started to take off—faster now—we were up on the step—we were trying to get off the water. I held my breath after each pounding spank as the pontoons skipped along from wave to wave. Weighed down with its heavy test load of fuel, the plane felt clumsy, like a duck with clipped wings. It met the coming wave quivering after each effort to rise. Now the spanks were closer together—quick, sharp jolts. I put my hand on the receiving set. It was shaking violently. Suddenly all vibration smoothed out. Effortlessly we rose; we were off; a long curve upward.—ANNE MORROW LINDBERGH, *North to the Orient*, pp. 38-41

Kinds of Paragraphs

WHEN A PERSON is writing, he is thinking of his material, of what he is saying, rather than of the form in which he is saying it. He is not interested in describing the kinds of sentences or paragraphs he is putting on paper. But for purposes of study it is useful once in a while to analyze what he has done and see if there are ways in which he can improve. The analysis is somewhat arbitrary, since the continuous communication is the important thing, but without it we cannot describe or discuss our writing in any detail. Sometimes conscious analysis will bring to light faults and make improvement possible, and often it will make clear exactly what we are doing.

The basis for classifying paragraphs is the kind of relationship that exists between the individual statements made. These statements, the raw materials of paragraphs, are either *details*—reference in words to things, people, feelings, real or imaginary events that can be specifically represented; or *ideas*—interpretations, opinions, general statements that our minds make. In writing, these statements stand one after the other but are related in such a way that they make a continuous communication.

There are three sorts of relation between statements: *chronological*, a relation through time; *impressionistic*, a relation that depends on the qualities of the writer's impressions; and *logical*, an objective relation depending on meaning that can be tested by anyone properly qualified in the material.

No one would sit down to write specifically a certain kind of paragraph, except as a practice exercise. The kinds are often found in combination, though one is usually more important and really controlling. But by an analysis of this sort some of the qualities and possibilities of writing can be emphasized and perhaps the way pointed to more effective presentation of our ideas because of the way they are formed into paragraphs.

1. Chronological paragraphs

Probably the most common, and certainly the easiest, movement in speaking and writing is chronological, the movement in narratives of real or imagined events. In conversation we give accounts of what I did, what we did, what they did; and we write accounts of personal experiences, autobiographies, biographies, explanations of how things are done, processes, and so on; or we may write fiction—short stories and novels.

1a. The time relation. The connection between statements in a chronological paragraph is usually simple. Time controls. One detail appears after another as they happened in time or as they are imagined to have happened. The verbs usually carry this sequence, and the continuity is made stronger by the continuation of the same subject from one sentence to another. The time may be emphasized and made more obvious by adverbs—*then, after this, before, soon, when, in a few days*—or by adverbial clauses: *When he got to the corner . . . . After the last dance . . . .*

*Exercise 4, p. 114

Indicating the verbs and adverbs of time in this opening paragraph of a short story shows how large a part time plays in narrative:

> Elizabeth Montgomery *woke up in the morning* wondering whether or not she *was* engaged. She *had been out* with Bob McEwen *the night before* and *at the end* there *had been* some spontaneous and apparently serious love-making. That is, she *knew* she *must have felt* pretty serious about it because *this morning* she *couldn't remember* where she *had put* her gloves. And *now* he *had left* for Chicago *for a few days* and he *had promised to write.*—SALLY BENSON, *People Are Fascinating,* p. 27

Similarly in the following paragraph from Ernest Hemingway's re-creation of a morning's hunting in Africa, the time

82

movement is emphasized by a few adverbs ("in the morning," "finally") and even more accurately by time clauses ("when we came out on the shoulder," "as the sun rose and lighted the opposite slopes," "while we watched"); but the actual sequence is carried simply by the verbs, each continuing the action that has been started. There is one explanatory interruption ("Animals on a plain can see so far that they have confidence . . ."), but almost every word shows us some picture or bit of action Hemingway has chosen to give from the morning's experience.

In the morning Karl and his outfit started for the salt-lick and Garrick, Abdullah, M'Cola and I crossed the road, angled behind the village up a dry watercourse and started climbing the mountains in a mist. We headed up a pebbly, boulder-filled, dry stream bed overgrown with vines and brush so that, climbing, you walked, stooping, in a steep tunnel of vines and foliage. I sweated so that I was soaked through my shirt and undergarments and when we came out on the shoulder of the mountain and stood, looking down at the bank of clouds quilting over the entire valley below us, the morning breeze chilled me and I had to put on my raincoat while we glassed the country. I was too wet with sweat to sit down and I signed Garrick to keep on going. We went around one side of the mountain, doubled back on a higher grade and crossed over, out of the sun that was drying my wet shirt and along the top of a series of grassy valleys, stopping to search each one thoroughly with the field glasses. Finally we came to a sort of amphitheatre, a bowl-like valley of very green grass with a small stream down the middle and timber along the far side and all the lower edge. We sat in the shadow against some rocks, out of any breeze, watching with the glasses as the sun rose and lighted the opposite slopes, seeing two kudu cows and a calf feed out from the timber, moving with the quickly browsing, then head lifted, long staring vigilance of all browsing animals in a forest. Animals on a plain can see so far that they have confidence and feed very differently from animals in the woods. We could see the vertical white stripes on their gray flanks and it was very satisfying to watch them and to be high in the mountain that early in the morning. Then, while we watched, there was a boom, like a rockslide. I thought at first it was a boulder falling, but M'Cola whispered.—ERNEST HEMINGWAY, *Green Hills of Africa*, pp. 170-72

Since narrative is usually of events that have happened or of a story that is told as though it had happened, it is usually written in the past tense. Occasionally for liveliness, especially when the passage is largely descriptive and records vivid feelings or vivid sense impressions, the present tense is used. This "historical present" is used by D. H. Lawrence in describing the bustle (note the verbs) and the sensations of his leaving Palermo:

> Our ship is hooting for all she's worth. An important last-minuter comes surging up. The rope hawsers are being wound clankily in. Seagulls—they are never very many in the Mediterranean—seagulls whirl like a few flakes of snow in the upper chill air. Clouds spin. And without knowing it we are evaporating away from the shore, from our mooring, between the great *City of Trieste* and another big black steamer that lies like a wall. . . . Slowly, slowly we turn round: and as the ship turns, our hearts turn. Palermo fades from our consciousness; the Naples boat, the disembarking crowds, the rattling carriages to the land, all fades from our heart. We see only the open gap of the harbour entrance, and the level, pale-grey void of the sea beyond. There are wisps of gleamy light—out there.—D. H. LAWRENCE, *Sea and Sardinia*, p. 41

*Tenses of verbs, § 3

As a rule the past tense should be used unless there is some definite reason for using the present; and meaningless changes in tense should be avoided.

1b. The unit of narrative. Since a narrative is usually continuous, breaking it into paragraphs is somewhat arbitrary. In most fiction and matter intended for rapid reading, the paragraphs are rather short. A new paragraph represents a new emphasis, a new focus of attention in the action, or a change in time, or movements of a different person (the real reason for paragraphing the speeches in a conversation). The following are typical paragraphs from fiction:

*Conversation

> There were a lot of people at the Shepherdsons' and the Shepherdsons' dog, Juniper, had crawled under the couch the way he always did when there was a lot of noise. The blond girl in the white satin dress was trying to coax him out. "Come Juniper," she called. "Come get the rats! Rats, Juniper!" But he only crawled farther under the couch, where he lay with his head on his paws and trembled.
>
> Mrs. Shepherdson came across the room with a strange man in tow. She walked across the room looking very determined, the way hostesses do when they have a lot of people on their hands. "Elise," she said, "I'd like you to meet Mr. Martin. He's from Minneapolis and he doesn't know anybody. So get up off the floor and take him under your wing, like a darling."
>
> Elise got up from the floor and brushed herself off a little. "Dog hairs," she explained. "He's shedding. Are you really from Minneapolis, Mr. Martin? Imagine!"

Mr. Martin said that he was, and they sat down on the couch together.

"I was engaged once to a man from Minneapolis," she told him. "Maybe you know him. His name was Sidney something. Let's see, it was Sidney Hitchcock or Babcock or something. Did you ever know anyone named Sidney Babcock?"

Mr. Martin thought a minute and then said he didn't believe he had.—SALLY BENSON, "Hotel Child," *People Are Fascinating,* p. 226

A writer of fiction may have longer paragraphs to emphasize continuity or singleness of impression. The following paragraph from a novel is full of consecutive details, the thoughts and feelings of the second wife who is looking at the room of her predecessor. It illustrates one of the chief advantages of fiction, that the writer can imagine his narrative more completely than can one who is writing about real people, who always escape his knowledge in some important respects. A story writer may know his people completely, not only their appearance, the things they do, their conversation, but even their thoughts and feelings, and these thoughts are part of the narrative.

I had expected to see chairs and tables swathed in dust-sheets, and dust-sheets too over the great double bed against the wall. Nothing was covered up. There were brushes and combs on the dressing-table, scent, and powder. The bed was made up, I saw the gleam of white linen on the pillow-case, and the tip of a blanket beneath the quilted coverlet. There were flowers on the dressing-table and on the table beside the bed. Flowers too on the carved mantelpiece. A satin dressing-gown lay on a chair, and a pair of bedroom slippers beneath. For one desperate moment I thought that something had happened to my brain, that I was seeing back into Time, and looking upon the room as it used to be, before she died. . . . In a minute Rebecca herself would come back into the room, sit down before the looking-glass at her dressing-table, humming a tune, reach for her comb and run it through her hair. If she sat there I should see her reflection in the glass, and she would see me too, standing like this by the door. Nothing happened. I went on standing there, waiting for something to happen. It was the clock ticking on the wall that brought me to reality again. The hands stood at twenty-five past four. My watch said the same. There was something sane and comforting about the ticking of the clock. It reminded me of the present, and that tea would soon be ready for me on the lawn. I walked slowly into the middle of the room. No, it was not used. It was not lived in any more. Even the flowers could not destroy the musty smell. The curtains were drawn and the shutters were closed. Rebecca would never come back to the room again. Even if Mrs. Danvers did put flowers on the mantelpiece and the sheets upon the bed, they would not bring her back. She was dead. She had been dead now for a year. She lay buried in the crypt of the church with all the other dead de Winters.—DAPHNE DU MAURIER, *Rebecca*, pp. 196-97

The paragraphs in biography and history and other narratives of fact, especially if they are first published in book form, are likely to be somewhat longer. The first of these paragraphs from an autobiography might have been broken into at least three, but Mr. Steffens was more interested in the total impression and the meaning of the action than in the drama itself. Lincoln Steffens had promised Israel W. Durham, one-time political boss of Philadelphia, to tell him just before his death what his "real sin" had been. In his last illness Durham had wired, "Come; you promised to," and Steffens tells the story of their meeting, which gives in dramatic form a fundamental point about American politics:

That interview—Durham's story pieced out with pertinent parts of other bosses' stories, the boyhood of Charlie Murphy, the Tammany boss, and President Roosevelt's description of Senator Matt Quay on his death-bed—I wrote all this as fiction under the title *The Dying Boss*. The plain facts are that Durham, weak and stricken, told me that he was ready, at last, to hear what his "real sin" was, and I said that it was disloyalty. He was shocked and incredulous. Since he held that loyalty was his chief and perhaps his one virtue, since he had never gone back on his friends, and—whatever else he had done, which was a-plenty—since he had been always a true, square friend, my charge was totally unexpected and hardly believable. And my argument, as it gradually convinced him, was devastating. He was a born leader of the common people, I reasoned; he had taught them to like and to trust him, even with their votes; he had gathered up and organized the power which lay in their ballots, their trust and their loyalty to him; and he, the good fellow, had taken his neighbors' faith and sovereignty and turned it into franchises and other grants of the common wealth, which he and his gang had sold to rich business men and other enemies of the people. He was a traitor to his own. He had asked for it straight, I gave it him—straight, and he got it. Not one word of evasion or excuse. He took it lying down, and all he said after a long, wan silence was: "Say, I sure ought to go to hell for that, and what'll they do to me? Do you think they'll set me on fire for—for what you said—disloyalty?"

I had to repair the damage I had done. I had to say something to reassure him; he looked as if he would faint. So I asked him what he did to fellows in his gang that went back on him. He said that he didn't do much; he let 'em go. Well, I answered, as brutally as I could put it, didn't he believe that his God was as merciful and forgiving as he, "Iz" Durham, was? He got that, too. He looked better, and he lingered longer than the doctors had predicted.—LINCOLN STEFFENS, *Autobiography*, pp. 418-19

The real function of chronological paragraphs is to represent the units of the action that the writer wishes to mark off, to emphasize.

1c. Common faults in chronological paragraphs. Chronological paragraphs, whether of fact or fiction, are the easiest of the three main types. No difficulty is likely except from a lack of detail, or from the unnecessary intrusion of general statements or interpretations that interrupt the narrative or from a change in point of view.

1. Lack of detail is fatal, because it is only by means of the small particular actions that we see what is going on. In the following from an account of a personal experience we are not told enough so that we can hear the girl's accent or picture the happening.

> Her accent was continental and pleasant to hear. I liked her almost immediately. I wanted to find out all about her life, her present journey, and her flight from Europe.
>
> The headlights of the bus pushed the night away and we were in Virginia. I called her Joan and she thought Herbie was a funny name. We talked like old friends who had been apart for years and had just met again. She was a Swiss who had fled with her family before the war was very old.

A boy who had told elaborately of preparations for a particular baseball game ended his paper with this paragraph, which gives a reader no clue at all to what really happened:

> The game itself did not prove to be an exceptional one. I know that I, for one, played in better games that summer and I might add I also played better games as an individual. Even so, it will be a very long time before I forget this great experience.

The reader wonders why the game will be so hard to forget.

2. As a rule the narrative should run continuously without being interrupted by comment or interpretation. If the comment is unavoidable it should be kept brief and so far as possible be done in terms of the narrative. The following paragraph has a crude interruption, here set inside brackets:

It was the seventh of August, 1940. My friend and I were hitching from one of the towns in the northern part of the state. Unlike most adventurers I did not notice the sky nor did I feel the impending danger. [I guess I don't make a very good hero. Now I must get back to my story.] After waiting a few minutes we were picked up by two men in an old Chevvie.

3. Change in point of view is generally unconvincing. Usually a paragraph of narrative should keep the same point of view, not shift from one actor or group of actors to another.

The four of us went in, laughing and pushing each other around. We sat in a booth in the back corner and noisily ordered our drinks. [Shift:] The bartender thought that he would be in for some trouble before long. He began to be very busy but kept throwing an eye in our direction. [Return to original point of view:] We kept up our racket and arranged for Eppie and Lew to stage a friendly little scrap.

2. Impressionistic paragraphs

The basis of the second type of paragraph relation lies in the writer's senses and in the associations already existing in his mind. To show this, simply ask two or more people to describe a scene. They may mention the same conspicuous details, but they will almost certainly put them in a different order, and they will choose and arrange differently the less conspicuous details. The selection and order depend on the interests and past associations of the writer, and it is these that make the paragraph a unit and not a mere enumeration of separate details. Without the unity that comes from an observer's mind we have merely a chaotic series of details that do not fuse into a picture, as in this bit from a story:

"Come on, kids, let's go out on the porch and make plans," suggested Jeanne. She was a tall blonde of seventeen, a couple of years younger than her five guests. Good teeth were prominent in the smile that was almost constantly on her small, round face. She grabbed Don Mumford's hand and half-pulled him along with her. Her actions and her slim figure were like her mother's.

2a. Descriptive paragraphs. Although a good deal has been written about a science or art of descriptive writing, the key to successful pictures in words seems to lie in the mind of the writer. So long as he puts down details that he recalls (or for fiction, that he imagines) more or less in the order that they

*Exercise 3, p. 114

impress him, he is probably safe. Systematic description, going, for instance, from top to bottom or from left to right in a scene, may be necessary in certain types of expository writing, as in reference works and handbooks; but for more general writing *the task is to focus the reader's attention first on what would strike an actual observer's attention and then to fill in the rest of the picture with details more or less in the way in which they would be observed.*

This means that conspicuous details will stand out, and those that have keen suggestiveness will stand out, and that many others will be run over quickly. The scene will be bounded in space, that is, it will be limited by the area to which the observer is directing his attention, but the relation between the details is not spatial. It depends on the senses, attention, and associations of the writer.

In the following descriptive paragraph, the individual statements are linked in part by pronouns and other typical machinery of paragraph continuity and in part by spatial words (*here and there, beyond*). In spite of some literary embroidery, the immediate sense impressions of Mr. Franck are the basis for the blending of sight and sound in the description of Cuzco, and its essential unity comes from the pattern the scene made in his mind.'

But more striking even than prehistoric ruins is the view of Cuzco from the foot of the inevitable wooden cross at the summit of Sacsahuama. So steep is the hill on this side, and so close to the town, that it seems almost to bulge out over it, and all the Imperial city lies spread out beneath, as from an aeroplane, its every plaza and patio in full view to its very depths, the activities of every family as plainly visible as if some magic wand had lifted away the concealing roofs. Here and there, even on a Sunday, an Indian in crude-colored garments and his pancake hat crawls along the fortress hill behind his oxen and wooden plow, with the Imperial city of his forefathers as a background. Beyond, the greenish valley of the Huatenay stretches away southward between velvety-brown, wrinkled hills, the four royal highways diverging from the main plaza as principal streets and sallying forth to the "Four Corners of the Earth" as directly as the configurations of the Andes permit. But always the eye drifts back to the city below, spread out in every slightest detail. Under the Incas it may have been "bright and shining with gold and gay with color, its long and narrow streets, crossing each other at right angles with perfect regularity, adorned with beautiful palaces and temples"; even to-day, under the rays of the unclouded Andean sun, it is a scene no mere words can bring to him who has not looked down upon it in person. The soft red of its aged tile roofs and the rich brown of its bulking churches leaves no need for golden adornment. The Sunday-morning noises come up distinctly—school-boys playing in the patios of monasteries, fighting-cocks haughtily challenging the world to combat, a weary bell booming a belated summons, the half-barbarous, half-inspiring screech of trumpets rising as a regiment of the garrison that keeps Cuzco loyal to "those degenerate negroes of Lima" sets out on a march; yet all blending together into a sort of pagan music that carries the imagination back to the pre-Conquest days of long ago.—HARRY A. FRANCK, *Vagabonding Down the Andes*, p. 452

The details may be chosen and held together for some mood or purpose of the writer, as for mild satire in the beginning of Margaret Halsey's view of Westminster Abbey:

The north transept of Westminster Abbey, by which you go in, is tall and shadowy, like a church, and has a churchly smell, but it is so stuffed with monuments and plaques that the traveler automatically begins to look around for price tags.—MARGARET HALSEY, *With Malice Toward Some*, pp. 47-48

Or they may be chosen and unified by some particular sense impression, as for color in this:

The brown earth turned dark and the trees glistened. The cut ends of the stubble turned black with mildew; the haystacks grayed from exposure to the damp, and on the roofs the moss, which had been all summer as gray as lizards, turned a brilliant yellow-green.—JOHN STEINBECK, *The Long Valley*, p. 222

In short stories and novels the descriptions of people are now less like posed studio photographs and more like candid camera shots. The details seem to be casually presented, and usually the character is doing something, so that the picture is relieved by bits of action and especially by his thoughts and feelings. In this way the reader meets the character more naturally.

The first of the two following paragraphs, from a short story, shows a small but revealing handful of impressions; the second, from a novel, a fuller portrait with more action. Note that both women are "described" in a definite time and place, and that the settings become quite "real."

Snow fell softly and the sidewalks were wet but Mrs. Rose Carey had on her galoshes and enjoyed feeling thick snow crunching underfoot. She walked slowly, big flakes falling on her lamb coat and clinging to hair over her ears, the lazily falling snow giving her, in her thick warm coat, a fine feeling of self-indulgence. She stood on the corner of Bloor and Yonge, an impressive build of a woman, tall, stout, good-looking for forty-two, and watched the traffic signal.—MORLEY CALLAGHAN, "An Escapade," A *Native Argosy*, p. 135

The man sitting beside Jenny continued to puff steadfastly at his pipe, lost in the news, holding mechanically in his further hand the return ticket which would presently be snatched by the hurrying tram-conductor. He was a shabby middle-aged clerk with a thin beard, and so he had not the least interest for Jenny, whose eye was caught by other beauties than those of assiduous labour. She had not even to look at him to be quite sure that he did not matter to her. Almost, Jenny did not care whether he had glanced sideways at herself or not. She presently gave a quiet sigh of relief as at length the river was left behind and the curious nervous tension—no more lasting than she might have felt at seeing a man balancing upon a high window-sill—was relaxed. She breathed more deeply, perhaps, for a few instants; and then, quite naturally, she looked at her reflection in the sliding glass. That hat, as she could see in the first sure speed-less survey, had got the droops. "See about you!" she said silently and threateningly, jerking her head. The hat trembled at the motion, and was thereafter ignored. Stealthily Jenny went back to her own reflection in the window, catching the clearly-chiseled profile of her face, bereft in the dark mirror of all its colour. She could see her nose and chin quite white, and her lips as part of the general colourless gloom. A little white brooch at her neck stood boldly out; and that was all that could be seen with any clearness, as the light was not directly over-head. Her eyes were quite lost, apparently, in deep shadows. Yet she could not resist the delight of continuing narrowly to examine herself. The face she saw was hardly recognizable as her own; but it was bewitchingly pale, a study in black and white, the kind of face which, in a man, would at once have drawn her attention and stimulated her curiosity. She had longed to be pale, but the pallor she was achieving by millinery work in a stuffy room was not the marble whiteness which she had desired. Only in the sliding window could she see her face ideally trans-figured. There it had the brooding dimness of strange poetic romance. You couldn't know about that girl, she thought. You'd want to know about her. You'd wonder all the time about her, as though she had a secret. . . . The reflection became curiously distorted. Jenny was smiling to herself.—FRANK SWIN-NERTON, *Nocturne*, pp. 14-15

The chief danger in descriptive movement, as in chronological, is that it will be interrupted by a different kind of material, by comment or by a general statement of fact, which will take the reader away from the picture that is being shown. To avoid this and any change in point of view, *simply imagine as you are writing that you are actually facing the scene and put down what you "see with your mind's eye."* Everyday writing offers so many opportunities for practice that a little attention should soon develop a sure handling of details. Putting a little more actual picture and scene into your letters, making the account a little fuller than a careless writing would make them, is a good way to start.

2b. Subjectively selected series of facts. Many paragraphs of facts are not built on a logical plan but represent some more informal associations in the writer's mind. The paragraph may be an enumeration of details that are held together by some feeling or attitude, by the recollection of some experience. The reader is led from one bit to another, surrendering himself to the train of association or to the succession of images, and if the writer's mind is interesting or important, the reader is pleasantly rewarded. This extract shows a rather elementary example of that type of movement:

*Exercise 2, pp. 113-14

> I believe that the most efficient people are seldom the most charming. For a journey of any length I believe a companion to be essential. I am dead against the current system of trial by jury. I do not like men who talk business during dinner or children who ask unanswerable questions. I find it increasingly difficult to lie successfully over the telephone.
>
> I prefer the soft, blue haze of twilight to the cold, harsh glare of dawn, and a night splashed with stars to both. I know of few people who are able to wear sudden wealth with grace. I am unable to subscribe to the modern passion for disguising a transatlantic liner as a combination teagarden-supper club, and believe there is nothing the least disgraceful about a ship's looking like a ship.—CHARLES G. SHAW, "How I Look at Things in General," *The New Yorker*, April 25, 1931

These seemingly random details suggest a definite point of view. Structurally they are related by the parallel form of the statements and by the continuance of the subject (*I*) and by the use of a series of verbs naming the writer's attitudes (*believe, am dead against, do not like, prefer . . .*). The paragraphs gain a sort of emphasis from the especially striking details that stand last.

A naturalist trying to give an impression of autumn cannot be logical, nor can he present a single particular scene. He will usually select impressions that have for him a special appeal and that can lead the reader to a similar understanding, as Mr. Peattie has done in this selection (one of three paragraphs on autumn):

Autumn is the blooming of the goldenrod all through the oak woods and across the fields. Autumn is the cricket's cry, the swarming of the monarch and the storms of the Lisa butterfly. It is the odor of leaf fires, the smell of crushed marigold leaves, of tansy, and the sharp terebinthine scent of walnut husks that look so apple green and leave so brown a stain.—D. C. PEATTIE, *An Almanac for Moderns*, (September 15)

The *New Yorker* frequently combines a series of "clues to the mystery of our time" from its random collection of clipings, letters, and publicity releases. The sheer interest of the individual items gives them a certain value, though the assembling is casual.

We would like to call attention this week to Deputy Warden Herman J. Ruthazer of the Raymond Street Jail, in Brooklyn, who says "Everybody's happy here since we put in the new cafeterias," and to the twenty-five Westchester horses who will carry on their backs the twenty-five horseback-riding air wardens who have volunteered for service; to Police Commissioner Valentine for ordering all milkmen in the city to be fingerprinted, and to Dr. Gilbert H. Fletcher, who, returning from Lisbon, says that the Nazis are circulating counterfeit American dollars in the occupied countries; to Jesse Jones, who received with equanimity the announcement that the Japanese Welfare Ministry is going to hand out a million rubber balls for young Japanese people to play catch with, and to Archibald MacLeish, who told a House committee that he has been able to discover only three non-Japanese in the country who can read and write Japanese; . . . and to the Daughters of the Union, who, when told that New York doesn't want a plaque to mark the spot where President Lincoln's body lay in state at City Hall before the burial in Springfield, announced that they would give the plaque to Springfield. Gentlemen, ladies, and horses, goodbye now.—*The New Yorker*, Apr. 25, 1942

3. Logical paragraphs

In impressionistic paragraphs the relation between statements is to a large degree personal and subjective. In logical paragraphs the relations between facts, details, opinions, and general statements are objective, in the sense that they can be demonstrated to others and that other people will see them in the same way. *The "logical" relations, such as equivalence, comparison, cause, effect, illustration, reason, are really the commonsense relations that we regularly see between statements.* We think automatically, but our thinking as it is edited for others can be analyzed by means of these relations. They may be indicated specifically (by *because, the reason for this is,* and scores of other words and phrases), or they may be implied or suggested. The only point is that a moderately careful reader should see the relation clearly, see the statements joined as the writer thinks them.

Most paragraphs of logical statement have a topic sentence which definitely states the main idea, or at least they have a purpose that is obvious. The type of development of a paragraph is the relation between the bulk of the individual statements and this controlling idea or purpose. More than one sort of relationship may be found in the same paragraph, in its various subordinate parts.

Examining paragraphs of various types can suggest the range of possibilities. It can also furnish a background against which you can compare and judge your own paragraphs.

3a. Restatement. Repetition of idea or restatement may be a method of developing or unifying a paragraph. Such repetition is chiefly for emphasis and clarity. Judicious repetition in different words, perhaps turning a general statement into a concrete statement, putting it in the form of a question, or translating it into a figure of speech often helps reach a reader more forcibly or helps reach more readers. One of the expressions will appeal to some, another to others.

In the paragraph below, Stuart Chase states six times and in a half dozen different ways the failure of words as a means of communication:

> Meanwhile, I had long been aware of the alarming futility of most of the literature dedicated to economic and social reform. As a young reformer I had organized meetings, written pamphlets, prepared lectures, concocted programs, spread publicity with enthusiasm. Those already inclined to my point of view attended the meetings, read the pamphlets, listened to the lectures, adopted the programs, but the apathy of the unconverted was as colossal as it was baffling. As the years went by it became apparent that I was largely wasting my time. The message—and I still believe it was a human and kindly message—[1] had not got through; [2] communication was blocked. [3] What we

reformers meant was not what our hearers thought we meant. Too often it was clear that we were not heard at all; [4] noises came through, but no meaning. [5] Few of the seeds I sowed bore out the ancient theory that the seed of truth, once planted, would surely sprout. The damn things would not come up. Why? [6] Why did Mr. Wilson's dubious "war for democracy" go over with a roar, while our carefully reasoned appeals drifted listlessly down empty alleys?—STUART CHASE, *The Tyranny of Words*, pp. 5-6

The italicized sentences in the following paragraph repeat three times Professor East's central idea:

The country has become much more socialistic than most people realize. Theoretically it is committed to a policy of free medical advice, and free mental training in the public schools. This program is partly logical and partly illogical. It is logical in that every citizen should be given the opportunity to realize on every physical and mental asset he possesses. It is illogical in that we treat all individuals as if they were Boston terriers, trimming their ears and teaching them identical tricks, so that they will fit a single given standard. *It would be much better, would it not, after patching up such physical disabilities as we may, to give each child all the education he can assimilate of the type for which he is fitted?* There is no point in trying to teach our twenty million morons to read and write. It is hardly worth while to prod another twenty million dullards through grammar school. It is foolish to lower high-school and college standards so that everyone who has a mere social urge for educational gloss is able to obtain it. *It would be a much better policy to reorganize the whole educational system in a way which would permit the establishment of specialized schools fitted to the different requirements of our variant population.* The progress of a people depends largely upon the upper 1 per cent. Dr. Cox has shown that the leaders of the world, the geniuses of various types who have made civilization, have been exceptionally intelligent as children. Intelligence tests have been sufficiently perfected to enable us to select such a group. Psychologists cannot guarantee that they will all be leaders; they can guarantee that the leaders will come from among them. *What greater service to humanity could a government perform than to select and train everyone who shows promise of outstanding ability, no matter from what walk of life he comes?*—EDWARD M. EAST, *Biology in Human Affairs*, pp. 189-90

3b. Definition. It is sometimes important to define a term that is essential to a paper. A formal definition or a quotation from a dictionary makes a stiff opening and should not be used if it is possible to explain the word's meaning by discussing what it stands for. The formal definition, like those in a dictionary, often leaves the reader still wondering exactly what the word means, at least what it means for him. A discussion, explaining the limits within which it is used and how it is not used, may be interesting as well as illuminating.

Even rather technical terms can be presented through discussion so that the reader will get their meaning and in addition have some perspective on the term itself, as in this definition of *nebulæ*:

> The astronomical term *nebulæ* has come down through the centuries as the name for permanent, cloudy patches in the sky that are beyond the limits of the solar system. The interpretation of these objects has frequently changed, but the name has persisted. It was once believed that all nebulæ were clusters or systems of stars; later it was found that some were composed of gas or dust. As new theories were developed, various new names were introduced, but in general the names did not survive. Only one revision has been permanent. Certain star-clusters, easily resolved with telescopes of moderate power, and obviously subordinate members of the galactic system, have been withdrawn from the list of nebulæ to form a separate and distinct class of objects.
>
> Today, the term *nebula* is used for two quite different kinds of astronomical bodies. On the one hand are the clouds of dust and gas, numbering a few score in all, which are scattered among the stars of the galactic system. These have been called *galactic nebulæ*. On the other hand are the remaining objects, numbering many millions, which are now recognized as independent stellar systems scattered through space beyond the limits of the galactic system. These have been called *extragalactic nebulæ*. The nomenclature is followed in this book with the exception that, since extragalactic nebulæ are mentioned so frequently, the adjective will be dropped. Therefore the term *nebulæ* will refer to extragalactic nebulæ alone, unless otherwise specified.—EDWIN HUBBLE, *The Realm of the Nebulæ*, pp. 16-17

Simple words can often be used and their meaning casually indicated without formal definition. In the first version of the following statement the reader's attention is focused on the word itself, and in the second version on the activity, where it really belongs:

> While I take the portable wheel at the bow, you make yourself useful by "shucking" clams. This is the fisherman's term for breaking open the clams and putting them into baiting form.

While I take the portable wheel at the bow, you make your-self useful by breaking the clams open and putting them into baiting form—shucking them, as the fishermen say.

An amateur's definition often does not tell enough and is too brief to focus attention squarely on the real meaning. In the next paragraph James Bryce takes time to make *tyranny of the majority* really mean something to his readers; then he discusses tyranny in the United States.

The expression "tyranny of the majority" is commonly used to denote any abuse by the majority of the powers which they enjoy, in free countries under and through the law, and in all countries outside the law. Such abuse will not be tyrannous in the sense of being illegal, as men called a usurper like Dionysius of Syracuse or Louis Napoleon in France a tyrant, for in free countries whatever the majority chooses to do in the prescribed constitutional way will be legal. It will be tyrannous in the sense of the lines

"O it is excellent
To have a giant's strength, but it is tyrannous
To use it like a giant."

That is to say, tyranny consists in the wanton or inequitable use of strength by the stronger, in the use of it to do things which one equal would not attempt against another. A majority is tyrannical when it decides without hearing the minority, when it suppresses fair and temperate criticism of its own acts, when it insists on restraining men in matters where restraint is not required by the common interest, when it forces men to contribute money to objects which they disapprove and which the common interest does not demand, when it subjects to social penalties persons who disagree from it in matters not vital to the common welfare. The element of tyranny lies in the wantonness of the act, a wantonness springing from the insolence which sense of overwhelming power breeds, or in the fact that it is a misuse for one purpose of authority granted for another. It consists not in the form of the act, which may be perfectly legal, but in the spirit and temper it reveals, and in the sense of injustice and oppression which it evokes in the minority.—James Bryce, *The American Commonwealth*, II, p. 339

An important element in a definition is making clear what the word does *not* mean, as John Dewey runs over various senses of the word *thinking* to define the particular sense (reflective thought) in which he is interested:

In its loosest sense, thinking signifies everything that, as we say, is "in our heads" or that "goes through our minds." He who offers "a penny for your thoughts" does not expect to drive any great bargain. In calling the objects of his demand *thoughts,* he does not intend to ascribe to them dignity, consecutiveness, or truth. Any idle fancy, trivial recollection, or flitting impression will satisfy his demand. Day-dreaming, building of castles in the air, that loose flux of casual and disconnected material that floats through our minds in relaxed moments are, in this random sense, *thinking.* More of our waking life than we should care to admit, even to ourselves, is likely to be whiled away in this inconsequential trifling with idle fancy and unsubstantial hope.

In this sense, silly folk and dullards *think.* The story is told of a man in slight repute for his intelligence, who, desiring to be chosen selectman in his New England town, addressed a knot of neighbors in this wise: "I hear you don't believe I know enough to hold office. I wish you to understand that I am thinking about something or other most of the time." Now reflective thought is like this random coursing of things through the mind in that it consists of a succession of things thought of; but it is unlike, in that the mere chance occurrence of any chance "something or other" in an irregular sequence does not suffice. Reflection involves not simply a sequence of ideas, but a *con*sequence—a consecutive ordering in such a way that each determines the next as its proper outcome, while each in turn leans back on its predecessors. The successive portions of the reflective thought grow out of one another and support one another; they do not come and go in a medley. Each phase is a step from something to something—technically speaking, it is a term of thought. Each term leaves a deposit which is utilized in the next term. The stream or flow becomes a train, chain, or thread.—JOHN DEWEY, *How We Think*, pp. 2-3

These examples show how it is possible to make a definition readable as well as clear and accurate. If a full definition is necessary, take plenty of space for it and make it a genuine part of the paper.

3c. Analysis. One of the most common methods for developing an idea expressed in a topic sentence at the beginning of a paragraph is to follow it with a series of facts. These details make a more or less complete analysis, that is, they break up the general statement into particulars.

The natural way to let a reader understand a situation, whether it is extraordinary or typical, is to give details of it. Here Mr. Chidsey gives us some "conception of the difficulties travelers met" in New York's great blizzard of 1888:

The actual fall in 53½ hours was 20.9 inches, or more than twice as much snow as had fallen all that winter, but this figure gives no conception of the difficulties travelers met. For the wind continued high, and the soberest observers reported drifts of fifteen and twenty feet. It was almost impossible to walk. A few hacks took to the streets, the drivers charging anything they could get and in some cases forcing whiskey down the throats of their horses in order to keep them alive. Surface cars struggled for a little while, and then stopped; many of them were literally buried. The Third Avenue Elevated Railway, not then electrified, ran a few trains downtown—one car each, with two or even three dinkey engines pushing it—but these too were stalled. In one of them, helpless between stations, were thirty men; but though they could not get down, they were so fortunate as to be in front of a saloon, and hot toddies were hoisted to them by means of a pail and a length of cord, so that the men remained tolerably happy for the fifteen hours of their captivity, and even were heard to sing. Sturdy little boys with ladders went from place to place letting people down out of second-story windows; generally they charged (this being in the days before Boy Scouts) fifty cents for the descent.—DONALD B. CHIDSEY, *The Gentleman from New York: A Life of Roscoe Conkling*, pp. 381-82

Mr. Adamic's analysis of the position of women in Montenegro is a typical paragraph of this sort.

The woman's position in Tsernagora is not much better than it was fifty years ago. Living in a patriarchal society which till lately was in constant state of war, they are treated by men as their mental and physical inferiors. They certainly do not compare favorably with the men either in looks or stature. As already said, they do all the hard work, just as they had been doing it through all the centuries of warfare, and about the only recognition they get for this comes in the form of contempt. Their men really respect them only as "mothers of Montenegrins" —that is, mothers of *male* Montenegrins. For a woman to give birth to a girl is not one-tenth the creditable achievement that it is to bear a boy. If she bears only daughters, she is a disgrace to her husband and treated accordingly. When I asked a man how many children he had, he said four, but I found later that he had six—he did not count his two daughters! When a son is born, the old-time, conventional Montenegrin father fires six shots in the air, whereupon all men who hear the shots exclaim, "May he be a hero! Luck to him!" When a girl is born no shots are fired.—LOUIS ADAMIC, *The Native's Return*, p. 141

The details in Sherwood Anderson's amusing (or tragic) analysis of the "things that can happen to a chicken" depend on the first sentence and are again bound together at the end of the paragraph.

99

One unversed in such matters can have no notion of the many and tragic things that can happen to a chicken. It is born out of an egg, lives for a few weeks as a tiny fluffy thing such as you will see pictured on Easter cards, then becomes hideously naked, eats quantities of corn and meal bought by the sweat of your father's brow, gets diseases called pip, cholera, and other names, stands looking with stupid eyes at the sun, becomes sick and dies. A few hens and now and then a rooster, intended to serve God's mysterious ends, struggle through to maturity. The hens lay eggs out of which come other chickens and the dreadful cycle is thus made complete. It is all unbelievably complex. Most philosophers must have been raised on chicken farms. One hopes for so much from a chicken and is so dreadfully disillusioned. Small chickens, just setting out on the journey of life, look so bright and alert and they are in fact so dreadfully stupid. They are so much like people they mix one up in one's judgments of life. If disease does not kill them they wait until your expectations are thoroughly aroused and then walk under the wheels of a wagon—to go squashed and dead back to their maker. Vermin infest their youth, and fortunes must be spent for curative powders. In late life I have seen how a literature has been built up on the subject of fortunes to be made in the raising of chickens. It is intended to be read by the gods who have just eaten of the tree of the knowledge of good and evil. It is a hopeful literature and declares that much may be done by simple ambitious people who own a few hens. Do not be led astray by it. It was not written for you. Go hunt for gold on the frozen hills of Alaska, put your faith in the honesty of a politician, believe if you will that the world is daily growing better and that good will triumph over evil, but do not read and believe the literature that is written concerning the hen. It was not written for you.—SHERWOOD ANDERSON, "The Egg," *The Triumph of the Egg*, pp. 47-49

3d. Illustration. One of the most valuable ways of bringing a general statement home to a reader, or even of making it clear, is to give an illustration, or two or three illustrations or examples. They may be brief, tucked into a sentence, or they may be so numerous or so fully told that they become a method of paragraph development. They may be formally introduced by some such expression as *for example* or *You can see this in—* or they can be, and preferably are, simply placed so that they obviously illustrate the general statement.

A fully developed incident in the following paragraph is an illustration of the general statement about Police Commissioner Valentine made in the first sentence—and it also serves as evi-

dence for the truth of the general statement. The illustration
is so complete that no comment is needed after it.

A suspicious mind and a talent for detecting a lie were of
invaluable aid to Valentine. One winter a patrolman reported
having rescued a man from drowning in Erie Basin. He was
enjoying a flurry as a hero when Valentine became skeptical.
The distance the policeman reported having swum in icy water,
towing a helpless man, seemed a trifle implausible. He called
the cop to Headquarters. They sat in Valentine's office and
chatted about swimming and the art of lifesaving. Valentine
arranged to meet him later at a Turkish bath and there ordered
him to strip and dive into the pool. The cop took off his uniform
but said he just wanted to sit in the steam room a while. Valentine was firm. The cop finally plunged in and in a moment or
two was floundering and yelling for help. Valentine, without
taking off his own uniform, jumped in and rescued him.—JACK
ALEXANDER, "Independent Cop," *The New Yorker*, Oct. 3, 1936

Professor Beard in these paragraphs uses brief references to
several situations to explain and illustrate the general statement
in the first sentence:

Assuming that relations exist between events, indeed convinced
by common sense and consensus, that they do exist, it follows
that in tracing relations we are led afar in space and backward
in time. This rule applies even to personalities and occurrences
apparently trivial in influence. The building of rayon factories
in the United States affects the living standards of Japanese engaged in producing silk worms. The simplest words used by a
mountaineer suggest the distant origins of the language he
speaks. Every personality, no matter how humble, every human
occurrence, however slight, has relations with other personalities
and occurrences contemporary and past.

Some of the relations are clear and can be easily traced to a
certain extent; for example, the relationships of family and race.
Others are complicated and elusive; for instance, the influence
of interested propaganda upon government policy and action.
But whether clear or elusive, we can never find a stopping place
when we try to trace them. A Baptist sermon in Atlanta, if we
seek to explain it, takes us back through the Protestant Reformation to Galilee—and far beyond in the dim origins of civilization. We can, if we choose, stop at any point along the line of
relations, but that is an arbitrary act of will and does violence
to the quest for truth in the matter.—C. A. BEARD, *The Discussion of Human Affairs*, pp. 68-69

A very common failing of amateur writing is leaving out, or
not bothering to put in, good illustrations of just what a general

statement means. Illustrations are one of the most useful methods of paragraph development, especially in discussions of ideas and general principles, adding to the interest and making the material more definite and meaningful for a reader. Often it is only from the illustrations that a reader discovers exactly what the generalization means and only through them that he can be led to think about the matter.

3e. Contrast and comparison. Comparisons and contrasts are useful for making ideas and situations more distinct, more interesting and emphatic. It is natural to set two or more things or situations or ideas side by side and discuss their likenesses and differences.

Sometimes evidence for a statement may be drawn from conspicuously contrasting sources, so that they are striking as well as to the point:

> When Mr. Gandhi visited London the reporters laughed at him for continuing to wear a loincloth. But who remembered to laugh at Lord Willingdon when he appeared, beneath an Indian sun, in tall hat, frock coat, and gray-striped trousers? I do not condemn the Viceroy's costume; it may have been politically necessary; it was right in London, but by all the rules of common sense it was as wrong in Delhi as was Mr. Gandhi's loincloth in London. Both gentlemen were, of course, giving political demonstrations; both were geographically wrong, and both were also artistically wrong.—RAMSAY TRAQUAIR, "Architecture and Geography," *The Atlantic Monthly*, Aug. 1938

This paragraph reveals Mr. Huxley's opinion of comfort by a series of comparisons and contrasts—old times and the present, comfort and beauty, England and other countries, physical and mental labor—and it ends with a figurative comparison:

> Having now briefly traced the spiritual origins of modern comfort, I must say a few words about its effects. One can never have something for nothing, and the achievement of comfort has been accompanied by a compensating loss of other equally, or perhaps more, valuable things. A man of means who builds a house today is in general concerned primarily with the comfort of his future residence. He will spend a great deal of money (for comfort is very expensive; in America they talk of giving away the house with the plumbing) on bathrooms, heating apparatus, padded furnishings, and the like; and having spent it, he will regard his house as perfect. His counterpart in an earlier age would have been primarily concerned with the impressiveness and magnificence of his dwelling—with beauty, in a word, rather

than comfort. The money our contemporary would spend on baths and central heating would have been spent in the past on marble staircases, a grand façade, frescoes, huge suites of gilded rooms, pictures, statues. Sixteenth-century popes lived in a discomfort that a modern bank manager would consider unbearable; but they had Raphael's frescoes, they had the Sistine chapel, they had their galleries of ancient sculpture. Must we pity them for the absence from the Vatican of bathrooms, central heating and smoking-room chairs? I am inclined to think that our present passion for comfort is a little exaggerated. Though I personally enjoy comfort, I have lived very happily in houses devoid of almost everything that Anglo-Saxons deem indispensable. Orientals and even South Europeans, who know not comfort and live very much as our ancestors lived centuries ago, seem to get on very well without our elaborate and costly apparatus of padded luxury. I am old-fashioned enough to believe in higher and lower things, and can see no point in material progress except in so far as it subserves thought. I like labour-saving devices, because they economize time and energy which may be devoted to mental labour. (But then I enjoy mental labour; there are plenty of people who detest it, and who feel as much enthusiasm for thought-saving devices as for automatic dishwashers and sewing-machines.) I like rapid and easy transport, because by enlarging the world in which men can live it enlarges their minds. Comfort for me has a similar justification; it facilitates mental life. Discomfort handicaps thought; it is difficult when the body is cold and aching to use the mind. Comfort is a means to an end. The modern world seems to regard it as an end in itself, an absolute good. One day, perhaps, the earth will have been turned into one vast feather-bed, with man's body dozing on top of it and his mind underneath, like Desdemona, smothered.
—ALDOUS HUXLEY, *Proper Studies*, pp. 296-99

Very often the actual subject of a paper is two people, things, events, situations, or ideas presented in relation to each other. Sometimes such a paper would be developed by giving a complete description of one and then passing to the other. But ordinarily this method makes a paper or a paragraph that breaks in the middle and fails to bring the actually related facts together. In comparing and contrasting the regulations of two colleges, for example, a writer might mention the cut system, eligibility rules, and grading system of one, and then the same features of the other. But usually it would be better to treat first the cut system of both, bringing to bear at one point all the description and discussion of that topic, and then to go on to the eligibility rules, grading system, and so on.

In Chapter 9 of *The Horse and Buggy Doctor*, Dr. Hertzler compares and contrasts the work of a surgeon under the primitive conditions of "kitchen surgery" with his work in the operating room of a modern hospital. Instead of giving an account of first one and then the other, perhaps following these with his opinion, he keeps both working conditions constantly before the reader, giving first some details of one and then of the other, with his opinion clearly stated or implied all along, as in this sample paragraph:

> I have interpolated the preceding in order to show that kitchen surgery had many advantages. Even the modest, intelligent, well meaning assistant can make himself a nuisance. Only one person can work at a time and while an assistant is doing something the operator is idle—that is his hands are, but his mind is thinking horrible thoughts. On the other hand if one operates alone in a kitchen his instruments are just where he placed them. One kept the instruments in the dishpan, took them out when needed, and put them back in again when he had finished with their use. They were always to be found in an area of a foot and a half, the diameter of the dishpan. There was no nurse to grab them, rub off real or imaginary blood and then place them somewhere else.—ARTHUR E. HERTZLER, *The Horse and Buggy Doctor*, pp. 221-22

One of the best ways to help readers see or understand something that lies outside their experience is to compare and contrast it with something familiar to them. A book on the ancient Greek drama begins by pointing out how it differed from the plays and the theater that we know:

> The ancient Athenian drama was in many respects unlike any kind of dramatic performance that we are accustomed to in modern times. The difference extended not only to the character of the plays themselves, and the manner in which they were presented upon the stage, but also to the circumstances under which the production took place. In order to form an accurate conception of the external features of the old Greek drama it will be necessary to dismiss from the mind many of the associations with which the modern stage is connected. In the first place, the luxury of having theatrical entertainments at every season of the year was a thing never heard of among the ancient Athenians. The dramatic performances at Athens, instead of being spread over the whole year, were restricted to the two great festivals of Dionysus, the Lenea and the City Dionysia. It is true that at these festivals the number of plays exhibited was large enough to satisfy the most enthusiastic playgoer. Several days in suc-

cession were devoted entirely to the drama, and on each day tragedies and comedies followed one another without interruption from morning till evening. But with the exception of the two festivals of Dionysus there was no other occasion on which plays were acted in the Athenian theatre. There were dramatic exhibitions in the various townships of Attica during the Rural Dionysia; but in Athens herself the drama was restricted to the two periods already mentioned. In fact, the ancient drama had much in common with modern musical festivals, in which at certain fixed seasons several days in succession are devoted entirely to music.—A. E. HAIGH, *The Attic Theatre*, pp. 1-2

3f. Cause and effect. Paragraphs are often developed by presenting in some detail the causes of the fact, event, or situation given in the topic sentence, or by giving its effects. This type of paragraph is especially common in discussions of social, economic, and political situations. The statements may be related by various specific connectives (*because, the cause of this was, the effect was, as a result, consequently*), or the relation may be apparent from the position of the statements.

In the first of the following paragraphs Mr. Laski gives the cause of what he believes is a weakness in American politics; in the second he lists a number of resulting effects:

Perhaps the most grave weakness in American political life today is the absence of a conservative philosophy. The Republican Party represents the impulses of interests on the defense rather than principles which are seeking the expression of action. The Democrats follow a leader whose inspiration is largely at variance with the traditions for which they stand, and who wins their support less because of the ends he seeks than because of the victories he secures. There has hardly been a time in modern American history when the divisions of party organization have had less relation to the divisions of American ideas.

That is an unhealthy condition for a number of reasons. It means, in the first place, that at election time the American people has no effective choice between rational alternatives; it knows the man whom it may place in the White House; it does not know what it may place him there for. It means, second, that while there is grave distrust of many of the purposes President Roosevelt is seeking to fulfil there is no coherent alternative to those purposes.—HAROLD J. LASKI, *Harper's Magazine*, Sept. 1937

In this paragraph from a protest against mismanagement in war, Mr. Montague puts first the effect, then the cause, and then returns to the effect (*And so . . .*).

The winter after the battle of Loos a sentry on guard at one part of our line could always see the frustrate skeletons of many English dead. They lay outside our wire, picked clean by the rats, so that the khaki fell in on them loosely—little heaps of bone and cloth half hidden now by nettles and grass. If the sentry had been a year in the army he knew well enough that they had gone foredoomed into a battle lost before a shot was fired. After the Boer War, you remember, England, under the first shock of its blunders, had tried to find out why the Staff work was so bad. What it found, in the words of a famous Report, was that the fashion in sentiment in our Regular Army was to think hard work "bad form"; a subaltern was felt to be a bit of a scrub if he worried too much about discovering how to support an attack when he might be more spiritedly employed playing polo; "The nobleness of life," as Antony said, when he kissed Cleopatra, was to go racing or hunting, not to sit learning how to forecast the course of great battles and how to provide for answering their calls. And so swathes of little brown bundles, with bones showing through, lay in the nettles and grass.—
C. E. MONTAGUE, *Disenchantment*, p. 196

3g. Reasons. Paragraphs are often developed by a series of reasons for a conclusion or decision or statement of opinion made in the topic sentence, which is likely in this type of paragraph to stand first. If the relationship of the reasons to this statement is clear, no connectives are needed, though in more complicated material or more formal treatment locutions like "The reasons for this are . . . This is true because . . ." may be needed.

The following paragraph gives a whole series of reasons for the statement which the writer makes in the first sentence:

And then, if you have failed not too awkwardly, you are usually more delightful as a companion than a better worker. Those who reach real success are likely to be constant workers. Even in their hours of recreation they frequently are preoccupied with some element of the thing they are engaged in doing. The successful man has less free time, and observes more punctiliously his self-set hours for withdrawing from companionship, than the failure. He can seldom be counted on for impromptu gaieties, since he is not unconsciously intent on finding any escape at all from the unsatisfactory conditions of his life. And, since he has none of the deep interior guilt which haunts the one who knows he is failing, he is under no compulsion to be winning. He reserves his humor and charm, his emotion and indulgence, for those whose lives are closely bound up with his by his own choice. So, except among his real intimates, he may have the name of being gruff and unapproachable, or too coolly civil. As long as you cannot bear the notion that there is a creature under heaven who can regard you with an indifferent, an amused or hostile eye, you will probably see to it that you continue to fail with the utmost charm.—DOROTHEA BRANDE, *Wake Up and Live!* pp. 54-55

Here Mr. Fadiman sketches his reasons for believing that "the trash of my generation was superior to the trash of today."

I say trash. Actually such books are "trash" only by standards which should not be applied to children's reading. They have the incalculable value that listening to perfectly inane adult conversation holds for children: they increase the child's general awareness. They provide admittedly rough paradigms of character, motivation, life experiences. That is why it seems to me that the trash of my generation was superior to the trash of today. I submit that *The Rover Boys in the Everglades* and *Frank on a Gunboat* are preferable to Superman and his kind on two counts: they were cleanly and clearly written, and their characters were credible and not entirely unrelated to the child's experience. When I was nine I could learn something interesting about life from even such highly colored affairs as the Frank Merriwell series, but I know that my son can learn nothing whatsoever of genuine interest (that is, which he can check against the expanding universe within himself) from the comics. I believe firmly that the current juvenile literature of the impossible is meretricious compared with the honest hackwork my own generation enjoyed. I also think that the kids are about ready to kick over this thriller fare in favor of something saner and more natural.—CLIFTON FADIMAN, *Reading I've Liked*, Preface, p. xvi

Since informational and critical writing is the bulk of college written work and a large part of all published matter, everyone should be able to compose accurate, connected, and effective logical paragraphs. The examples in this section have been grouped according to type for convenience of description and analysis, but more important than classification is the aim to present material fully and interestingly in any sort of appropriate and well-composed paragraph. It is probably not going too far to say that anyone who can write good paragraphs can— or can learn to—write good papers.

Exercises

The following exercises are given to emphasize the kinds of paragraphs and to give practice in composing different types.

1. Study carefully each of the following paragraphs. Classify it as Chronological, Impressionistic, or Logical (predominantly). If you decide it is Impressionistic, determine whether it is predominantly description or a subjectively selected series of facts. If you decide it is Logical, classify it as one of the seven types of Logical Paragraphs. Write a short analysis of the paragraph, picking out any details, phrases, stylistic devices, or the like which help to gain the effect.

1. On the morning of July 4, 1927, the routine of Sing Sing Prison was disturbed by a tragic accident. The inmates were taking their exercise in the prison yard overlooking the Hudson River, when a canoe bearing three young men with supplies and equipment for a picnic came unsteadily down the river, the surface of which was roughened by a fresh wind. When near the prison pier the canoe capsized. Convicts who saw the incident moved, as if by impulse, toward the three figures who were struggling in the water. Apparently unable to swim the youths were clinging to the sides of the overturned craft and calling for help. Six of the prisoners volunteered, even begged with tears in their eyes, for permission to swim out to the rescue; but the keepers, who carried rifles in their hands, would not allow it. According to the warden himself, the guards had to threaten to shoot the prisoners in order to keep them back. One by one the victims, their strength ebbing and their cries dying away, sank into the river and disappeared. It was reported that the incident produced a profound depression throughout the prison, dampening the holiday spirit which might otherwise have prevailed.—FLOYD H. ALLPORT, *Institutional Behavior*, p. 49

2. If we hadn't looked it up, we wouldn't have believed that practically two years elapsed between the torpedoing of the Lusitania and President Wilson's announcement of a state of war, or even that there were three full months between the bombardment of Fort Sumter and the Battle of Bull Run. Periods of undeclared war tend to shrink or even vanish in retrospect; the date when conflict first became inevitable and the date when it finally became actual soon follow one another without an appreciable interval in the mind. Perhaps some miracle, nowhere visible at the moment, can keep this nation at peace, but if things work out the way we think they will, the brief armed truce that marked the spring and summer of 1941 will shortly be forgotten. It won't be long before people will be

recalling that the President made a speech proclaiming a national emergency and later on that very week the guns began to roar. —*New Yorker*, June 7, 1941

3. His lips were thick, and so was his long, straight nose. His hands, clasped before him on the table, were enormous and muscular; and their fingers, pallid by comparison with the brown of his face and hands, looked parboiled, as though left overlong in water. Beneath his large eyes the flesh was puffy; and his shoulders, sloping down from a bull-like neck, filled his buckskin hunting shirt so solidly that the leather might have been shrunk to fit them. The breadth of his chest and upper arms gave him the look of holding a deep breath.

He wore a tight little infantryman's hat which had a sort of semicircular black plate or visor cocked straight up in front, as if to protect the wearer's forehead from bullets or blows; and a curved ornament which I thought was leather rose from the back and swept over the cap's top like a squirrel's tail. The eyes that stared at me from beneath that upstanding black visor were the color of the round gray pebbles that lie along our Maine beaches, scoured by the surf.—KENNETH ROBERTS, *Northwest Passage*, p. 84

4. A college practice field, except for occasional bursts of noise from the normal young men engaged in working out, has very much the atmosphere of a classroom. The squad, for a good part of the time, will be broken up into smaller groups. One will be linemen, another backs, another passers and receivers. They will go over and over certain plays, with the assistant in charge of the particular group breaking in every now and then and, in a classroom voice, explaining mistakes, asking questions and once in a while demonstrating.—ROBERT F. KELLEY, *The New York Times*, Oct. 14, 1941

5. When I was a little boy our city seemed to me an old city, that had been there always. My memory goes back to 1905 perhaps, 1906 certainly. Even then I can remember a cemetery that was almost full, and streets whose stone pavement was worn out. Cable car and trolley tracks which had been paralleled by more modern equipment lay rusting in the ground. The two steel bridges across the river had been built to replace older wooden bridges. Near my father's office were old buildings, their steps worn concave by climbing feet, their brick and stone walls dingy and ruinous. Brick, stone, and steel had decayed and worn out, even in 1905. Obviously, even then, the city must have been very old. I never thought that less than a century or two had gone into the maturing of it. Even when I was taught in school the real date of the first settlement, I did not fully believe it. My mind memorized the date, but the city was nevertheless

an old city where generations of people had been born, grown old, died, and filled an old graveyard.—HARRISON PLATT, *No Encore*

6. This simplicity is best illustrated from pidgin, which is English meat with Chinese bones, as we say in China. There is no reason why a sentence like "He come, you no come; you come, he no come" should not be considered as clear as the more roundabout "You needn't come, if he comes, and he needn't come if you come." In fact, this simplicity makes for clarity of expression. Moon, in *Dean's English*, quotes an English Somerset farmer as testifying before the judge: "He'd a stick, and he'd a stick, and he licked he, and he licked he; if he licked he as hard as he licked he, he'd a killed he, and not he he," and this seems to me a much more sensible way of talking than one with the Germanic case-distinctions. For according to the Chinese, the difference between "I lick he" and "he lick I" is perfectly clear without the subjective-accusative complex, and the adding of the third person singular ending "s" is as superfluous as it is already proved to be in the past tense (I had, he had; I went, he went). Actually lots of people are saying "us girls" and "them things" without ever being misunderstood or losing anything except a meaningless "class" which has nothing to do with beauty of expression. I have great hope that English and American professors will one day bravely and respectably pronounce a "he don't" in the classrooms, and that the English language may one day become as sensible and clear as the Chinese, through the influence of pidgin.—LIN YUTANG, *My Country and My People*, pp. 81-82

7. If the Moon was formed from a big bulge on the surface of the Earth, some interesting conclusions can be drawn concerning the materials of which it consists. As we have mentioned, our Earth consists of a number of shells, with the heavier materials in the central regions and the lighter ones on the surface. Modern geophysics recognizes the existence of three major shells. The outer crust of the Earth consists of a layer of granite (with an average density 2.7 times that of water) extending to a depth of from 50 to 100 kilometres. This granite layer rests on a layer of heavier volcanic material, known as basalt, which is probably several thousand kilometres deep and reaches almost half-way to the centre of the Earth. Still farther down we find a molten core, consisting mostly of iron and other heavy metals. The presence of this metallic core, with a density of about 10 (probably even higher), is responsible for the fact that the mean density of the Earth, as estimated from its known total mass and volume, is about 5.5, that is, more than twice the density of the rocks found on its surface. This separation of materials is due to gravity, of course, and must have taken place when the Earth

was still entirely liquid, permitting easy circulation between the centre and the surface. Thus, when the big tidal bulge separated from the Earth, it probably took with it large quantities of molten granites and basalts, but only a very small amount, if any, of the heavy metals from the central regions. Consequently, we must expect that the mean density of the Moon would be considerably lower than that of the Earth and only slightly higher than the densities of granites and basalts. This expectation is splendidly confirmed by observations that give the value of 3.3 for the mean density of the Moon. Thus, in contrast to the Earth, *our Moon must be of stony structure throughout its entire body.*—GEORGE GAMOW, *Biography of the Earth*, pp. 43-44

8. When you are engaging in silent reading, you do not look at each letter separately, and very often not even at each word. Many ideas are expressed not by any single word but by a series of words which together make what is called a phrase. Thus, the idea expressed in the phrase "in a day or two" is not contained in any one of the words, but in the entire phrase. If you read each word separately you do not get as well or as rapidly the meaning that the author intended you to get. Look at the sentence: "We shall reach Yellowstone Park in another two days if we drive 200 miles each day." There are really five ideas in this sentence, although there are sixteen words: "We shall reach" is one idea; "Yellowstone Park" is another; "in another two days" is the third; "if we drive" is the fourth idea; and "200 miles each day" is the last. When you read this sentence you should read not sixteen words, but five ideas—or five phrases. —C. GILBERT WRENN and LUELLA COLE, *How to Read Rapidly and Well*, p. 3

9. I suppose, like any nasty old frustrated writer, I have had to secure my revenge somehow. Perhaps that accounts for the persistent monotonous reiteration of my belief that most young American novelists (the ones who *do* get published) simply do not know their trade. I don't care what the richness or depth of their experience may be; they do not know the rules of rhetoric. The English language is a magnificently flexible instrument, but it asks of every writer that he use it with a certain regard for its possibilities and its limitations. The savage, spontaneous young people who rush their novels into print every year are superior to these possibilities and these limitations. It is true that they get by for a while on a certain childish freshness, a certain apparent originality. Then they are forgotten. But in the meantime they have cluttered up the book market, wasted the time of readers, and certainly contributed nothing to the clarification or development of sound literary standards. I hope this does not sound too righteous; it's so sore a point with me that I find it hard to be gently humorous. Every man in addition to his formal

religion has a private religion, consisting of a set of ideas, or a hobby or perhaps, like Dubedat in *The Doctor's Dilemma,* a group of heroes. I have that feeling about the English language. I don't mean its great masters, but the tongue itself. I am myself a most indifferent wielder of English, but a sinner is not debarred from worship. And I think that, in our own strange, wild, headlong period, reverence for the language is growing rarer and rarer. When it is not present in professional writers, in those who owe their very being to it, I get depressed, and so, I think, do all those who really love the tongue they speak.—CLIFTON FADIMAN, *Reading I've Liked,* pp. xxxvi-xxxvii

10. We are less bored than our ancestors were, but we are more afraid of boredom. We have come to know, or rather to believe, that boredom is not part of the natural lot of man, but can be avoided by a sufficiently vigorous pursuit of excitement. Girls nowadays earn their own living, very largely because this enables them to seek excitement in the evening and to escape "the happy family time" that their grandmothers had to endure. Everybody who can lives in a town; those who can not, have a car, or at the least a motor-bicycle, to take them to the movies. And of course they have the radio in their houses. Young men and young women meet each other with much less difficulty than was formerly the case, and every housemaid expects at least once a week as much excitement as would have lasted a Jane Austen heroine throughout a whole novel. As we rise in the social scale the pursuit of excitement becomes more and more intense. Those who can afford it are perpetually moving from place to place, carrying with them as they go gayety, dancing and drinking, but for some reason always expecting to enjoy these more in a new place. Those who have to earn a living get their share of boredom, of necessity, in working hours, but those who have enough money to be freed from the need of work have as their ideal a life completely freed from boredom. It is a noble ideal, and far be it from me to decry it, but I am afraid that like other ideals it is more difficult of achievement than the idealists suppose. After all, the mornings are boring in proportion as the previous evenings were amusing. There will be middle age, possibly even old age. At twenty men think that life will be over at thirty. I, at the age of fifty-eight, can no longer take that view. Perhaps it is as unwise to spend one's vital capital as one's financial capital. Perhaps some element of boredom is a necessary ingredient in life. A wish to escape from boredom is natural; indeed all races of mankind have displayed it as opportunity occurred. When savages have first tasted liquor at the hands of the white men, they have found at last an escape from age-old tedium, and except when the Government has interfered they have drunk themselves into a riotous death. Wars, pogroms, and persecu-

tions have all been part of the flight from boredom; even quarrels with neighbors have been found better than nothing. Boredom is therefore a vital problem for the moralist, since at least half the sins of mankind are caused by the fear of it.—BERTRAND RUSSELL, *The Conquest of Happiness,* pp. 59-60

11. For a day or two the place looked so like an overflowed Arkansas town, because of its currentless waters laving the very doorsteps of all the houses, and the cluster of boats made fast under the windows, or skimming in and out of the alleys and byways, that I could not get rid of the impression that there was nothing the matter here but a spring freshet, and that the river would fall in a few weeks and leave a dirty high-water mark on the houses, and the streets full of mud and rubbish.—MARK TWAIN, *Innocents Abroad,* p. 283

12. The collapse of France shows that it is not censorship but bad information that causes the greatest confusion. For twenty years, military experts had assured the world that the French had the finest army in Europe. The German air force and mechanized troops were fine, too, but the French had trained longer and they had built their Maginot Line. The German attack took the world by surprise not because the French censorship had prevented correspondents in France from writing the truth as they saw it. The German attack took the world by surprise because almost nobody in France or abroad knew how inadequate the French army was as compared with the German. The decadence of the French people, the "Fifth Column," the "strategy of terror," the Fascist sympathies of some of the "200 families" played a part, but the central truth was that the French armed forces suffered a crushing defeat which took the Germans themselves by surprise. Literally nobody knew the facts about the inadequate French preparations.—QUINCY HOWE, *The News and How to Understand It,* pp. 207-208

13. When I was a kid band-concerts were held in Union Park. That was when Flo Jacobson had a reputation as a sweet singer, that was when music publishers hired her to plug their numbers at the concerts. She wore a big white floppy hat, stood on the platform, and sang the new songs. I copped a handful of navy beans from the store when my father wasn't looking, and at the concert George Hurrel and I tossed the beans at the band, aiming for the brass instruments. When the music was soft you could hear those hard navy beans hit the cornets and trombones, then go rattling to the wooden floor. One night a cop caught us, but that's another story, and a long sad one at that.—ALBERT HALPER, "Young Writer Remembering Chicago"

2. Write an impressionistic paragraph giving a selection of your likes or dislikes or both so as to suggest (but not to state)   *Pages 92-93

the general direction of your taste. For a suggestion see the selection by Charles G. Shaw on page 92.

*Pages 88-89

3. Write a descriptive paragraph on one of the following topics or a similar one as assigned: the building (exterior) in which the class meets; the opening kickoff of a football game; a specific campus restaurant at a specified time of day; a campus statue; a specified campus figure (anyone from the president to the old-clothes man); a picture or other feature of the classroom; the campus as a whole. After the class has been divided into groups of four or five, students in each group can work on the same topic. This exercise has a double point: to give practice in writing descriptive paragraphs and to bring out the difference between details observed and selected by different people with the same opportunity for observation.

*Pages 82-83

4. In not more than one page give a clear synopsis of a movie which you have seen or a book which you have read. Work it out in a direct time sequence. (Both books and movies frequently begin part way through the story and later cut back to give earlier events.)

5. Write five or six topic sentences. Decide on the best method of development. Write two paragraphs developing two of your topic sentences.

CHAPTER 5

Sentence Form

1. **Definition**
2. **Sentence elements**
   a. Main elements b. Secondary elements c. Third elements
   d. Appositives e. Connectives
3. **Order of sentence elements**
   a. The typical English sentence b. Inverted order c. Position
   of modifiers
4. **Coordination and subordination**
   a. Conjunctions b. Relation between clauses c. Subordination
   and sentence movement d. Sentences classed by their clauses
5. **Parallelism in sentence form**
   a. Successful parallelism b. Faulty: Shifted constructions
6. **Incomplete sentences**
   a. Verbless b. Subjectless c. Fragmentary
7. **Run-on sentences**
   a. Successful: Contact clauses b. Unsuccessful: Comma fault
8. **Writing and revising sentences**

A COMPLETE TREATMENT of sentences would include the largest part of grammar, at least the whole of *syntax*, which treats of the relations between words as they are used in speaking and writing. This chapter takes up a selection of topics on sentences, the ones that seem most important for review and emphasis at the college level and the ones most immediately concerned with the activity of writing. These topics serve also as a foundation for considering in Chapter 6 various qualities of sentences that give greater effectiveness and interest to writing. *Grammar

1. Definition

No one has yet manufactured a completely satisfactory definition of *sentence*. If we define it as an independent expression having a subject and a verb, we are faced with a number of obviously good sentences lacking one or the other of these

115

elements—though most will have both. If we define it as a group of words expressing a complete thought, we sooner or later have to admit that there is no standard for knowing when a thought is complete. Some years ago a German wrote a book, *Was ist ein Satz?* (What Is a Sentence?), in which he showed the inadequacy of more than a hundred existing definitions—and then made up his own, equally inadequate.

But we are in a quite human, if slightly humbling, situation in which we have to discuss sentences. We know that there are certain small units of communication that stand by themselves, that at least *grammatically are independent of each other.* For their full *meaning* we may need sentences that come before or after, but their elements do not depend on other sentences for their grammatical standing. Spoken sentences are characterized by certain stresses and usually by a pause at their end, and written sentences are marked by periods, question marks, and exclamation marks. The words in a sentence also stand in some definable relation to each other, though sometimes it is slight. *This relationship between words is the grammatical basis of the sentence.*

The variety of expressions that we call sentences is enormous. Children's first sentences are often of only one word: *Up* means "Take me up"; *Me* may mean "Give me some of that too." Grown-ups have a number of one-word sentences: exclamations (*Oh! Welcome!*); others like *Go. Why?*; *Yes* and other answers to questions ("How many were there?" *Three*). There are numerous two-word patterns: *He laughed. Come here. You did!* But most sentences are longer, several words in some fairly systematic organization, and so varied that even a long chapter such as this cannot describe them all. Each has a form that can be described in grammatical terms. To convey our meaning they have to be in some common pattern. Since listeners and readers have definite expectations, we should use the common, typical forms, and we should avoid some forms because they are frowned upon by users of Good English. We learn the usual forms of sentences from listening to and imitating other speakers and writers and from study in school, and we use them pretty successfully in communicating with others.

*Declarative
sentences

*Questions

*Exclamations

*Commands
and requests

It is fair enough to say that a *written sentence is what a person with some experience in the language intentionally puts between end stops.* Professor Ballard says, "It is as much of my full purpose as I care to reveal at the very moment—as much of my meaning as I wish to deliver in one handful." Miss Rickert uses more learned words for the same idea: A sentence is ". . . a deliberately separated phase of the thought continuum; to the ear set off by a longer pause than obtains at any point within it; to the eye by an end punctuation mark."[1]

*Exercise 1, pp. 142-43

These attempted definitions suggest that sentences are to a considerable extent a matter of judgment, certainly of choice among a great variety of possibilities. In fact they are so individual that sometimes a writer does not see why someone else objects to a particular one he has written. But the more we know about the typical sentence forms, the easier it is to describe and examine our specific sentences and come to an agreement about them.

Miss Rickert's definition can help us judge whether sentences are successful or not, and can help us find reasons for our opinions. Unsuccessful sentences do not represent the writer's apparent purpose, his view of his subject matter, or they fail to advance the reader's understanding of the subject, or they may even confuse him. The students who handed in the following sentences were not paying attention to their writing:

1. He has a very strong will, once his mind is made up no one on earth can change it, he is rather stubborn at times, but for the most part he tries to see the other fellow's point of view.

(The main trouble with this is not that three grammatically complete statements are run together with nothing stronger than commas between them, but that the conflicting statements have not been built together so that a reader can understand the relationship between the stubbornness of the person described and the sympathy with which the last clause credits him.)

2. Lady Beaconsfield affectionately called him "Dizzy" and she did everything in her power to make him the success he was.

(Combining a nickname and a wife's help in building a statesman's career can only make a reader smile. He cannot make the leap between the ideas as they are presented, and the writer shouldn't ask him to.)

3. My first course in math was taken at Riverside High School in Milwaukee. This was first-year or elementary algebra.

---

[1] Janet R. Aiken, A New Plan of English Grammar (New York, 1933), Chapters 1 and 17; Ballard, Chapter 11; Bloomfield, Chapter 11; Otto Jespersen, A Philosophy of Grammar (New York, 1924), Chapters 8 and 22; Rickert, Chapter 4.

117

(The reader feels that he is not getting his money's worth from the individual sentences: My first course in math, elementary algebra, was taken . . .)

4. There were also several groups which were campaigning for Landon in this election. These groups in the election of 1932 were for the most part unheard of.

(Of course there were several groups campaigning for Landon; the first sentence has not advanced the writer's idea at all. Perhaps he meant: Several groups that campaigned for Landon were almost unheard of in 1932.)

5. I am writing with regard to a notice posted on the bulletin board at Middlebury College, from which I will receive a bachelor of arts degree in June.

(In a letter applying for a job the phrase concerning graduation is too important to trail as a subordinate statement to something about a bulletin board.)

Unsuccessful sentences are of course not confined to student papers; many find their way into print. The writer of the following paragraph does not seem to have been paying the attention to his sentences that we have a right to expect in a professional author. The short units of expression, their jerkiness and lack of connection make the paragraph difficult reading.

Another illustration: flying. When automobiles were struggling into use, Northcliffe had little newspaper influence. He did his best to make England realize that the invention and perfection of the gasolene motor would change all problems of transport and road-making; that the automobile was not a toy. England was obstinate. England lagged behind France and America, only later made up for lost time. When flying begins, he is at the top of his power. He forces everyone to follow what is being done. He speeds up the improvement of machines by giving prizes for notable flights. Flying makes rapid headway. England has been forced to take interest in it. England is in the van of progress.

Now read the two following passages, taken almost at random from a magazine and from a biography, and see how each sentence advances the subject, how the separate points are tied together, how the reader is guided from one sentence to the next:

There are more beautiful women and better actresses in Hollywood than Marlene Dietrich. But no other embodies so perfectly that elusive combination of qualities—variously defined as glamour, personality or, even, color—which added to less subtle requisites makes a beautiful actress a Star. Marlene Dietrich is not so good a tragedienne as Greta Garbo. She is inferior as a fashion plate to Constance Bennett, and less potent at the box office than Shirley Temple. What they are not she is—the ultimate refinement of a rare and delicate artifact, the distilled essence of a Movie Actress.—*Time*, Nov. 30, 1936

A man who accepts a religion without being religious lets himself in for more hardships than one would suppose. My father persisted most manfully in going to church; and he usually entered its portals at peace with the world and settled himself down contentedly in his end seat: but somehow before very long his expression would darken, as his hopes of hearing a sensible service little by little were dashed; and he came out in an inflamed state of mind that could not have been good for him.

The Episcopal service in general he didn't criticize; it was stately and quiet; but the sermon, being different every Sunday, was a very bad gamble. And once in awhile there would be an impromptu prayer that he would take great offense at. Sometimes he disliked its subject or sentiments—if he chanced to be listening. Sometimes he decided it was too long, or its tone too lugubrious. I remember seeing him so restive during a prayer of that kind, that—although the entire congregation was kneeling in reverence—he suddenly gave a loud snort, sat up straight in his pew, and glared at the minister's back as though planning to kick it.—Clarence Day, *God and My Father*, pp. 17-18

2. Sentence elements

The relation between the words in a sentence may be shown by several grammatical means, means that have evolved for various reasons in the long history of English and that we automatically understand. In "Jimmie's shoes" and "They saw him" the relation is shown by *form*, by the case ending *'s* and the case form *him*. English does not use this means very much, since its nouns and verbs have so few forms, compared, say, with German. In "The game went badly" we know that *badly* modifies the verb *went* because of its adverbial form in *-ly*; in "She felt bad" *bad*, an adjective, modifies *she*. Words are also held together by *word order*, by being in the usual position we have come to expect and to understand. In "The eagle was attacking the fishhawk" our experience has taught us that *eagle* is the subject of *was attacking* because it precedes the verb, and that fishhawk is the object because it follows the verb. Our adjectives usually come before the nouns to which they refer, and though

*Genitive case

*Pronouns

*Predicate adjectives

119

we can say "a hot summer" we know that in "That summer hot weather came in July" *hot* relates to *weather*.

A word may be related to the rest of the sentence by being in a subordinate construction, in a phrase or in a clause. In each of these the word group is an element of the sentence. In "The beginning of the term" *term* is related to *beginning* by the preposition *of*. In "The first day after the term began" the clause *after the term began* modifies *day* as if it was a single word, obviously related through the conjunction *after*, and *term* takes its place in the sentence through its place in the clause.

We use our language thoughtlessly and without conscious attention to such grammatical matters, but we cannot describe or discuss our writing in any detail without analyzing our sentences, by seeing and naming the relationships that exist between our words. In brief sentences the relations are usually clear, but in longer ones they are often obscured though the frame of the sentence and the relations themselves remain the same.

For convenience in labeling the parts of sentences we can indicate the elements by letters and indicate three main levels of relation and two others, apposition and connection.

2a. Main elements. The typical English sentence is composed of a *subject* (s), the starting point of the statement, and a

verb (v) or *linking verb* (LV) or "copula" (*be, become, feel, seem*). The meaning of the verb may be completed by an *object* (o) or an *indirect object* (IO), and the meaning of a linking verb is completed by a *complement* (c).

The subject, verb, and object form the frame of the typical sentence, to which other elements stand in some definite relationship that can be described in grammatical terms.

The following examples show the main elements in ordinary patterns:

     s   v   o
Mrs. Pennoyer | bought | a dozen eggs.

   s   LV   c
Harold | felt | tired.

               s   LV   c
The highest ranking student | becomes | valedictorian.

                        s
That the others might have some trick plays |

           v   IO
  had never occurred | to them.

s   v   o
He | said | that they ought to know better.

*Noun clauses

*Phrases
*Clauses
*Adjectives,
use
*Adverbs, use

(Note that in the last two sentences the subject of one, *that the others might have trick plays*, and the object of the other, *that they ought to know better*, are clauses with subjects and verbs of their own, but that they have the construction of a single word as an element of the sentences of which they are a part.)

2b. Secondary elements. Words, phrases, and clauses that are not one of these main elements may be related to the sentence by modifying one of the main elements (The *highest ranking* student). These secondary elements may be indicated by italic letters: adjective elements modifying the subject (*ms*), or modifying the object (*mo*), or the complement (*mc*); adverbial elements modifying the verb (*mv*).

<pre>
        ms   s   v   o
Coming into the open, | he | could see | the tracks |
        mv
    more plainly.
            mv   s   v
When he came into the open, | he | could see
        o   mv
    the tracks | more plainly.
        ms   s   ms
The high school | orchestra, | which was directed by Mr.
            v   mo   o   mv
    Appley, | played | two numbers | between each act.
</pre>

The sentence as a whole is often modified by a word or group of words, a *sentence modifier* (*sm*):

<pre>
    sm   s   v   o
Certainly, | he | knew | it. (This differs from "He certainly
    knew it," in which certainly modifies knew.)
                sm   s   LV
If we take motive into account, | the crime | does not seem |
    c
    so serious.
</pre>

2c. Third elements. Other words may be related to the pattern of the sentence by modifying these secondary elements (The *local* high school orchestra, *more* plainly). Since their relationship to the secondary elements is like that of secondary elements to the main, there is no need for a separate symbol for them, but if it is necessary to indicate the relationship, another *m* (for *modifier*) can be used:

<pre>
    mms   ms   s   v   mmv   mv
The local high school orchestra | played | unusually well.
</pre>

121

There may be further degrees of modification (An almost / completely / accurate / description), but since the fundamental relationship is the same, it is rarely worth while regarding them as a separate rank in describing or diagramming the movement of the sentence.

*Apposition   **2d. Appositives.** Some words repeat the content and function of other words, are in *apposition* (*a*) to other words:

> s   sa   v   c
> The word *company* | may be | either singular or plural.
> mv   mva   s   v   o
> Then, while we studied, | they | played | the radio.

*Prepositions   **2e. Connectives.** Prepositions that introduce phrases and conjunctions that introduce clauses are not elements of the
*Conjunctions and articles there referred to   whole sentence but of the constructions in which they occur. The phrase or clause as a whole is an element of the sentence. If a conjunction relates a sentence to the one before, it is an element of the sentence and can be indicated as a *sentence connective* (*sc*).

> PHRASE: *between* each act
> CLAUSE: *when* the party broke up
>   ms   s   sc   LV
> SENTENCE CONNECTIVE: This plan, | however, | seemed |
> C
> useless.

3. Order of sentence elements

The effect of a sentence depends in part on the order in which its elements stand. The more elaborate the sentence is, the more important is the way it is built up.

3a. The typical English sentence. The typical order of the main sentence elements is: subject—verb—object or complement,

> s   v   o
> Sixty students | got | permission to leave early.
> s   LV   c
> Ash Wednesday | is | the first day of Lent.

No matter how many modifiers may be in the sentence, its basic pattern will ordinarily be s—v—o.

The typical order of sentence elements is so much a part of English grammar that we really identify subjects and objects, except when they are pronouns, by their position before or after the verb respectively (Jim [s] beat Frank [o]). This sense of posi-

122

tion is responsible also for such informal usage as *who* instead *who, § 2
of *whom* when as an object it precedes the verb or preposition
controlling it. (*Who* [in writing usually *whom*] was he with?)

3b. Inverted order. One standard departure from this typical
s-v-o order is *inversion,* in which the complement, or an
emphatic modifier of the verb stands first, followed by the verb
and the subject standing last (c-v-s). Or the object or complement may precede the subject and verb (o-s-v).

   o   s   v   *mv*
This book | he | was now reading | for the third time.
   c   s   v   *ca*
Foolish | he | was,] just plain foolish.
  mv   v   s   *ms*
First | came | the faculty | in academic costume.

Inversion is the usual order in questions that are not introduced by an interrogative pronoun:

   v s   o   *mv* v s   o
Does he think he can fool us?   Where did you get it?

An emphatic modifier often is the reason for inversion:
  mv   v   s   o
Only then did he realize what he had done.

3c. Position of modifiers. The English habit of placing modi- *Word order, § 3
fiers close to the words they modify is another important part
of grammatical word order. *Subordinate elements should clearly
refer to the words they modify.*

FAULTY ORDER	RIGHT ORDER
But the principal disapproved of the petition and enforced the law which he had made with the aid of the hall squad.	But the principal disapproved of the petition and with the aid of the hall squad enforced the law which he had made.
The jury convicted the defendant of assault and battery after deliberating two hours.	After deliberating two hours the jury convicted the defendant of assault and battery.
After eating breakfast, my mother sent me off to school.	My mother sent me off to school after I had had my breakfast.

*Participles, § 2

These matters of order are a matter of grammar, because they
affect the meaning of a sentence. Order of elements are also
matters of style, giving variety and emphasis. These uses are
discussed in Chapter 6, §§2 and 4, pages 155 and 165.

4. Coordination and subordination

Since a majority of sentences contain more than one clause, the means by which relation between clauses is shown is an important part of grammar. The relation should be clear to the reader and it should represent the writer's intention, that is, the relation that exists in his thought and that another can be led to see. In traditional English grammar there are two levels

of relation between clauses: they are of equal importance, that is, *coordinate*, or one is less important than the other, that is, *subordinate* to it. We usually identify the kind of clause by the connective which introduces it.

4a. Conjunctions. (1) *Coordinate clauses* are joined by: CO-ORDINATING CONJUNCTIONS: and, but, for, nor (and not), or, yet

CORRELATIVE CONJUNCTIONS: both . . . and, either . . . or, neither . . . nor, so . . . as, not only . . . but [but also], whether . . . or

CONJUNCTIVE ADVERBS: accordingly, also, besides, consequently, hence, however, indeed, namely, nevertheless, so, and some others

2) *Subordinate clauses* are related to the main clause of the sentence by a number of connectives:

SUBORDINATING CONJUNCTIONS: The most common are:

after	because	since	when
although	before	so that	where
as	how	though	while
as if	if	till	why
as long as	in order that	unless	

RELATIVE PRONOUNS: who, which, that, what

4b. Relation between clauses. The most important fact is that connectives represent the relationship between *ideas*; the exact meaning of the connective (cause, time, contrast, condition, and so on) is more important than subordination or coordination. Incidentally the type of clause shows by its grammatical level the relative importance of the statements as the writer regards them.

The general principle is that the more important, the principal statements should be in independent clauses, and the less important should be in subordinate clauses or in phrases. When a main statement is made subordinate or a less important one made into a main clause, we have "upside-down subordination."

A few inexact sentences, with possible revised forms, will illustrate how careful subordination can make statements more accurate.

INEXACT	REVISED
She had always liked singing and dancing and so she decided to learn tap-dancing and get a job.	Since she had always liked singing and dancing, she decided to learn tap-dancing and get a job.
The system of scrubbing sports has long been a tradition on the campus and I have found that scrubbing a sport means doing anything and everything.	I have found that the system of scrubbing sports that has long been a tradition on the campus means doing anything and everything.
Illustrations were given in every case and it was easily understood, which made it all the more interesting.	Illustrations were given in every case so that it was easily understood and all the more interesting.
Throughout it all I sat back and read and slept, and trusted to the discretion of my mother the clothes and equipment I needed.	Throughout it all I sat back and read and slept, trusting to the discretion of my mother the clothes and equipment I needed.
Mr. Oglethorpe, who was the original proprietor of Georgia, was a man who believed that every man had the right to defend his honor.	Mr. Oglethorpe, the original proprietor of Georgia, believed that every man had the right to defend his honor.
The Stanley Steamer looked like one of those cars of the nineties in every way except its wheels, and they were changed so as to use pneumatic.tires.	The Stanley Steamer looked in every way like one of those cars of the nineties except for its wheels, which were changed so as to use pneumatic tires.
Often a grave will contain no burial goods. Others might contain a few tools or beads. The latter is the more usual.	Although often a grave will contain no burial goods, usually one will contain a few tools or beads.
He may have attended both of the preceding classes, and by chapel time he begins to feel the desire for a respite from mental work.	If he has attended both of the preceding classes, by chapel time he begins to feel the desire for a respite from mental work.
He was recovering quite nicely when he had a relapse.	When he was recovering quite nicely, he had a relapse.

4c. Subordination and sentence movement. The use of subordinate clauses is a mark of an accurate and mature style. Children are said to subordinate about fifteen per cent of their statements, while mature writers subordinate about half of theirs. Sentences with subordinate elements are not only more accurate; they give greater variety and more exact emphasis than a series of coordinate statements.

The following brief quotation contains six subordinate clauses. The loss from translating them into simple declarative sentences shows something of the advantages of subordination.

STATEMENTS SUBORDINATED	WITHOUT SUBORDINATION
The contention that democracy is *per se* identical with mediocrity is a wanton assumption considering the fact that democracy, until it is realized economically as it has not yet been in capitalistic countries, has not been tried at all. Until it is tried economically it is too early to tell what the common man may contribute to uncommon achievement in literature and art and thought.—IRWIN EDMAN, *Four Ways of Philosophy*, p. 155	It is contended that democracy is *per se* identical with mediocrity. This is a wanton assumption. Democracy not realized economically is not democracy. In capitalistic countries this has not been tried at all. [The statements of Mr. Edman's second sentence are so closely interrelated that they cannot be broken down into separate statements in this fashion.]

Subordination is the principal means of avoiding or overcoming choppy sentences:

ORIGINAL PARAGRAPH	STUDENT'S REVISION
We made our second stop at a hotel on the top of the mountain. This hotel, six thousand feet above the sea, was equipped with modern conveniences. We were grateful for the limeade at twenty cents and the rhum at twenty-five cents. The lack of ice wasn't noticeable. Any drink would seem cool at 102°. The flower garden around the hotel was a welcome relief after the barren road we had traveled. The hotel had a banana plantation of about twenty-five trees.	At the crest of the mountain, 6000 feet above sea level, with the temperature at 102°, we welcomed drinks of limeade (20c) and rhum (25c), which were cooling even though they lacked ice. These drinks were served on the terrace of a modern hotel that overlooked a flower garden and a banana plantation of twenty-five trees, a scene that offered a pleasant relief from the barren road we had traveled.

The final adjustment between main and subordinate statements is one of the concerns of revision.

4d. Sentences classed according to their clauses. The most usual classification of sentences is according to the number and the kind of clauses they contain.

1) SIMPLE: having one independent subject-verb statement, though the subject or the predicate may be compound and any element may be modified by words and phrases, but not by a clause (which would make another subject and verb statement).

*Simple sentences

> Constant change is the outstanding characteristic of a live language used by an intellectually alive people.—C. C. FRIES, *American English Grammar*, p. 6
>
> WITH COMPOUND SUBJECT: Many historical *differences* and some sectional *differences* have become also social differences. —*Ibid.*, p. 11

*Compound subject

> WITH COMPOUND PREDICATE: The first *used* the study of systematic or formal grammar, *aimed* at a knowledge of rules, and *demanded* much practice in classification, analysis, and parsing.—*Ibid.*, p. 23

*Compound predicate

> WITH PARTICIPIAL PHRASE: *In referring to Hitler's failure to win friends and influence people in the United States* I have judged his propaganda in terms of its immediate results.— QUINCY HOWE, *The News and How to Understand It*, p. 203

2) COMPOUND: having two or more main statements but no subordinate clauses:

*Compound sentences

> WITH COORDINATING CONJUNCTION: Strikers, reformers, plutocrats, and sociologists will be no more, *and* the world will be delivered from the Idle Poor and the Busy Rich.—DON MARQUIS, *The Almost Perfect State*, p. 91

*Coordinating conjunctions

> WITHOUT CONNECTIVE: Each set of language practices is best in its own special sphere of use; one will necessarily differ from the other.—C. C. FRIES, *op. cit.*, p. 9

*Contact clauses

3) COMPLEX: having one main statement and one or more statements in subordinate clauses:

*Complex sentences

*Clauses

> [Main clause:] It assumes [noun clause:] that the most important facts concerning any words, forms, or constructions of language are the circumstances [adjective clause:] in which they are usually used, [adverbial clause:] because these words, forms, or constructions will inevitably suggest these circumstances.— C. C. FRIES, *op. cit.*, p. 24
>
> [Main clause:] Maturity consists in understanding [noun clause:] what is possible to one's own nature, given the nature of things.—IRWIN EDMAN, *Four Ways of Philosophy*, p. 281

*Compound
sentences, § 4

4) COMPOUND-COMPLEX: having two or more main clauses and one or more subordinate clauses:

> The families of the wealthy, especially those whose wealth has continued for several generations, ordinarily mix but little with the families of unskilled laborers; and the families of college professors even in a small city have usually very little social life in common with the families of policemen and firemen.—C. C. FRIES, *op. cit.*, p. 10

5. Parallelism in sentence form

5a. Successful parallelism. Since a sentence is a unit, all ways of maintaining and showing this unity are important. Besides the order of elements and use of specific connectives, parallelism is one of the most useful ways of holding sentence elements together. *Parallelism means that elements that have the same relationship to the statement are expressed by words in the same grammatical construction.* Two or more locutions of the same grammatical rank and in similar phrasing (adjectives, nouns, verbs in the same form, clauses or whole sentences of the same kind . . .) are said to be parallel. Such constructions are natural to the writer when they represent accurately his view of his material, and they are convenient to the reader, since they suggest by their form this relation that the writer intends.

*Parallelism
and
balance,
p. 159

Elaborate parallelism is a trait of style, but elementary parallelism is a trait of grammar, because it primarily shows relationships between parts of the sentence. Various elements in the following sentences are held together by parallelism.

> During three periods of liberal pressure from outside the Court, Mr. Chief Justice Hughes voted ‖ liberal forty-one times,
> ‖ reactionary ten times.
> IRVING BRANT, *The New Republic,* July 28, 1937

(The parallelism would have been violated if the last phrase had been "with the reactionaries ten times.")

> I shall not begin with
> ‖ any general definition of
> ‖ what is and
> ‖ what is not poetry,
> ‖ or any discussion of whether poetry need be always in
> ‖ verse, or any consideration of the difference
> ‖ between the poetry-verse antithesis
> ‖ and the poetry-prose antithesis.
> T. S. ELIOT, *The Use of Poetry and
> the Use of Criticism,* p. 5

We should || collaborate with all of them on routine matters in a fair spirit,

keep every engagement entered into with them to the letter, and

show calmness and official reserve in the face of provocative gestures so long as they remain gestures only.

H. F. ARMSTRONG, *We or They*, p. 44

The good life is one || inspired by love and || guided by knowledge.

BERTRAND RUSSELL, *What I Believe*, p. 28

She walked slowly, big flakes || falling on her lamb coat and || clinging to hair over her ears . . .

MORLEY CALLAGHAN, *A Native Argosy*, p. 155

Parallel clauses help tie parts of a thought together and are one of the simplest ways of showing the reader that they are equal in the writer's mind. Note that parallel clauses usually begin with the same connective or with other words that are obviously parallel—the binding is in the first few words:

The teacher must realize

|| that usage varies from the grossly illiterate to the most precise of literary distinctions,

|| that the line between permissible and nonpermissible uses is by no means fixed, and

|| that the correction of expressions accepted by a high percentage of linguistic experts is a sheer waste of time.

An Experience Curriculum in English, p. 241

|| Although some were shouting, || like the men and women on the pier

|| although some were hysterical, || like the men and women crowding around the plank,

|| although some were dazed,

|| there was a difference between them and the persons who awaited them.

LEANE ZUGSMITH, *Home Is Where You Hang Your Childhood*, p. 65

5b. Failure in parallelism: Shifted constructions. Failure to use similar or parallel constructions for ideas in similar relationship violates conventional English grammar. Inconsistent constructions make for difficult reading. Whether they are from ignorance of the possibilities of the language or from careless, hasty writing, they should be avoided.

*Shifted constructions

129

Some common shifted constructions are:

1) IN POINT OF VIEW. (*a*) *Shift of subject*:

SHIFTED: His admiration for Paderewski is that of any pupil for his master and has had many pleasurable visits with his old friend.

CONSISTENT: He admires Paderewski as any pupil does his master and he has had many pleasurable visits with his old friend.

SHIFTED: First the book is read, and after that you are required to write a synopsis of it.

CONSISTENT: First you read the book and then you write a required synopsis of it; [or] First you are required to read the book and then to write a synopsis of it.

b) *Shift from impersonal to personal statement*:

SHIFTED: The first two years of college are practically wasted. A freshman studies a random collection of courses in several departments, French, English, a history course, chemistry or mathematics. In his sophomore year he takes "introductory courses," though he doesn't know what they introduce him to. It is only in his junior year, I think, that he really begins his education.

IMPROVED: The first two years of college, I think, are practically wasted. . . .

SHIFTED: After the initial schism was made in the Catholic Church, the various ideas of what we should believe concerning our Past took many strange and divers paths; most of them, however, having the common denominator of history as a state of progress. It is to some of these ideas that we now turn, with all due humility and full recognition of my own insignificance in comparison with the giant intellects which produced them.

TO IMPROVE: Drop the apology altogether or use a formula like "Let us now turn to some of these ideas."

c) *Shift from negative to positive statement* or the reverse:

SHIFTED: Poems should not exceed 40 lines and prose articles over 800 words.

CONSISTENT: Poems should not exceed 40 lines and prose articles should not exceed 800 words. (Or omit second "should not exceed.")

2) IN VERBS. (*a*) *Shift between active and passive verbs*:

SHIFTED: The lines passed [active] the reviewing stand in good order but a few moments later they were seen [passive] grinning and uneven and out of step.

CONSISTENT (both active): The lines passed the reviewing stand in good order but a few moments later they were grinning and uneven and out of step.

b) *Shift between participles and other parts of verb:*

SHIFTED: Do you approve letting children run wild and doing anything they want to?

CONSISTENT: Do you approve letting children run wild and do anything they want to?

SHIFTED: Pupin continues writing in his steady manner, never or hardly ever changing his sentence structure, but proceeds [Change to: proceeding] with his usual long and direct sentences.

SHIFTED: His style does become monotonous after reading the book awhile, but as he progresses rapidly, not staying on any one incident too long, he does write interestingly; therefore not needing [therefore he does not need] much sharp conversation or variation of sentences.

c) *Shift between moods:*

SHIFTED: First take [imperative] a good look around and then you should decide [indicative] which section you want to aim for.

BOTH IMPERATIVE: First take a good look around and then decide which section you want to aim for.

(Other shifted constructions are discussed in: *Comparison of adjectives and adverbs §5, *Coordinating conjunctions §2, *Reference of pronouns §§1 and 3, *Tenses of verbs §3.)

6. Incomplete sentences

As we have already said in sections 1 and 2 of this chapter, a sentence is a grammatically independent statement and the typical, the usual English sentence has a subject and predicate. There are, however, a few types of sentence that lack one or the other of these two main elements.

6a. Verbless sentences. There are several types of sentence without a main verb that are common and in good if rather limited use in all levels of speaking and writing. The verbs are not "left out"; they are not thought, spoken, or written. The statements are complete and independent without them.

1) EXCLAMATIONS, from *Ouch!* and other monosyllables to *What a mess!* and on to complicated phrasing of direct feeling.

2) ANSWERS TO QUESTIONS, from *Yes* and *No* and *Not if I know it,* to specific answers to definite questions:

And what was the philosophy behind the Sherman Act and the Clayton Act? *Individualism, pure and undefiled.* "The New Freedom" *as President Wilson phrased it in literary language.*

"Break up the trusts and let each tub stand on its own bottom."
That was the cry among little business men.—C. A. BEARD, *The
Myth of Rugged American Individualism*, p. 14

3) DESCRIPTIVE DETAILS, ADDED MODIFIERS. Often in passages
that are chiefly descriptive, especially if the details are given
as impressions, the only verb possible would be a colorless *is*
or *are* or *has* or *have*. This is suppressed without loss of meaning and with gain in economy and sharpness.

And after all the weather was ideal. They could not have had
a more perfect day for a garden-party if they had ordered it.
Windless, warm, the sky without a cloud. Only the blue was
veiled with a haze of light gold, as it is sometimes in early summer.—KATHERINE MANSFIELD, *The Garden Party*, p. 59

There was one in particular of Mother looking very roguish
and chic in her voluminous dress, sitting way up on top of a tall
and insolent camel, with two big black men in white turbans
standing off at one side. *No other member of the party around.
Not a soul in sight but the black men and Mother.* Father
looked at that photograph often and groaned about it at night,
and kept shouting things to himself about "the ends of the earth."
—CLARENCE DAY, *Life With Father*, p. 116

The fat old porter knocks. Ah, me, once more it is dark. Get
up again before dawn. *A dark sky outside, cloudy. The thrilling
tinkle of innumerable goat-bells as the first flock enters the city,
such a rippling sound.* Well, it must be morning, even if one
shivers at it. And at least it does not rain.—D. H. LAWRENCE,
Sea and Sardinia, p. 35

Often in passages portraying a character's thought the verbs
are omitted, increasing the speed and naturalness of movement:

Principles—he mused—*au fond* were pocket; and he wished the
deuce people wouldn't pretend they weren't! *Pocket, in the deep
sense of that word, of course, self-interest as members of a definite
community.* And how the devil was this definite community, the
English nation, to exist, . . .—JOHN GALSWORTHY, *The White
Monkey*, p. 3

4) APPOSITIONAL SENTENCE. The sentence in which an adjective or other modifier is set beside its noun without benefit
of verb is very common.

An understatement, this.—S. E. MORISON, *Harvard College in
the Seventeenth Century*, p. 320
No verb no predication.—P. B. BALLARD, *Thought and Language*, p. 83

Easy enough to argue that the increased estate taxes are de-voted to governmental social programs in the public interest.

Hard to drive out the fear of politics in the administration of public philanthropy.—*Nation's Business*, Dec. 1936

Appositional sentences often serve as transitions:

So much for the proviso "English." Now for a more important proviso, that of "period or periods."—E. M. FORSTER, *Aspects of the Novel*, p. 21

5) CLAUSES AND PHRASES. Occasionally a phrase or subordi-nate clause, adverbial or adjective, stands alone as a sentence. These are usually light (*Which is another story. Not that it matters.*) or almost formulas; or sometimes a *because*- or a *which*-clause is set off by itself for emphasis:

There we are; now let us classify them. *Which he does.*—E. M. FORSTER, *Aspects of the Novel*, p. 27
Marks! Your marks had to be up to a certain standard. You had to get good marks to get promoted. *Into the next grade. Into high school. Into college.* Marks counted.—JOHN R. TUNIS, *Ladies' Home Journal*, Sept. 1938

Such sentences are rare, for usually participial phrases and subordinate clauses suggest by their very form that they are dependent upon what precedes or follows and should rarely be left standing as sentences. See *6c* below.

6b. Subjectless sentences. Sentences without subjects are much less common than sentences without verbs. There are a few of a traditional pattern like *No sooner said than done* and commands and requests (imperative sentences):

Don't let me ever hear you say that again. Please try.

Other subjectless sentences are confined almost entirely to nar-rative in which the subject is easily understood from the con-text, or to very informal and familiar writing. The most com-monly omitted subject is *I*, which receives very little stress in speaking. This type of sentence is most appropriate to repre-senting dialog in stories or in informal sketches of people: *I, pronoun, §§ 2, 3

They took no interest in civilized ways. Hadn't heard of them, probably.—CLARENCE DAY, *Life With Father*, p. 30
"Guess I can live on the town if I've a mind to. Been paying taxes for thirty years and more."—ERSKINE CALDWELL, *We Are the Living*, p. 219
You needn't be alarmed about the water's having fish in it. Means it's on the alkaline side.—*The New Yorker*, Oct. 30, 1937

6c. Fragmentary sentences. Most other types of incomplete sentences are unsuccessful and to be avoided. A sentence part that is carelessly or ineffectively punctuated as a whole sentence is called a *fragmentary sentence.* It is usually the result of the writer's carelessness, or of his not being sufficiently conscious of the relation between parts of his statements, or, very often, merely of lack of practice in writing. *Prepositional phrases, participial phrases, and subordinate clauses show by their form as well as by their incomplete meaning that they are parts of other constructions and are not meant to stand alone.* Because readers rightly expect the form of statements to represent the actual relation between their parts, editors and teachers expect most sentences to fall into the typical s-v-o pattern.

Here are specimens of three common types of fragmentary sentences with suggested remedies. All of them show by their form that they are dependent elements, not stable enough to stand alone.

1) PARTICIPIAL PHRASES

Looking carefully through his water glass he finds a liner deep in the quicksand, lying on her side. *The nearest porthole being twelve feet down.* He anchors his boat, takes a wrench and dives down to the porthole and tries to break it.

National elections and student elections in the high school I attended may be compared as closely as an object and its own photograph. *The only difference being in size.*

At the end of each reporting period each subject was marked numerically, on the basis of one hundred. *The Deportment column covering all the social habits of the child.*

2) SUBORDINATE CLAUSES

At the time my old rowboat and three horsepower motor seemed to be a high speed job to me. *Although it only attained a speed of about twelve miles an hour.*

IMPROVED FORMS

Looking carefully through his water glass he finds a liner deep in the quicksand, lying on her side, her nearest porthole twelve feet down. He anchors his boat, takes a wrench, dives down to the porthole and tries to break it.

National elections and student elections in the high school I attended may be compared as closely as an object and its own photograph; the only difference was in size.

At the end of each reporting period each subject was marked numerically, on the basis of one hundred. The Deportment column covered all the social habits of the child.

IMPROVED FORMS

At the time my old rowboat and three horsepower motor seemed to be a high speed job to me, although it only attained a speed of about twelve miles an hour.

2) SUBORDINATE CLAUSES

Leather-Stocking was first drawn as an old man and his youth described last of all. *While the other periods of his life were filled in in a very erratic order.* Yet he is the same character from beginning to end.

Green Mansions is a weird, wandering story, the main part of which is taken up with description of the South American jungles. *While the characters, who provide a beautiful romance of the tropical forests, seem incidental.*

IMPROVED FORMS

Although Leather-Stocking was drawn first as an old man and the other periods of his life were filled in in a very erratic order, his youth the last of all, he is the same character from beginning to end.

Green Mansions is a weird, wandering story, the main part of which is taken up with description of the South American jungles. The characters, who provide a beautiful romance of the tropical forests, seem incidental.

Contrast these two *because*-clauses, one of which seems stable because it is in direct answer to a question, the second not stable because it directly explains the preceding statement and should be related to it:

SUCCESSFUL: Why? Because service and ethics are service and ethics, and the business of business is business.

UNSUCCESSFUL: Finally another season came to an end but this had been a more happy one for me. Because I now had my own boat and I thought I was on my way to bigger and better outfits.

3) BRIEF EXPLANATORY ENUMERATIONS, especially when introduced by a phrase like *"such as"*:

After these cards have been run through, the firm knows what volume of business has been done during the week in each of the departments. Such as tobaccos, candies, canned fruits, fresh produce. [Simply join to the preceding sentence, using a comma after *departments*.]

WEAK FRAGMENT

When I first arrived all was quiet, but soon men began to gather with their dinner pails. Some on foot, others in wagons, and the higher class in Model T Fords.

IMPROVED FORM

When I first arrived all was quiet, but soon men began to gather with their dinner pails, on foot, in wagons, and the higher class in Model T Fords.

Most fragmentary sentences like these are careless, and a writer revising his paper with attention and care would not let them stand.

In deciding whether or not to let an incomplete sentence stand in your writing, apply the principle of appropriateness and consider the types of reputable incomplete sentences described in this section. Certainly remove those that are careless and that suggest by their form that they should be built on to neighboring sentences. In rather formal writing, an incomplete sentence that is not of a generally recognized pattern like an answer to a question or an exclamation is usually out of place. In informal writing there is somewhat more leeway, but still you should remember that most readers are more or less offended by departures from the typical English sentence patterns.

Teachers and students will not always agree on whether a particular incomplete sentence is legitimate or a fragment, any more than professional writers and editors of publishing houses agree on such matters. But the classifications we have suggested should make it possible to agree on grounds of effectiveness and appropriateness. Unformed sentences are a handicap to a reader and a mark of a careless or immature writer. You should make sure that the sentences you let stand represent an accurate grouping of your ideas and show the relation existing between those ideas.

To guard against careless incomplete sentences, some teachers ask students to indicate that one is intentional by putting a star or the word *intentional* in the margin. That is one way to play safe.

7. Run-on sentences

Two or more main clauses written with only a comma between them (or even, in particularly careless writing, with no mark at all between them) are called a run-on sentence. Judged by their grammatical form the two statements could be separate sentences. Whether or not they should be written as two sentences or revised in some other way depends in part on current practices in punctuation and sentence form, but more on the relations between the statements themselves.

7a. Successful run-on sentences: Contact clauses In books and articles by writers of high standing we find run-on sentences— and they have been passed, furthermore, by editorial copy readers. Here are a few:

*Contact clauses

> Men are said to be partial judges of themselves. Young men may be, I doubt if old men are.—T. H. Huxley, *Autobiography*.
> She loved Marise, nobody had a nicer little girl, nor a prettier.— Dorothy Canfield, *Rough-Hewn*, p. 135

The theatre was dark, the second show was over.—THOMAS WOLFE, *Look Homeward, Angel,* p. 275

This is to be our vision of them—an imperfect vision, but it is suited to our powers, it will preserve us from a serious danger, the danger of pseudo-scholarship. . . . They are gateways to employment, they have power to ban and bless. . . .—E. M. FORSTER, *Aspects of the Novel,* pp. 22, 24

Such sentences have always been common in speech ("Hurry up, we'll be late"—spoken without dropping the voice after *up*) and recently, with the increasing colloquialness of written style, they have become more common in writing. One of the best ways to test such a run-on sentence is to speak it aloud in a natural tone. If your voice drops as it does at the end of a sentence, it is a comma fault and should be written as two sentences or revised to some other form. If your voice does not drop ("They had to take him out finally, he was crying so loud") and if the two clauses read naturally with no more pause than ordinarily stands between two clauses of the same sentence, it may be a good sentence. Such a relationship between clauses without an expressed connective has been called *parataxis* and *asyndeton,* but we are using a simpler name for it, suggested by Professor Jespersen: *contact clauses.*

Besides this oral test, you should consider the closeness of the relation between the ideas of the two clauses. The punctuation between two contact clauses should represent the writer's intention. Taking a run-on sentence as a question of punctuation and intending to make the punctuation represent the writer's intention, a comma, a semicolon, or a period is possible. A period marks the largest degree of separation, two statements that the writer wishes to keep separate. A semicolon between them means that to the writer the statements are not closely related, but still the relation between them is closer than that between either of them and the statement preceding or following. A comma should mean that they are very closely related and that they can be spoken as one genuine sentence.

Besides the relation between the thought of the two clauses, you should consider their appropriateness to other features of your writing. You should remember the widespread prejudice against them, and that editors do not often let them stand in matter they are to publish. *Run-on sentences are almost always inappropriate in formal English,* which is usually conventional and avoids colloquial constructions. Two contact clauses in the midst of a rather fully and formally developed passage will ordinarily seem a let-down, a bit of carelessness. *They are rare, too, in discussions of ideas,* even when they are rather informally written, because exposition primarily shows the relationships between statements and that means ordinarily linking them by specific connectives. Occasionally the relationship is obvious, or some other trait of style, especially parallel construction, makes running together natural:

> That is why, in the rather ramshackly course that lies ahead of us, we cannot consider fiction by periods, we must not contemplate the stream of time.—E. M. FORSTER, *Aspects of the Novel,* p. 28

They are most useful in easy, rapid narrative (factual or imaginative), in which the clauses are relatively short, approaching the short turns of actual speech, and in which relationships can be rapidly grasped without the aid of connectives. In fact connectives would ordinarily bring an unneeded note of formality into such narrative.

These principles can usually help a writer decide in revising his manuscript whether he should let a run-on sentence stand or should rewrite it. A sentence like "After stepping back to survey his work, he finds that the steps are not even, another brick must be put under the bottom one" would not be noticeably bettered if it was made more conventional by adding a second *that:* "After stepping back to survey his work, he finds that the steps are not even, that another brick must be put under the bottom one." Nor, in a definitely informal context, would a more elaborate version of this sentence be an improvement: "Gosh, I thought, if anything more can happen to us, bring it on, I can stand anything now."

7b. Unsuccessful: Comma fault. A carelessly run-on sentence is variously referred to as a Comma Blunder, a Comma Fault, or Comma Splice. In the following "sentence" three locutions with a subject and complete verb (and so capable of standing as separate sentences) are run together:

> Their future looked pitifully black, they were working and getting nowhere, instead of profiting by their labors they were losing.

Since in reading these aloud your voice drops at the end of each, they should be written as three sentences or else rewritten in some other form:

> Their future looked pitifully black. They were working and getting nowhere. Instead of profiting by their labors they were losing.

After their seven years of school English, college students should have no difficulty in knowing when they have a grammatically complete sentence or when they have joined two of them. The students who turned in these were probably not paying attention to their work:

> Hitler has no children, if he did, they would have little chance to succeed their father.

> We burned wood then and he always made a great deal of noise with the lids, you could hear him all over the house.

> In the autumn of 1930, forty-eight persons were shot by an order of the Gay-Pay-oo, among this group were many distinguished professors and specialists.

Probably most of the comma faults in student writing occur because the writer has made two sentences grammatically complete in form for what should be a main and a subordinate statement with the relationship between them clearly indicated.

One of the commonest types of comma fault has a personal or demonstrative pronoun (*he, it, they . . . this, that . . .*) used instead of a relative pronoun (*who, which*):

UNSUCCESSFUL	IMPROVED
The Ranger's crew is made up of 26 professional sailors, most of them are of Scandinavian ancestry.	The Ranger's crew is made up of 26 professional sailors, most of them of [most of whom are of] Scandinavian ancestry.
While a boy lives at home he is dependent on others, they help him out of his difficulties and provide at least for his necessities.	While a boy lives at home he is dependent on others who help him out of his difficulties and provide at least for his necessities.

Many comma faults are due simply to separating ideas that should be fused into one statement:

UNSUCCESSFUL	IMPROVED
This last piece of work was very difficult, the hack-saw blades grew hot and broke.	This last piece of work was so difficult that the hack-saw blades grew hot and broke.
One part receives the stimulus from outside and transmits the impulse to the cell, this is known as the dendrite.	One part, known as the dendrite, receives the stimulus from outside and transmits the impulse to the cell.
The pressmen were a good natured bunch who seldom complained about their conditions, instead they usually joked about them.	The pressmen were a good natured bunch who more often joked about their conditions than complained.

139

Another common type is when a second verb is used in a construction that does not require it:

Unsuccessful	Improved
Then came the speeches, some of them were very amusing while others were very serious.	Then came the speeches, some of them very amusing, others very serious.

In each of these the thought seems to be single and rightly put in one sentence but the connection between parts of the thought was not shown exactly enough. Of course very often sentences profit from more drastic revision than is shown in these examples.

Sometimes a conjunction can be properly inserted that would make the sentence compound:

Unsuccessful	Improved
The rules governing the freshmen aren't wrong, the method of enforcing them should be corrected.	The rules governing the freshmen aren't wrong, but the method of enforcing them should be corrected.

Only once in a while will the easiest (laziest) change, repunctuating with a period or semicolon, make the sentence really any better. A semicolon between the two clauses is often suggested, but it would not have helped materially any of the sentences given above and usually should not be used unless there is a connective. Sometimes a dash will mark the abruptness of the break in thought, but in most styles dashes should be kept for more special uses.

*Dash

The vigilantes did not bother with courts which might cause a wait of six months for satisfaction, instead they hung their men as close to the scene of the crime as possible and left the body there as an example.	; better here
The long days of Front and Market streets were a thing of the past, the store now opened for business at eight in the morning and closed at six-thirty, including Saturdays.	Probably better as two sentences
Business today does not wait for a young fellow to learn, if the new employee does not seem fitted for the job another is found to take his place.	; or . depending on emphasis desired

140

In reading all of these you drop your voice at the comma, which shows that the clauses have the form and value of two separate sentences. *The point to consider is whether the ideas are closely enough related to stand properly in a single sentence, and then whether the relationship has been shown.*

To guard against carelessly run-on sentences (comma faults), some teachers ask students to mark contact clauses they wish to leave by a star or the word *intentional* in the margin. As with incomplete sentences, this is a good way to play safe.

8. Writing and revising sentences

It is much easier to describe sentences than it is to make suggestions for writing them effectively. One reason is that we are not conscious of individual sentences in speaking—and shouldn't be in writing. We can figure out the plan of a paper before writing, and we can see the general form of a paragraph in our mind before putting it on paper. But sentences are best written without too much conscious attention—*and then revised*.

The points that have been made in this chapter should be applied in revision, when you read over what you have written and can consider matters of form without interfering with your thinking. Some conscious practice, as in exercises, is useful to focus attention on different phases of sentences and to give practice in remaking them. Then you can do the same to your own sentences, if they need it. Gradually your first draft sentences will improve and less revision will be necessary.

If you have got as far as college without picking up the fundamental patterns of English sentences, you should make up for lost time in a hurry. College students and college teachers shouldn't waste their time on sixth-grade work. But no matter how correct your sentences may be, there is still chance for further growth in other qualities.

Practice in writing will show most effect in increased skill in composing mature, meaningful sentences. Letters, papers in all courses as well as in the composition course, even short impromptu bits jotted down and thrown away will help. One of the surest ways to grow in these details would be to write something every day, even if it wasn't more than half a page, and glance it over for sentence form. Any practice in writing you can give yourself will show in increased control of sentences.

Exercises

*Pages 116-17 1. Study the following definitions of a sentence:

1. The word *sentence* means (1) a group of words composed of a subject (with or without adjuncts) and a predicate (with or without adjuncts) and not grammatically dependent on any words outside itself (e.g., "I will go," "I, being the person best acquainted with the situation, will go as soon as the carriage which I ordered has come"); or (2) two or more such groups joined by coordinating conjunctions or presented in such a way as to show that they are to be taken as a unit.—E. C. WOOLLEY, *New Handbook of Composition*, p. 310

2. A group of words so related as to convey a completed thought with the force of asserting something or of asking, commanding, exclaiming, or wishing, and marked at the close, in writing, by a period, question mark, or exclamation point.— *Webster's Collegiate Dictionary*, 5th ed.

3. The sentence is a complete communication in words, containing a verb of independent rank, with its subject.—JANET R. AIKEN, *A New Plan of English Grammar*, p. 14

4. A sentence is a (relatively) complete and independent human utterance—the completeness and independence being shown by its standing alone or its capability of standing alone, i.e. of being uttered by itself.—OTTO JESPERSEN, *Philosophy of Grammar*, p. 307

5. It seems wiser for the grammarian not to attempt any scientific definition of the sentence, but to rest content with some approximate description, such as the statement, for example, that sentences are the separate structural units into which thought is broken as it proceeds step by step in a sequence of expression.—GEORGE P. KRAPP, *The Knowledge of English*, p. 247

6. So a sentence is the discourse between two points; the two points being consecutive full stops.—BALLARD, *Thought and Language*, p. 59.—It is as much of my full purpose as I care to reveal at the very moment—as much of my meaning as I wish to deliver in one handful.—*Ibid.*, p. 65

7. A "complete" thought, or what we may call a sentence-thought, is therefore any idea or group of ideas that is felt as answering to one impulse of attention. Not its amount of meaning but its being felt as *directed* is what makes it complete.— A. D. SHEFFIELD, *Command of Sentence-Patterns*, p. 24

8. From this point of view, the sentence may be regarded as a section of the stream of thought having such an extent and logical coherence of parts that it may be grasped as one unitary conception in much the same way as a quincunx or a triangle or a square of dots is grasped.—PILLSBURY AND MEADER, *The Psychology of Language*, p. 261

142

9. A sentence is a group of words which have some connection in meaning. Between the sentence signals—the capital and the period—these words state something that makes sense for a reader or listener. *Sentence sense* means merely the ability to "feel the wholeness" of meaning in the statements you are reading or writing.—SALISBURY AND LEONARD, *Making Sense*, p. 55

10. . . . a deliberately separated phase of the thought continuum; to the ear, set off by a longer pause than obtains at any point within it; to the eye by an end punctuation mark.—EDITH RICKERT, *New Methods for the Study of Literature*, p. 111

a) In 2 and 3 what is a *completed thought*? Would a definition involving this phrase fit equally well a simple sentence, one clause of a compound sentence, a whole compound sentence?

b) Do these definitions lead you to believe that a sentence is primarily a psychological (thought) unit or a grammatical unit depending on the presence of certain grammatical functions such as subject and verb? Consider Definitions 1, 4, 6, and 9.

c) Why is a sentence difficult to define?

d) Can you make a satisfactory definition? If not, do you think you have, nevertheless, a fairly good working idea of what a sentence is?

e) Some of these definitions agree with the doctrine given in §1 of this chapter; others do not. Pick what seems to you the best of each group and write a discussion, pointing out their good points and also their weaknesses or flaws.

2. For each of the following paragraphs make an analysis of the clauses similar to that in the article *Complex sentences.

If there is in the universe any organism whose reactions are completely predictable, it is the New York cop. We could have warned those volunteer firemen who tried to help out last week with the fire down on Thirty-fourth Street that one of the cops present would say, "That armband don't mean anything to me— ga wan, get back!" and that another would say, "Ga wan, ya more nuisance than ya worth!" To explain to a cop, whose mind is full of his own murky ideology, whose every energy is devoted to his war with the civilian population, that there is now another war on, that the city conceivably might be bombed, that if it is bombed there will be more fires than the regular Fire Department can handle, that the volunteer firemen will then be our only hope of saving the city, and that it is a good idea for them to get some experience before the emergency—this is a chore which we, for one, would not care to undertake. It is our observation that all abstract discussion of citizens' rights or duties is met by the jolly roundsmen with a simple, reticent "Ga wan!"

We predict that when the bombs start falling, the cops will react by laying about with their billies, and our advice is to stay home if you don't want to be run in.—*The New Yorker*, Mar. 7, 1942

Lest you feel that you are to be overburdened with superstructures of plot which might in their mechanism destroy a feeling of life reality in your work, remember that all composition is rigidly governed by systems of syntax, grammar and rhetoric; however, just as after a few years out of school you write without *thinking* of grammar, because you have learned it and "forgotten" it (use it subconsciously instead of consciously), so will you, after learning the rules of plot, use plot subconsciously and intuitively.— JACK WOODFORD, *Plotting*, p. 37

It was a long rough road we had traveled together, friends from the first, sometimes understanding, often misunderstanding. Yet in all that time I can remember no major issue on which we had disagreed. A remark overheard, a headline, a glimpse through the window of the dingy little bar, and I would look over at him, and he would raise his eyebrows to look across at me. Had I not been so numb with misery on account of the brutal injustices in Spain, I should have been more deeply depressed when the Hôtel du Caveau closed its door. Madame Marie, frightened and loyal, could not keep it going. She took her sick husband to their house in Montmorency where quietly, in isolation and the hope for France he never could relinquish, Henri Julliard started slowly to die, a little day by day, as shells and bombs from Italy and Germany raked the helpless bodies of Spanish patriots, as the clubs of police and the bayonets of Senegalese battered and pricked the outraged French workers, as the day came nearer when no Frenchman could raise his head, when Liberty, Equality and Fraternity were stripped from the public buildings, when the land that had been civilization's darling became the orphan of rampant violence.—Elliot Paul, *The Last Time I Saw Paris*, pp. 362-63

3. The system of sentence analysis in §2 is easily enlarged to show the relation between elements of subordinate clauses. The whole clause can be enclosed in brackets, its elements marked with the same symbols as those of main clauses, and the relation of the clause as a whole to the rest of the sentence marked above.

The examples that follow will show the method at work:

   sm   *s*   *v*   *mo*   *o*
In the first place, | the club | doesn't have | enough members.

                           *m*v
s   *v*   *s* *v*   *mo*   *o*
Any sentence | can be analyzed | [if you use sufficient patience

and don't go | into unnecessary detail.]

A substitute | for rubber | [which would really take | its place]

had not been developed.

We | wondered | [when you would come.]

According to the system shown in §2, diagram the following passages:

The college cannot directly create the student's philosophy. Americans, young and old, are slow to accept dogmatic dicta and dislike to have their opinions formed for them. The college, however, can create the atmosphere and inspire the teaching force from which such a philosophy may emerge. While the undergraduate is suspicious of rhetoric and bombast, he is sensitive to a sincere and reasonable appeal. Clarify the issues, explain the dangers our American ideals face, emphasize the obligation to leadership which rests upon him, and the undergraduate will respond to the call.—CHARLES SEYMOUR, "War's Impact on the Campus," *New York Times Magazine*, September 29, 1940

In Louisiana he had a wife and three children. One day his wife petulantly asked him why he did not kill a hawk that was after her chickens. He was a marvelous shot. He could shoot a twig under a squirrel a hundred yards off and then with another shot kill the squirrel as it and the severed twig fell. On the day his wife urged him to kill the hawk, he picked up his gun and walked out in shirtsleeves. Something more than two years later he returned. "The hawk kept flying," were his only words of explanation. Then he left for the West, where the bears grow bigger.—J. Frank Dobie, "Mister Ben Lilly," *Saturday Review of Literature*, May 16, 1942

4. Study the sections on incomplete sentences in this chapter (§ 6a, § 6b, § 6c). In the following sentences make the alterations in wording or punctuation necessary to improve those which seem to you incorrect or ineffective. Whether you change a passage or leave it as it is, write a clear statement of your reasons.

1. It seems wrong that a few executives should be paid more than a hundred thousand a year. While other men are trying to support families on fifteen dollars a week.

2. The citizens demand real police protection. Where they need it. When they need it. Whenever they need it.

3. When statistics show that more than three quarters of the criminals sentenced to prison are under twenty-three, they reveal something in our system of crime-prevention definitely bad. Something still worse, when they show that more than half of these men are rearrested within two years after their release. The complete futility of prison both as a preventive and as a cure.

4. The time will come when men will no longer listen to the promises of political messiahs. When they will no longer sacrifice their comfort and prosperity for a State which in return gives empty words. When they will again demand some measure of liberty.

5. Finally, after the receipts were all in and the expenses had been met, the carnival netted a profit of more than eight hundred dollars. Which was what the committee had hoped for.

6. New York has a population of more than seven million. Being in one city one eighteenth of the population of the whole country.

7. In the last analysis, the success or failure of the eggs-in-one-basket city manager plan, despite varied arguments from advocates and opponents, will always depend on just one factor. The city manager.

8. The modern apartment offers many services and conveniences but is often bad for health. Lacking the sunlight and fresh air which destroy bacteria and help to prevent such diseases as tuberculosis.

9. "Do you believe that half a million men should be kept out of all productive industry to serve in the army in peace time?"

"Yes, because if these men were not in the army the Government would still have to support an equal number of the unemployed."

*Exercises, p. 252

5. Follow the same directions as in Exercise 4.

1. A real disappointment, a blow which Frances had dimly expected but still could not take without crying a little.

2. Row after row of vines, which were loaded with grapes at that season, stretching away as far as the eye could follow them.

3. The scene was aimlessly gay. Some couples strolling by the parapet, slowly back and forth; a few dancing; but most of them sitting at small tables near the dance floor.

4. Being poor at a given moment is easy enough to accept, but the prospect of being poor always may break a man's spirit.

5. All the old people moving, moving to that famous climate, hoping for a little more comfort, a little more sunshine, a little more ease after they had worked themselves out on the Middle Western farms.

6. Finally the engineers found a way to eliminate the noise. A beam of light which replaces the needle.

7. Ducks, hundreds of ducks, headed north! Spring was finally coming.

8. The room always looked restful. Low, informal chairs, cool gray walls, curtains with just a border of dull rose to break the gray, and always a feeling of space and graciousness.

9. This country is like the Arizona desert. But wilder and more barren.

10. So much for the economic problem.

6. In the following passage make an analysis of the sentences, noting particularly the order of sentence elements and the use of incomplete sentences. Try expressing the same ideas in a paragraph composed mainly of segregating sentences in typical order. Does the writer gain anything except complexity by the form he has chosen?

The gulf between the two conceptions of life is indeed deep and wide. Here, not absolute freedom certainly but great and precious freedom—freedom to think, to believe, to disbelieve, to speak, to will, to choose. There, not some freedom, but none— nothing but obeisance, body, mind and soul, before the iron will and upstretched arm of a restless, infallible master. But what makes us speculate so somberly on the possibility of maintaining tolerable relations between these two worlds is not just that dictators and their entourage of made-to-order philosophers, bogus scientists, subservient courts and dictated press hold different conceptions from ours about everything which we consider of importance. After revising histories, philosophies, bibles, and law codes they have proceeded to a revision of the dictionary itself. As a result, intercommunication across the abyss has become almost impossible. And with all means of argument, explanation and accommodation swept away, there grows up on both sides a not unjustifiable belief in the inevitability of a prolonged struggle for supremacy and survival.—HAMILTON F. ARMSTRONG, *We or They*, pp. 3-4

7. In the following passages, pick out the compound sentences, contact clauses, and comma faults. Discuss the appropriateness of each one, and revise those which you consider inappropriate.

1. (a) Ferguson can write educated, formal prose when he wants to, he seldom wants to for more than a phrase or two. (b) He never lets the language master him, he masters it and makes it do what he wants it to. (c) The somersaults he makes it take are at least unusual. (d) Some of them are just the result of natural exuberance, some pay deference to the technical lan-

guage of the stage, some are deliberately calculated for the contrast and timing of the comedian.

2. (a) Many readers, especially professional men, prefer biography to any other form of reading, they like to read about people, to meet them, so to speak, and find out about them. (b) Fictional characters in novels, even though they are usually composites of several real people and are made to seem lifelike, do not please them. (c) They are not real, the novelist is free to handle them as his imagination directs. (d) The biographer is bound by what really did happen, his characters have to act not as they might but as in life they did. (e) Any problems they meet in a biography they met as actual people, and their solutions have a validity for readers greater than the novelist's imagined solutions to fictional problems.

*Coordination and Subordination, p. 124

8. The following paragraph has been revised so that both important and unimportant ideas are given approximately equal emphasis. Recast and combine the sentences, adding connectives where desirable, so as to stress important ideas and subordinate less important ideas.

Now I don't believe in the factory's producing happiness. I have said this before. I am, nevertheless, willing to believe in it. You do believe in happiness resulting from steam power. Show me one or two examples of it. Show me your own happiness from it. I can show you examples of happiness without it. I can show you millions of happy people. These people are made happy by their own industry. I can show you farms in Bavaria, Switzerland, the Tyrol, and similar places. These men and women are happy. They have no mechanical power. Show me one happier English family. It has the products of the steam engine. I can be convinced by any sort of evidence. Bring me the testimony of one or two English families. Perhaps you can't do that. Can you convince them? Perhaps actually they are happy. They may not realize it. They claim not to be.—Adapted from Ruskin, "Fors Clavigera"

*Exercises, shifted constructions, p. 253

9. Analyze the structure of the following paragraph, pointing out all parallelism, all deliberate repetition. Notice also the variety of sentence movement and of order of sentence elements. This passage was written about 80 years ago. Can you find anything in the sentence structure or movement which shows its age?

It is almost too much to expect of poor human nature, that a man capable of producing some effect in one line of literature, should, for the greater good of society, voluntarily doom himself to impotence and obscurity in another. Still less is this to be expected from men addicted to the composition of the "false or malicious criticism," of which Wordsworth speaks. However, everybody would admit that a false or malicious criticism had better never have been written. Everybody, too, would be willing to admit, as a general proposition, that the critical faculty is lower than the inventive. But is it true that criticism is really, in itself, a baneful and injurious employment; is it true that all time given to writing critiques on the works of others would be much better employed if it were given to original composition, of whatever kind this may be? Is it true that Johnson had better have gone on producing more *Irenes* instead of writing his *Lives of the Poets*; nay, is it certain that Wordsworth himself was better employed in making his *Ecclesiastical Sonnets*, than when he made his celebrated *Preface*, so full of criticism, and criticism of the works of others? Wordsworth was himself a great critic, and it is to be sincerely regretted that he has not left us more criticism; Goethe was one of the greatest of critics, and we may sincerely congratulate ourselves that he has left us so much criticism. Without wasting time over the exaggeration which Wordsworth's judgment on criticism clearly contains, or over an attempt to trace the causes—not difficult I think to be traced—which may have led Wordsworth to this exaggeration, a critic may with advantage seize an occasion for trying his own conscience, and for asking himself of what real service, at any given moment, the practice of criticism either is, or may be made, to his own mind and spirit, and to the minds and spirits of others.—MATTHEW ARNOLD, "The Function of Criticism at the Present Time"

CHAPTER 6

Qualities of Sentences

---

1. **Sentence weight**
   a. Segregating sentences b. Aggregating sentences c. Length of sentences today
2. **Variety in sentence movement**
   a. Varying position of secondary elements b. Inverted movement c. Interrupted movement d. Loose and periodic sentences e. Parallelism
3. **Sentence economy**
   a. Removing deadwood b. Direct phrasing c. Long and short constructions d. Reducing predication
4. **Sentence emphasis**
   a. Mechanical devices b. Intensives c. Repetition d. Separation of elements e. Position
5. **Sound and rhythm**
   a. Euphony b. Figures of sound c. Rhythm
6. **Good sentences**

THE PRECEDING CHAPTER discusses chiefly grammatical points, matters of fundamental form that are to be considered in nearly all sentences. It is necessary, for instance, for the subject and object to be clear and the modifiers rightly placed. The form of a sentence should appear stable and intentional to the reader and lead him to a direct understanding of its meaning. But there are a number of more variable qualities of sentences in which a writer has more leeway, more freedom for personal choice. He may make his sentences long or short, direct or involved, emphatic, rhythmical—he may use or not many facilities of the language, as his habits or taste or purpose suggest. These are not matters of grammar but of style. They raise questions of appropriateness and effectiveness rather than of correctness. It is in these qualities that one writer's sentences differ from another's. An examination of these will show all sorts of possibilities for growth in effectiveness and individuality of writing.

1. Sentence weight

The most obvious, and perhaps the most fundamental, of these characteristics is length, because a conspicuous and basic difference between sentences is in the amount of substance they contain. Some writers tend to give a detail or two in each sentence; others build several details together into longer, more complex sentences. The shorter type, which tend to isolate details, are *segregating* sentences; the longer type are *aggregating* sentences.[1] A writer naturally uses a variety of sentence patterns, but usually he tends, intentionally or not, toward one or the other of these types.

1a. Segregating sentences. The shorter type of sentence is characteristic of most newspaper writing, of much business writing and advertising, of familiar writing, as in diaries and letters, of most stories, and of many discussions of ideas in both books and magazines. At the worst, these sentences become choppy and jerky, breaking the ideas into too small units for a reader to follow conveniently. At the best, the ideas come directly, follow each other naturally, as they were thought, or at least as they would be spoken.

*Exercise 4, p. 179

Here are two examples of segregating sentences. The first is from a journal. The 8 sentences range from 1 to 17 words in length, averaging just under 10. The clauses are short and uninterrupted, one statement following another as in conversation:

> Oct. 7th, Monday—Morning. Overcast and bleak. The sea looks icy. It is the coldest it has been. We are expecting the Piercys to lunch, but I doubt if they will come. Stephen thinks *Yes* so we are keeping big fires going in the dining room and sitting room. I cut and arranged all fresh flowers, but my hands almost froze while I was outside. Ellison's ears and nose are scarlet, and his eyes watering, but he keeps saying, "*This* isn't cold."—ELIZABETH ETNIER, *On Gilbert Head*, p. 115

In the following paragraph, a discussion of an idea, the sentences range from 5 words to 69 in length, but over half of them are between 8 and 17 words, and they average 16. Except in the two longer sentences, the ideas are analyzed, almost presented singly: "The word dresses the stage. The word brings on the actors. The word supplies their look, their clothes, their gestures." In a different style these might be fused into one sen-

---

[1] E. H. Lewis, *The History of the English Paragraph* (Chicago, 1894), especially p. 56; Rickert, Chapter 4.

tence, but here they appropriately stand as three. The paragraph is a well connected chain of reasoning.

> The first fact which everyone knows is that radio is a mechanism which carries to an audience sounds and nothing but sounds. A radio play consists of words and word equivalents and nothing else. There is no visible actor disguised to assume a part. There is no stage-set contrived to resemble a place. There is only the spoken word—an implement which poets have always claimed to use with a special authority. There is only the word-excited imagination—a theater in which poets have always claimed peculiar rights to play. Nothing exists save as the word creates it. The word dresses the stage. The word brings on the actors. The word supplies their look, their clothes, their gestures. The more packed and allusive the word, the more illuminating its rhythms, the more perfectly is the scene prepared, the more convincingly is the play enacted. On the stage, verse is often an obstacle because the artifice of the verse and the physical reality of the scene do not harmonize: it is for this reason that verse is easily accepted on the stage only where the scene is made remote in time and therefore artificial to begin with, or where the verse is blurred out and made to sound as much as possible like prose. But over the radio verse is not an obstacle. Over the radio verse has no visual presence to compete with. Only the ear is engaged and the ear is already half poet. It believes at once: creates and believes. It is the eye which is the realist. It is the eye which must fit everything together, must see everything before and behind. It is the eye and not the ear which refuses to believe in the lovely girlhood of the middle-aged soprano who sings Isolde, or the delicate, water-troubling slenderness of the three fat Rhine maidens ridiculously paddling at the ends of three steel ropes. With the eye closed or staring at nothing verse has every power over the ear. The ear accepts, accepts and believes, accepts and creates. The ear is the poet's perfect audience, his only true audience. And it is radio and only radio which can give him public access to that perfect friend.—ARCHIBALD MACLEISH, *The Fall of the City*, Preface

1b. Aggregating sentences. Longer sentences, in which several contributing details are presented as a unit, are characteristic of formal styles, especially of discussions of ideas; they are also fairly common in fiction, especially in descriptive passages, and in newspaper leads, where an attempt is made to summarize the most important information of a news item in the first sentence or two. The following examples show how naturally several details may be fused into a unit if they appear closely related, parts of a whole, to the writer. The first has 97 words.

*Exercises 2 and 3, pp. 178-79

Owing to the fact that England simultaneously received the reformation, the renaissance, and this notion of a gentleman's education, there was brought about an unwilling compromise between gentility and learning, a rubbing of shoulders between the poor scholar and the squire's son, that has made the English and American college what it is today: the despair of educational reformers and logical pedagogues, the astonishment of Continental scholars, a place which is neither a house of learning nor a house of play, but a little of both; and withal a microcosm of the world in which we live.—S. E. Morison, *The Founding of Harvard College*, p. 56

The second sentence, of 90 words, is more simply constructed, since its length comes chiefly from enumeration:

In general it may be stated, without further attempt at proof, that the basic feature of the new economic system that must be built is the provision in ample quantities to all the populace of the basic material needs, food, clothing, shelter and other present-day necessities and reasonable luxuries, as a community responsibility similar to the provision of a postal service, water, police and fire protection, education, parks and national defense; and that this involves public ownership of the basic means of production and distribution, and a controlled monetary mechanism.—Alfred M. Bingham, *Insurgent America*, pp. 4-5

In the second sentence of the following three (of 57, 129, and 42 words), Mr. Sitwell wished to keep the contrast between Shakespeare's and Dickens' England in a single unit, and the sentence, long as it is, carries out his intention.

Indeed if England were suddenly to be submerged by the steely arrows of her rain beneath her grey waves, and no vestige of her left save the works of two authors, Shakespeare and Dickens, yet our country would continue to have a very real existence in the minds of those who learnt to read this dead language. Shakespeare would be the guide to her permanent and rustic life, to that ideal country of green, deep lanes and high green banks, of wild flowers and oaks and elm trees, of scented limes and mysterious murmurings in the woods at night, and the old grey walls of hall and cottage, buttressed against time and padded with moss and lichen: Dickens, to that dark moment of sudden wealth when, within a few decades, her cities, losing all proportion to the landscape out of which they had grown, had swollen to elephantine and meaningless dimensions, having as many people as in former ages had composed entire nations, while the smoke of her chimneys blackened the sky above her, and all her streams were sullied with the filth of her factories. And this, even if it be not as pleasant, is a very real side of England: and one that seems, withal, as if it may wholly destroy our older and more traditional life with its entangling apparatus of road, railway, and bungalow.—OSBERT SITWELL, *Trio*, pp. 89-90

1c. Length of sentences today. In current writing the sentences are notably shorter and more direct than they were two or three generations ago.[1] A passage from *The New Yorker* "Talk of the Town" averaged 29.1 words to the sentence; one from a short story by Katherine Mansfield averaged 18. Typically the sentences in current expository writing average in the high twenties, with longer sentences found in discussions of ideas and in formal styles; shorter ones are found in newspapers, rapid narrative, and informal writing. Children begin writing short sentences and gradually increase their length and complexity until as college students they approximate those of professional writers, as shown in this table:

*Exercise 1, p. 178

AVERAGE NUMBER OF WORDS TO THE SENTENCE

4th grade	11.1 words	High school freshmen	17.3
6th grade	12.	sophomores	17.8
7th grade	13.5	juniors	18.
8th grade	15.2	seniors	19.8

University freshmen 19.9
upperclassmen 21.5
Professional writers 20.9

M. J. STORMZAND and M. V. O'SHEA, *How Much English Grammar?* p. 19

A student whose sentences were growing in maturity would show a rough correspondence with these figures, though the figures given for university students and certainly for professional writers may be a little lower than is typical.

The figures we have given are averages; the actual sentences in series would show considerable variety. In a book review (Granville Hicks' review of Robert Frost's *Collected Poems*, in *The New Republic* for Dec. 3, 1930) in which the sentences ranged from 11 to 64 and averaged 28¼, they stood in this order: 17, 13, 23, 15, 26, 46, 46, 21, 64, 29, 36, 19, 40, 26, 27, 18, 32, 13, 19, 30, 32, 26, 28, 22, 11, 18, 48, 22, 22. Although a writer usually has a definite tendency to one or the other type of sentence, he

---

[1] For comparison see L. A. Sherman, *Analytics of Literature* (Boston, 1893), Chapter 19, "Literary Sentence-Length in English Prose," and following chapters.

will vary considerably: In the volume of short stories *Winner Take Nothing*, on pages 12 and 13, Mr. Hemingway's sentences run from 1 to 21 words, with an average of about 8½, but in a different story (pages 63-65), they range from 16 to 133 words with an average of 49.

You should know whether in general you tend to build your material into aggregating sentences or tend to present it in smaller units, in segregating sentences. Then in revising a particular paper you should see whether your sentences present your material in the units in which you see it and wish the reader to see it.

If your sentences in an expository paper average less than 20 words or more than 30, you should look at them to make sure, if the figure is low, that you are building your details together into mature sentences or, if the figure is high, that the sentences are clear and appropriate to the material. There is no special virtue in either long or short sentences, but length is sometimes a symptom of other qualities.

2. Variety in sentence movement

Series of sentences of about the same length and of the same general pattern are monotonous. The four below (which were written as a paragraph in a review) are not only of the same length; their structures are practically the same.

s	v	o or c	LENGTH IN WORDS	LENGTH IN SYLLABLES
It	takes	great courage to write on ideas.	8	11
They	are	such treacherous things.	5	7
They	are	a constant source of dispute.	7	9
They	defy	successful exposition.	4	10

Varying the length helps avoid such monotony, but even more important is varying the form, the order and kinds of elements fashioned into the sentences. The range of possible sentence movements is so large that here we can point out only a few of the general types.

2a. Varying position of secondary elements [modifiers]. Since the regular s-v-o order of English sentences is generally followed, the chief source of variety is the many possible positions for modifiers. Because the subject is usually a conspicuous and emphatic word, a series of sentences beginning with their unmodified subjects tends to become monotonous. If modifiers of the subject or of the whole sentence occasionally stand first, the monotony is broken. Notice the different movement of these openings:

> The attempts were failures.
> The first serious attempts were failures.
> In spite of their seriousness, the first attempts were failures.
> Although he worked with great seriousness, his first attempts were failures.

An occasional sentence beginning with a long phrase or with a subordinate clause takes the stress away from the subject and makes for variety. Similarly the sentence may end with the object, or with a modifier of the object, and phrases and clauses can fall between the elements.

A passage of sentences that are conspicuously modified will show how far the conventional s-v-o order may be concealed by modifiers of the various elements:

> Opening at an $11 top, running well over two hours, costing more than a million and (to ensure getting this back) press-agented for months ahead as the greatest marriage that was ever married between (among) William Shakespeare, Max Reinhardt, William ("Fog Over Frisco") Dieterle, Felix Mendelssohn, Bronislava Nijinska, James Cagney and a good sprinkling of Warners' best California baked hams—being all this, [s] the film "A Midsummer Night's Dream" [v] demands [o] a certain amount of attention that will never be justified in terms of pure entertainment. At its many screenings there [v] will be [s] no lack of Ah's and Oh's, [s] culture clubs [v] will have [o] discussions, [s] newspaper critics [v] will put on [o] their Sunday adjectives; but [s] the picture [v] is [c] fairly tedious, being twice the average running time, and there [v] is going to be [s] a powerful minority of American husbands who will get one load of the elves and pixies, and [v] feel betrayed away from their stocking feet and sports page, and [v] say as much, violently.
> —Otis Ferguson, *The New Republic*, Oct. 16, 1935

2b. Inverted movement. A less common means of varying the sentence pattern is *inversion*, in which the order of the main elements departs from the usual s-v-o. A complement or an emphatic modifier of the verb stands first, followed by the verb and then the subject (c-v-s, *mv*-v-s); or a complement or object may precede the subject and verb (o-s-v).

> mv v   s ms
> Then | came | the greatest treat | of all.
>   o   s   v mv
> This job | he | kept | six years.

      c   s   LV   *m*s
A bargain | it | was, | at that price.

This sort of inversion is not very common and ordinarily is not used unless the words put first really deserve special emphasis. It is a mannerism of *Time* magazine ("Singular was the U.S. attitude in one respect"), which *The New Yorker* has critically parodied, "Backward ran the sentences until reeled the mind."

2c. Interrupted movement. As a rule we do not put words between the major elements of a sentence except short modifiers that are closely related to one of the words (as in "He does *not always* pay his bills promptly"). If the modifiers are long or not very closely related to the principal words, the movement of the sentence is interrupted:

> This background of crusades and crimes, *with imaginary castles and gallows in the distance,* shed a kind of glamour on the lives of these mild Quakers, who, *in spite of the Quaker ban on worldly fiction,* must, *it appears,* have been reading *Waverley Novels* on the sly. And was it not for them all perfectly authentic? Had not one of them crossed the Atlantic and made a special pilgrimage to Scotland, and there, *on the spot, when visiting the estate of this family,* been overcome by a profound conviction of its truth? . . . . What genealogist could demand, what documents, *the family felt,* could provide, more convincing evidence than that?—LOGAN PEARSALL SMITH, *Unforgotten Years*, pp. 6-7

In the last sentence the feeling of interruption is increased by the second subject and verb that stand between the first verb of the sentence and the object:

      s   v1   s2
What genealogist | could demand, | what documents, | the
   sm   v2   o
family felt, | could provide | more convincing evidence than that?

Such interruptions give variety to sentences, but they also make slower and sometimes even difficult reading. They are more characteristic of conspicuously formal style than of current informal style, in which such modifiers are likely to precede or to follow the main sentence elements.

2d. Loose and periodic sentences. A sentence in which the meaning is not completed until the end is called *periodic;* a sentence which continues after the main statement is complete is called *loose.*

[Periodic] He who starts on a ride of two or three thousand miles may experience, at the moment of departure, a variety of emotions. [Loose] He may feel excited, sentimental, anxious, carefree, heroic, roistering, picaresque, introspective, or practically anything else; but above all he must and will feel a fool. [Loose] It is like sitting down to read the Faërie Queen right through, only worse. [Periodic] Not yet broken in to the stately unhurrying tempo of the caravans, not yet absorbed in the life of the road, he finds, in the contrast between the slowness of the first short stage and the hugeness of the distances before him, something keenly ridiculous. His imagination and his sense of drama reject so little a beginning to so great an enterprise. [Loose] His mind is full of the immensity of his ambitions; his body, sitting on a horse, makes the first move towards their fulfillment at a pace which is often exceeded by old ladies in bath chairs. He feels a fool.—PETER FLEMING, *News from Tartary*, p. 107

Loose sentences are characteristic of our conversation, in which we typically add subordinate statements after the main statement. Periodic sentences are somewhat more formal. The reader's or listener's attention is suspended until the end; he has to hold the complete sentence in mind rather than let later elements blot out the earlier parts. The danger of periodic sentences is that they may seem unnatural; the danger of loose sentences is that they may be unemphatic. We could wish that the last clause of the following sentence was omitted or tucked away somewhere in the unemphatic middle:

It is becoming a commonplace to say that in thought and feeling, or at least in the language in which they are expressed, we are living in some bygone century, anywhere from the thirteenth to the eighteenth, although physically we belong to the twentieth century.—JOHN DEWEY, *Individualism Old and New*, p. 13

The two following sentences are loose and would be as natural to conversation as to writing.

One rather felicitous definition runs as follows—"Culture is what is left over after you have forgotten all you have definitely set out to learn"—and in this sally you get at least a useful warning against associating culture too closely with the academic paraphernalia of education.—JOHN COWPER POWYS, *The Meaning of Culture*, Preface

For Pope was merely repeating St. Thomas, who had written twenty volumes to reassure a world on the verge of doubt—twenty volumes to say that it was really right that things should be wrong, God only knows why.—CARL L. BECKER, *The Heavenly City of the Eighteenth-Century Philosophers*, p. 67

The loose sentence above could be stopped comfortably at three different points (after *St. Thomas, verge of doubt, should be wrong*), and yet it is a complete and satisfying unit.

The following sentence is periodic:

An intelligent and experienced observer of affairs at Washington has said that all political questions which he has heard discussed in Washington come back ultimately to problems connected with the distribution of *income*.—JOHN DEWEY, *Individualism Old and New*, p. 97

This periodic sentence is perfectly natural, yet by postponing the crucial phrase till the end it holds attention all the way and gives an intensified emphasis to *the distribution of income*.

There is no reason to strive for either loose or periodic movement, especially in a generally informal style made up largely of segregating sentences. By far the larger number of sentences, written as well as oral, are loose. For this reason, especially if the style is somewhat formal, an occasional sentence in which the meaning is not completed until its end contributes not only suspense but variety.

2e. Parallelism and balance. (1) PARALLEL MOVEMENT. In Chapter 5, § 5 we learned that putting parts of the sentence that are of equal value in the same (parallel) construction was one way of making the sentence a unit. More elaborate parallel movement becomes an element of style and stands out sufficiently among the more casually constructed sentences to give a note of variety. It is more characteristic of formal than of informal writing. *Page 128

The following elaborate and rather conscious examples of parallelism control the movement and rhythm of their passages, but still the parallel locutions are sufficiently varied in length and form so that they do not seem monotonous:

We attain to heaven	by using this world well,
	though it is to pass away;
we perfect our nature	
not	by ending it
but	by adding to it
	what is more than nature,
	and directing it towards aims
	higher than its own.

CARDINAL NEWMAN, *On the Idea of a University*

159

Don Andrés de Ribera, the Viceroy of Peru, was the remnant of a delightful man, broken by ‖ the table,   (Nouns, all ob-
‖ the alcove,   ject of prepo-
‖ a grandeeship and sition *by*)
‖ ten years of exile.

As a youth ‖ he had accompanied embassies to Versailles and
    Rome;
‖ he had fought in the wars in   (Coordinate
    Austria;   clauses of similar
‖ he had been in Jerusalem.   pattern)

He was a widower and childless of an ‖ enormous   (Adjectives)
‖ and wealthy
      woman;

he had collected ‖ coins a little,
‖ wines,
‖ actresses,   (Series of nouns, all objects
‖ orders and   of *collected*)
‖ maps.

From the table he had received the gout; (Coordinate clauses
from the alcove a tendency to convulsions; with similar openings)

from the grandeeship a pride so ‖ vast and (Adjectives)
‖ puerile

that he seldom ‖ heard anything that was said to him and
‖ talked to the ceiling in a perpetual mono-
    logue;
from the exile, oceans of boredom,
   a boredom that was so pervasive that it was like pain—

he ‖ woke up with it and   (Compound predicate)
‖ spent the day with it,

and it sat by his bed all night watching his sleep.
        THORNTON WILDER, *The Bridge of San Luis Rey*, p. 170

2) BALANCED SENTENCES. When the parallel locutions, especially clauses, of a sentence are noticeably equal in length and similar in movement, the sentence is called *balanced*. Even in a plain style, balanced sentences are fairly common for emphatic statements and especially for comparisons and contrasts:

Those who are naturally proud and envious
    will learn from Thackeray to despise humanity;
those who are naturally gentle, to pity it;
those who are naturally shallow, to laugh at it.—JOHN RUSKIN,
Sesame and Lilies

The busy years hastened away; the traces of Time's unimaginable touch grew manifest; and old age, approaching, laid a gentle hand upon Victoria. The grey hair whitened; the mature features mellowed; the short firm figure amplified and moved more slowly, supported by a stick.—LYTTON STRACHEY, *Queen Victoria*, p. 374

They have been educated to achieve success; few of them have been educated to exercise power.—WALTER LIPPMANN, A *Preface to Morals*, p. 66

3. Sentence economy

Economy in writing means leading a reader to your exact meaning without unnecessary handicaps to understanding. Few, simple, exact words are its basis, but the pattern in which the words stand has a good deal to do with it. The fewest words and simplest constructions are not always the most economical, for they may oversimplify the message, or they may limit its readers to those who are practiced in following a compact style. But *unnecessary* words and *needlessly* complicated expressions cannot be economical. Expressions that contribute nothing to meaning actually detract; if there are many of them they will weigh down the sentences and may even conceal meaning. Unnecessarily full constructions also lead to boredom. For amateur writers the chief way to economical expression is to remove offending expressions in revision until after a while they fail to appear even in the first draft. If you train yourself to be sensitive to waste in expression, you will soon learn to avoid being wasteful.

3a. Removing deadwood. *Deadwood* is a convenient label for a lazy word or phrase that *adds nothing to the meaning of a sentence*.[1] A bit of deadwood can be omitted, at least with slight change of phrasing, with no loss at all in meaning and with positive gain in neatness. Note the bracketed phrases in these sentences:

*Exercise 7, p. 179

Every thinking person these days seems inclined to agree [with the conception] that the world has gone mad.

Anyone acquainted with violin construction knows that the better the wood is seasoned, the better [the result will be as far as] the tone of the instrument [is concerned].

An efficient high school system [of today] should include adequate provision for manual training.

To my surprise the damage was not as bad as I had expected [it to be].

[1] This trait of style is called *jargon* in Sir Arthur Quiller-Couch's *On the Art of Writing* (New York, 1916), pages 100-26.

161

[It was] during this time [that] the greatest number of cases came down.

[There is] only one excuse [that] is acceptable, [and that is] "I have a class this hour."

It was the first time [in my life] I had seen Niagara Falls.

The part played by tradition in the civilization and culture of a people is nowhere more fully exemplified than in [the matter of] student influence in China and Latin America.

At the end of an hour and a half we arrived at [the spot where] the red flag [was situated].

The following statistics [serve to] give a good idea of the effects of tobacco:

When the stain is dried, the entire surface of the desk is steel-wooled to take off any excess stain [that may be present].

He kept things moving at breakneck speed throughout [the entirety of] the performance.

A common type of dead phrase is the addition of *color* to a word that can mean only color ("green in color"), *number* to a number ("nine in number"), *shape* to a definite form ("rectangular in shape"), or locutions like this:

The architecture [of the houses] and the landscaping [of the grounds] whisper a word of town pride to the passers-by.

A few words are particularly common—and doubly bad in that they not only add useless weight but often take the emphasis from more important words:

nature: He was never popular because he was awkward [by nature].

variety: During the past spring and summer there has been a noticeable dearth of A pictures and not many more pictures of [the] class B [variety].

character: The second was quite different [in character].

These things, though [of a] useful [character], were not what he needed most.

happen: [It happened that] we were within three months of being the same age.

case: While this probably would be true in some cases, I do not think it would be true of the average case. ["While this might sometimes be true, I do not think it would be typical"—or something like that.]

Many of them have been put to death in individual cases [Many individuals have been put to death], and the whole race has been disfranchised and expelled from their professions.

line: He had always thought he would do something along agricultural lines [in agriculture].

*happen

*case

162

This particular nuisance in writing is one of the easiest to correct and prevent. Just drawing a line through the unnecessary words while revising will take out a particular bit of deadwood, and after you watch for such expressions a little while, they just stop appearing even in first drafts. Such elimination is one of the easiest ways to begin the attack on fuzzy writing.

3b. Direct phrasing. Besides avoiding words that contribute nothing to the meaning of a sentence a writer needs to watch for expressions that use *too many* words for conveying a single notion, that is, *he should avoid circumlocution.* The fewest words are not always the best form, but a conspicuous number of roundabout expressions result in flabbiness. They make the writing seem immature, and tire a reader.

*Wordiness

See also
*Repetition,
§ 1.

Wordy	Revised
It has some of the best ski trails in the country and as far as the other cold weather sports are concerned, they have them too, along with one of the most fashionable hotels in the country.	They have a very fashionable hotel, all the cold weather sports, and some of the best ski trails in the country.
During the time that she was in Los Angeles, she had at least six different jobs.	While she was in Los Angeles, she had at least six different jobs.
We must realize the fact that the producer's hand is felt at every stage of producing a picture.	We must realize that the producer's hand is felt at every stage of producing a picture.

*Voice, § 4

Here are some typical examples of circumlocution:

> *destroyed by fire* means *burned*
> *come in contact with* usually means *meet* or *know*
> *the necessary funds* usually means no more than *the money*
> *in this day and age* means *today*
> *the sort of metal they use for plating the shiny parts of automobiles* might mean *chromium*

Because in speaking we often use more words than are necessary, we need to be especially careful in our writing, where circumlocution is more conspicuous.

3c. Long and short constructions. English offers a choice between a long and short way of expressing a number of relationships. Relative clauses frequently do not show a relative pronoun: "the experience *we had*" is as good as "the experience

*Function
words, § 2

*Ellipsis
*Clauses, §2

that we had." Not all clauses have verbs: *"If possible,* come a little early," or *"If it is possible,* come a little early." The conjunction *that* may or may not be used: "We like to think *that* our scholarship standards are higher than yours" or "We like to think [   ] our scholarship standards are higher than yours."

In the shorter forms nothing is omitted; merely a different pattern is being followed. As Professor Curme says, "Fuller expression would be incomplete expression, for it would mar the thought, take something vital away from it."

The choice between these forms is a matter of style, to be determined by appropriateness. Formal English uses relatively few of the short expressions, tends to fill out all constructions. Informal English uses them more freely, very much more in speaking than in writing ("We better go" instead of "We'd [We had] better go"). Familiar conversation, as well as general vulgate usage, dispenses with much of the apparatus of formal grammar:

> "Dance Friday." "You going?" "No. You?" "Don't think so."

In revising a paper it is usually possible for a writer to tell from the movement of the passage whether or not he should make his constructions more complete. In ordinary informal writing a fairly frequent use of the short forms makes for naturalness.

*Page 124

3d. Reducing predication. An "idea"—a small part of our meaning—may be expressed in one of four grammatical units: in a word, a phrase, a subordinate clause, or a full sentence. The form ought to be roughly proportional to the value of the idea, important ones in the longer and more weighty forms, less important ones in the more economical ones. In the following example of the scale of expressions, we would probably all agree that the first was the most appropriate, the most economical for an adequate expression of the notion:

WORD: The snow *blanketed* the countryside.
PHRASE: The snow, *like a blanket,* covered the countryside.
CLAUSE: The snow, *which lay like a blanket,* covered the countryside.
SENTENCE: *The snow lay like a blanket.* It covered the countryside.

*Subject
and
verb, §3

Obviously the chief difference is between the first two, which contain no verb, and the last two, which contain verbs, or *predications.* Modern style tends to use fewer predications, fewer clauses, than English style of a century ago. One mark of amateur writing is the use of a predication for an idea that a more practiced writer would reduce to a phrase or a single word.

AMATEUR	MORE ECONOMICAL
Labor was quick to realize the advantages of this new form of passive resistance, and *before the succeeding year rolled around,* no less than two hundred sit-down strikes had been reported.	Labor was quick to realize the advantages of this new form of passive resistance, and *within a year* no less than two hundred sit-down strikes had been reported.
A few of the fellows *who were less serious* would go to a bar *where they would have a steak dinner and a few glasses of beer.*	A few of the *less serious* fellows would go to a bar *for a steak dinner and a few glasses of beer.*
I *am a native of Florida* and am very glad to write on this subject.	*Since I am a native of Florida,* I am very glad to write on this subject. Or: *As a native of Florida,* I am very glad to write on this subject.
We taxied back and forth in front of the starting line, waiting impatiently for the sound of the gun *which would mean that the race was started.*	We taxied back and forth in front of the starting line, waiting impatiently for the sound of the *starting* gun.

Of course as we write, we can't always be stopping to ask ourselves, "How much is this idea worth?" But in revising papers, especially in the early stages of our writing experience, it is occasionally worth while to see if we have made the expressions more full than necessary to express our complete meaning. Writing can be made so compact that it is bare and hard to follow, but few beginning writers need to worry about that. They need to be encouraged to use a more tidy, more economical style. Length in a paper does not come from piling up *words* but from piling up *material,* ideas, and especially details of observation that convey your meaning. Proper economy comes from trying to say more in a given number of words.

4. Sentence emphasis

The emphasis in a piece of writing comes principally from the use of strong and distinctive words and from a progressive arrangement of statements in paragraphs and of the paragraphs in the whole. But sentences contribute to this general impression, and the general methods of order, proportion, and mass also apply to them. Economy that we have just discussed is an important factor, for wordiness keeps the meaning from standing out as it should, as the writer intends it to stand. In this section we shall look at some of the more specific means to sentence emphasis.

*Emphasis

4a. Mechanical devices. Writing and printing have various mechanical means—underlining (italics), capitals, emphatic punctuation—for stressing words and passages. These devices are used by amateur writers often in an attempt to make up for deficiencies in style or content and usually result in what is known as the "forcible-feeble," as in this speech, a crucial one in the novel from which it is taken:

*Underlining
*Capital letters, § 10
*Schoolgirl style

> "*I go on through!*" he repeated earnestly. "I have suffered— but I know that I am Destiny's darling! . . . *You* have suffered but *you, too, can carry on through!* . . . Take it from me! I know! In spite of all the little detainments, disappointments, disillusionments—*I get the lucky breaks! I get the signal to go forward!* I have been delayed—long—long—long—but—at length—*I get the* GREEN LIGHT!"

With increased skill in writing, a person relies less and less on these mechanical devices. He depends more and more on distinctiveness of expression, position, and other rhetorical means of showing that one statement is more important than another.

4b. Intensives. There are several ways of emphasizing meaning by the use of special words, particularly in colloquial language. A speaker can stress a *too* or *very* or *much* so that it will have a good deal of force (and the activity of the stress gives him a certain physical satisfaction). On paper these intensives are less convincing, in part because the tone of voice is lacking and, at least in careful prose, in part because written style is likely to use words more accurately than oral—approaching the ideal speech Mark Rutherford accredited to Mary Mardon:

> There was no sort of effort or strain in anything she said, no attempt by emphasis of words to make up for weakness of thought, and no compliance with that vulgar and most disagreeable habit of using intense language to describe what is not intense in itself.—HALE WHITE, *The Autobiography of Mark Rutherford*, p. 50

A number of adjectives and adverbs are primarily intensives: *much, very, such, too, highly, certainly, extremely, tremendously.* . . . They may be used for a just emphasis, but they usually suggest an oral stress and are often out of place in writing. Too many of them suggest the schoolgirl style. Most small profanity belongs in this category, the words beginning with the letter *d* allowing a satisfying stress and bite and not contributing otherwise to meaning.

*very

*Schoolgirl style

In writing, quite often a statement would actually be stronger if the intensive was omitted or if the oral type of sentence was changed to a written form:

> We had [such] a lovely time at your party.
> Everybody was [so] tired after the holiday round of parties.
> In pushing the product the slogan has [surely] been [unquestionably] of paramount importance.

The colloquial superlative, used to indicate a considerable degree of a quality instead of the greatest, is a typical intensive in conversation, but not so appropriate to writing:

*Comparison of adjectives and adverbs, § 5e

> She had the nicest manners [for *nice* or some more exact adjective].
> He is a most important figure in the book [an important figure].

The pronouns in *-self* are idiomatic intensives in all levels of usage:

*himself, herself

*myself

> He picked the flowers himself.   I must see Catherine herself.

Lately *personally* and *in person* have been used as a substitute for *himself, herself,* and so on, especially in business English and in slang or familiar conversation.

> It turned out to be Jimmy in person.   He picks the necessary vegetables for dinner out of his small personal garden [out of his own garden].

There are many other colloquial and informal intensive idioms with pronouns (and some compounds, like *he-man*):

> But, if we consider how we *all of us* attain what limited measure of a command of metaphor we possess . . .—I. A. RICHARDS, *The Philosophy of Rhetoric,* p. 90

There are scores of words of rather intense meaning—*thrill, intriguing, devastating, passion*—all of which have their necessary and legitimate uses and all of which are likely to be used to emphasize some feeling that does not really deserve such a vigorous word.

The use of such intensives should be a matter of appropriateness, especially of appropriateness to the subject. But often, particularly in speech, their appropriateness to the person who is using them is more important. At their best they may represent a vigorous and emphatic personality; at their worst they show insensitiveness to the values of words. If they are overused, they are sure to result in a weakening of statements.

4c. Repetition. (1) UNHAPPY REPETITION. Using necessary words several times in a short space is often unavoidable, but repetition of words is unpleasant when the writer has a wide possible choice. Such repetition may be the result of small vocabulary, but most of it is due to plain laziness or inattention to writing—certainly to a lack of revision. Both small vocabulary and carelessness are back of the five *beautiful's* (not to mention one *beauty*) in this:

> The landscape is beautiful. There are myriads of beautiful, stately trees, which contribute greatly to the beauty of the place in every season of the year. There are also many beautiful wild flowers and other pretty forms of undergrowth. The climate and the absence of smoke and dust of the city makes it very easy to cultivate a beautiful lawn, with flowers and shrubs. The lake is a wonderful part of the landscape. There are many beautiful views in different times of the day and season.

More typical of careless repetition are such sentences as these:

> This dam was without doubt going to be the largest [dam] in the world.
> [The problem of] feeding her ever increasing population is one of Japan's most acute problems.

Repetition of whole phrases is likely to be more objectionable, because naturally a group of words attracts more attention:

> The next morning we noticed the river had risen considerably and was flowing at a very fast pace. We decided to resume our journey immediately, and soon we were once more traveling down stream, but this time at a much faster pace [even faster].

The writer of that either has an insensitive ear or else he did not read his paper over. We feel sure it was carelessness when we find this a little later:

> Twice I thought our canoe would surely upset, and I could see the fellow sitting in the middle [of our canoe] was scared to death.

Especially to be watched is repetition of the same word in two different senses, easy to do in English because of the number of meanings many words carry:

My marks showed a marked improvement.
No President in time of war has dared to fight the powerful financial interests of this country who have interests in the belligerent countries.

Such repetitions as these are easily attended to in revision by simply drawing a line through the less essential word or phrase, or replacing it with a pronoun, or rephrasing in some more economical way.

A slightly different form of careless repetition is doubling the meaning of a word or part of a word unnecessarily. We write *continue on* when *continue* is enough, *repeat again* when we mean merely *repeat*.

The modern college student [of today]
In this modern melting pot, I found people [there] who were unacquainted with the English language.
I believe that colleges should offer scholarships but they should not offer only athletic scholarships [alone].
the [resultant] effect
undergraduate students (*Graduate students* is necessary because not all graduates become students.)
He told us that if everyone was free Thursday evening [that] we would meet then.
Dams have been built with [about] four or five sluices in them. [*Four or five* is indefinite enough without the *about*.]
I know many officers who try to give you any *possible* assistance that they *can*.
First we should understand what *equipment* and *paraphernalia* are necessary for this sport.

The remedy for all this loose, careless repetition is the same: careful revision. Reading a paper aloud is perhaps the surest way to catch such lapses, since our ears will sense more than our eyes.

2) SUCCESSFUL REPETITION. Repetition of words and repetition of ideas in other words are useful stylistic devices. Repetition may help hold a passage together, it may emphasize ideas, and it may suggest emotion.

*Restatement, p. 94

A controlled repeating of important key words is useful in keeping the reader's attention focused on the subject. It is especially useful in binding sentences together and in holding paragraphs together. Writing of the Supreme Court, you will have to mention the Supreme Court frequently and it is often better to say *Supreme Court* than to hunt for trite synonyms (like *the highest tribunal*). Simply see that the sentences are economically constructed to avoid unnecessary repetition and that pronouns are used where they can be conveniently written.

The repetition of *name* and *choose* and *select* binds together the thought of this paragraph and emphasizes its meaning:

> Therefore, in every fresh application of a name we can discern two acts: first, the choice of a detail in the thing named, and second, comparison in that detail of the thing named with other things. These two acts are always in a certain sense one, for it is the memory that makes the choice. Naming things is like cutting doughnuts: here is an undifferentiated mass of dough, upon which the cutter, which remembers the character of other doughnuts, descends and makes after that character a definite excerpt. Exactly thus a word descends into a general impression and selects out a clear experience. It selects an experience similar to the ones which it remembers. But since in this process sometimes the act of selecting, and sometimes the act of remembering, is emphasized, we can divide names accordingly into two classes. There are names which predominantly choose, and names which predominantly compare. The words *shaggy* and *lazy*, for example, *choose* a feature of the horse, but they leave those memories with which it is to be compared, undefined. *Pot-bellied* and *strawberry roan*, on the other hand, not only choose the part and the color, but they also declare the comparison to a remembered pot and a remembered strawberry. All names are of one or the other of these two types.—MAX EASTMAN, *Enjoyment of Poetry*, p. 40

Repetition of phrases and constructions is often a matter of emotion, feeling, and may contribute to rhythm.

In the first of the following examples the repetition of *big* suggests a tone of irony; in the second the repeated sentence (which is frequently repeated in the course of the story) becomes a refrain:

> When a big oil man, a big radio man, and a big education man met in the offices of N. W. Ayer & Son, the big advertising people, and closed a deal whereby Atlantic is to pay Yale twenty thousand dollars for the exclusive right to broadcast Yale's home games, including, as the *Times* put it, "the privilege of mentioning oil during intermissions," one of the major problems of American civilization was solved.—*The New Yorker*, Sept. 19, 1936

170

Night after night Tom watched the sheep upon the downs with empty hollow sockets, till his dead hair grew and covered his poor dead face, and hid the shame of it from the sheep. And the wind blew and blew.

Sometimes on gusts of wind came some one's tears, and beat and beat against the iron chains, but could not rust them through. And the wind blew and blew.—LORD DUNSANY, *A Dreamer's Tales*, p. 160

Such repetition is rare, of course, and confined to imaginative writing. Mr. Eastman's repetition in the paragraph on the page opposite is more typical of factual writing. No writer needs to fear repeating the key words of his subject, and rightly used they will add emphasis to his discussion.

4d. Separation of elements. In speaking, one of the most used and most effective means to emphasis is a pause. It allows what has just been said to sink in, or if the voice is suspended, it throws emphasis on what is to follow. It is difficult to transfer this effect to the written page, but something of its value can be had by keeping constructions separate.

The most emphatic separation of course is into individual sentences, if the ideas deserve it:

> You do not revise dogmas. You smash them.—RANDOLPH BOURNE, "What Is Opinion?" *The New Republic*, August 18, 1915

Internal punctuation, commas and especially semicolons, keep statements separate and tend to force a pause even in quick eye reading:

> One remembers the old stories of invisible kingdoms where princes lived with ladies and dragons for company; and the more modern fairy-tales in which heroes drift in and out of dimensions more complex than the original three.—JOHN STEINBECK and EDWARD F. RICKETTS, *Sea of Cortez*, p. 80
>
> There are three ways of seeing animals: dead and preserved; in their own habitats for the short time of a low tide; and for long periods in an aquarium.—*Ibid.*, p. 189

(Commas could have been used, instead of semicolons in those two sentences.)

In a series of parallel words or constructions, repeating the conjunctions or prepositions may add emphasis to the individual elements. Contrast the movement of the two versions of these sentences:

The collecting buckets and tubes and jars were very full of specimens—so full that we had constantly to change the water to keep the animals alive.—*Ibid.*, p. 78

The collecting buckets, tubes, and jars were so full of specimens that we had constantly to change the water to keep the animals alive.

In the course of a lifetime of voyaging he went to China, to India, to all parts of Africa, and even to the Arctic.

In the course of a lifetime of voyaging he went to China, India, all parts of Africa, and even the Arctic.

An abrupt break in the direction of the thought movement may make for sharp emphasis, especially in informal writing.

A hardness about this technicolor epic makes it difficult to enjoy all the way through—the eventual hardness of the theater seat.

Just when you were beginning to get adjusted to Olsen and Johnson's out-patient clinic of the psychiatric ward, *bang*, you had fifty pounds of ice in your lap.

4e. Position. The most important means of emphasis is *position*, ordering the words and parts of the statement so that the stress falls unmistakably on the exact words you want it to. The most emphatic position is the end of a sentence, and the next most emphatic is the beginning.

Since the subject of a sentence is usually an important element, it properly has the initial emphasis, although often some other element deserves first position. The frequent use of "anticipatory subjects" (*there* is, *there* were, *it* is) is consequently weakening:

*there is, there are

Anticipatory subjects	More emphatic
There are many people who read history to raise their self-esteem.	Many people read history to raise their self-esteem.
There is some evidence pointing to the gradual disappearance of hazing in our colleges.	Some evidence points to the gradual disappearance of hazing in our colleges.

*Voice, § 3

*Page 156

Departures from the normal word order, as described in §2 of this chapter, are usually prompted by a desire for emphasis on the words put first:

Charles he had beaten twice, but never his brother.
And last of all came the man they had expected would be first.

172

> This we have; this you cannot give us; but this you may so easily take away.—G. Lowes Dickinson, *Letters from a Chinese Official*, p. 38

The ends of sentences deserve more attention. As Professor Wendell put it, sentences should "end with words that deserve distinction." Since we cannot foresee the ends of our sentences in speaking, we are likely to add various unemphatic elements and in general let them run downhill. In writing we have the opportunity to revise our sentences and give them more definite form.

Unemphatic	More emphatic
The first forty minutes passed quickly enough, but we began to squirm in our seats when a second and then a third speaker appeared.	The first forty minutes passed quickly enough, but when a second and then a third speaker appeared we began to squirm in our seats.
We were surprised to hear him talk so glibly about electricity and motors, knowing as we did that he had never looked at a machine in his life.	Since we knew that he had never looked at a machine in his life, we were surprised to hear him talk so glibly about electricity and motors.

It is easy to avoid such lapses from firm expression, and it is easy and natural, with a little practice, to end sentences strongly. This means often putting elements in an order of *climax*, that is, arranging words, phrases, clauses, or sentences in an order of increasing value. The increase may be in mere physical length, for usually in a series of phrases or clauses the longest is put last. The increase may be in force of sound or distinction of phrasing. Or the increase may be in complexity of meaning or of emotional or ideal value. The scale of value of course is the speaker's or writer's; it is his sense of the importance of the various bits of his idea represented by the climax.

Here is a conventional climax pattern, with the last of the three parallel phrases the fullest in expression and the most important for the writer's purpose at the moment:

> They come from an intellectual level where conformity seems the highest of goods, and so they lack the primary requisite of the imaginative author: the capacity to see the human comedy afresh, to discover new relations between things, to discover new significances in man's eternal struggle with his fate.—H. L. Mencken, *Prejudices, Fifth Series*, p. 177

The climax in the following sentence represents the writer's emphasis, since she is most interested in the word *confusing*:

> To be young is always a difficult, dangerous, and confusing business—but it can seldom have been so difficult, so dangerous, and above all so confusing, as in England during the first ten years of the twentieth century.—ANN BRIDGE, *Enchanter's Nightshade*, p. 38

Climax is the natural order for arranging the items of a series unless there is some necessary or logical reason for another order. Failing to use a climactic order results in a weak sentence or, if the last member of the series is conspicuously less important than the preceding, in definite anticlimax. Anticlimax is usually a sign of careless or thoughtless writing:

> It spoiled the rest of the summer for the boys and disappointed them terrifically.

> No degree will be conferred or certificate given unless the applicant shall have sustained a good moral character, settled all college bills, and returned all books and paid all fines to the library.

Intentional anticlimax is one of the sources of humor:

> "Because Luxembourg is divine," he said, his eyes lighting. "I spent a most wonderful vacation there a year or two ago. It is a cameo, a miniature. It is a little country and everything in it is little: the inns, the mountains, the waiters, the people, the prices [anticlimax]. It is divine!"—IRWIN EDMAN, *Philosopher's Holiday*, p. 65

*Phrases, § 2

*Prepositions, § 3d

> If we often speak of Miss Dorothy Thompson, it is because we think she is the most wonderful of mortal women, greater than Garbo, greater than Mrs. Harrison Williams, greater than all the Quintuplets put together.—*The New Yorker*, Sept. 24, 1938

Emphasis, like most sentence qualities, is to be tested in revision, when a writer takes the role of reader and tries to make his words represent to someone else his own view of his subject. Finding ways of making this emphasis is one of the most challenging parts of writing.

5. Sound and rhythm

Although prose is not expected to appeal to the ear in the same way that poetry does, unpleasant sounds or combinations of sounds are a slight handicap in reading, even in silent reading, and more pleasing sounds often add a positive pleasure. Sound is not such a conspicuous trait of prose now as formerly, when reading aloud was more in vogue. The average news story is planned for eye reading only and is a form of punishment when read aloud, and so is much writing that is not journalistic. But a pleasing sound is a characteristic of most satisfying prose. Reading aloud is one test of good prose and should add something to the reader's enjoyment.

5a. Euphony. *Euphonious* means pleasing to the ear. Euphony depends in part on avoiding unnecessary harsh sounds (too many *g's*, *dg's*, and so on), groups of consonants that are hard to pronounce (as in "backed to the door" and "propelled by the repeated and seemingly needlessly brutal remarks and jabs of the detectives"), and combinations of easily confused sounds (like *s* and *sh*: "This seething mass of shiny sea shells began to wrestle and box"). Such jerky, choppy rhythms are awkward, and so also are too many conspicuous unstressed syllables ("seemingly needlessly").

Becoming too conscious of euphony is likely to result in a rather light and perhaps not sufficiently strong movement; but it is important to read one's papers aloud and to remove conspicuously harsh or feeble expressions.

These few sentences show euphony, and also adjustment of the sounds to the subject matter, from the smooth, lingering syllables of the opening to the more emphatic and rougher movement at the end:

> A rose in a moonlit garden, the shadow of trees on the turf, almond bloom, scent of pine, the wine-cup and the guitar; these and the pathos of life and death, the long embrace, the hand stretched out in vain, the moment that glides forever away, with its freight of music and light, into the shadow and hush of the haunted past, all that we have, all that eludes us, a bird on the wing, a perfume escaped on the gale—to all these things we are trained to respond, and the response is what we call literature. This we have; this you cannot give us; but this you may so easily take away. Amid the roar of looms it cannot be heard; it cannot be seen in the smoke of factories; it is killed by the wear and the whirl of Western life.—G. Lowes Dickinson, *Letters from a Chinese Official*, p. 38

5b. Figures of sound. The repetition of the same or similar sounds is a factor in binding words together, as well as of giving immediate pleasure in reading. Rime, which is so important in unifying verse, is out of place in prose, where a noticeable rime sound is usually offensive. But an occasional and natural use of some of the other figures of sound may serve to bind together words and phrases.

*Alliteration   One of the commonest of these is *alliteration*, the same sound at the beginning of words or of stressed syllables within words:

> the shadow and *h*ush of the *h*aunted past
> the *w*ear and *w*hirl of *W*estern life

Alliteration runs riot in much light writing and in advertising slogans ("a wispy, waspy waistline"), and, used more sparingly, it is characteristic of a good deal of formal writing.

*Assonance   *Assonance*, similar vowel sounds in syllables that have different consonant sounds, is quite common in prose:

> a perfume esc*a*ped on the g*a*le

*Rhythm, § 1   **5c. Rhythm.** We do not need to go into an elaborate study to realize that prose has a definite, if varied, rhythm, that stresses differ in intensity and in number and in combination.[1] Two lines from the Dickinson passage show considerable difference:

$$\overset{x}{\text{the}} \overset{\prime}{\text{move}}\overset{x}{\text{ment}} \mid \overset{x}{\text{that}} \overset{\prime}{\text{glides}} \mid \overset{x\,\prime\,x\,x}{\text{forever away}}$$

$$\overset{x}{\text{but}} \overset{\prime}{\text{this}} \mid \overset{x}{\text{you}} \overset{\prime}{\text{may}} \overset{x}{\text{so}} \overset{x\,x}{\text{easily}} \mid \overset{\prime}{\text{take}} \overset{x\,\prime}{\text{away}}$$

Rhythm, § 2   A conscious concern for rhythm is dangerous unless you want to write patterned prose. But you can at least avoid long series of unstressed syllables that will give a weak or flabby effect; you can avoid tacking on a phrase after a movement has reached an effective stable point; and you can make sure that the stresses do not become monotonous.

Probably the fundamental difference is between a simple movement that suggests the rather casual rhythm of conversation and the more elaborate and varied rhythm that suggests formal or eloquent or "literary" prose.

Some of the general differences between these two movements will be felt in reading aloud two such contrasting passages as the following:

> Walter had just turned the corner of Charles Street into Seventh when he saw her. She was standing a little way up the block talking to a fellow in a black overcoat and a black felt hat, and just the way they were standing—the fellow leaning back against the wall of the building there and she crowded close against him, looking up at him—was enough to let Walter know the kind of talk they were having. Almost without thinking, he stopped and stepped back a pace down Charles, out of

---

[1] The best treatment of prose rhythm is Norton R. Tempest, *The Rhythm of English Prose* (Cambridge, England, 1930).

176

sight around the corner.—ROBERT M. COATES, "The Net," *Short Stories from the New Yorker*

United with his fellowmen by the strongest of all ties, the tie of a common doom, the free man finds that a new vision is with him always, shedding over every daily task the light of love. The life of Man is a long march through the night, surrounded by invisible foes, tortured by weariness and pain, towards a goal that few can hope to reach, and where none may tarry long. One by one, as they march, our comrades vanish from our sight, seized by the silent orders of omnipotent Death. Very brief is the time in which we can help them, in which their happiness or misery is decided. Be it ours to shed sunshine on their path, to lighten their sorrows by the balm of sympathy, to give them the pure joy of a never-tiring affection, to strengthen failing courage, to instill faith in hours of despair. Let us not weigh in grudging scales their merits and demerits, but let us think only of their need—of the sorrows, the difficulties, perhaps the blindnesses, that make the misery of their lives; let us remember that they are fellow-sufferers in the same darkness, actors in the same tragedy with ourselves. And so, when their day is over, when their good and their evil have become eternal by the immortality of the past, be it ours to feel that, where they suffered, where they failed, no deed of ours was the cause; but wherever a spark of the divine fire kindled in their hearts, we were ready with encouragement, with sympathy, with brave words in which high courage glowed.—BERTRAND RUSSELL, "A Free Man's Worship," *Mysticism and Logic*, p. 56

Most modern writing is closer to the plain style of the first of these, but its range and possibilities are great. If you feel that your writing is in a rut, reading aloud passages that appeal to you—and that you can read in a natural tone of voice—may help you realize more fully the potentialities of your writing and add to its other qualities some of the pleasure that comes from a fitting rhythm.

6. Good Sentences

Talking about qualities of sentences one by one and in such detail makes writing seem much more complicated and perhaps even artificial than it really is. All of our discussion has been intended to show some (it has by no means covered all) of the possibilities of this simple and unavoidable unit of speech and writing. Granted some experience in talking and writing, the surest way to good sentences is familiarity with what you intend to say and confidence that you can say it so that someone else will be glad to read it. This will let you write rapidly, so that the ideas will really move and will seem to follow each other naturally. Your sentences serve the fundamental purposes of communication.

If for some reason you have not had much practice in purposeful writing, you can profit by study of the points in these two chapters, by attentive reading of good prose, and by some conscious experimentation and certainly by careful revision of the sentences that come haphazardly. Gradually—sometimes rapidly—the general texture of your sentences will change, for the better. Analysis as we have been discussing it is not an end in itself. Remember that the aim is not any one pattern but a varied and pleasing style that will not only convey your meaning but will be appropriate to it and to your hoped-for readers and to yourself. Write naturally and merely tidy up your first efforts in the light of what experienced writers have found to be the effective qualities of good sentences.

Exercises

1. In a run of at least twenty consecutive sentences from one of your recent papers determine and write down the following facts: (a) length of the sentences in words: the shortest, the longest, the average number of words per sentence; (b) types of sentences: the number of simple, compound, and complex; (c) the number of coordinating conjunctions used between clauses, the number of subordinating conjunctions, of conjunctive adverbs, of relative pronouns, of clauses without a connecting word. After you have made this analysis, write a paragraph telling what you discovered about your sentences, making any comparison that occurs to you with the sentences of other writers or with the ideas given in this book. If you commonly use segregating sentences, you will probably use a small number of connectives; if you use aggregating sentences, you will use more.

*Pages 154-55

2. Write a theme in three sentences. See how much you can pack into each sentence without losing its movement, trying to make each one at least fifty words long. The result will be a tour de force, but the performance will show something about sentence connectives.

*Pages 152-53

3. Recast the paragraph by Archibald MacLeish on page 152, changing segregating sentences to aggregating. Leave out none of the ideas. You will have to add connectives and make small changes in wording; do not make unnecessary changes in wording. At present there are twenty-three sentences averaging 16.08

words. Aggregating sentences should reduce the number to 7—10, and raise the average number of words to more than 40.

4. Recast the paragraph by Osbert Sitwell on page 153, chang- *Pages 151-52
ing aggregating sentences to segregating. As it stands the paragraph contains three sentences averaging 76 words. Segregating
sentences should give roughly four times as many sentences
averaging about a quarter of the original length.

5. Find and bring to class a passage of a paragraph or two in
which the sentences appeal to you as effective. Prepare and
write out comments on them, noting especially length and variety, inverted or interrupted movement, position of modifiers,
parallelism, and emphasis.

6. Find a few isolated sentences that strike you as notable:
(a) the best sentences of several different types, (b) the flattest
and dullest that you find in a regular publication (books, magazines, or newspapers). Comment on the reasons for their effectiveness or ineffectiveness.

7. Cut out the deadwood in the following passage. Occa- *Pages 161-63
sionally small changes in wording may be necessary, but usually
you need only strike out the useless words.

> There are many students who have trouble handing in their
> compositions punctually on time. It is not that the work is too
> hard. In the case of the ordinary paper, the average student can
> write it in about an hour to an hour and a half. Every student
> can give this long a quantity of time to his work. The trouble, in
> respect to most students, is due to the fact that they postpone
> doing the work too long until it is too late. If it should happen
> that they have delayed until they have only forty minutes of time
> left, it is hardly possible that they can spend the hour or more
> necessary. In the case of some of them, they spend enough time
> to be sufficient for writing a paper in thinking up ingenious but
> useless excuses that do not work with the professor.

8. In the following paragraph find all the repetition and be *Pages 168-71
prepared to discuss its effectiveness. Notice, too, repetition of
idea with variation of wording. The sentences are segregating,
most of them very short. Write an analysis of the movement
of the sentences, noting inverted movement, interrupted movement, parallelism, or other qualities of the sentence movement.

> There were three waves of migration on this continent and
> the second was always the cattlemen. Ahead of the cattle went
> the trappers and Indian traders, leaving a creek's name or a
> marked tree or a few bones in a huddle of last year's oak leaves.
> Behind the cattle came the farmers. It was the farmers' plows

that edged the drovers westward. And it was the grass by which the drovers went. At the close of the seventeenth century the free range lay around the cowpens on the outskirts of the tide-water settlements of Virginia. A few years later it was in the uplands of the Piedmont. By the middle of the eighteenth century an officer in Braddock's army saw the cowpen men near the headwaters of the Potomac where that stream comes down from Cumberland and makes a gateway to the West. A few years after that there were droves of razorbacks and sheep and cattle in Kentucky. Then the cattle frontier reached Ohio: at the close of the War of 1812 travelers in the Pittsburgh country met droves of thousands of cows and swine from the interior of that region bound for Pennsylvania to fatten for the Philadelphia market. After that there were cattle on the prairies, then across the Mississippi, then at the edges of the Plains. There were always cattle out ahead of the plows. And for the simplest reason. Beef and pork and mutton were the only crops in that land without roads which could take themselves to market.—ARCHIBALD MacLEISH, *A Time to Speak*, p. 176

9. The following passage is taken from a student description of a wedding reception. Write an analysis of the sentence movement and the sentence structure. Study, if possible, the emphasis. Then rewrite the passage so as to secure variety and emphasis.

The reception line was in the living room. The bride was in white satin with a soft, white veil hanging loosely down the back. On her head was a little white cap. A young boy with wavy hair and glasses got to the bride and hesitated as to what he should do. His face got red; he wanted to kiss her. She helped him by sticking out her cheek. He gave her cheek a little peck. A tall man, with his 'tails' hanging very loosely, came up to the line. His brown eyes gleamed under his shaggy eyebrows as he kissed the bride. She joked and chatted with him. When he shook the groom's hand, he wished him all the happiness in the world. The bride had to bend way over to kiss a little boy in blue knickers. She kissed him on the forehead and sent him off with a pat on the head. He wanted to come back and get another kiss, but his mother took him by the hand.

10. The following paragraph, which consists of a single sentence, is an extreme but interesting example of aggregation. Compare it with the passage in the preceding exercise. Write out an analysis of its use of parallelism, repetition, alliteration, rhythm, and devices for securing emphasis.

Other Americans have like myself listened to League debates, compact of declarations, appeals, warnings, reservations; have talked with elected leaders in the capitals and corners of Europe —thousands of them, literally, in these eighteen years—some perfunctory and pompous, some cynical and witty, some bombastic and tearful, some dignified, a few generous, two or three prescient and serene; have watched elections and plebiscites, café riots and strikes; have sat on countless terraces reading the conflicting reports of countless cabinet crises; have seen kings wade in trout streams, kneel rigid at midnight mass, open parliaments, lie in state; have watched so many kinds of men march—shouting or grim, desperate for bread, in delirium for freedom won, in relief for freedom lost; have had private exhibitions of this dictator's magnetic eye and squared shoulders, special auditions of that one's wet and crescendo speech, as showy as a skyrocket and as convincing; have heard amplifiers blare and crowds thunder—Piazza Venezia, Red Square, Pariser-platz, Puerta del Sol, Ringstrasse—windows shuttered in fear or cascading flags and carpets and flowers; have huddled in attics with ex-Premiers around a gas-ring and a plate of speckled cakes; have seen wreaths fade on monuments and barbed wire rust in the undergrowth by quiet streams and chimneys smoke where new guns and gases are made.—HAMILTON FISH ARMSTRONG, "We or They," pp. 1-2

11. Study the qualities of the sentences in some of the illustrative paragraphs, such as the one by Otis Ferguson on page 156, by Joseph Conrad in *Heightened style, and by John Steinbeck in the same section. The outline on page 150 will suggest topics for special study.

12. Study and analyze a passage of your own writing in the same way.

13. Revise a passage from one of your recent papers, so as to gain in sentence variety, economy, and emphasis and to improve the rhythm and sound. Hand in both your original version and your revision.

CHAPTER 7

The Meaning of Words

1. **The supply of words**
   a. The English vocabulary b. The individual's vocabulary
2. **Denotation: The core of a word's meaning**
   a. Concrete words b. Relative words c. Abstract words
3. **Connotation: The suggestion of words**
   a. Meaning from context b. Synonyms
4. **The responsible use of words**
   a. Mistaken words b. Vague words and phrases c. Unfair or unintended connotation
5. **The usefulness of dictionaries**
   a. Kinds of dictionaries b. Uses of a dictionary
6. **Increasing your vocabulary**
   a. Transferring words from recognition to active vocabulary b. Learning new subjects c. Adding individual words

ANYONE WHO is even temporarily concerned with his speaking and writing becomes interested in words and their ways. His curiosity naturally turns to their meaning and to the various ways in which they are used; he becomes conscious of some words that he lacks but really needs and of some that he partially knows. This book might have begun with a discussion of words, since they are the fundamental elements of speech and writing. But if our purpose is communication, we are first aware of ideas expressed consecutively, of words as they stand in individual statements (sentences) and in groups of statements (paragraphs). In fact they do not properly exist by themselves but only as they are put to some use. It seems more natural to consider first those wholes and later to look more closely at the qualities of the single words of which they are composed. This and the following chapter discuss various points about the meaning and use of words, about what they do and do not accomplish for us in our attempts to tell others something or to understand what others say.

1. The supply of words

1a. The English vocabulary. The exact number of English words is not known and cannot be exactly known. The unabridged dictionaries now contain about 500,000 entries, the Second Edition (1934) of *Webster's International* advertising 600,-000. Many of these are for compound words (*livery stable*) or for different derivatives of the same word (*rare—rarely*), so that the *Oxford English Dictionary* breaks down its entries into these categories: Main words—240,165, Subordinate words—67,105, Special combinations—47,800, Obvious combinations—59,755, Total—424,825. Of course most of the "main words" are given with more than one "meaning" and some with dozens of different meanings.

The dictionaries contain thousands of obsolete words to help us read the older literature. But on the other hand they do not attempt to cover completely many groups of words that can be drawn upon, especially slang, localisms, trade names, and the colloquial technical words of the various trades and occupations; and words used only occasionally by scientists and specialists in many fields. Besides these there is the fringe of foreign words that may be borrowed temporarily (*raison d'être*, *Weltanschauung*) and others that can be made up for special occasions (like *unparlorable*) but are not used often enough to become a part of the regular stock of the language. Spencer Armstrong says (*How Words Get into the Dictionary*, p. 29):

> However, it is no flight of fancy to state that there are between 1,000,000 and 1,250,000 words in our language today. At least two-fifths of these are ultrascientific terms used only in the recesses of the laboratory; they are not to be found in standard dictionaries and figure in special glossaries of the sciences to which they belong.

New words are being constantly added to the vocabulary— Mr. Armstrong estimates at the rate of about 3000 a year or as many as 5000 in years of special activity such as war. Radio broadcasting alone, he says, has put 5000 words into the large dictionaries.

"The circle of the English language has a well-defined centre but no discernible circumference," says the Preface to the first volume of the *Oxford English Dictionary*. The words of the well-defined center, perhaps 200,000 of them, we may meet in our reading, especially if it is broad enough to include both older and modern literature, and some scientific fields. And these same words make the reservoir from which as speakers and writers we draw the raw materials of our expression.[1]

1b. The individual's vocabulary. It is hard to tell what portion of this store of words an individual uses. It used to be fashionable to say that a grown person of average social standing used only a few hundred words, but actual counts have shown that children soon pass the mark that was set for adults. More recent studies and estimates put the vocabulary of an average adult at more than 10,000 words—and some guesses put that of an educated person as above 50,000. A person with a definite occupation probably has at least 10,000—think how many objects with names (and names for their qualities and for what they can do) there are in any store or factory or even in a kitchen or a barn! Reading and higher education add other words to those picked up from daily experience, and Mr. Armstrong thinks that a college graduate "should have command of upwards of 20,000 words." The number of words in general use is steadily increasing. New machines and new products increase the number used in practical affairs as the increase of general and theoretical knowledge adds to the vocabulary of the educated person. Mr. Lawrence E. Nelson estimates that a reader today needs a vocabulary one-third larger than he did in 1840.[2]

*Exercise 1, p. 208

However many words a person may "know," he will know them in different ways. The figures of the preceding paragraph refer to his *recognition vocabulary*, the words that he will understand more or less accurately in reading or listening but that he may or may not use. This recognition vocabulary is usually regarded as roughly three times as large as his *active vocabulary*, the words he will use easily in speaking and writing. Very little is known about the relation between these two active vocabularies, the spoken and the written. They may be about the same in size but include different words: A good many words of ordinary conversation would not appear in writing, and many, used in writing, a person might not use in his conversation. The vocabularies of public address and of writing would be more alike than those of writing and familiar conversation.

[1] References: Spencer Armstrong, *How Words Get into the Dictionary* (New York, 1933); Kennedy, Ch. 10, "The Modern English Vocabulary"; *Oxford English Dictionary*, Prefaces to Vols. i and x; Robert L. Ramsay, "Taking the Census of English Words," *American Speech*, 1933, viii, 36-41.

[2] References: Kennedy, § 84 and the sources there referred to; Lawrence E. Nelson, "In Defense of Ezra," *The English Journal*, 1938, xxvii, 513-17; *Word Study*, Feb. 1939, pp. 5-8.

In the following paragraph of academic prose some of the words illustrate possible distinctions between a recognition and an active vocabulary. They are italicized for later discussion.

Two sorts of experience are recognized as having *worth*, or as capable of having it, an *active* and a *passive;* one is *creation* or control, and the other *appreciation*. These are not strictly separate experiences, but rather *"aspects"* of experience, yet they are practically *separable* to a large degree. The worth of active creation or control is a kind of appreciation; usually, the worth of the experience of activity depends more or less upon a feeling of worth toward or appreciation of some "result" brought about. But though the two things are usually more or less *associated* and overlapping, we are all familiar with extreme cases in which on the one hand the feeling of worth is nearly or quite purely passive and on the other the worth of an activity is nearly or quite independent of the character of the result. The literature of *value*, like that of science, shows a *bias* for *monism*, so there is a tendency to reduce all value to *"contemplation"* or to the "joy of being a cause," according to the *temperamental predilections* of the particular writer, but a *candid* observer must accept both, and all sorts of mixtures of the two.—FRANK H. KNIGHT, "Scientific Method in Economics," *The Trend of Economics*, edited by R. G. Tugwell, p. 230

Probably most college students would recognize and understand more or less accurately every word in this passage, except perhaps *monism*, though some would have trouble defining *predilections*. A good many would recognize but would not ordinarily use *aspects, separable, associated, bias* (though they would use *biased*), *contemplation*, and perhaps *temperamental*. *Passive, creation*, and *appreciation* they might use in writing but ordinarily would not use in their conversation unless they were trying to "make an impression." The words *worth* and *value* are common enough, but not in the senses in which they appear here: *worth* is here a noun instead of, as more commonly, an adjective ("worth so much"), and *value* is used in a philosophical sense. Probably most students would not use *candid* outside the currently popular phrase *candid camera*. It is quite proper that many of these words remain in the average person's recognition vocabulary; it would be for the individual to decide whether he could conveniently use *bias* or *candid* or *monism* or any of the others. But it is important to recognize that there are different strata in everyone's vocabulary, no matter what its size is.

2. Denotation: The core of a word's meaning

The words we use and the words we recognize have got their meaning from the way they have been and are being used by people in speaking and writing. *A word "means" what it stands for to the speaker or writer, listener or reader, what in their experience or imagination or feeling it refers to.* The object or class of objects, act, situation, quality, idea, or fancy to which a word refers is called its *referent* (ref'ər ənt), and by representing this referent a word gets a core of meaning, its denotation. In dictionaries the ways in which a word is generally used are recorded, stated in other terms, as *Washington pie* is defined in Webster: "Layer cake with a cream filling or with a fruit-jam filling." But this definition in other *words* is not the meaning of *Washington pie* but an effort to direct the reader to a recollection or imagination of the word's referent. Its meaning is not the words of the definition but the food.

One way to show that meaning is *not in the word* is to consider some words that are used in various senses. To take common examples: What is a *knot?* a *cut?* a *seal?* a *play?* What do you do when you *play* or *strike*, or *fly*, or *fall?* A *knot* may be a tie of some sort in a rope, a group of people, a spot in a board, a tough problem, the measure of a ship's speed. The meaning is not in the word but in what it refers to. What it does refer to is usually clear from the sentence in which it is used, that is, from its *context*. It is so difficult to say how much we understand from a given word and how much from its context that it is not very profitable to consider the meaning of isolated words.

*Linguistics

The division of linguistics that studies the meaning and changes of meaning of words is called semantics, or semasiology. In the last few years this field has been particularly active, under the leadership of C. K. Ogden, I. A. Richards, Count Alfred Korzybski, and others. These men have added much to our knowledge and understanding of words and the ways in which they are used and misused. In this short account we can only suggest some of the more obviously useful facts of semantics.[1]

[1] The most readable and practical introduction to semantics is S. I. Hayakawa, *Language in Action* (New York, 1941). This and other elementary treatises, such as Irving J. Lee, *Language Habits in Human Affairs* (New York, 1941), can lead a reader to the more difficult original works. There are useful chapters in general books on language: Bloomfield, Chapter 9; Kennedy, Chapter 13; Greenberg, Chapter 15. Thurman W. Arnold, *The Folklore of Capitalism* (New Haven, 1937), especially Chapter 5, and H. R. Huse, *The Illiteracy of the Literate* (New York, 1933) are more popular applications of semantics.

Definiteness of meaning varies considerably among different words, depending in part on the exactness with which they bring to mind specific referents. Three classes of words will show this varying definiteness. Other groups could be made according to some trait of their meaning, but these are enough to suggest that there are different relations between words and what they stand for and that the problem of using words exactly is more complex than it might seem at first thought.

2a. Concrete words. First and most definite are specific concrete words whose meaning is established by more or less regular reference to actual objects. *Chair*, for example, has a definite core of meaning because it is used to apply to a kind of seat. Even though people might disagree over a particular untypical chair—one might be called *stool* or another might be called *sofa*—almost always the meaning of *chair* would be definite enough for one's purposes. *Morris chair, rocking chair, ladder back chair* are more definite in their reference. The specific image that a word raises in the minds of different people will vary somewhat: at a given moment *robin* may mean to one person *robin-pulling-at-a-worm*, to another, *robin-on-a-nest*, to another, *robin-crying-rain*, but in each there is a core of meaning for *robin*. A word with which a person has had no experience (perhaps *spandrel, tenon, farthingale, rickrack*, or *tachistoscope*) will have no meaning for him. *Exercise 13, p. 211

A speaker or writer would not as a rule use these concrete words without a fairly definite knowledge of their core of meaning; a reader or listener will either know this meaning, be able to approach it through a dictionary definition or other reading, ask someone who knows, or learn it by observation. It is lucky for all of us that such a large part of our vocabulary consists of these fairly exact words.

2b. Relative words. Words that name qualities also have a fairly definite core of meaning, or at least a direction of meaning, but their reference in a given instance depends a good deal on the experience and intention of the user. *Red*, for instance, runs from orange to violet and for a reasonably definite meaning needs to be qualified by another word, *light, dark, orange*. To a person in "the upper brackets," a family with $1500 a year might be *poor*, but to a person on relief that family might be *well off*. Similarly, *warm, heavy, thick, rough, pretty, honest, beautiful, tall* are relative in meaning. Some attempts have been made to make possible an exact or standard sense for some of these words, as in the color scale for exact naming of colors in art or in physics, standardized weights and measures, or in definitions by law of words like *drunk* and *speeding* so that they can be used in courts.

In using these descriptive words, especially those that record our attitudes and judgments, the most important thing is to remember the various degrees, the exact shading that it is possible to express. In ordinary conversation we don't make many distinctions. A person is *wet* or a *good egg* (or whatever the equivalent slang is this year), a show is a *flop* or a *wow*, a novel is *fascinating* or *disgusting*. Our fraternity mates—or members of our political party—are *honest, generous, loyal,* and so on; our rivals are ———? Actually we know, and when we are trying to talk accurately we say, that they fall somewhere between the extremes. We and our acquaintances are neither saints nor double-dyed villains but somewhere between. Can we say just about where? To try is challenging and a step toward civilized living—as well as a triumph in the use of words.

2c. Abstract words. Even more difficult to use accurately are abstract words, which do not have specific referents against which their meaning can be checked. The most definite abstract words refer to acts or relationships or directions: *trading, murder, cost, citizenship, nation, height.* They have definite meaning simply because English-speaking people generally agree in the way they are used. Other abstract words are collective, that is, they stand for a gathering of individuals— *college, swing music, the administration* (of a college or of the United States). They summarize one or more common traits belonging to a number of particular people or things or situations and have a pretty definite core of meaning but may be used with very different values. The real danger in such words is that often as we use them we lose sight of the individuals for which they stand. "The *youth* of our country" may actually keep us from seeing the millions of young people referred to and may let us or lead us to make statements that we never would if we visualized clearly even a dozen of them. *Capital,* for instance, means employers and investors collectively, and *labor* stands for workmen. But ordinarily as they are used, there is no notion of people suggested; they may be used as words of praise or blame, so that feeling would be more important than reference to any group of living persons.

Many other words do not have referents even as commonly agreed upon as those. The meaning of such words as *beauty, art, the good life, culture, evil, education, Americanism* is a

*Page 223

188

complex of reasoning and feeling that varies from person to person. An adequate definition of any such word would be an essay, and its meaning would depend on the past experience, the emotions, and the general outlook of the person making it. Obviously understanding is difficult here, because the listener or reader has a different experience, different feelings, and a different philosophy so that the difficulty is at least doubled.

We cannot expect that more or less haphazard people, as we all are, will always use these words exactly, but we should be prepared for their exact use whenever possible. *One way to do this is to translate our meaning into other terms and by giving two or three versions reach some sort of exactness and hope through one or the other to meet the reader's expectations.* As speakers or writers our intention is to lead a listener or reader not just to words but to consciousness of objects or ideas in a real or imagined world. To do this *we can give wherever possible specific, concrete examples of what we mean.* The fundamental sin is using words that do not "refer to something," do not, that is, have meaning.

A more general safeguard is to realize the range of meaning that abstract words have and make clear where in this range our immediate intention falls. The word *poetry,* for example, is often a stumbling block to mutual understanding because it ranges through at least three general senses. It may mean no more than composition in verse; it may be used collectively to mean a body of particular poems; or it may mean an idealized form of writing, that is, poems having certain characteristics that we respect or are fond of. (The *Oxford English Dictionary* and the *Century Dictionary* are particularly useful in pointing out such ranges of meaning.) Obviously for exact and reasonable communication it is highly important that a speaker or writer knows where in the range of meaning of abstract words his core of meaning falls and that he makes this clear to his listeners or readers. Trying to attain fairly exact communication is one reason for the prevailing *concreteness* of modern style.

3. Connotation: The suggestion of words

The denotation of a word is (more or less) informative and factual and is what we ordinarily mean by its "meaning"; it is what a dictionary definition tries to lead us to. But this meaning is somewhat affected by the circumstances in which the word has been generally used and by the particular context in which it occurs. This suggested quality, as distinct from the central core of meaning, is called its *connotation*.

*Exercise 5, pp. 209-10

Looking at a few groups of words having substantially the same denotation will bring out this quality and show why one could not be indiscriminately substituted for another.

childlike (approving); *childish* (derogatory)

saliva (factual, slightly formal, with scientific suggestion); *spit* (the usual word but to many people "an ugly word")

killed in battle (factual); *died a hero's death* (honorific); *slain by the enemy* (emphasis shifted to the baseness of the act)

antique (generally approving); *old-fashioned* (factual, though often suggesting disapproval); *passé* (lightly derogatory)

drunk (in general use); *intoxicated* (more polite); *under the influence* (euphemistic—minimizing); *pie-eyed, soused, stinko* (not necessarily derogatory in meaning but suggesting light or slangy speech)

appendectomy (professional); *appendicitis operation* (slightly formal); *had his appendix out* (colloquial)

reporter (factual); *journalist* (slightly pretentious); *newshawk* (usually with slight derogatory note); *legman* (shoptalk)

slender (factual, tending to approval); *thin* (factual, tending to disapproval); *skinny* (disapproving); *sylphlike* (poetic, formal); *svelte* (fashionable)

handkerchief (factual); *hanky* (children's talk or humorous); *snotrag* (low); *kerchief* (archaic)

mongrel (factual); *cur* (derogatory); *feice* (local)

The connotations of these words suggest an attitude or a feeling of the person using them and would arouse a similar (or perhaps an antagonistic) attitude or feeling in most readers or listeners. The context in which the word has been generally used, the level of usage it comes from, and the general social attitude toward its referent and toward the people who generally use it (gangsters, politicians, businessmen, teachers, children, seamen . . .) all contribute to the suggested qualities. The value of slang and of much profanity is more in the suggestion of the words than in their denotation. The connotation of these words may change as they or their referents move up or down in social esteem. *Methodist* started as a word of dispraise but is now simply factual, the name of a church, or often a word of esteem. *Propaganda* only a few years ago meant a means of spreading a truth or a faith, but it now implies spreading falsehood or at least an unfair presentation of information.

3a. Meaning from context. Besides these connotations that are more or less permanent characteristics of words, there are more immediate connotations that come from context, from the way they are used at a specific time or from the other words around them. In speaking we can alter or even invert the usual meaning of a word by the tone of voice or facial expression or gesture. We can call a person a liar in such a way that he will know he is being flattered. In writing the tone is set by the general style and by the tenor of ideas expressed. *War*, for example, may refer simply to a historical event, or it may be used with suggestions of bravery or of suffering or of chicanery. *Democracy, communism, monarchy* are primarily words for types of social organization, but they may carry also suggestions of loyalty or hate. The full possibility of meaning of many words cannot be indicated by a dictionary; consider what would be omitted in a standard definition of such words as *fascism, income tax, ball game, quintessence, the founding fathers* (of the United States), *scab, the forgotten man, horse and buggy era.*

Besides these widespread connotations and those that are clear in the context, there are often special associations a word may have for a particular person, a suggestion that his past experience or his temperament or his ideals or his imagination has given it for him. In impersonal writing such associations are usually suppressed, but in familiar writing and in fiction and especially in poetry they play a prominent part.

Making use of the connotations of words gives writing a quality of style that is called *suggestion*. The reader is carried beyond the literal meanings, senses the feelings of the writer, and comes to believe in him as a real person. Amateur writers tend to rely too much on impersonal denotations and to squeeze out of their writing this personal quality. In the following paragraph from "A Death in the Country," Mr. Benét uses only ordinary words, but he suggests a definite scene and the emotion of a man remembering the funeral of his mother.

*Abstract and concrete words

Well, he wasn't looking forward to a pleasant time. He felt fagged and on edge already. There was work for the active partner of Norman, Buckstone, and Carroll in his brief-case, but he could not get down to the work. Instead he remembered, from childhood, the smell of dyed cloth and poignant, oppressive flowers, the black wisp tied on the knocker, the people coming to the door. The house was full of a menace—full of a secret—there were incomprehensible phrases, said in a murmur, and a man in black gloves who came, and a strangeness behind a shut door. Run out and play, run out and play; but there was no right way to play any more—even out in the yard you could smell the sweet, overpowering flowers—even out in the street you could see the people coming and coming, making that little pause as they saw the black wisp. Beautiful, they said, she looks beautiful; but the glimpse of the face was not mother, only somebody coldly asleep. Our sister has gone to dear Jesus . . . we shall meet on that beautiful shore . . . but the man spoke words, and the harsh box sank into the hole, and from it nothing arose, not even a white thing, not even silver vapor; the clay at the sides of the hole was too yellow and thick and cold. He's too young to realize, said a great many voices—but for months nothing was right. The world had stopped being solid, and people's smiles were different, and mother was Jesus' sister, and they gave her clothes away. Then, after a long time, the place was green again and looked just like the other graves, and the knife in your pocket was a comfort, going out there Sundays in the street car.—STEPHEN VINCENT BENÉT, *Thirteen O'Clock*, pp. 257-58

3b. Synonyms. *A synonym is a word of nearly the same meaning as another.* Often the real difference between them is in the connotation. There are very few pairs of interchangeable words. Even names of specific things, like *rhubarb—pieplant, kerosene—coal oil, delphinium—larkspur,* differ, for though they refer to the same objects, their connotations differ, because one of the pair is used in a definite part of the country, or by a specific group of people, or under certain circumstances, so that one cannot be regularly substituted for another. English is especially rich in words of slightly different shades of meaning: *joke—jest; obedient—dutiful—yielding—compliant—obsequious; multitude—throng—crowd—mob.* Because of these differences in connotation, merely trying to escape repetition of a word is not a sufficient motive for using a synonym. It is better to avoid unpleasant repetition by the use of pronouns or by recasting the sentence.

*Repetition, p. 168

When a writer looks for a "synonym," he is really looking for a word of nearly the same meaning as the one he has in hand but one that can give his meaning in the particular sentence more exactly. The important point, then, in looking at two or more words of similar meaning is to know how they *differ*.

Some synonyms should be looked for before writing the first draft; others after the first draft is written. If a writer knows that he is going to discuss a subject with which he is not very familiar, he can think over the words (really the material of the subject) and can sharpen his sense of the necessary words before he begins to write. If he expects to need words for colors, or for the qualities of poetry, or for the parts of a radio, he can gain control of them before he sits down to put his words on paper.

But as a rule testing the exactness of words is a matter of revision. He can see then the context in which they are to stand and can test them for exactness of meaning, for appropriateness to the subject and to the readers, for their degree of formality or informality. Sometimes he can find a single word to take the place of a long phrase; sometimes he can replace a general or ambiguous word with one of specific meaning, as *funny* might be *amusing, laughable, odd, queer, different, peculiar*; or *walk* might be replaced by a more descriptive word. Sometimes the change is to bring a word in line with the level of usage of the rest of the paper, choosing one either more or less formal: *want—wish—desire; roomy—spacious; fast—rapidly.* Sometimes it is a matter of finding the exact name for something that the writer has seen but has never named in one word, like the small platform on which an orchestra conductor stands (*podium*), or a part of a landscape (perhaps a *mesa*, or a *hogback*, or an *arroyo*).

The prime source of synonyms as of other words is conversation and reading. A person usually has a plentiful and ready supply of words in the fields in which he is really at home. Cultivating a habit of observing and using words in discussion is the best background for making the choice of exact words easy.

There are also various tools at hand. Dictionaries group words of similar meaning and indicate the general distinctions between them. There are also several books of synonyms, especially F. S. Allen, *Synonyms and Antonyms* (New York, 1921), and Roget's *Thesaurus of English Words and Phrases* (in two recent revisions, New York, 1922, and New York, 1936).[1] This *Thesaurus* (thi sô′rəs) is probably the most used book of synonyms. It lists words by topics, in parallel columns giving words of opposite meaning, and offers a wide range from slang to formal and even obsolete words. It does not give definitions of the words, so that its chief use is to remind a person of words that he recognizes but does not use readily. In this way it is very useful in bridging the gap between one's recognition vocabulary and one's working vocabulary. It is often helpful in revising a paper.

---

[1] See also S. Stephenson Smith, *The Command of Words* (New York, 1935), Chapter 6.

4. The responsible use of words

The preceding sections show that exactness in the use of words is difficult. Words are only roughly accurate in their meanings because human beings are not exact, or at least are exact only as the result of special training or of some immediate necessity. If a person wishes to deceive, language offers him the means; by intentional misuse of words or by an irresponsible manipulation of the emotional suggestion in words a "propagandist" (or anyone else) can distort truth and make error prevail, at least for a time.

But in spite of some selfish and even evil intentions, an honest attempt at communication can be made to succeed. Our semanticists may even make us too suspicious of words. The difficulty is not so much in the words as in the intent of the person using them or the lack of a responsible purpose. Honest failure in communication is possible because of careless or unhappy choice of words, and sometimes we fail to make full use of the facilities of our language. But a sincere effort to convey material we are really familiar with can succeed.

Absolute exactness is not always desirable. A person who in conversation is overexact or overcareful is likely to become a bore, sacrificing immediate appeal to precision. Often in a poem so much depends on the connotation of the words that several "meanings" are possible, and properly enough so long as a reader does not insist that his interpretation is necessarily the one the writer intended. In simple explanation or statements of fact, especially in scientific writing, the words are likely to be used for their central core of meaning. In attempts to persuade and in any sort of emotional speech, the connotation counts for more. Even exaggeration or words of relatively little specific content, like *un-American*, are typical of vigorous statements of opinion. In the following sentences *failure, fantastically impossible,* and other expressions show this emotional use of words, which convey Mr. Nock's half-truth not in precise but in emphatic terms which will deceive no one.

*Exercise 11, p. 211

New York State spent half a million dollars on a three years' study of its system by a commission including thirty men of national reputation and seven college presidents; and the report made public on the day I write this shows that while New York's system is as good as any in the country, or even better, it is for all essential purposes virtually a total failure. It is a failure for the same reason that the American educational system is everywhere a failure; it fails because it is condemned to the fantastically impossible task of making silk purses out of sows' ears. The commission did not report this fact, probably because it is fundamental, insuperable, and unpleasant. All similar investigations have blinked it, no doubt for the same reason; but the naïve policy of the ostrich will not alter facts, and this is the primary fact of the situation.—ALBERT JAY NOCK, "College Is No Place to Get an Education," *The American Mercury*, Feb. 1939

In contexts where exact words are necessary or desirable, as in most factual writing and in college writing, there are three typical faults to be guarded against:

4a. No meaning: Mistaken words. Sometimes a word is used for a meaning that it has not acquired in its previous history:

> How are the coaches outwitting their *prototypes* [*competitors?*]?
>
> An educated man seems to have an expression signifying shrewdness, *comprehensibility* [*understanding?*], and originality, which no other person can quite match.

Usually, as in the last sentence (note the *signifying*), such errors occur when a writer is attempting a level of usage in which he is not at home or when he confuses two words of similar sound (*temerity—timidity, flaunt—flout*). Confusion is especially likely to occur between words of opposite meaning (*imply—infer*). Confusions in writing of words that sound alike (homonyms) are a matter of spelling rather than of meaning. Even if the context makes the meaning clear, as it often does, such inaccuracies are a mark of carelessness or of imperfect education.

*flaunt—flout
*imply—infer
*Homonyms

The remedy for this sort of error is to stay within your known vocabulary or to check with a dictionary words of which you are not quite sure.

*affect—effect

4b. Too little meaning: Vague words and phrases. Sometimes words are used that are too general to convey an exact meaning. They are more characteristic of conversation than of writing: Counter words like *fine, bad, good* in writing should usually be replaced by more definite adjectives, and even words like *interesting* or *important* frequently stand for some particular sort of interest or importance that could better be named, so that the reader's thought could be brought nearer to the writer's intention. Many phrases could be replaced by single exact words with a gain in economy and sometimes in definiteness:

*Counter words

> The men with axes would then trim off the branches while the men with large crosscut saws cut the *large part of the tree* [*trunk*] into sixteen-foot lengths.

Last year in a nearby city an *occupant* [*prisoner*] in the county jail escaped.

The other thing that *I have in mind* [*My other intention— hope—plan?*] is to go to ·France.

*Page 239

4c. Too much meaning: Unfair or unintended connotation. Exaggeration is a legitimate form of expression, but often words are too intense for a writer's meaning. Perhaps a *most* should be *many*, or a superlative should be reduced to a less extreme statement, or an *only* or *nothing but* should allow for other possibilities. Or extreme words like *unique, intriguing, thrill* should be replaced by words that are merely descriptive.

*Exercises 9, 10, and 17, pp. 210 and 212

Epithets that are emotional rather than descriptive (*fascist, communist*) should be used with special care, and usually an expansive emotional patch, like the following description of the content of a volume of poems, should be avoided entirely:

There will be a vivid color and vibrant pulse of life about it. And the pen of each contributor will touch a chord of desire in the readers' heart of thoughts trooping across its pages, gripping with an inward fire of intensity a vast imaginative tapestry of the beauties of America. By sparkling streams and in green hills there will be found undiscovered places to dream and it will be warm and impressive in human emotion.

The best remedy for such writing is to keep looking at the subject and to resolve to present it as it really is. This will help a writer express himself in words that are relatively exact in meaning.

5. The usefulness of dictionaries

The most useful tool for a writer, in or out of a composition course, is a good dictionary. Nowhere else can he find so much information about words and their use, and nowhere else, if he is really interested in his language, can he find so much curious, incidental, and even amusing information about words. The more he refers to his dictionary and browses in it, the more his powers of communication can grow.

But dictionaries are primarily for reference. They answer questions about the meaning of words so that the student can read with more understanding. They settle doubts (or arguments) about single words. And they help a writer decide on the most accurate and effective word or phrase to use. *A writer will use his dictionary most in revision and should get the habit of turning to it frequently while revising a paper and preparing the final copy.*

5a. Kinds of dictionaries. (1) GENERAL DICTIONARIES. There is no such thing as "the dictionary," which can be quoted to settle any question about words. There are a number of dictionaries, all (except the scholarly historical dictionaries) commercial ventures—that is, the editors compile the best book they are capable of and able to prepare with the money allowed by the publisher. ($1,500,000 was appropriated for making the second, 1934, Webster International.) Dictionaries consequently vary, and choosing one to satisfy a person's needs is difficult. Dictionaries obviously vary in three fundamental respects (as well as in minor matters like typography and arrangement of entries), in *date, size,* and responsibility of *editing.*

a) Date. Words are continually being added to the general stock of the English langauge, other words are used in new senses, words drop out of use, spellings and pronunciations change. Words set in motion by new discoveries in science and by new inventions send us to a dictionary more often than any other class. For this reason date of compilation—not of printing—is important. To find this date look at the earliest date of copyright on the back of the title page. Many dictionaries offered at low prices or given as premiums are new printings of old dictionaries and are of less use because of their age. It is probably more profitable in the long run to buy a recently revised dictionary of the "college" size, with about 140,000 entries, than one with three times the number but perhaps twenty years old. In consulting dictionaries in libraries you should look for one recently revised.

b) Size. For serious work with words it is necessary to go to a recent "unabridged" dictionary, which will have upwards of half a million entries. These are expensive and rather cumbersome, so that for most people the smaller size, costing usually from $3.50 up, according to binding, is more generally useful. The more uncommon words are left out in the abridgment but those needed for most reading and writing are included. Still smaller dictionaries, down to the pocket sizes, and those intended for use in lower schools, may be handy for checking spelling, but they are not sufficient for college work.

c) Editing. Date and size of a dictionary are easily determined, but it is very difficult to judge the editing of such a complex work. Responsible editing makes the dictionary really useful, gives it what "authority" it may possess. That is, it should not be a compilation from existing word books but from a vast accumulation of actual recorded uses of words. It should

*Exercise 6, p. 210

*Change in language

be based on an enormous file of recent quotations from all sorts of writers from all over the English-speaking world. This raw material then should be worked over by trained editors who digest the evidence of use into the dictionary's brief articles.

d) Current English dictionaries. There are several useful American dictionaries of English:

The Webster Dictionaries (International, second edition, 1934, and Collegiate, fifth edition, 1936) are probably preferred by most users who are primarily interested in literature and the English language. They are carefully edited, rather conservative dictionaries. Their definitions are sometimes rather hard to follow. They pay more attention to the origin of words than the other dictionaries and put first in a series of definitions the original meaning of a word, which may not be its current meaning. These genuine Merriam-Webster dictionaries should not be confused with others bearing the Webster name but based on old editions. These ersatz Websters carry on their title page, usually in very small type, the statement "This Dictionary is not published by the publishers of Webster's Dictionary, or by their successors."

The Standard Dictionaries (unabridged, desk, and college sizes) pay somewhat more attention to technical words and admit new words more readily than the Webster. They list the simplified spelling forms. They use two pronunciation keys, a system of diacritical marks and the International Phonetic Alphabet, which sometimes confuse people who do not use a dictionary frequently. Their synonyms are clearly distinguished.

The New Century Dictionary (two volumes, 1938 edition), uses a somewhat simpler pronunciation key than most dictionaries and gives unusually full and intelligible definitions of words, reinforced by frequent quotations.

The Winston Simplified Dictionary and others have stressed typographical arrangement and less technical definitions.

In consulting a general dictionary a person should go to a recent, good-sized edition of one of these. And in buying one, he should buy the largest, most recent edition that he can afford.

2) SPECIAL DICTIONARIES. Dictionary making (lexicography) is a highly specialized art, or applied science, and the general dictionaries are supplemented by a considerable number of special word books and several more are now being compiled.[1]

---

[1] M. M. Mathews, *A Survey of English Dictionaries* (New York, 1933), is a history of English dictionaries.

a) *Historical dictionaries.* The *Oxford English Dictionary* in ten large volumes is the great storehouse of information about English words. It traces the various forms of each word and its various meanings with dates of their first appearance and quotations from writers illustrating each. There is a *Supplement* giving material on new words and evidence on earlier words not found in the original work. Besides being the standard authority on the history of English words, the *Oxford English Dictionary* is useful in reading older literature to find exactly what a word meant at a particular time in the past. An abridgment, the *Shorter Oxford English Dictionary,* in two volumes, is on the same plan and is very useful for interpreting past literature.

*Exercise 14, p. 211

The *Dictionary of American English* now appearing is on the same plan as the *Oxford,* giving the histories of words as they have been used in the United States. An entry begins with the first use of the word found in American writers and continues, giving quotations, to the present. In this way it supplements the linguistic information of the *Oxford* and is of special usefulness in reading American writers.

Besides these there are dictionaries for Old English and for Middle English, and other period dictionaries are being compiled, like the *Dictionary of Early Modern English* (1500-1700).

b) *Dialect dictionaries.* Besides Joseph Wright's *English Dialect Dictionary* (6 volumes), giving words in the various dialects of England, there are a number of special word lists from different regions, in books and in periodicals like *Dialect Notes* and *American Speech.* Eric Partridge's *Dictionary of Slang* is a historical dictionary of English and American slang from early to recent times. Work is being done on the *Linguistic Atlas of the United States and Canada* which will eventually appear with very full accounts of the use and movements of certain words in this country.

c) *Dictionaries in special subjects.* Because the general dictionaries cannot give the complete vocabulary in specialized fields of work, they are supplemented by a growing group of dictionaries in special subjects, like the following:

Alsager, C. M., *Dictionary of Business Terms* (1932)
Ballentine, J. A., *Law Dictionary* (1930)
Dorland, W. A. N., *American Illustrated Medical Dictionary* (1932)
Farrow, E. G., *Dictionary of Military Terms* (1918)
Jackson, B. D., *Glossary of Botanic Terms* (1928)

Other general dictionaries will be found listed, with critical notes, in I. G. Mudge, *Guide to Reference Books* (6th edition; Chicago, 1936), pp. 51-85, and dictionaries of special subjects, p. 86 ff.

5b. Uses of a dictionary. Obviously, to get the most out of a dictionary, its owner needs to know what various matters it includes. He should look through its table of contents to see what units of material there are besides the main alphabetical list of words. He should see if it contains a supplement of new words. He should read a page or two consecutively to see how words and phrases are handled, and he should try pronouncing some familiar words to see how the pronunciation key works. A few pains taken learning to use a particular dictionary will be more than repaid by its increased usefulness.

Although we think of dictionaries first as giving information about spelling, pronunciation, and meaning, they contain several other types of facts also.

*Chapter 10, p. 267

1) SPELLING. A word is entered in a dictionary under its usual spelling. As a rule a writer can come close enough to this usual spelling so that he can find a word he is in doubt about, but sometimes he has to keep in mind other common spellings of a sound—so that if he fails to find *gibe* he will look

*Exercise 7, p. 210

under *jibe*. When usage in spelling is divided, two spellings are given for the word. The one the editors believe is more common is usually put first: *hemoglobin, haemoglobin; although, altho.* Ordinarily a writer will take the first of the two forms unless the second for some reason is more appropriate to other traits of his writing. The spelling entries in a dictionary give the division of a word into syllables and so show where words should be divided at the ends of lines as in *mor ti-*

*Division of words

fi ca tion, dis par ag ing ly. They also give the spelling of compound words, showing whether the editors have found them most often as two words, as one word, or with hyphen. Most dictionaries recommend the use of more hyphens than are necessary, certainly for informal writing. The introductions to most dictionaries contain general discussions of English spelling.

*Pronunciation

2) PRONUNCIATION. Dictionaries respell words in specially marked letters to show their pronunciation. The exact sounds represented by the symbols are shown at the bottom of the page and are further explained in a general discussion of English pronunciation in the preface. (The one in the Webster dictionaries is especially full and informing.)

200

ac·cli′mate (ă·klī′mĭt; ăk′lĭ·māt), *v. t. & i.* [F. *acclimater*, fr. *à* to + *climat* climate.] To habituate, or cause habituation, to a climate not native; to acclimatize. — **ac·cli′mat·a·ble** (ă·klī′mĭt·à·b'l), *adj.* — **ac′cli·ma′tion** (ăk′lĭmā′shŭn; ăk′lĭ-), *n.*

cer′ti·o·ra′ri (sûr′shĭ·ō·rā′rī; -râr′ī), *n.* [From *certiorari* to be certified; — a term in the Latin form of the writ.] *Law.* A writ from a superior court to call up for review the records of an inferior court or a body acting in a quasi-judicial capacity.

phi·lat′e·ly (fĭ·lăt′ĕ·lĭ), *n.* [F. *philatélie*, fr. Gr. *philos* loving + *ateleia* exemption from tax (*telos*).] The collection and study of postage stamps, stamped envelopes, etc., of various issues; stamp collecting. — **phil′a·tel′ic** (fĭl′àtĕl′ĭk), **-tel′i·cal**, *adj.* — **-tel′i·cal·ly**, *adv.* — **phi·lat′e·list** (fĭ·lăt′ĕ·lĭst), *n.*

quay (kē), *n.* [OF. *kai, cay* (F. *quai*).] A stretch of paved bank or a solid artificial landing place made beside navigable water, for convenience in loading and unloading vessels.

From *Webster's Collegiate Dictionary*, Fifth Edition,
G. & C. Merriam Company

The Standard dictionary shows the same pronunciation of the word in two different sets of symbols:

cer″ti-o-ra′ri, 1 sūr′shi-o-rē′rai; 2 çĕr′shi-o-rä′rĭ, *n. Law.* A
phi-lat′e-ly, 1 fĭ-lat′ĭ-lĭ; 2 fĭ-lät′e-ly, *n.* The study and collection
quay, 1 kĭ; 2 kē, *n.* A wharf or artificial landing-place where

From the *College Standard Dictionary*,
Funk & Wagnalls Company

Dictionaries are somewhat imperfect guides to pronunciation because their prime source of material is published books and articles, and actual speech is harder to record, especially in a large country. Usually full or "platform" pronunciation is given, which if followed completely would give a person's speech a slow and somewhat stilted sound. Often rapid speech results in shorter vowels than the dictionaries indicate, and stress varies with the position of a word in a phrase. Furthermore our dictionaries do not recognize sufficiently the variations in American pronunciation, usually giving New England or eastern pronunciations most weight.[1] But people learn the common words from hearing them and can rely on dictionaries for pronunciation of the unusual ones.

*Exercise 9, p. 210

Dictionaries show divided usage in the pronunciation of many words, as in the Webster examples of *acclimate* shown above. As a rule a person should use the pronunciation most common among the educated people of his community, for example *ant* or *änt* as the pronunciation of *aunt*.

*Pronunciation, §2

3) DEFINITION. The definitions of words of course take up the bulk of the space in a dictionary. The definitions of unusual words help the reader get the full and actual sense of a passage that treats material new to him. Dictionaries

[1] See George P. Wilson, "American Dictionaries and Pronunciation," *American Speech*, 1938, xiii, 243-54.

carry many dialect, obsolete, and archaic words to help in reading English writers such as Burns and Shakespeare. Scientific, technical, slang, and provincial words are generously included, although by no means all words of these classes are given.

For a writer the dictionary definitions are most useful in checking the meaning of words he is almost sure of, but not quite. When he is revising a paper, he needs to make sure that some words mean what he thought they meant when he put them in the first draft, and he wants to make sure that they stand a good chance of meaning to his reader what he intends them to. Very often he will need more information for this purpose than a dictionary can give because of its limited space and must go to an encyclopedia or other work.

It is not so much the meanings of uncommon words, like *hackbut, pyrognostics,* or *zymurgy,* that a writer needs as the meanings of those near but not quite at the center of his vocabulary. Almost any series of dictionary entries will illustrate these words and the scope and method of dictionary definition:

check'row' (-rō'), *n.* One of a series of rows, as of corn, dividing land into squares between which a cultivator may be operated. — *v. t.* To plant in checkrows.	Word from particular occupation.
Ched'dar cheese, *or* **Ched'dar** (chĕd'ẽr), *n.* A smooth-textured pressed cheese, orig. made at Cheddar, England.	
chedd'ite (chĕd'ĭt; shĕd'ĭt), *n.* [From *Chedde*, town in Haute-Savoie, France.] A blasting explosive consisting essentially of a mixture of a chlorate or perchlorate with an unctuous substance, as castor oil.	Full understanding here may mean looking up *chlorate* and *perchlorate*.
cheek (chēk), *n.* [AS. *cēace, cēoce.*] **1.** The fleshy wall or side of the face below the eye and above, and to the side of, the mouth. **2.** Usually *pl.* Something suggestive of the human cheek in position or form; as: **a** A side, or upright, as of a door or gate. **b** One of the projections on each side of a mast, supporting trestletrees. **c** One of two corresponding sides, as in a tool; as, the *cheeks* of a vise. **3.** In general, side. **4.** *Colloq.* **a** Impudent or saucy talk or behavior. **b** Cool confidence; audacity. — *v. t. Colloq.* To address or face with cheek.	Sense 1, original, literal meaning. 2, extended meanings, applied to things having something in common with the human cheek. Used in occupations. 3, generalized meaning. 4, figurative meaning.
cheek by jowl. With heads together; in close intimacy.	Phrase with special meaning.
cheek'y (chēk'ĭ), *adj.; CHEEK'I·ER* (-ĭ-ẽr); -I·EST. **1.** *Colloq.* Brazenfaced; impudent. **2.** Having well-developed cheeks, as a bulldog. — **cheek'i·ly,** *adv.* — **·i·ness,** *n.*	Other parts of speech from *cheek,* some with special meanings.

From *Webster's Collegiate Dictionary*, Fifth Edition, G. & C. Merriam Company

Definition is a difficult problem for the editors of dictionaries, and perhaps at present is the least satisfactory part of their work. Their great need for saving space makes many definitions cryptic, meaningless to anyone but a specialist. The newer dictionaries have made some progress in simplifying definitions, making their meaning clearer to the average person. Compare these definitions of *housemaid's knee* taken from three different sources:

WEBSTER: A swelling due to an enlargement of the bursa in the front of the patella.

COLLEGE STANDARD: An enlarged bursa in front of the knee that afflicts housemaids or others who kneel in working.

WINSTON: a swollen condition of the knee joint, caused by continued kneeling.

Recently, too, dictionary makers have tended to clarify the meaning of words by showing their use in illustrative phrases or sentences. In particular such phrases and sentences have been added after abstract words, or to show the use of a word with different prepositions and in certain verbal patterns.

There are three points to remember in using dictionary definitions. (*a*) A dictionary does not *require* or *forbid* a particular meaning of a word but *records* the uses that have been found for it. Now and then a word is in the process of acquiring a new meaning or somewhat altering its usual sense. (*b*) The dictionary definition is for the most part a record of the denotation of a word and often cannot give its connotation. For this reason it is safest not to use a word unless you have heard or read it and so know it in part from experience, at least what suggestion it carries if it is not a simple factual word. (*c*) Finally and most important, the words of the definition are not the meaning of the word, but they, and perhaps an illustration, are to let you see what in the world of objects or ideas the word refers to.

4) LEVELS OF USAGE. Words that are unlabeled in a dictionary are supposed to belong to the general vocabulary; other words are labeled *dialectical, obsolete, archaic, foreign, colloquial, slang, English, United States,* or are referred to some field of activity—*medicine, law, astronomy, baseball, manufacturing, electricity, philosophy.* *Levels of usage, p. 11

These labels are rough guides to levels of usage, but a writer should bring his own observation and judgment to bear on individual words. Many that carry no label are rarely used (*curtilage, moot* . . .) and would mar informal writing. In general the editors' point of view is rather conservative, and many words marked *Dial.* or *Colloq.* would fit perfectly well into most writing. It must be clearly understood that these labels are intended to be descriptive terms and are not intended to prohibit or even to discourage the use of the words so labeled. *Colloq.* means that the word is characteristic of cultivated conversation rather than of formal writing; *U.S.,* that the word is in good use in the United States but not in England or other parts of the English-speaking world. *Colloquial and written English

5) SYNONYMS. Most dictionaries gather words of similar meanings into a group and show in what ways they are alike and in what ways different:

> **dis-pute′,** 1 dis-piūt′; 2 dĭs-pūt′, *v.* [DIS-PUT′ED[d]; DIS-PUT′-ING.] **I.** *t.* **1.** To question; challenge; controvert. **2.** To argue about; discuss. **3.** To strive or contend for; contest. **II.** *i.* **1.** To debate; wrangle; quarrel. **2.** To compete, as for a prize. [< F. *disputer*, < L. *disputo*, < *dis-*, apart, + *puto*, reckon.]
>
> Syn.: antagonize, argue, battle, combat, contend, contest, controvert, debate, discuss, oppose, quarrel, question, reason, wrangle. Persons may *contend* either from mere ill will or self-interest, or from the highest motives: "that ye should earnestly *contend* for the faith which was once delivered to the saints," *Jude* 3. To *controvert* is to *argue* wholly on the negative side, urging considerations against an opinion, proposition, or the like. One may *argue* and *discuss* without an opponent. We may *question* or *discuss* a proposition without reference to any one's advocacy of it, but to *contend, debate,* or *dispute* implies an opponent. A dispute may be personal, fractious, and petty; a debate is formal and orderly; if otherwise, it becomes a mere "wrangle." Compare ARGUE; CONTEND; QUESTION; REASON. —**dis′pu-ta-bl(e**[r], *a.* That may be disputed; controvertible; doubtful.—**dis″pu-** or **dis-pu″ta-bil′l-ty,** *n.*—**dis′pu-tant.** **I.** *a.* Engaged in controversy; disputing. **II.** *n.* One who disputes.—**dis″pu-ta′tion,** *n.* **1.** The act of disputing; controversy; discussion; argumentation. **2.** A rhetorical or logical exercise; a scholastic debate. Syn.: see ALTERCATION.—**dis″pu-ta′-tious,** *a.* Characterized by or pertaining to dispute.—**dis″pu-ta′tious-ness,** *n.* **dis-pu′ta-tiv(e**[s]‡. **-ly,** *adv.*—**dis-put′er,** *n.* **dis-pute′,** *n.* **1.** A controversial discussion; a verbal contest. **2.** An altercation; wrangle; quarrel.
> Syn.: see ALTERCATION; FEUD; QUARREL.

From the *College Standard Dictionary*,
Funk & Wagnalls Company

*Chapter 8, p. 213

The discrimination of synonyms is often more helpful in selecting the right word to use than the definition.

6) LINGUISTIC INFORMATION. The part of speech in which a word is generally used, whether a verb is used transitively or intransitively is indicated, as well as the principal parts of verbs, plurals of nouns, and any other distinctive form a word may as- *Exercise 2, p. 209 sume. The origin of the word, how it got into English, is usually given. Sometimes this is merely a statement of the language from which the word came into English (Italian, Latin, Japanese . . .), and sometimes it is a more complicated chain of origin and change of form, as in the Webster Collegiate statement on *Origin of words *course,* tracing it from Latin, through Italian and French, to English:

> **course** (kōrs; 70), *n.* [From F. *cours* (OF. *cors, curs*), fr. L. *cursus,* and fr. F. *course,* fr. It. *corsa,* fr. *correre* to run; both fr. L. *currere, cursum,* to run.]

From *Webster's Collegiate Dictionary,* Fifth Edition,
G. & C. Merriam Company

The *Oxford English Dictionary* and the *Dictionary of American English* are historical works, tracing through dated quotations the changes in form and meaning of a word. The introductions to many dictionaries contain histories of our language and valuable information on spelling, pronunciation, and other traits of language.

7) MISCELLANEOUS INFORMATION. Most dictionaries contain some reference material not strictly needed in a book of definitions, such as lists of places and prominent historical figures, abbreviations, foreign words and phrases. Formerly these items were run in lists in the back of the volume, but the tendency in recent dictionaries has been to put them in the main alphabet.

6. Increasing your vocabulary

"But my vocabulary is so small" is one of the commonest excuses of students in composition courses and of older people who have some intention of speaking or writing. They seem to think that if they had more words they could write, and they often sound as though having a small vocabulary was a bodily affliction, like near-sightedness or hay fever, and to be got over by wearing glasses or by some miracle of medicine.

If their vocabularies really are small, that is only the symptom and not the real disease, for words cannot be considered apart from their meaning and usefulness. A small vocabulary means either that they do not have the information they think they have or, if they do, that they do not talk about it and perhaps even do not think about it. People may have moods and feelings (or "affective states" as psychologists say) without the words to tell of them, but they do not have facts or ideas without the words to tell of them because these do not exist in their minds apart from the words. The only exception would perhaps be sense impressions, a particular shade or tint, an odor, something seen or heard or sensed, for which they lack an accurate name; though if the image is clear enough in their memories, they can usually find some way of describing it at least roughly.

Not everyone needs the same words. The ones it is necessary to be concerned about are those that you need for a more complete understanding of subjects that you are actually dealing with or thinking about or that you might reasonably expect to use in talking or writing.[1] One trouble with learning "a word a day" is that very often the additions are not particularly useful. A published word-a-day scheme suggested learning these words:

obdurate   contiguous esoteric   implacable turgid   lucent
amenable   corporeal   sedulous   lassitude   tortuous   exemplary

---

[1] The correlation between size of vocabulary and practical success is discussed in Johnson O'Connor, "Vocabulary and Success," *The Atlantic Monthly*, Feb. 1934 (reprinted as the Introduction to his *English Vocabulary Builder* and elsewhere).

These are all good English words that will occasionally crop up in the more highbrow books and magazines. But they are hard to work into ordinary conversation because they belong to the formal level of the language, and they really are not needed anyway, even in writing, because everyone already has perfectly good words for the same ideas: *obdurate* is *hard, harsh, hard-hearted, stiff-necked, stubborn* . . . and *amenable* may mean either *liable* or *yielding, submissive* . . . and so on.

There are more natural and more effective ways of adding to your stock of words.

6a. Transferring words from recognition to active vocabulary. Your recognition vocabulary grows chiefly through reading, to a much less extent through listening and observation. Some of these words that you recognize but do not use would be convenient in your active vocabulary. Little is gained by adding words that exactly translate what you can already say. It is more important to practice using words that let you say something you couldn't say without them or that let you say something more exactly than you now can. The way to get words you recognize in reading into your active vocabulary is to use them, perhaps by taking some special pains, by talking and writing more, and especially by talking or writing more exactly.

Occasionally in your reading, especially in college, pay particular attention to these words, especially when the reading is about a subject that you might well write or talk about. Underline or make a list of words you find in reading that you feel a need of and look up the less familiar ones in a good dictionary. And then before very long make it a point to use some of them in speaking or writing. After you have used a word two or three times, it will be yours always.

A book of synonyms or the synonym entries in a dictionary may help carry a word from your recognition to your active vocabulary. It is not always safe, from such a list, to use a word that you have never seen before, because you will probably not know its exact connotation. But very often a synonym list will remind you of a word you have seen or heard and in this way help bridge the gap between your two vocabularies.

6b. Learning new subjects. The most natural way to learn new words is by learning something new, whether it is from observation or conversation or from a magazine article or a college textbook. You can't take facts or ideas away with you unless they are in verbal form. The easiest way to increase your vocabulary is by acquiring groups of words from new experience. You will learn several in visiting a printing plant for the first time; a person who learns to drive a car will pick up a number of new words. There are words from every experience, from every job, every sport, every art, every book (most authors have vocabularies of their own), from every field of thought and study. Consider the words that would be added to a person's vocabulary from a newly acquired interest in radio, in printing, in sailing, in music, in the poems of Archibald MacLeish, in astronomy, in biology.

*Exercises 3 and 4, p. 209

To make these new words your own, tell someone about what you have just learned, talk the subject over with someone who is also interested in it, or try to teach it to someone who knows nothing of it, or write about it. Some of you may come from families where father is in the habit of telling the family at dinner whatever he has just heard or read. Sometimes it isn't too interesting for the family, but it's very good for father, for he is impressing the facts on his mind, and very often he is using new words that will become a permanent part of his vocabulary.

In college a student's vocabulary increases enormously and at all levels. He comes to use the words of the college organization (*registrar, curriculum, honors courses, schedule, conflict* . . .); he picks up the colloquial and slang vocabulary of the campus (*dorm, poly sci, home ec, pan hell,* and perhaps some not so widely used, like *prelim* or *tunk*); he may take up a new sport or some other activity and so acquire more words; and the courses he takes will add several times as many words as the other pursuits of college life, some of them technical and of restricted use, many of them of more general application. Acquiring the vocabularies of biology or sociology or history is a very important part of the respective courses; certainly you can't go far without the names of the facts and ideas taken up. The words should be accurately learned *the first time they are met:* scrutinized for their spelling, pronounced as they are in class or as a dictionary specifies, and studied for their exact meaning. Probably a good deal of trouble in courses comes from imperfectly acquiring, only partly understanding, the specialized words when they are first met. Once they are understood, they should be used. Many of them will be called out in recitation or examination or term papers, but using them casually in conversation, even humorously if they can be made to carry a joke, or using them in talking over the course work with another will help impress them on your mind and make them come forth more easily. In this way you will acquire those thousands of words which the statistics on vocabulary credit a college graduate with.

6c. Adding individual words. Besides these two most common processes for adding words to your vocabulary, it is possible to acquire individual words that appeal to you. The typical process is seen in picking up slang: you hear the word, and it appeals to you, and you use it, perhaps for its own sake. The same holds for more serious words. Playing with them is a good way to make them your own, unless your attempt at humor is going to seem strained.

Conversation and casual reading will give a good many useful words, perhaps most of them fitting in general situations rather than in special fields of study. They may be words a little off the beaten track but accurate and expressive—*livid, echelon, prink, eupeptic*—the language is full of such words that can make your writing more exact or more vivid. They are the ones to salvage from the vast number that pass through or near your consciousness in the course of a day. An objective test, like the Inglis Vocabulary Test or the Michigan Vocabulary Profile, may suggest some particular regions where you could profitably extend your stock of words.

The essential point is that you are not merely "increasing your vocabulary." You are acquiring more meaningful and useful words, increasing your powers of understanding, extending your range of interests, as well as adding to your command of the enormous supply of English words in order to think, speak, and write in the manner of educated people.

Exercises

*Pages 184-85

1. Check the following list of words to see how many you now use in speaking and writing and how many you would recognize in reading but would not use. Look up the others in a good recent dictionary. How many of these might prove useful to you?

baroque	derisive	histrionic
bathos	doghouse	ineffable
bicameral	entrepreneur	ineluctable
beige	eclectic	innuendo
cacophony	euthanasia	jardiniere
camouflage	fink	labiodental
claustrophobia	flexor	lutecium
cliché	fugue	miasma
chatoyant	gambrel	morphology
catholic	ganglion	madder (noun)
corvette	hedonist	myopia
decalcomania	hegemony	noggin

208

nutria	peroration	snide
ocarina	riparian	sonde
peplum	riprap	swatch
odium	scherzo	totalizator
poliomyelitis	semantics	tourmaline

2. In a large dictionary look up the origins of a group of words, making note of how they are formed, from what languages they came into modern English, or any change of meaning that may have taken place or of any interesting facts in their history. The following is a sample list: *Pages 204-205

agoraphobia	gypsy	silhouette
bergschrund	hydrophobia	sincere
camera	influenza	sinus
canard	inoculate	starboard
chauvinism	lieutenant	surrealism
checkmate	lunacy	taboo
cicerone	monkey wrench	torpedo
cinema	nostril	tycoon
davenport	parachute	ukulele
echelon	peninsula	verdigris
fascism	piano	vermicelli
filet mignon	radio	vitamin
galvanize	schizophrenia	whiskey

3. Reread § 6b, "Learning new subjects." Learn something that is new to you—by reading or by observing (as by visiting, say, a printing plant or a museum) or by talking with someone. Write a paper reporting what you have learned and at the end make a list of the new words you have used and a comment on whether or not they might be used in your future speaking or writing. *Pages 206-207

4. Prepare a list of words on a special subject with which you are familiar but which might be strange to your classmates, such as the "points" of a dog or horse, darkroom equipment, tools and process of etching, music or harmony, knitting, dress materials, chess, restaurant cooking, surveying, or aviation.

5. The following groups are synonyms, but none of the words have exactly the same connotations. Discuss the connotations of the words in each group. *Pages 190, 192-93

village, hamlet, tank town
arrangement, conspiracy, plot, deal
yclept, called, named, denominated
fixer, mediator, go-between, intermediary
slaughterhouse, abattoir, shambles
narcotics, drugs, dope

needy, indigent, poor, destitute, impoverished, broke, underprivileged
nag, horse, steed, jade, charger
reactionary, conservative, Tory, mossback
ersatz, imitation, substitute
tired, worn out, all in, exhausted, weary

6. Write out the following information about the dictionary
you own or usually use.

*Pages 197-98

Title
Publisher
Date on title page
Date of original copyright (on back of title page)
Number of words listed (approximate)
  Does it have a supplement of new words?
  Does it have a separate biographical or geographical section?
  Does it have a discussion of spelling and pronunciation?

7. Give an alternate spelling for each of the following words
and indicate by a check the spelling preferred in your dictionary.

*Page 200

mold	rhyme
analyze	thorough
archeology	instalment
sceptre	counsellor
skeptical	vitamine

8. Look up the following words and copy them with the symbols used by your dictionary to indicate their pronunciation. If
two pronunciations are listed, which is more familiar to you?

*Pages
200-201

hegemony	interest
chassis	Mojave
controvert	omega
inexpert	predilection
modulation	conflict

*Page 196

9. The following headline appeared in an American newspaper after Congress had passed the bill authorizing certain
reorganizations in the government:

CONGRESS PASSES DICTATOR BILL

Comment on this headline. Was there in fact a bill officially
given this title? What would be a newspaper's purpose in giving
it such a name if it was not its official title?

10. In a radio forum on free speech and censorship a speaker
said that free speech (not involving military information)
would be unmolested unless it was a disturbance of the peace,

in which case it would be prosecuted like any other disturbance of the peace. Comment on this statement's use of words and its meaning.

11. Study the following passage. Look up any unfamiliar words in the dictionary. The dictionary definitions will not help you to understand their use in any of the phrases in quotes. From a week's reading of the newspaper, make up a list of words of your own which the newspaper uses in special senses *for or against us,* or at least for or against something. Does this use of words make for accurate communication? For colorful reporting? For false emphasis or misconception of something? *Pages 194-96

War, always the schoolmaster, has recently been giving us a stiff little course in semantics, the lessons arriving each day, neatly printed in the newspapers. Take a word beginning with "a," for example. Take "annihilation." It doesn't mean, as it used to, that everybody got killed, unless, of course, you happen to be talking, as a journalist, about your enemy. If you're talking about your own side, it means that the organization of a combat unit is temporarily disrupted. "Retreat" is another one: a strategic shortening of the lines if your side is moving backwards; a probable debacle if it's the other side. For a time we thought we had "skirmish" securely in its place, a military expert having told us, with a light shrug, that anything inflicting less than a thousand casualties could be called only that. Then "smash" came along ("U.S. Smashes Jap Drive") and turned out to be a matter of only seven hundred casualties, although, rather modestly, the Chinese merely "repulsed" a Japanese drive on the same day to the tune of fifty thousand. We are comforted to know that, as the war goes on, we'll always be able to count on the newspaperman, jotting down history on the run, to tell us when a verb is for us or against us.—*New Yorker,* Jan. 24, 1942

12. Study and be ready to discuss the connotation of words in the paragraph by Otis Ferguson on page 228.

13. Study the following words, classify as abstract, relative, or concrete, and be ready to discuss the range of meaning of each of the following in their various meanings. *Pages 187-88

literature	outstanding
boring	sixth columnist
success	harmony
centimeter	value

14. Study an article of some length in the Oxford English Dictionary (full-sized edition) which runs to some length (Sug- *Page 199

gested words: *do, gentle, treasure, eye, gage, can*). Bring in a short history of the word, its origin, shifts in its spelling, meaning, and function, and any interesting developments which it has undergone.

*Origin of words

15. Using a full-sized dictionary, find the original meaning of each word, and for compounds the root meaning of each element in the compound. What is the current meaning of each word? Try to figure out and write down the evolution of the root meaning to the current meaning.

flag (verb)	bromide	shorthand
creeping bent	briefcase	monkey wrench
stop (noun)	type (verb)	cabinet (gov't)
copy (technical)	machine tool	phaeton
lantern-jawed	parterre	strike (labor)
stand-in	transmission	spare (bowling)
sub-marginal	(automotive)	bedlam
(econ.)	tandem	

16. The following list contains phrases common in the current language, used in books, songs, movies, or radio programs, but not covered by dictionaries. Explain the meaning of each and try to explain its origin, giving special attention to any word or words not used in their dictionary sense.

Newspaper headline—Small Business Gets Washington Runaround

Song title—You Can't Brush Me Off

Song title—I've Got You Under My Skin

Book title—Whistle Stop

Book title—Fashion Is Spinach

Radio program—The Dog House

Radio program—What's Cookin'

Movie title—Ball of Fire

Political note—Alphabet Soup

Headline—Gold Star Mothers Meet

Review—It Laid an Egg

*Pages 194-96

17. Find and bring in one or two passages illustrating too much meaning. Also one or two displaying a responsible use of words. Be prepared to discuss individual words in the passages.

Qualities of Words

BESIDES THEIR FUNDAMENTAL work in carrying our meaning, words also have qualities that add to or detract from the appeal a speech or article makes, that increase or diminish its readability or its listenability. From the point of view of meaning, these qualities are part of the words' connotation; from the point of view of impression (or artistry), they are a part of style. For this chapter at least Jonathan Swift's statement holds: "Proper Words in proper Places, makes the true Definition of a Style."

"Proper words in proper places" carries us back to the principles of appropriateness developed in our chapter on Good English, appropriateness to the subject, to the reader or listener, and to the writer or speaker. These principles apply to all phases of our use of language but are easiest to demonstrate in a discussion of words. Obviously the words spring primarily from the subject and must fit it. Discussing a machine we have to name its parts, describe its functions, and so on, either in technical or popular terms; discussing baseball we naturally have to talk about *bases* and *bats* and *pitchers* and *shortstops* . . . , probably in a rather racy manner; discussing the influence of newspapers there are *editorials* and *headlines* and *leads* and *propaganda* and

*Page 39

213

Associated Press and *paid advertising* . . . , and the tone would probably be serious. But there will be a number of words not specifically demanded by the subject, that one writer might use and another not. In these some balance is to be struck between the reader's expectation and the writer's usual habits of expression. This chapter is concerned with some of the problems of this balance, considering first some hindrances to a clear meeting between the two parties in their attempt at communication and then some of the traits of words that can add not only to a reader's understanding but to his pleasure.

1. Words that weaken

Most ideas are not particularly complicated or difficult; certainly most that college students treat of are not. Such ideas ought to be presented so that they make a direct appeal to the readers for whom they are intended. But the style in which they are expressed is often something of a handicap and especially in amateur writing is likely to make the reading more tiring than is necessary. In Chapter 6 we discussed *deadwood*, expressions that added nothing to the meaning of a statement. Here we look at three sorts of words that may convey meaning but that kill the interest of a reader, at least of one with wide enough experience to have any genuine taste or judgment. These are *Trite words*, *Euphemisms*, and *Big words*.

*Deadwood, p. 161

1a. Trite words. A *trite expression* (or a *cliché* or a *hackneyed word*) is a phrase that is overused. It is obvious that certain necessary functional words—*a, the*, the prepositions, the conjunctions—do not wear out. More important, the actual names of things and acts and qualities do not wear out; and formulas like *How do you do* and *Yours truly* may be used over and over without attracting any real attention at all. Expressions that deserve to be called trite are something more than the direct, natural expression. We can call for *bread* as often as we need to—but *staff of life* is quite a different matter, linguistically. It is a figure of speech, once bright and perhaps even startling, now actually threadbare and hardly serving a weak attempt at humor.

We should not be too severe about triteness in ordinary conversation. The common expression, even if it is figurative, has its place. (Havelock Ellis says "You cannot avoid using *clichés*, not even in the very act of condemning them.") But when they become a conspicuous trait of a person's writing, he had better watch out. Many trite expressions are a symptom that the writer is in a rut or that he lacks knowledge in this particular subject, or at any rate isn't taking care or showing interest in the actual writing. A reader will sense this—and a writer should sense it first and prevent it. "There is nothing improper in such phrases from the point of view of correctness," says Professor Krapp (*A Comprehensive Guide to Good English*, p. xvi), "but from the point of view of style they are worse than incorrect— they are evidence of an effort and a failure to attain animation and originality in expression . . . the wordy expression makes no special bid for attention, whereas the trite expression is sup- posedly ingenious and worthy of note."

*Exercise 1, p. 247

What sort of expression should a writer who wants to avoid the charge of *trite* look for? Most trite expressions will be found to be outworn figures of speech, frayed quotations, attempts at a gentility that the idea does not deserve, or phrases that some- how are found intact more often than is pleasing, especially journalistic combinations of adjectives and nouns.

1) WORN OUT FIGURES OF SPEECH:

Father Time	tide of battle	flowing with milk
history tells us	irony of fate	and honey
darkness overtook us	commune with nature	trees like sentinels
better half [wife]	crack of dawn	run like a flash
mother nature	bolt from the blue	

a watery grave (. . . from a watery grave—that is, from drowning) order of the day (Seasickness was the order of the day.)

Make your own list. A good deal of slang that is wearing out belongs also in this category.

Especially in expressions of sentiment and emotion we would do better to remain literal than fall back on these ancient figures: "An icy chill seized him at the pit of his stomach. What could he do? He was caught like a rat in a trap." How did he really *feel?*

2) FRAYED QUOTATIONS. Shakespeare has so many magnifi- cently quotable lines that a writer who confines himself to the most used (All the world's a stage—Uneasy lies the head— To be or not to be—Not wisely but too well) makes his readers guess he has never actually read Shakespeare or he could make fresher choices. The Bible is similarly sinned against, though so many of its phrases have passed into the common language that it is not always fair to label them trite.

*Echo phrases

If you want to illustrate a point by quotation, it is safest to take one from your own reading rather than to rely on these stock expressions.

3) EUPHEMISMS. Many readers now are particularly sensitive to verbal attempts to bring our rather stern and rowdy existence in line with "the finer things of life": *honest toil—marts of trade—keep body and soul together—gentle reader*. These and many others are not only euphemisms, as discussed on page 218, but trite as well.

4) ORTHODOX EPITHETS. Some adjectives are found too often before the same nouns; some adverbs become linked to particular verbs. This is particularly a trait of what we have called *journalese*, where phrases seem to become traditional and later to lose touch with actual observation.

*Newspaper
English, § 2

This sort of triteness (and other sorts as well) Frank Sullivan recorded in his "Cliché Expert" series in *The New Yorker*. In this extract the Cliché Expert, Magnus Arbuthnot, is discussing his calling:

Q—Mr. Arbuthnot, you are an expert in the use of the cliché, are you not?

A—Yes, sir, I am a certified public cliché expert.

Q—In that case would you be good enough to answer a few questions on the use and application of the cliché in ordinary speech and writing?

A—I should be only too glad to do so.

Q—Thank you. Now, just for the record—you live in New York?

A—I like to visit New York but I wouldn't live here if you gave me the place.

Q—Then where do you live?

A—Any old place I hang my hat is home sweet home to me.

Q—What is your age?

A—I am fat, fair, and forty.

Q—And your occupation?

A—Well, after burning the midnight oil at an institution of higher learning, I was for a time a tiller of the soil. Then I went down to the sea in ships for a while, and later, at various times, I have been a guardian of the law, a gentleman of the Fourth Estate, a poet at heart, a bon vivant and raconteur, a prominent clubman and man about town, an eminent—

Q—Just what is your occupation at the moment, Mr. Arbuthnot?

A—At the moment I am an unidentified man of about forty, shabbily clad.

Q—Now then, Mr. Arbuthnot, what kind of existence do you, as a cliché expert, lead?

A—A precarious existence.

Q—And what do you do to a precarious existence?

A—I eke it out.

Q—How do you cliché experts reveal yourselves, Mr. Arbuthnot?

A—In our true colors, of course.

Q—Now, Mr. Arbuthnot, when you are naked, you are . . .

A—Stark naked.

Q—In what kind of daylight?

A—Broad daylight.

Q—What kind of outsider are you?

A—I'm a rank outsider.

Q—You are as sober as . . .

A—A judge.

Q—And when you are drunk?

A—I have lots of leeway there. I can be as drunk as a coot, or a lord, or an owl, or a fool—

Q—Very good, Mr. Arbuthnot. Now, how brown are you?

A—As brown as a berry.

Q—Ever see a brown berry?

A—Oh, no. Were I to see a brown berry, I should be frightened.

Q—To what extent?

A—Out of my wits.

Q—How about the fate of Europe?

A—It is hanging in the balance, of course.

Q—What happens to landscapes?

A—Landscapes are dotted.

Q—How are you attired in the evening?

A—Faultlessly.

Q—What goes with "pure"?

A—Simple.

Q—The word "sundry"?

A—Divers.

Q—What are ranks?

A—Ranks are serried. Structures are imposing. Spectacles are colorful.

Q—Thank you, Mr. Arbuthnot. What kinds of beauties do you like?

A—Raving beauties.

Q—How generous are you?

A—I am generous to a fault.

Q—How is corruption these days?

A—Oh, rife, as usual.

Q—How do you point?

A—I point with pride, I view with alarm, and I yield to no man.

Q—What do you pursue?

A—The even tenor of my way.

Q—Ever pursue the odd tenor of your way?

A—Oh, no. I would lose my standing as a cliché expert if I did that.

Q—As for information, you . . .

A—A mine of information.

Q—What kind of mine?

A—A veritable mine.

Q—What kind of cunning do you affect, Mr. Arbuthnot?

A—Low, animal cunning.

Q—And when you are taken, you are taken . . .

A—Aback.

Q—I see. Well, Mr. Arbuthnot, I think that about covers the ground for the time being. I'm sure we're all very grateful to you for your coöperation and your splendid answers, and I think that everyone who has listened to you today will be a better cliché-user for having heard you. Thank you, very, very much.

A—Thank *you*, Mr. Steurer. It's been a pleasure, I assure you, and I was only too glad to oblige.

> FRANK SULLIVAN, "The Cliché Expert Takes the Stand,"
> abridged from *The New Yorker*, Aug. 31, 1935

We should not of course slow up our first writing by stopping to find original phrases, but we should be sensitive enough to triteness to remove it from our copy in revision. The remedy is nearly always the same: to look squarely at what we are talking about and present it simply and as exactly as possible.

1b. Euphemisms. A *euphemism* is a pale or comfortable word or phrase used instead of the more common or abrupt name for some discomfort or suffering, or for something presumed to be offensive to delicate ears. The substituted expression may be more vague, less harsh in sound or connotation, than the more exact and literal term it displaces; it is often abstract, semi-learned, or a Latin derivative instead of the native English word.[1]

The most excusable euphemisms are those intended to soften the misfortunes of life. Though they remind us of the taboos of primitive languages, at their best they are a sign of fundamental kindness: *pass on* or *pass away* for *die*, *laid to rest* for *buried*. In intimate human relationships, in letters and in conversation with bereaved people, these are a sign of human sympathy; but their use in impersonal relationships, in journalism or literature, will usually make for weakness. *The Style Book* of *The Detroit News* tells its writers (p. 75):

> Write simply, *he died*, and not *passed away, shuffled off this mortal coil, gave up the ghost*, or any similarly amateurish phrase.

[1] J. M. Steadman, Jr., "Affected and Effeminate Words," *American Speech*, 1938, xiii, 13-18, gives a number of such words from students' lists. See also Edwin R. Hunter and Bernice E. Gaines, "Verbal Taboo in a College Community," *American Speech*, 1938, xiii, 97-107.

There is no occasion for clothing the incident of death in a panoply of words, nor should birth be written of except simply. Do not say, *A little stranger was ushered into a cold world*, but *A child was born*. In writing of vital statistics—death, birth, marriage—be content to state the facts without unnecessary embellishment. Forget about the stork, the grim reaper, Hymen and Cupid.

The largest group of euphemisms has rather a moral than an emotional backing, for it consists of substitutes for many short abrupt words, the vigorous monosyllabic names of certain physical functions and social unpleasantness. One of the aspects of "Victorianism," as it is generally understood, was this rather remote vocabulary. For years *sweat* was taboo among "the upper classes" as both verb and noun, replaced by *perspire* and *perspiration*. *Spit* became *expectorate; drunk* was *intoxicated*, and even *drink* (the verb) tended to become *imbibe* in all uses. Teeth were *extracted* instead of *pulled*. *Story* took the place of *lie*, or in various dialects it was *whopper, fib, misrepresentation*. Both *stink* and *smell* gave way to *odor, belly* to *abdomen*, and so on. *Exercise 2, p. 247

One of the conspicuous traits of modern style has been to discard these euphemisms and return to the "short and ugly" (to some people) words of the common language. Some realistic novelists seemed motivated as much by naughtiness and a desire to shock as by artistic accuracy but they have now won almost complete freedom, for themselves and for others. A number of the less serious euphemisms survive only in a playful dialect—*avoirdupois* and *embonpoint* for *weight* or *stoutness, limbs* for *legs*, though the humor is usually more intended than successful.

Euphemisms show one side of the relation between language and social attitudes. They represent timidity sometimes but more often a conscious seeking for "respectability," the kind of respectability that brought down the satire of Bernard Shaw and many younger writers. People who would never say *damn* could say *P. D. Q.* without qualms. At a more serious level newspaper euphemisms like *companionate marriage, love child, social diseases*, allowed certain virtuous people to talk about matters they would never have mentioned by their more common names. The recent recognition of the seriousness of venereal diseases, for example, has led to consistent campaigning by doctors for more direct discussion, so that most papers have taken *syphilis* from their blacklists.

At present there is a conspicuous group of euphemisms found in the treatment of social situations, especially by conservative writers. *Workers* become *our industrial army*. What in 1893 was known as *hard times* is now called a *depression* and a slighter falling off of business a *recession*. Those *out of work* or *jobless* are the *unemployed*, perhaps the victims of *technological unemployment* (an accurate but distant noun); and the *poor* are the *underprivileged*. We cannot always avoid using these words, but it is necessary for a writer to keep clearly in mind the specific unhappiness and suffering they name.

A third group of euphemisms has developed in "the business world": *Funeral director* for *undertaker, tonsorial artist* (now humorous) for *barber, reconditioned* for *second-hand, public relations counsel* for *press agent, laundress* for *washerwoman, paying guest* for *lodger* or *boarder*—and we are even *guests* on the more luxurious trains. Specific industries have two dialects of their own, their necessary technical vocabulary and a euphemistic one for the customers (or "clients"). *The New Yorker* carried the story of a young man just taken on to receive complaints in a firm that dealt in oil burners. He noted down his first day a customer's complaint that his burner had exploded. " 'Young man,' said his superior, breathing fire, 'you won't get very far in this business until you learn that we do *not* have explosions. We have puffbacks.' "

Except for these journalistic and commercial terms, and some taboos of the radio networks, the movies, and newspapers, the temper of the times is now against euphemisms in writing; and unless circumstances actually demand a substitute for the ordinary names of things and situations, a writer should call a spade a spade—simply of course and without unnecessary emphasis. Fowler's advice is right: "Euphemism is more demoralizing than coarseness."

1c. Big words. We are using the term *Big words* to cover several common faults of writing that come from an unhappy use of words. The words may not all be long or uncommon (*deem, doff, dwell* are big words in the sense of this article), but they are big in that they are *too heavy for their place*.

There is little objection to long words when they are called for by the subject and are appropriate to the reader and come naturally to the writer, that is, are the words in which he thinks. They are the only and necessary names for many ideas and for many things, and they must be used in much technical, scientific, and professional writing—though they may be overused even in the writing of specialists. *Sphygmograph, schizophrenia, Pleistocene* all have their place, though it is a restricted place. (If one of these words becomes needed in ordinary speech, a shorter form or a substitute arises, as *TNT* did for *trinitrotoluene.*) Some longer words may be needed, especially in formal writing, for rhythm or for their connotation: *immemorial, multifarious, infinitesimal, anticipation.*

Here we are looking at big words which do not fit, that are too heavy or too pretentious for the subject or for the writer. They are often written thoughtlessly or to show off, but they are often written also in a serious attempt to "improve" one's expression. *Exercise 3, p. 247 The writer fails to realize that he will improve his writing by more exact and more suggestive words (which may or may not be longer than those he ordinarily uses) rather than by words that are merely more elaborate. Just translating one's thought from the ordinary words in which it occurs into longer or more pretentious ones does not improve writing. As Fowler puts it in his article on "Long variants": " 'The better the writer, the shorter his words' would be a statement needing many exceptions for individual persons & particular subjects; but for all that it would, & especially about English writers, be broadly true. Those who run to long words are mainly the unskilful & tasteless; they confuse pomposity with dignity, flaccidity with ease, & bulk with force."

Gelett Burgess has written an eight-page plea for the use of short words without using a single word of more than one syllable. He begins:

> This is a plea for the use of more short words in our talk and in what we write. Through the lack of them our speech is apt to grow stale and weak, and, it may be, hold more sham than true thought. For long words at times tend to hide or blur what one says.
>
> What I mean is this: If we use long words too much, we are apt to talk in ruts and use the same old, worn ways of speech. This tends to make what we say dull, with no force or sting. But if we use short words, we have to say real things, things we know; and say them in a fresh way. We find it hard to hint or dodge or hide or half say things.
>
> For short words are bold. They say just what they mean. They do not leave you in doubt. They are clear and sharp, like signs cut in a rock.—GELETT BURGESS, *Short Words Are Words of Might*, Chap Book No. 2 of the College English Association

It is natural for a person to feel that his own speech is not good enough to use in public appearances and in writing. It is true that our day-to-day language is not good enough—but the remedy lies in improving and extending the best features of our speech, not in assuming an unnatural language, as formal words and idioms are likely to be for most students and for many others. The goal of much English teaching has been development of a formal style, and conscientious students have dutifully translated their material into such passages as this, in which a girl introduces us to a fat man oiling a lawn mower at some historic shrine that she does not bother to name or place:

> As we approached one of the beautiful historic buildings of western New York as yet unscarred by time's relentless talons and having about it an intangible aura of antiquity, we observed a man of over ample proportions kneeling beside a lawn mower to lubricate its creaking wheels. The act lent a jarring and anachronistic note to the peaceful scene.

This sins against good English on all three counts: first, the material is a simple picture which is obscured by such phrases as *time's relentless talons, intangible aura of antiquity, a jarring and anachronistic note*—not to mention the man *of over ample proportions lubricating the lawn-mower*. Second, the writer did not visualize her readers. Ordinary people are bored by such formality and the intelligentsia is not fooled by the affectation. Third, and most important, it is not appropriate to the writer, an alert and intelligent girl—who shortly after began to write more naturally.

"Official English" of governments and institutions is often made ridiculous for its big words. As Prime Minister, Winston Churchill has tried to reduce the pompousness of official documents, and President Roosevelt poked fun at this OCD order:

> Such preparations shall be made as will completely obscure all Federal buildings and non-Federal buildings occupied by the Federal Government during an air-raid for any period of time from visibility by reason of internal or external illumination. Such obscuration may be obtained either by blackout construction or by termination of the illumination.

He suggested translating this to:

> Tell them that in buildings where they have to keep the work going, to put something across the window. In buildings where they can afford to let the work stop for a while, turn out the lights.

We may never write with charm, but at least we can have the decency to use simple, direct, meaningful, natural words.

Some of the commonest words that are usually out of place are:

advent	domicile	peruse
behold	dwell	reside
congregate	metropolis	stated (for said)
deem	nuptials	termed
doff, don	participate	transpire

You can easily add other words to this list—perhaps from your own writing.

*Long variants

The remedy for this type of big words is simple: Read aloud to yourself what you have written and if you find it conspicuously different from the way you would *tell* the same thing to a friend, consider the words carefully and see if you can't use the simpler, informal words that are natural to you—and let no others stand in your copy except for very good reason.

2. Abstract and concrete words

The names of persons, animals, objects, materials, places—in general "things" that can be seen and touched—are concrete: *banker, payee, oak, delphinium, police dog, chromium, water, island.* The names of qualities, conditions, actions, summaries of particular facts, and so on are abstract: *goodness, honesty, pep, oomph, fear, height, culture, beauty, infancy, sophistication, system, singing.*

*Denotation. p. 186

It is easy to identify such clear-cut examples, but there are many words which are abstract or concrete according to their use: *youth—a youth; force—forces* (soldiers); *painting—a painting; sprinkling—a sprinkling* (as of pepper). For a number of words the classification as abstract or concrete cannot be made outside of their context and indeed is not really significant: *music, war, word.* The names of actions—*racing, stalking, striding*—are grammatically abstract but since they suggest a picture they may seem as vivid as concrete words; but in general, abstract words do not suggest a picture and are less colorful than concrete words. This is especially true of divided and borderline words: *youth* is not so clear cut as *boy, young man, student; forces* are not so easily visualized as *army, soldiers,* or *troops.*

2a. Abuses of abstract words. Abstract words are for *ideas,* for opinions, generalizations, summaries of experience. One of the less happy traits of much current writing is the use of abstract words where words that suggest a picture would fit better. A movie company, going about the very practical business of getting people to come to a movie, composes a paragraph without a single concrete word in it except, perhaps, *audiences*:

> We confess to a belief that this is a significant and inspiring event in the history of the American cinema—an extraordinary adventure in entertainment. And therefore we prefer that the first audiences be the dominant cultural group in the community.

We find these abstractions even in novels, which are supposedly *pictures* of people doing things:

> An American countess, once a Broadway star, sororized with an artist's model in citron and red, and fraternized with a group of men *whose sartorial and tonsorial eccentricities proclaimed their dedication to art.*

> The place was too crowded to permit of much *terpsichorean evolution.*

This use of abstract words is closely related to the use of scientific and pseudo-scientific words instead of more common ones. Students in the upper college classes, after courses in physics, biology, economics, sociology, education, and so on, sometimes have to struggle to write their native language. Customs have become *mores*, jails and prisons *penal institutions*, various twists of personality are *complexes*, opinions are often *reactions*. These are useful words and people with literary educations are likely to be unduly suspicious of them; but since they lack suggestion they are best left to their respective fields of study when in non-specialized writing there is a common word for the same idea.

Using such technical terms and imitations of technical terms is one of the principal temptations of thoughtful and well-educated writers, one for which Malcolm Cowley criticizes Lewis Mumford in a review of Mumford's *The Culture of Cities*:

> Mumford is entirely too fond of fancy words with Greek or Latin roots. Sordor, geotect, resorption, sessile, vermicular, encystment, plexus, nexus, locus, polynucleated, perduring, depauperated: the effect of words like these is to distract attention from the subject under discussion and to center it on the style. Mumford hates a heavily ornamented façade in architecture; why does he tolerate it in his own prose? But there is more involved than a mere question of ornament. Savages believe in the magical properties of words; they think that enemies can be slain and cattle and wives made fruitful by finding the proper incantations. There is a vestige of this belief in every writer, I suppose, but in Mumford there is more than a vestige. When he dislikes some feature of our civilization—for example, trailer

camps—he slays it with epithets hurled like thunderbolts. "Mechanical escapism, as embodied in the trailer and the trailer camp, is one of those ludicrous examples of ideological miscegenation of which the modern world is full: the neurotic offspring of romanticism and mechanics, . . ." But people will go on riding in trailers for all of Mumford. Ideological miscegenation is often good fun.—MALCOLM COWLEY, *The New Republic*, April 20, 1938

Aloof style among people with ideas is one reason why ideas do not spread more rapidly. Ideas exist only in words and if the words are foreign to large numbers of people, those people can't "think" and some of the blame lies with writers who make thinking unnecessarily hard. H. T. Webster, whose cartoons show that he knows the language people use, sums this fact up:

And I doubt if we'll ever get far with currency stabilization or other international economic adjustments until economists begin abandoning the argot of celestial mechanics.

The trouble with the Better Minds is that They Don't Speak Our Language.—*The Forum*, Dec. 1933

2b. Appropriate uses of abstract and concrete words. The point for writing is that *specific facts, narratives of experience, and application of ideas to particular situations should be written in concrete terms; general ideas, summaries of experience, and opinions of all sorts need abstract words—but even they will reach a wider audience and be more emphatic if they can be thrown into concrete terms.* Often a writer makes his point in both abstract and concrete terms, gaining in emphasis from the repetition and appealing to different readers through the different qualities of the two sorts of words.

In the following abstract paragraph there are hardly half a dozen concrete words: *capitalist, coffee crops, cornerstone* (used figuratively), *consumers, Alice in Wonderland, doctors.* The abstractions here are good English, fitting to the author (a professor of philosophy), to the audience and readers (originally the selection was a lecture in a college series, and was later published as a book for people interested in general ideas), and to the subject (an opinion about a whole social system).

For quite apart from the questionable morality of the profit system or the moot question whether a society without some form of the profit motive could become a permanent development, there remains a less debatable consideration. The capitalistic economy has as the cornerstone of its logic not the profit motive but the profit system. If the capitalist economy does not work even in the way of steadily producing profits for capitalists, it would seem urgently to call for revision. Even the layman is by this time familiar, often through bitter personal experience, with the gruesome tale of economic collapse, collapse that recurs in cycles and seems fated at each cyclic recurrence to become more serious. Capitalism depends on expanding markets, which in the nineteenth century were findable, as were raw materials, in hitherto industrially unexploited regions of the world. A more efficient technology demands more buyers for its products. The pyramided concentration of wealth, the saturation of markets, the inability of consumers to buy, the surpluses which must be sold at panic prices or destroyed—one recalls the destruction of bumper coffee crops in Brazil—the consequent unemployment, the increase in technological unemployment with the development of new machinery; these are all symptoms of a permanent disease of our present economy, a disease which 1929 simply made painfully dramatic, as the World War had made clear the consequence of rivalry for markets and raw materials. A system that repeatedly fails to provide profits for the entrepreneurs, and with its cycles of unemployment and its increasing burden of apparently permanently unemployed fails to insure minimum decency of life or security for the employed—only Alice in Wonderland could quite approve the logic of such an arrangement; only a loose user of words could call it a system or a success. No wonder that doctors and witch-doctors have been called in to cure it! No wonder that the uneasy rich and the impatient poor look hungrily for a Messiah!—IRWIN EDMAN, *Four Ways of Philosophy*, pp. 135-36

*Imagery

The nouns in the following paragraph are almost all concrete. They show a more popular—and here a more intense—criticism of one phase of the same industrial system.

Indeed there is much to be said on both sides. Watching a tractor save the labor of fifty men; a steam shovel dispensing with picks and shovels and aching backs; a pulmotor bringing a dead man back to life; a silver airplane against a blue sky—one can only rejoice in the utility and the beauty which the machine has brought. But when one realizes that a fleet of not over five hundred of those silvery beauties, each with a bomb suspended beneath it, is readily capable of utterly destroying a civilization, such as that of England, in something like two hours' time; when one views the dour and besotted ugliness of the Pittsburgh industrial district; when one reads of little girls scalped by machinery while working on the night shift in Chinese cotton mills—the hymn of thanksgiving somehow sticks in one's throat.—STUART CHASE, "The Good and Evil of the New Industrialism," *Current History*, July 1929

2c. Their place in current style. Nineteenth-century English style made wide use of abstract and general words, even when the subject was simple; modern style is in part a reaction against this and, except in academic and formal English, is notably concrete. Gilbert Murray described the old-fashioned way of introducing students to Latin and Greek this way:

> Nearly all of us approach the classics through an atmosphere of education, with its concomitants of dictionary and grammar, its unnatural calm, its extreme emphasis upon dutifulness and industry, and the subtle degradation of spirit produced by its system of examinations.—*The Rise of the Greek Epic*, p. 6

A writer today with Gilbert Murray's vigor of mind would omit *concomitants*, say *school* instead of *education*, and translate *its unnatural calm, its extreme emphasis upon dutifulness and industry* into two or three specific details that would make us feel the boredom of a routine classroom. He would use a few more words but they would be shorter, more concrete, and would make us feel the situation more acutely.

The unnecessary use of abstract and big words in an article definitely limits its currency, makes it unduly formal for situations in which informal English would be expected and more effective.

Recent writers on semantics are vigorously calling attention to the loose use of abstract words, especially those charged with feeling. *Capital* instead of *businessmen*, *labor* instead of *workingmen*, *depression* for *hard times*, *faculty* for *teachers* all tend to substitute a vague, distant idea for a vivid realization of particular people. The following paragraph represents only a shadowy notion of the writer's idea (What is *beauty*, an *inalienable heritage*, a *natural right, cosmic necessity?*):

*Page 188

*Exercise 4,
pp. 247-48

> Beauty is man's inalienable heritage; it is one of his natural rights, on a par with his right to life, liberty, and the pursuit of happiness. Modern civilization has denied him this right, giving him instead much ugliness of thought and act and environment. I do not think that this birthright can be restored to him except by concrete and operative religion. Religion, by cosmic necessity, brought art, which is the precipitation of beauty, into being. After four thousand years it became negligent of its trust; now if it will it can open the road, not as the only path, but as one of many, an alienated world may come back to old loyalty and to a better way of life.

The writers today who appeal most immediately to us write concretely. This selection, the beginning of an article on music

227

and musicians, minces no words, brings us close to the writer, to his motive for writing, and to his subject:

> They buried Bessie Smith just the other day. She was a great handsome chunk of a woman and still so much in her prime you'd never dream her fifty years; but they picked her out of an automobile smash-up in Memphis and put her in the ground, and now there is nothing left of Bessie, who was the great girl they called the Empress of the blues. And so I think it is a good idea to speak about the good musicians who are left, as quickly as we can, while they are still among us.—OTIS FERGUSON, "Piano in the Band," *The New Republic*, Nov. 24, 1937

And this concrete comment is more illuminating than many more sweeping, more general comments on our "civilization":

> There is a detailed account of the softening of society in the current *Harpers*, by Roy Helton. Mr. Helton propounds the theory that the sex of civilization has changed, from male to female. Our world, he says, is entirely female dream—shelter, comfort, advantages for the young. Here again is a contradictory situation. A female society, although decadent, nevertheless offers the only hope of a warless world. War in a woman's world is unthinkable, simply because women are bored stiff by the destructive machinery which men find exciting and amusing. Last week we happened to be in the country and our host was blowing up some rocks on his place. The presence on the premises of dynamite was highly stimulating to every male. The workmen themselves were keyed up and would gladly have worked all day without pay for the privilege of taking part in an explosive program. The foreman was as eager as a boy; he loved everything about dynamite—the caps, the long coil of wire, the battery with the throw switch, the red flags to stop traffic, the brush dunnage, and the long, important warning cry of "Fi-i-ire!" Small boys showed up from nowhere and took an active part, inspecting the charge, racing about, and jumping up and down wildly. There wasn't a female in the bunch. The reaction to dynamite of the female members of the household was that dynamite was something to be got over as soon as possible. Not one of them had ever seen a dynamite cap, or wanted to. They lacked that curious inquiring and alert spirit which makes men the great destroyers and the great builders they have turned out to be.—*The New Yorker*, Sept. 7, 1940

*Analysis, p. 98

Abstract words are necessary for discussing general ideas, summarizing facts, and giving opinions, though even in such subjects concrete words can help. Concrete words seem to be closer to the writer's thoughts and feelings, they are easier for a reader to grasp, and they control the reader's thoughts more exactly than general terms can. College students must read a good deal of abstract writing in their courses but they should remember that their own writing is often of specific, intimate matters and should be as concrete in style as their subjects allow.

3. Figurative use of words

3a. Use of figures. Words have their original, fairly exact, literal meanings; they can also be borrowed to apply to other matters that have something in common with this original meaning—they can be used figuratively.[1] A *table* may be not only a piece of furniture, but food served. A fraternity is a *house*. *Head* has its original, literal meaning as a part of the body but is applied to the highest or foremost or principal part of a wide variety of things—of a screw, nail, pin, army, the force of a stream of water, bay, news story, stalk of grain, hammer, bed, golf club, beer, boil, barrel—not to mention parts of a number of machines and the leaders of all sorts of institutions and governments and movements. Ordinary speech is full of these figures: we *play ball* even when we work with others; we may *chime in* by adding our voice to others'; we may see a tree as a *tent* in summer or as a *skeleton* in winter. Figures are the basis of much slang—a person may be (like) a *peach*, a *prune*, a *wet blanket*, a *good egg*, a *five minute egg*, a *flat tire*. In this way words may extend their meanings by being used figuratively; the figurative sense may become in time a new, regular meaning.

We all use words figuratively, use "figures of speech." We can hardly speak a minute without using some figures. And practically all writing, except perhaps works of reference and purely scientific or scholarly papers, makes some use of figurative language. It is one way to make meaning more interesting, more exact, more complete, or more intense. In the plain style dominant now in factual writing, figures of speech are used only occasionally, but they still play a part. Here we have a paragraph of direct, literal words until the last sentence is intensified by a rather conventional but vigorous figure—"take it out of their skins":

> The bandits in the mountains were all men like Meng's uncle —poor peasants, or disbanded or deserted soldiers who had once been peasants. They had chosen between the army with its prof-

---

[1] References: Rickert, Chapter 3; McKnight, Chapters 14-17; Fowler has articles on the individual figures of speech, as do other reference works on writing and on literature.

fered bowl of rice; the uncertain life of ricksha or wharf coolies in the Coastal towns; emigration to Nanyang where wealth came to one man in a million only and slavery to the rest; or banditry, which meant to them "robbing the rich to give to the poor." Such men took to the mountains in small or big bands. They would not rob their own villages, but it was easy to descend upon strange towns and villages where none of their kin lived, robbing and burning. Despite the armed gendarmes that guarded the two rich families in Meng's native village, these families were known to pay a regular secret tribute to bandits from distant districts; by such means only did they keep their homes over their heads. But this tribute they in turn took out of the skins of the village.—Agnes Smedley, *Chinese Destinies*, p. 47

This paragraph from *Time* shows that ordinary vigorous exposition may include a number of figures:

One day last week a black cloud *rolled in* [metaphor] from Lake Erie toward Conneaut, Ohio, dropped from its *belly* [metaphor] a thin, whirling column which touched the dark water, *churned up* [metaphor] a *fountain* [metaphor] of spray. This towering waterspout, more than 3,000 ft. high, moved in over the *fringe* [metaphor] of the town, where it began to behave *like a tornado* [simile]. It smashed windows in a score of houses, ripped off a porch, reduced a chicken coop to *matchwood* [exaggeration], hurled a bevy of screeching fowl high into the air. *Prancing* [metaphor] into the Nickel Plate Road yards, the funnel sucked up some heavy cans of calcium carbide, flung one 300 yd. against the side of a coal tower. After 20 min. the twister was lifted back into its *mother* [metaphor] cloud, drenching the ground with water as it rose.—*Time*, Aug. 10, 1936

In imaginative writing figures play an even larger part. They are more used in realistic writing than might be expected:

He dozed. The train *clicked on* [imitative word], stopped, jolted. He waked and dozed again. Someone *shook him out of sleep* [metaphor] into a primrose dawn. Among unshaven puffy faces *washed lightly over* [metaphor] as though with the paling ultimate stain of a holocaust, blinking at one another with *dead* [metaphor] eyes into which personality returned in secret opaque *waves* [metaphor]. He got off, had breakfast, and took another accommodation, entering a car where a child waited hopelessly, crunching peanut-shells under his feet as he moved up the car in a stale ammoniac odor until he found a seat beside a man. A moment later the man leaned forward and spat tobacco juice between his knees. Horace rose quickly and went forward into the smoking car. It was full too, the door between it and the jim crow car swinging open. Standing in the aisle he could look forward into a diminishing corridor of green plush seat-backs topped by hatted *cannonballs* [metaphor] swaying in unison, while *gusts* [metaphor] of talk and laughter *blew back* [metaphor] and kept in steady motion the blue acrid air in which white men sat, spitting into the aisle.

He changed again. The waiting crowd was composed half of young men in collegiate clothes with small cryptic badges on their shirts and vests, and two girls with painted small faces and scant bright dresses *like identical artificial flowers surrounded each by bright and restless bees* [simile]. When the train came they pushed gaily forward, talking and laughing, *shouldering* [metonymy] aside older people with gay rudeness, clashing and slamming seats back and settling themselves, turning their faces *up out of laughter* [metaphor], their cold faces still *toothed with it* [metonymy], as three middle-aged women moved down the car, looking tentatively left and right at the filled seats.—WILLIAM FAULKNER, *Sanctuary*, pp. 201-202

3b. Qualities of figures of speech. Since figures of speech are likely to be a little conspicuous, they need to be used with care, so that they make a genuine contribution to understanding or to the appeal of the passage. It is better to do the best possible with literal words unless a happy and accurate figure comes to mind. These qualities need to be considered:

1) APPROPRIATENESS. Since figures are used to make the passage in some way more effective, they should be appropriate. They should be accurate enough to contribute to the meaning in some way and they should be in tone with the subject and style. This is out of key:

> In learning more about him I found that he was just about the kindest man I have ever met. He had the heart of an elephant and the mind of a genius.

And these seem too tremendous to suggest even voracious reading:

> He sank his teeth into the throat of the book, shook it fiercely until it was subdued, then lapped up its blood, devoured its flesh and crunched its bones. . . .

But the metaphors in this add interest and color to Mrs. Lindbergh's picture:

> But the next morning we were *giants again in seven-league boots*. The engine, roaring anew after a few hours' work in calm water, lifted us easily into the air. Once more the harbor *dwarfed to Japanese-garden proportions*. The trees became *moss*;

the thatch-roofed house, *a child's toy*. And these tiny *doll-like figures* in a miniature boat, waving *match-stick arms*—who were they? Of course, the singing sailors.—ANNE MORROW LINDBERGH, *North to the Orient*, p. 173

2) NATURALNESS. Each of the figures should seem to come naturally from the way the writer sees his subject—to be the sort that he might use in his conversation. They should not be tacked on or used just to be different or "to make an impression,"—they should bring the reader closer to the writer's actual sense of his subject. There are many figures, especially colloquial comparisons (*tired as a dog, lap of luxury* . . .), which are pretty threadbare, but which still work when we're not too fussy about the effect we are making on our listener. But in writing we should be more careful. "Trees that stand like sentinels" is an example of the lazy, trite, and really useless figure. Trees of course do stand like sentinels sometimes—but it would not occur to most of us to say so if we hadn't heard the phrase before, and our repetition of it doesn't help our subject or do credit to our style. More conspicuous still are tags of literary figures (like *the arms of Morpheus* and *Mother Nature*) which wore themselves out long ago—so long ago that they can hardly be used any more even in fun. Either stock or forced figures keep us from seeing the picture clearly and tend to make a reader doubt a writer's sincerity. Some of the more pretentious and less scrupulous advertising loses its effect because of use of extreme figures: "A joy package of surprise ribboned with rainbow laughter."

Struggling for freshness usually brings on either these trite figures or strained ones. The figures to use are the ones that come naturally to your mind when you are trying to give an exact account of the subject. They do not need to be unusual, but should fit in their context and sound as though you were actually thinking them.

The figures in this paragraph not only help illuminate Mr. Ferguson's point but sound as though they came naturally from his way of seeing things. Each of the italicized phrases could either be omitted or translated into literal words; but if you try it you will see the loss.

Before the newspapers got hold of it, the term "swing" in its best sense was a musician's *shortcut way* of saying that the music *had come alive*, that its phrases ran beautifully together *like foothills* and *filled the world*. There is no word for this transformation *from the passive to the active voice*—or little conscious appreciation of it either, for the more complex music becomes and the farther we get from its sources, the more dependent we are on "interpreters." Music has two lives: first the concept in somebody's head and heart, second the expression. In between it is *a mummy*, because for all its intricacies, notation can't do more than tell you *where to dig for the body*. It has a great passive beauty even on the flat page of the score, it is true, and any *ham* [borrowed here from its application to actors] symphony orchestra could hit a couple of clean chords from the "Egmont" overture and *bring your heart up to your shoulders*. But virtuosity becomes too greatly prized (the highest soprano, the fastest cadenza) and *pedestrianism* too easily tolerated in *a field where few can walk at all*. And so we have these versions that make you suspect Bach *shot thirty-second notes into the score with a machine gun*, and that music in general could be added up *like a column of figures*. One thing does not run into another; each note being written down and so fixed, *like a fly on a pin*, they play it that way with triumphant tenacity. Whereas music should always flow *as beautifully as words in the speaking voice*.—OTIS FERGUSON, "Benny and the Budapests," *The New Republic*, Oct. 5, 1938

3) CONSISTENCY. If a figure is continued through more than one phrase, sometimes it becomes "mixed"—becomes inconsistent in some way:

As he passed to greater wealth and newer offices he closed the door forever upon the stepping stones by which he had risen.

The sophomore who wrote "My father is a limb in a chain of the business cycle" couldn't have been thinking about his father—or about his writing.

Mixed figures are often used intentionally as a sort of easy but sometimes effective humor—like those attributed to Samuel Goldwyn ("They're always biting the hand that lays the golden egg") or this from *Jurgen:*

"Indeed, it is a sad thing, Sylvia, to be murdered by the hand which, so to speak, is sworn to keep an eye on your welfare, and which rightfully should serve you on its knees."—JAMES BRANCH CABELL, *Jurgen*, p. 124

As a rule a figure should not be carried very far, but occasionally, especially in interpretations, one may dominate several sentences or a paragraph, as the "breaking up of the Victorian ice" in this:

To be young is always a difficult, dangerous, and confusing business—but it can seldom have been so difficult, so dangerous, and above all so confusing, as in England during the first ten

233

years of the twentieth century. Those years were witnessing the
earlier stages of a change-over from one social order to another, a
change which was completed by the War. The Victorian ice
was beginning to break up, but a great deal of it was still fairly
solid, especially away from the centre of the stream, along the
banks and in the backwaters. Even there, however, the movements of the central currents were disturbingly felt. Cracks began to shoot through family life, and the firm Victorian faith in
the inevitability of family affection; large chunks of the cruder
forms of religious belief broke off and were carried away; ominous shivers ran through the sanctity of marriage, filial obedience,
the complacent acceptance of social inequality, and other solid-
seeming structures. Above all the moral conventions, those delicate tacit assumptions of what constitutes desirable behavior, on
which each generation stands, were in motion—they shifted
under your feet; pushed by some unseen force, they tilted sideways, and threatened to plunge you into unknown waters.—ANN
BRIDGE, *Enchanter's Nightshade*, pp. 38-39

3c. The most common figures. Some beginning writers are
cautious and avoid everything but literal statements, though
their conversation is probably full of metaphors and similes and
other figures. There is no satisfactory writing without some
adventuring in ways of expression. If a figure really adds something to the subject, either in meaning or in tone, and if it is
appropriate, natural, and consistent, your reader will welcome it.
A good many different figures of speech can be identified—over
two hundred have names, most of them given by the ancient
Greek rhetoricians and far from easy for us to handle. It is not
so important to be able to identify or call them by name as it
is to realize that there are these various ways of giving color
to writing.

Anyone who is writing or who is discussing writing needs to
know a few of the particular figures.

The following figures of speech and related traits of style are
treated in this book, those marked * in alphabetical articles,
and those with pages in the chapters:

In this chapter are discussions of the four most common types of figures:

Metaphors, similes, analogies
Metonymy
Irony
Exaggeration and understatement

1) METAPHORS, SIMILES, ANALOGIES. The most common figures of speech are the various types of comparisons, and very common they are, in both speaking and writing. Conversation uses many metaphors and similes, old standbys such as *red as a rose, go like a shot, a cold shoulder, tower of strength*; the somewhat newer expressions from slang—*a wet blanket*, people *an inch deep*, get a *load* of this, *pulled his punches*; and fresher, special inventions that are more appropriate in writing. It is easy to borrow words from one field of thought or work and make them fit in another—like *fadeout, close-up*, from the movies, *asset, liability* from business, and so on. *Exercise 7, p. 248*

Metaphors and similes are characteristic of all writing except routine exposition. They serve the purpose of all proper figures of speech, making the writing more exact, more concrete, more alive and interesting.

Metaphors and similes and analogies all make comparisons, but the three figures differ in form and in fullness. An analogy is usually a rather full comparison, showing or implying several points of similarity. A simile makes a comparison exact, labels it by an introductory word, *like* or *as*. A metaphor is the shortest, most compact of these comparisons; in it the likeness is implied rather than stated explicitly. Typically the writer asserts that one thing *is* another (in some respect), or suggests that it acts like or has some of the qualities of something else, as in the examples below:

But meaning is an arrow that reaches its mark when least encumbered with feathers.—HERBERT READ, *English Prose Style*, p. 16

And up we had climbed until we were face to face with those giants, snow-streaked, and the bright fog sitting on their shoulders.—ANNE MORROW LINDBERGH, *North to the Orient*, p. 154

[A simile would be . . . those mountain peaks, *like giants* . . .]

. . . the tracks of field mice were *stitched* across its [the snow's] surface in the morning.—JOSEPHINE JOHNSON, *Winter Orchard*, p. 307

. . . for the waves cast by a *pebble of thought* spread until they reach even the nitwits on the shores of action.—IRWIN EDMAN, *Four Ways of Philosophy*, p. 100

Two *well-upholstered* ladies leaving the Broadhurst Theatre . . . —*The New Yorker*, April 9, 1938

The difference between a metaphor and simile is merely one of phrasing: where the metaphor implies the likeness a simile says specifically that one is like the other, using the words *like* or *as*. A literal statement of similarity is not a simile—"the Congress is like a state legislature" is plain statement of fact. A comparison in which two objects differ in most respects but still may be strikingly alike in some one respect that is important to the writer's immediate purpose is a simile:

. . . . woods *like Persian rugs* where Autumn was commencing. —WILBUR DANIEL STEELE, "Bubbles"

Elaborate similes descended from those of Homer and Vergil are now out of fashion and confined to formal writing:

And Rustum to the Persian front advanced,
And Sohrab arm'd in Haman's tent, and came.
And as afield the reapers cut a swath
Down through the middle of a rich man's corn,
And on each side are squares of standing corn,
And in the midst a stubble, short and bare—
So on each side were squares of men, with spears
Bristling, and in the midst, the open sand.
MATTHEW ARNOLD, *Sohrab and Rustum*

Current similes are more direct, less drawn out than those descended from classical literature:

He knows the unfortunate penchant of black bass of the same size for trying to swallow each other, *like competing labor unions*. A. J. LIEBLING, *The New Yorker*, Feb. 5, 1938

What seems to be lacking in the older prose is the sense of the uninterrupted flow of the mind: Bagehot, for example, appears to cut off this continuum, shall we call it, into arbitrary lengths, *as we slice chunks off a cucumber*.—BONAMY DOBRÉE, *Modern Prose Style*, p. 225

And yet if the new generation were fed exclusively upon the best of scientific writing it is doubtful whether they would be conditioned against war. For such great impulses as the dangerous, competitive life are, of course, emotional and spring from ancestral regions into which the logic of facts penetrates *like a bullet which shoots through the trunk of a tree leaving only a hole which the living tissues quickly close.*—H. S. CANBY, "War or Peace in Literature," *Designed for Reading*, p. 89

Similes should not attract too much attention to themselves and should be appropriate to the subject and really add something to the reader's sense of it.

An analogy compares one idea or situation with another. Inappropriate and inexact analogies are distressing:

If it is generally agreed that the abolition of all navies would greatly benefit the world, why cannot we also say with an equal amount of justification that common abolition of the most expensive forms of advertising would greatly benefit business?

But swiftly sketched analogies often bring home or emphasize an idea:

By what process of reasoning can a man who is quite conversant with the separate meanings of *put*, of *up*, and of *with* ever infer that *to put up with* means *to endure*? We might as reasonably expect the person who has discovered the several properties of carbon, hydrogen, and oxygen to infer from them the amazing properties of alcohol. In neither case do the elements afford a clue to the nature of the compound.—P. B. BALLARD, *Thought and Language*, p. 168

Most firearms carry a little higher than they are aimed. But not the pen. With that, aim just above the target; and a little to the left.—CHRISTOPHER MORLEY, *The Saturday Review of Literature*, Sept. 24, 1938

Sometimes when a writer is not watching his work he will run together two figures that are inconsistent. These are commonly referred to as *mixed metaphors* and are responsible for many boners. *Boners

The new measure took a firm foothold in the eye of the public.

The mixing may not be so contradictory as this, but it may bring close together figures that are incongruous:

We opened our hearts to the proposal, but we were slapped in the face for our trouble.

Obviously, to be effective, comparisons should be accurate and fresh—or at least individual. The ones quoted in this discussion are not startling, but neither do they instantly remind the reader of the times he has found them before. *Mother Nature, a sea of clouds, snow like a blanket, trees like sentinels, eyes like*

237

limpid pools are trite and show that the writer is echoing his reading and not drawing upon his own observation.

2) METONYMY AND SYNECDOCHE (me ton′i mi, si nek′dō kē). These two figures of speech substitute for the exact name of something the name of something closely associated with it. Strictly, synecdoche gives the name of a part when the whole is meant (so many *mouths* to feed, a *sail* in the offing, plant employing sixty *hands*), or of a whole for a part (*Minnesota* won [the team won], the *army* adopts a policy). But synecdoche is now generally regarded as a type of metonymy, the use of one word for another that it suggests:

> THE MATERIAL FOR THE OBJECT MADE OF IT: *rubber* for footgear made of rubber, or for automobile tires; *glass* for tableware or a window

> THE MAKER OR SOURCE FOR THE THING MADE: *Shakespeare* for Shakespeare's plays; *England* meets *America* in the Davis Cup matches

> ANY NAME CLOSELY ASSOCIATED WITH THE OBJECT: *in the red*; *capital* and *labor* for employers and workmen; men *in the upper brackets*, for wealthy men; a *dish* for something to eat; "*3 Miles* of Boys March on Fifth Av."; play to the *grandstand*

Metonymy is not only a common figure of speech (common in both formal literary and in colloquial usage) but it is one way in which the meanings of words change. Long use of *the crown* for *the king*, *the heart* for *courage* or for *sympathy* and hundreds of other similar words has given them definite secondary meanings, separate senses in dictionary definitions.

*Humor
*Sarcasm

3) IRONY. Irony is implying something markedly different, sometimes even the opposite, from what is actually said. Light irony is a form of humor, severe irony is usually a form of sarcasm or satire—though exact definition in such matters is impossible and unfruitful.[1]

Irony may be in a passing phrase or developed in a longer passage. *The New Yorker* ends a comment on a patented paper napkin that cannot slip away:

> Life, you see, gradually approaches a sort of homely perfection, all the little inconveniences ironed out, only the large grotesqueries remaining unchanged from year to year—war, poverty, melancholia, and the lethal fumes from internal combustion.— *The New Yorker*, Aug. 14, 1937

[1] See Fowler, "Humour, wit, satire, sarcasm, invective, irony, cynicism, the sardonic."

"We made two dollars," Merle told her, "off nineteen steers. The cattle business is very good. Next year we might try twenty and buy a big dish-mop in the fall."—Josephine Johnson, *Now in November*, p. 222

When one thinks of Mr. Morgan selling his paintings and his yacht and even his home, one understands the pulsing heart which beats even in the breasts of the mighty. If Mr. Morgan is content to surrender his estates, it is more than a little trying to hear the complaints of an Arkansas share-cropper who has deliberately failed to meet his payments on his cabin and is asked to give it up.—Robert Forsythe, *Redder Than the Rose*, p. 112

William Saroyan means exactly the reverse of the advice he seems on the surface to be giving about the use of unessential adjectives:

But rules without a system are, as every good writer will tell you, utterly inadequate. You can leave out "utterly" and the sentence will mean the same thing, but it is always nicer to throw in an "utterly" whenever possible. All successful writers believe that one word by itself hasn't enough meaning and that it is best to emphasize the meaning of one word with the help of another. Some writers will go so far as to help an innocent word with as many as four and five other words, and at times they will kill an innocent word by charity and it will take years and years for some ignorant writer who doesn't know adjectives at all to resurrect the word that was killed by kindness.— William Saroyan, Preface to *The Daring Young Man on the Flying Trapeze*

A common form of irony consists in pointing out a contrast in events in which someone has unwittingly done or said something that conflicts with his proper character:

"You must come," Mrs. Merrill said. "It's going to be very gay. And that's what most of us need nowadays—gaiety." An almost fanatic look came into her eyes, and it seemed to Miss Miriam Folsom that if Bertha Merrill ever got her hands on a little gaiety, she would shake it until its teeth rattled.—Sally Benson, *People Are Fascinating*, p. 189

4) Exaggeration and understatement. Exaggeration is a figure of speech (also called *hyperbole*) when it is not intended to deceive but to emphasize a statement or situation, to intensify its impression. Exaggeration may mean choosing a word of broader or more intense meaning than literal accuracy would call for (like *perfect* for *excellent*, or *mob* for *people*, or

starved for *hungry*), or it may be a more complex exaggeration of statement:

> But the feelings that Beethoven put into his music were the feelings of a god. There was something olympian in his snarls and rages, and there was a touch of hell-fire in his mirth.—H. L. MENCKEN, "Beethoven," *Prejudices: Fifth Series*, p. 89

> These little self-contained flats were convenient; to be sure, she had no light and no air, but she could shut it up whenever she liked and go away.—JOHN GALSWORTHY, *The Man of Property*, p. 224

Exaggeration is one of the most common colloquial figures, crystallized in many phrases: "dead tired," "thrilled to pieces," "I'm all ears," "a thousand thanks." Such standard phrases pass off well enough in ordinary conversation but often seem trite on paper.

A too free use of superlatives or of intense adjectives is weakening and should be avoided:

> Within the limits of Colorado, New Mexico, Arizona, and Southern California there are four centers of sublime and unparalleled scenic sublimity which stand alone and unrivalled in the world.

Exaggeration is a frequent source of humor, both literary and popular. A mass of American anecdotes and tall tales hinge on the figure—as in the yarn told of Kit Carson (and probably of others) that in the Valley of Echoes in Jackson County, Wyoming, it took eight hours for an echo to return, so that he would shout "It's time to get up" as he went to bed and the echo would wake him up in the morning. The Paul Bunyan stories make a cycle of popular exaggeration.

The figure is as much a part of more sophisticated humor and satire:

> Englishwomen's shoes look as if they had been made by someone who had often heard shoes described, but had never seen any, and the problem of buying shoes in London is almost insoluble—unless you pay a staggering tariff on American ones. What provokes this outburst is that I have just bought a pair of English bedroom slippers and I not only cannot tell the left foot from the right, but it is only after profound deliberation that I am able to distinguish between the front and the back.
> —MARGARET HALSEY, *With Malice Toward Some*, pp. 99-100

*Negatives

Understatement is the opposite of exaggeration and often a form of irony. It may mean stating an idea in negative terms

240

(litotes) or a statement in less strong words than would be expected: "Dempsey was not a bad fighter."

> And as he still came toward her, she darted at his legs and threw him. It had been years, thirty or more anyway, since Dr. Hopkins had been thrown off a raft and he had lost the knack. Being thrown off a raft is not an organized sport.—SALLY BENSON, *People Are Fascinating*, p. 71

> The submarine's communications may be feeble, as Mr. Howard says, but a U-boat commander certainly knows whether his torpedoes missed or hit. He is one guy who isn't in doubt as to immediate results, and, ordinarily, he doesn't get around to regular reading of American newspapers.—ARTHUR ROBB, *Editor and Publisher*, March 7, 1942, p. 36

4. Allusion

Besides treating his main subject a writer usually has space for some incidental matter—to add interest, to explain more clearly, to emphasize what he is saying. Some of this incidental matter will be *allusions*, brief references to literature, to history, to things, to people and what they do. In part these allusions are added content, contributing to the development of the subject. But since they are voluntary additions of the writer, to a considerable extent their purpose is stylistic—a way of saying something that could have been put differently—and may properly be included as a phase of the choice of words. Certainly their effect is very largely one of style.

*Exercise 9, p. 249

4a. To literature, written and oral. Many people who write are rather bookish, deeply and widely read, and so interested in what they have read that allusion to it naturally appears in explanation of other matters. (They may use quotations, too, but we are talking of a less formal use of reading.) Speeches from two Shakespearean plays are referred to here:

> *There is nothing new in heaven or earth not dreamt of* [Hamlet] in our laboratories; and we should be amazed indeed if *tomorrow and tomorrow and tomorrow* [Macbeth] failed to offer us something new to challenge our capacity for readjustment.— CARL L. BECKER, *The Heavenly City of the Eighteenth Century Philosophers*, p. 23

William Beebe refers to a Poe story in describing the life-cycle of a tiny animal:

> Poe wrote a memorable tale of a prison cell which day by day grew smaller, and Opalina goes through much the same adventure.—*Jungle Days*, p. 22

It is easy to overdo literary allusion, either by using too trite and commonplace references or by using so many that the writer seems to give up his proper work to other writers. The following paragraph will strike some people as uncomfortably bookish. Mr. Newton has chosen for his immediate purpose to allude freely and obviously to things which others have written:

> I have recently been reading old Montaigne. The French essayist died in 1592. Shakespeare had not then written his greatest plays, yet Montaigne was complaining that the world had seen its best days, that things were not as they used to be; and he believed it, too, for an honester man than Montaigne never lived. The English have a comic weekly, *Punch*—it has been functioning now for almost a hundred years; someone said, long ago, that it is not as good as it used to be—to be met by the rejoinder that it never was. There will be cakes and ale again—and ginger hot in the mouth, too. I have had mine and you will get yours and enjoy them, but you must be patient, diligent, and not too easily discouraged. A famous philosopher once said that most apprehension is needless pain, that the things we fear most never happen. There was a song sung by some of us during the war, the refrain of which was, 'It's a terrible, terrible, terrible war, still it's better than no war at all.' And so I say of the world. But, in the words of Walt Whitman, 'I sing myself.'—A. EDWARD NEWTON, "Newton on Blackstone," *Atlantic Monthly*, Jan. 1937

But familiarity with books can be used quite nonchalantly. How many titles of recent books can you recognize in this sentence?

> In "We Saw It Happen" they write personal history as they please along the transgressors' way inside Europe and along the headlines and deadlines beat that stretches from West Forty-third Street to Tokyo.—CHARLES POORE, *The New York Times*, Nov. 25, 1938

Allusion to written literature is more characteristic of formal English than of informal, which is apt to borrow from proverbs, current phrases, advertising ("that good Gulf weather"), and the great stock of colloquial phrases ("more possibilities than a pig bank has pennies").

Homely, everyday phrases can be used to advantage in any informal discussion:

> The thing for the faculty of the University to do is to *take it easy*. Don't get excited. *Walk, don't run to the nearest exit* and *enjoy life in the open*. In a few months the sun will shine,

water will run down hill, and *smoke will go up the chimneys* just the same.—WILLIAM ALLEN WHITE, *The Emporia Gazette*

And allusions to familiar formulas can be turned to fresh account:

All of Stratford, in fact, suggests powdered history—add hot water and stir and you have a delicious, nourishing Shakespeare. —MARGARET HALSEY, *With Malice Toward Some,* p. 65

4b. To history. We often allude to outstanding events in the past: to Waterloo, Elba, the Rubicon, and to the lives and characters of important persons:

The voice of duty speaks differently to Savonarola, to Cromwell, to Calvin, to Kant and to the contemporary communist or fascist.—IRWIN EDMAN, *Four Ways of Philosophy,* p. 292

Detailed historical reference is rather characteristic of formal writing; brief reference to better known events characterizes informal writing.

More characteristic of current writing is allusion to current events, persons in the public eye, immediate affairs:

Neither King George nor Queen Elizabeth has lived a life in which any event could be called of public interest in the United Kingdom press and this last week was exactly as most of their subjects wished. In effect a *Calvin Coolidge* entered Buckingham Palace with *Shirley Temple* for his daughter.—*Time,* Dec. 21, 1936

One difficulty with such casual allusions is that time makes them hard to identify—a reason why Shakespeare's plays and other older literature need explanatory notes. This was written in 1921:

Suppose a young man, just out of college and returned to his moderate-sized home town in Ohio (*why not Marion?*), honestly tries to make those contacts with the national culture which Mr. Sherman so vigorously urges him to make.—HAROLD STEARNS, *The Bookman,* March 1921

"Why not Marion?" is meaningless to young people today, and many of their elders will have forgotten that it was President Harding's home town, often referred to in 1921. But missing the allusion does not interfere with the appeal of the passage. As with other such references if a reader does recognize the allusion, he has an added pleasure.

It is possible to give a tactful explanation of an allusion, as the opening of the second sentence interprets the allusion of the first sentence in this:

> Right under my eye is *the mellow muddy river that Theodore Dreiser's brother sang,* long ago. *On the banks of the Wabash* I see a huge pile of discarded cars, rust-rotted fragments of machines, shanties paintless and broken-roofed, the homes of human discards among the industrial refuse.—WALDO FRANK, *The New Republic,* Nov. 4, 1936

Such topical allusions are best for immediate consumption, and since most of us are not writing for the ages, they are quite fit. They help make a piece sound as though it was written in the present and as though its writer was awake to what was going on.

4c. To life. One of the most fertile kinds of allusion, and one that is open to everybody, is to the things that people do, the things around us, bits from our work, our sports, our hobbies. It was natural for Simeon Strunsky, a newspaperman, to write, "On Broadway nature uses her fattest type-forms." The directness of modern style encourages such direct allusions to the life around us, as in this bit from a discussion of teachers' oaths:

> But, it is said, teachers have great influence on the young; and we must be sure that the young are under proper care. Very well. If we are to insure the patriotism of those who have influence over the young, let us do so. Let us begin with parents and have them take an oath to support the Constitution. Let us include newspaper men, and especially the designers of comic supplements. Let us line up all the movie stars. Let us insist on an oath of allegiance from radio performers. If the teachers are to be required to take an oath, Amos and Andy should be required to salute the flag and sing the "Star Spangled Banner" twice a day.—ROBERT MAYNARD HUTCHINS, *No Friendly Voice,* pp. 122-23

Besides their real function of adding something to the meaning, allusions also suggest the personality of the writer, if he is not posing, because the allusions that naturally occur to him come from his past experience and are brought to mind because they are interesting to *him.* One reason that many themes seem so depersonalized is that students often leave out these allusions —even take them out after they have naturally strayed into the first draft. We should expect that a student who likes to read Ernest Hemingway or *Time* would occasionally refer to something he had read; or that one interested in dogs or sailing or jazz or classical music or the life of Napoleon would occasionally bring in a bit from one of these interests to point up another subject. If an allusion doesn't fit, it is easily taken out in revision; if it does fit, the paper will have just so much more meaning and life, and the words will have not only meaning but a greater depth of connotation.

5. Colorless vs. lively words

The qualities of words that we have been discussing contribute chiefly to the life and force of writing, in a word to its readability. Completely colorless and impersonal writing is often desirable and even necessary, as in scholarly papers, but it makes a less deep impression and must limit the readers to those already having a concern for the subject.

*Academic writing

*Scientific and technical writing

The following paragraph is quite accurate but quite colorless—and very few people could read through the fifteen page pamphlet from which it comes.

> Our way of life is menaced today and we are concerned about its defense. The first step in the defense of democracy (as we realize more readily in times of crisis, though it was just as true in easier days of security) is to ensure an understanding and appreciation of its essential values and of the obligations it entails. So many young people have grown up thinking of the advantages of democracy in terms of their personal liberty to do what they like, and so devoid of any sense of the claims of democracy upon their service, that we are now able to see clearly how seriously our educational institutions have been failing to transmit our ideals and to play their part in developing the attitudes and loyalties on which our free society depends for its very survival.

One of the outstanding traits of modern writing is the range and vigor and suggestiveness of the words used. We do not need to go to works that make primarily a literary appeal to find this. Here are paragraphs from two rather journeyman factual books, one an account of an expedition collecting marine specimens (and ideas), the other a survey of recent American painting. The writer's attention in each is firmly centered on his immediate subject, but he has not switched off the rest of his mind. He takes words and instances as he finds them, puts them to work, and conveys not only his ideas but a sense of life. An outstanding trait of each is the *range* of the vocabulary, from casual colloquial words to rather technical.

There is one great difficulty with a good hypothesis. When it is completed and rounded, the corners smooth and the content cohesive and coherent, it is likely to become a thing in itself, a work of art. It is then like a finished sonnet or a painting completed. One hates to disturb it. Even if subsequent information should shoot a hole in it, one hates to tear it down because it once was beautiful and whole. One of our leading scientists, having reasoned a reef in the Pacific, was unable for a long time to reconcile the lack of a reef, indicated by soundings, with the reef his mind told him was there. A parallel occurred some years ago. A learned institution sent an expedition southward, one of whose many projects was to establish whether or not the sea-otter was extinct. In due time it returned with the information that the sea-otter was indeed extinct. One of us, some time later, talking with a woman on the coast below Monterey, was astonished to hear her describe animals living in the surf which could only be sea-otters, since she described accurately animals she couldn't have known about except by observation. A report of this to the institution in question elicited no response. It had extincted sea-otters and that was that. It was only when a reporter on one of our more disreputable newspapers photographed the animals that the public was informed. It is not yet known whether the institution of learning has been won over.—JOHN STEINBECK and EDWARD F. RICKETTS, *Sea of Cortez*, p. 180

Another irritant contributing to the drift of the American artist into his present state of forthright nationalism was his old grievance against the European portraitist, usually a third-rate member of the pretty-pretty school of eyelash affixers, who crosses the Atlantic to batten on portrait commissions from the culturally illiterate. These "artists" are merely commercial limners, skillful in surface flashiness and clever masters of the technique of publicity and social flattery. Americans who try to click heels with them usually end up on an elbow. The news and society reporters (not the art critics) give them yards of publicity with photographs dramatizing their records among European royalty. A visit to Washington would produce sittings from Congressmen, a member of the Cabinet or even the President—every American ruler since 1912, except F. D. R., patiently sat to some foreign painter, for "reasons of state." After a year among our dollar aristocrats, the "artist" would carry back across the Atlantic with him as much as $50,000—his departure attended by the futile curses of better but less suave American portraitists. It is a condition that obtains even today. American taste in the upper brackets being what it is, our lords and ladies of breeding and position like to feel that the same brush that painted Duchess Thisque or Countess Thatque can be hired by Mrs. Smith to outshine Mrs. Jones.—PEYTON BOSWELL, JR., *Modern American Painting*, p. 73

Certainly a college student, alive and thinking, can aim to express his ideas with similar life.

Exercises

1. Turn back to the "Cliché Expert" (page 216) and study Mr. Arbuthnot's answers. Think not of the words but of the actual object, condition, or action to which the words refer. Then consider the cliché in relation to it. Does it express what you really think? E.g. *daylight*, not the word but the condition. Do you think of it as *broad*? *Farmer*, not the word, the man. Does *tiller of the soil* suggest him vividly? Be prepared to discuss ten or fifteen of the clichés in the passage and to suggest words or phrases which express with some accuracy what you actually think.

2. Collect a list of euphemisms from your reading. Ads and business pages in your newspaper make good sources. Carefully vague statements by leaders of business, labor, government and so on are also good. Be prepared to translate the euphemisms you collect into "short and ugly" words. *Pages 218-20

3. Translate the following horrible example into language of ordinary size and weight. Try to explain why it is horrible. *Pages 220-23

The spirit of autumn lures all humanity into the great outdoors. Then peace reigns throughout the forest spaces. The stifling heat, the oppressive humidity, the clouds of insatiable insect life that beset the summer wayfarer in the woods and glades have vanished, banished by the cool breath of fall. Already the sly fingers of Jack Frost have touched the foliage, working their subtle alchemy to tint it with bright hues. Although here and there a stalwart of the forest, prematurely stripped of its leafy cloak, rears itself starkly ready to withstand the blast of winter, for the most part the trees still wear Joseph's coat of many colors. The few forest creatures to meet the observant eye of the autumn pedestrian are scurrying about gathering some last morsels to augment the hoard on which they will subsist after the woodlands fall into their long repose under a blanket of gleaming white. Such a landscape cannot but bring balm to heal nerves worn and frayed by the stresses and strains of urban existence.

4. Statements made in the same form may have very different force. (1) One may be literally true. "The motor delivers 1200 h.p." (2) Another may be literally inaccurate but express an idea which may be accepted as an ideal or a goal to be approximated. "Every American will give generously to this charity." (3) Another may be not literally true and express

*Pages 227-28

only the speaker's feeling, his approval or disapproval. "All capitalists, labor leaders . . . are crooks." (4) Or a statement may be between any two of these. Discuss and classify the following statements. In what sort of writing would each be appropriate?

1. An Aryan is a person supposed to be descended from the prehistoric group of people who spoke the Aryan language, from which the Indo-European languages have descended (adapted from *Thorndike-Century Dictionary*).
2. The Japanese are pure yellow Aryans.
3. Differences in IQ are generally believed to reflect differences in innate intelligence.
4. All men are created equal.
5. Conciliation prevented a strike.
6. Compromise would be rank appeasement.
7. A calory is a measure of heat.
8. The warmth of his personality attracted everyone.
9. Tragedy is a higher art than comedy.
10. Mt. Whitney is not quite a hundred feet higher than Mt. Rainier.

5. Rewrite the passage by Gilbert Murray on page 227 substituting concrete words for the abstracts wherever possible. You will have to think of specific objects to replace the abstracts, but not so narrowly specific as not to suggest the situation covered by the abstracts.

6. Although in most of your writing concrete words will be more appropriate than abstracts, you will occasionally want to use some abstracts. A little practice will not hurt you. Rewrite the passage by Stuart Chase on page 226 substituting abstracts for concretes where you can. Do not exaggerate.

7. Pick out the similes and metaphors in the passage by Virginia Woolf on page 546 and in the selection from *John Brown's Body*, page 563. Write out as well as you can the idea suggested by each comparison, using words literally. Be prepared to discuss whether the idea is expressed more accurately with or without the comparison, and whether an idea can take on apparent depth or significance by suggestive rather than literal expression.

*Pages 235-38

8. Develop the description suggested by one of the following opening sentences, or a similar one of your own composing, into a paragraph or two. Think of a real person, place, or situation. Make all your details as concrete and specific as you can. Especially choose nouns that name specific objects, verbs that show exact specific actions, and adjectives that make the picture more definite.

1. At half past three a peasoup fog closed in.
2. Quillan looked as if he would go down before the end of the round.
3. Rows and rows of barracks stretched the whole length of the camp street.
4. The moon was just swinging up over the trees.
5. That dress would give any girl confidence.

9. Identify and explain as many allusions as you can in one of the following: passage by H. F. Armstrong on page 181; passage by James Thurber on page 552; passage by Margaret Halsey on page 554. *Pages 241-45

10. Analyze and comment on the qualities of words in your latest paper.

11. Write a description of a person or a place you know well, making it as concrete as possible, and avoiding colorless adjectives such as *nice* or *good*.

CHAPTER 9

Grammar: "Minimum Essentials"

1. Sentence errors
2. Shifted constructions
3. Spelling
4. Punctuation
5. Questions of word forms
6. Agreement
7. Misrelated modifiers
8. Idiomatic constructions

"ENGLISH GRAMMAR," Professor Curme says, "is the English way of saying things." It includes the forms of words, their cases and tenses, their use in phrases and sentences. There are, as we saw in Chapter 1, several varieties of usage, different levels of grammar, some of which are appropriate to educated people and some that are not. A college student or a college graduate intends to speak and write Good English, that is, to use the language as others of his class do in carrying on public affairs. In most respects he does so. But there are some forms and some constructions that are especially likely to raise questions, and some that may raise questions even for professional writers. About the more elementary of these, college students cannot plead ignorance, for they have been harped on and drilled on in seven or eight years of earlier schooling. If a student leaves the apostrophe out of the genitive of a noun, or confuses *its* and *it's* or uses pronouns inaccurately, it is almost always from carelessness, or at best from lack of practice in speaking and writing as educated people do. Since these lapses from Good English are so conspicuous that no one with any pretense to education can afford to make them, learning to avoid them is often spoken of as mastering the "minimum essentials" of our language.

If you have reached college without forming the habit of using the language expected of you, your first responsibility in a composition course is to make up for lost time. You must take the responsibility, for no one can take it for you. A teacher can

*Page 11
*Funda-
mentals

250

only indicate what you should do—he cannot go beyond that. Only your desire to take your proper place in society, or pride in your own accomplishment, can lead you to do now what you should have done long ago.

The steps in becoming sure in these "minimum essentials" (and more complicated matters, too) are definite and simple:

1. *Be sure you know what is appropriate to Good English; know the form or phrase or construction that is most generally used by educated people.* You learn this by listening to conversations and to talks, by reading in books and magazines, by looking points up in a good dictionary or in a reference book such as this one. If you have some difficulty with fundamental matters, such as those enumerated below in this chapter, you certainly should not worry about matters in which practice differs, like the use of hyphens, or of the subjunctive. Moreover, do not worry about matters that are no longer considered so important as they once were, like the "split infinitive" or a "preposition at the end of a sentence." Keep your eye on the practices that are important and know what is expected of you in those.

*Split infinitive
*Prepositions, §3d

2. *Practice on the points that you have not mastered,* as you would practice a play in a sport or the use of a tool that you wanted to become adept in. Exercises in textbooks can give an opportunity for this practice. More important is revising your papers according to the corrections and criticisms made on them, and most important of all is revising your papers before they are handed in. If you know that you are not sure of some particular points—reference of pronouns, spelling, run-on sentences, for example—go over your paper looking for that particular point. Taking the responsibility for your own usage in this way is the quickest road to genuine improvement, and to getting full credit for the progress you are making.

The points that are usually considered "minimum essentials" are treated in other chapters and in the alphabetical articles in this book. The list given here is to call your attention to the most commonly needed essentials, showing where the full treatment is to be found. The list will help you get acquainted with this book and can be used as guidance for review of these elementary questions of usage. Each item in the list is followed by a group of exercises to be used as a check to see whether you know each point, or as drill if you do not.

All these exercises can be assigned as written exercises for homework, or as oral or written classroom exercises as the instructor prefers.

251

1. Sentence errors

*The most serious offenses against good English are uninten-
tional fragmentary sentences* (sentences that lack a main verb:
"He had never played in a real game. Although he had been on
the squad for two years") *and comma faults* (two or more grammatically independent sentences punctuated with only a comma
between them: "They didn't venture out too far, fish were plentiful within three miles of shore"). For "Fragmentary sentences,"
see Chapter 5, page 134. For "Comma faults," see Chapter 5,
page 138.

*Exercises 4
and 5,
pp. 145-47
1a. Fragmentary sentences. Some of the following sentences
are improper fragments. Recast or repunctuate those sentences
which need repair, telling why you did or did not change them.

1. It is rather interesting to note that John Tunis reports that
50 per cent of the Harvard 1911 class admitted in 1936 that
their occupations had not turned out as they had hoped at the
time they were graduated from college. Twenty-five per cent
wishing they had chosen some other career.

2. Dr. Grantham's literature courses drew 35 per cent of the
votes; economics and political science polled 12 per cent each;
and Dr. Fowler's comparative religion course drew 11 per cent.
So much for percentages.

3. According to 65 per cent of us, the college 20 years ago was
not too idealistic. Although 26 per cent believe it was.

4. I am afraid I can't say anything about constructive statesmen in western Europe in 1939. Now if you had said destructive!

5. If a beaver dam or a bird's nest is part of nature, why
aren't the things man creates? The Empire State Building, for
instance.

6. Many boys go to college from sheer momentum. Not being
able to think of anything else to do.

7. Nearly three quarters of the reading reported is non-fiction. If the lists are actually representative, about a third of this
being biography.

8. Perhaps, when the long crisis is past, we can settle down
to a few years of normal living. What we used to think of as
normal.

9. The power locked in the atom will run a million factories.
If it can be unlocked.

10. Whereas some six million tons of shipping were destroyed.
Eight million tons under construction more than offset the loss.

*Exercise 7,
pp. 147-48
1b. Comma faults. Some of the following sentences contain
comma faults. Recast or repunctuate those sentences which
need repair, telling why you did or did not change them.

1. Briggs did not exactly want to contribute, he had been maneuvered to a position where he could not refuse.

2. Dignity and caution both told him to stop, he wasn't listening.

3. Ricchetti's serves a beautiful shrimp cocktail, the sauce being exactly as hot as the average customer can stand it.

4. The schedule called for launching in July, the ship hit the water in late April.

5. He said that we ought to bar German and Italian music, since we never did play Japanese music he didn't mention that specifically.

6. The concerto has really only one recommendation, it is difficult, extremely difficult.

7. The decision may be right, may be wrong, it doesn't matter. An umpire loses all control if he lets a player change his mind for him.

8. All her temperamental outbursts had a perfectly obvious purpose, in spite of the director or anyone else she wanted her own way.

9. Maybe we have gone soft. *A primrose is a primrose* got Wordsworth's Peter Bell a bad reputation, *a rose is a rose is a rose* only makes us smile at Gertrude Stein.

10. A man like Boss Tweed he respected, he had some admiration for anything on a large scale.

2. Shifted constructions

Similar constructions should be in parallel form, so that sentences do not shift from active to passive voice, from personal to impersonal, or shift subjects unnecessarily: "One minute there are small farms, and in the next you are riding on a street walled with twenty- and thirty-story buildings." For "Shifted constructions," see page 129, and *Shifted constructions.

*Exercise 9, pp. 148-49

Rearrange or recast the following sentences to get rid of shifted constructions and to make elements parallel which are parallel in idea.

1. One should buy all the bonds he can afford, and they can be bought almost anywhere.

2. An interne is not awakened by casual noises; he can snore peacefully through people talking, lights flashing, or bells ringing; but the call bell tinkling his special ring will pull him out of a deep sleep.

3. Tires should be checked for pressure at least once a week, and you should move them to different wheels once every month or two, in order to get the best service.

4. Almost over the airport, the plane faltered, went into a

spin, began to leave a thin trail of smoke; then flames burst out.

5. Like Caesar, Clare Boothe came and looked—beautiful; all but Dorothy Parker, me, and a few other hardy souls were promptly conquered.

6. What Kieran and Adams can't answer, Levant can; an encyclopedia and a bond are paid for the question all three can't answer.

7. Listening to opera in the dark is certainly less strain on the culture seeker than to stand uncomprehendingly in the bright light and on the hard floors of an art museum.

8. Actually, the effect of cigarette smoke on the human system is not thoroughly understood: doctors have blamed all sorts of disease on it, it has been denounced by reformers, but science has proved little about it.

9. In the ground forces enlistments are not desired, but you will still be welcomed into the Air Corps if you have the qualifications.

10. Perhaps one should not complain, but I would like a little more recognition.

3. Spelling

A writer should spell common words accurately and be reasonably careful in spelling unusual words. See Chapter 10, page 267, and the exercises on page 275.

4. Punctuation

A writer should use punctuation marks so that they make his meaning clear. For the commonest problems of punctuation, see Chapter 11, page 276, and for further details the articles on the individual marks, *Comma, *Quotation marks, *Semicolon, and so on; and articles *Restrictive and non-restrictive, and *Series. Additional exercises appear on page 285.

4a. Punctuation—restrictive and non-restrictive. Some of these sentences already have adequate punctuation. Others contain non-restrictives, appositives, or interrupters which should be marked off with commas. Punctuate where necessary. Be ready to discuss cases of divided usage.

1. His opinion in spite of all their arguing was exactly what it had been.

2. The winter he pointed out would bring increased suffering to the unemployed and put additional strains on relief agencies.

3. Rubber which has been used can be reworked but never regains its original elasticity.

4. California Oregon and Washington which are on the coast have problems different from those of the inland states.

5. Kit Carson in Saroyan's play *The Time of Your Life* is a very different character from Kit Carson the famous Indian fighter and scout.

6. Roger Williams who founded the Rhode Island colony was a student of Indian languages.

7. The cub although obviously hungry refused to eat.

8. The constant motion up and down up and down was making him sick.

9. Red the fashionable color that spring is trying to many complexions.

10. They rode up whooping and yelling and tied their horses to the rail.

4b. Series. Punctuate the following sentences, if they need it.

1. Monotonously chanting Chicken ham and cheese sammitches sammitches chicken ham and cheese sammitches the train butcher moved slowly down the aisle.

2. If you are overweight if you have flat feet if you suffer from indigestion and insomnia still you may not be beyond the help of physical training or the reach of the Draft Board.

3. The undeviating precision of Chrono Watches results from a combination of advanced design the highest quality of materials and superb craftsmanship.

4. Leaping diving making short rushes at the ship the porpoises swarmed around us for two hours.

5. You knew that Jimmy was being initiated; you and Helen and Betty were only trying to make him feel sillier.

6. Waxed rouged and polished an orange has exactly as much juice as it started with.

7. A city Democrat Al Smith always made political capital of language of the people by the people and for the people especially for the people.

8. Rough tough McLaglen struggles with the part of a smooth slick crooked promoter and finds it heavy going.

9. Your job is to act innocent and ignorant whatever you see whatever you hear.

10. The records are kept in a special vault protected against fire smoke water and even intense heat.

4c. End punctuation. Supply the appropriate end punctuation.

1. How Mark Wakefield led his party safely across the glacier in the fog and darkness not even he can explain

2. How did the saying *As Maine goes, so goes the nation* originate

3. I asked what your plan is

4. What a failure that program turned out to be

5. Would you please turn down your radio

6. Although he had not really answered my question, what more could I say

7. How they laughed

8. Do you believe the trouble can be completely cured

4d. Quotes with other marks. Punctuate the following sentences, putting the italicized passages in quotes. Place the quotes in the conventional American relation to other marks of punctuation.

1. How many people really mean it do you suppose when they say *I would rather die than eat parsnips*

2. *No man* he remarked judicially *is permitted to marry his widow's sister*

3. *Yours sincerely* may mean *sincerely;* just as often it means the direct opposite

4. Even when you know Professor Spooner meant *Let me show you to a seat* when he said *Let me sew you to a sheet* it takes a second to figure out *She had a half warmed fish in her heart*

5. Turning up his collar he whispered *This tree is wet through. Shall we try the next one*

6. *A mouse* she screamed making a neat vault on to a chair

7. *This is the first time* he grated sourly *that I ever remember seeing three heels on one pair of shoes*

8. Without turning his head he tossed a short *Hiya pal* at me as he went by

9. *I would not ask a dog to eat this steak* Mr. Mullin said, sadly laying down his knife *not even a fierce young dog*

10. *Wouldn't you have done exactly the same thing* he asked the judge

5. Questions of word forms

The forms of English words have been so simplified (compare its declensions and conjugations, for example, with those of German) that only a few give any real trouble. These are mostly forms in which vulgate usage differs from that of Good English, as in some pronouns, the principal parts of some verbs, or instances in which two similar forms are confused. The following articles describe most of the forms of English words, with special emphasis on those that are untypical or bothersome: *Genitive case (The possessive form of nouns); *Plurals (of nouns); *Pronouns (their classes and forms); *between you and me; *himself, *myself (used as subjects); *It's me; *who, whom.

5a. Genitives and plurals. (1) Change the countries to citizens of the countries.

After Perry turned professional, even though France, Germany,

England, and the United States entered strong teams, Australia dominated the Davis Cup matches.

2. Show that Travis caught three, not one fish, and missed a chance to shoot two, not one moose.

On his vacation in Canada, Travis caught a bass that weighed three pounds and a half and spoiled a chance to shoot a moose by slipping and falling into the lake.

3. Add a word to show that the slide rule belonged not to Jim but to his boss.

Jim broke his slide rule.

4. Make the people plural.

A woman and a child died in the lifeboat from exposure.

5. Make the possessives plural.

A woman's shoes usually have higher heels than a girl's.

6. Make the time two hours.

An hour's walk will get you there.

7. Make the letters plural.

In old books an s looks like an f.

8. Make the plants singular.

Gladioli are planted by the gate.

9. For Smith substitute Jones. Make the picnic plural.

All the Smiths like a picnic.

10. Express the time in centuries.

The painting was dark with two hundred years' grime.

5b. Cases of pronouns. Choose the correct form in each sentence. If you believe that more than one form could be used, indicate the level at which each would be appropriate.

1. The principal asked Jim and (I, me) to take charge of the meeting.
2. (Who, whom) do you want to see?
3. Nobody is more generous than (he, him).
4. They didn't expect it to be (I, me) calling at that hour.
5. Was it (they, them) who invented the idea?
6. I like her mother better than (she, her).

7. The winning margin came through (he, his, him) winning the shot-put.

8. Between the bus and (whoever, whomever) wanted to ride on it was a strip of deep mud.

9. (Who, Whom) do you think will be eliminated?

10. After the boat left, there were only (we, us) two on the island.

11. I think (he, his, him) taking charge prevented a very serious panic.

12. All three of us, Mary, Dick, and (I, my, me), climbed into the front seat.

13. They all laughed but (he, him).

14. We all laughed except (he, him).

15. "It's (he, him), it's my Dad," the boy shrilled.

16. (Who, Whom), we asked each other, would do a thing like that?

17. Between (we, us) and the old man, who loved his grapes much better than (we, us) children, a hot feud broke out every season.

18. Was it (they, them) you meant?

19. We suspected (he, his, him) to be the thief.

5c. Tenses of verbs; voice. *Principal parts of verbs; *Tenses of verbs; *shall—will, should—would, *lay—lie, *set—sit; *Voice

a) Rewrite the following sentences, adding an auxiliary *have* or *has* to the verb in each main clause below and making any other changes necessary to make the sentences consistent.

1. The F.B.I. knew the identity of two of the counterfeiters almost from the beginning, and they set a trap to catch the ringleader.

2. Fifty times a day one of us runs to the window to find out what the noise is.

3. Mumps and chicken pox broke out in the camp.

4. By the time the cast memorize their lines, the jokes begin to wear thin.

5. Ten seconds after the alarm rings the big truck slides out of the fire station.

6. The same little old man with a beard sat at the same corner table with what might have been the same cup of coffee every time I dropped in after the show.

7. They chose to run the risk of traveling by plane.

8. They drank cup after cup of coffee but finally they grew sleepy in spite of it.

9. For hours they drank beer and sang songs in moderately close harmony.

10. Man did not spring from the apes, but both presumably came from a common ancestor.

b) Answer the following questions, using a verb consisting of a single word.

1. When you were in high school, did you ever run the 440?
2. Did you ride all the way with three in the front seat?
3. Did the discovery of the marked money lead to his arrest?
4. Did anyone know that the ambassador would be on the plane?
5. Do the radio voters actually choose the songs?

c) Answer the following questions, using a verb consisting of some form of *have* and the past participle.

1. Did the phone ring for me since you have been here?
2. Did you ever swim in a cold mountain stream before sunrise?
3. When you were a little boy, did you ever catch your trunks on a rough spot on a slide and tear out the seat?
4. Did you ever buy anything at a pawn shop?
5. Didn't Mary write even one letter to you while she was in California?

d) Choose the proper verb, remembering that *lie, sit,* and *rise* are intransitive, *lay, set,* and *raise* transitive.

1. The route to Key West (lays, lies) almost straight across the shallow sea on a series of fills and bridges.
2. The excavation was abandoned, and the tomb was left (laying, lying) open and empty.
3. The Mayan pyramids had (laid, lain) buried in the jungles for uncounted centuries.
4. The rank jungle growth had tried to thrust the stone apart, but the great blocks were so closely set that it could only (lie, lay) a cover of humus over them.
5. Before their astonished eyes the barren little valley (laid, lay) as empty as a cup.
6. A section of the stage (raises, rises) with two pianos on it.
7. The high spring tides (raise, rise) the water level up to the third floor of the docks there.
8. The beam of a searchlight flashed into the sky and (raised, rose) high into the mist, a beacon for the groping airliner.
9. For seven innings the Cleveland batters were (sat, set) down without a hit.
10. The flag should be (raised, risen) as soon as the sun has (raised, risen).

259

e) Change passive verbs to active verbs, making other changes necessary on account of that change.

1. The manager is heartily hated by all his employees.
2. Owen was thrown through the windshield by the force of the collision.
3. It was proved by the F.B.I. that the fire was started by saboteurs.
4. The land is bled white by a few years of continuous cotton growing, but year after year cotton is put in by indifferent share-croppers.
5. The mile was won by a darkhorse, Keene, in the surprising time of 4:09 flat.
6. The general, it was hinted by most of the commentators, was forced to resign not because of ill health but because of Hitler's displeasure.
7. In February the orchestra in perhaps the finest performance in its distinguished career was led by Stokowsky.
8. Because of a broken wheel, wrecked in the take off, the landing was made critically dangerous.
9. America is being made conscious of distance by the shortage of cars and accessories.
10. Mrs. Drewry was held in contempt of court three times in one afternoon's session.

5d. Adverbs and adjectives. *Adverbs, types and forms, §3, *-al ly; *Adjectives, types and forms, §2

Choose the appropriate adjective or adverb form. If more than one form could be used, give both and say something about the circumstances under which each might be appropriate.

1. The dog barked, the phone rang, and the baby cried (louder and louder, more and more loudly).
2. On the still night air the scent of apple blossoms drifted (sweet, sweetly).
3. Without any additional machinery, the factory can turn out parts much (quicker, more quickly) than it has been doing.
4. With high octane gas the motor starts (easy, easily) and runs (good, well) even in subzero weather.
5. Your arguments always sound (convincing, convincingly) even though there is usually a catch in them.
6. The office staff were quick to volunteer that they had been treated (fair, fairly).
7. If you want to enjoy some fine mountain scenery, drive very (slow, slowly) when you come out of the canyon.
8. You don't look as if you felt very (good, well).

9. In cutting out the neckline, Grace (accidently, accidentally) cut her finger and stained the material with blood.

10. As the motor warmed, it stopped popping and began to run (steadier, more steadily).

6. Agreement

6a. Agreement of pronoun and antecedent. *A pronoun agrees with its antecedent in number, gender, and person.* See *Reference of pronouns, *every and its compounds, *collectives, *none.

a) Rewrite the following sentences changing each verb to the singular. Make other changes which naturally follow, taking particular care that all pronouns are appropriate to their antecedents. In any cases of divided usage, give both and indicate the level which you think appropriate for each.

1. Both teams have their minds made up to win.

2. Those bulbs are some which were developed at the Agricultural School.

3. The less people listen to rumors, the less they are frightened by them. (Use *a person* for *people*.)

4. All you men will receive your notifications in the morning mail.

5. We, who knew him best, had had no warning sent to us of his intentions.

6. All contestants draw their starting numbers out of a hat.

7. We have all had our feelings deeply stirred by an unprovoked attack on our territory. (Use *everyone*.)

8. Will you all move your chairs out of the path of the movie projector. (Use *everyone*).

9. Those kinds of roses lose their leaves in a frost, but they are not much hurt.

10. The F.B.I. have their ways of finding out what suspected persons have been planning.

b) Follow the same directions as in the preceding exercise.

1. The jury, through their foreman, gave their verdict of "Not guilty."

2. All optimists are convinced that the clouds over them are lined with sterling silver.

3. The company were lined up behind their captain.

4. All the men affected feel that their being chosen was fair.

5. First come a group of novels, and all of them are on the same theme.

6. All officers must furnish their own equipment and uniforms.

261

7. None of the books are radical in their teaching.

8. All parents favor their own children.

9. The audience were pleased and gave their applause generously.

10. The first couple were Jim and Betty Lou, and both were radiant.

6b. Subject and verb. *A verb agrees with its subject in number and person.* See *Subject and verb; *Collective nouns; *one of those who; *there is, there are.

a) Rewrite the following sentences, making the indicated changes and any others which these make necessary.

1. Omit *a collection of*: There was a collection of forty French moderns in the exhibit.

2. Change *in addition to* to *and*: The state sticker in addition to the federal revenue stamp brings the total tax to eight cents a package.

3. Change *Sociology* to *Economics*: Sociology is now the most popular course in the University.

4. Change *its* to *their*: The orchestra responds perfectly to its leader's direction.

5. Change *Neither* to *Both*: Neither of the tenors has a very good voice.

6. Change *This* to *These*: This deer is just beginning to grow antlers.

7. Change *Northwest* to *Oregon, Washington, and Idaho*: The Northwest, with all its vast area, comprises only one division of the Bureau.

8. After *He* add *is one of the people who*: He hates vegetables.

9. After *One* add *of the two*: One has to lose, since they can't both win.

10. Change *America* to *Americans*: America will accept no such future.

b) Follow here the directions given for the preceding exercise.

1. Change *one* to *people*: The more one has, the more he wants.

2. Change *or* to *and*: What you want or what you think you can get is a question that you must settle in advance.

3. Change *The whole family* to *Everyone*: The whole family were gathered in the kitchen.

4. Change *All* to *Each*: All the ushers wore little red badges on their caps.

5. Change *One* to *None*: One of the bears is tame.

6. After *always* add *a pile of:* There are always books by the bed.

7. After *crowd* add *of cadets:* There is always a crowd around the soda fountain.

8. Take out *a variety of:* There was usually a variety of pies for dessert.

9. Change *Anyone* to *Everybody:* Anyone knows that television is being perfected.

10. Begin *with several other boys:* Jim is driving to New York Saturday.

7. Misrelated modifiers

A phrase or clause should clearly modify the word the writer intends. A common fault is a misrelated participle, as in "Turning away from an unproductive soil, the sea provided the Scotch with income for centuries" instead of "Turning away from an unproductive soil, the Scotch for centuries made their living from the sea." See *Dangling modifiers; *Participles, § 2; *Word order, § 3.

7a. Dangling constructions. Some of the following sentences contain dangling modifiers. Revise those sentences which need revision so as to eliminate the dangling modifiers.

1. Climbing a ladder and taking off the shade, the trouble turned out to be only a burned out bulb.

2. Nonchalantly smoking a cigarette, his hands automatically found the chords and beat out the rhythm.

3. Having been practically brought up in a sailboat, the yawl's crankiness when closehauled gave no trouble.

4. Angered by what was certainly a violation of their code, the Indians were sullen and smoldering.

5. Using an oil base, the paint can be built up thickly, so as to give an almost three-dimensional effect.

6. After hearing the Franck Symphony, practically anything will sound dull.

7. Flattered, although he had done nothing to be proud of, George began to swell out his chest and show off.

8. Using alcohol, specimens keep practically indefinitely, but the colors, especially of tropical fish, quickly fade and change.

9. Hit in the neck by a squashy snowball, memories of those distant winters in Wisconsin came crowding back.

10. Looking at Williamsburg, now so perfectly restored, the past seems very close.

7b. Dangling or misplaced modifiers. You are asked to make one or more changes in each of the following sentences. Read the directions for each item carefully and write down the revised sentence, making the change asked for and other alterations that are then necessary, but do not make more alterations than are necessary.

1. Add the idea of *to fly safely* at the end of the sentence: Cadet Franklin's training is still insufficient.

2. Begin *Coming out of the subway*: A solid row of skyscrapers faced us.

3. Begin *Fresh from the tropics*: The intense cold made him suffer.

4. Add *to float*: A ship's volume must be greater than the volume of an equal weight of water

5. Show that the pistol belonged to the guard on duty: The guard's pistol had a broken firing pin.

6. Begin *To arbitrate fairly*: Local standards of living and wage scales must be studied.

7. Begin *To save themselves work*: Many inventions have been developed in the textile industry.

8. Begin *Entering the airlock*: The air pressure which has filled the diver's blood with abnormal amounts of oxygen is gradually reduced.

9. Begin *Fishing off Florida*: A big sailfish struck the hook.

10. Add *to get cold in the water*: The layers of fat on his body are too thick.

7c. Misplaced modifiers. Recast all sentences in which the meaning is ambiguous or misleading.

1. Reporters found the men who had been almost frozen in the ship's galley drinking hot coffee.

2. She wore a tiny bouquet on her shoulder which was made of yellow rosebuds.

3. No one noticed that some of the ballots were missing until they were counted.

4. The wind driven waves washed away a house surging over the breakwater.

5. The captain had learned the trick he was going to use in an earlier encounter with a submarine.

6. Using several pen names, the two editors had almost written every article in the magazine.

7. There is a complete record of all fires started by saboteurs in the fire marshal's desk right now.

8. Backed by a spontaneous wave of sentiment, Congress voted a wide extension of the Draft.

9. The great seas impressed even the Coast Guardsmen as they crashed on the rocks.

10. The company was looking for a man with a car to interview rural clients.

8. Idiomatic constructions

Some words are joined to other words by particular prepositions or adverbs (interested *in*, interested *by* . . .). See *Prepositions, §3; *ability (to); *agree to, agree with; *compare—contrast; *different, and other specific articles.

The idioms in expressions of comparisons are specific ("The prices vary as much as if not more than the quality"). See *Comparison of adjectives and adverbs, §5.

8a. Prepositions in idioms. In each sentence a blank represents an omitted preposition which would complete the idiom. Fill in the preposition.

1. At Haliewa they spent the whole morning in a glass-bottomed boat, fascinated ...... the marine plants, the coral formations, and the brilliantly colored fish.

2. After his sister's elopement, Drake developed a strong distaste ...... publicity.

3. He seems to be completely indifferent ...... public opinion.

4. Some students have trouble adjusting to college because it is fundamentally different ...... high school.

5. The old heating system was not adequate ...... both the original building and the new wing.

6. Six Justices concurred ...... Justice Robinson's opinion.

7. He is capable ...... making up the whole story as a joke.

8. He was simply waiting, hoping ...... something to happen which would take the responsibility off his shoulders.

9. After the prize was awarded, it was discovered that whole pages of the winning essay were identical ...... a pamphlet published ten years before.

10. The union will not agree ...... the proposition offered by the management.

8b. Idioms in comparison. Make the change suggested in each sentence and any other alterations made necessary by this change.

1. Change *three* to *two*: *Afterglow* is the most subtle of Travers' three novels.

2. Add the idea that flying may be safer. Transatlantic flying is just as safe as steamer travel.

3. Give Herman more than one opponent: Herman will be the more dangerous in the final sprint because he has greater endurance than his opponent.

4. Make the mule more adept than a horse: A good mule is just as strong and as adept at applying his weight as any horse.

265

5. Make Mrs. Winters exceed in bulk anyone you ever saw. Mrs. Winters was an exceedingly fat woman.

6. Make the adjectives superlative: Of the four puppies, Timmy was always sleepy and indolent.

7. Make the adverbs, except *always*, comparative: When he was excited, he always drove fast and recklessly.

8. Make him even more vicious than a snake: This gunman, Morse, is as sly and vicious as a snake.

9. Make Tommy the most intelligent: Tommy stands out as intelligent in a group of remarkable children.

10. Insert a phrase to make a contrast between the actual situation and the situation which might be expected: Strangely enough, there have been fewer suicides since the country went to war.

The list of problems in idiom could be indefinitely extended. The following illustrate a few of the commoner idioms that raise questions: *Double negatives; *kind, sort; *kind of [a], sort of [a]; *like—as; *Gerund.

Following the usage of educated people in such items as these is only the beginning of writing Good English, but before you can go on, you must be sure of these. Fortunately any one person is likely to be troubled by only a few of the expressions listed here and for the majority they would be merely a review. Anyway they are soon mastered after they have been called to one's attention. Reading the set of themes that begins on page 307 will bring up a number of problems of usage in the context in which they occurred.

Spelling

IT IS NOT EASY to get a language down on paper. It exists first and fundamentally as speech, and for the most part, writing is a representation of what we say. In English we try to represent our speech with an alphabet of twenty-six letters, three of which—*c* (or *k*), *q*, and *x*—merely duplicate the work of other letters. The twenty-three active letters singly and in combinations like *th*, *ea*, *sh* have to record words employing some forty sounds. The difficulty is greatest in the vowels: *a*, for instance, spells the vowel sounds of *lay*, *lap*, *far*, *fare*, *was*, not to mention untypical words like *many* and sounds without definite character as the second *a* in *comparative*. This means that one may with very good reason be uncertain of the conventional spelling of a word that is familiar in speech.

1. Inconsistencies in English spelling

Besides the limitation of the alphabet there is even greater difficulty keeping pace with a changing pronunciation. English spelling was stabilized chiefly by the printers of the fifteen and sixteen hundreds, and though it has changed considerably since then, it has not kept abreast with the spoken forms. This fact accounts for many of the more strange English spellings: *meat* and *meet* once represented different sounds; *colonel* was pronounced in three syllables, col-o-nel; the *gh* in *night*, *though*, and other words was sounded, as it still is in Scotland. The

curious group including *bough, cough, though, through* is
largely explained by different pronunciations in different English
dialects—the pronunciation of one word comes from one dialect,
of another from a different dialect, but the original spelling is
kept.

The English habit of borrowing words generously from other
languages is responsible for such groups as *cite, sight, site*, and
hundreds of words that do not follow conventions of English
spelling—*bureau, croquet, hors d'oeuvre, khaki, onomatopoeia*.
We have even borrowed foreign tricks of spelling some sounds,
as in *gu*ard and *qu*een.

These facts suggest that, though English spelling cannot be
defended, both its general confusion and the form of a particular word can be explained by reference to the history of the
language.[1] This does not help us spell a given word, but it does
help us understand why the difficulties exist, why our spelling
can be made the butt of so many jokes and furnish curiously
spelled rhymes for limericks.

1a. Spelling change. Students of the language are united in
their belief that spelling should represent our spoken words
more accurately. Thirty years ago Professor Lounsbury wrote his
English Spelling and Spelling Reform in the belief "that the
English race will not be content to sit down forever with a system of spelling which has nothing to recommend it but custom
and prejudice, nothing to defend it but ignorance, nothing but
superstition to make it an object of veneration." A completely
phonetic spelling is unlikely, and even if one was set up, it
would soon become antiquated, because pronunciations (the
real forms of words) would continue to change. But many of
the inconsistencies could be removed and many silent letters
dropped. Laymen who have mastered the present spelling object to change. They feel that it would be tampering with our
literary heritage—not realizing, for example, that the spelling
of the current Shakespeare texts has been modernized by editors.
The sweeping changes suggested by devotees of "spelling reform" have naturally made a good many people afraid of all
change.

---

[1] Henry Bradley, *Spoken and Written Language* (Oxford, 1919); W. A.
Craigie, *English Spelling* (New York, 1927); Kennedy, Chapter 7 and
section 128; Thomas R. Lounsbury, *English Spelling and Spelling Reform*
(New York, 1909); Robertson, Chapter 8. The section "Orthography" at
the front of the Webster dictionaries, especially the International size, contains a great deal of information about English spelling.

But in spite of opposition many changes in spelling have taken place and are taking place. The *u* has been dropped from words ending in *-our* (*colour—color*) in the United States, and it is being dropped in England. *Economic, public, poetic* once ended in *k*; words with *ae* are being spelled with *e* (*anaesthetic—anesthetic*), and so on. These gradual and almost imperceptible changes are more in keeping with the spirit of English than a wholesale "reform" would be.

A writer now has a choice of simpler spellings in some hundreds of words. The choice he makes between forms will depend upon his feeling of appropriateness. Formal writers are consistently conservative in spelling. Informal writers make use of the shorter forms more readily. At present scientific and business English are most open to changes in spelling. In familiar writing many people are more adventurous than in writing intended for strangers. Most professional writers will be conservative, as most readers will expect them to be. But anyone seriously interested in furthering the gradual simplifying of English spelling will find many occasions on which he may appropriately exercise his mite of influence by using simpler spellings and familiarizing readers with such forms. These will be more widely accepted as readers become accustomed to seeing them.

The essential point is for a person to realize how generally the shorter form is used and then to decide whether he wants to be adventurous or not. *Altho, tho,* and *thru* are in general use in business and advertising and in familiar correspondence and have been adopted by enough periodicals so that they are included in recent dictionaries as alternate forms. *Nite* and *naborhood,* on the other hand, are not found outside advertising and familiar writing, and *brot* or *thot* have not even reached the advertising columns. In many words (*catalog—catalogue, program—programme, esthetic—aesthetic* . . .) usage is divided, and the shorter forms are becoming the more usual.

When usage is divided in spelling a given word, ordinarily choose the simpler or more natural form. For a surprising number of words, two spellings are current and are recorded in dictionaries. A person who wishes his style to appear formal may adopt older or more complex forms, but most people writing today, and certainly anyone who has difficulty with spelling, will ordinarily prefer:

1. The more modern of two equally reputable spellings of common words: *center, mold, sirup, today* rather than *centre, mould, syrup, to-day.*

2. The simpler form of a specialized word if it has attained currency among the people who use it most: *anesthetic, catalog, medieval, program, sulfur* rather than *anaesthetic, catalogue, mediaeval, programme, sulphur*.

3. American rather than British spellings (though both spellings are usually current to some extent on both sides of the Atlantic): *color, labor, pajama, story* (of a building), *traveler*, rather than *colour, labour, pyjama, storey, traveller*. Of course in spelling British proper names or in direct quotation, British spelling should be kept, as in "the Labour party."

1b. Uniform spelling. The present emphasis upon uniformity and correctness in spelling is due partly to historical and partly to social causes. In the eighteenth century there was a special drive for uniformity in various matters of language. After the appearance of Samuel Johnson's dictionary and later of Noah Webster's, spelling received special emphasis. In the United States, in schools, Webster's blue back speller—over 60,000,000 copies of which were sold in the nineteenth century—helped make spelling one of the main jobs in school. The spelling lesson was something definite; the goal was well defined in the dictionary and spelling book; progress toward it could be marked. There is now over a century of this school pressure behind the desire for uniformity in spelling.[1]

Another enforcement of uniformity has come from printers and publishers, who naturally wish for consistency in what they print and so usually revise manuscripts according to the dictionaries or according to their own stylebooks based on the spellings of the dictionaries. Dickens and others of our celebrated writers were "poor spellers" whose copy was corrected by editors. Recently book publishers have come to allow a writer a little freedom in his choice of spellings, but periodicals normalize the spelling in the manuscripts they print.

Back of the schools and the editors there is a more general social demand for uniformity. Mistakes in spelling are easily noticed, even by people who would have difficulty with some of the more complex matters of language. It is a convenient test of literacy and even of respectability. "English orthography [spelling]," says Thorstein Veblen, ". . . is archaic, cumbrous, and ineffective; its acquisition consumes much time and effort; failure to acquire it is easy of detection. Therefore it is the first and readiest test of reputability in learning, and conformity to

---

[1] Allen Walker Read, "The Spelling Bee: A Linguistic Institution of the American Folk," *PMLA*, 1941, 56:495-512.

its ritual is indispensable to a blameless scholastic life" (*The Theory of the Leisure Class*, p. 399). In a country like ours where people pass from one class to another, even such a seemingly small matter as spelling is made a part of the initiation to the class that carries on public affairs.

The real reason for "learning to spell" is that educated readers expect to see words in the standard forms. Good spelling is, consequently, an important—if the most superficial—trait of Good English.

2. Suggestions for improvement in spelling

It is social insistence, then, rather than any fundamental linguistic requirement that makes accurate spelling a requirement of good English. And in spite of its admitted difficulty, fairly correct spelling is possible for anyone, though if he has reached college age without having acquired the knack, it will mean work. The goal for "a poor speller" is not to spell perfectly but to spell well enough so that his copy will not attract unfavorable attention—and to know how to check possible errors. The most fatal mistake is to give up, to enjoy poor spelling as a hypochondriac enjoys poor health.

If you have really serious difficulty with spelling, it will pay to do some general reading, focusing on the individual words. Keeping lists of your own spelling problems and working on them is more important than using lists made up by others. Copying short passages that contain words you need to use helps fix them in mind, and writing down from dictation is even better. This lets you write the word in its context and so helps accustom you to putting it in a natural setting.

Here are a few general suggestions, followed in the next section by more specific ones on particular groups of words:

2a. Make sure of the words you use frequently. Words like *shining, dining room, dormitory, separately, huge, accidentally, quantity* it is inexcusable to misspell. Probably most such slips that occur in college papers are due to carelessness, to hasty copying, or to not proofreading the final copy. That makes them even more objectionable than misspelling uncommon or difficult words. Errors of this sort can be cleaned up by paying attention or by writing them over correctly a few times. Sometimes pronouncing them carefully will help; for instance if you tend not to sound the first *t* in *quantity*. If you miss common words you should keep a list of your mistakes and go over them often until you master them. A little time spent this way will pay real dividends.

2b. In learning new words, get both the spoken and the written forms at the same time. In college most new words come from textbooks or other reading. Making a word your own is chiefly a matter of attention to its sound and its looks. Pronounce a new word distinctly, visualizing its syllables; if it is at all difficult, study it carefully and then say it without looking at it; then write it down, and compare with its printed form. Then continue saying and writing it a few times until you are sure of it. Focus on the word's appearance by holding a pencil point under it. Underline new words, if they are going to be important to you, so that they will stand out on the page and thus help you remember their exact form. Modern methods of teaching reading—for meaning only, seeing only key letters in words—tend to make visualizing of words difficult and actually handicap a person's spelling, however much they may help his reading. At times it is necessary to counteract the habit of rapid reading so as to really *see* the individual words and even the letters of the words, to fix them in mind.

This method of learning the spelling of a new word holds also for correcting errors you may have fallen into. But it is important not to add to that collection of errors. Paying careful attention to the sound and the sight of a word will in time fix it in your memory so that it will always come right.

2c. Make it easy for yourself to look up the spelling of words you are not sure of. A moderate sized dictionary, the "college" size in most makes, will have all the words you will need, and it is not so full as to make searching hard. Even the pocket dictionaries may be adequate for spelling lists, if not for finding the meanings of words, though they are not likely to be up-to-date. Some word lists, if large enough, may help with common words. One of the most compact is the index to Roget's *Thesaurus of English Words and Phrases*, which is especially easy to use because it has several hundred words on a page and no extraneous material to get in the way.

Above all, don't rely on roommates or other persons who may happen to be around. Their guesses are often no better than yours.

2d. Spelling is to be attended to in revision. This is the most important general advice to remember. Don't stop when you are writing to look up a word or even to worry about it. You will almost certainly lose something more important if you do— the trend of your thought, the movement of your sentence at least. Mark it in some way (with a ? or a check mark) if you are suspicious of the way it looks, and then check up on all spellings together while working over what you have written. In revision also check carefully for careless spellings. A teacher can sympathize with misspelling difficult words or new words, but hardly with *quiet* for *quite* or *their* for *there*. Careful reading of a paper just for the spelling is the best advice for anyone who is likely to make mistakes.

3. Groups of words

One of the useful things to do in studying spelling is to group together words that have some trait in common (a vowel, an ending) or that show a habit of English (like doubling the final consonant under certain conditions). Everyone groups some words in ways that help him remember their form.

Here is a list of articles in Part Two of this *Guide-Index* that treat specific spelling problems.

The articles in this list marked † give the most useful rules or suggestions for mastering large groups of common words.

-able, -ible (desirable, legible)
Accent marks in spelling (as in words from French, like *café*):
    See *Foreign words in English §§ 3*b*, 4, and *Accents.
-ae, -oe- (esthetic, ameba)
† -al ly (politically, incidentally)
American and British usage (color, colour; theater, theatre)
-ance, -ence (attendance, existence)
Apostrophe (Bob's picture, the companies' charter)
-cal, -cial (musical, judicial)
Capital letters
† -ce, -ge (peaceable, courageous)
Contractions (didn't, he'll)
Dieresis (reëxamine)
† Doubling final consonants (refer—referred)
† E § 5 (silent or mute *e*) (changeable, likeness)
-ed (exceptions to rule)
† -ei-, -ie- (achieve, feign, receive)
en-, in- (encourage, inquire)
-er, -or (debater, objector)
-er, -re (luster, scepter)
Foreign words in English (chauffeur, ersatz)
† Homonyms (words pronounced alike but spelled differently: plain, plane; altar, alter)
Hyphen (re-enter, father-in-law, forty-seven)
in-, un- (incapable, unedited)
-ize, -ise (apologize, advertise)
-le words (meddle, nickel)

-or (-our) (honor, Saviour)
-ough (-augh) (although, cough)
Plurals (beauties, birches, heroes, knives)
re- (reform, re-form)
Silent letters (debt, night)
† Slurred vowels (comparable, repetition)

Besides these general articles there are a number of brief comments on particular words, such as *all right, *fiancé, *glamor, *species. For common words offering special problems, it is usually worth while to see if the alphabetical section of the *Guide-Index* carries a specific article.

4. A brief spelling list

Here are about 100 common words that are frequently misspelled. Are you sure of them?

accelerate	definite	laboratory
accidentally	describe	led
accommodate	description	library
acquainted	develop	loneliness
across	difference	loose (lüs)
affect	dining room	lose (lüz)
all right	disappeared	
altogether	disappoint	Mediterranean
apologize	dormitory	miniature
appearance		minute
argument	effect	misspell
article	eighth	
association	embarrassed	noticeable
athlete	existence	noticing
attendance	experience	
audience	extracurricular	occurrence
auxiliary		omitted
	familiar	optimist
	fascinate	
benefited	finally	propeller
brilliant	freshman class	psychology
Britain		
business	government	quantity
	guard	quiet
		quite
	hindrance	
calendar	huge	really
chosen		received
collegiate	incidentally	recommend
conscience	initial	religious
conscious	intramural	repetition
curriculum	irrelevant	

rhythm	subsidizing	undoubtedly
roommate	suppose	until
	suppress	
sacrifice	surprise	vegetables
seize	syllable	visible
separated		
shining	temperament	weather
similar	tragedy	whether
skis	truly	wholly

A much fuller list of words will be found in the article *Spelling.

Exercises

1. In your spelling notebook set up headings for classifying groups of words, and under appropriate heads list words that cause you trouble. For example: *-ance, -ence (-ant, -ent); *-able, -ible; *E §5 (e dropped or retained before ending); *-ei-, -ie-; *Doubling final consonants; *y or i before an ending.

2. Study *Homonyms. Make up a list of your own. Write sentences that illustrate the different meanings and spellings of ten pairs.

3. Make up a list of words often confused with other words, although not true homonyms (formerly, formally; quite, quiet). Write illustrative sentences to show meaning and spelling.

Punctuation

PUNCTUATION MARKS are one means of helping us get our exact meaning on the page. They do more than mark such obvious facts of language as "This is a sentence," "This is a question." They help us separate words (and thoughts) and so present them distinctly to a reader; they help group and keep together related ideas; they set off certain words for emphasis. Their use affects the tempo of writing: Too many marks may slow the reader to the point of exasperation, and too few may make him go over a passage two or three times to gets its probable meaning. The writer who wishes his work to appear to the best advantage will give close attention to its punctuation.[1]

Most marks come naturally. Even in a hastily written first

---

[1] The most thorough modern study is George Summey, Jr., *Modern Punctuation—Its Utilities and Conventions* (New York, 1919). In many respects it needs revision to represent practice today, but it is a realistic treatment based on a study of actual publications.

Current English Usage, Part I, summarizes a number of opinions on various disputed uses and gives a suggestive statement of principles on pages 72-92.

The stylebooks of publishing houses treat punctuation. The University of Chicago Press *Manual of Style* (10th Ed.; Chicago, 1937) is thorough, representing the usage of a conservative house. John Benbow, *Manuscript & Proof* (New York, 1937), directions for writers and compositors of the American Branch of the Oxford University Press, is brief but perhaps the most sensible of the stylebooks.

draft the writer will feel the natural grouping of his ideas sufficiently to mark the sentences and most of the subordinate
elements in some reasonable way. But punctuation is not completely automatic, even with practiced writers. The boy who put
at the end of a class theme "Not time to punctuate" was partly
right, for punctuation needs careful checking in revision. Most
of the suggestions about the use of particular marks made in this
chapter and in the alphabetical articles in Part Two are to be
applied in revising papers rather than in writing the first draft.

The practices of punctuation are set by the editors of books
and periodicals, who draw up statements of their usage in style-   *Stylebooks
books and change the manuscripts they print to conform to
these rules. Though the practices vary somewhat between publications, they agree on most points. English teachers try to
encourage students to follow the more important and agreed
upon of these uses. Since readers have come to understand
punctuation marks as signals in interpreting what they read, it
is to a writer's interest to know and to follow the usual conventions and also to know where he has opportunity for choice.

1. Open and close punctuation

There are two general tendencies in punctuation that need to
be understood before considering specific items of usage. Some
writers appear to use as many marks as they can, and some use as
few as possible. These two tendencies are called *close punctuation* for the full pointing and *open punctuation* for the
sparse pointing. Time has something to do with styles of punctuation. Nineteenth-century usage preferred close punctuation,
made necessary and appropriate by the dominant complex types
of sentence. The current trend of most editors and even more
of most writers is toward open punctuation.

Sentence movement is the controlling factor, since more complex (not necessarily longer) sentences need more points and
heavier points (semicolons for commas) to guide the reader;
shorter and more direct sentences need fewer. A writer's tempo
also has bearing, since punctuation marks have the effect of
slowing up the reading; a swiftly moving style, especially in
narrative, needs few marks.

Besides the need for fewer marks in simple and direct sen-
tences, there are several situations in which usage is divided and   *Comma, §2
the marks are optional, as between the next to last and last   *Series
members of a series: *red, white, and blue* or *red, white and blue*.[1]

[1] R. J. McCutcheon, "The Serial Comma Before 'And' and 'Or,'" *American Speech*, 1940, xv, 250-54.

In close punctuation the mark is used in such a place; in open it would usually be omitted.

The last word in close punctuation is shown in this sentence from Thomas Clap, an eighteenth-century president of Yale, who obviously intended to set off each phrase in his exposition:

> Yale-College in *New-Haven;* does not come up, to the Perfection, of the Ancient Established Universities, in *Great Britain;* yet, would endeavour, to Imitate them, in most things, as far, as the present State, will admit of.

Not many have carried punctuation to that extent, and even President Clap gave up the experiment. A more typical example of a rather close punctuation follows, with a parallel revision showing a more open form:

CLOSE	OPEN
Now the chief literary and dramatic vice of the scientists and philosophers, is that they seldom begin at the point of the reader's or hearer's interest. Here, for example, is a book on botany. It begins with a long account of the history of botany, and continues with an even longer account of the general principles of the science. But what do you, or what do I, want to know about the feeble beginnings of botany? We want to know—provided, of course, that we want to be something more than the ladylike botanists who know only the names of flowers —we want to know what the problems of botany are; in what direction botanical research is tending; what differences all this botanical research makes anyway; why it is worth studying.	Now the chief literary and dramatic vice of the scientists and philosophers is that they seldom begin at the point of the reader's or hearer's interest. Here for example is a book on botany. It begins with a long account of the history of botany and continues with an even longer account of the general principles of the science. But what do you or what do I want to know about the feeble beginnings of botany? We want to know, provided of course that we want to be something more than the ladylike botanists who know only the names of flowers, we want to know what the problems of botany are, in what direction botanical research is tending, what differences all this botanical research makes anyway, why it is worth studying.

The first sentence in a brief review of a novel from the (London) *Times Literary Supplement* shows how direct sentence movement removes the need for internal points:

Cardiac failure has been so often used as a device that the reader's own heart sinks slightly on learning in the first chapter that John Raymond was given six months to live by a Harley-street specialist.

Fiction writers, for whom straightforward movement is naturally important, have more leeway in punctuation than factual writers. A passage from John Dos Passos' *The Big Money* shows how open punctuation tends to help the impression of movement; more marks would make the passage appear more formal and make it move less swiftly:

Margo felt funny driving out through the avenues of palms of Beverly Hills sitting beside Sam Margolies. He'd made her put on the old yellow eveningdress she'd bought at Piquot's years ago that Agnes had recently had done over and lengthened by a little French dressmaker she'd found in Los Angeles. Her hands were cold and she was afraid Margolies would hear her heart knocking against her ribs. She tried to think of something funny to say but what was the use, Margolies never laughed. She wondered what he was thinking. She could see his face, the narrow forehead under his black bang, the pouting lips, the beaklike profile very dark against the streetlights as he sat stiffly beside her with his hands on his knees. He still had on his white flannels and a white stock with a diamond pin in it in the shape of a golfclub. As the car turned into a drive towards a row of bright tall frenchwindows through the trees he turned to her and said, "You are afraid you will be bored. . . . You'll be surprised. You'll find we have something here that matches the foreign and New York society you are accustomed to." As he turned his face towards her the light glinted on the whites of his eyes and sagging pouches under them and the wet broad lips. He went on whispering squeezing her hand as he helped her out of the car. "You will be the most elegant woman there but only as one star is brighter than the other stars."—JOHN DOS PASSOS, *The Big Money*, p. 407

All this suggests that before one can worry intelligently about a specific mark of punctuation in his writing he needs to know something about his style in general, whether it is rather involved and formal, requiring the support of a number of marks, or straightforward and relatively simple, not needing them. A theme reader's experience is that most college students write rather directly, or soon learn to, and that they come to college with a tendency to close punctuation that is not appropriate to their writing. Most of them should probably follow a rather open style, using marks—except in a few stereotyped places where readers will expect them—only to emphasize the structure and meaning of the sentence. Benbow's advice (*Manuscript & Proof*, p. 85) is sound: "In general, omit all punctuation which does not add to clearness."

2. The meaning of the punctuation marks

The punctuation marks can be divided into groups according to their principal uses. Detailed description of the use of each mark and examples will be found in the alphabetical article on each in Part Two.

2a. End stops. Used principally to indicate the end of sentences:

*Abbreviations
*Money
*Questions
*Exercises, p. 255
*Indirect Question

*Exclamation mark

. Period, at the end of statements (and after abbreviations, in sums of money, and so on)

? Question mark, at the end of questions (whether the question is a whole sentence or a part of a sentence); not used after indirectly quoted questions: He asked if we wanted to come. (Contrast: He asked, "Do you want to come?")

! Exclamation mark, at the end of an exclamation or other vigorously stressed sentence (and also within a sentence after a single word exclamation)

——Long dash, after a statement that is interrupted, as in conversation

. . . Ellipsis, after a statement that is left uncompleted, or a speech that is allowed to die away.

2b. Internal marks. Used to separate or to indicate the relation between elements within a sentence:

*Dates

, Comma, the most common mark and with the greatest number of specific uses. It has a number of conventional routine uses, as between the day of the month and year in dates (December 27, 1941), between town and state, county, or country (Chicago, Illinois; Chicago, Cook County, Illinois), and so on. It is used as a mark of slight separation of words, phrases, and clauses. The most common problems in the use of commas are discussed in § 3*a-d* of this chapter.

; Semicolon, a mark indicating separation between elements greater than that marked by a comma and slightly less than that marked by a period. See § 3*e* of this chapter.

: Colon, a mark of anticipation, pointing to what follows. It is used after the salutation of a business letter, and to introduce formal quotations, explanatory statements, or series too long to be prefaced by a comma.

— Dash, a mark of separation, more intense than a comma. It is used when the construction of a sentence is abruptly broken or to indicate a note of surprise or feeling. It is used too often in amateur writing as a substitute for a comma.

( ) Parentheses, or curves, used to inclose explanatory statements not built into the construction of the sentence

[ ] Brackets, used to indicate matter that has been inserted in quotations and as parentheses within parentheses

2c. Quotation marks. Used to inclose speeches of real or imagined conversation and short excerpts from printed matter.

' ' Single quotation marks   " " Double quotation marks

Either may be used as the mark of quotation. If there is a quotation within a quotation, the marks are alternated:

> "The first eight I called on answered 'Not prepared,' " Miss Stoddard complained. Or:
>
> 'The first eight I called on answered "Not prepared," ' Miss Stoddard complained.

2d. Miscellaneous marks. Occasionally regarded as marks of punctuation:

' Apostrophe, used in the genitive case of nouns and to indicate omission of letters in contractions, also in forming plurals of single letters or numbers: 9's, c's *Genitive case*

- Hyphen, used in spelling some compound words and to indicate division of words at the end of lines in copy *Division of words*

* Asterisk, to mark some special use of a term

{ } Brace, to combine two or more lines, as in tabulations

∧ Caret, to mark an omission in copy

. . . . Leaders, spaced periods to guide a reader's eye across a page *Underlining*

_____ Underlining, for emphasis, to indicate italics of print, as in the titles of books and periodicals. *Titles of books, articles, etc.* *Ships' names*

3. Common problems in punctuation

Most of the slips in punctuation that teachers have to mark in themes come from carelessness, not from ignorance: a period instead of a question mark at the end of a question, the close quotes left out after a quotation, and so on. Careful proofreading of the final manuscript should reduce such errors to a minimum.

Some mistakes in punctuation come from uncertainty of what the usual practice is. The various uses of each mark are fully discussed in the entry on it in the alphabetical part of this *Guide-Index*. Here are brief discussions of the most common problems.

3a. Commas to avoid. There is a temptation to put commas in some places where they actually interfere with reading, that is, where they keep apart elements that should run consecutively.

Modifiers

*Comma,
§5*a*

1. Do not separate a simple subject from its verb, or a verb from its object, or a preposition from its object.

> Boys who are supposedly wild [no comma] should not be sent to a strict preparatory school.
>
> All my hobbies and inclinations [no comma] came at last into their own.
>
> Everyone is crying [no comma] "Economize." ("Economize" is a direct object, not a quotation formally introduced by a verb like *He said*.)
>
> He would not have done it except [no comma] that everyone was daring him to.

But see
*Comma,
§2*b*,
Adjectives
in series

2. Do not separate a short adverb from the words it modifies or an adjective from its noun.

> Soon [no comma] we were at the gym and in less time than usual [no comma] were in our uniforms.
>
> It was a rather cool [no comma] May night.

3. Do not separate a conjunction from the clause it introduces:

> The girls almost always did the assignments, but [no comma] the boys usually tried to bluff.

3b. Restrictive and non-restrictive modifiers. When a word, phrase, or clause following the word it modifies limits the meaning of that word, restricts its meaning, it is called *restrictive* and is not set off by a comma. When such a modifier merely adds a descriptive detail, gives further information, it is called *non-restrictive* and is set off. Usually there is a slight pause or change in tone of voice in saying the non-restrictive modifier but not in saying a restrictive one.

*Comma, §3,
Restrictive
and non-
restrictive

1) RESTRICTIVE—NO COMMAS

*Exercises,
p. 254

> Boys *who are supposedly wild* should not be sent to a strict preparatory school. (Not all boys are supposedly wild.)
>
> This atmosphere is completed when you are greeted by the doorman *dressed up like a Keystone Cop*. (His costume is the distinctive feature.)
>
> His friends *Jock and Harry* were the first to arrive. (He had other friends.)
>
> A freshman has a chance to see all that is going on at a fraternity *when he receives an invitation to dinner*.

2) NON-RESTRICTIVE—COMMAS USED

> Another time Frank spent an unforgettable week with his father, *who had broken a leg and was unable to go to the office*. (He had but one father.)
>
> His best friend, *Jock*, was the first to come. (He had but one best friend.)

A student [Restrictive clause follows; no comma] *who has gone four years to a prep school attending study hall six nights a week* suddenly finds himself in college, [Non-restrictive clause follows; comma] *where studying must be done on his own.*

Note that when a non-restrictive modifier stands in the middle of a sentence, there should be a comma *before* and *after* it.

3c. Commas between clauses. (1) Usually a long adverbial clause (or phrase) that precedes the main part of the sentence is set off by a comma: *Comma, § 1

When we lost the fourth of the six games, we just about gave up.

Because so much of the land has been taken for farms, regions where birds and wild animals can live have been greatly reduced.

[Phrase] In a society in which social standing is not hereditary, a person's job is the chief sign of his status.

2) Clauses of a compound sentence are generally separated in formal writing by a comma. In informal writing such clauses are separated if they are long or if the grammatical subject is changed. Usually if the clauses are connected by *but* or *for* a comma is used.

Most textbooks have tended to encourage close punctuation, and students sometimes seem to see how many commas they can put in.

There are recognizable dialects in the United States, but they show fewer differences than would be expected in a country of such size.

Yet this is not a characteristic test, for the same reaction is given by several other aromatic compounds.

3d. Commas to prevent confusion. A comma is used to prevent any probable confusion or hesitation in reading. *Comma, § 7

After all, the students had gone quietly.

They had to hurry, for their dinner had been long on the table.

He came up sputtering and blubbering, as usual looking like nothing else but an overgrown baby seal.

3e. Semicolon and colon. The distinction between the semicolon and colon is simple. The colon points to what follows, introduces or anticipates something, as the text of a letter following the salutation *Gentlemen:*, or a long or formal quotation (Mr. Bristow said in part:), or any other anticipatory expression: *Colon

Then come the fellows in charge of the various departments: the soda fountain, ice cream, the grill, and the clams.

There is one thing that I am very sure of now: at this stage of his experience he should have followed my advice.

*Semicolon

A semicolon, on the other hand, is a mark of separation, almost as full as a period. It is not needed except in rather long and complex sentences, or when one or more of the elements have commas within them, or when coordinate clauses are not closely connected:

Most words need modifiers to make their meaning more exact; they need connectives to tie them to other words.

For *pumpkin*, two levels of pronunciation are recognized: formal, pump′ kin; colloquial, pung′ kin.

In formal papers for college courses and in theses formal usage should be followed; in informal college papers, like many themes, either style may be used, as the instructor prefers.

*Exercises, p. 256

3f. Marks in combination. Occasionally questions arise over the order of two marks of punctuation that follow the same word.

*Parentheses, §5

A punctuation mark belonging to a part of a sentence that includes a parenthesis comes *after* the second curve:

There are several words of foreign origin that keep their original plural forms (like *alumnae, alumni, analyses*), and many that have two forms (like *appendix, cactus, formula*).

*Quotation marks, §4b, c

Most publishers put a comma or a period inside the closing quotation mark, regardless of whether it belongs to the quotation or to the sentence as a whole:

"In the beginning," he said—meaning probably "two years ago."

*Quotation marks, §4

Exclamation points and question marks stand inside the quotation marks if the quotation is an exclamation or a question, outside if the including sentence is the exclamation or question:

Then suddenly he shouted "Get out of here, all of you!"
You don't mean that he actually said "You're another"!
She asked, "Won't you please try to do it for me?"
Did she say, "Please try to do it"?

The articles on the individual punctuation marks contain more discussion and more illustrations of these uses, as well as of others.

The best way to use this book when you have a question of punctuation is to look up the *Index* article on the particular mark that you think is most likely to fit; if that does not answer your question, look up the mark that seems to you next most likely. *And remember that this testing of punctuation marks belongs in the revision stage of your writing.*

Exercises

1. The punctuation marks have been removed from the following passages, and you are asked to put in marks that will make them meaningful. First glance through a passage, to get an idea of its content and of its general movement. Decide whether open or close punctuation is appropriate to it, and what your own tendency is in punctuation. Then copy the passage, inserting punctuation marks and capital letters and paragraph breaks but making no other changes. Write in the margin of your paper the reason for each mark, or be ready to tell why you used it.

1. Erich Leichen who had been a parachute jumper and stunt man ever since the war stepped into the little frame hut that was the office of the downtown air service he said hello brothers and reaching for a magazine that he had already looked at a dozen times sat down on the back seat salvaged from a 1914 cadillac that was now doing duty as office furniture the little fellow with clear blue eyes who was president and only pilot of the one plane air service stopped pecking at the second hand typewriter in front of him and raising his feet from the floor gave the desk a shove with one hand and spun around three or four times in his noisy swivel chair hot isnt it erich and erich only grunted in reply

2. i want my photograph taken i said the photographer looked at me without enthusiasm he was a drooping man in a gray suit with the dim eye of a natural scientist but there is no need to describe him everybody knows what a photographer looks like sit there and wait he said i waited an hour i read the ladies companion for 1912 the girls magazine for 1902 and the infants journal for 1888 i began to see that I had done an unwarrantable thing in breaking in on the privacy of this man's scientific pursuits with a face like mine after an hour the photographer opened the inner door come in he said severely i went into the studio sit down said the photographer i sat down in a beam of sunlight filtered through a sheet of factory cotton hung against a frosted skylight the photographer rolled a machine into the middle of the room and crawled into it from behind he was in it only a second just time enough for one look at me and then he was out again tearing at the cotton sheet and the window panes with a hooked stick apparently frantic for light and air then he crawled

*Conversation

*Quotation marks with other marks

285

back into the machine again and drew a little black cloth over himself this time he was very quiet in there i know that he was praying and i kept still when the photographer came out at last he looked very grave and shook his head the face is quite wrong he said i know i answered quietly i have always known it he sighed i think he said the face would be better three quarters full im sure it would i said enthusiastically for i was glad to find that the man had such a human side to him so would yours in fact i continued how many faces one sees that are apparently hard narrow limited but the minute you get them three quarters full they get wide large almost boundless but the photographer had ceased to listen he came over and took my head in his hands and twisted it sideways i thought he meant to kiss me and i closed my eyes. —STEPHEN LEACOCK, "With the Photographer," *Behind the Beyond,* pp. 53-55

3. the university of north missouri lawrence missouri registrars office september 25 1938 mr a h smith 48 south street goshen maine my dear mr smith your request for a catalog has been duly received by this office we regret very much to inform you that our supply of the current edition of the catalog has been completely exhausted if there are any specific questions which you would like to have answered we shall be pleased to do so through correspondence kindly regard this office always at your service very truly yours george walstead registrar.

*Letters, Business

4. and for my part i will try to punctuate this book to make it easy for you to read and to break it up with spaces for a pause as the publisher has asked me to do but this i find very extremely difficult

for this book is the talking voice that runs on and the thoughts come too and come and go to illustrate the thoughts to point the moral to adorn the tale

oh talking voice which is so sweet how hold you alive in captivity how point you with commas semi colons dashes pauses and paragraphs—STEVIE SMITH, *Novel on Yellow Paper,* pp. 37-38

5. that subject is closed my decision stands its final instead of replying i settled myself down in an easy chair hooked a leg over one of its arms and lit a cigarette i took my time about it and although the expression on his face never varied he must have been starting to burn inside he couldnt stand anyone refusing to kowtow to him or not being sufficiently impressed by his presence and authority i took a deep drag exhaled slowly with audible satisfaction and spoke the subject was closed i said.—SIDNEY MARSHALL, *Some Like It Hot,* p. 171

*Pages 277-80

6. when all the marked words and expressions have been transferred to cards perfect the alphabetical arrangement and combine the subentries in alphabetical order under each main entry wherever there are a number of page references for one

item such figures should appear in numerical sequence the entire series of card entries may be typewritten on sheets with carbon copy for the convenience of the printer in setting be careful to show capitalization punctuation and indentions—A *Manual of Style,* Tenth edition. University of Chicago Press, pp. 176-77

7. this he observed severely to himself as he lanced his way with the ferrule of his stick through a brigade of yelling students was the higher education in new york he sighed his silver eyes tender behind the lenses of his *pince-nez* for possessing that acute faculty of observation so essential to his business of studying criminal phenomena he could not help but note the tea-rose complexions the saucy eyes and the osier figures of various female students in his path his own alma mater he reflected gloomily paragon of the educational virtues that it was might have been better far better off had it besprinkled its muscular classes with nice-smelling co-eds like these yes indeed—"The Adventure of the African Traveler," *The Adventures of Ellery Queen,* Ellery Queen, p. 1

2. Study the punctuation of some of the illustrative passages in the *Guide-Index* articles, considering the marks in relation to other traits of style, and giving reasons for the use of all marks *Pages 277-80 that attract attention or of the omission of marks that could have been used. Suggested selections: Marquis W. Childs, pages 417-18; John Dos Passos, pages 492-93; Donald B. Chidsey, page 193.

3. Make an analysis of your recent papers to see if there are any recurring problems of punctuation that bother you. Then see how far you can go toward settling these problems by reference to appropriate articles in Part Two of this *Guide-Index.*

4. Re-examine the punctuation of your recent papers. Is it consistently open or close? Is it appropriate to other qualities of your style of writing?

The Writing Process

WRITING is either hard or easy, as a person makes it. For most people who have not written very much, the chief difficulty is uncertainty as to what they should do. Worry takes more out of them than work. They try to see the completely finished paper at the very start of thinking about it, perhaps even before the topic is definite in their minds, usually before the material has been got together and lined up. At that stage they cannot even worry intelligently about the paper, much less see their way to working profitably on it.

For writing a paper is work, and it should be gone about in a workmanlike manner. There is no mystery about it (unless you find yourself doing very much better than you expect to do) and, as in all jobs, there is a definite series of steps. Each step has its characteristic problems and makes its characteristic contribution to the finished paper. The beginning of wisdom in writing, and of freedom from loose worry, is in seeing these various stages clearly so that each can be attacked by itself and the paper advanced in an orderly and profitable fashion.

This *Guide and Index* is primarily intended to help you with the smaller, more detailed problems of writing—paragraphs, sentences, words, phrases, points of grammar and style, and so on. But since these exist only as parts of whole papers, a natural background for their discussion is an account of the process of writing.

STAGES IN WRITING A PAPER WITH THE CONTRIBUTION OF EACH STAGE

1. THE WRITER'S BACKGROUND—A reservoir of general and specific information, habits of expression, etc.
2. FOCUSING ON A SUBJECT—Definition of topic, listing of problems involved and of possible sources of information
3. GATHERING MATERIAL—Notes (in mind or on paper) from memory, observation, interview, reading, speculation
4. EVALUATING AND SELECTING—A tested and selected body of information to be presented in the paper
5. PLANNING THE PAPER—A synopsis or outline of the paper
6. WRITING THE FIRST DRAFT—Tentative copy of the paper
7. REVISING—Necessary changes in material, corrections and improvements in the words, sentences, paragraphs
8. PREPARING THE MANUSCRIPT—The completed paper, ready for readers or for printing
9. SEEING THE MANUSCRIPT INTO PRINT—The printed copy

Writing a paper can be divided for convenience of discussion into nine stages, shown in the accompanying table. Any such analysis must be somewhat arbitrary because of the variable conditions involved in a particular article—the writer's habits and background, his purpose, the complexity of the material, the length proposed, and the time at his disposal. In a letter to a friend the stages are telescoped and can hardly be identified, but in writing a letter applying for a job each may be painfully distinct. The questions and problems of all the stages taken together are enough to swamp a person, even a professional writer, but by taking one step at a time each can be disposed of, and an orderly, workmanlike process can replace the jumble of worries.

Making due allowance for the telescoping of some of these steps and for the varying weight given each because of the differences between writers and between specific pieces of writing, we may take them as typical of most writing activity. They are confessed more or less definitely in many descriptions of their work made by professional writers. An experienced feature writer tells how he turns out articles:

> First, I fix upon the particular aspect of the particular subject which I wish to treat. Second, I outline the questions which require to be answered in treating this subject. Third, I supply from my own resources what part of the answers I can. Fourth, I complete my answers by additional study and by personal investigations—inquiry from competent persons, or personal visits to whatever places may be necessary. When all the questions are answered satisfactorily, the material is ready to be organized and written out.—PAUL SCOTT MOWRER, in H. F. HARRINGTON, *Modern Feature Writing*, p. 37

*Forms of discourse

*Factual and imaginative writing

Our list of stages applies primarily to the process of turning out an expository article, like a magazine article or course paper, but the steps are not so very different for the "creative" sorts of writing, though the process may be more difficult to watch. In stories, for example, there is usually an outside stimulus that turns the writer's mind to a theme, or person or situation, a period of gathering material, either from memory, from observation, or (as for a historical novel) from a period of specific research. The material crystallizes into some form, perhaps from seeing a climax or a purpose; and then there is writing and revision and preparation of copy. In describing the writing of one of his stories, Irvin Cobb shows that his background played a larger part than it would in most factual articles, but several steps of the process are given:

> It will not require many words for me to give you the genesis of my story: *The Belled Buzzard.*
>
> One morning I was returning in a motor-boat to my father-in-law's summer cottage on Tybee Island, Georgia, after a fishing trip to the mouth of the Savannah River. On a sand-pit a flock of buzzards fed on a dead shark. The sight of them, with their ungainly, flopping movements, their naked heads and their unwholesome contours, set me to thinking. My mind went back to the stories I had heard in a country newspaper-office in Kentucky of that hardy annual of rural correspondents, the belled buzzard. To myself I said that here a man might find material for a short story.
>
> That same day I got the notion for my beginning and picked on a name and a personality for my principal character. The following day, I think it was, my climax came to me, all in a flash.

I was busied for the moment with other work but when I returned North, a fortnight later, and went up to the Adirondacks, I sat down and wrote the yarn in about four days of fairly steady grinding. The *Post* printed it and it became perhaps the best known of all my serious stories.—In T. H. UZZELL, *Narrative Technique*, p. 292

It is useful for an amateur writer to look at his writing habits, especially to find the stages that he does best, enjoys the most, and to find the stages that give him difficulty. Realizing which these last are (and something of the feelings that accompany them) will show where to work for improvement. One student in a composition course diagnosed her case this way:

1. General interest in some subject.
2. Collecting and reading material or concentrated thinking—expansion.
3. Rest.
4. Deducing some idea.
5. Attacking it any way, some way—to get a start.
6. First draft. Bad, very bad. All sorts of irrelevant ideas crop up. No sense to anything. Despair absolute.
7. Dutifully hanging on to some thread.
8. A sudden inspiration. New viewpoint of the whole thing.
9. Shaping an outline.
10. With outline in mind and in *sight* beginning fresh copy.
11. Gradual and painful progress. Matter of discrimination. Pulling in all relevant material. Arranging material so that it will bear upon a POINT. Translating into language my deductions.
12. Finally an end.

Am in habit of thinking slow (perhaps chaotically)—writing slow—and usually get stuck at points #5 and #6—and very often cut the whole process off right there—result: all sorts of blasphemous statements.

A more detailed discussion of the typical activity and some common problems of each stage will help you prepare to attack your own writing tasks with confidence and a sensible program of work.

1. The writer's background

You don't start writing any paper from zero, and though your background may not be exactly a step in writing, it is so fundamental that it must be considered. Probably the subject and some of the subject matter, certainly your general attitudes and ways of thinking, as well as the words and habits of expression that you have accumulated, will be put to use in writing any

*Appropriateness to speaker or writer, p. 47

*Affectation

291

given paper. Out of this background, of course, comes the entire material for a good many papers—accounts of earlier experiences in school, in sports, with books, with people, from travel, hobbies, jobs; from it ought also to come the point of view—the way you look at your subject—without which the paper is likely to be impersonal and dull. This background should also furnish some individual words and personal phrases, illuminating figures of speech and illustrations, incidents, information, bits of color and life that can contribute to the main subject in small but important ways.

*Figurative use of words, p. 229

*Allusion, p. 241

Your background is steadily growing and the value of new experiences and ideas can be increased by combing your memory to bring to light half-forgotten experiences and enthusiasms, considering past and present together, and bringing your whole mind to bear on your writing. If you do this, your papers will sound as though they were written by a living person, not by an automaton, and they will, furthermore, sound as though they were written by you, not by anyone else.

2. Focusing on a subject

The first step in producing a particular piece of writing is to focus your attention upon some field of knowledge or experience, or upon some definite topic. This is done almost automatically when you decide to write a letter to someone—Mother, Father, Fred, or Janet. A great deal of the writing in the world is assigned or so closely controlled by circumstances that the writer has relatively little choice. A professional writer makes an article out of material that he has on hand or that he gathers because he is especially interested in it or has special opportunities for getting it, or he is assigned a subject and gathers material with which to develop the article. In college some topics are assigned and must be made the best of, but usually you have a list from which to choose, or a specified type of paper is assigned for which you can select the exact content. If you make yourself write on a distasteful subject, you have handicapped yourself at the start. So far as possible take subjects that you do or could or would like to *talk* about.

2a. Subjects from the writer's experience. Your experience, no matter how limited it may seem to you, will have some bits that are not common to everyone, and anyway the parts that really interest you can be made interesting to others, in writing as in conversation. Your family, the people you have known, either as individuals or as groups or types, your school experiences, your jobs, hobbies, sports, the places you have lived in or visited, your opinions and ideas, all offer material. It will be useful early in a composition course to think over your more interesting experiences and make notes of those that are promising for future use in papers.

Often the choice of subjects in college should grow out of your desire to extend your experience, to know more than you do about something in history, literature, economics, biology . . . wherever your interest has been aroused. Except in course papers that call for routine summaries of material, choose a subject in which you will not be merely hashing over some stereotyped material or just rewriting something you have read. Take a subject to which you can make some contribution, no matter how small, in attitude or opinion, in illustration or application drawn from your experience.

*Chapter 13, p. 319

2b. Subjects for investigation. When the paper is to be based on research, you should choose a subject that you have some curiosity about, that you have some reason for wanting to know about, so that you will feel that you are learning something worth your attention as well as preparing a paper. Everyone would like to know a little more about scores of subjects, subjects that come up in conversation (What is the BFF? a sharecropper? What are the Nuremberg laws? What is the Atlantic Charter exactly?) or that have been touched on briefly in a course. There are the whole fields of history, of science, of literature, of social organization to choose from. Following a topic in books and periodicals will produce the material for an informal paper or for a research paper with footnotes and bibliography.

*Page 322

2c. Limiting a subject. Sometimes a writer chooses a subject that is too small for the length of paper he is attempting, so that he has to build it out by going into considerable detail or by touching on closely related matters. But ordinarily students choose subjects that are much too large. College papers are short; even one of 1000 words would fill only one newspaper column, or be a quarter as long as the typical magazine article, or a little over two pages in this book. The purpose of a paper is to illuminate a reader, to give him some special information or ideas, not just to remind him that the subject exists. Choose one that can be handled adequately in the length expected. There is not much point in writing 1000 words—or even 5000 words—on Benjamin Franklin, but something could be done in a short paper with some phase of Franklin's career, his work as post-

293

master general, his part in the founding of the University of Pennsylvania, his relations with some person, his life in Paris, or perhaps with an attempt to sketch from his letters the great number of things he worked on in a single year. Similarly "peace" and "war" are too large topics for discussion; the subject should be narrowed to some particular phase—the opinions of a certain social class or group, the use of radio in war, the effect of a treaty or some such particular act, the work of some person, something about the emotions of people in peace or in war.

Once your attention is fixed on a subject, the material already in mind begins to gather and to help you foresee what other information may be needed and where it may be found. For long papers a working bibliography of books and articles that may be

*Final choice of subject, p. 323

of use is part of this preliminary analysis. Sometimes the subject cannot be definitely narrowed down until after some material has been gathered. If you are not sure exactly what the aim of the paper is, try to define it in a sentence or two, or in a question that will be answered by the paper. This will give something to tie to in the later stages of work.

At the end of this stage, you should know pretty definitely what the paper is to be about and have some idea of how and where you will get the material that is to go into it. Obviously the earlier you decide these questions, the more time you will have for the later stages of the paper. It is too late to decide what you will write about when you sit down to put words on paper, and waiting for a subject to come to you then is a waste of time.

Focusing early on a subject that interests you and that you believe can interest your readers makes the later stages of the writing process easier and the final result worth while.

3. Gathering material

The material for letters and short papers on personal experiences may seem to come spontaneously, but often even for this writing a little time given to jogging the memory may be well spent. *By far the largest part of the time given to the composition of more elaborate papers will be spent in assembling material.* Scientific and scholarly works may represent the accumulations of a lifetime. This stage is the most likely to be neglected by a writer in a hurry—and he may wonder why he has trouble in writing a paper when the simple fact is that he hasn't the material to put down.

Material comes from memory, from observation and experiment, from interviews with people, from reading and study, from reasoning and speculating on what one has learned in all these ways, and from imagining scenes and actions, as for stories. It is hard to direct one's memory—though thinking about some past experience for a time, then later recalling it again, and so on at intervals, often brings back details that at first were forgotten. Similarly the bits of action for a story can be built up by thinking at frequent intervals of the imaginary people and actions, each time adding some details. Sources of material outside the writer's mind can be more consciously directed and skill in handling them can be cultivated. In particular a person's command of the direct sources of original material—observation, experiment, interviews—can be greatly improved by attention and by practice. A writer's chief distinction often comes from small bits of information which he has actually reported, and the interest and value of many papers rest on the amount of first hand detail they carry. The technique of research in laboratories and in documents and books has been carefully developed by scientists and scholars and one of the functions of higher education is to teach these methods. Even though our "reason" may work less accurately than our fact-finding faculties, common sense and practice in forming opinions, as well as training in logic and other college courses, can improve reasoning ability. A writer's own opinions, hypotheses, and generalizations are evolved by examining and comparing and reflecting on the data he has got from other sources. It is safe to say that nothing of importance can be written without some speculation showing through.

For short papers on simple and familiar subjects, of course, the material is carried in the writer's head though often scratch notations are a help—and they keep bits of material from slipping away. Detailed material needs a body of written notes.

4. Evaluating and selecting the material

Since the material when assembled is of varying reliability and of varying importance for the particular paper to be written, it should be gone over, sorted, and evaluated. This is a stage for questions. Is this statement accurate? Is this book reliable—in its facts, in its reasoning? Have I enough material for the paper proposed? Have I tried all the best sources? Can I get more material by talking with someone? Have the important phases been covered? Which are the most important facts and conclusions for my paper? Which are of secondary importance?

*Originality

*Evaluating material, p. 335

295

It will help you in visualizing the paper as it will finally stand if you compose a definite statement—not a title, but a sentence—of the subject as you see it after the material has been gathered and thought about. Suppose you have built model airplanes and are to "write about it." Several different papers could be written in this general field. You could describe their building in detail; you could record your own experiences, your failure or successes; you could tell of it as a hobby, and of the pleasure you and your friends got from it; you could emphasize the knowledge you gained; you could discuss the government's wartime encouragement of model building. The main point is that you shouldn't try to cover all these, unless the paper is to be quite long and stand as a thorough treatise. A sentence statement of a purpose for a particular paper might be: "The hobby of building model airplanes is instructive and in wartime has become genuinely useful." That statement would define your approach—not personal, though your experiences would be your source of details, but topical. It suggests that you might touch briefly on the hobby phase to gain interest and make contact with a reader, and then select facts about different models, identifying some types, perhaps with diagrams, and stressing especially the wartime use of the models. It would let you examine your miscellaneous material in the light of a definite purpose, help you decide to discard some and highlight other points; it serves as a touchstone for deciding whether a certain bit of material belongs in the paper or not.

This sort of evaluation is especially necessary in approaching well-known or commonplace subjects. It is not enough to take a general subject like "Learning to Drive a Car." You have to consider "In these days when almost everyone knows something about automobiles, what can I write that may possibly be of use or interest to some readers?" The result of such a question would probably be a narrowed and more explicit subject based on some of the material, perhaps coming down to "Learning the traffic regulations" or "Preparing for winter driving." Lack of some such exact sense of the topic is the cause of many failures in writing.

In making this survey of your material, it is helpful to sort out *essential* points that must be included and *contributing* points that may be used or not, perhaps for illustration, depending on circumstances in the actual writing.

The result of this stage should be a sifted body of material with which you are thoroughly familiar, brought in line with the purpose of the paper, selected after considering its interest and accuracy and importance for your purpose.

5. Planning the paper

While you are criticizing and selecting the material your paper is to present, you are thinking about the order in which the various points should probably stand. The plan—whether a picture in mind, some scratch notes, or a formally prepared outline—is a record of the order in which you expect the material will be arranged. Here for the first time you begin to face the reader, to consider his expectations and to see how they can be met.

Primarily the plan grows out of the material you have to present to your reader. You get ideas for planning a paper as you gather material, and you probably make one or perhaps several tentative outlines while you are accumulating it, and certainly while you are selecting and evaluating it. These may show gaps in the material that you need to fill in. A narrative paper can be planned early, since all that is required is for you to visualize the little climaxes or incidents that will divide it into stages. But drawing up the actual working outline, or revising a tentative outline to use as the working plan, is a relatively late stage in the writing process.

*Outline form

After you have reviewed and selected the material to be presented, the next step is to see the material in a series of blocks or stages. If it isn't easy to see what the main topics are, try listing the various small bits of material and putting side by side or in columns or on separate sheets of paper the ones that have something in common. Some people are helped by drawing squares on a sheet of paper and putting similar or related matters in the same square.

The labels over these squares or the main steps you have seen in the material are the main heads of a plan or outline. Typically a paper will have from three to five main stages or heads within the outline. *A paper with only two is likely to break in the middle, unless it is very short.* If it is a paper of 1500 words or so, five points would average only 300 words apiece—and 300 words does not say very much. Magazine articles of 6000 words rarely have more than five or six main divisions. The real process of *composing* is gathering ideas together, grouping them so that a reader can follow easily, and *any outline of more than five main heads should be examined carefully to see if the material has really been put together or if perhaps too much isn't being attempted for a short space.*

297

The small special points of the material can next be arranged under the main heads to which they belong. Sometimes they will form natural groups of related points, which will stand under subheads in the outline.

After the main blocks are determined, their order can be decided on. A typical expository article should increase in value as it goes along. The last stage should be more important, more meaningful, more intense, or more interesting than the preceding—for some reason or other it is the point you want the reader to get as the most emphatic. Try then to see your paper as a series of waves of increasing height, that is, of increasing value, not necessarily of increasing length. The beginning has the double duty of attracting the reader's interest and getting him really into the subject. The last point is the one he is to carry with him. In between, the topics can be arranged according to any reasonable plan that will advance the subject.

*Beginning
paragraphs,
p. 67

*Concluding
paragraphs,
p. 70

The plan that this examination of your material gives can then be compared with your notion of the perfect paper on the subject or with somebody else's idea of how the paper should go—just as a check on the judgment you have shown.

Some written notes, though not necessarily a formally numbered outline, will be a great help in the actual writing. In fact it will remove most of your remaining worries, for there is nothing more discouraging than to have to pause in the middle of rapid writing to wonder if this point really goes here. But it is necessary to remember that a paper cannot always be completely visualized ahead of writing, that any preliminary outline is a working plan, the best way you can see to lay out the material before you begin to write. Even the most perfectly numbered outline should be changed in the process of writing if there is good reason to change it.

After the paper is written, the plan should be adjusted to the actual development of the paper. Then, if it is to be made a part of the submitted manuscript, it should be cast in one of the standard forms described in the article *Outline form.

6. Writing the first draft

Of course some writing has been going on in the last three steps, but actual consecutive writing appears here as the sixth step in developing a paper. And if the preliminary stages (whether they took only a few minutes of concentrated thinking or weeks of reading and study) have been well done, the writing should be free from worry, perhaps even a pleasure.

Most papers that a person is taking seriously need to be written out in a first draft and then revised and written over. After the material has been gathered and a plan made, either in rough notes or in an outline, you can concentrate all your energies on expression. A long paper can be broken up into stages and each stage concentrated on and written more or less by itself. This removes the strain of trying to keep a great deal of material in mind at once.

*Writing paragraphs, p. 58

You shouldn't wait too long to get an ideal opening—this is really a sort of procrastination. The paper must be started some way if it is to be written, so that it is better to make a tentative start, the best that suggests itself at the moment, and change it later. After a few pages you will find that you are writing better, and many times a good opening will be found by simply crossing out the first paragraph or two. If the material has been well laid out, it is relatively easy to concentrate on one stage at a time and not lose energy by trying to think of everything at once.

This doesn't mean that the first draft should be careless, but simply that it is a means and not an end. For most people the first draft should be a rather rapid writing down of the material of a paper. The paper will have more life and will represent your sense of your material more closely if it is written rapidly than if you pause to perfect each sentence before going on to the next. It is usually fatal to stop to look up spelling or to check mechanics at the time of writing. Save a little time for revising so that you can make a business of tending to such small matters. Leave plenty of space in a first draft between lines, between paragraphs, and in margins to allow for working over the expression.

It is probably better to make the first draft a full telling of your material, since it is always easier to take out unwanted matter than it is to expand topics that have been done too sketchily.

Besides a good stock of material, the feeling of *being ready to write* is the best guarantee of a good paper. This is the prime result of careful work in the early steps.

7. Revising

Few people work so precisely that their first draft will represent the best they are capable of. Freed from the problems of actual composition, you can go over your work and bring it up to a desired standard of uniformity. This criticism and reworking should bring the paper to an accurate expression of your view of the subject and prepare it for a reader.

In revising, the writer takes the point of view of a reader or critic as far as he can and looks at his work to see how it will read or, if it is a speech, how it will sound. This means testing for material, for plan, and for style and the mechanics of writing.

7a. Material. A check for material is necessary to make sure that enough has been put in the paper to gain its intended purpose. Often the writer is so familiar with the topic that he forgets to put in enough details to inform or interest the readers. Occasionally there will be too much included, but not often. The first question then is, Is the material complete enough for my purpose? Does it need more examples, details? Do the facts given need more interpretation? Were my sources the best which could be obtained? The accuracy of the statements should be checked; if the writer is uncertain about anything, the uncertainty should be acknowledged by words like *perhaps, probably, I think.* The interpretations and opinions should be examined once more for their reasonableness and convincingness.

*Page 81

Trying to take the reader's point of view will result in sounder and more illuminating papers. A writer should always think, Would I like to read this paper? Could I profit from reading it?

7b. Plan. Reading the almost completed paper will test its plan. Is space wasted at the beginning? Will the first few sentences appeal to a reader and make him want to continue? Is it clear what the subject is from the beginning (or near the beginning)? Is the subject advanced by clear-cut stages, and is the relation between one stage and the next clear? That is, can a reader pass from one paragraph or group of paragraphs to the next without losing the thread? A paragraph which sounds like a new start, sounds as though nothing had been said already, needs attention. Does the conclusion leave the reader with the point the writer wants him to carry away? Is it distinctively written? Many times irrelevant matters are brought in at the last or the writing goes flabby or signs of haste are obvious. The beginning and ending of any paper need special attention in revision.

*Page 67

*Transitions between paragraphs, p. 65

*Concluding paragraphs, p. 70

*Chapter 2, p. 35

*Removing deadwood, p. 161

7c. Mechanics. Finally the paper should be examined for the small matters that can so easily mar what is fundamentally a good job. Do the paragraphs hang together? Are the sentences correct and are they direct and effective? Is the style fairly consistent, that is, either dominantly formal or informal, the colloquialisms (if there are any) appropriate? Can any deadwood be removed? Are the words as exact and meaningful as possible?

* "Minimum Essentials," p. 250

Can the paper be read aloud easily and clearly? Finally the accuracy of spelling, punctuation, and other mechanical matters, as well as the various references, should be checked.

Reading a paper aloud is a particularly good investment of time. In reading aloud the writer must read more slowly than with the eye alone and will not only catch unhappy phrases and sentences but will see more of the details, especially of punctuation and spelling. A person who makes a good many mistakes will sometimes find them more surely if he reads with a pencil point running just below the line of writing to help keep his eyes focused. It is a good idea for a writer to give a paper a special reading, looking just for his known weaknesses—the joints between paragraphs, or spelling, or meaning of words, or whatever he feels he is not sure of. Such concentration in revision will go a long way toward clearing up special difficulties.

A dictionary and a handbook should be especially useful in revision, since they will help answer many particular questions.

On page 303 is the beginning of the first draft of the radio speech given by President Roosevelt on the evening of April 14, 1938.[1] It shows the care with which a writer revises his copy and how a speech or an article may grow in revision. Some of the President's changes are stylistic, as when he changes the formal and distant "to add certain observations by way of simplification and clarification" to "to talk with you about them," or when he changes the abrupt "has received a setback" to "has received a visible setback."

Others are elaboration of points. Between the original first and second sentences he made an addition (indicated by A1) of two brief paragraphs on the appropriateness of his theme to Holy Week, ending ". . . and that it is not inappropriate to encourage peace when so many of us are thinking of the Prince of Peace." This adds a note of feeling and leads indirectly to the main topic. Other changes are in the direction of accuracy, as the "six" to "seven," and others are defensive, as changing "Spring of 1933" (when he was President) to "beginning of 1933" (when President Hoover was still in office). Insert B, about 200 words, elaborates and makes more personal the reasons for the government's delay in undertaking relief measures, and includes

---

[1] The President's speech will be found in newspapers of April 15, 1938. There is a discussion of the style of this and others of President Roosevelt's speeches by S. T. Williamson in *The New York Times Magazine* of May 1, 1938. Elmer Adler, *Breaking into Print* (New York, 1937), reproduces a number of manuscript pages by well-known writers, showing their revisions.

the material crossed out at the bottom of the page:

> But I know that many of you have lost your jobs or have seen your friends or members of your families lose their jobs, and I do not propose that the government shall pretend not to see these things.
>
> I know that the effect of our present difficulties has been uneven; that they have affected some groups and some localities seriously, but that they have been scarcely felt in others. But I conceive the first duty of government is to protect the economic welfare of all the people in all sections and in all groups. . . .

The page offers an excellent example of revision that improves style, adapts the material and the presentation more definitely to the audience, and carries out the writer's purpose more accurately.

8. Preparing the manuscript

The final step in writing a paper is preparing a manuscript for another person to read. This may be simply making a fair *Page 338 copy of a first draft, or, as in research papers, it may involve footnotes and a bibliography. Whether it is a letter, a class paper, or a copy of an article or book for publication, the aim is the same, to make a manuscript that reads easily and represents the writer's decent pride in his work. One reason for legible copy in writing courses is the mass of papers an instructor reads.

8a. Materials. The materials for copy have now been pretty well standardized. Paper 8½ by 11 inches is almost universally used, except in legal documents. For longhand copy the conventional "theme paper" having lines about half an inch apart is best. Odd sizes do not handle or file well and narrow lined note-*Typewritten book paper makes hard reading. For typewritten copy use a copy fair grade of bond paper. Certainly all papers that allow the writing to show through are discourteous to readers. Handwritten manuscripts should be in ink. Pale ink defeats the purpose of legibility and colored inks are regarded by many as in bad taste; black or blue black is the best. A good black record typewriter ribbon and clean type make a readable typed page. A magazine sometimes adds to a rejection slip "One reason for the rejection of this manuscript is the typing, which is too faint for the editor to read."

In longhand copy the ascenders and descenders of letters like *b, l, f, g* should not be allowed to cut across letters on the line above and below, and letters easily confused (*a-o, n-u*) should be made clearly. The letters of a word should be held together so that the reader's eye can grasp the word at a glance.

DRAFT #1

RADIO SPEECH

Five months have gone by since I last spoke to the

people of the Nation about the state of the Nation. ~~Five~~ *A a i A*

years ago we faced a very serious problem of economic and

social recovery. For four and a half years that recovery

proceeded apace. It is only in the past ~~six~~ *seven* months that

it has received a *visible* setback. *A A 2.*

This recession has not returned us to the disasters

and suffering of the ~~Spring~~ *beginning* of 1933, ~~but it is serious~~ *B*

~~enough for me to talk with you about it tonight in the same~~

~~spirit and with the same purpose which I employed in talks~~

~~from the White House in the earlier years.~~

Therefore *I have* Today ~~I~~ sent a Message of far-reaching importance

to the Congress. I want to read to you tonight certain

passages from that Message, and to ~~add certain observations~~ *talk with you about them,*

by way of simplification ~~and clarification.~~

Each of you is conscious of some aspect of the

present recession; it has affected some groups and some

localities seriously; it has been scarcely felt in others.

And let us agree at the outset that this recession is not

to be compared in fundamental seriousness with the great

depression of 1929 to 1933.

From *The New York Times*. Used by permission of, and arrangement with, *The New York Times* and Mr. Stephen T. Early, secretary to the President.

*Division of
words

8b. The page. 1. Leave comfortable margins on all pages. A good right margin will not only improve the looks of a page but will reduce the number of words that have to be divided at the end of lines. An inch and a half at the left, an inch at the right, an inch and a half at the top and an inch at the bottom are typical margins. Very short papers should be centered on the page.

2. Typewritten copy should be double spaced. An extra space can be left between paragraphs but is not necessary. More useful is an extra line left between the main stages of a paper.

3. Paragraphs are indented about an inch in longhand and from five to eight spaces in typescript.

4. Only one side of the sheet should be used.

5. Pages should be arranged in their proper order (it is surprising how many times they are not in order), and pages after the first should be numbered, preferably in the upper right hand corner and in Arabic numerals (2, 3 . . .).

*Titles of
themes

6. The title should be centered on the top line in longhand manuscript and about two inches from the top in unlined paper and the text begun about an inch below. A title should not be underlined or set in quotation marks unless it is an actual quotation. No end punctuation is necessary unless the title is a question or exclamation. Since the title is not a part of the body of the paper but is rather a label put upon it, the first sentence of the text should usually be complete in itself and not refer back to the title by a pronoun.

7. Common practices that should be avoided are:

Indenting the first line on a page when it is not the beginning of a paragraph.

Leaving blank part of the last line on a page when the paragraph is continued on the following page.

Putting punctuation marks at the beginning of a line. A mark belongs with the word that it follows, not at the beginning of the next construction.

*Submitting
manuscript

8c. Endorsing manuscript. Manuscript to be submitted for publication carries the writer's name and complete address in the upper left-hand corner of the first page.

Most course papers in college are folded vertically (up and down) and endorsed near the top of the outside front fold, as the instructor may direct. Most teachers want to have available:

Student's name
Topic, title, or assignment of paper
Date submitted

Other facts, such as the number of the paper, the name and section of the course, or the instructor's name may be put below these three lines. Clear and uniform endorsement of such manuscripts is a real convenience to the teacher who must handle the papers.

If the papers are to be handed in flat, this endorsement should be on the back of the last sheet or on a special title page as the teacher directs. Sheets should be held together by paper clips that can be slipped off, not by fasteners that pierce the paper or by pins, hairpins, or string.

8d. Corrections in copy. The final copy should be made as accurate as possible but later corrections are sometimes necessary. If there are many or if they are complicated, the page should be done over. If they are relatively small, like inserting a letter or a word, or substituting a single word, this can usually be done neatly without damaging the page.

Words that are to be struck out should have a line drawn through them. (Parentheses have other uses.) Words to be added can be written in the margin or between the lines and a *Caret caret ($\wedge$) inserted at the place where they belong.

The goal is a clean, legible copy that can be read by another. Reading this final copy aloud rather slowly will be a good last check to make sure that mistakes have not slipped in in the copying.

9. Seeing the manuscript into print

The manuscript form is the final state of most college writing, but some of the papers in composition courses find their way into campus periodicals. Anyway, since the goal of much writing is publication and since a college graduate is almost certain to write something that will see publication of some sort, he should know something of this last stage. It may be merely a final check preparatory to mimeographing or some other informal sort of *Proofreading publication. Or it may be an elaborate process of editing, revi- *Stylebooks sion at the suggestion of an editor, and proofreading, before the *Type words are finally published in periodical or book for general circulation.

10. Craftsmanship in writing

Perhaps our sketch of the writing process doesn't seem to pay much attention to the gliding of the pencil on paper or the click of typewriter keys. The actual work of putting words on paper is a result of other effort and its success depends completely on the earlier steps. And many people find their pleasure in these

305

earlier steps and in the finished product rather than in the physical activity of writing, as one of our most skillful English writers testifies:

> In a sense, every kind of writing is hypocritical. It has to be done with an air of gusto, though no one ever yet enjoyed the act of writing. Even a man with a specific gift for writing, with much to express, with perfect freedom in choice of subject and manner of expression, with infinite leisure, does not write with real gusto. But in him the pretence is justified: he has enjoyed thinking out his subject, he will delight in his work when it is done.—MAX BEERBOHM, "A Pathetic Imposture," *Yet Again*, p. 77

At any rate, writing is an activity, something we do. And the ideal of a writer can best be put in terms of the craftsman's ideal, of handling tools and materials well. The *materials* in writing are the facts, opinions, ideas, imaginings, and feelings that you want to put in readable shape for others. The *tools* are the sounds, words, and constructions of the English language. The materials for the most part lie outside the scope of this book, which presents a partial description of the tools and some suggestions for their handling.

In handling these tools we can't do better than stress the craftsman's ideal of good materials worked upon honestly with the right tools. Sherwood Anderson presents this ideal as it applies especially to writers of fiction but in a way that can be extended to all writers:

> Consider for a moment the materials of the prose writer, the teller of tales. His materials are human lives. To him these figures of his fancy, these people who live in his fancy should be as real as living people. He should be no more ready to sell them out than he would sell out his men friends or the woman he loves. To take the lives of these people and bend or twist them to suit the needs of some cleverly thought out plot to give your readers a false emotion is as mean and ignoble as to sell out living men or women. For the writer there is no escape, as there is no real escape for any craftsman. If you handle your materials in a cheap way you become cheap. The need of making a living may serve as an excuse but it will not save you as a craftsman. Nothing will save you if you go cheap with tools and materials. Do cheap work and you are yourself cheap. That is the truth. —SHERWOOD ANDERSON, *The Modern Writer*, p. 39

This applies equally to writers who may be simply reporting what they have seen or sketching their ideas or giving their opinions.

306

In many of the pages of this book we may seem to get rather far from ideals. But in discussing the meaning of words, the patterns of English phrases, even relatively mechanical matters like punctuation and spelling, our motive is to help you present your materials more effectively, to help in your work as a craftsman in writing to satisfy the craftsman's ideal of a good job well done.

Exercises

1. Write a description of the way in which you write, noting exactly, for example, how you go about writing a letter, a theme, or a paper for some other course. What stages in the writing give you the most pleasure? The most difficulty? How can you overcome the difficulties? *Pages 291-92

2. Consider your past experience as subject matter for papers. Do not plan an autobiography, but make up a list of specific matters that it would interest you to write about and that might interest others. Consider places you have lived in or visited; trips taken; people you know; jobs you have had; sports, hobbies, reading, plays, movies; ideas and opinions; anything at all. *Pages 292-93

3. Select a few particular topics from your list (Learning to Fish, My First Night in Camp . . .) and write down what you would need to do in the various stages of writing a paper on each. *Pages 293-94

4. Select from your experiences two subjects that you think would make good papers of 500 words each; one that would make a paper of about 1200 words. Could any of these be developed into longer papers? *Pages 294-96

5. Study an article from a magazine or a book of readings and try to discover the various sources of material used by the writer. How much of it seems to have been gathered at first hand? How much value do the opinions and reflections of the writer contribute?

6. Make an outline of an article in a magazine or a volume of readings. Use one of the methods suggested in *Outline form, §1.

7. Make a list of all the points you might possibly put into a paper drawn from your experience. Jot them down as they occur to you. Later arrange the topics, discarding some and grouping the rest into an outline from which you could write a paper. Hand in both the rough and the finished draft. *Pages 297-98

8. Make a topic outline for your next paper. Check it carefully for matters of form described in *Outline form, §2.

9. Make a list of the changes you made in revising a paper,

*Pages
299-303

grouping them under material (adding, omitting), plan, grammatical and mechanical matters (spelling, punctuation, sentence movement . . .). Which of the weaknesses corrected are generally characteristic of your writing? Can you think of specific ways to eliminate them?

10. The following papers are a small set of themes received from an assignment to write a paper of about 600 words that would give a reader information about something of which the writer had special, first-hand knowledge.

Read a paper through once to get a general impression of its material and arrangement. Then make a list of the words or phrases or sentences that you think deserve special comment, identifying the locution by indicating the line in which it occurs, as, from the first paper:

> Line 4   soda-jirker Sp   Correct: soda-jerker

Note places that you think especially successful. By reference to articles in Part Two of this book note, wherever helpful, real mistakes or ineffective spots—spelling, punctuation, use of words, sentence structure, paragraph movement, or anything you think might be improved.

Write a statement commenting on the successful and unsuccessful qualities of the paper, giving the writer any advice you think he might profit by in revising this paper or in improving future work. Consider the interest and value of the subject, the method of development (use of details and so on), the organization, specific matters of style and usage. Assign a grade, in the system used at your institution, that will show in your opinion the relative merit of the papers. They range from unsatisfactory to excellent.

1. BLACK AND WHITE, PLEASE

"Black and White."

"Yes, Sir." In the space of approximately twenty seconds the customer has his soda in front of him. Continually throughout the day the three or four soda-jirkers are putting out sodas, 5 frappes, milk-shakes, and many other soda-fountain combinations.

A crew of sixteen work in the Frank Foster Stand on Jackson Beach from one end of the bar to the other. Not all jirking sodas because even specialization is present in such a simple trade as the roadside refreshment business. Clam man, grillmen, ice-cream 10 scoopers, soda jirkers, chefs, and stock manager are all included in the crew of sixteen. Salaries range according to the position and responsibility that one holds. The manager and assistant manager naturally are the highest paid as they have to know the racket throughout. Next in line comes the stock manager. He has charge of receiving all the stock, and taking invintory every Sun- 15 day night. Then are the fellows in charge of their various departments, the soda-fountain, ice-cream department, the grille, and the clams. Specialization occurs in that each man is assigned to one of the departments in which he is most efficient. Naturally there are one or two of the help that are able to work in all the 20 departments.

The ice-cream scoopers are usually the greenhorns learning the trade. They do all the lugging of the ice cream cans when the load comes in on the trucks, and usually all the dirty work in cleaning up around the stand. Cries of "Sorry! All out of maple- 25 nut," "Chocalot up" are heard continually from the ice-cream section throughout the rush that usually lasts for at least three hours a night.

A little further down, the grill men are actually sweating water as the heat around the frier-elators and grille usually reaches well 30 above 100 degrees. "Mustard and relish on your frankfurt, sir," "Half a pint of clams and french fries, please" are heard from that end of the bar. Each one doing his particular job such as toasting the rolls, cooking the frankfurts, and pasting them. Or breaking the clams while the other cooks them.   35

The work at the soda-fountain is a little bit more complicated. Usually there are four men who work on this fountain as it is a double one. As well, the men have to take care of the dining room service and the bar service. Two men take care of service while the other two take care of the bar. Here these men put up 40 everything from a soda to a Banana Royal and Parfaits. By closing time the bar is a filthy mess which means another hour's work or so before the help can quit for the night. When everything is set for the next day, all leave for a few hours sleep before cries of "Coffee Ice Cream Soda," "Have you any Raspbery Sherbert," 45 "Four frankforts with Mustard," and "A quart of clams" start all over again from morning to night.

2. This Caulking Problem

To be sure there is a right and a wrong way to do everything, and unfortunately some things done wrongly result in bad affects in one form or another. The caulking of a boat is no exception to this rule. A good caulking job is easily done, and if successful, makes it possible for the boatman to enjoy a carefree and unwor- 5 ried season. However if the poor yachtsman fails to use proper materials, or an insufficient amount of time, of course it can but be expected that a leaky hull and perhaps a mid-season layup will be in order.

10 The job in itself requires nothing but time, patience, and but a limited amount of skill. Luckily enough the materials are comparatively inexpensive, consisting mainly of caulking irons, hammer, reamer, caulking cotton and perhaps a little caulking compound. The process can be classified into really two big steps,
15 the first being to clean out the seams, removing the old cotton and paint, and the second being the replacement of old cotton with new. This in itself presents no problem, as it's merely a matter of knack. The whole process is simply to ream out the seams, being careful to get out all the old cotton, then taking
20 some new cotton, rolling it up into thin strands, and with hammer and iron, inserting these strands, firmly between the seams. However in this there is danger; danger of putting so much cotton in the seam that it can't close up properly after the swelling process is started, which results either in a split bottom plank or
25 bent ribs. To avoid this, the boatman must see to it that his seams are filled with cotton to the extent that it can't be pushed out easily with a knife, but not to firmly imbedded so that even a reamer has difficulty in removing it. Rather than this, a solution to the problem can be found by using a limited amount of cotton,
30 and by placing as a background, more or less, of the cotton a little non-hardening caulking compound. This completes our caulking job.

If possible, the engine should be left out of the boat at the launching. This for the simple reason that the chances are ten
35 to one that if the boat is caulked really properly, it will sink, and stay under water for at least a two day period. In this period, from the time the bottom first hit the water to the time the boat is rehauled up on the ways, the seams will have had time to swell, swell to the extent that the cotton is made sufficiently tight to
40 keep the hull dry, and to the extent that the soft compound, which formed a temporary filling, had been completely pushed out of the seams. Of course in the case of larger boats, this method of temporary sinking is impractical, and can be remedied by placing the boat on strong supports, and filling the bottom
45 with from two to three inches of water, enough to do the swelling from the inside out. It will be found that the above method is perhaps more desirable than the other yet conceived. It permits the hull to swell without the danger of buckling, and it makes for stronger seams, since all the caulking is cotton, and none the
50 soft compound.

3. SWIMMING

Swimming as a sport started about forty years before the war, and since then it has sprung up to be the leading pleasure in the water world. As a result of the thousands of people that swarm to the beaches and lakes, many different sports were started all

involving swimming. I'm not going to describe about anyone par- 5
ticular thing in swimming, but am going to describe certain things
about swimming and the sports that have swimming as a base.

Speed swimming started forty to fifty years before the war,
when Harvard University had a swimming meet with a small college from the south. As a result of this meet, many men origi- 10
nated different styles of their own which started swimming, as a
sport, to the top of the atheletic world. Speed swimming is entirely different than any other kind, in that it takes more energy
and stamina to stay with it. Speed in the water is based especially
on the form of a person. If a man is slow, rides high or low in the 15
water, and has no rhythmic leg kick, he is not suited for the
speed world. If on the other hand, a man is quick reacting, rides
level in the water, and has a rhythm, he is worth considering. To
make a speed swimmer, many months are needed to teach him
these fundamental traits. New leg kicks are shown him, new arm 20
strokes are demonstrated, and different ways of breathing illustrated. As soon as these fundamentals are learned, he starts training to perfect these strokes. These are just the first important
laws that go into the perfection of a speed swimmer.

In the year 1931, the swimming coach of Yale University intro- 25
duced a game into the swimming world known to all as "Water
Polo." In spite of the fact that it is the roughest and most daring
game known it has become the rising thing in the water world.
Played much the same as basketball, only in the water, each team
tries to advance the ball to its opponents goal. It was played 30
mostly among the older groups, but was later taught in boys
camps to see how a youngster handled himself in the water. Today
it has become a nation wide sport, and is now played in some
girls colleges.

Due to the mad rush of the American people to the beaches 35
and lakes, the most helpful enterprise was established; namely
"The American Red Cross Life Saving." Due to so many drown-
ings in the past, this organization was started chiefly to teach the
person what to do in case of an accident. It was chiefly taught
to life guards at the beaches, but soon became a government law 40
that everyone should know something about the service. To-day
it is taught in camps and schools as well as in clubs and
Y.M.C.A.'s. This service is divided into three units. First, the
Junior Life Saver, taking in the children from the age of twelve
to sixteen, the Senior Life Saver, taking the ages from sixteen to 45
twenty, and the Examiners from the age of twenty to the end.
All members are given tests which are renewed every one or two
years. This is the greatest thing that has sprung from swimming,
and the one most used.

Before the World War, a certain group of men got together and 50
formed what is known today as "The Olympic Games." These

311

games are held in a different country every four years to determine
which country is best in the field of sports. Here was where swimming reached its peak. Dashes, long distances, and relays were
55 the events that were run off. Time records were established from
these games, individuals became interested, and new records were
sought for. Due to these games and the interested coaches, swimming mended its way into the heart of every college.

These are only a few of the sports that were derived from
60 swimming. Aquaplaning, serf boarding, and diving are others
that were started and had swimming as its base.

4. It's Not As Bad As You Might Think

Most people have seen an auto-trailer, but because the majority have never lived in one or have never even had a good
look at the inside of one, the feeling is that they contain only a
few things, and that only those who have little money ever travel
5 in them. In attempting to clear up or correct this erroneous thinking, I will try to paint a picture of the inside of one of these
streamline covered wagons, and then give some of the benefits
derived from owning one.

Using as an example a trailer that sells for about three thousand
10 dollars, we'll see what they jam into its small space. In the rear,
immediately after coming through the backdoor, we would find

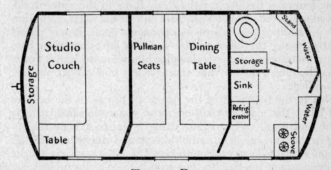

TRAILER DIAGRAM

the kitchen, a unique arrangement in that everything is in an
arm's reach. There is no walking from one cupboard to another
or back and forth from the sink to the stove, as is necessary in
15 most houses. In a trailer everything is compact, and yet all the
kitchen necessities are there. We find a table-high combination
cooking and heating stove across from the porcelain sink. On
the walls are cup-boards, and two twenty-gallon steel water tanks
are stored away in the rear wall. To the right of the backdoor,
20 small I will admit, is a toilet, but although there is a mirror and
a shelf in the room also, there is no wash basin, for the sink in

the kitchen is used for bodies and dishes alike. The modern trailers will have a small electric refrigerator, however you'll still find many that have only a box-like affair that uses ice.

Coming forward a little we will find a compartment, com- 25 prised of closets and pullman seats, that is used as a sitting-room in the daytime. This same room, during meals, can be converted into a dining-room by moving the seats forward and by pulling down a table which lies flat against the wall that separates this room and the kitchen. These seats make up into a six foot 30 double-bed, as does the studio couch that is in the next compartment. Both of these couch-bed affairs run crosswise and just fit into the space allotted to them. Also in this third compartment, to the side, is a small table and a straight chair for writing.

The trailer is equipped with electric lamps and wall connec- 35 tions, a radio, from six to eleven safety-glass windows, and two roof ventilators. In every available space there are closets or small shelves, the latter being connected to the walls in such a way that they can fold back and lay flat—as does the table in the middle compartment, out of the way—when they are not in use. 40 The majority of trailers, by the way, are now constructed of steel, with about an inch and three-quarters of dead-air space in the walls for insulation. Also I should mention that a trailer in the price-field that I have been speaking of, is about twenty feet long, a little over six feet wide, and a good six feet high.   45

Of course this description has been of the enumerating type, but what I'm trying to stress to the reader is that a great deal is contained in this little space, in this house-on-wheels. In fact, almost everything that is needed for a couple of weeks vacation is included in some nook or corner.   50

5. Used Car Lot

A long white arbor covered with a gaudy yellow-and-black awning; a little shanty off to the side, with a mammoth sign overhanging its provincial whiteness— Smoky traffic roars by, leaving trailing wisps of stinking smoke. Dribbles of pedestrians slowly stroll along and idly gape at the shining stock on hand of Brad- 5 ley's Used Cars.

Beneath the protecting canvas, the front line or "show cars" waited for prospective customers. Late Cadillacs, sporty Fords, Buicks and other popular makes showed off their merits here. Back of these stood late model cars, not as expensive as their 10 brothers in front. The rear line had the "bargains," cars that any salesman would be glad to get rid of for fifty or a hundred dollars.

George, a conservative, well-dressed college man, disposed of the first line stock for prices ranging from $500 to $1000 or more. 15 Fisher's stand was the middle line. Hard-bitten and a good busi-

313

ness man, he could handle the toughest prospects easily. Hagar, a flashy, loud, fellow took care of the last line, commonly called "jalopy row."

20 The cars of the first two lines received 15 or 20 repair operations. Motor work, fender straightening and touch-up jobs were necessary on all. New tires were never put on. Instead, the originals were retreaded by a vulcanizing process which cost about $6 and lasted for 10,000 miles. Tires not badly worn had their treads 25 regrooved by a red-hot cutting tool. Retreads looked like new tires and regrooves seemed slightly worn to the suckers. To compensate for the seeming paradox of a 15,000 mile car riding on excellent tires, the mileage would be cut down to six or seven thousand. Every car in the lot had its mileage turned down at 30 least 1/3 of its original distance. Sharp-eyed mechanics always made mileage and tire conditions agree. Turning mileage down is a common practice in businesses of this sort, despite stringent laws to the contrary. It was a "well-if-he-does-it-I-can-do-it" situation. Other operations were merely check-ups. Wheel align- 35 ment, windshield wipers, upholstery and pedal pads came under this heading. At an expense of 15 cents, new pedal pads could be put on, checking any possibility of the prospect's guessing how far or how hard the car really was driven. Inexpensive checking of small points paid profits in the end. The last line of cars re- 40 ceived only a motor tuning and a polish, but surprizing enough, were a lucrative investment. The company's price policy answers this possible inconsistency.

Salesmen were paid $25 straight salary plus a 2% commission on sales. On the front of every car was a cardboard tag sup- 45 posedly bearing the car's record number for the company's books. It was, however, a code by which the salesmen could determine the price they should get and the price they could take for that particular car. A number such as 665705 meant: get $675 but take $650, the second, fourth and sixth numbers being the "get" 50 price; the first, third and fifth, the "take" figure. If a salesman sold over the top asked figure, the difference was split between him and the company. Therefore, on the third line of cars, where running condition instead of age was a prime necessity, prices wholly out of line from the true value were received. Because 55 of a great turn-over of third line cars, the company realized a larger percentage of profit on the "jallopies" than on the first line automobiles.

This used-car lot was sponsored by an organization which sells over a million cars a year, so it was by no means a fly by night 60 affair. Although no sloppy repairs were done, and no highly crooked deals were tolerated, there was just a slight suspicion that the company was getting the best of the customer on every

314

deal. This company, however good or bad, is representative of many similar organizations in the United States.

6. Electrolysis in Cosmetology

In studying the structure of hair we find that it grows thru the skin in a tube like pore, technically known as the follicle. At the bottom of the follicle are the hair papilli cells, and it is from the papilli that the hair gets the nourishment that causes it to grow. Since the papilli is the only source of nourishment it is logical 5 that only by completely destroying it that the growth of the hair can be stopped permanently.

For this purpose in a beauty shop, a multiple electroylsis machine, that is many needles, usually twelve, is used. The needle is made of platinum about three-quarters of an inch long and a 10 slightly bit thicker than a hair. The source of electrical current is a dry cell battery and the wiring is such that the needles carry a negative charge, which as we know will disintegrate body tissue. A single red wire carries a positive charge and is used to complete the circuit. 15

The first step in use of this machine is sterilization not only of the needles but of all objects that come in contact with the patient. A sterilizing lotion other than alcohol is used for this purpose. Alcohol will retard the chemical decomposition and also causes the pores to contract making it difficult to insert the 20 needles.

It is essential that the patient is in a comfortable position so that the muscles and nerves are relaxed. Taunt muscles make insertion of the needles difficult and it is impossible to work on a patient under nerveous strain. The operator, too, must be in a 25 comfortable position as standing and bending soon becomes very tiresome.

Placing the needle into the follicle is not a difficult task as one uses a derma-lense and gives consideration to the natural growth of a hair. Hair follicles naturally grow at a slant of twenty-five 30 to forty degrees. The needle is inserted in a straight line along the angle of growth. Pressure is not used at anytime to force the needle as such action will cause the needle to pierce the follicle, enter the skin tissues, cause pain, and miss the papilla. The needle will slide easily into the follicle, so that when placed at 35 the wrong angle it will pierce the skin warning the operator of incorrect insertion. There will always be a slight resistance when the needle reaches the papilla thereby signifying to the operator that the proper designation has been reached. After the first needle has been placed the second is then inserted, not to close 40 to the first as this would centralize the disintegration and cause

315

a slight pain. As other needles are inserted the current is stepped up.

When the last needle is inserted the first hair treated is usually
45 ready to be removed. Never allow a needle to be inserted over two or three minutes. The hair is lifted out with a tweezer and if the disintegration is complete the hair will come out freely. If there is any resistance it is a sign that the follicle has not been completely destroyed and the needle should be reinserted to continue the
50 action.

After removing a needle a substance will come to the surface, this is the decomposed cells, it should be removed immediately as it will become hard upon reaching the air and form a scab called an *escher*. Formation of eschers will prolong healing and
55 if picked off by the patient will most likely leave a scar. The liquid will also be on the needle and should also be wiped off immediately or it will crystalize and make reinsertion impossible. This liquid trapped under the skin will be carried off through the body's waste system.
60 After the treatment hot towels should be applied in order to open the pores allowing most of the liquid to escape thru the skin and to stimulate circulation and in that way carry off the trapped waste. Cold towels should follow the hot ones to insure a cleansing and rapid closing of the pores so that eschers cannot
65 form. An astringent lotion should be applied after the cold towels to complete the action.

7. BAKING BREAD IN MASS PRODUCTION

Although bread is the basic food in one's meal, and has been for hundreds of years, there are thousands of people ignorant of how bread is really made due to the fact that to-day almost everyone is dependent upon the modern bakery. No longer is it nec-
5 essary for the housewife to add to her hardships in preparing a meal to have to bake bread daily when for a small sum it is possible to purchase each day enough fresh bread to supply a moderate size family. Therefore, as so many are dependent upon our modern bakeries, the following is a description of the process by which
10 large size bakeries follow in the production of thousands of loaves.

The first operation naturally is the getting to-gether of the proper ingredients, consisting of flour, yeast, milk, sugar, salt, malt extract, shortening, and water, and all bakeries make sure
15 that the ingredients they purchase are of first class standard. Having obtained these the making of the white bread, otherwise known as pan bread, can begin. There are two methods, one known as the Sponge Dough Method, and the other as the Straight Dough Method. The Sponge Dough Method is where
20 the making of the dough is divided into two sections. A quantity

316

of flour, water, and yeast are thoroughly mixed and left to thoroughly develope, after which it is put back into the dough mixing machine and re-mixed with the balance of the ingredients, namely, sugar, milk, salt, malt extract, and shortening, where it is again left to raise until it is thoroughly matured. It is then 25 ready to be made up into the loaves of bread of whatever size is wanted. The Straight Dough Method is where the entire ingredients are put into the mixer to-gether and mixed in one operation, the dough left to develop until such time as it is ready for sealing into the required size loaves. 30

In the process so far a very important function is taking place, that is fermentation, and there is nothing left to guess work, as the dough is thoroughly checked from time to time as to the proper temperature, and all ingredients are exactly and precisely scaled according to the formula used. 35

After the dough is thoroughly developed it is taken and put into the Dough Dividing Machine which divides the dough into pieces according to the weight required. From this it goes into another machine, which rounds it up into a ball, and it is left to further develop for another ten or twelve minutes. Its next 40 course is into the Moulding Machine which shapes it into a loaf of bread to go into the pan. After the loaf is in the pan it is left to further develop until it is about twice its original size, and then it is put into the oven to bake.

Again the use of the termometer is very necessary to see that 45 the oven is of a proper temperature to bake the loaf, which takes about thirty to forty minutes, according to the size of the loaf, and the larger loaf naturally requires a longer time to bake than the smaller one.

After the loaf is baked it is left to cool naturally, and when cool 50 it is put into the Slicing Machine, and directly from the Slicing Machine into the Bread Wrapping Machine. This operation of slicing and wrapping the bread is done without touching the loaf after it is put into the slicing machine. This operation has been a big help to the public, because much complaint originally came 55 to the bakers, due to the bread being crumbly, which many times was not the fault of the bread, but was because of the poor knives used in the process of slicing the bread. The length of time from the first mix of all the ingredients to the wrapped loaf is approximately seven hours. This again would vary in many varieties, 60 according to the type of bread baked.

In conclusion it might be stated that in bakeries of to-day the question of guess work is entirely eliminated. Many Bakeries use laboratory tests of all ingredients, and are continually sampling different grades of flour. Many bakers blend a flour grown in the 65 southwest, a flour most commonly known as Winter Wheat Flour, and a flour raised out in the Dakotas, Montana, and Min-

nesota which is a Spring Wheat Flour. The Winter Wheat is
sewn in the fall of the year, left in the ground all winter, and is
70 harvested very early in the summer. Whereas the Spring wheat is
sewn in the spring of the year and matures at a little later time
than the Winter Wheat Flour. These two flours are of a different
character and a proper blending of the two is very important.
But either one of these flours will bake a very good loaf of bread,
75 if and when used seperately.

The Research Paper

A COLLEGE LIBRARY is for fun and for work. It furnishes an almost limitless number of books and periodicals for leisure reading, and for study its accumulation supplements the laboratories, lectures, recitations, conferences, and textbooks in the main work of education—that of furthering the intellectual development of teachers and students.

The college library is not fundamentally different from the school and public libraries you have already been using, though it may well be larger and more complexly organized and furnished with a greater number and variety of specialized works. It has its standard organization, its staff of specialized librarians, stated hours, rules for the circulation of books, a system of classifying and arranging books to which the key is the card catalog, the stacks full of the books themselves, and various special locations of particular kinds of works. All these a student needs to know, for a self-reliant use of the library is absolutely necessary to carry on college work. This training is necessary too for later life. A college graduate isn't expected to know everything, but he ought to know how to find out about almost anything.

For your leisure use of the library you need to know its general rules, how to find books through the card catalog, the location of the recent periodicals, the new-book shelf, the fiction section, the location of any particular sort of book that specially interests you, the provisions for browsing and casual reading, the most comfortable chairs and the best lighting. You need also to know the difference between ordinary rapid reading and careful study, that is know when to read fifty to a hundred pages an hour, getting the gist of a story or of some light book, and when to read thoroughly, digesting carefully for some definite purpose all that the writer says.[1]

This chapter does not deal with leisure reading, but with one phase of library *work*, as it applies to writing a paper for which the material is entirely or largely drawn from reading, called variously a term paper, or source paper, or research paper.

1. Purpose of a research paper

A research paper is a record of study in some special field, scientific, social, historical, literary. Genuine or "original" research is the discovery and discussion of material that has not been generally known; undergraduate research is usually based on published information that has been gathered by someone else. *It is primarily a record of intelligent reading in several sources on a particular subject.*

Since a good deal of college work is acquiring and becoming able to discuss the information and ideas of others, a standard method of discovering material, making notes of it, and presenting it has been developed. Preparing a research paper gives practice in using this method. The research paper in composition courses often emphasizes method and form and so prepares a student for later papers in other courses. Advanced work in literature, history, and the social sciences especially depends on this sort of study, and in sciences a laboratory experiment is often supplemented by research in what has been previously

---

[1] For helpful suggestions for the former see C. Gilbert Wren and Luella Cole, *How to Read Rapidly and Well* (Stanford University, 1935), and for the latter, Mortimer J. Adler, *How to Read a Book* (New York, 1940), Part 2.

done. The same methods, more elaborately developed, are the basis of graduate work in the various professional schools, the means by which theses and dissertations and monographs are manufactured. These methods of research are also the basis of many sorts of reports and industrial studies. A glance at the "learned journals" in a college library will show that there are periodicals in every field of knowledge which contain research articles written by specialists, usually for other specialists. Such articles are produced by these research methods and presented in what is only an extension of the form described in this chapter. A freshman "research paper" is a start on the road of scholarship that extends through the advanced courses in college to the work of professional people who are steadily adding to the knowledge and understanding of the past and the present.

Besides offering training in research methods, a paper of this sort shows the various stages of the writing process very clearly. Because of its length each stage becomes of particular importance. A mistake in choice of subject will make all later work a chore; gathering the material is by far the largest part of the task; selecting material and planning the paper are conspicuous because of the amount there is to be said; and the form of manuscript requires special attention because of the footnotes and formal bibliography. Each stage takes time and judgment and gives an opportunity to observe and practice various methods of composition.[1]

At first thought the writer's contribution to a research paper seems slight. The material is from sources outside his experience, the style is impersonal and rather formal, and the intention is primarily to inform rather than to entertain or to move. But actual work on a paper shows how large a part the individual really plays. He chooses the subject, in line with some interest of his own. He not only uncovers the material, often using considerable ingenuity, but he must use his judgment constantly in selecting which of dozens of facts fit his purpose. This purpose he has defined for himself, and he arranges his points in a plan that will accurately emphasize his sense of their relative value. The methods of gathering material have been worked out by thousands of research workers who have pre-

[1] Because of the size of the job and the length of time needed to complete it, the best procedure is to read this chapter rapidly to get a general idea of what will be expected in the different steps of the process and then to study each section and do the appropriate exercises as each step becomes due.

ceded him, the form of the manuscript has been standardized, but the actual content represents the writer's interest and judgment at every step.

Furthermore, a research paper is not necessarily a series of facts alone. Facts must be *interpreted*, for only the most common knowledge can stand without some comment on its meaning. Questions of causes, of results, of importance are not settled by recording information; a mind must work on the data to find the proper relationship between them and to see their meaning in perspective. No one can gather and present intelligently the materials of a research paper without leaving his mark on them.

The main purpose of a research paper, from the point of view of a composition course at least, is to give training in college writing, in gathering, reflecting on, organizing, and putting in readable form material gained from study. But much of the interest as well as the profit for the writer comes from the material itself, from learning something new and becoming a bit of an authority in a small field.

2. Subjects

You can write a research paper on almost any subject, but if you let yourself choose "almost any subject" at random, you will be sorry. Such a paper is a long job and will become a bore or at least a waste of time unless you take a subject that interests you, that will add something useful to your stock of knowledge.

2a. Choosing a field. The natural way to begin choosing a subject for a research paper is to consider a field in which you are really interested. It may be business or medicine or engines or dress design . . . or anything else. It may be a field that you are studying in another course, chemistry or history or social science or a language; any course touches briefly on subjects that you would like to know more about, raises questions that it does not fully answer.

Your own experience has raised many questions that can be answered with a little study. You may have worked in a chain store, or merely traded at one, and wondered about the organization of chain stores, or how much of the country's business they handle, or the reasons for special taxes on them in some states. You may be interested in some person, living or dead, and want to know more about him. You may have wondered about some past event mentioned briefly in the news—the Chaco War, the Know-Nothing Party, the Open Door Policy in China. You may play a saxophone and want to know some-thing of its development and rise to popularity. You may be interested in some recent development in technology: synthetic rubber, the pseudo-bass circuit in small radios, sulfanilimide and related remedies ...; or in some organization: Quakers, the Asso-ciated Press, government agencies of information and censor-ship, exactly what the C. I. O. is. The range of possibilities can only be suggested. Books and periodicals can furnish informa-tion about them all to be used in writing a research paper.

A good type of paper can be developed by taking an opinion you hold or think you hold and doing some reading to find evidence for it. You may approve or disapprove of some of the projects included under "socialized medicine," or of hazing in colleges, or of the closed shop, of radio supported by public assessment rather than by advertisers, or of any one of scores of problems, simple and intimate or complex and socially im-portant. Although starting with an opinion may lead to selec-tion only of material that fits your case, as in a debate, an honest attempt to find sound factual reasons is a useful project —and may result not only in a better based opinion but a more thorough understanding of the problem.

Although any topic is possible, there are some that you should be warned against. It is good sense to avoid topics that are too commonly used, that do not represent a genuine individual choice, the kind that students fall back on as a last resort— the history of baseball, control of venereal diseases, swing vs. classical music. Your instructor can tell you what topics he has found students take thoughtlessly or that in his experience have worked out badly. Topics for which the material is uncer-tain, like treatment of cancer, or for which the material is likely to be biased, are difficult because you need unusual judgment to handle them.

2b. Final choice of subject. Some of the topics just mentioned are specific enough to be treated in papers of two or three thousand words, but most have been *fields* that contain many specific subjects for particular papers. They need to be limited to something that can be treated adequately in the length of paper to be written, treated with enough detail so that you can really illuminate a reader, so that you do something besides enumerate the commonplace facts that most people already know. After a little general reading in the field you can focus on a particular subject, always bearing in mind the length you are to approximate. Better than taking "the Associated Press"

*Limiting a subject, p. 293

323

would be to take its origin, or its present organization and services; instead of "airplanes" or "aviation," the safety devices in airplanes or the possibility of air freight lines. Sometimes the library yields information on some phase more readily than on another. Perhaps you will find a topic just to one side of the one you started on, perhaps not "sources of pigments for oil painting" but "tempera as a medium of painting."

As quickly as possible you should obviously narrow your subject to one that is workable, usually while gathering your working bibliography or at least in the very early stages of note taking. Your instructor can offer suggestions for the final selection of a topic, especially if you have indicated the sort of material you would like to work in. Thoughtful and early attention to the choice of subject will make all later stages of the work easier and more profitable.

3. The working bibliography

After you have tentatively chosen a subject for your research paper, the next step is to canvass the available sources of material. You will probably read first some brief general treatment of the subject, perhaps in an encyclopedia or other reference book, to orient yourself. But before you concentrate on gathering material you need to compile a working bibliography of references that you hope will have material for you and that you expect to consult. It is wise to make this list before actually starting to take notes, to make sure that enough material on the specific subject is available in the library. This preliminary survey of materials saves time and worry in going about the actual reading and allows for intelligent selection of books and articles to be read. Finding several promising references shows that you will be able to go through with the subject and adds to your confidence in the work.

3a. Materials. Research workers have adopted or developed standard forms and materials to use in keeping track of references and notes. Everyone should have a consistent method of taking and keeping the notes from which he works. For casual work, notebooks and odd sheets may do, but for large and important jobs, such as the typical research paper, and for training in research methods, the most flexible and easily expandable materials are the standard filing cards or slips, either 3x5 or 4x6 inches. The 4x6 size is probably more convenient, since it can hold more than the 3x5 and allows for more generous spacing and labeling of material. A *separate bibliography card should be prepared for each reference* and later as many note cards of material from the reference as your purpose requires will be added to your file of material for the paper.

3b. Form of bibliographical entries.

The purpose of the bibliography card is to record all the facts about the reference that you will need to identify it, to find it in the library when you are ready to use it, and to make the formal bibliography that will stand at the end of the paper (described on pages 343-344). Each card consequently should carry these facts:

The subject of the work listed, best kept in the upper left-hand corner

The author's name, with last name first. If the book is edited, put the editor's name, followed by *Ed.*

The title of the article (in quotation marks) or of the book (underlined to represent italics)

The *facts of publication:*

Of a book, the city and date, and the name of publisher if it is needed for any reason

Of a magazine, the name of the magazine (underlined), the year, the volume, the pages covered by the article

Of a newspaper story, the name of the paper (underlined), the date, the page, and the column number if you wish

The library call number and location—for future convenience

Any other facts that relate to the reference as a reference, such as the particular pages of a book that treat your specific subject, or a comment on the value of the book

There are three chief types of bibliography cards: those made for books, for magazine articles, and for news stories. Each type has certain matters of form that should be carefully observed. The arrangement of the necessary facts on each type of bibliography card is shown in the specimens reproduced on the next page.

3c. Keeping bibliography cards.

Your bibliography cards should be kept in alphabetical order according to author (or first important word of the title if there is no author given). If there are only a few they can be held together with a paper clip or kept in an envelope or an expanding pocket file that can be bought for either of the standard size of cards. For large accumulations there are boxes and filing drawers of various sizes.

Students always ask how many references they should have for a paper. Graduate research is expected to show *all* the pertinent material. Undergraduate papers are supposed to represent a fair covering of the subject. No paper should be written relying on only one or two sources, but of course for a short paper

325

that must be done in a limited time a student can easily be weighed down by too much material. Papers that run from 2000 to 5000 words have typically from six to fifteen or twenty sources, depending on the nature of the subject and the length and thoroughness of the work.

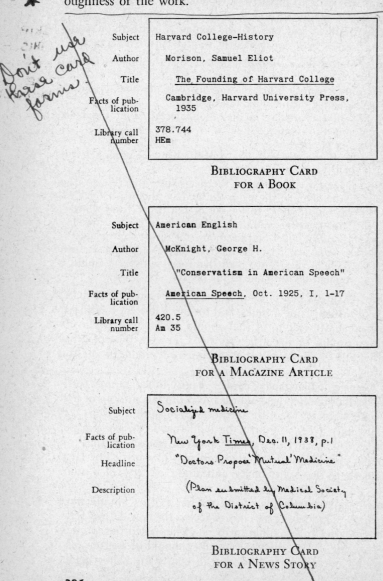

Don't use these card forms

Subject	Harvard College—History
Author	Morison, Samuel Eliot
Title	The Founding of Harvard College
Facts of publication	Cambridge, Harvard University Press, 1935
Library call number	378.744 HEm

BIBLIOGRAPHY CARD
FOR A BOOK

Subject	American English
Author	McKnight, George H.
Title	"Conservatism in American Speech"
Facts of publication	American Speech, Oct. 1925, I, 1-17
Library call number	420.5 Am 35

BIBLIOGRAPHY CARD
FOR A MAGAZINE ARTICLE

Subject	Socialized medicine
Facts of publication	New York Times, Dec. 11, 1938, p.1
Headline	"Doctors Propose 'Mutual' Medicine"
Description	(Plan submitted by Medical Society of the District of Columbia)

BIBLIOGRAPHY CARD
FOR A NEWS STORY

4. Sources of references

Almost everyone starts work on a subject with one or two sources in mind, such as a discussion in a textbook, or a magazine article, or the name of a writer or of a book that treats the subject. Very often these first readings give references to other works, and notes on them make a natural starting point for the working bibliography. Besides such informal starts there are standard sources of references which should be consulted.

4a. The library card catalog. The library card catalog lists books by *author*, by *title*, and by *subjects* treated. If you know the name of a man who has written on your subject, look up his name in the card catalog of the library. Look up also the *subject heading* that you are writing about, remembering that your exact subject may not be given but that there may be one that will include it. You may not find the heading *Skyscraper* but may find under *Architecture* or *Building construction* books that will touch on skyscrapers. The library subject card below (T. S. Eliot is the subject) and the working bibliography card show what should be taken down and what should be omitted.

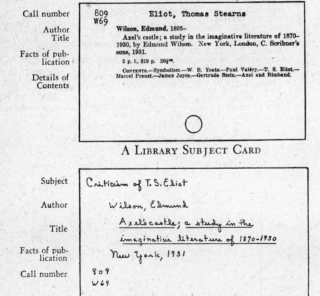

A LIBRARY SUBJECT CARD

A BIBLIOGRAPHY CARD
BASED ON THE LIBRARY SUBJECT CARD

4b. Periodical indexes. Next to the card catalog the most important source of references is the *Readers' Guide* and other periodical indexes.

1) THE READERS' GUIDE. This reference source gives under author entries (1, 2, and 5 in the illustration below) and under subject entries (3, 4, and 6 in the illustration) references to articles in some 200 current magazines. It can give references up to the preceding month and is consequently one of the most valuable sources for topics that are of current importance. The abbreviations used by the *Guide* should be filled out as they are taken down, so that there will be no future question about what they mean and so that they will be in the form expected in the final bibliography. The abbreviations are explained in a list at the beginning of each issue.

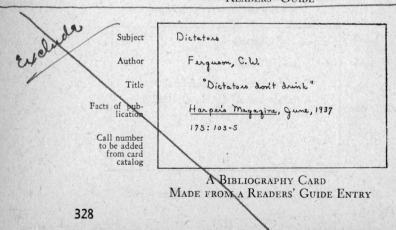

1. DEWEY, Thomas Edmund
     Pay up and shut up. Vital Speeches 3:498-501 Je 1 '37
2. DE WOLFE, Elsie (Lady Mendl)
     Modern regency. Arts & Dec 46:34-6+ My '37
3. DIABETES
     Restoration of carbohydrate oxidation in diabetic tissue in vitro. E. Shorr. bibliog f tab Science ns 85:456-8 My 7 '37
4. DIAMONDS
     Diamonds and joy. il Time 29:86+ My 17 '37
5. DICKSON, Harris
     Haunted lake. Collier's 99:72+ My 29 '37
6. DICTATORS
     Dictators don't drink. C. W. Ferguson. Harper 175:103-5 Je '37
     Dulce et decus pro dictatore. M. Ascoli. Am Scholar 6 no3:365-71 '37
     Liberalism and dictatorship; prospects for democracy. W. R. Castle. Vital Speeches 3:463-6 My 15 '37
     U.S. or them? Time 29:69-71 My 17 '37

DIVISION
Experimen
of the q
Sch J 3'

DIVORCE

Swedish d
Je '37

No to agur
DIX, Lester
     Library in
       62:447-50
DOAN, Gilbe
     Our sons s
       '37
DOBIE, Edi
     Preparatio
       My '37
DOCTOR Fa
DOCUMENT

TYPICAL ENTRIES IN THE
READERS' GUIDE

Subject	Dictators
Author	Ferguson, C. W.
Title	"Dictators don't drink"
Facts of publication	Harper's Magazine, June, 1937
	175: 103-5
Call number to be added from card catalog	

Exclude

A BIBLIOGRAPHY CARD
MADE FROM A READERS' GUIDE ENTRY

2) OTHER MAGAZINE INDEXES. There are a number of periodical and other indexes in various fields that are very useful for beginning work on a research paper. The ones marked with a † in this list are the most generally useful and should be known by everyone:

> *Agricultural Index* 1916– Indexes magazines and bulletins
>
> *Annual Magazine Subject-Index* 1908– Indexes about 150 periodicals, some in special fields, especially history
>
> *Art Index* 1929– Indexes periodicals and museum bulletins
>
> *Dramatic Index* 1908– Articles and books relating to the stage. Published also as Part ii of the *Annual Magazine Subject-Index*
>
> *Education Index* 1929– Articles, books, reports, and pamphlets dealing with education
>
> *Essay and General Literature Index* 1900– Subject and author index to published volumes of essays
>
> *Index to Short Stories*– Author and title index to stories in books and magazines
>
> †*Industrial Arts Index* 1913– Subject index to material in engineering, technical, and business periodicals, books, and pamphlets
>
> *International Catalogue of Scientific Literature* 1902– An annual index volume in each of seventeen scientific fields ~~Not in Pitt~~
>
> †*International Index to Periodicals* 1907– Indexes about 300 periodicals from various countries; includes historical, literary, political, and scientific subjects
>
> †*Poole's Index to Periodical Literature*– Articles from American magazines, 1802-1906
>
> *Portrait Index* 1906– Lists portraits in books and magazines. The *Readers' Guide* notes portraits in its entries ~~Not in Pitt~~
>
> †*Public Affairs Information Service* 1905– "Public Affairs" is liberally interpreted; a valuable source
>
> *Quarterly Cumulative Index Medicus* 1927–
>
> †*Readers' Guide to Periodical Literature* 1907– Indexes about 200 American magazines
>
> *Song Index* 1926– Indexes 12,000 songs in collections
>
> *Writings on American History* 1906– Indexes books and periodicals ?

Almost every field of study is now represented by a monthly or annual index to current material.

3) THE NEW YORK TIMES INDEX. Most libraries have *The New York Times Index*, which appears monthly and runs back to 1914. Though this indexes specifically *The New York Times*, it will serve as an index to other papers on matters of general importance because it gives the dates of events which would presumably be covered in all papers of the same date. Through

1936 or

329

this index it is possible to find many speeches and important documents as well as accounts of happenings.

4c. Bibliographies in special fields. Besides these periodical indexes there are often annual bibliographies in the learned journals in special fields and there are many bibliographies in one or more volumes that survey a complete field. Most of these are more elaborate than a student needs for his practice research paper but when he begins to work in detail in a particular field he should know any special bibliographies that lie within it. This type of work is represented by the following samples:

> *Select Bibliography of Chemistry* (H. C. Bolton), 1899-1904
> *Geologic Literature of North America, 1785-1928* (J. M. Nickles), 1931
> *Guide to Historical Literature* (G. M. Dutcher and others), 1931
> *Cambridge Bibliography of English Literature*, 1940, 3 volumes
> *Contemporary British Literature* (J. M. Manly and Edith Rickert), 1935
> *Contemporary American Authors* (F. B. Millett), 1940
> *Bibliography of Writings on the English Language . . . to the End of 1922* (Arthur G. Kennedy), 1927
> *Guide to Reference Books* (I. G. Mudge), 6th ed., 1936, and supplements

4d. Reference works. The reference department of a library has a large number of general and special works with which to answer questions. Often it is a good plan to see what one of these has to say about your subject before you do any extensive searching, because its article can help you find your way around more intelligently. The articles almost always refer you to authoritative specialized works so that they are a good starting point for compiling a bibliography. (The second step then is to see if the books referred to are in your library.)

1) GENERAL ENCYCLOPEDIAS. Everyone needs to use these great storehouses of information. They are frequently revised and you should make sure that you are using the most recent edition available.

> *Encyclopaedia Britannica*, 14th edition, 1936; later issues have some alterations and additions
> *New International Encyclopaedia*, 2d edition, 1930
> *Encyclopedia Americana*, 1936

2) SPECIAL ENCYCLOPEDIAS. Less well-known but even more important for college work are the encyclopedias and general reference works that have been compiled in various individual fields. Their articles can usually go into further detail than those in the general encyclopedias can, and the approach is more specialized. These works are usually shelved in the reference department of the library but are sometimes kept with other books in their respective fields. An early acquaintance with those in subjects in which you expect to work will be valuable. Some of the best known are:

Agriculture: *Cyclopedia of American Agriculture* (Bailey), 1908-09, 4 vols.

American government: *Cyclopedia of American Government* (McLaughlin and Hart), 1914, 3 vols.

American history: *Dictionary of American History* (Adams), 1940, 6 vols.

American literature: *Cambridge History of American Literature* (Trent and others), 1917-21, 3 vols.

Art: *Bryan's Dictionary of Painters and Engravers*, 1903-05, 5 vols.

Harper's Encyclopedia of Art, 1937, 2 vols.

Biography (American): *Dictionary of American Biography*, 1928-36, 20 vols.

Who's Who in America, biennially since 1899

Biography (British): *Dictionary of National Biography*, 1885-1937, 63 vols. and supplements

Who's Who, British, annually since 1849

Business: *Encyclopedia of Banking and Finance* (Munn), 1937

Chemistry: *Thorpe's Dictionary of Applied Chemistry*, 1937

Education: *Cyclopedia of Education* (Monroe), 1925, 3 vols.

English literature: *Cambridge History of English Literature* (Ward and others), 1907-27, 15 vols.

History: *Encyclopaedia of World History* (Langer), 1940

Cambridge Ancient History (Bury and others), 1923-34, 16 vols.

Cambridge Medieval History (Bury and others), 1911-32, 7 vols.

Cambridge Modern History (Ward and others), 1926, 13 vols.

Music: *Grove's Dictionary of Music and Musicians*, 1927-28, 5 vols. and supplements

Philosophy and Psychology: *Dictionary of Philosophy and Psychology* (Baldwin), 1910, 3 vols.

Religion (and related subjects): *Catholic Encyclopedia*, 1907-22, 15 vols. and supplements; *Dictionary of the Bible* (Hastings), 1898-1902, 5 vols.

> Encyclopaedia of Religion and Ethics (Hastings), 1908-1927,
> 13 vols.
> Jewish Encyclopedia, 1901-06, 12 vols.
> Science: Hutchinson's Technical and Scientific Encyclopaedia
> (Tweney and Shirshov), 1936, 4 vols.
> Van Nostrand's Scientific Encyclopedia, 1938
> Social Sciences: Encyclopedia of Social Sciences (Seligman and
> Johnson), 1930-35, 15 vols.

General and special dictionaries are described on page 197 in
Chapter 7.

3) YEARBOOKS, ETC. For facts and (especially) figures, there
are numerous series of annual publications that are valuable for
the information they contain and for what they can direct you
to. A few are:

> The American Yearbook (facts about the United States), 1910
> to date
> Commerce Yearbook (U. S. Department of Commerce)
> The Statesman's Yearbook (Political and industrial information
> about the British Empire and other nations) 1864 to date
> World Almanac and Book of Facts, 1868 to date. (This is the
> one general reference work that an individual can afford to
> own and anyone with a serious interest in affairs can hardly
> afford to be without.)

Besides these specific sources that must be covered, there will
always be chance references. Almost every article or chapter
will mention something else on the subject or give some clue
that can be followed up. Talking with people who work in the
field will produce suggestions. The sources of material spread
out like a fan—one source leads to another, and, if you work
long enough in a field, friends and sometimes even strangers
may give you clues without being solicited. Because one reference leads to another, it is usually safe to start work on a
subject if you can turn up two or three references at the beginning. Systematic work and ingenuity, following up hunches of
where material will be found, will almost always enable you
to find enough to finish the job.

Since one reason for the assignment of papers is to train
students in methods of research work, you should do as much
as possible without asking for help. The library has reference
librarians and assistants, but they should not be bothered until
you have exhausted your own resources or unless a problem
has come up in tracing a reference or locating a book that you
cannot solve by yourself.

5. Gathering material: Note taking

Most research workers take their notes on the 3x5 or 4x6 slips or cards because they are flexible—they are easy to handle and to sort—and because they can be indefinitely accumulated and can be kept in good order by the use of guide cards that have tabs on which subjects can be written. Even for a small job, such as a course research paper, they are the most convenient materials. Students should accustom themselves to using them.

5a. Form of notes. The three essential parts of the contents of a note card are:

The material, the facts and opinions to be recorded

The exact source, title and page number, from which they are taken

A label for the card, showing what it treats

It is usually a waste of time and effort to take notes in numbered outline form. It is important simply that the material be clearly noted and clearly labeled. A handy form of hanging indention, in which the second and succeeding lines are indented, is shown in the specimen below, which works well for typical material that can be taken in blocks. If the data is made up of a number of small particular facts, some scheme of tabulating should be worked out.

Keeping track of the exact source will tax almost any note taker. Remember that the final paper will have footnotes referring to the exact page from which the material comes, and work out some system for keeping track of the title and page. Some note takers put these facts at the bottom of the card, but it is easy to forget to write them down after the card has been written.

Source

Label   First Harvard Commencement   Morison, Founding of Harvard Coll

Notes with page references

257   1st Harvard commencement Sept. 23, 1642
    Gov. Winthrop, his guard, the magistrates of the Colony come from Boston by ferry or barge

258   By 9 or 10 a.m. audience on benches in the college hall. 9 in graduating class. Splendid formal procession. (Details given)

259   Long extemporaneous prayer in Latin; Latin salutatory oration; one of the graduates gives oration in Greek; exercises in Hebrew
    Adjourn at 11 for dinner and strolling in the college yard.

SPECIMEN NOTE CARD

It is safer to record the source first. The specimen card shows a convenient form. In the upper right corner put the author's name and a short form of the title—just enough to make reference to the full bibliography card easy and sure. In the left margin, opposite the note, put the exact page on which the material was found. Inclusive pages (as 87-114) are not to be used unless the note actually describes or summarizes what those pages say. Later cards from the same source can be numbered 2, 3, 4. . . .

The subject of the card is most conveniently placed in the upper left corner, where it can be instantly seen. It should label the subject of the material on that particular card. This procedure not only identifies the card itself but makes it possible to sort the cards in preparation for outlining and writing the paper.

Notes need not be taken in full sentences—words, phrases, topics are enough. It is not often worth while to copy notes. They are means to an end (a good paper), not works of art themselves. Take workable notes, in ink, as you do the reading, and don't bother about copying them except for some very good reason.

5b. Suggestions for taking notes. Usually it is best to read the article or chapter through rapidly first to see what it contains for your purposes. Then go over it again, taking down the necessary notes. From the first few references you will need to take a good many notes, but after you have accumulated quite a bit of material, perhaps a long reference will give only a few additional facts.

Rules for what to take cannot be laid down. Your judgment will improve as you go on, and the guidance of teachers in special subjects is almost necessary at the start. Here are two general points that will apply to all topics:

1) *Distinguish between the author's facts and his opinions.* Label the opinions "So-and-so thinks. . ." In general pay most attention to the facts presented (unless of course your topic is about opinions, as for instance in a paper on "What Reviewers say of Hemingway's short stories"). You will need the facts as the basis of your own opinions, and you will need them in writing your paper as material and as evidence for your own opinions.

2) *Distinguish carefully between direct quotation and summary of your writer's material—and take as little quotation as possible.* Quotations should be carefully marked by quotation

marks. They should be taken only for good reason: unusually important material, crucial for your paper; a striking statement you may want to quote in your paper; controversial or difficult material that you need to think about before deciding exactly what it means for your subject. Almost everything else should be digested in your own words and so reduced to the scale of the paper you are writing.

Accurate notes are one of the chief tools of scholarship, and early and careful practice in taking them is excellent training that may be useful in all college courses and in a great many jobs after graduation.

6. Evaluating material

Since composing a research paper is in large part an exercise of judgment, it is important to evaluate the sources being used. "I found a book in the library that said . . ." is a confession of careless work; *the point is to find the best books, the most recent authoritative material on the subject.* Most of us cannot evaluate references until after we have done a good deal of work in a field and we must at first fall back on the opinions of others. In reading several sources you are likely to find remarks about other sources—that so-and-so is the recognized authority, or that so-and-so has misused certain figures, and so on. These should be noted and if they seem reasonable should be taken into account in using the material.

For recent books it is often possible to find a review that will be some indication of the book's value. Many reviews in newspapers and general periodicals deal with the interest rather than the accuracy of a book, though they sometimes discuss this too. The best sources for reviews of serious works are the learned journals of the appropriate fields: the *American Historical Review* for historical works, and so on.

After you have worked awhile on a subject you are in a position to evaluate a good deal of the material yourself, and your serious opinion of the value of articles and books should influence you in choosing which to use.

Notes of criticism are part of the bibliographical division of the work and should be entered either on the bibliographical card or on a separate card to be kept with it.

Sources are often classed as *original* and *secondary*. An original source is a first record of certain facts or the closest that a person writing now can come to the subject he is discussing; a secondary source is something written by someone else using the original sources. In a paper on a literary subject, for instance, the original sources are primarily the works written by the man you are discussing, or letters, diaries, and so on that he wrote or that were written by others who knew him; secondary sources are what a critic or historian has written about the man and his work. In a science, original sources are usually records of observation or experiments made by some person; secondary sources are based on these records. In history, original sources are records of all sorts or responsible reproductions of them, letters, diaries, documents, and remains, such as coins, tools, buildings; secondary sources are a "historian's" account based on these evidences. Textbooks and reference works are all secondary sources.

Graduate research relies chiefly on original sources. Undergraduate papers are drawn principally from secondary sources, but a student who is trying to do a thorough job should try to use some original sources. He certainly should come as close as he can to the first record of the facts he is to use. In choosing material to present he should try to find the closest and most reliable material he can.

7. Planning the paper

After the material has been pretty well gathered, the work of planning and writing is not essentially different from that of any other type of paper. Since the material is gathered from study instead of from memory or observation, it seems more objective; you can review it easily by reading the notes over; you find it easier to think about it as *material* and do things with it. If you have taken your notes well, with only closely related facts on a single card, you can sort into piles the cards that contain facts belonging together. As in any paper, the main divisions grow out of the material you have to present—it is this material grouped into a few stages.

Review
Planning the
paper, p. 297

Because of the amount of material and the length of the paper to be written, you will have to make some sort of outline before writing. You should try to group the material in from four to six stages—not more unless the paper is unusually long. To check the plan, and to make it possible for your instructor to examine it and make suggestions, you should cast it in one of the standard forms of outline.

*Outline
form

If you have the time, it is wise to keep the outline around for a day or two and look at it closely to see if it is a real grouping of the facts and ideas you are to present, one that your reader can follow easily and one that represents your understanding of the material and your intended emphasis.

8. The first draft

By this time you should be thoroughly familiar with your material. Even though you have been reviewing it as a whole and thinking it over in the last two steps, it is a good idea to read your notes through once or twice to get them freely in your mind. Then you can deal with them easily, without just transcribing from note cards to paper.

This review of the material will also help you get it into your own words, to get it away from the form in which you found it and to get it into the proportion in which it belongs in your paper. Digesting the material into your own words is important. If you are inclined to be lazy or hasty (or—as happens once in a great while—dishonest), you will tend to follow your sources too closely. It is the intention of the assignment that you are to take information from various sources and work it over into a form of your own. You are supposed to digest it and not just reproduce it. Direct quotation should be kept to a minimum, used only for striking or very important matter, and should always be indicated by quotation marks or, if it is more than a sentence or two, by being indented in the copy. The quotations should be brief; often a part of a sentence will be all that is worth quoting and the rest of the material will be summarized in your own words. The purpose of this advice *Plagiarism is not just to "prevent copying" but to encourage the proper method for producing a paper of this sort, which is to learn something new from reading and then write about it.

Because the finished paper is to give credit in footnotes to the sources from which you have taken your facts, you will have to work out some way of keeping track of the sources in the first draft. One simple way is to put in parentheses after a statement an abbreviated form of reference to the source used. For the first note on the specimen on page 340 this might be:

A House Committee on Veteran's Affairs was constituted, with Royal
C. Johnson, a Legionnaire, Chairman (Duffield, 260).

Or the reference may be put in the margin opposite the statement it applies to. Then when you make your final copy you can present the data in the proper footnote form.

The traditional style of research papers is formal and imper- *Choice sonal. It is not usually necessary for the writer to refer to him- between self at all, and if it is made, the reference should be brief. But personal and impersonal writing does not have to be stupid. It simply means impersonal that you put down your material as compactly and directly as styles, p. 43 possible. You will often find yourself writing more concretely and more compactly than the sources you are using.

9. Footnote form

Any paper that is based on a study of the writings of others should acknowledge the sources used. It is only common courtesy (or decency) to give credit where credit is due; it is a sign of scrupulousness to tell the sources of specific statements, so that a reader can judge for himself the evidence they are based on; and it allows an occasional interested reader to turn to the sources for further information with a minimum of effort. College students are expected to draw their materials from varied sources, and a frank acknowledgment of sources actually used in a paper is not only businesslike—it will raise an instructor's respect for the student who makes it.

In rather informal papers the sources may be given in a note at the beginning or at the end of the paper:

> The material for this paper was taken from Marquis W. Childs, *Sweden—The Middle Way* (New Haven, 1936).

Or the source may be thrown in parentheses following an important statement, or built into a sentence:

> (Marquis W. Childs, *Sweden—The Middle Way*, page 68). . . .
> Marquis W. Childs says in *Sweden—The Middle Way*. . . .

In formal academic papers—reports for courses, term papers, theses, dissertations—it is conventional to give exact references to sources of material in footnotes. The forms used at different institutions and in different "learned journals" vary slightly in mechanical details, but the aim of all is the same—*to record in some brief and consistent form the author, title of work, facts of publication, and exact page from which each quotation and each essential fact is taken*. The style suggested in this article covers the ordinary problems of using footnotes in the usual college paper.

9a. Handling footnotes. (1) *Footnotes are needed:* For all direct quotations except well-known bits from the Bible or other literature that are used for style rather than content, *and for all important statements of facts or opinions that are taken from written sources*. The writer is the best judge of the importance in specific passages. Obviously figures, dates, descriptions of situations, opinions, interpretations, and the like that are presented to advance the theme of the paper need a stated source.

Material from conversation, from lectures, from any source that a reader cannot turn to is acknowledged in the text of the paper or in a prefatory note. The source of a diagram, table, or illustration is not given in a footnote but under the title directly beneath the diagram (See example on page 9).

If two or more sources contribute to the same information, they may be put in one footnote, separated by semicolons:

[1] Stuart Robertson, *The Development of Modern English* (New York, 1938), pp. 516-20; Charles C. Fries, "The Periphrastic Future with *Shall* and *Will* in Modern English," PMLA, 1925, xl, 963-1024.

2) *The reference figures* are placed slightly above the line at the end of a quotation or *after* the statement whose source is being given. A reference mark may be put after the first important statement in a paragraph with the understanding that the material that follows is from the same source until a new reference mark is given. But it is now more usual in undergraduate papers to put the reference mark at the end of the material from a particular source, typically at the end of a paragraph (as in notes 1 and 3 in the specimen page following).

3) *Reference symbols* (* § †) are no longer used in scholarly work, though they may be used in articles or periodicals in which few footnotes occur. Rather the notes are numbered either from 1 up on each page of manuscript or from 1 on through a paper or article or through each chapter of a book. The latter scheme is now more used than the page by page numbering.

Although the number of sources referred to in a paper must vary with the type of subject and the kind of sources used, typically a student research paper will show from two to four footnotes to a page of typewritten manuscript.

4) In the completed manuscript, footnotes may be put directly following the line in which the reference mark appears, separated from the text by lines:

The first theater in Boston was not opened until 1794, but

4 A. H. Quinn, A History of the American Drama from the Beginning to the Civil War (New York, 1923), p. 115.

long before that Harvard students had been acting plays in their rooms. The diary of Nathaniel Ames, who graduated in . . .

Or the footnotes may be grouped at the foot of the page as shown in the specimen. The first method is sometimes preferred when the copy is being sent to a printer, but the second is easier to prepare and more usual. With a little practice enough space can be saved at the bottom of the page to contain the needed notes.

A House Committee on Veteran's Affairs was constituted,[4] with Royal C. Johnson, a Legionnaire, Chairman.[1]

The number of lobbies in Washington today is a difficult fact to discover because of the secrecy attached to many of them. Frank Kent in 1930 placed the number having headquarters in Washington at 145. Of that number he said 60 were really effective with sufficient financial or voting strength back of them to compel consideration.[2] About the same time E. P. Herring listed 423 organizations with permanent representatives in Washington.[3] It seems probable that the number is even higher today. Some say there are 750 regular lobbyists and when a tariff bill is introduced more flock in from all over the country.

Recent developments in the methods of these lobbyists have been toward an ever-increasing use of indirect methods, and one authority says "It can fairly be said that the most effective lobbying is being done through the use of the indirect methods."[4] These can be roughly divided into three classes: prompting constituents to bring influence on their legislators, campaigning for the election of the "right" legislators, and direct moulding of opinions of the public.

To prove to legislators that if they do not vote a certain way they will offend constituents at home, lobbyists instigate a flood of letters and telegrams that descends upon representatives from their districts. It comes in all forms, much of it clearly revealing that it was prompted by pressure groups. On one occasion a Senator received ten telegrams addressed to Charles H. Thomas when his middle initial was S.[5]

The American Legion lobbyists use this method of pressure more effectively than any other group.

> Occasionally a legislative crisis comes, and then the Legion
> machine shows its full strength. From the Legislative Committee
> of the Legion goes forth a telegram to forty-eight State Command-
> ers of the Legion who relay it to twelve thousand Legion Post Com-
> manders throughout the country who in turn pass it on to seven
> hundred thousand Legionnaires. The telegram reads like this: Use
> every legitimate means to see that the Senate passes the Blank
> Bill with enough majority to override a presidential veto. Use
> letters, telegrams, and radio to bring pressure on your Congress-
> men and Senators.[6]

1 Marcus Duffield "The American Legion in Politics," The Forum, 1931, LXXXV, 260.
2 Frank R. Kent, The Great Game of Politics (New York, 1930), p. 259.
3 E. P. Herring, Group Representation Before Congress (Baltimore, 1929), p. 276.
4 E. B. Logan, "Lobbying." The Annals of the American Academy of Political and Social Science, 1929, Supplement to vol. CXLIV, p. 61.
5 Ibid., p. 13.
6 Duffield, p. 260.

Page from a student research paper

9b. Form of footnotes. There are many small particular matters of form in the handling of footnotes, and no discussion of the subject treats them all. The most common and important for undergraduate papers are these:

1) The *author's* name is given with first name or initials first. (In entries in a bibliography, the last name comes first.)

2) The *title of a book or magazine* is underlined.

3) The *title of a periodical article* is put in quotation marks.

4) The *first time a book is mentioned* in a footnote, the facts of publication, city and year (and if desired, the publisher's name between the city and year) are given. The first time a magazine article is referred to, the year, volume number (in Roman numerals), and page are given.

9 Lyon G. Tyler, Williamsburg, the Old Colonial Capital (Richmond, 1907), p. 224.
10 Thomas H. Eliot, "Funds for the Future," The Atlantic Monthly, 1938, CLXII, 225.

5) For *later references* to the same source, a short form is used, enough to identify the particular work in the bibliography:

Author's last name alone if not more than one work by the same man is being used:

11 Tyler, p. 239.

Author's name and a shortened form of the title if more than one source by the same man is used:

12 Tyler, Williamsburg, p. 236.

For a magazine article, the author's name and the magazine and page are enough:

13 Eliot, The Atlantic Monthly, p. 227.

6) *Ibid.* means in general "in the same place" and in a footnote means "in the same book or article." It is used, underlined, to refer to the work cited in the immediately preceding footnote.

14 Robert S. and Helen M. Lynd, Middletown (New York, 1929), p. 44.
15 Ibid., p. 162.

Ditto marks are not used in footnotes.

7) Occasionally other matter—an added fact, a statement of a different opinion—is included in footnotes, but this sort of thing should be kept to a minimum. In college students' work it is well to confine footnotes to references to sources.

8) The following *abbreviations* are commonly used in footnotes. Those that come from Latin (like *ibid.*) are usually underlined to represent italics.

art.—article

c. or *ca.* (*circa*)—about a given date (c. 1480)

ch. or chap.—chapter; chaps.—chapters

col.—column; cols.—columns

ed.—edited by; edition (2d ed.)

f.—following (one following page); ff. (more than one following page: p. 286 ff.)

ibid. (*ibidem*)—in the same work, as explained in §6

l.—line; ll.—lines

MS.—manuscript

n. d.—no date (used when the date of publication of a work cannot be found)

n. p.—no place (when place of publication cannot be found)

n. s.—new series (of a periodical: *Science,* 1925, n. s. xlii, 418)

p.—page; pp.—pages (p. 162; pp. 162-68)

tr.—translated by

vol.—volume; vols.—volumes. (*vol.* and *p.* are not used when figures for both are given: vol. III; p. 682; but—III, 682)

The following abbreviations were formerly in general use but are less common now:

cf. (*confer*)—compare (now usually replaced by the English: see)

et al. (*et alii*)—and others (used instead of giving all the names when a work has several authors; now *and others:* C. W. Young and others)

infra—below (referring to something discussed later in the article)

loc. cit. (*loco citato*)—in the place cited (referring to a previous indication of source)

op. cit. (*opere citato*)—the work cited (sometimes used instead of repeating the title of a work: Tyler, *op. cit.,* p. 256; but now a shortened form of the title is more usual: Tyler, *Williamsburg,* p. 256 as explained in §5)

passim—in various passages (referring to a matter discussed in several places in a given book or article)

q. v. (*quod vide*)—which see (sometimes used to suggest consulting a work, now more generally replaced by *see*)

seq. (*sequentes*)—following (replaced by f. and ff.)

supra—above (referring to something already discussed in the article)

vide—see (now replaced by the English word)

9) When the material used is taken at second hand from a work, both the original source and the source from which it is taken should be given.

16 William Caxton, Preface to <u>Eneydos</u> (1490), quoted Albert C. Baugh, <u>A History of the English Language</u> (New York, 1935), p. 241.

10) Law cases are cited according to the following form:
The plaintiff's name, *v.* (= *versus*, against), the defendant's last name, the volume number of the reports in which the case is given, the abbreviations for the report series, the page on which the case begins, and the year in which the decision was rendered:

    17 Lochner v. New York, 198 U. S. 539 (1905)

For further details of the less common reference problems see The University of Chicago Press, *Manual of Style* (10th ed., Chicago, 1937); S. F. Trelease and E. S. Yule, *Preparation of Scientific and Technical Papers* (Baltimore, 1936); or the form of footnotes used in the better scholarly journals of the field in which you are writing.

Any description of the form of footnotes makes their use seem harder than it really is. If you have good notes that have the exact sources of their facts clearly recorded, it is relatively simple to keep track of the necessary sources in the first draft and then to place them in the final manuscript in the proper form.

10. The final bibliography

A finished research paper has a bibliography of the sources actually used in its writing—which does not mean that all the items consulted will be listed but only those which have given material. This is partly a record of work done but principally it is to help a reader identify exactly the works used and cited in the footnotes.

The form of bibliographies has been pretty well standardized so that author, title, facts of publication, and if desired a word of criticism can be given economically and systematically. There are various minor differences recommended by different publishers or different universities. For instance, the three main parts of the bibliographical entry may be separated by periods or by commas:

    Abelson, Paul. The Seven Liberal Arts. New York, 1906.
    Abelson, Paul, The Seven Liberal Arts, New York, 1906.

The period at the end of the line is unnecessary and often omitted.

Sometimes the name of the publisher is given between the place of publication and the date:

    Kennedy, Arthur G., Current English, Boston, Ginn and Company,
    1935
    Kennedy, Arthur G. Current English. Boston: Ginn and Company,
    1935

In some bibliographies the items are grouped under headings "Books," "Periodicals," "Miscellaneous," but this practice is not so common as formerly; now all items are usually run in one series. If the publishers are given, their names may be placed between the place and the date of publication, in parentheses or between commas. These are small matters; the important point is that the various items should be clear and the entries consistent.

This short bibliography shows a simple and workable form:

BIBLIOGRAPHY

Ames, Nathaniel, "Diary," <u>Dedham Historical Register</u>, 1890, I, 9-16, 49-52, 111-119 [A group of periodical articles]

Matthews, Albert, "Early Plays at Harvard," <u>Nation</u>, Mar. 19, 1914, XCVIII, 295 (Or: 98, 295) [A periodical article]

Quinn, A. H., <u>A History of the American Drama from the Beginning to the Civil War</u>, New York, 1923 [A book]

<u>Records of the Linonian Society</u> 1768-1790, MS in Yale University Library [Unpublished material]

Tyler, L. G., <u>Williamsburg, the Old Colonial Capital</u>, Richmond, 1907 [A book]

All the items are arranged in one alphabetical list, according to the authors' names. When there is no author, the work is best listed by the first important word of the title: *Records* comes between *Quinn* and *Tyler*. Specimen bibliographies are at the ends of some articles in this *Guide-Index* (*Colloquial and written English) and there is a general bibliography with brief descriptive notes on pages ix-x.

A student should look at the form of bibliographies in the books and articles he reads and should make careful note of the changes from the form presented in this article that are suggested by his teachers.

11. The completed paper

Since writing a research paper is in part an exercise in method and form, you should follow carefully the practices suggested in this chapter and any changes or additional points given by your instructor. Otherwise you are not profiting by the training offered or preparing yourself for later academic papers.

Typically the completed paper would comprise these units (Those in brackets are optional):

Title page, giving the title of the paper, writer's name, the date submitted, and any other information asked for.

[*Preface*: In a preface the writer talks about his work. Usually you will not need a preface, but if you wish to thank someone for special help, or to call attention to some unusual material, or to note some point that you wanted to but were unable to treat, state the points briefly in a preface. A preface stands on a page by itself.]

Outline: Make the type of outline directed. Be sure that it is brought in line with any changes in your original plan made in the actual writing of the paper. Check its form by reference to the article *Outline form. The outline can serve as a table of contents if you give at the right the page on which the treatment of each main topic begins.

Text of the paper: This is the final copy of your paper, complete with footnotes, with any diagrams or other illustrative material. Put the title at the top of the page and follow the manuscript form usually expected of you. Before making this final copy, go through §9 of this chapter once more to make sure that your footnotes follow the form suggested there. [*Diagrams, graphs, etc.]

Bibliography: On a separate page give in the form suggested in §10, page 343, your final bibliography, the list of books and articles actually used in writing your paper. If you want to, make brief comments on the sources, at least indicating the most useful ones.

[*Appendix*: Occasionally a paper needs some rather long table of statistics, too long to work into the body of the paper, or a long quotation, as from a treaty or other document that much of the paper is based on. Such matter can be placed in an appendix.]

Exercises

1. The following list is made up of subjects too unspecific and too broad for successful treatment in a research paper of moderate length. They are fields rather than subjects. Pick out two or three which interest you, study them, and work out for each one at least one subject which you could handle in a research paper. [*Pages 322-23]

> Racing rigs for sailboats
> Gliders and sailplanes
> Reed instruments in orchestral music
> The Amateur Owners and Pilots Association
> The photoelectric cell
> Plastics and light metals

The forty-hour week
Swing records
South American wars for independence
Ethiopia
Anesthetics
ASCAP
Federal housing vs. private construction
Basic English

*Pages 323-24 **2.** List two subjects, either from question 1 or entirely of your own invention, on which you would be satisfied to write a research paper. State why you are interested in each subject. Other than general reference works, do you know in advance any particular source? Does each subject seem to you likely to produce a paper of the right length, or does it need narrowing or enlarging?

3. Locate in your library the following: the card catalog, the Library of Congress catalog (if it is open to the public), the encyclopedias, *Pages 327-32 *The Readers' Guide, The Dictionary of National Biography,* and the *Dictionary of American Biography.* If possible, find out something about the meaning of the reference symbols in your library's card catalog system.

4. Make out about half a dozen bibliography cards on the subject *Pages 325-26 which appealed to you most in Exercises 1 and 2. Try to get some for articles in periodicals as well as for books. For suggestions about the form of your cards, see page 327.

5. Check the value of one of the books for which you made *Pages 335-36 out a card in Exercise 4, following the methods outlined in §6, page 335. Find out what you can about the author as well as about the book.

6. Find out who wrote the article in the *Encyclopaedia Britannica* on your subject and find out what you can about him.

7. Look up one of the following men, using the sources indicated for each. Write a paper of 300 to 500 words, taking as your subject *not* the biography of your man but significant *differences and disagreements* between the sources you use. Be on the lookout for emphasis on creditable or discreditable episodes and for implied or explicit estimates of the character and historical importance of your man, as well as for disagreements over what might be considered matters of fact.

John Paul Jones: *Dictionary of National Biography, Encyclopedia Britannica,* and *Appleton's Cyclopedia of American Biography.*
Fra Filippo Lippi: *Encyclopaedia Britannica, Catholic Encyclopedia,* and Robert Browning's poem, "Fra Lippo Lippi."

Warren Gamaliel Harding: *Americana Encyclopedia, Dictionary of American Biography,* and *Encyclopaedia Britannica.*
Henry IV of France: *Encyclopaedia Britannica* and the *Catholic Encyclopedia.*
Savonarola: *Encyclopaedia Britannica* and the *Catholic Encyclopedia.*

8. Hand in an outline of the research paper you are planning *Page 336 on the subject which you have chosen and for which you have completed a preliminary gathering of material.

9. Put the following references to source material into con- *Pages 341-42 sistent footnote form as they would appear in a research paper. Keep them in the present numerical order.

1. To pages 425 and 426 of a book by Allan Nevins called American Press Opinion, published in 1928 by D. C. Heath and Company, Boston.
2. To an editorial in the Boston Traveler on December 2, 1940, entitled The Responsibility of the Press.
3. To pages 309 and 310 in a book called Press Time. The book has a subtitle: A Book of Post Classics. It was issued by the New York Post but the exact date is not given.
4. To page 39 of the book mentioned in 1.
5. To pages 110 to 114, inclusive, of the same book.
6. To an unsigned article called The Versailles Treaty which appeared in The Nation on April 26, 1919.
7. To an article called How to Read Editorials, written by Roscoe Ellard. This article was published in 1937 in the National Council for the Social Studies' seventh yearbook, which was called Education Against Propaganda, published in New York.
8. To an article entitled Letters to the Editor As a Means of Measuring the Effectiveness of Propaganda, written by two men, H. Schuyler Foster, Jr. and Carl J. Friedrich and printed in The American Political Science Review for February 1937, pages 71 to 79. This issue of the magazine was part of volume 31.
9. To pages 317 to 324 of the second volume of The Prairie Years by Carl Sandburg, published in 1926 in New York by Harcourt Brace and Company.

10. Put the items in the preceding exercise in proper form and Pages 343-44 order for a bibliography.

PART TWO

INDEX TO ENGLISH

THESE ALPHABETICAL ARTICLES contain the following types of information:

1. **Grammatical points**—Definitions and examples of usage of such matters as *Case, *Conjunctions, *Plurals, *Principal parts of verbs

2. **Discussions of particular words and phrases,** with recommendations for usage, such as *continual—continuous, *fiancé, fiancée, *get, got, *like—as, *route, *shall—will, *so . . . that, *very

3. **Page references** to subjects discussed in the preliminary chapters

4. **General articles** treating subjects somewhat more limited than those of the preliminary chapters, such as *American and British usage, *Colloquial and written English, *Foreign words in English, *Pronunciation

5. **Articles designed especially for theme correction,** with abbreviations for use on themes suggested in the margin, such as *Adjectives, use, *Dangling modifiers, *Reference of pronouns

To make these articles most useful, read first Chapter 1, Varieties of English, and Chapter 2, Good English, as a background for the specific suggestions made. Then read a few consecutive pages to see those general principles applied and to get the feel of the articles and some notion of what they can do for you in guiding your usage in actual speaking and writing.

An asterisk (*) before a word or phrase means that that word or phrase is entered alphabetically elsewhere in the *Index*, and that further information will be found there.

References to the sources most used in gathering the material for this book are usually made to author's name only. The exact titles of these sources will be found on pages ix, x.

A full discussion of the symbols by which pronunciation is represented appears in the article *Pronunciation §3.

A THE pronunciation of *a* is hard to pin down in English, because the letter represents several different sounds and because these sounds that it typically represents are also spelled in a number of other ways. A has three principal sounds, described in sections 1 to 3 below, and several that are less common:

1. "Long *a*" (ā), as in *ale, fable, hate.* This sound is also commonly spelled *ei* or *ey* (*neighbor, veil, obey*), and *ea* (*break*), and *ai* or *ay* (*maid, pay*). A following *r* considerably alters the long *a* sound however it is spelled, as in *fare, share, precarious, hair, prayer, wear.* In unstressed syllables long *a* loses some of its *a* quality (contrast the first *a* with the second in *vacation*) and is sometimes called "half long *a*." Since its changed value comes naturally from the reduced stress, no separate mark is needed for this sound (vā kā′shən).

2. "Short *a*" (a) as in *fat, ladder, detach.* This is a very common English sound, and especially common in American pronunciation. Short *a* in unstressed syllables, like other unstressed vowels, tends to lose its distinct sound and to become the "slurred vowel" represented by ə: *against* (ə genst′).

3. "Broad *a*" (ä), as in *far, larger, father,* and in *hearth* and the first syllable of *sergeant.*

4. "Intermediate *a*" in a troublesome group of words called the "ask words" because the sound is sometimes referred to as "*a* as in *ask*." The fact about *ask, aunt, bath, can't, grass,* and a number of other words is that their pronunciation varies with different people of very good standing all the way from short *a* to broad *a* with many intermediate stages. In certain parts of New England, especially around Boston, and in a few other American cities, and among people who have been influenced by the pronunciation of these places or that of southern England, broad *a* (chäns, fäst, päth) is used, but most Americans use short *a* (chans, fast, path), or a sound very close to short *a*. Usage is divided on the pronunciation of these words, and a person should use whichever sound is

native to him or is used by the circle in which he lives and not try to use a different sound which he assumes to be more correct but which he is almost certain not to use consistently. In this *Index* these sounds are marked as short *a* (a) with a reference to this paragraph (*A §4).

5. A frequently spells the "open *o*" sound, especially before *l* plus a consonant, and after *w*: *all, ball, tall,* W*alter, warm.* In our pronunciation key this sound is represented by ô (ôl, bôl, wôrm). The *a* in *was, quality, wand, water,* and other words is equivalent to short *o*.

Reference: W*ebster's International,* "A Guide to Pronunciation," §§76-96

a- A- as a prefix from Greek meaning *not* is used in forming many words in the formal and scientific vocabularies:

amoral   asexual   asymmetrical   atypical   achromatic

It is usually pronounced ā (ā si met′ri kəl) though "short *a*" is heard, especially in *amoral* and *achromatic.*

A prefix *a-* from various Old English origins is found in many words (*abed, aloud, asleep*) and survives in vulgate English in phrases like *going a fishing, a hunting.* See dictionaries for details of origin and use.

a, an **1.** The choice between *a* or *an* depends on the initial sound of the following word:

A is used before all words beginning with a consonant sound, that is, before all words spelled with initial consonants except silent *h,* as in *hour,* and before words spelled with initial vowels that combine consonant and vowel sounds, as in *eulogy, unit:*

a business   a European trip   a D   a usage

A*n* is used before all words beginning with a vowel sound, including words spelled with initial silent *h* (see *H):

an apple   an F   an hour apart   an honor

Questions sometimes arise over words beginning with *h* but not accented on the first syllable, as in *histo′rian, hotel′.* Formerly this *h* was not pronounced, so that *an* was used; but now that the *h* is pronounced, some people continue to say *an hotel′, an histor′ical event* (but *a his′tory*). A *hotel′, a histor′ical event,* and so on are more common and generally preferred pronunciations.

2. Repeating *a* or *an* before each noun of a series tends to keep the various words distinct and make the expression emphatic: *a pen, a sheet of paper, and an envelope* (*a pen, sheet of paper, and envelope* would be less emphatic).

3. There is a tendency to join *a* to a few common words in writing. *Awhile* is written as one word, but not *a lot.*

For *a half hour, half an hour,* etc., see *half. For *kind of a, sort of a* see *kind of [a], sort of [a].

a, b, and c Usage is divided between using and not using a comma before the *and* that precedes the last word of a series of three or more parallel words (a green, white, and yellow flag—a green, white and yellow flag). For discussion and examples see *Series.

Ab **Abbreviations** (CORRECTION: Write out in full the abbreviation marked.)

1. APPROPRIATENESS. Abbreviations belong most appropriately to manuals, books of reference, business and legal documents, scholarly footnotes, and other works in which saving space is important. They also fit in familiar writing—notes for our own use, letters to friends. In literature and most formal writing, abbreviations are held to a minimum, though modern informal style is much less strict in this than older style.

Shoptalk, familiar conversation, and slang use many abbreviations for the names of things frequently mentioned: *t.b.* (*tuberculosis*), *d.t.'s* (*delirium tremens*), *b.o.m.* (newspaper: *business office must*), *b.f.* (*boyfriend*), *g.f.* (*girlfriend*).

2. STANDARD ABBREVIATIONS. *Dr.,* *Mr.,* *Mrs.,* *Messrs.* are always abbreviated when used with a name. A number of abbreviations, such as *St.* (*Saint*), *a.m.* and *p.m.,* S.E.C., T.V.A., and abbreviations for other government agencies are generally used. In formal writing, titles like *Reverend, *Professor, President, and Senator would not be abbreviated at all, but in most writing they are found abbreviated *when initials or given names are used:* not *Prof. Hylander,* but *Professor Hylander* or *Prof. G. W. Hylander.*

English still has many abbreviations of Latin words:

A. D.	*Anno Domini*—in the year of our Lord (*Centuries)
cf.	*confer*—compare (for which *see* may be used)
*e.g.	*exempli gratia*—for example
*etc.	*et cetera*—and so forth
*ibid.	*ibidem*—the same (used in footnotes)
*i.e.	*id est*—that is

Such abbreviations are not italicized, unless there is special reason for italics (as when *ibid.* represents the title of a book), since they are regarded as English words. Less commonly used abbreviations from Latin (*c.* or *ca.* [*circa,* about, used in uncertain dates], *seq.* [*sequentes,* following]) are usually italicized.

Dictionaries contain special lists of abbreviations at the back or else explain their meaning in the main list of words.

For abbreviations used in footnotes of research papers, see "Form of footnotes," p. 341.

3. PERIOD WITH ABBREVIATIONS. Naturally a writer intends to use a period after an abbreviation and omitting it is a careless slip, but a pretty common careless slip.

Some publishers do not use a period after an abbreviation that is to be followed by a colon, as *i.e:* and only one period is used when an abbreviation falls at the end of a sentence.

There is a growing tendency today not to use a period after an abbreviation that ends with the last letter of the word abbreviated: *Dr, Mr, Mrs, vs, Wm.* This is more common in British than in American usage.

Periods are frequently not used with the abbreviations of names of government agencies (*WPA, NYA, FBI, OGR*), and of other terms if the abbreviation is generally used instead of the name (*OGPU, PMLA*), and of phrases like *mph, hp, kwh, rpm* in scientific contexts or when used with figures (*780 rpm*).

Compare *Contractions, *Clipped words.

ability (to) The idiom with *ability* is *to* and an infinitive (*ability to do,* not *of doing*):

He has the ability to design beautiful buildings.

The idea is often better expressed by an adjective or verb:

He is able to [He can] design beautiful buildings.

Or the notion of ability can be implied in direct statement of accomplishment:

He designs [is designing] beautiful buildings.

Ablative case The functions of the ablative case of Latin are performed in English by preposition phrases: *from home, at the bay.* *Case

able to *Able to* is sometimes crudely used instead of *can:*

> CRUDE: This is not able to be done because of lack of time.
> GOOD ENGLISH: This cannot be done because of lack of time.
> Or: They are not able to do this because of lack of time.

-able, -ible The common and useful suffix *-able,* meaning "able to," "liable to," and so on, is hard to spell because in a number of words *-ible* is found. The point to remember is that *-able* is by far the more common form and that it should be used also in *coining occasional words like *jumpable* or *come-at-able.*

1. This list contains a few of the many words in *-able*:

abominable	hospitable	laughable	serviceable
admirable	imaginable	lovable	sizable
advisable	improbable	movable	suitable
applicable	incurable	noticeable	teachable
changeable	indefatigable	peaceable	tolerable
comfortable	indispensable	perishable	unbearable
comparable	inevitable	preferable	unbelievable
desirable	inseparable	presentable	unmistakable
detestable	intolerable	profitable	unspeakable
eatable	justifiable	pronounceable	usable
excusable	knowable	receivable .	

2. The following rather common words have *-ible*:

accessible	discernible	indelible	repressible
admissible	divisible	inexhaustible	responsible
audible	edible	intelligible	revertible
combustible	eligible	invisible	risible
compatible	fallible	irresistible	seducible
comprehensible	feasible	legible	sensible
contemptible	flexible	negligible	submersible
convertible	forcible	perceptible	suggestible
corruptible	horrible	perfectible	suppressible
credible	impassible	permissible	susceptible
destructible	impossible	plausible	tangible
digestible	incredible	possible	terrible
dirigible	indefensible	reducible	visible

3. Several words are found with either *-able* or *-ible*. The more common form is put first:

collapsible—collapsable	collectable—collectible
gullible—gullable	preventable—preventive
reversable—reversible	

See Fowler, "-able, -ible."

about (at about) *At about* is a common colloquial doubling of prepositions: "I got there at about three o'clock." In writing ordinarily choose the more accurate of the two: "I got there *at* three o'clock," or "I got there *about* three o'clock." *About* is usually the one intended.

The same applies to the colloquial *at around*.

above *Above* is primarily used as a preposition (*above* the clouds) or adverb (the statements made above—*above* modifying the verb *made*). Its common use as an adverb, as in "The story told above" (that is, on the same page or on a preceding page), would be avoided by most writers in favor of "The story I have told . . ." or some such expression.

The use of *above* as an adjective (the above statements) or noun (The above is confirmed . . .) is better limited to business writing and reference works. This sentence shows how crude *above* as a noun may sound in an inappropriate context:

> In answer to the above I would say that the children didn't grow up with the right parents.

Reference: Pooley, pp. 115-16

Absolute phrases Absolute phrases are not built into the basic structure of a sentence but rather modify the sentence as a whole: "*The narrows passed*, we went along at a good speed." (Contrast "Having passed the narrows, we went along at a good speed," in which *having passed* modifies *we*.)

Such absolute phrases are not idiomatic English and are usually awkward. The natural construction would be a clause, "When we had passed the narrows, we . . ."

For fuller discussion see *Participles §4, *Infinitives §4, *Latin and English §3.

absolutely In speech *absolutely* has become generalized to mean "very" or "quite": "He is absolutely the finest fellow I know"—and in slang means simply "yes." It is sometimes a useful word to put force into dialog but would be out of place in most writing, except in its original meaning of "completely, unconditionally."

Abstract and concrete words (CORRECTION: Try to change the ab- *Abst* stract expressions marked to concrete ones.)

Nouns that name qualities, conditions, actions, summaries of particular facts are abstract: *love, civilization, danger, age, flying.* They contrast with concrete nouns, which name persons and things that can be seen and touched: *girl, schoolhouse, tree.*

Abstract nouns are necessary in discussing ideas, but are often used where specific, concrete words would be more exact and forceful, as in this sentence:

> Cleanliness of apparatus, particularly glassware, is of utmost importance to insure against the entry of any substance other than that for which the search is being conducted.

For discussion of the use of abstract words, see "Abstract and concrete words," p. 223. For discussion of their meaning, see "Concrete words," p. 187, and "Abstract words," p. 188.

Academic degrees *Degrees

Academic writing One conspicuous trait of academic writing—that is, the publications of teachers and scholars and others engaged in research and in originating ideas—is its documentation, the devices of bibliography and footnote reference that give the sources of material used in preparing the paper. Scrupulousness in use of materials and in giving exact references to those materials sets scholarly writing off from popular books and articles. For form see "Footnote form," p. 338; "The Final Bibliography," p. 343.

When scholarly articles and monographs deal with particular points of research—the results of experiments, of historical research, of special investigation in any field—they naturally show the specialized vocabulary, compactness, and impersonality of *scientific and technical writing. Less specialized academic writing is dignified and almost necessarily in a formal style.

Partly because many works by professors and research workers are written more impersonally than they need be, "academic" is often used to describe writing that is unpleasantly abstract, distant, and dry, and to describe the style of many textbooks and of some other books supposedly for general reading that do not show sufficient adaptation to the desired readers. But such failures in communication should not hide the importance of much academic writing. Very often the men engaged in discovering new facts, in originating interpretations of facts, are not particularly interested in popularizing them and leave that task to others. Their writing is adapted to a rather limited audience but their ideas may be carried to a wider audience by other writers more interested in or better adapted to reaching a wider circle.

This passage presents an idea clearly and exactly for a limited group and suggests some of the typical traits of academic writing of the better sort:

> An expert is a person who, in some special field of knowledge, has a technical competence not possessed by ordinary persons. He has the knowledge that is necessary to adjust means to ends. He can diagnose changes or predict results if certain postulates are made. An engineer can calculate the strength of materials required if a bridge is to bear some given load. A specialist in maternity welfare can indicate the steps it is desirable to take in order to reduce the death-rate in childbirth. An expert in naval armaments can state the thickness of armour-plate required to resist the entrance of projectiles hurled against it. A motoring engineer can devise a car most likely to avoid danger of skidding on a greasy road-surface. In the great society, we could not for a day preserve its scale of living unless there were countless men and women applying their knowledge to the solution of these problems.

But the fundamental issues of society are not the kind of problem the expert is accustomed to handle. They require not specialisation so much as the power to coordinate. They involve judgments of value, predictions about psychological impact, which are the product not of expert technique, but of a certain divine common sense which has no necessary connection with it. It is, of course, true that common sense, even when divine, is helpless without the results of expert knowledge; but the converse proposition is even more important. For the vices of specialisation are of an ultimate quality. There is always the danger that the specialist will over-emphasise the proportionate importance of his results to the total which has to be attained. Sailors can never be safely left in control of a naval department. Doctors have a dangerous tendency to see the population not as normal human beings, but as potential patients. Efficiency engineers very largely forget the psychological factor in their equations. Mr. F. W. Taylor's famous comparison[1] of a certain type of man with the unresisting ox omitted the unfortunate refusal of that type to remain permanently oxlike in character. The problems which the statesman has to decide are not, in the last analysis, problems upon which the specialism of the expert has any peculiar relevance.—HAROLD J. LASKI, *Democracy in Crisis*, pp. 171-72.

[1] *Principles of Scientific Management*, p. 359

See "Formal English," p. 25.

Accent Accent is the increased force given to certain syllables in speaking. In this *Guide-Index stress* is used rather than *accent*.

See *Pronunciation §4, *b* and *c*, *Rhythm, *Noun and verb stress.

Accents French words in English sometimes keep the accent marks with which they are spelled in their original language:

ACUTE: café outré attaché fiancée
CIRCUMFLEX: crêpe tête
GRAVE: frère suède

The accent marks are regularly used in formal writing and formal publications. In informal writing those that are not needed to indicate pronunciation (as *café* is) and generally in newspapers, the marks are dropped. Both fete and fête, role and rôle are found, for instance. See *Foreign words in English, and for particular words consult a recent dictionary.

accept *except

Accidence *Inflection and the specific articles referred to there.

accidental, accidentally Watch the spelling (and pronunciation) of *accidentally*, which is an *-al-ly word.

accordingly *Conjunctive adverbs

Accusative case A noun or pronoun that is the object of a verb (or verbal [participle or infinitive]) or of a preposition is in the accusative (or objective) case. The personal pronouns, except *you* and *it*, have separate forms: *me, her, him, us, them; whom* is the accusative of the relative and interrogative *who* (but see *who—whom*). Nouns do not have a special form for the accusative; the case is identified by position usually following the verb or preposition.

Besides being a direct object, the accusative is used as a predicate accusative in such sentences as these:

The meeting elected John Henry [direct object] chairman [predicate accusative].
They all thought Margaret [direct object] the better poet [predicate accusative].

The subject of an infinitive is in the accusative case (It was almost impossible to get *them* to do it) and often of a verbal noun (They were surprised at the vacation beginning so soon).

Nouns in the accusative case are often in an adverbial construction, especially of time, amount, extent:

This course runs *a full semester.*
Other times she'll howl *all night.*
This model costs *ten dollars* more.

For further details of the uses of the accusative case, see *Objects; *Infinitives § 4; *Gerund § 2; *It's me; *Who, whom.

act In the sense "to behave, bear oneself as being or as if being" (Webster), *act* is a *linking verb, so that its meaning can be completed by an adjective:

He acts old.   He acts older than he is.   He acts wise.

Active voice A verb is in the active voice when its subject is the doer of the action: "Jimmy's father *gave* him a car" as contrasted with the passive verb in "Jimmy *was given* a car by his father." See *Voice and *Passive voice.

ad *Ad* is the clipped form of *advertisement*, has only one *d*, and should not be followed by a period. Like other *clipped words it belongs to informal and familiar speech and writing.

address Verb stressed on second syllable: a dres′ or ə dres′; noun's stress divided: a dres′ [ə dres′] or ad′res; ad′res is most used in the word's commonest sense, the address of a letter, package, etc.:

Mr. Thorpe was to address (a dres′) the meeting.

Mr. Thorpe then addressed (a drest') the meeting.
Mr. Thorpe's address (a dres' or ad'res) was almost an hour long.
The letter's address (ad'rəs, FORMAL a dres') was illegible.

Addresses When the various parts of a person's address are written on the same line, they are separated by commas:

Miss Louise Finney, 48 Adirondack View, Middlebury, Vermont
Mr. Davis was a native of Carroll County, Va., and a graduate of the College of William and Mary.

For addresses in and on letters see *Letters § 1, *b* and *c*.

Adjective clauses An adjective clause is a subject-and-verb construction that modifies a noun or pronoun. Many such clauses are introduced by relative pronouns, *who, which, that:*

The man *who lived at the head of the street* has moved away. (Clause modifies *man.*)
People *who live in glass houses* shouldn't throw stones. (Clause modifies *people.*)
The belief, *which he had held from boyhood,* gradually slipped away. (Clause modifies *belief.*)
Animals *that live in caves* lose their powers of sight. (Clause modifies *animals.*)

One of the oldest, most economical, and neatest constructions, particularly characteristic of English, is the adjective clause without an introductory word (See page 163):

The one *I caught yesterday* weighed three pounds. (Clause modifies *one.*)
The girl *I left behind me* . . . (Modifies *girl.*)

Adjective clauses can perform all the functions of adjectives. See *Adjectives, types and forms, *Restrictive and non-restrictive.

Reference: Curme, *Syntax*, Chapters 13, 14

Adjectives, types and forms An adjective modifies a noun or pronoun, that is, in some way makes its meaning more exact: a *black* spider, *those* men, *certain blind* interests.

1. TYPES. Adjectives are of three general types: (*a*) *Descriptive adjectives*, the most common type, modify the noun by naming a quality or condition of the object it names: a *gray* shutter, *vivid* colors, *difficult* words, a *laughing* girl, the *wrecked* car.
b) *Limiting adjectives* point out in some way the object named or indicate quantity or number: *this* vase, *his former* address, *several* books, *their* ambitions, *seventy-five* seats, the *nineteenth* day, a *double* dose, *any* woman.

359

c) *Proper adjectives,* derived from proper nouns, originally are limiting adjectives: *French* possessions, the *Puritan* colonies—but often become descriptive: *French* culture, *Puritan* manners. Sometimes they mingle both functions, as *Elizabethan* in *the Elizabethan drama* both limits drama to a period and brings to mind qualities of a group of plays.

Often a proper adjective is used so frequently in a merely descriptive sense that it loses its relation to the proper noun from which it came and becomes a simple descriptive adjective, written without a capital: *bacchanalian, pasteurized, diesel, india* ink, *paris* green.

2. FORMS OF ADJECTIVES. Many adjectives have come down from an early period of the language (*high, handsome, civil*) and many have been made and are still being made by adding a suffix to a noun or verb. Some *suffixes that are still active are:

-able (*ible*)—translatable, dirigible
-ed—sugared, and usually in adjectives that are compound words: four-footed, well-lighted
-escent—florescent
-ese—Burmese, journalese
-ful—playful, soulful
-ish—darkish, womanish
-less—harmless, fearless
-like—birdlike
-y—cranky, dreamy, squiffy, corny

3. POSITION OF ADJECTIVES. According to its position in a sentence, an adjective is either attributive or predicate:

Attributive adjectives are placed next to their nouns, usually preceding as in the *tiny* brook, *horseless* carriages. Sometimes there is good reason for placing an adjective after its noun:

a good plan *gone* wrong (Participle as adjective)
a woman *sweet, simple, home-loving* (Two or more adjectives in formal usage often follow.)
the outfit *complete* [For emphasis]
court *martial,* attorney *general* (Following French patterns)
a plan so *complicated* no one could follow it [The adjective modified by other words]
a *white* cap, *small* and beautifully *made* (Avoiding an awkward piling up of adjectives before the noun)

Predicate adjectives come after some form of the verb *be* or some other linking verb (*taste, feel, turn,* . . .), except in inverted sentence order (Silent was the night).

The day is *warm.*   That pie smells *good.*
The train was *crowded.*   For a while I felt *bad.*

See *Linking verbs.

4. COMPARISON OF ADJECTIVES. A greater degree of the quality named by an adjective is shown by adding -*er* or -*est* to the adjective or by placing *more* or *most* before it:

POSITIVE	COMPARATIVE	SUPERLATIVE
learned	more learned	most learned
warm	warmer or more warm	warmest or most warm

For further examples and discussion of use see *Comparison of adjectives and adverbs.

5. ADJECTIVE CLAUSES. Clauses may be used as adjectives:

Everyone *who approves of this* will please raise his right hand.
That was the summer *that we went to Yellowstone.*
He asked the first man *he met.*

For further examples and discussion see *Adjective clauses, *Clauses §1, *Restrictive and non-restrictive.

6. OTHER PARTS OF SPEECH AS ADJECTIVES. One of the outstanding traits of English is the use of nouns in the adjective function: a *glass* jar, the *Chamberlain* government, a *hurry* call, *store* bread, the *high school* course, the *horse and buggy* days. *Parts of speech
Participles are the adjectival parts of verbs: a *coming* man, a *deserved* tribute.
Prepositional phrases often function as adjectives:

a bird *with a long bill* (= a *long-billed* bird, a descriptive adjective)
a bird *in the hand* (a limiting adjective)

7. ADJECTIVES USED AS NOUNS. By using an article words ordinarily used as adjectives may be made to function as nouns: *the just, the rich, the unemployed, a high* (of weather) *an* all-time *high, a* new *low.*

References: Kennedy, §§ 52, 105; Curme, *Parts of Speech*, Chapters 3, 11; *Syntax*, Chapters 5, 13, 14, 25

Adjectives, use Adjectives should add something to the exactness of a writer's statement or to the definiteness of his picture. As Herbert Read puts it, "appropriate epithets may be either exact or happy." In *briny* ocean, the *briny* does not add, because all oceans are briny; *stark* does not add much to the meaning of *tragedy*, or of *madness* either. Very general adjectives like *good* or *bad* or *beautiful* or *wonderful* do not as a rule add; the reader wants a more specific detail, a particular sort of *good* (*generous, affable, efficient* ...). Many adjectives that are exact enough have been used too often with certain nouns (*fond* farewell, *beady black* eyes) and are merely trite. Because most people do not use carefully exact adjectives in conversation, they often fall back on these flat and stale modifiers in writing—and professional writers sometimes fall back on them too (*Newspaper English §2; Trite words, p. 214).

A writer may try too hard to make a picture exact. Most of the adjectives in the following paragraph are exact, that is, they add clearly to the meaning. But there are too many of them; the writer has been too conscientious. The passage would be more readable if those in brackets, and perhaps others, were taken out.

In a hotel dining room there is not the [*clamorous,*] *raucous* bedlam of its *immediate* surroundings, but a *refined, subdued* atmosphere, pervaded by *distinct,* faintly *audible* sounds. The orchestra, with a barely *perceptible* diminuendo, concludes the [*melodic,*] *slow-tempo* arrangement, climaxed by the [*beautiful*] strains of the "Merry Widow" waltz—*rising, falling, fading* with *plaintive* supplication. Then later, while a *modern, rhythmic* melody is being played, the *hushed* clash of cymbals, the [*musical*] tinkle of the chimes, and the *softened* blare of brass blend harmoniously with the [*pulsing,*] *vibrant* voice of the *featured* soloist, only to be anticlimaxed by the *perfunctory* applause of the diners. The [*constant,*] *relentless* shuffle, shuffle, shuffle of *dancing* feet becomes *monotonous* with its [*endless*] repetition and *imperceptible* variation, while *trite* conversation is often interrupted by the *affected* voice of the *solicitous* waiter. The whispers and [*gay*] laughter, the *discordant* clatter of dishes upon trays, and the [*careless*] scraping of chairs blend into the room's *distinctive* personality.

Such a passage is treated with irony by William Saroyan in the preface to *The Daring Young Man on the Flying Trapeze:*

All successful writers believe that one word by itself hasn't enough meaning and that it is best to emphasize the meaning of one word with the help of another. Some writers will go so far as to help an innocent word with as many as four and five other words, and at times they will kill an innocent word by charity and it will take years and years for some ignorant writer who doesn't know adjectives at all to resurrect the word that was killed by kindness.

But a sensible and sensitive use of adjectives is necessary. In most exposition the first requirement of adjectives is exactness; they must answer the needs of the material, like the italicized words in this paragraph:

Many counselors on *public* relations had *one* foot in commerce and the other in politics—even *international* politics. The most *eminent* figure in *this* class was the *late* Ivy Lee. It seems a pity that he died silently, leaving behind, so far as anyone knows, no *real* record of *his* activities. The *candid* reminiscences of Ivy Lee would be as *useful* to a *future* historian as Pepys' Diary— and perhaps as *interesting* to the student of *human* souls. He began his *larger* career as counselor for *certain Rockefeller* interests. He was *careful*, nevertheless, not to identify himself with the Rockefellers or *any other* group, so leaving himself *free* to serve *all* clients. He had a hand in an agitation for recognition of Russia as a means of increasing our *export* market. Indeed, he may have directed *this* campaign. So, too, when an element among the bankers decided that cancellation of *European war* debts would benefit *American* finance, they used Lee's talent for sweetening *unpopular* causes. And in the *last* year of his life he was advising the *new German* government on ways and means for making *Nazi* principles and methods less *hateful* to the *average American* citizen.—WILL IRWIN, *Propaganda and the News*, pp. 267-68

In writing that makes a definite attempt to capture the feelings and sensations of the reader, the adjectives must be exact (as they are in the following paragraph) but they must also deserve the epithet "happy"; that is, they must seem to fit and at the same time to contribute an accent, to lead the reader to the writer's feeling; perhaps they may make an imaginative appeal. In describing an actual experience Ernest Hemingway presents a picture rather than a series of facts:

In the *five* days I saw a dozen or more *kudu* cows and *one young* bull with a string of cows. The cows were *big, gray, striped-flanked* antelope with ridiculously *small* heads, *big* ears, and a *soft, fast-rushing* gait that moved them in *big-bellied* panic through the trees. The *young* bull had the start of a spiral on *his* horns but they were *short* and *dumpy* and as he ran past us at the end of a glade in the dusk, *third* in a string of *six* cows, he was no more *like* a *real* bull than a *spike* elk is like a *big, old, thick-necked, dark-maned, wonder-horned, tawny-hided, beer-horse-built* bugler of a bull-elk.—*Green Hills of Africa*, p. 138

Notice that the relatively insignificant *glade, dusk*, and *trees* are not modified but that the gait is *soft, fast-rushing*. The gait needed to be described; the dusk and the trees are merely part of the background.

Adjectives sometimes tend to make a slow movement in writing, partly because many of them have a falling rhythm; that is, the stressed syllable is followed by one or more unstressed syllables. They may contribute to a leisurely, relaxed effect:

The sheltering trees only emphasized the ashen deadness of the wrinkled clapboards.

Too many of them may result in an excessively slow movement.

Carl Sandburg has been credited with advising a writer, "Think twice before you use an adjective." This is probably sound advice for anyone who is writing a good deal and tends to let thoughtless adjectives slip in. But it is also important for a writer to fix his eye on his subject and write about it as he really sees it. Without stuffing in adjectives he should fill in the qualities that are needed for the reader to recreate the picture or idea for himself. The adjectives then should be at least exact, and some of them may be happy.

Reference: Aiken, Chapter 10
Compare *Adverbs, use.

Adjunct An adjunct is a modifier (as adjective of noun, adverb of verb), or a word or group of words that completes the meaning of some sentence element, as the object of a verb, or a predicate adjective. See *Modifiers.

adult Pronunciation divided: ə dult′—ad′ult.

Adverbial clauses Subject-and-verb constructions may serve as adverbial modifiers:

After the ball was over . . .   He came *because he had to*.
When we got up we found it raining.
He anchored *where the fish were supposed to be*.

See *Adverbs, types and forms; *Adverbs, use; *Clauses.

Adv **Adverbs, types and forms** (CORRECTION: Give the adjective marked an adverb form [as, change *real* to *really*, *considerable* to *considerably*. See §3 below].)

An adverb modifies a verb (He came *fast*, He loved *not wisely* but *too well*), an adjective (*absolutely* perfect), an adverb (*too* well, *quite* rightly), or a whole clause or sentence (*Possibly* you are right). Adverbs may be classed in two ways:

1. CLASSED BY FUNCTION: (*a*) Simple adverbs, modifying a single word or sentence element:

He will come *today*. (Modifying verb *come*)
She was *over* sixty. (Modifying adjective *sixty*)
Almost immediately we saw them. (Modifying adverb *immediately*)

b) Sentence adverbs, modifying whole sentences:

Perhaps he will come today. *Unfortunately* there were no more left.

c) Conjunctive adverbs, which connect clauses and also modify their meaning:

Consequently we agreed to call the matter closed. They were, *however*, by no means convinced.

See *Conjunctive adverbs.

d) Interrogative adverbs, introducing questions:

When did you begin to feel this way?
Where was the car when you first saw it?

2. CLASSED BY MEANING. Adverbs have a wide variety of meanings and can be variously grouped. A convenient grouping follows:

a) How? (Adverbs of manner)

alike so well worse keenly openly painstakingly

b) When? In what order? (Adverbs of time and succession)

afterward when finally late lately never soon

c) Where? (Adverbs of place and direction)

below far north there upstairs

d) How much? To what extent? (Adverbs of degree and measure)

all almost less little much quite completely equally

e) Why? (Adverbs of cause and purpose)

consequently therefore

f) Yes or no. (Adverbs of assertion, condition, and concession)

yes no certainly doubtless not perhaps possibly surely truly

SLANG, VULGATE: O.K. nix absolutely

g) Introductory and parenthetical adverbs

accordingly furthermore however

3. FORMS. Some adverbs have forms that have developed from Old English forms without a special adverbial sign: *now, quite, since, then, there, where*; but most adverbs are adjectives or participles plus the ending *-ly*: "He rowed *badly*"; "She was *deservedly* popular"; "*Surely* you heard that."

There are a number of adverbs with the same forms as adjectives, most of them going back to Old English adverbs that ended in *-e* (an ending which has disappeared) instead of to those that ended in *-lice* (which gives us the current *-ly*). Some of these are:

better	early	hard	much	smooth
cheap	even	high	near	straight
close	fair	late	right	tight
deep	fast	loud	second	well
doubtless	first	low	slow	wrong

Most of these also have forms in *-ly* too, so that we can write "He sang loud" or "He sang loudly." The *-ly* forms are likely to be preferred in formal English and the shorter forms in informal and familiar writing. The shorter forms are often more vigorous than the longer:

Go *slow*.   Don't talk so *loud*.   It was so windy that I had to hold on *tight* to the iron stand to keep from being blown off the summit.

In vulgate English the *-ly* forms are not so much used and people say "It came *easy*," "He talked *big*," "It was **real* good," "The fire burns *bright*." *Special* and **considerable* are frequently used instead of *specially* and *considerably*. This fact is responsible for many errors in English and a beginning writer should be especially careful to use a proper adverbial form rather than these vulgate forms.

4. COMPARISON OF ADVERBS. A greater degree of the quality named by the adverb is shown by adding *-er* or *-est* to an adverb or by placing *more* or *most* before it:

POSITIVE	COMPARATIVE	SUPERLATIVE
hard	harder	hardest
slow	slower	slowest
slowly	more slowly	most slowly

Most adverbs of more than one syllable are compared with *more* and *most*. See **Comparison of adjectives and adverbs.

5. Other constructions are used as adverbs. Nouns may be so used (See **Accusative case, **Genitive case §2):

He came *every morning*. He plans to stay *a month*.

Phrases may have the functions of adverbs (**Phrases §3):

He came *in the morning*.
After the examination he had stopped studying.

Clauses may act as adverbs (**Adverbial clauses):

When it came time to go, he didn't know what to do.
He stayed on and on *because he didn't know how to leave*.

References: Kennedy, §54; Curme, *Parts of Speech*, pp. 73-86

Adverbs, use What has been said about the use of adjectives (**Adjectives, use) can be said again about the use of adverbs: Adverbs, too, should be either exact or happy or both. When an amateur writer wants to portray rapid or violent action, he is quite likely to make too free a use of adverbs and kill the whole effect. In this paragraph we would be relieved—and see the picture more clearly—if the writer had abandoned his adverbs:

Shrill horns scream *threateningly*. Automobiles careen *wildly*. Giant buses lumber *dominantly* along. Policemen shout *warningly* and then *desperately*. Pedestrians scurry across the broad avenue. And then more squeaky, impatient cars, more terrifying trucks, and more lumbering buses.

Some writers tend to qualify too much, to make a statement and then draw part of it back with such words as *probably*, *apparently*:

I shall [probably] try to read your paper tonight.

It is better to choose the most accurate word available and use that.

Many of the longer adverbs are unemphatic because they are unstressed toward the end, and when two or more of them come close together they make a clumsy or unpleasant sounding phrase. The repetition of the *-ly* is especially enfeebling:

. . . she sang *resonantly*, if *slightly nasally*, between the towering walls of the adjacent buildings.

They each respond to recurrent temperamental differences, and to analogous though *chronologically distantly* separated social conditions.

Sometimes writers use an adverb plus an adjective or a verb when an accurate adjective or exact verb would be neater and just as expressive.

Scholarships should be kept for those who are *studiously inclined* [that is, for those who are *studious*].

When no one was looking I took the goggles and *swiftly made my way* out of the store. [Even *hurried* would say as much and a verb like *scurried* might say more.]

Reference: Aiken, Chapter 11

Adversative connectives Connectives that link two statements in opposition: *but*, *but then*, *however*, *notwithstanding*, *on the other hand*, *still*, and *yet* are some of the more common ones in current usage.

advertisement Ad vẻr'tiz mənt is winning out over ad'vər tīz'mənt and is now the more common pronunciation, though both are heard.

Advertising style *Business English

adviser, advisor Advis*er* has been the more common spelling, but the *-or* form (from analogy with advis*ory*) is being increasingly used. Either is correct.

-ae- (æ), -oe- (œ) Words from Greek and Latin that contain the digraphs *-ae-* and *-oe-* have been for a long time variously spelled in English. (Most printers do not now use the ligatures—the two letters made together, æ, œ—except in works dealing with the ancient languages.) Both *-ae-* and *-oe-* are pronounced as though written *e* (either long or short). Many words have been simplified in the past: *economics, encyclopedia, pedagogy, penal* were formerly *oeconomics, encyclopaedia, paedagogy, poenal.*

The present trend is to hasten this simplification. Medicine, for instance, has adopted many of the simpler forms, like *anesthetic.* The long series of words beginning with *haem-* (meaning "blood") now preferably begins with *hem-* (*hematic, hemoglobin, hemorrhage* . . .), and so on. The American Historical Association long ago adopted *medieval.* The dictionaries now give such words as *ameba, cesura, dieresis, esthetic, subpena* either as preferred or alternate spellings. For a particular word consult a recent authoritative dictionary. More formal styles tend to keep the older form with the two letters, more informal styles to use the simple *e.*

Latin plurals in *ae* of course still keep the two letters: *alumnae, antennae, formulae.* See *Plurals §4.

In Greek and Latin proper names the two letters are kept: *Boeotia, Caesar, Oedipus.*

affect, effect Since most people make no distinction in pronouncing the first vowel of these words, the spelling is likely to be confused.

Affect, a rather formal word, is always a verb, meaning to "influence" or "put on" (compare *affectation*):

This will affect the lives of thousands.
He affected a stern manner.

Effect is most commonly a noun, meaning "result":

The effects of this will be felt by thousands.
What would be the effect of doubling the amount?

Effect is also a verb in formal English, meaning to "bring about":

The change was effected peaceably.

Affectation We pick up our language as children by imitating the speech of people around us, and we change our language later in life by imitating what we hear others say or what we find in reading. So long as these changes furnish us with more varied and more exact ways of saying things, they are proper and necessary, and represent a healthy growth. But sometimes we are led to adopt different pronunciations or different words or different constructions not so much to make our speech more effective as to make it more elegant, or even for the effect of the language itself rather than the effect of what it is conveying. Such changes are affectation and are unpleasant.

Affectation is most easily spotted in pronunciations. In some parts of the United States bēn (for *been*), rä'ŦHĕr, and ī'ŦHĕr are common pronunciations, but consciously·adopting them is affectation in regions where bin, ra'ŦHĕr, or ē'ŦHĕr are usual. For many people expressions like the following are affectations: *aren't I—one should, shouldn't one—*Briticisms like *no end—that which* for *what.* Using slang except for humorous effect is an affectation for a person who dislikes it.

The line between natural and affected speech is hard to draw, since it depends chiefly on motive. In general, picking up expressions not commonly heard from the educated people of a community is dangerous. Increasing the expressiveness of one's speech is praiseworthy, but just trying to be "different" will usually result in bad English. The way to avoid affectation is to consider the appropriateness and expressiveness of language and to shun "big words."

See Chapter 2, Good English, p. 35; *Pronunciation § 2.

aggravate In formal English *aggravate* means "to intensify or increase something unpleasant," as to *aggravate suffering* or *a wound* or *a crime.* In familiar usage *aggravate* means to "annoy" or "irritate": "I was never so aggravated in my life." The same distinction is made with the noun, *aggravation.*

Aggregating sentences Sentences in which several details are built together are called *aggregating,* as contrasted with shorter *segregating* sentences which usually have one or two statements. See "Aggregating sentences," p. 152.

Agreement (CORRECTION: Make the pronoun or verb marked agree grammatically with the word to which it is related [its antecedent if it is a pronoun, its subject if it is a verb].)
Certain parts of speech which vary in form for gender or number should agree when they stand in relationship to each other:

1. *Subject and verb* agree in number (The *man is* old—The *men are* old) and person (*I go* tomorrow—*He goes* tomorrow). *Subject and verb, *Collective nouns

2. A *pronoun* agrees with its *antecedent* in gender (The *man* found *his* keys—The *girl* found *her* keys), and in number (The *boy* had lost *his* way—The *hikers* had lost *their* way). *Reference of pronouns, *each, *every

3. A *demonstrative adjective* usually agrees with its *noun* in number (*That kind* is inexpensive—*These shoes* cost more than the old ones). See *Demonstrative adjectives, *that §5, *this, *kind, sort.

Because of the greatly simplified inflections of English, agreement is a relatively simple matter: our nouns have only two case forms and our verbs have one form except in the third person singular of the present tense and the past tense is the same throughout. The chief cause of failure in agreement is that we do not hold our grammatical patterns in mind very well. If several words intervene between the two that should be in agreement we seem to forget the way we started out. This is especially true if the subject is a collective noun, or if we start with a singular subject and several words, some of them plural, come before the verb, so that we are tempted to use a plural verb.

For other problems of agreement see *Apposition and *Tenses §2.

agree to, agree with One agrees *to* a plan and agrees *with* a person.

ain't Used in place of *isn't, aren't, hasn't,* or *haven't, ain't* is vulgate English only.

As a familiar contraction for *am not, ain't* is a different problem. Spoken English really needs a contraction for the first person. *Amn't* is unpronounceable. *Aren't* is often used, especially in England: "I'm making real progress, aren't I?" and this usage seems to be increasing in the United States. In familiar speech many people say *ant,* not *ānt,* and very generally shorten *aren't* to *ant* (ant ū gō'ən? for *Aren't you going?*). But the expression is never appropriate in formal and informal English.

In representing conversation in writing, we should recognize that *ānt* or *ant* is the spoken form, and spell the expression *ain't.*

Reference: *Current English Usage,* pp. 122, 127-28

airplane—aeroplane for several years these two words competed for general usage, but in the United States at least *airplane* is both the official and popular form. *Aeroplane* (pronounced both ā'ər ō plān' and ār'ō plān) is more commonly used in England.

a la A *la* is regarded as an English preposition, meaning "after," "according to":

a la Whistler   a la *The New Yorker*

In formal writing and modish advertising (as of cosmetics and fashionable clothes), the accent mark is usually kept (à *la*); elsewhere it is written *a la.* We do not use the other French forms, à *l'* and *au.*

alamode (whether meaning "in the fashion" or referring to ice cream or pie) is usually written as one word and without the accent mark. The French form (*à la mode*) is found less often.

alibi In formal English *alibi* means "a defense on the ground of having been in another place"; in familiar and colloquial English, *alibi* refers to any excuse.

all and its compounds The following words and phrases need watching:

all ready [adjective phrase]: At last they were *all ready* to begin.
already [adverb of time]: They had *already* begun.
*all right [adjective phrase]: The seats seemed *all right* to me.
alright [occasionally so spelled in familiar writing when used as an adverb of affirmation]: *Alright*, we'll forget it this time.
all together [adjective phrase]: We found them *all together* in an old trunk. There were six *all together*.
altogether [adverb, equivalent to *wholly*]: That's *altogether* another matter.

Alliteration Alliteration is the presence of the same sound at the beginning of a series of words or of stressed syllables within words. Besides contributing to the pleasure that a reader may find in the similar sounds, alliteration serves to bind the phrase, sometimes a series of phrases, into a unit:

the crowded, cloistered colleges of Oxford.—PAUL ELMER MORE
. . . ran over the starry smoothness of the lagoon, and the water between the piles lapped the slimy timber once with a sudden splash.—JOSEPH CONRAD, "The Lagoon," *Tales of Unrest*, p. 199

Alliteration is one of the figures of sound that contributes to the musical effect of poetry, though not one of the most important:

Here I am, an old man in a dry month,
Being read to by a boy, waiting for rain.
T. S. ELIOT, "Gerontion"

In ordinary expository prose conspicuous alliteration is usually out of place because it tends to attract attention to the expression and away from the idea. Its use in formal and elevated prose, especially in prose with an oratorical or poetic background, is more appropriate.

At present alliteration is one of the chief weapons of advertising sloganeers, and makers of flashy titles, who simply push to a conspicuous point the natural binding power of the figure:

If you see it in the Sun it's so.   Potatoes Promote Prosperity
Corinthian Carpet Cleaners   Mealtime Magic with Milk

Alliteration is also characteristic of humorous verse and prose and of any mannered writing on the light side:

> Tell me, what is a man to do
> When the *l*ady his *l*ife is based upon
> *L*ikes to be *w*ooed but *w*on't be *w*on?
>
> OGDEN NASH, *Hard Lines*, p. 58

Sad, serene, and somewhat silly, *The Garden of Allah* belongs to that dignified class of pictures which reviewers customarily praise for the music and photography.—*Time*, Nov. 30, 1936

Compare "Figures of sound," p. 175.

all (of) *All* is frequently followed by *of* in many constructions where the *of* is not necessary and might not be used in formal writing:

All [of] the milk was spilled.   They passed all [of] the candidates. You can't fool all of the people all of the time.

All of is usual with a pronoun:

All of them went home.   They wanted *all of it* but got only half.

all right—alright *All right* is the spelling of both the adjective phrase (He is all right) and the sentence adverb, meaning "yes, certainly" (All right, I'll come).

Alright is a natural analogy with *altogether* and *already*, but at present is found only in advertising, comic strips, familiar writing, and, very rarely, in fiction. It will be worth watching to see if *alright* makes its way into typical informal English. Meanwhile, be on your guard.

Allusion An allusion is a brief, incidental reference to literature, history, general experience, current events, or popular sayings, used to add interest and increase understanding of the main subject. The following sentence from a short story shows several allusions:

The sense of it, and of us all on that lighted ship in the dark sea, sailing together for a few days, heaven only knew [popular phrase] where and why, made me lapse off into a reverie of this queer, improper world of ours, that is really no place for a lady [popular phrase], but that after all is something for to admire and for to see [Kipling]— where some of us are whited sepulchres [conventional literary allusion], and some of us are lined with pink [reference to an anecdote told earlier in the story], and few of us can help it, and the best souls get put down as *persona non grata* [originally from diplomatic vocabulary], and funny stories lie behind cold official facts, and people may be as absurd as hippopotamuses and yet——H. G. DWIGHT, *Stamboul Nights*, p. 310

The use of allusions in writing is discussed on p. 241.

allusion—illusion *illusion

-al ly English has a number of adjectives with the (Latin) endings -*al* and -*ical*: *fatal, final, medical, historical, political.* Usually an adverb is made by adding -*ly* to this ending. This should be remembered in spelling these words.

accidental	accidentally	incidental	incidentally
political	politically	practical	practically

Several adjectives ending in -*ical* show a tendency to drop the -*al*: *alphabetic, biographic, geographic, grammatic, philosophic,* are becoming more common, following the course of *academic, frantic, emphatic, poetic,* and others that have already shed the final syllable. The use of nouns in -*ic* as adjectives (a *music* festival) adds to this group, in appearance at least.

almost See *most for use of *most* for *almost*.

also is a weak connective; ordinarily *and* will do its work better:

He came with tents, cooking things, *and* [better than *also*] about fifty pounds of photographic equipment.

See *Conjunctive adverbs.

alternative comes from the Latin *alter*, "the second of two"; some formal writers, in deference to the word's origin, confine its meaning to "one of two possibilities," but it is commonly used to mean one of several possibilities, and is so defined in dictionaries.

although *Although* and *though* connect with the main clause an adverbial clause of concession, that is, a statement in opposition to the main statement but one that does not contradict it. *Although* is more likely to introduce a clause that precedes the main clause, *though* one that follows:

Although the rain kept up for almost three weeks, we managed to have a pretty good time.
We managed to have a pretty good time, though [although] the rain kept up for almost three weeks.

There is no distinction in meaning between *though* and *although*.

Often one of two clauses connected by *but* can be thrown into an *although* clause with greater accuracy of meaning and with greater variety in the sentence pattern:

We had rehearsed that act time and time again, but we all missed our cues the first night.

Although we had rehearsed that act time and time again, we all missed our cues the first night.

The spelling *altho* has made more headway than *tho* and *thru*, and is quite appropriate in familiar writing but would not be used in formal writing, and not often in informal writing.

See *but. Reference: Curme, *Syntax*, pp. 332-40

altogether See *all and its compounds.

alumnus In spite of their clumsiness four Latin forms of this word are kept in English:

One male graduate is an	*alumnus* (ə lum′nəs)
Two or more male graduates are	*alumni* (ə lum′nī)
One female graduate is an	*alumna* (ə lum′nə)
Two or more female graduates are	*alumnae* (ə lum′nē)

By common practice *alumnus* and *alumni* are used for graduates of coeducational institutions. Because of this complication of forms, *graduate* and *graduates* are increasingly used. *Alum′* is used colloquially in some institutions.

a.m. and p.m. These abbreviations (for *ante meridiem*, "before noon," and *post meridiem*, "after noon") are now usually written in small letters except in headlines and tables. They are most useful in tables and lists of times. In consecutive writing they are used only with figures for specific hours: "from 2 to 4 p.m."

M. is the abbreviation for noon: "12 m." There is no corresponding abbreviation for midnight.

Amb **Ambiguity** (Correction: Make the meaning you intend unmistakable.)

Although inexact writing is common enough, actually ambiguous writing, in which there is possibility of confusing two meanings, is relatively rare. The context usually shows which of two possible meanings must be taken. The most common sources of actual ambiguity are:

1. Inexact reference of pronoun, especially in *indirect discourse:

He told his father he had been talking too much.

Such a sentence usually needs reforming, perhaps as:

"I've been talking too much," he told his father.
"You've been talking too much," he said to his father.

See *Reference of pronouns.

2. Squinting modifiers, that is, modifiers that may refer to either of two words or constructions:

I said *when the game was over* that I would go.
[When the game was over I said that I would go, or, I said that I would go when the game was over.]
Some people *I know* would go there anyway.
[Some people whom I know . . . or, Some people would go there anyway, I know.]

3. INCOMPLETE IDIOMS, especially in comparisons:

"I like Alice as well as Will" might mean "I like Alice as well as Will does," "I like Alice as well as I do Will," or "I like both Alice and Will."

See *Comparison of adjectives and adverbs.

4. YES OR NO AFTER NEGATIVES. *Yes* or *no* often needs to be made clearer with a clause answering a negative question or commenting on a negative statement.

You haven't any more red ink, have you? [Answer, "Yes, I have" or "No, I haven't."]
Let's not use such a long quotation. [No, let's not.]

American Since it is inconvenient to form an adjective or a compound in *-man* from *the United States, American* is ordinarily used. It is obviously inexact, since Canadians and Mexicans are as American as we are. But it is no more inexact than many other words and is generally used in this sense. Perhaps we can take an Englishman's judgment:

The use of *America* for *the United States* & *American* for (*citizen*) *of the U. S.* is open to as much & as little objection as that of *England* & *English*(*man*) for *Great Britain* (& *Ireland*), *British*, & *Briton*. It will continue to be protested against by purists & patriots, & will doubtless survive the protests.—H. W. FOWLER, *Modern English Usage*, p. 18

Use *the United States* rather than *America* as the name of our country but use *American* as the adjective and the name of an inhabitant.

American and British usage There are several reasons why the English spoken and written in the United States differs from the English spoken and written in England. The English language was brought to North America in the seventeenth and eighteenth centuries, and since that time the language used on both sides of the Atlantic has changed noticeably, and naturally in somewhat different ways. For the past few generations the first-hand contacts between Americans and Englishmen have been confined to a handful of the upper classes of both nations (in contrast to the

rather frequent movement back and forth among the citizens of
the British Empire), so that there has been little chance for the
pronunciation of one to affect the other. The people live under
different governments, are brought up under differing educational
systems. Social stratification, affecting the ideals and habits of
large classes of people, is considerably different. In spite of the mutual circulation of books and periodicals, visits of lecturers, professors, and ministers, and interchange by way of the movies and
the radio, many of the factors that tend to keep a language unified
and to keep the speech of the British possessions close to that of
England cannot operate very effectively between England and the
United States.

The differences have led to interesting emotional attitudes on
both sides. There has been considerable arrogance. Britishers
scorn what they like to call "vulgar Americanisms," partly from
dislike of different language customs, partly from a feeling of
superiority in customs and manners: The maker of the glossary
to the London edition of Sinclair Lewis' *Babbitt* went beyond simple definition when he wrote for *ice cream soda* "Ice cream in soda
water. A ghastly American summer time drink." Fowler says that
the realization that Americans had dropped the *u* from words in
-*our* stopped the British from making the same change. Many
Americans look upon British accent and vocabulary as ludicrous or
at best snobbish. The average American's dislike for Briticisms
has been intensified by the imitation of British usage by some
Americans, who have affected both British pronunciations and
British words.

As to written style, in recent years the vigor of our literature has
done much to give American English standing abroad, and the
movies are carrying their version. Thirty years ago the Fowler
brothers wrote in *The King's English*, "Americanisms are foreign
words, and should be so treated"—and they treated them so with
gusto. Ten years ago Ernest Weekley wrote "The foreign language
which has most affected English in our own time is contemporary
American." In 1938 Eric Partridge put as a subtitle to *The World
of Words* "An Introduction to Language in General and to English and American in particular." H. W. Horwill's *Dictionary of
Modern American Usage* (Oxford, 1935) is further evidence of a
serious regard for our language, attempting to describe the American vocabulary for the English people without belittling it and incidentally telling us a good deal about British usage.

In the written language some spelling differences stand out.
The British tend still to prefer -*re* to -*er* in words like *center* and

theater, though they use both forms; they still keep -*our* in a number of words, though they are gradually simplifying; they use *x* in a few words like *inflexion*; they tend to double more consonants, as in *traveller*, *waggon*; and there are various individual words that differ, such as *tyre* (automobile *tire*). But these distinctions do not affect a large number of words, and actually usage on most of them is divided in both countries. They are just enough to show that a book is of British or American origin but they do not interfere with reading except among patriotic fanatics of one country or the other. They really are one of the better arguments for allowing more individual freedom in spelling, but offer a problem to a publisher who wishes to circulate a book in both countries.

In the United States for a number of years students have been at work discovering and describing our speech. The magazine *American Speech* (founded in 1925) has published specific observations of usage and more general articles. Professor George Philip Krapp's *The English Language in America* (New York, 1925) and John S. Kenyon's *American Pronunciation* (Ann Arbor, 1935) are scholarly works. The four editions of H. L. Mencken's *The American Language* (New York, 1919—) have given a sturdy defense of American as against British usage. Mencken is not quite fair in that he usually pits the American vulgate against formal British, but his main point, the existence of a distinct popular speech in the United States, is well proved. Now the publication of the *Dictionary of American English* is presenting the most complete and accurate record of our words yet made.

There are of course several varieties of English in use on both sides of the Atlantic, and Great Britain presents a greater variety than the United States, in part because of sturdy remains of older dialects in the various counties, in Scotland, and in Wales, and in part because of mannerisms of various upper groups, as "the Oxford accent." Among Englishmen and Americans of about the same degree of education and similar social position, differences in pronunciation are likely to be particularly striking. There are different values for the vowels, differences in particular words like the British trā (*trait*), prō cess, con tents', lef ten'ənt for *lieutenant*, ral'i for the American rô'li (*Raleigh*), and in general a more rapid speech and tendency to slur syllables (such as -*ar* in *dictionary*). The slower, fuller pronunciation by Americans seems wasteful and provincial to a Britisher.

Everyone knows some of the differences in vocabulary in certain common words: In England an *elevator* is a *lift*, *radio* is *wireless*, *crackers* are *biscuits* (*cakes* and *muffins* are also different from those in America), *dessert* is fruit after the sweets, a *sit-down strike* is a *stay-in strike*, a *run* in a stocking is a *ladder, daylight saving time* is *summer time, installment buying* is the *hire-purchase system, white-collar* workers are *black-coat* workers. From the group word *tin can* the British have taken *tin*, while Americans have chosen *can*. A *truck* is a *lorry*, an *automobile* is a *motor car* (though both are compromising on *car*), *gasoline* is *petrol*, sold in a *gallon* of five quarts. A *billion* is a thousand million in America (and France) and a million million in England (and Germany).

There is a vulgate speech in both England and America, a vast array of slang that baffles readers on the opposite side of the Atlantic, and many colloquialisms that belong to each. *No end* and *ráтнér'* are supposed to identify an Englishman as clearly as *guess* or *reckon* is supposed to identify an American—in a book. One reason for careful study of the differences between the two speeches was the increased vogue of realistic fiction, which necessarily made use of more colloquial English and more colloquial American. In fact, the increased informality and colloquialness of modern prose in both England and the United States tended to emphasize the distinctions between the two, and probably went a long way toward general recognition of differences.

The grammar of the popular levels of English and of American differs somewhat—contrast the speech of ordinary people in novels of the two countries. But in the formal writing of the two there is less difference in grammar than in vocabulary. Collective nouns are more likely to be plural in British usage (*the government intend*); British writers differ in small matters like the position of *only*, the proper preposition with *different*, and distinguishing *like* and *as*. (See Stuart Robertson "British-American Differentiations in Syntax and Idiom," *American Speech*, 1939, xiv 243-54.)

A fairly long catalog of such minor differences between these two branches of English could be drawn up, but their importance should not be exaggerated or allowed to obscure the fundamental fact that the resemblances far outnumber the differences, and that the speech of the two countries represents two different strands of the English language. With patience a citizen of one country can understand the speech of the other, and with tolerance for small differences one can read the other's books and periodicals without trouble. An Englishman should write for Englishmen and an American for Americans. Too much concern for an "American language" may be mistaken patriotism. It is better to regard our speech as one of several branches of the great English language.

For an American there is no virtue in consciously cultivating British pronunciations or adopting British words and idioms. If he uses generally accepted American English he will reach his proper public, and if what he writes is interesting or important enough he can reach English readers too.

Many particular entries in this *Index* note differences between British and American usage. Anyone who wishes to look further into the matter can refer to the books mentioned in this article, or he can begin with the shorter discussions in Kennedy or McKnight or other books on English.

among *between

amount, number *Amount* is used of things viewed in bulk, weight, or sums; *number* is used of things that can be counted:

an *amount* of milk [but a *number* of cans of milk]
an *amount* of beets, corn, oats, wheat [but a *number* of bushels or carloads of any of these]
a *number* of seats, a *number* of people, a *number* of mistakes
an *amount* of money, an *amount* of humor

ampersand is the name for the **&** sign (originally a linking of the letters of *et*), called also *short and*. Its primary use, obviously, is to save space. It is used chiefly in business writing and in reference works. In addressing firms, use the form they habitually use (. . . and Company or . . . & Company), and in quoting, follow your original carefully.

Anacoluthon (spelled also *anakoluthon*; pronounced an'ə kō-lü'thon; plural *anacolutha*) is the learned word for changing from one grammatical construction to another within the same sentence. Some common types of anacolutha are described as shifted constructions on p. 129.

Analogy (Figure of speech) See "Metaphors, similes, analogies," p. 235.

Analogy in language *Analogy* is the name for the natural tendency in users of a language to make their speech more regular by forming new words like some existing ones, bringing old words closer together in form, or bringing constructions in line with familiar patterns. It is easiest to watch analogy in the attempts of children to master their language. Before they learn the forms conventionally used by grown-ups, they manufacture forms like those they are familiar with: Most children for a time say *mans* before they learn to say *men*; they experiment with verb forms, usually making verbs regular, *singed* for *sang* or *sung*, *digged* for *dug*, or they may say *dag* instead of *dug*.

Analogy is the force that has disposed of many irregularities in the main body of the language. Out of various plural forms used in Old English, -*s* has won in all but a few words and analogy is still bringing more words to that form, like **formulas*. Words occasionally are changed in spelling by analogy, as the -*b* was rather recently added to *crumb* and *thumb* from analogy with *comb, dumb*, and so on. *Cole slaw* is often replaced by *cold slaw*. **Adviser* is now changing to *advisor* from analogy with *advisory* and words like *inspector, distributor*. *Alright* is slowly making its way from analogy with *already*. (See **All right.*) New words are formed on analogy with old ones, like *avigation, aerobatics*. Since **who* is the form that usually stands before a verb, as its subject, people ordinarily say *who* instead of *whom* when the object precedes the verb (*Who* were you with?).

See **Change in language, **due to*, the words starred in this article, and various other examples of analogy treated in particular *Index* entries.

Reference: E. H. Sturtevant, *Linguistic Change* (Chicago, 1917), p. 38 ff., Ch. 6. See also the indexes of most works on language for their treatment of analogy.

Analytic and synthetic forms When the form of a word is altered to show some difference in meaning or function, the derived form is called *synthetic*; when some other word is put with the main word to express the changed meaning, the new form is called *analytic*. English shows both methods in comparing adjectives and adverbs and in its possessive:

SYNTHETIC:	quiet	quiet*er*	quiet*est*
	lovely	lovel*ier*	lovel*iest*
	a horse*'s* hoof; the king*'s* subjects		

ANALYTIC:	quiet	*more* quiet	*most* quiet
	lovely	*more* lovely	*most* lovely
	the hoof *of* a horse; the subjects *of* a king		

English verbs are generally analytic in conjugation:

| *he has said* | (contrasted with the Latin *dixit*) |
| *he will love* | (contrasted with the Latin *amabit*) |

Analytic forms probably make a language somewhat easier to learn, since there are fewer separate words to keep in mind, and they make it possible to emphasize the signs of the various forms: I will' come.

*Comparison of adjectives and adverbs §§1 and 2; *Genitive case §§1 and 2; *Verbs

-ance, -ence (-ant, -ent) Two of the most troublesome groups of words in English spelling are those ending in *-ance* (*-ant*) and *-ence* (*-ent*). Most of them are nouns and adjectives descended from verbs of different Latin conjugations whose vowel signs are generally represented in these endings. There is no difference in our pronunciation of the endings—both get the slurred vowel ə (də fen′dənt). There is a slight tendency to level the two in the direction of the ending with *e*, but for the present all we can do is learn the individual forms by memory or frequently consult a dictionary.

Here are some of the commoner words of these types:

-ance, -ant

Noun	Adjective
attendance, attendant	attendant
balance	[balanced, balancing]
defendant	defendant [defending]
descendant	descendant or descendent
expectance, expectancy	expectant
extravagance	extravagant
forbearance	[forbearing]
incessancy	incessant
intolerance	intolerant
perseverance	perseverant
reluctance	reluctant
repentance	repentant
resemblance	[resembling]
resistance	resistant
significance	significant
tenant, tenancy	tenant
tolerance	tolerant
vigilance	vigilant
warrant	[warranting]

-ence, -ent

Noun	Adjective
antecedence, antecedent	antecedent
competence	competent
confidence	confident
consistency	consistent
dependence (-ance)	dependent (also dependant)
existence	existent
independence	independent

-ence, -ent

Noun	Adjective
innocence	innocent
insistence	insistent
obedience	obedient
persistence	persistent
presence	present
prevalence	prevalent
prominence	prominent
reverence	reverent

A group of nouns end in -ense:

dispense   expense   offense   pretense   suspense

and 1. *And* is a *coordinating* conjunction, that is, it connects elements of equal grammatical value:

ADJECTIVES: a pink and white apron; a blue, green, and white flag
ADVERBS: He drove fast and a little carelessly.
NOUNS: trees and shrubs; trees, shrubs, and plants
VERBS: I found the book and opened it at the exact place.
PHRASES: in one ear and out the other
SUBORDINATE CLAUSES: While the boys were swimming and [while] the older folks were resting, I was reading.
COORDINATE CLAUSES: The first generation makes the money and the second spends it.

Care needs to be taken that the elements are really of equal value. Some temptations to connect wrongly unequal elements are:

a) Main verbs and participles:

Three or four men sat on the edge of the lake with their backs to the road, [and] apparently watching the ducks.

b) Main and subordinate clauses (*which §2):

A contract has been let to install new copper work on the Post Office [and] which will require 4500 pounds of lead coated copper.

2. *And* is often overused in amateur writing, used where no connective is needed, or where some other connective would be more accurate:

All the passages inside the muskrats' house tended to head upward and we pushed the traps far enough in to reach dry ground. [Since all the passages . . ., we pushed . . .]
At prep school we had certain hours for study and during that time [during which time] the dormitories were quiet.
The freshmen have a number of required courses and [but] the upperclassmen almost none.

3. In current writing, especially informal writing with rather short sentences, *and* often stands at the beginning of sentences:

> You cannot permit investment bankers to manage trusts without permitting all of them to do it. And you cannot open it to the good ones without opening it to all. And in practice, the least trustworthy will be the first to rush in to employ this facile instrument of money control.—JOHN T. FLYNN, *Scribner's Magazine*, July 1937

If this usage becomes conspicuous, some of the *and*'s should be dropped or two sentences put together as a compound sentence.

4. In some compact writing *and* is omitted between series of items. Judiciously used this omission makes for economy, but used very frequently it is a mark of a "telegraphic" style which is usually inappropriate for general writing. Three *and*'s would be possible in this sentence:

> An expert at making points of dogma crystal clear, Father LaBuffe had a blackboard handy, [∧] covered it with white, red, green, [∧] yellow chalk marks demonstrating the meaning of the Trinity, Original Sin, Transubstantiation, [∧] Incarnation.—*Time*, Sept. 27, 1937

These *Index* articles involve *and*: *Compound predicate, *Compound sentences, *Compound subject, *Conjunctive adverbs, *Coordinating conjunctions; *between you and me, *which (*and which*); *Series (punctuation before *and* in a series of three or more items)

and etc. is a careless redundancy, since *etc.* (*et cetera*) already contains *and* (in the Latin *et*). See *etc., et cetera.

and/or is primarily a business and legal locution. It is useful when three alternatives exist (*both* circumstances mentioned or *either one* of the two): *fruit and/or vegetables* means "fruit and vegetables," or "fruit or vegetables."

The use of *and/or* in general writing is objected to by many people because of its business connotation, but it is sometimes found:

> There is something in the power of "great" personalities, but to found a theory of history on it is to deny the demonstrated existence of surrounding circumstances which condition and/or determine the conduct of leaders, heroes, and dictators.—C. A. BEARD, *The Discussion of Human Affairs*, p. 107

And alone often means *and/or* or *or*, and would be interpreted so:

> Adjectives and adverbs are usually placed near the words they modify. [Whichever is used stands near the word it modifies.]

and which *which §2

angle *Angle* is often *deadwood and suggests a vulgate or business phrase that is out of place in general writing:

> In a preparatory school the masters go at the matter from a different angle [that is, *differently*] and make the same kind of literature more enjoyable.

Anglicization The process of making foreign words into English words. See *Foreign words in English.

Antecedent An antecedent is the word or statement to which a pronoun or pronominal adjective refers. It may stand before or after the pronoun:

> We did not hear their call again and when we found the Thompsons they were almost exhausted. (*The Thompsons* is the antecedent of the pronominal adjective *their* and the pronoun *they*.)

For relations between antecedents and their pronouns see *Reference of pronouns.

antenna In zoölogy the Latin plural *antennae* is usually kept, but this is too foreign a form for most of us in talking about radios, so that the regular plural form of the radio antenna is *antennas*.

anti-, anti The prefix *anti-*, meaning "against" in its various senses, is hyphened only before root words beginning with *i* and before proper nouns:

anticlimax	antifreeze	antimonarchic	antisocial
anti-imperialistic	anti-intellectual	anti-British	anti-Semitic

Anti- is pronounced an'ti or often, more emphatically, an'tī.

Anti is a colloquial and informal noun, meaning "a person opposed to something"; plural *antis*.

> The supporters of the plan spoke amid boos from the antis.

Anticipatory subject See *there is, there are.

Anticlimax Arrangement of a series in order of descending importance of the elements. It may be intentional, as a form of humor (as in Pope's "Men, monkeys, lap-dogs, parrots, perish all"), or unintentional because of a lapse of judgment that should be corrected. See p. 174.

Antithesis *Antithesis* means contrast. For paragraphs developed by contrast, see "Contrast and comparison," p. 102.

Antonym An antonym is a word that means the opposite of another word: *hot, stingy, boring* are antonyms of *cold, generous, entertaining*. Most books of synonyms also give antonyms, as do the synonym entries in dictionaries.

any, and compounds with any 1. *Any* is used primarily as an adjective (*any* member of the family; *Any* dog is a good dog), but also as a pronoun (*Any* will do).

In comparisons of things of the same class, *idiom calls for *any other*: "This book is better than *any other* on the subject"; but: "I think a movie is more entertaining than *any* book" (Not the same class of things).

2. COMPOUNDS WITH *any*: Anybody, anyhow, anything, and *anywhere* are always written as single words. *Any* rate is always two words: "At *any rate*." *Anyone* is written as one word when the stress is on the *any*, and as two when the stress is on the *one*:

Anyone (en'i wun) would know that.
I'd like *any one* (en i wun') of them.

Anyway is one word when the *any* is stressed (I can't do it en'e wā) and two when the stress is about equal: *Any* way (en'i wā') I try, it comes out wrong.

Anybody is colloquial and informal; *anyone* is rather more formal.

3. PRONOUNS REFERRING TO *anybody, anyone. Anybody* and *anyone* are singular and take singular verbs: Anybody [Anyone] feels bad at times. They are referred to by *one* or more often by *he, his, him*: Anybody knows what he deserves.

Informally *anyone* and *anybody* often are treated as collectives and are referred to by a plural pronoun:

. . . and a top that goes up and down without anybody losing their temper.—THORNTON WILDER (letter), *Theatre Arts*, Nov. 1940, p. 821

Compare *every and its compounds; Fries, p. 50.

4. VULGATE FORMS. *Anyhow* is colloquial and vulgate for *anyway* (He couldn't do it *anyhow*) and *any place* for *anywhere* (He wasn't *any place* I looked). *Anyways, anywheres* are vulgate for *anyway* and *anywhere*.

Aphorism *Epigrams

Apostrophe (') (CORRECTION: Insert an apostrophe where it belongs in the word marked; or, take out a wrongly used apostrophe.) *Apos*

1. The most common use of the apostrophe is in spelling the *genitive (possessive) case of nouns and of the indefinite pronouns (*anyone, nobody, someone*—See *Pronouns §8):

Dorothy's first picture   The companies' original charters
Everybody's business is nobody's business.

Special examples of possessive form are discussed in *Genitive case.

2. The apostrophe is also used to show the omission of one or more letters in contractions: *can't, I'm, I'll, it's* [*it is*]. See *Contractions.

3. An apostrophe is generally used in plurals of figures, letters of the alphabet, and words being discussed as words:

three *e*'s   the 1920's   The first of the two *that*'s

There is a growing tendency to omit this apostrophe:

> The legendary Miss Millay, the feminine Byron of the 1920s . . .
> —Louis Untermeyer, *Modern American Poetry*, p. 485

4. In representing colloquial speech, an apostrophe is used to show that certain sounds represented in the usual spelling were not spoken:

Good mornin'   He was goin' to see fer himself.
"An' one o' them is the new schoolmaster," he shouted.

This is a legitimate use, but too many apostrophes make a spotted page and confuse the reader. It is better to suggest occasional malpronunciations than to try to represent them conscientiously. *Conversation

5. Apostrophes are not used in the genitive of the personal pronouns (*his, hers, ours, theirs*) or to apologize for a commonly used simplified spelling form (*altho*, not *altho'*; *thru* rather than *thro'*).

appearing Inflated (or falsely formal) for *looking*:

a comfortable looking [better than *appearing*] street
a fine looking [better than *appearing*] house

appendix The English plural *appendixes* is rapidly overtaking the Latin *appendices* and is the better form except in quite formal usage.

Apposition, Appositives Apposition is a method of modifying a noun or other expression by placing immediately after it an equivalent expression that repeats its meaning:

Alexander [appositive:] *the Great*
The word [appositive:] *apposition* means "putting beside."

Appositives are either close (restrictive) and not set off by commas, or loose (non-restrictive) and usually set off by commas (*Restrictive and non-restrictive):

CLOSE: Washington *the Capital* is a symbol of democracy and America. Washington *the city* is a symbol of almost everything that sincere and thoughtful men know is wrong with democracy and

America.—ALDEN STEVENS, "Washington: Blight on Democracy," *Harper's Magazine*, Dec. 1941, p. 50

LOOSE: Literary critics have repeatedly called attention to the pathetic fallacy, *the reading of emotion* in emotionless things, the angry thunder, the benign sunshine.—IRWIN EDMAN, *Four Ways of Philosophy*, p. 29

CLOSE (RESTRICTIVE, LIMITING)	LOOSE (NON-RESTRICTIVE, DESCRIPTIVE)
Coach Bradley	Our coach, Bradley,
My aunts Mary and Agnes (He had more aunts.)	My aunts, Mary and Agnes, . . . (He had only two.)
The fact *that he had been over the road before* gave him an advantage.	This fact, *that he had been over the road before*, gave him an advantage.
Fletcher the grocer	Fletcher, our grocer, . . .
William the Conqueror	William I, conqueror of England, . . .
	Wisdom, the property of few, . . .

An appositive agrees with its headnoun in number and case:

He called the two of us, *John and me* [objects].
The two of us, *John and I* [subjects], were going together.

Reference: Curme, *Syntax*, pp. 88-92

Appropriateness The doctrine of this book is that Good English is based on appropriateness in the language to the subject and situation, to the reader or listener, and to the writer or speaker. For discussion, see pp. 39-50.

apt *likely

Arabic numerals Our ordinary numbers, 1, 2, 647. See *Numbers.

Archaic Words and constructions formerly common in the language but now going out of use (*methinks, goodly, aye, thou*). See "Archaic English," p. 4.

Areas of usage See "Levels of usage," p. 11.

are or is? When the subject and object or complement are of different numbers the verb agrees with the subject. (These tracks are a pretty good road—A pretty good road is made by these tracks.) See *Subject and verb § 2e.

arise Situations may *arise*, but not people, except in poetry. See *rise. Compare *wake.

around *round—around

Articles *a, an; *the

-ary For pronunciation of words ending in *-ary* (*dictionary* and so on) see *Pronunciation §4c.

as *As* is one of the most versatile words in English and one of the most frequently used. Some of its more frequent uses at present are:

1. AS AN ADVERB:

OF DEGREE: I came *as* soon as I could.
INTRODUCING APPOSITIVES: I regard him *as* our greatest pitcher. There were several kinds of shellfish, *as* scallops, oysters, crabs, lobsters. (This last use is informal.)

2. AS A PRONOUN: In formal English usually with *same* or *such* as antecedent:

We were in the same row *as* the others were.
It was such a day *as* one rarely sees.

Also as a common vulgate relative pronoun, taking the place of *who* and *that:* "Everyone *as* has his ticket can go in."

3. AS A PREPOSITION: "in the position of, in the role of":

She had a job *as* stenographer.   He was in the cast *as* Mercutio.

In the colloquial construction "I don't like him as well *as her*," (meaning "I don't like him *as well as I like her*") *as her* may be construed as a prepositional phrase: "Who would want to go with such a poor skater *as* me? (Formal usage would often have ". . . with such a poor skater as I [am].")

There is a growing tendency to use *as* instead of *like* as a preposition:

Madame Curie loved radium as [*like* preferable] a child.

4. AS A CONJUNCTION: *As* occurs most commonly as a conjunction, introducing several kinds of clauses.

DEGREE OR MANNER: . . . as far *as* I could.
TIME=WHILE: *As* I was coming in, he was going out.
ATTENDANT CIRCUMSTANCE: He told stories *as* we went along.
CAUSE: *As* it was getting dark, we made for home.

Such a handy word is of course much used in speech, which often prefers *counter words to more exact ones. But the very variety of possible uses makes *as* a problem in written English. It is necessary in comparisons (We went as far *as* he did) and for attendant circumstance (*As* we walked along he told us stories) though *while* is preferable if the emphasis is on the time or the action (*While* we were walking along he told us stories).

As is weak in the sense of *because*. Usually *since* or *because* would be better in writing and certainly would be better in formal English:

COLLOQUIAL: *As* it was almost time to go, we were getting more and more exasperated.

MORE EXACT AND EMPHATIC: *Since* it was almost time to go, we were getting more and more exasperated.

Because it was almost time to go, we were getting more and more exasperated.

References: Curme, *Syntax*, pp. 269-71; *Parts of Speech*, pp. 78-82, and index references in both volumes

as . . . as 1. In double comparisons we sometimes fail to complete the first construction with a second *as*:

He is fully as tall [∧] if not taller than his older brother.

This reads more smoothly if completed:

He is fully as tall *as*, if not taller than, his older brother.

But since the interrupted sentence movement is undesirable in informal English, it is usually better to complete the first comparison and then add the second:

He is fully as tall as his older brother, if not taller.

2. In negative comparisons formal English sometimes prefers *not so . . . as*:

The winters are *not so* long or so cold *as* they used to be.
The winters are *neither so* cold *nor so* long as they used to be.

Informal English does not as a rule make this distinction:

The winters are *not as* long or as cold *as* they used to be.

Which idiom is to be used depends on the formality of the context.

as if (as though) In formal English the subjunctive is used after *as if* or *as though*:

He acted *as if* [*as though*] *he were* losing his temper.

In informal English the subjunctive would not always be used:

He acted *as if* [*as though*] *he was* losing his temper.

See *Subjunctives.

as or like For the conflict between *as* and *like* (I can't swim *as* I used to—I can't swim *like* I used to), see *like—as.

Aspect of verbs Grammarians have recently begun to study in English verbs a characteristic called *aspect*, the means by which we show whether the act is a whole, completed, and regarded as a fact (*Terminate* or *punctual aspect:* "She *swam* half a mile that afternoon"; "He *fell asleep* in spite of himself"), or whether the act is continuing (*Durative* or *progressive aspect:* "She *is swimming*"; "He *was falling asleep* in spite of himself"). Anyone interested in the matter can turn to the brief treatments in Kennedy, pp. 303-304; Curme, *Parts of Speech*, pp. 232-37; *Syntax*, pp. 373-88; and then go on to the references mentioned there.

Assonance Rhyme is the correspondence in two syllables of the vowel sounds and the consonants (if any) following them (*leaf—sheaf, lake—wake*); assonance is the like sound of vowels in syllables having different consonants (*brave—vain, lone—show*). Assonance is a common and effective sound element in verse and is also common in prose, especially in emotional or heightened prose:

> "that id*ea*l country, of gr*ee*n, d*ee*p lanes and high gr*ee*n banks."—
> OSBERT SITWELL, *Trio*, p. 89

Asterisk (*) Except in reference works, the asterisk or star is not used so much now as formerly, because it is a conspicuous mark and attracts more attention than is necessary.

1. Asterisks are sometimes used to indicate a rather long omission in a quotation, as of a stanza or more from a poem, or a paragraph or more from prose, though now a line of spaced periods is more in favor. *Ellipsis

2. In fiction a group of asterisks has been used to suggest that action is not given or to indicate passage of time between movements of a story, but here again a line of spaced periods or extra space between the movements is more common. *Ellipsis

3. In works which have very few footnotes, an asterisk may be used as a reference mark, placed after the statement calling for the note and again at the beginning of the footnote.

4. In this book, where frequent cross references are helpful, the asterisk has been adopted to avoid unpleasant repetition of the word *See*, and to make cross references in running text.

as to *As to* is often a clumsy substitute for a single preposition, usually *of* or *about:*

> Practice proves the best teacher as to [*in, for, of*] the use of organ stops.
> If the question contains words as to the exact meaning of which [of whose exact meaning] you are uncertain, by all means get out your dictionary.

athlete, athletic, athletics Watch your spelling of these, and help your spelling by pronouncing them in clearcut syllables: ath'lete, ath let'ic, ath let'ics.

When *athletics* refers to sports and games it usually takes a plural verb and pronoun:

> Our athletics *include* football, basketball, and baseball.

When *athletics* refers to skill or activity it usually takes a singular verb and pronoun:

> Athletics *is* recommended for every student.

Attributive An adjective that stands next its noun is attributive (a *blue* shirt, a shirt, *blue* and *clean*), as contrasted with a predicate adjective that is related to its noun by a *linking verb (The shirt is *blue*).

Author card, Authorities See "The working bibliography," p. 324 and "Sources of reference," p. 327.

autobiography *biography

Auxiliary verb A verb used with another verb to form a phrasal tense, voice, or mood is called an *auxiliary verb:*

> I *am* going.   He *will* go.   They *were* lost.   He *should* watch out.

Be, do, have are the commonest auxiliaries; *can, may, shall, will, must, ought, should, would, might* are frequently used as auxiliaries; *get, let, need,* and *used* sometimes function as auxiliaries. See *Index* entries on these verbs and the general article *Verbs.

awful In formal English *awful* means "inspiring with awe." In familiar and vulgate English it is a general utility word of disapproval—"ugly, shocking, ludicrous" (*awful* manners, an *awful* run in my stocking). As a result of this contamination the word is seldom used in careful writing; *awe-inspiring* has taken its place. *Awfully* is an example of *Schoolgirl style.

awhile, a while *Awhile* is an adverb (*awhile* ago). Strictly a prepositional phrase, in which *while* is a noun, should be in three words (*for a while, in a while*), but *awhile* is sometimes found.

Awkward (CORRECTION: Rewrite the passage marked.)   *Awk*
A rather general word of disapproval conveniently used in correcting themes. It may refer to clumsy, *absolute phrases, unnatural *word order, unnecessary *repetition of a word or phrase, uncomfortable *reference of pronouns, *split infinitives, or other unfortunate phrasing.

B The letter *b* is chiefly conspicuous in English for its frequent appearance as a *silent letter and therefore a possible snare in spelling and sometimes in pronunciation. Many silent *b*'s, especially after *m*, represent *b*'s that were pronounced in Old English but perhaps have not been generally sounded for hundreds of years: *climb* (klīm), *comb* (kōm), *limb* (lim). The *b* is pronounced in the formal or archaic *clamber* and in *limber*. A *b* has rather recently been added in *crumb* and *thumb*. Other silent *b*'s represent sounds that were in the Latin ancestor words but that had been dropped as the words passed through Old French: *debt* (from *debitum*), *doubt* (from *dubitare*), *subtle* (from *subtilis*). Some of these *b*'s were re-inserted by Renaissance scholars because they wished to tie English closer to Latin: Chaucer wrote *det* but we cannot.

When *b* comes next to *p* the two sounds sometimes are assimilated to one: *cupboard* (kub′ərd), *subpoena* (sometimes sə pē′nə).

Back formations *Origin of words § 3d

bad, badly *Bad* is an adjective of varied application:

a bad man	a bad night	bad weather	a bad light
a bad cold	a bad accident	bad news	a bad taste

In "I feel bad about it," "She looks bad," *bad* is a predicate adjective. See *Linking verbs.

Badly is an adverb used to describe the manner of the action named by the verb:

He draws badly.   The starter has always worked badly.

Worse, worst, the comparative and superlative of *bad*, of course come from a quite different root. They were first used in comparing *evil* and *ill*, and when *bad* acquired the meaning of those words, *worse* and *worst* were used for it too.

Bad grammar *Bad grammar* is used as a term of reproach and is applied to all sorts of locutions from "I ain't got none" to supposed confusions in the use of "shall" and "will." Our attitude toward such locutions may be less severe if we recognize their sources. Some people feel that these expressions are sins against good English, that they are lapses from a standard. Generally they are expressions from a different dialect, often from colloquial or vulgate speech, that occur in the midst of more formal English. The objection to them is not that they are sins against "grammar," for most of them are perfectly conventional ways of expression in their appropriate dialect, but that when they appear in a different setting, they are *inappropriate*, and consequently to be avoided. Other instances of inappropriate grammar are due to imperfect mastery of a construction usual in a given level as in various *shifted constructions. See Chapter 2, Good English.

Balanced sentences Sentences in which two parts are of conspicuously similar length and form. See "Balanced sentences," p. 160.

Barbarism is a term used to describe a word that is irregularly formed or that is not in good use, like *irregardless* and *preventative*. See *Long variants, *Origin of words § 3.

Basic English The increased use of English as the language of trade and travel in all countries and the need for a simplification of English for teaching to foreigners has led to several attempts to compile a short list of necessary, universal words and a minimum selection of the grammatical forms of our language.

The most widely discussed of these simplifications was worked out by C. K. Ogden and is called Basic English. He compiled a list of 850 words which he regarded as *basic* for conversation, and proposes that they be taught all over the world and used as the foundation of an international language. The words would be used according to a simplified English grammar. *Robinson Crusoe* and other books have been translated into Basic, and some elementary textbooks are written in Basic.

The list of words and the grammar are open to various criticisms. Relying on roundabout phrases to express simple ideas and especially relying on *verb-adverb combinations will puzzle many foreigners. The individual words are simple enough, but the meanings of such combinations as *look up* (in a book), *look up to, come over, feel for* are not derived from the combined meanings of the single words. Nevertheless the attempt to make English more widely current is worth watching.

References: Kennedy, §§ 129, 130; Ogden, C. K., *The System of Basic English*, New York, 1934; Aiken, Janet R., *Commonsense Grammar*, New York, 1936, Ch. 20; Fries, C. C. and Trevor, A. A., *English Word Lists*, Washington, 1940.

be 1. FORMS. The English verb *be* has forms from three originally separate verbs (as in *are, was, been*) but we use the verb so much that the various forms give little trouble:

PRESENT: I am, you are, he is; we, you, they are
    OBSOLETE: thou art
PRESENT SUBJUNCTIVE: I, you, he, we, you, they be
PAST: I was, you were, he was; we, you, they were
    OBSOLETE: thou wast or wert

PAST SUBJUNCTIVE: I, you, he, we, you, they were
  OBSOLETE: thou wert
INFINITIVE: be; PRESENT PARTICIPLE: being; PAST PARTICIPLE: been

Some old forms survive in stock phrases ("the powers that *be*") and in the vulgate, as in "You ain't [sometimes *be'n't*] going, *be* you?" The vulgate also continues to use *was* in the plural ("*Was* the Adamses there?"), which would have been good informal usage 200 years ago. This levels the past tense to one form (*was*), as it is in all other English verbs.

2. AS A LINKING VERB: *Be* is the most common *linking verb, linking, without adding specifically a meaning of its own, a subject and a predicate nominative or adjective:

Jerome was the secretary. [Predicate nominative]
She is sick. [Predicate adjective]

With the finite parts of *be* the predicate noun or pronoun is in the nominative case in written English:

It was *he*. [Colloquial: It was *him*.]

It's I is formal for colloquial and familiar *It's me*. *It's me
When the infinitive has a subject and complement, both are in the objective form:

I wanted *him* to be *me*.

When the infinitive has no subject, formal usage has a nominative as the complement (I wanted to be *he*) but informal usage would more often have an accusative (I wanted to be *him*).

3. AS AUXILIARY VERB. Forms of *be* are used with the present participles of other verbs to form the progessive tense form:

I am asking   he was asking   you will be asking

Forms of *be* with past participles form the passive voice:

I am asked   you will be asked   he was asked

In colloquial English, a form of *be* is often used in two different functions, as linking verb and as auxiliary:

COLLOQUIAL: They were ready and getting into the car.

In formal English the form of *be* should be repeated:

FORMAL: They were [linking verb] ready and were [auxiliary] getting into the car.

4. AS VERB OF COMPLETE PREDICATION. *Be* is a verb of complete predication when indicating states or positions:

He *was* at home anywhere.   The fire *was* just across the street.

394

In the sense of "exist," "live" (Hamlet's "To be, or not to be," "Can such things be?") *be* is now rather rare but can be used sometimes with strong effect:

> You have heard nothing of your wife and your children. They do not know if you are dead or alive or blinded. You do not know where they are, or if they are.—DOROTHY PARKER, *The New Yorker*, Feb. 5, 1938

For use of subjunctive forms ("If I were you . . .") see *Subjunctives; for agreement with subject when predicate noun is of different number ("The broken twigs were proof . . . ," "The proof was the broken twigs") see *Subject and verb; see also *ain't, *It's me.

beau Plural *beaus*, or, formally, *beaux*; pronounced bōz.

because introduces a subordinate clause giving the reason for the independent statement:

> Because we were getting hungry, we began to look for a convenient restaurant.

Since and *as* can be used in such clauses, but they are less definite, more casual, and are more characteristic of easy speech than of writing:

> In a small rural school these young children have to stay for the rest of the day's session, because [more definite than *as* or *since*] there is no one to take them home.

For, which also introduces reasons, is a more formal word, rather rare in conversation and informal writing. It also has often the sense of giving evidence for the statement, for the writer's knowledge of the fact stated, rather than for its cause:

> INFORMAL: I know he is reliable, because I have traded with him for years.
> MORE FORMAL: I know he is reliable, for I have traded with him for years. ["He is reliable because I have traded with him for years" would not make sense.]

See *reason is because . . . for use of a *because* clause balancing the noun *reason*. See also *for.

become *Linking verbs

been Pronounced bin, rarely bēn in the United States but more commonly in England.

Beginning paragraphs (CORRECTION: Revise the opening paragraph to make it lead more directly into your subject and if possible to arouse your reader's interest.) *Beg*

For discussion of qualities of beginning paragraphs and examples, see "Beginning paragraphs," p. 67.

beside—besides *Beside* is a preposition referring to place, "by the side of," as in "beside the road," "beside her," and is used figuratively in a few rather formal idioms like "beside the point," "beside himself with rage" (*Beside* is less commonly used as an adverb, with the meaning of *besides*).

Besides is an adverb or preposition meaning "in addition to" or "except":

> We tried two other ways besides [adverb].
> Besides our own members, . . . [preposition]
> He said that his wife was a regular farm wife who helped him milk the cows besides raising five fine healthy children [preposition].

It is used colloquially as a conjunctive adverb:

> He didn't think that he ought to get into the quarrel; besides, he had come to enjoy himself.

between, among *Among* implies more than two objects:

> They distributed the provisions among the survivors.

In its most exact use, *between* implies only two:

> They divided the prize between Kincaid and Thomas.

If *between* is used of more than two, it suggests the individuals involved more than the situation:

> The family of seven hadn't a pair of shoes between them.

Reference: Pooley, pp. 120-22

between you and me Since the object of a preposition is grammatically in the accusative case, the correct form is *between you and me, for you and me, to you and me* (or when the pronouns are objects of a verb, "He will take *you and me*").

Among people with dangerously little learning the form is often *between you and I*—reversing the usual colloquial tendency to use *me* (as in *It's me), perhaps because the speakers remember the prohibition against *It's me* and carry over the taboo to a different construction.

Bible, bible *Bible*, referring to the Christian Scriptures, is capitalized but not italicized: "You will find all that in the Bible, and more too." *Bible* in the sense of an authoritative book or (informally) a book much consulted or quoted, is not capitalized: "Gray's *Manual*, the botanist's bible, . . ."

The usual form of particular references to parts of the Bible is:

the Old Testament   the New Testament (capitalized but not italicized)

The Ten Commandments are in Exodus xx (or: in Exodus 20).

The Ten Commandments are in Exodus 20:3-17.

I Corinthians 4:6

The adjective *biblical* is not capitalized.

Bibliography   A bibliography is a list of books and other published material consulted in writing a paper (a final bibliography), or to be consulted in gathering material for a paper (a working bibliography).

Details of form and method of both bibliographies are given in Chapter 13, The Research Paper:

"Form of a working bibliography," p. 324.

"Sources of bibliographical references," p. 327.

"Form of final bibliography," p. 343.

Big words   (CORRECTION: Use a simpler, more natural word instead of the formal or heavy one.)   *Big W*

Modern writing uses direct and ordinary words instead of "bigger" ones—*home* rather than *domicile, think* or *believe* rather than *deem, happen* rather than *transpire,* and so on. For full discussion of big words and suggestions for avoiding them see "Big words," p. 220.

biography   Pronounced bī-og′rə fi (or bi-, not bē-). A biography is the life of a person written by some one else; an autobiography is the life of a person written by himself.

Blanks for names and dates have gone out of fashion. The present style is all for specificness. Don't write "In 18—" but, if the exact date isn't to be given, "About sixty years ago."

Similarly, "Mr. ——" or "Mr. X" or "A man whom I shall call Mr. Wheeler, though that is not his name" would be avoided. Real names are used wherever possible, or if they cannot be used, the avoidance is made as inconspicuous as possible by "A man," "Someone," or some such expression.

Blend   A word made by fusing two words often with a syllable in common: paratroops, cinemactress, beautility, snoopervise. *Origin of words § 3b.*

Until a blend has made its way in the language, as *electrocute* (for *electric* and *execute*) has, it is more appropriate to informal than formal writing.

blond, blonde   As a noun, *blond* is used of a man, *blonde* of a woman:

He is a blond.   She is a blonde.   a peroxide blonde (or blond)

In its adjective use, the -e is gradually disappearing and in informal writing, at least, *blond* can always be written. Some write *blonde* when it refers specifically to a woman (a blonde Helen) and *blond* elsewhere, including *blond hair*.

Brunet, brunette are in the same situation: masculine noun *brunet*, feminine noun *brunette*, with perhaps a tendency to use *brunette* as the adjective (to help represent the accent on the second syllable).

Probably two such common words will gradually lose their French spellings and be written like English words with only one form.

-body *Anybody, everybody* are single words. See *any and its compounds, *every and its compounds.

Boners Confusion of two similar words, mistaken constructions, combinations of ideas that don't belong together have always been a source of fun for everyone except the persons who made them. Volumes of these boners have been gathered and several periodicals run specimens that they find in other publications. Here are a few that have cropped up in themes:

My papers have a decided tendency toward longevity.
He is descended from one of the most virulent [really *poisonous?* or merely *virile?*] families in the U. S. A.
Jean is no plastic saint.
For the lowly freshmen are moved by sediment rather than by intellect in their voting.
The arduous loves of movie stars are not always convincing.
Many times I started for the library to do some research on Gestalt's psychology.
[Of the cross country team, running on back roads:] Not even the sharp stones can dampen their spirits.

Keep your eye out for boners in manuscript and in print and get what fun you can from them—but most of all scan your own writing to catch them before they come to anybody else's attention.

book refers especially to the contents, *volume* to the physical appearance. A *book* may be in two or more *volumes*.

book These compounds with *book* are spelled as one word:

bookbinder	bookmaker	bookshelf
bookbindery, etc.	bookmark	bookshop (book shop)
bookcase	bookplate	bookstore
bookkeeper	bookseller	bookworm

As two words:

book end	book learning	book review

born, borne 1. The past participle of *bear* in most of its senses is *borne*:

> They had *borne* this poverty without complaining.
> The ship was *borne* along by a fast breeze.
> The ship, *borne* along by the breeze, was soon out of sight.

Bear in most of these senses is somewhat formal; *endure* or *carry* would be more common.

In the sense of "give birth to," the past participle of *bear* is spelled *borne* except in the (very common) passive when not followed by *by*:

> She had *borne* five children.
> Of the four children *borne* by his first wife . . .
> He was *born* in 1891.   A *born* liar.
> The children, *born* in Chicago . . .

2. In autobiographical papers, writers often become self-conscious or humorous in giving the fact of their birth: "I saw the light of day first on June 28, 1924"; "No planets blazed on the night of June 28, 1924, when a squally infant appeared in the home of Mr. and Mrs. . . ." None of these is any improvement over the simple and natural statement "I was born June 28, 1924."

Borrowed words *Foreign words in English; *Origin of words § 2

both *Both* is a favorite colloquial way of emphasizing two-ness:

> The twins were both there. They are both alike. Both Harry and his brother went.

Strictly speaking, all these *both*'s are redundant and would not be used in formal English. They usually fit in informal or colloquial English. But a sentence like "The both women got along well enough together" is a localism for "The two women got along well enough together."

both . . . and *Correlative conjunctions

bourgeois Pronounced bür′zhwä, sometimes bür zhwä′. Singular and plural are pronounced the same. The noun *bourgeoisie* is bür′zhwä zē′ or bür′zhwə zē′.

Brace { } is the mark used to group two or more lines of writing. Its use is chiefly in technical writing, especially in tables and formulas. Examples of braces will be found in *English language and the Levels of usage table on p. 13.

Brackets [ ] Brackets are rarely used in general writing and are not in the standard typewriter keyboard, but in much academic and professional writing they have specific and convenient uses.

Brackets are primarily editorial marks, used to show where some explanation or comment has been added to the text, especially to quoted matter:

> The preposition *due to* is not more incorrect than the preposition *owing to*, which is approved by the same dictionary [the *Concise Oxford Dictionary*], but it is not yet so thoroughly established in the language.—G. O. CURME, *Syntax*, p. 561

> and by the Accounts thereof, made up by Mr. Peirce, Master of the said ship, and [*torn*] Agent for Mr. Craddocke, one of the Owners; being al[*torn*] by Mr. Peters . . .'—S. E. MORISON, *The Founding of Harvard College*

If the torn word had been filled in by the editor, the conjectured letters would be in brackets: being al[lowed] by Mr. Peters . . .

In quoting material, *sic* in brackets is sometimes used to indicate that an error was in the original: "New Haven, Conneticut [sic] . . ."; or a correction may be inserted in brackets: "When he was thirty-eight [Actually he was forty-three] he published his first novel."

Brackets are used, though now rarely, as parentheses within parentheses. They are likely to be found particularly in legal documents or in footnotes to theses, etc.

In this *Index*, brackets are used in examples of faulty writing to inclose words that might better be left out, or to suggest an improved expression:

> Throughout [the course of] the year I read such books as *Oliver Twist* and *Boots and Saddles*.
> The continuously moving belt makes a noise *similar to* [*like*] a cement mixer.

breath noun, breth; **breathe** verb, brēᴛʜ:

> a *breath* of air   the air we *breathe*

Brevity See discussion of economy, p. 161, and *Wordiness.

Britain Remember the spelling.

British usage *American and British usage

broadcast The past tense and past participle of *broadcast* are both *broadcast* and *broadcasted*, with the first more common.

Broad reference A pronoun referring to a preceding idea rather than to a particular antecedent is said to have a broad reference. See *Reference of pronouns §1.

bunch In formal English *bunch* is limited to objects that grow together or can be fastened together (a bunch of carrots, roses, keys) and to expressions like "a bunch of cattle." Colloquial and informal English holds to the older usage of *bunch*, applying it to a small collection of anything—including people.

bureaucracy Pronounced bū rok′rə si; sometimes bū rō′krə si; *bureaucrat* pronounced būr′ō krat.

burst The principal parts of *burst* are *burst, burst, burst:*

One *bursts* almost every day. Two tanks *burst* yesterday. One tank had *burst*.

Bust is vulgate in the sense of "smashing" or "exploding" or "breaking out." It is slang in the sense of "going broke" but good English in "*busting* a bronco" or "*busting* a trust."

It was the idea of busting the trusts and imprisoning their officers that roused the crowd.—N. A. CRAWFORD, *The Ethics of Journalism,* p. 65

bus has plural *buses* or *busses*, the first more common American usage.

Business English (CORRECTION: The word marked would be appropriate in business writing but not in the place you have it. Change to one from the general vocabulary. [See last paragraph of this article.]) *Bus*

The writing of business English has attained a very high standard of mechanical form. The layout, spacing, and paragraphing of most business letters and reports are excellent, reflecting the skill of professional typists; and the skill of layout men and printers is available for printed matter.

But the usage and style of these business communications vary considerably. Most firms at present pay a good deal of attention to the style of their written and printed matter. The old clichés—*in re, the above, Yrs. of 23d inst, rec'd and contents noted, and oblige*—have practically disappeared. Naturally all degrees of formality and informality are found. The prime virtues of good business writing are *directness* and *adaptation to reader*. Giving information about goods, arranging methods of payment, even encouraging sales, all profit from straightforward writing. Adapting the style to the reader is especially difficult in writing advertising and business letters, since usually the writer is not acquainted with his reader and in spite of elaborate market analyses may not visualize him right. If the letter is sent broadcast, there is the difficulty of making it *seem* personal when it really cannot be personal. But for most purposes "business English" is merely good English applied to the specific needs of industry and trade.

At present a good deal of business writing is informal—not only in the attempts to get the back-slapping approach on paper, but also in its naturalness, or even colloquialness. Like our realistic novelists, business people have adventured into a simple style and have handled English with the freedom a living language deserves. They have pioneered in the much needed shortening of our spelling. Business writers have used all the native resources of the language in making new names and in brightening style—outright coinages like *kodak, vaseline, fabrikoid,* blends like *servicenter, unisteel, sunoco,* compounds and respellings like *cutex, denticuring* (preventive dentistry), *tudor* (cars), *lubritory, valetaria* (a laundry). Though many such words are ludicrous or overcute or in poor taste, some are expressive and are normal language developments. They are much better than attempts at false dignity (*client* for *customer, favor* for *letter, the business world* for *business, cheque* for **check*) and the silly exaggeration of a good deal of advertising—seen most clearly in movie ads ("Garbo in the strong arms of Robert Taylor . . . truly a lifetime of thrilling romance in one shining moment of ecstasy!").

The question of fitness arises when certain words with obvious business connotation are used in other contexts. Some are frequently borrowed and are useful: *deal, asset, feature, bank on,* and *take stock in* are common colloquial usage. But many people, who perhaps do not like to be reminded that they live in a society primarily commercial, are offended by *advise, *angle, *and/or, *contact, *realtor, receptionist, selling point.* Such words are out of place in formal writing and in discussions of ideal rather than practical affairs; but in informal writing business locutions are often useful. H. S. Canby used ordinary business terms to point up a comment on current literature:

> No; public taste, ease of publication, variety of interest, even editorial capability, have all risen with the intellectual development of the country; only the professional writers, as a class, have not progressed. They have become astonishingly clever, as clever as the mechanism of a Ford; but as a class they have not moved ten feet towards literature. *They have standardized their product without improving the model.—Saturday Papers,* p. 56

See *Letters; *Reports; "Euphemisms," p. 218; "Shoptalk," p. 24. The various textbooks on business English give details of the use of English (and psychology) in business situations.

Business letters *Letters

business world Inflated for *business* or *business men:*

> The bookkeeping course interested me because I expect to enter the business world [because I expect to go into business].

but *But* is the natural coordinating conjunction to connect two contrasted (adversative) statements of equal grammatical rank. It is more natural than the heavy and formal **however* or **yet.* (See also **although.*)

1. The locutions connected by *but* should be of equal grammatical weight:

ADJECTIVES: not blue but green.
ADVERBS: He worked fast but accurately.
PHRASES: He didn't come in the forenoon but in the early evening.
CLAUSES: We just rested the first day but the second we got down to real work.
SENTENCES: Enigma of the semitropics, the Rio Grande defied the best engineering minds of two countries for a century. But $10,-000,000 in flood control work has harnessed the treacherous stream.

For comments on *but which* see **which* §2.

2. The statements connected by *but* should be actually in opposition:

> He knows vaguely that the nation is not much good any more; he has read that the crust of the earth is shrinking alarmingly and that the universe is growing steadily colder; but he does not believe that any of the three is in half as bad shape as he is.—JAMES THURBER, *My Life and Hard Times,* Preface
> He supported a wife and three children on this pittance *and* [not *but*] he seemed very proud that he wasn't on relief.
> Our view was limited to about twenty yards down Tuckerman Ravine; [not *but*] beyond that everything was in clouds.
> It was murder cruel and brutal, but that crime on that April afternoon in 1920 was to become the most widely known crime of a generation. [That cruel and brutal murder on an April afternoon in 1920 was to become . . .]

3. *But* should be used efficiently, carrying its real meaning. It should not be doubled by a *however* which can add nothing:

> The students wanted to extend the Christmas vacation a day beyond New Years, but [however] the Administration couldn't see their point of view.

A **double negative with *but* is found only in vulgate usage:

FORMAL: There are but three eggs left.
INFORMAL: There are only three eggs left.
VULGATE: There aren't but three eggs left.

4. *But,* like **and,* often stands at the beginning of sentences in informal styles, especially if the sentences are short.

5. Two clauses connected by *but* should ordinarily be separated by a comma. The contrast in idea suggests the use of punctuation even when the clauses are relatively short.

> I couldn't get the license number, but it said something about the New York World's Fair.

But is part of the clause in which it stands and should not be separated from it by a comma. A parenthetical phrase following the *but* may of course be set off by commas ("Two commas or none"):

> His speech was supposed to be extemporaneous, but he had really been practicing it for a week.
> His speech was supposed to be extemporaneous, but, to be quite truthful, we must add that he had practiced it for a week.

6. Minor uses of *but* (*a*) As subordinating conjunction, after *no doubt,* in questions with *know,* and in a few other constructions:

> It cannot be doubted but the strain had told on him. [Formal; more usual, *that* or *but that*]
> There is no doubt but [or *but that,* or more formally, *that*] he had tried his best.
> Who knows but everything will come out right?
> Nothing would do but I must spend the night with them.

b) As a preposition, equivalent to *except:*

> We didn't get anything but a couple of shad.
> No one could have done it but me.

Formal grammarians—and a very few speakers—would prefer to regard *but* in this sentence as a conjunction introducing an elliptical clause: "No one could have done it but I." Nevertheless, "but me" is now common idiomatic English.

c) As a rather formal adverb, equivalent to *only:*

> If he but stops to think, he can bring together these reactions to form an image of himself.

References: Fowler, article "but"; Kennedy, p. 539; Curme, *Parts of Speech,* index references

but that—but what *But that* is the usual conjunction in written English:

> He didn't know but that [vulgate: but what] the other car could still turn out.

FORMAL: I don't doubt that he will come.
INFORMAL: I don't doubt but that he will come.
VULGATE: I don't doubt but what he'll come.

C In Old English *c* represented two sounds: Usually it was *k—cruma,* "crumb," *cempa,* "warrior," *cyning,* "king"; but before *e* or *i* it often represented *ch* (*ceosan, ciepan, cild*). This second sound is spelled *ch* in Modern English: *choose, cheap, child.* It was the Norman Conquest that really complicated *c,* for it brought in many French words in which *c* was sounded *s.* Today *c* is an unnecessary and divided letter, doing work that could more certainly be done by *k* and *s.* Many words spelled with *c* must be respelled with *k* or *s* to show pronunciation: sit'i (*city*), sel (*cell*), fōrs (*force*), kōld (*cold*), kum (*come*), ärk (*arc*).

Before *e, i,* or *y, c* is regularly pronounced *s: cent, civil, cynic;* before *a, o, u,* and any consonant but *h, c* is regularly *k: can't, coffee, cute, fact.* Marked with a cedilla, as in *façade, c* has the *s* sound before *a, o,* or *u.*

When followed by a *y* sound (which may now be lost in the word), *c* represents *sh: ocean* (ō'shən); *conscience* (kon'shəns); *special* (spesh'əl).

C is silent in *czar, indict, muscle,* and a few other words.

Before *e* or *i,* *cc* spells *ks: accident, occident, success;* otherwise it is *k: acclaim, accommodate.*

See *ch.

-cal, -cial Words ending in *-cal* (*critical, historical, musical, political* . . .) are sometimes confused by careless writers with those ending in *-cial* (*artificial, beneficial, judicial* . . .). *-al ly

calculate, guess, reckon *Calculate* (cut in vulgate to kal'klāt or even to kal'āt), *guess, reckon* are localisms for the *think, suppose, expect* of good English. (Which is the word in your region?)

can—may (could—might) 1. IN FORMAL ENGLISH. In formal English careful distinction is kept between the auxiliary *can* when it has the meaning of ability, "being able to," and *may,* with the meaning of permission.

You may go now. He can walk with crutches. You may if you can.

The distinction makes possible the classic dialog at many tables:

"Can I have some more meat and potato?"
"You *may* [with a withering accent] have some more meat and potato."

May also indicates possibility:

He may have the one.

2. IN INFORMAL AND COLLOQUIAL ENGLISH. In less formal usage *may* occurs rather rarely except in the sense of possibility:

It may be all right for her, but not for me.

Can is generally used for both permission and ability:

Can I go now? You can if you want to.
I can do 80 miles an hour with mine.

This is in such general usage that it should be regarded as good English in speaking and in informal writing.

Can't almost universally takes the place of the awkward *mayn't*:

Can't I go now?   We can't have lights after twelve o'clock.

3. MIGHT AND COULD. *Might,* originally the past of *may,* and *could,* the past of *can,* are now used chiefly to convey a shade of doubt, or a smaller degree of possibility:

It might be all right for her, but it wasn't for me.
It might have been all right for her, but not for me.

Adverbs are likely to be used instead of *may* or *might* in such constructions, especially for the past tense:

Perhaps it was all right for her, but not for me.

Could also suggests doubt or qualified possibility:

Perhaps I could write a poem, but I doubt it.
I could do 80 miles an hour in mine, too.

Be able to tends to replace *can* and *could* when the idea of ability needs emphasis:

I am able to live on my income.

cannot, can not Usage is divided; both forms are common; *can not* is perhaps slightly more formal (or emphatic) and less common than *cannot.*

can't help (but) This idiom illustrates differences between various levels of usage:

FORMAL: I *can but feel* sorry for him.
INFORMAL: I *can't help feeling* sorry for him.
FAMILIAR, VULGATE: I *can't help but feel* sorry for him.

The last is so commonly used in speaking and writing that perhaps it should be regarded as good English. *Current English Usage* (p. 130) says it is disputable "and cannot be called definitely wrong."

Capital letters (CORRECTION: Capitalize the word marked, for one _Cap_ of the reasons shown in this article; or, if the word marked is written with a capital, make it a small letter.)

*Proofreading marks can be used for correcting themes. Three lines under a small letter means: make this a capital. A slanting line drawn through a capital means: make this a small letter.

march 15   He came from West of Buffalo.

Certain uses of capitals, as at the beginning of sentences or for proper names, are conventions followed by everyone; certain others show divided usage or are matters of taste. In general, formal English tends to use more capitals than informal English, and newspaper usage tends to cut them to a minimum.

This article summarizes the principal uses of capitals in current writing. Further discussion and examples will be found in the articles marked by asterisks.

1. SENTENCE CAPITALS. The first word of a sentence is capitalized. In *quotations, the first word of a quoted sentence or part of sentence is capitalized, but when the quotation is broken, the second quoted part of a sentence is not capitalized:

> He said, "The first time I came this way almost none of the roads were hard surfaced."
> "The first time I came this way," he said, "almost none of the roads were hard surfaced."
> He said, "Perhaps," and went on.

Complete sentences that stand in *parentheses are capitalized always if they stand between other sentences; but if they stand within sentences they usually are not.

> The men were very stiff and self-conscious in their swallowtail coats (the dinner jacket had not been invented), bulging shirt fronts, white kid gloves (which often smelled of naphtha), and the enormously high "poke" or "Piccadilly" collars. . . .—E. ALEXANDER POWELL, _Gone Are the Days_, p. 138

A complete sentence standing after a *colon would not be capitalized if it was short and closely connected to the preceding words, but usually would be if it was long or if for some reason the writer wanted to emphasize it or keep it distinct:

> Charles Sumner wanted to know his opinion on European law journals: what should he say?—H. S. COMMAGER, _Theodore Parker_, p. 109

> Possible explanation: The nestlings were struck by an eastern Arctic storm which only the older birds were able to escape.—_Time_, Nov. 7, 1938

2. PROPER NAMES. Proper names and abbreviations of proper names are capitalized: names of people, places, races (Indian, Negro, Caucasian), languages (French, Latin), days of the week, months, companies, *ships, institutions, fraternities, religious bodies, historical events (the Revolutionary War), documents (the Constitution), *Course names.

The names of the *seasons (*summer, fall, midwinter . . .*) are not capitalized except for emphasis or stylistic reasons.

The points of the compass (*north, south . . .*) are not capitalized when they indicate direction, but are usually capitalized when they denote a region (though this practice is now declining):

His grandfather had come west in 1849.
He was much more popular in the West than in the East.

Army, Navy, and so on, are capitalized when they refer to the organized forces of a particular nation: United States *Army,* the British *Navy.*

Proper nouns that have become common nouns (*tweed, sandwich, burnsides, plaster of paris*) are not capitalized, nor are proper adjectives in senses that no longer suggest their origin: *Paris fashions* [fashions originating in Paris], but *paris green.*

3. LINES OF POETRY. The first letter of a line of poetry is capitalized unless it was originally written without a capital, as in the second example below:

These lovely groves of fountain-trees that shake
   A burning spray against autumnal cool,
Descend again in molten drops to make
   The rutted path a river and a pool.
        ELINOR WYLIE, "Golden Bough"

   Ecstatic bird songs pound
   the hollow vastness of the sky
   with metallic clinkings—
   beating color up into it
   at a far edge,—
        WILLIAM CARLOS WILLIAMS, "Dawn"

4. *TITLES OF ARTICLES, BOOKS, ETC. The usual convention is to capitalize the first word, all nouns, pronouns, verbs, adjectives, and adverbs as well as prepositions that stand last or contain more than four (sometimes five) letters:

With Malice Toward Some   *The Book of a Naturalist*
You Can't Take It with You   *Pity Is Not Enough*

5. THE PRONOUN *I* IS CAPITALIZED (not from any sort of egotism, but simply because a small *i* was likely to be lost or to become attached to other words). The exclamation *O is capitalized, but not *oh* unless it begins a sentence or is to be especially emphasized.

6. NAMES OF RELATIVES, INDIVIDUALS. Names of members of one's family (my Father, my Brother Wren—or my father, my brother Wren) are often capitalized in familiar writing as a mark of courtesy. A title and also nouns standing for the name of a person in a high position are capitalized: "The Colonel was there"; "The President spoke."

7. REFERENCES TO DEITY. *God, Jesus,* nouns such as *Saviour,* and pronouns referring directly to a sacred figure are capitalized— though practice is divided on the pronouns:

Webster for the first time in an English Bible rendered Jesus's saying as He said it.—HARRY R. WARFEL, *Noah Webster,* p. 411

As we think of him [God], do we think of what he has done or what he can do for us? Do we love him so much that we would keep him for ourselves?—S. K. YEAPLE, *Your Money and Your Life,* p. 30

Pronouns referring to pagan deities—Zeus, Jove, Venus . . . are not capitalized.

8. STREET, RIVER, PARK, ETC. Usage is divided over capitalizing such words as *street, river, park, hotel, church* when they follow a proper name. Typically, books and conservative magazines would use capitals; more informal writing, in many magazines and most newspapers, would not:

FORMAL: the Mississippi River   Thirty-second Street
INFORMAL: the Mississippi river   Thirty-second street

9. ABSTRACT NOUNS. Abstract nouns are likely to be capitalized, more often in formal writing than in informal, when they are personified or when they refer to ideals or institutions: "The State has nothing to do with the Church, nor the Church with the State."

10. STYLISTIC CAPITALS. Some writers, usually in a rather formal style, use capitals as a form of emphasis, to lead the reader to stress certain words a little or give them more attention:

MY MISSION

But when in modern books, reviews, and thoughtful magazines I read about the Needs of the Age, its Complex Questions, its Dismays, Doubts, and Spiritual Agonies, I feel an impulse to go out and comfort it, to still its cries, and speak earnest words of Consolation to it. —LOGAN PEARSALL SMITH, *Trivia,* p. 34

car is a satisfactory and economical solution of the contest between *automobile, auto, motor car,* and other terms for "a gasoline propelled pleasure vehicle."

Card catalog See "The library card catalog," p. 327.

Cardinal numerals The numbers used in counting—*one, two, three, sixty-eight* . . .—are called *cardinal numerals. Ordinal numerals* indicate order or succession: *first, second, third, sixty-eighth* . . .

Cardinal and ordinal numerals are grammatically construed as adjectives or pronouns.

For their use and representation in writing see *Numbers.

C Carelessness (Correction: Correct the obvious and apparently careless mistake marked.)

Conferences with students on their themes show that well over half the mistakes and slips that an instructor has to mark are due not to ignorance but to carelessness. Everyone is liable to careless lapses in hasty work. But a course paper is not supposed to be hasty work; it should represent the best you are capable of. Slips like *it's* for *its* (or the other way around), *detract* for *distract*, most comma faults and fragmentary sentences, and scores of others are due to lack of attention in the final stages of preparing a paper. An instructor can sympathize with lack of knowledge but not with lack of care; in fact, he should refuse to read an obviously careless paper.

One of the best investments is in a careful reading of your final manuscript. It will make the paper more presentable (and worth a better grade), as well as give you the satisfaction that comes from seeing a job through to the best of your ability.

Caret ($\wedge$) An inverted v-shaped mark put in a line of manuscript to show that something between the lines or in the margin should be inserted at that point:

```
        Yes, they were smart, but there wasn't any reason why they
                    because
  shouldn't be, all they did was study.
            ^
```

This is a respectable way to revise papers and should be used to improve a paper to be handed in or to make a correction suggested by an instructor, though too frequent use shows lack of care in the preliminary writing and revision.

In reading proof the matter to be inserted is put in the margin. *Proofreading

Case One of the ways in which the relation may be shown between a noun or pronoun and another element in a sentence is by case. In languages like Latin and German whose nouns and pronouns (and adjectives too) are fully declined, the case endings of the nominative, genitive, dative, and accusative (and ablative in Latin) are important clues to meaning. In English, case is a much less useful factor in grammar. Our adjectives do not take any endings; nouns are reduced to two forms, a genitive and a common form that serves for all other relationships (*soldier's—soldier*), and the personal pronouns are reduced to three, a nominative, genitive, and accusative (*I—my—me*).

We express the relation of nouns and pronouns to other sentence elements through *word order* (an accusative object following its verb or preposition, for example) and by means of *prepositions* (*to Fred* instead of a dative). The few problems in case that we have come chiefly from the surviving accusative form of pronouns (*It's me, *Who—whom*).

This *Index* has articles on four cases to call attention to the few functions in which the case forms are significant, to note problems in usage that are due to case forms, and to make possible some comparison between English and the languages which rely more definitely on case to express relationship between words:

*Nominative (or subjective)—the subject of a verb, complement of a linking verb

*Genitive (or possessive)—indicating not only possession but various adjectival and adverbial relations

*Dative—principally notions of interest or location or "indirect objects"

*Accusative (or objective)—the object of a verb or preposition

Fuller accounts of the grammatical points involved will be found in the articles on the various functions indicated: *Subject and verb, *Objects, *Infinitives § 4, *Linking verbs, *Gerund § 2; and *Genitive case, *Nouns, *Pronouns, *Word order.

For more complex treatments of problems of English cases, see Kennedy, pp. 465-67; Jespersen, Chapter 14 (the two-case system); Curme, *Parts of Speech*, pp. 127-36 (the four-case system).

case Some of the commonest bits of *deadwood in writing are various locutions with the word *case*. They are wordy and keep the real person or situation or thing (whatever the "case" stands for) one construction away from the reader.

These quotations, some from student papers, some from published articles, show how easy it is to let an unneeded *case* slip into careless writing.

Drinking went on very moderately except in a few scattered cases. [Written of a convention. The "cases" would be delegates?]

Perhaps it is because I like fiction to have happy or at least satisfactory endings that I disliked these books. In not one [case] was I satisfied with the ending.

. . . but that does not happen to be the case [but that isn't true]. In many cases a corporation may wish to carry on only one type of business and in such a case it is necessary for such a charter to be obtained in a state where this particular line of work is to be carried on. [If a corporation is to carry on only one type of business, it must secure a charter in the state in which it will operate.]

catalog—catalogue Spelling divided, with the shorter form gaining. Nearly half the colleges now use *catalog* as the name of their annual bulletin of announcements.

Cause Statements of cause are usually found in clauses introduced by *as, *because, *for, *since. See the articles on these connectives.

Cause and effect For discussion and example of paragraphs developed by showing the relationships of cause or effect between statements, see "Cause and effect," p. 105.

ce-, ge- A few special spelling problems arise from the use of *c* for the sound of *s*, and of *g* for the sound of *j*. Ordinarily *c* has the sound of *s* before *e* and *i* (*cent, city*) and of *k* before *a, o, u* (*catch, corner, cute*).

A word ending in *-ce* (pronounced *s*) or *-ge* (pronounced *j*) keeps the final *e* before suffixes beginning with *a, o,* or *u* to indicate the pronunciation: *courageous, noticeable, peaceable.* Before a suffix beginning with *e* or *i* the final *e* is dropped: *diced, noticing, encouraging.*

Usually a word ending in *c* (pronounced *k*) adds a *k* before an ending beginning with *e* or *i* or *y* so that it will still be pronounced *k*:

colic, colicky   picnic, picnicked, picnicking

See also *-ei-, -ie-.

Cedilla A mark under the letter *c* (ç) to show that it has the sound of *s* before *a, o,* or *u*. *Façade* is the most common English word spelled with a cedilla. Other words with cedillas are *Provençal, garçon, aperçu, soupçon.*

center around (or about) *Center around* (The story *centers around* the theft of a necklace) is a colloquial idiom. The formal idiom is *center on* or *upon.*

Centuries Remember that the fifth century A. D. ran from the beginning of the year 401 to the end of the year 500, the nineteenth century from January 1, 1801, through December 31, 1900. That is, to name the century correctly, add one to the number of its hundred. You can figure this out by remembering that you live in the *twentieth* century.

Partly because of the frequent errors made in this scheme of indicating centuries, the informal practice of naming the hundred is becoming more and more used, even in formal writing: the seventeen hundreds, the nineteen hundreds . . .

Dates before Christ are figured like those after: The first century B. C. runs back from the birth of Christ through 100, the second century from 101 through 200, the fifth century from 401 through 500, and so on.

The abbreviation A. D. (*anno Domini,* in the year of our Lord) is written before the year: A. D. *1943.* Strictly it should not be used with centuries, since it means "in the year . . .," but actually it is by historians (the fifth century A. D.). B. C. (before Christ) follows the year: *431* B. C.; *the fifth century* B. C.

certain Deadwood in This *certain* person, just one *certain* thing . . .

cf. For Latin *confer;* sometimes used in footnotes for *compare, see* a given reference for other or further facts.

ch *Ch* spells the sound *tsh* (pronunciation symbol *ch*), as in *arch, bachelor, chatter, check, cheese, child, church.* When the sound is not at the beginning of a word, it is often spelled *tch* (*batch, watch*) and *ti* in such words as *question, Sebastian.* Compare also *righteous* (rī'chəs) and *literature.*

In some words rather recently taken in from French, *ch* has the French sound of *sh: champagne, chagrin, mustache, machine.*

In a number of words from Greek, *ch* is sounded *k: chemist, chimera, chorus, echo.*

Change in construction See "Shifted constructions," p. 129, and *Shifted constructions.

Change in language (oral and written) Since language exists only as it is used, and since it is used by people as a tool rather than as an end in itself, it is subject to change. Occasionally changes are relatively sudden and far reaching, as after an invasion by a nation with a different language, but ordinarily they are slow and casual, the accumulation of slightly different pronunciations, casual or designed changes in the meanings of words, gradual changes in grammatical forms and constructions. English shows many changes during the hundreds of years that we are able to study it. (See *English language). When we think of the millions of varied people using our language and of the wide territory over which they are spread, the wonder is that change is not more rapid. The spread of school systems, the wide circulation of books and periodicals, and the radio all tend to slow up change somewhat, but the English language is still changing. One of the fundamental principles of linguistics is recognizing that this change is natural and unavoidable in language.

Attempts to direct the course of English have not been very successful. The development of formal grammar in the eighteenth century affected the speech, or at least the writing, of a small and influential group but left untouched the great majority of users of the language. The simplified spelling movement has had much less effect than we should expect from such a sensible and needed effort. Today advertising is the chief source of spelling change, although some teachers and nearly all linguists believe that our spelling should be modified. In general, schools and publishing houses have taken a pretty firm stand against change, some of them even now presenting usage of the middle nineteenth century. It is possible that this will not always be true. As Professor Sturtevant put it:

> In the past such efforts [of teachers] have usually been directed against a usage that was supposed to be an innovation, but there seems to be no reason in the nature of the case why the school should not some day be enlisted in an effort to improve the language.— *Linguistic Change*, p. 177

A person interested in writing needs to be aware of the naturalness and necessity of change in his language and should cultivate the habit of watching the small signs of change that he hears and sees in speech and writing. He needs also to decide whether he is going to oppose change, to welcome it in all its forms, or to try to discriminate, adopting in his own work only those new words and forms and constructions that seem to be more convenient and more expressive than older forms. Following the direction in which English has already been moving (as the increase in nouns making their *plural with -s) is a good general principle to follow.

Several discussions in this *Guide-Index* treat points of change in current English. Reading them will suggest what to watch: Meaning of words (in Chapter 7), *Origin of words, Spelling (in Chapter 10), and specific articles like *all right—alright, *-al ly, *due to, *like—as, *shall—will.

The study of the changes that have taken place in English and the reasons for them is fascinating, and ample materials exist for carrying it on. The *Oxford English Dictionary* gives the history of individual words from their first appearance in the language, recording their changes in form and in meaning. Histories of the language, like those by H. C. Wyld, Albert G. Baugh, and Stuart Robertson, tell the story in detail. The general and orderly process of change is described in Otto Jespersen, *Language,* Part iv, and in E. H. Sturtevant, *Linguistic Change* (Chicago, 1917). See also Bloomfield, Chapter 20 ff.; Kennedy, Chapter 14.

chaperon Sometimes found with a final *e* but most commonly *chaperon.* Pronounced shap′ər ōn.

Chapters Chapters are usually numbered in Roman numerals, though Arabic numerals are being increasingly used. In bibliographies and copy, lower case Roman numerals (i, ii, x . . .) are now more common in referring to chapters than are capitals (I, II, X . . .).

In formal book style, references to titles of chapters are quoted. In most writing they are simply capitalized.

> FORMAL: Kennedy, Chapter xiv, "Improvement of the English Language"
> INFORMAL: Kennedy, Chapter 14, Improvement of the English Language

Charts *Diagrams, graphs, etc.

check—cheque *Cheque* is the regular British spelling but its use in the United States is formal or pretentious. It is used by some banks in advertising as a prop to dignity.

Chinese Preferred by natives of China (and others) to *Chinaman, Chinamen,* because of the belittling connotation of those words. Say *a Chinese, the Chinese.* In compounds *Sino-* (sī′nō or sin′ō) is used: *the Sino-Japanese War.*

Choppy sentences See "Segregating sentences," p. 151.

cinema The regular British term for moving pictures. It has made little headway in the United States.

Circumlocution is the use of several words for an idea that might be conveyed by one. See "Sentence economy," p. 161, and *Wordiness.

Cities The name of the country or state need not be given with the name of well-known cities: Athens, Berlin, Chicago, Hollywood, London, New York, Rome, San Francisco. Many American cities and towns bearing the same names need identification if used in writing that is to circulate outside their states: Athens, Georgia; Berlin, New Hampshire. *Proper names; *Comma § 8*b*

claim In formal and informal English *claim* means to demand something due or regarded as due (as, to claim an inheritance), or to assert as a fact or right (as, to claim descent), or to demand (as, to claim attention).

In informal and vulgate English *claim* means more often simply "assert": "He claims he is the fastest runner here."

Clauses 1. A clause is an element of a compound or complex sentence that ordinarily has a subject and a finite verb. (But see §2.) By means of a conjunction or of an implied connection the clause construction is related to the rest of the sentence. A simple sentence, like "The bird flew higher and higher in slow easy circles," is not called a clause.

Compound sentences have two or more coordinate clauses, of grammatically equal value, connected usually by *and, but, for,* or another *coordinating conjunction.

[First clause:] Then Italy, in February, was finally persuaded to sign the Non-Intervention Pact, [Second clause:] and a few days later twenty thousand Italian soldiers landed at Cadiz.—*Kaltenborn Edits the News,* p. 48

Complex sentences have at least one main clause, grammatically capable of standing alone, and one or more subordinate clauses, joined to the main clause or clauses by *as, because, since, when,* or some other *subordinating conjunction, or by a relative pronoun, *that, who, which.*

[Main clause:] There are, besides, certain differences in the domestic and foreign policies of the two democratic nations [Subordinate clause:] which influence their behavior in the Spanish situation. —*Kaltenborn Edits the News,* p. 48

Subordinate clauses are classified according to the grammatical function they serve in the sentence: *Noun clauses* are subjects and objects of verbs or objects of prepositions:

[Subject:] *That herons fed at night* was not news to him. No one knew [Object:] *which way they had gone.*

Adjective clauses modify nouns:

The man *whom they met* [or, The man *they met*] did not return. The cement road turned into a macadam road, *which in time turned into a clayey unsurfaced road.*

Adverbial clauses add notions of time, place, cause, effect, concession, etc:

When they finally got that straightened out, it was too late to go on. They were discouraged, *because the harder they tried, the less he seemed to understand.*

The following paragraph contains a number of clauses. Subordinate clauses are labeled in brackets preceding each:

We grow familiar in time with the style of the great writers, and [Adverbial] when we read them we translate them easily and unconsciously, [Adverbial] as we translate a language we are familiar with; we understand the vocabulary [Adverbial] because we have learnt to know the special seal of the creative person [Adjective] who moulded the vocabulary. But at the outset the great writer may be almost as unintelligible to us [Adverbial] as though he were writing in a language [Adjective] we had never learnt. In the now remote days [Adverbial] when "Leaves of Grass" was a new book in the world, few [Adjective] who looked into it for the first time, however honestly, but were repelled and perhaps even violently repelled, and it is hard to realize now [Noun] that once those [Adjective] who fell on Swinburne's "Poems and Ballads" saw at first only picturesque hieroglyphics [Adjective] to which they had no key. But even to-day how many there are [Adjective] who find Proust unreadable and Joyce unintelligible. [Adverbial] Until we find the door and the clue the new writer remains obscure. Therein lies the truth of Landor's saying [Noun] that the poet must himself create the beings [Adjective] who are to enjoy his Paradise.—HAVELOCK ELLIS, *The Dance of Life,* p. 164

2. VERBLESS CLAUSES. The typical clause has a subject and verb, but just as there are verbless sentences (See p. 131), there are clauses without finite verbs. They are of three types:
a) Elliptical clauses, in which the verb can be supplied from another part of the sentence or can be added with certainty because of the frame of the sentence:

I don't believe it any more than you. [Supply: *do,* or *believe it.*]
When [Supply: *he was*] sixteen, he had gone to work.

b) Locutions with the value of clauses but containing participles or infinitives (which may also be construed as participial or infinitive phrases) rather than finite verbs:

Having done all my errands [= After I had done all my errands], I began to look for amusement.
He hoped *to do* [= He hoped that he would do] the whole job in a month.

See *Infinitives §4, *Participles §§3 and 4.
c) Genuine "abridged clauses" in which no verb element stands (or ever has stood). These should not be construed as elliptical clauses, since no verb ever enters the speaker's or listener's mind. Two familiar sayings illustrate the abridged clause:

The more, the merrier.
The better the day, the better the deed.

See "Sentence elements," p. 119, "Order of sentence elements," p. 122, and *Complex sentences, *Subordination, *Restrictive and non-restrictive.

Reference: Curme, *Syntax*, Chapter 10

Cl **Clearness** (CORRECTION: Make this statement clear to a reader by fuller statement or by making the words more exact or by straightening out the grammatical construction.)

Clearness is one of the fundamental virtues of writing, perhaps the fundamental virtue, but it is a little hard to discuss. No accumulation of small virtues or banning of particular faults will produce essential clearness. It is true in writing that pronouns should match their antecedents, that verbs and subjects should agree, that constructions should not be wantonly shifted. These are traits which, though often ignored in speech, require care in writing.

True, clearness will be gained not so much by attention to these details as by determination to convey to the reader the ideas and feelings you wish him to find in what you say. Clearness is the fundamental virtue of writing because it enables writing to carry out its fundamental purpose, communication. But writing has other purposes too—influencing people, entertaining them—and expression also has other virtues. Even in exposition, where clearness is the first demand, it is not the only one. Preoccupation with clearness for its own sake will produce writing that is clear—but also cold and dry. Without clearness a paper will certainly be bad, but with clearness it may not be particularly good. There are overtones demanded by certain situations, there are special considerations of the sensibilities of readers, there are small signs of the writer's own sense of the matter, even his sense of himself. All of these elements may detract in some small way from immediate clearness and yet add importantly to a complete understanding of the whole and so be intrinsic to good English.

Many of the articles of this *Index* discuss small contributions to clearness. Give them the attention they deserve but remember that clearness comes really from habits of thought.

Cliché A worn-out word or phrase. See "Trite words," p. 214.

Climax Climax is the arrangement of a series of words, phrases, clauses, or sentences in an order of increasing value and usually of increasing length. See "Position," p. 172.

Clipped words Words made by dropping a syllable or more, typical of shoptalk and familiar speech, and often finding their way into the general vocabulary: *ad, bus, exam, home ec, gas* (for *gasoline*), *phone.* Many, like *gent, prof,* are out of place in writing. *Origin of words §3c

coach As a verb used either with persons (teams) or with the name of a sport as object:

He coaches baseball.   He coached a winning team that fall.

Cognate *Cognate* means "related, of the same family." It is applied to languages that are from the same stock, as Spanish and French are both descended from Latin. *Cognate* is also applied to words in different languages which are modern forms of some one word in an older language: German *Wasser*, English *water*.

References: Kennedy, §80; the origins of words given in dictionaries, especially in the *Oxford English Dictionary*

Coherence (CORRECTION: Make the relation between the parts *Coh* of this sentence or between these sentences or paragraphs exact and clear to a reader.)

Coherence—the traditional name for *relationship, connection, consecutiveness*—is a difficult and necessary virtue in writing. It is necessary because a reader does not have the same mind as the writer, does not see the same relationships, and consequently must be led through a line of thought, guided from one stage, from one sentence, to another. It is difficult because a coherent piece of writing is a triumph over natural human casualness; it represents an editing of a writer's thought so that it can pass over to others' thought.

Coherence is the name of a quality of finished writing and is to be checked finally in revision. A writer cannot be always worrying about the connection between his statements while he is at work, but careful planning will make coherence more likely. Unless he is mentally ill, there is always some relation between a person's consecutive "thoughts," but the relation may be entirely personal. Carefully thinking over material before beginning to write should help prepare a coherent paper, especially if some sort of plan, arranging the different stages in a natural and sensible order, is drawn up. But coherence must be tested after writing. The writer must sit as reader, go over his copy as impersonally as he can to see if what he has written not only hangs together for him but will, so far as he can judge, hang together for those he wants to read it. He should ask himself, "Is the relation between these statements clear? Can a reader pass from this sentence to the next, from this paragraph to the next, without feeling a break?"

A natural arrangement of material is not enough for this; there must often be signs of the relationship between sentences and paragraphs. These signs, and various suggestions pointing toward coherence, and examples of successful and unsuccessful attempts at coherence are discussed in this *Guide-Index,* especially in *Connectives, Chapters 3 and 4 (Paragraphs) and 5 and 6 (Sentences), *Reference of pronouns, "Planning the paper," p. 336.

Coining words Making up a word for a particular statement (like *was-ness*) or for general use (like *fabrikoid*) is called *coining,* and the word made is called a *coinage.* For discussion and examples see *Origin of words §§1 and 2.

Coll **Collective nouns** (CORRECTION: Revise according to the principles of this article the agreement of verb and/or reference of pronouns to the collective noun marked.)

1 A collective noun is a noun whose singular form names a group of objects or persons or acts. Some common collective nouns are:

army	contents	herd	*public
*athletics	*couple	jury	remainder
audience	crowd	mankind	rest (= remain-
band	dozen	majority	der)
class	flock	*number	row (of trees)
*committee	gang	offspring	team
company	group	*politics	

When a writer means the group as a whole, a collective noun takes a singular verb and singular pronoun; when he means the individuals of the group, the noun takes a plural verb or pronoun:

The crowd that *has* been noisily engaged in finding *its* seats *settles* down and the incessant murmur of voices slowly quiets.

The crowd that *have* been noisily engaged in finding *their* seats *settle* down and the incessant murmur of voices slowly quiets. (The first form is preferable.)

The first *couple* on the floor *was* Tom and Janet.

One day when we were near where the old *couple were* living, we dropped in to see *them.*

2 *Obviously a collective should not be treated as both singular and plural in the same context:*

The *company was* organized and immediately sent out *its* [not *their*] representatives.

Mess is over and the guard have [not *has*] a busy morning ahead of them [not *it*].

There is often a temptation to use a collective noun and try to keep it singular when the meaning really calls for a plural construction. Often the writer slips unconsciously from singular to plural in such a passage:

Into the church troops the entire town, seats itself on the uncomfortable wooden benches and there remains for a good two hours, while an aged curé preaches to *them* [consistency demands *it*] of their [*its*] wicked lives and awful sins.

[This might better have started "Into the church troop all the people, seat themselves . . ."]

In making inconsistent constructions consistent, the first member is fully as likely to need to be changed as the second, as in the sentence above about the church.

3 The plural of a collective noun signifies different groups:

The audiences of New York and Chicago differed in their receptions of the play.

4 In measurements and amounts a plural noun is often followed by a singular verb:

Eighteen inches is half a yard.
About 80 pounds of carbon bisulphide is [or *are*] added.

*Subject and verb § 2; *every and its compounds § 1

References: Curme, *Syntax*, pp. 539-40, 50-51; Fries, pp. 48-50, 54, 57-59

Colloquial and written English (CORRECTION: The colloquial expression marked is inappropriate to the context in which it stands. Change it to one more formal, in line with the general style.) *Colloq*

1. COLLOQUIAL ENGLISH. Colloquial means conversational, used in speaking. Since the speech of people varies with their education, work, and social status, there are obviously many different types of colloquial English, from the rather bookish speech of some professors and others through the "cultivated colloquial" of fairly well educated persons, to the "low colloquial" of the majority of everyday people, which makes up the vulgate level of English. The bulk of conversation is informal, and consequently *colloquial* suggests informal rather than formal English. It need not, however, mean the speech of uneducated people, and in this book applies to the language spoken by people of some education and social standing, to language that can be safely used except on decidedly formal occasions.

Dictionaries mark words *Colloq.* to suggest that in the editors' judgment they are more common in speech than in writing. Many people take this label to mean that the dictionary frowns upon the use of these words, but the Webster definition of *colloquial* shows that this is not true:

> acceptable and appropriate in ordinary conversational context, as in intimate speech among cultivated people, in familiar letters, in informal speeches and writings, but not in formal written discourse (*flabbergast; go slow; harum-scarum*). Colloquial speech may be as correct as formal speech.

The three colloquial expressions that are given as examples prove that Webster is not using *colloquial* as a word of dispraise or even of suspicion, for though *flabbergast, go slow,* and *harum-scarum* suggest speech rather than formal writing, they are accurate, expressive, useful words, to be used with confidence in most situations.

Speech is of course the basis of a language, and writing is to a large degree a representation of speech. We learn to speak unconsciously by imitating our elders, and somewhat later we learn to write, but consciously and under the direction of teachers, so that the great majority of people never come to be quite at home "on paper." They do much more talking than writing, and for some, speech may be almost their only language.

Many educated people, especially in the professions, get most of their information from periodicals and books, so that the written language naturally colors their speech. In certain limited areas, especially the upper levels of scientific, scholarly, and philosophical fields, and in some literature, the primary relation between oral and written language is reversed. The subjects are rarely spoken of, even by specialists, and almost never are in familiar speech. Here the written forms are the norms, imitated in speech.

The language taught and to a large extent used in schools in the past has been written and formal. Dictionaries are based primarily upon the written language, and the pronunciations they give are those of formal public address. The grammars have also been based chiefly on written literature and, except the more recent reference grammars, have ignored the spoken. With more work in oral composition and an increasing attention to spoken English in language work, there is now less of the attempt to make students talk as their elders write and more of a tendency to give colloquial English its due place. Since a language really lives as it is spoken, it is not healthy when the written language gets out of touch with the colloquial.

2. Appropriateness of colloquial English in writing. The chief problems come in the appropriateness of colloquial locutions in writing.

a) *In familiar writing.* Obviously, familiar writing, as in letters to friends or in personal notes for our own use, is and should be close to speech, to the writer's speech. Contractions, clipped words, short cuts in constructions all help bring the writer close to his reader, and their number and use will depend upon the extent to which he uses them in his speech.

b) *In informal English.* Informal written English is closely related to colloquial English. It is based upon speech rather than upon traditional written literature. It is not a mere setting down on paper of casual, lazy, careless speech, but it is a refinement of good talk, especially of the words and the movement of good talk. Some people hesitate to let their writing become colloquial because they think it means cheapening it, reducing it to the level of prevailing speech. But the basis of a person's writing is his own speech, not somebody else's. He takes as the starting point for his growth in writing his own way of talking rather than the writing of others.

c) *In formal English.* More serious questions arise in formal writing, in impersonal discussions of facts and ideas, as in college papers, and in articles and books for special and rather restricted groups of readers. Although formal English now has a wider range than it did, still its background is really the written English of a generation or so ago and in so far as it is influenced by speech it is by the speech of the platform rather than of conversation.

Once in a while a contraction is used for the sake of rhythm, even in formal writing, and in vigorous formal writing there is now a wide range in words that will include some characteristically colloquial. But in general, formal English relies on words that have made their way in writing, and its constructions are usually filled out, not shortened as in speech. In these days it is not necessary to avoid colloquialisms altogether, but they should be appropriate and not attract attention to themselves.

3. Some differences between colloquial and written English. The early stages of preparing a talk for an audience or a paper for readers are pretty much the same. The subject is chosen to fit the situation and to appeal to the intended readers or listeners; material is gathered to carry out the subject; and the plans of a good talk and of a good article do not materially differ. If there are differences in these stages they probably come because it is harder for a writer than for a speaker to keep his future audience in mind; a speaker knows that he will face a definite group of people and finds it easier to work directly for them from the very beginning.

In later stages, and in the actual presentation of the material, there are some unavoidable differences, more or less obvious.

a) Obvious differences. Pronunciation, the enunciation and stressing of words, belongs to speech; spelling, only to written language. Handwriting or typing may correspond in a poor way to the bodily presence of a speaker, but in printed articles and books even that touch of individuality is lost. Instead of the pauses and stresses of speech, writing has the feeble substitute of punctuation, italics, and so on, and really the writer relies more on the quality of his words, on repetition and word order, than on these mechanical signs of emphasis. The contractions of the colloquial language may be carried over to informal writing, but abbreviation is primarily the method of shortening written words. For the loss of the oral means of emphasis—gesture, facial expression—the writer must again rely on a resourceful use of words.

b) Pace and rhythm. A speaker can control the pace of his listeners—he can make his words (and his statements) come slow or fast as he wishes. A writer cannot control the speed with which his readers will go over his material. Some readers will read too slowly and make too much of small matters; others will race over the pages and miss much, perhaps even essential points. Of course, listeners cannot be made to take in what they hear, but in so far as they do, they will be going along with the speaker at his pace. The pace of printed prose will be much less evident, though it does vary between writers. Some prose seems written for slow reading, because of "hard" or perhaps merely exact words, because of indirect sentences, unfamiliar turns of expression; other passages suggest rapid reading, because of familiar and simple words, short, direct sentences. Even the printing can help, as in the short lines of newspaper columns.

Similarly the rhythm of a passage may be suggested even in print. The impression of a speaker depends in part on his rhythm, on the heaviness and frequency with which he stresses his words. This rhythm represents the speaker and guides the listener in understanding what he says. The natural speech rhythms of, for instance, New Englanders, Southerners, Scotsmen, and Londoners differ conspicuously. Even though the rhythm of speech can only be suggested on the printed page, a writer can convey rhythm to the page. Rapid silent reading catches little of it, but slower reading, in which the words may be almost pronounced, will usually sense it. One reason why much stereotyped writing, such as reference books and news writing, is colorless and unpleasant to read —and cannot be read aloud with pleasure—is that the writer has

suppressed so completely his natural speech rhythm (*Rhythm).
c) *Vocabulary.* One characteristic of the spoken vocabulary is
usually unsatisfactory on the written or printed page—the rather
loose use of words. In talking we often get along with general
words, rarely trying to find exact adjectives in describing something
or in giving our opinions. We fall back on *good, bad, pleasant,*
perhaps even on *nice,* and express the degree of our meaning by
tone of voice, gesture, or facial expression. In writing we need exact
words to make up for the oral support that we give vague words
in conversation. It might be better if we used more exact words
in conversation, but searching for words while we are talking is
likely to take the life out of our speech and may make it seem formal and aloof. Very often the added exactness of writing does not
mean using rare words, but just more exact ones, as in this simple
descriptive statement:

At the top of the pole crouched a shivering gray kitten, mewing
faintly and clinging desperately to the wood with her claws.—WILLA
CATHER, *O Pioneers,* p. 5

But the typical specific words of spoken English have more useful qualities. They are likely to be shorter and to stand closer to
experience. We would usually speak of *words* rather than of
vocabulary, bugs than of *insects, jobs* than of *positions.* We like
expressive words like *harum-scarum* and *flabbergast;* we *sponge* on
our relatives; we think someone is *no great shakes.* We are likely
to use *verb-adverb combinations instead of specific verbs: *give in*
for *surrender, give up* for *sacrifice.* To *pepper and salt* is a good
colloquial verb, and so is to *keep an eye out for.* Most people's
speech includes some localisms, slang, and vulgate expressions. A
good talker is likely to take whatever words fit his meaning and
his mood, without ordinarily questioning their ancestry or social
status.

d) *Sentences and syntax.* Spoken sentences are usually shorter
than written, or if they are long, it is because one statement is
added to another rather than because clauses are carefully built
together with subordinating conjunctions and manipulation of
word order. In speaking, we must, like Henry Ward Beecher,
plunge into a sentence, "trusting to God Almighty to get us
through it." We are likely to split constructions, to shift in the
middle of a sentence, to let the agreement of verbs follow the meaning rather than grammatical requirements, and so on. Speech goes
rapidly by and is not carefully scrutinized for details of expression.
In writing, the words lie on the page and can be analyzed. A
writer is therefore more careful. Since he has the opportunity to

revise, as the speaker does not, he is usually held responsible for a fairly strict following of the conventions of the level of usage in which he is writing.

The closeness of written literary English to the colloquial language of the time has varied from period to period. In the nineteenth century the two were conspicuously far apart—consider Arnold and Ruskin, and even more the rank and file of lesser writers, such as Sir Arthur Helps. The last fifty years in England and the last thirty in the United States have seen a closer approach of written to spoken style. The colloquial vein in modern writing is very strong. It fits in fiction, in intimate narrative, and in much general exposition, as these two brief extracts show:

I don't know why Father and Mother chose Irvington to go to, that summer. There were lots of other places to go where we boys could have enjoyed ourselves better, but we weren't consulted of course, and we'd have been surprised if we had been.—CLARENCE DAY, *Life With Father*, p. 41

If you have the sort of money that runs to seagoing yachts or even to shiny mahogany runabouts your opinion of outboard motors—if any—is probably low. Likely you carry an outboard-powered dinghy or tender, and any time you drop anchor in a sporting harbor like Nantucket or Boothbay you are sure to see a couple of fussy little boats with outboards clamped to their sterns, kicking up a great wake and bouncing around like shag dancers. If someone invited you to go out for a ride in an outboard you might go, the same way you might condescend to take a ride in the subway to see how the other 99 per cent lives, or the I'll-have-fun-if-it-kills-me way you might put on torn overalls for one of Elsa Maxwell's parties. But you wouldn't take outboards seriously. If they came up in the course of a conversation you would either look as though you'd never heard of them, or you would guillotine them with a contemptuous "Oh, those."—"The Put-Put," *Fortune*, Aug. 1938

Writing like this is not only highly readable but it can be used to convey a wide range of information, thought, and feeling. Probably the most practical as well as the most honest thing for a beginning writer is to study his own speech and see how far it can serve as the basis for his writing. "One would like to think," says Mr. Bonamy Dobrée, "that all of us will come to the stage of refusing to write what we would not, indeed could not, say."

See also *Conversation and Chapter 1, Varieties of English.

Anyone wishing to study the relationship between colloquial and written English will find further material (and varying opinions) in these: Abercrombie, Lascelles, *Colloquial Language and Literature*, Society for Pure English Tract xxvi (Oxford, 1931); Bradley,

Henry, *Spoken and Written English* (Oxford, 1919); Curme's *Parts of Speech* and *Syntax* pay special attention to colloquial forms and constructions; Dobrée, Part iv; Knott, Thomas A., "Standard English and Incorrect English," *American Speech*, 1934, ix, 83 ff.; Sherman, L. A., *Analytics of Literature* (Boston, 1893), 285-86, 311-12, and index references; Woolbert, C. H., "Speaking and Writing—A Study of Differences," *Quarterly Journal of Speech*, 1922, viii, 271-85; Wyld, Henry C., *A History of Modern Colloquial English* (New York, 1920), and *Historical Study of the Mother Tongue* (New York, 1906).

Colon (:) The colon is a mark of anticipation, directing attention to what follows. It is a formal mark and usually emphatic. Its use contrasts to that of the semicolon, which is a stop, almost a period. Students do not use as many colons as they should, and often use a semicolon instead of one: *Colon*

> Yesterday I received a clipping from home, the essence of which is as follows: [not ;]

The principal uses of the colon are:

1. After introductory expressions, as in the preceding line, and after the salutation of formal letters:

Dear Sir: (Contrast the comma in informal letters: Dear Fritz,)

It is generally used to anticipate quotations in factual writing (not in fiction), especially if the quotation is a complete grammatic unit and runs to more than one sentence. Whether or not a colon is appropriate with shorter quotations depends in part upon the formula with which it is introduced. If the quotation is closely built into the sentence, a comma is usual (*says,* in the quotation below); if the introduction is more formal, a colon is usual (below, *was added:*).

> A card made out at 10:45 P.M. on Nov. 4, 1928, says, "Arnold Rothstein, Male, 46 years, 912 Fifth Avenue, gunshot wound in abdomen, found in employee's entrance, Park Central Hotel, 200 West Fifty-sixth Street. Attended by Dr. McGovern, of City Hospital. Removed to Polyclinic Hospital. Reported by Patrolman William M. Davis, Shield 2943, Ninth Precinct." Two days later the word "fatal," in parentheses, was written in after the word "abdomen," and a second report, with more detail, was added: "Rothstein apparently had been engaged in card game with others in Room 349 on third floor of Park Central Hotel when an unknown man shot him and threw revolver out of window to street. Body found by Lawrence Fallon of 3164 Thirty-fourth Street, Astoria, employed as house detective for the hotel."—MEYER BERGER, *The New Yorker*, Nov. 26, 1938

427

2. A colon is used between clauses when the following one is either an illustration of the first, a restatement in different terms, or sometimes an amplification of the first:

The supposition that words are used principally to convey thoughts is one of the most elementary of possible errors: they are used mainly to proclaim emotional effects on the hearers or attitudes that will lead to practical results.—H. R. Huse, *The Illiteracy of the Literate*, p. 21

Lazy minds give up in despair: "I can't write anyhow," say students to me year after year; they mean that they won't think.—Barrett Wendell, *English Composition*, p. 136

The complaint against philosophy from the point of view of society appears in substance to be that it is either useless or pernicious: useless when the philosopher thinks about "timeless" things, pernicious when he thinks critically of the times in which he lives.—Irwin Edman, *Four Ways of Philosophy*, p. 96

3. There are a few conventional uses of the colon, though they vary among publishers:

a) Between hours and minutes expressed in figures

11:42 a.m.   3:28 p.m.   (or: 11.42 a.m., 3.28 p.m.)

b) In formal bibliographies and formal citations of books:

Between author and title—Stuart Chase: *Men and Machines*
Between place of publication and publisher—New York: Holt, 1930
Between volume and page—*The Atlantic Monthly*, 160: 129-40

In these three positions a comma would often and perhaps usually be found.

4. By some writers colons are preferred where most would use commas or semicolons:

It [a castle] is a shut place that commands by its shutness the open place about it. A castle is builded of the stone of its world: it rises from the stone of its world: it *is* the stone of its world. A castle is austere toward the world which it defends. It is invariable, forbidding: its strength is that of a perpetual shutting-out of all which lies outside it. Sun beats on the castle wall: inside it is dark. Moon melts its bastion and bathes its county blue: it is harsh and rigid. Water and wind make song of the green hills: the castle is silent. It is the lord of its county because it is apart from it. A castle is hot in a cold land: a castle is cold in a hot land: a castle is high in a low land: a castle is full in a land of dearth: a castle is dry in a land of verdure.—Waldo Frank, *Virgin Spain*, p. 108

This is a matter of taste rather than of correct punctuation. The mark usually attracts some slight attention to itself when used this way.

5. *After a colon either a capital or a small letter may be used.* The capital is more usual when the matter following the colon is in the form of a complete sentence, a small letter when it is a subordinate element. That the deciding factor is largely the closeness of thought relation between the two parts of the sentence is suggested by the following quotations from a single article:

> Thus the task of democracy has always been a twofold one: to prevent political privilege from reëstablishing itself, and to make peaceful settlement of disputes possible in a society without privilege.
>
> Those who believe that fascism is simply a tool which Big Business created as soon as it found democracy dangerous overlook one important fact: the opposition of Big Business to democracy is much older than fascism.
>
> The ways in which the kings settled social disputes were very different, in spirit as well as in technic: The kings of France, after having subdued the rebellious nobles, protected the social privileges of the nobility to the point of subjecting both citizens and peasants to cruel oppression; the kings of Prussia, who occasionally liked to be called "kings of beggars," without fully living up to the implications of that title, tried to restrict exploitation of the masses; so, much earlier, did Elizabeth of England.—CARL LANDAUER, in *The American Way*, by D. C. Coyle and others

6. *When a colon follows an abbreviation* the period of the abbreviation is usually omitted: *i.e:* rather than *i.e.:*

colonel is a good example of a spelling that has survived a change of pronunciation. The word, from the French, had two parallel forms, *colonel, coronel,* each pronounced in three syllables. In 1701 Daniel Defoe could write:

> Yet who the hero was, no man can tell,
> Whether a drummer or colonel [kol ə nel'].

For 150 years the word has been pronounced kêr'nəl, from the *coronel* form, but spelling has kept *colonel.* An enlightened attitude toward spelling would iron out such a confusion.

column, columnist Usual pronunciation kol'əm, kol'əm nist or kol'əm ist. Vulgate kol'yum, kol'yum ist is often used humorously and increasingly for a newspaper "column" and is sometimes represented in the spellings *colyum, colyumist.*

combine *Combine* (kom'bīn) as a noun came into use either from the verb *combine* (kəm bīn') with the characteristic change in stress (*Noun and verb stress), or perhaps as a back formation from *combination.* It is not in good use in the abstract senses of *combination,* but is good colloquial English for a group of people

429

joined together for business or political gain and usually implies either shady or forceful activities. *Combine* is the right name for the machine that reaps and threshes in the field.

Comma **Comma** (,) (CORRECTION: Insert or remove a comma at the place marked in accordance with one of the sections of this article.)

About half the total number of punctuation marks used in writing are commas and probably the question "Should there be a comma here?" is the most common question we ask in revising our manuscript. The question is hard to answer because the comma is a light mark without any special tone or meaning of its own, as the colon and dash so conspicuously have, and yet it is tremendously useful in clarifying our meaning. "It is, perhaps, humiliating," Mr. Dobrée says, "to think that the placing of a comma may be much more important than any of your ideas."

Fundamentally a comma is a mark of slight separation. The separation is very slight indeed in the conventional uses (as in dates), but in most instances it is just sufficient to keep words or phrases distinct and so make them more easily understood, and often to throw a slight emphasis on what follows. Typical modern prose does not need so many commas as nineteenth century prose did because its sentences are shorter and more direct. The following passage shows typical modern practice in use of commas. At the end the reason for each comma is noted, and some places are pointed out where commas might have been used but were not.

Just as we were leaving [a paper factory], [1] I saw two little boys sweeping an immense, [2] dusty litter down a long corridor. They must have been fourteen, [3] which is the age for leaving school in England, [3] but they were small enough to be taken for nine or ten. They glanced at us apathetically [4] and then went drearily on with their sweeping. Their faces were almost blotted out with fatigue [5] and they moved like sick old men. I touched Mr. Higginson on his pin-striped sleeve [6] and asked him how many boys of that age were employed in the plant, [7] but either he did not hear me over the noise of the machinery [8] or he pretended not to. There is a curious distinction, [9] incidentally, [9] between English and American conservatives. It lies in their hearing. If an American reactionary has his attention called to subhuman living conditions, [10] he answers with great heat [11] that those people spend all their money on radios and fur coats. The British Tory, [12] on the other hand, [12] smiles radiantly and replies, [13] "We *have* been having frightful weather, [14] haven't we?" That is the principal difference, [15] I think, [15] between the two civilizations—Americans make an unconscionable noise and clatter in their running away from life, [16] whereas the English have been running away from it for so long, [17] they do not even know that it is there.—Margaret Halsey, *With Malice Toward Some,* p. 226

1 Comma separating an adverbial clause that precedes the main clause

2 Comma between two parallel adjectives, both modifying *litter;* contrast *sick old men* below

3 Two commas setting off a non-restrictive adjective clause

7 Comma separating coordinate clauses connected by *but*

9 Two commas setting off the parenthetical modifier *incidentally*

10 Comma separating an adverbial clause that precedes the main clause

12 Two commas setting off the parenthetical *on the other hand*

13 Comma preceding a quotation

14 Comma separating two clauses of a compound sentence

15 Two commas setting off the parenthetical *I think*

16 Comma between two coordinate clauses of a compound sentence; formal writing would have a semicolon here because the connective is a *conjunctive adverb (whereas).

17 Comma separating the main clause from a following subordinate clause. If the connective *that* had been written introducing the subordinate clause, probably no comma would have been used: "whereas the English have been running away from it for so long [that] they do not even know that it is there."

A writer using close punctuation, that is, using as many marks as he could, would probably put commas at 5 and 8, separating pairs of coordinate clauses, but since the clauses are short and closely connected in thought, the comma is not necessary and is properly omitted here. Some writers might put a comma at 4 and 6, separating the two verbs that have *they* and *I* as subjects. Unless the verb and object locutions are very long, it is better to omit such a comma. Open punctuation rightly omits a comma at 11, though one might be used in close punctuation.

In straightforward narrative the punctuation is likely to be even more open than in expository writing, and commas are often omitted that would be used in exposition. They might interrupt the movement and seem to make the narrative move slower than the writer wishes. In these first few sentences from a short story, Morley Callaghan might have used commas at the points marked:

All the way home from work that evening [,] Thomas Boultbee thought of Easter Sunday which was only two days away, and of his young wife, Elsie [,] who had died of pneumonia and been buried in the last winter month. As Thomas Boultbee started to climb the stairs to his apartment [,] he felt very lonely. His feet felt heavy. By the time he got to the landing [,] he seemed unreasonably weary [,] and he rested to take a deep breath.—Morley Callaghan, "Rocking Chair," *Now That April's Here,* p. 139

Uses of the Comma

The following list of uses of the comma outlines the treatment in this article. The numbers and letters refer to sections and subsections. Brackets mean that a comma should be avoided.

1. Between clauses
   a. Between rather long coordinate clauses, especially those connected by *but, not, for*
   b. After subordinate clause or long phrase preceding the main clause
   c. Before a subordinate clause following the main clause and not closely related to it

2. In lists and series
   a. Between units of a list or series (*Series)
   b. Between coordinate adjectives in the same relation to their noun
   c. [Not between two words or phrases joined by *and*]

3. Around non-restrictive modifiers (*Restrictive and non-restrictive)

4. Around interrupting and parenthetical elements
   a. Around interrupting constructions
   b. Around conjunctive adverbs not standing first in their constructions

5. With main sentence elements (s-v-o)
   a. Sometimes after a long or heavily modified subject
   b. [Not between a short subject and its verb]
   c. [Not between verb and its object]
   d. [Rarely between compound predicates]

6. For emphasis and contrast

7. For clearness
   a. Before words of two possible functions (*for, but*)
   b. To prevent a noun being taken as an object
   c. To prevent wrong interpretation
   d. To separate consecutive uses of the same word

8. In conventional places
   a. In dates   b. In addresses
   c. After salutation of informal letters   d. In figures
   e. With degrees and titles   f. With weak exclamations
   g. [Not to show omissions of a word]

9. With other marks of punctuation
   a. [Not with a dash] (*Dash §6)
   b. With parentheses (*Parentheses §5)
   c. With quotation marks (*Quotation marks §4, *b* and *c*)

The examples on pages 430 and 431 suggest that though rules can be given for the use of some commas the actual practice of writers varies considerably. Except for uses that are quite conventional, writers go largely by the feel of the sentence, its movement and emphasis. Studying the punctuation of good recent prose that has about the same movement that you would like your writing to have is particularly useful in getting the right feeling for placing commas.

As a general thing college students use too many commas, more than the simple material and the direct movement of their sentences need. Most textbooks and most teachers have tended to encourage close punctuation, and students sometimes, especially the more conscientious students, seem to see how many commas they can put in and so give their writing a slow movement that it doesn't deserve. The boy who wrote this sentence was taking no chances:

Naturally, the first thing he does, after his interest is aroused, is to attempt to construct a small receiving set of his own.

No one of those commas is wrong but no one of them is necessary, either, and without them the sentence moves more easily—and more appropriately to a simple account of experiences in amateur radio:

Naturally the first thing he does after his interest is aroused is to attempt to construct a small receiving set of his own.

The general advice of this book, then, is to use commas where the reader will expect or need them, but beyond this to use them only when they actually contribute to the understandability of the sentence. Where choice is possible, the final decision will often depend on fitness to other factors of style: The formal writer will always tend to use more commas than the informal. Partly because the use of commas depends on the movement of a passage, it is better not to pause in writing the first draft to decide about putting in a comma. *Commas should be attended to in revision, when the context can help decide questions of appropriateness.*

The following sections on uses of the comma are intended to help you decide what uses are appropriate in your writing.

1. BETWEEN CLAUSES. (*a*) *Between coordinate clauses.* A comma is not needed when the clauses are short and closely related in meaning:

A solid retaining wall held the structure horizontal [ ] and a walled-in ramp, which was parallel to the front of the building, dropped down to a side street.

Numerous ex-summer homes had been converted into "hotels" [ ] and their employees met every incoming boat.

Especially in easy narrative a comma is likely not to be used:

The elevated rushed into an underground shaft [ ] and in the hollow, re-echoing roar only the high runs of the sax could be heard.

A comma is used when the clauses are rather long and when it is desirable to emphasize their distinctness, especially if the clauses have different subjects.

The frozen steel edges shrieked as they bit into the ice-covered turns, and the driving sleet slashed against their goggles and jackets with such force that it was impossible to keep clear vision, to say nothing of protection for their bodies.

Obviously in a great many sentences it makes no real difference whether a comma stands between the clauses or not, so that appropriateness to the general movement of the passage is the main reason for using or not using one:

Most of them have no good reason for not going out for the teams and they often admit that laziness is the real reason.   [or]
Most of them have no good reason for not going out for the teams, and they often admit that laziness is the real reason.

A comma is generally used between two coordinate locutions joined by *but* or *not*, to emphasize the contrast:

I can remember mother telling me that a book was one's best friend, but I couldn't understand how anyone could feel that way.
I told him that I was ready to pay my half of the bill, but that didn't satisfy him.
The sympathizers with these plans are to be pitied, not blamed.
Grammar is not nowadays a matter of rules for correct usage, but a knowledge of how sentences are constructed.

Compare §6.

A comma is generally used between clauses connected by the conjunction *for*, to avoid confusion with the preposition *for*:

CONJUNCTION: They are obviously mistaken, *for* all intercollegiate sports are competitive.
PREPOSITION: The English teacher had assigned us "Treasure Island" [ ] *for* a book report.

Compare §7.

For commas between complete clauses that could stand as separate sentences, see "Run-on sentences," p. 136, *Comma fault. *b) After a subordinate clause (or long phrase) that precedes the main clause of the sentence.* If a clause or phrase preceding the main clause of the sentence is long or if it is not closely connected with the main clause, it should be followed by a comma:

If that lake wasn't frowning at something or other that night, I'll drink it down to the last drop.

Although willing to use his athletic ability, he wouldn't study hard enough to become eligible.

If an alumnus walked into a fraternity house and called our generation of students a bunch of softies, he would be telling the awful truth.

Ever since 1803 when Chief Justice John Marshall threw down the gauntlet to President Thomas Jefferson in the decision of Marbury vs. Madison, the Supreme Court has undone the work of Congress and the executive.

When the preceding clause or phrase is short and closely related in thought to the main clause, there is usually no comma following it. This is especially true in narrative writing, as shown in the passage from Morley Callaghan previously quoted.

In my opinion [ ] these youthful marriages are justifiable in every respect.

When we had all gathered near the fence [ ] we could see that they were bums.

Today [ ] American youth has more opportunities for success than ever before.

When appropriations are before the House he continually checks the Democrats' expenditures. [A close relationship between the statements]

When the subject of the subordinate clause is the same as the subject of the main clause, there is less need for the comma:

When *he* came in *he* brought news of another wreck.
When *I* came in, *he* was sitting up.

c) *Before a subordinate clause that follows the main clause.* A comma usually stands before a subordinate clause (or long phrase) that follows the main clause if it is not closely related in thought. If it is an essential modifier of the main statement, the comma is often omitted. The writer's sense of the closeness of the connection between the two statements must be the guide unless actual misunderstanding could arise from omitting the comma.

The bantams are used to hatch and rear the young pheasants [,] because the old pheasants aren't very fussy with their young.

Last spring the best miler in college failed to run [,] because he was too lazy to practice.

Kemal Ataturk's death came as a blow to a nation of 14,000,000 people, although he reformed their social customs, their religion, and their economics with dictatorial zeal and speed.

2. LISTS AND SERIES. (*a*) The comma is the natural mark to use *between the units of enumerations, lists, series* (unless the units

435

are long or contain commas within them, when semicolons would be used—*Semicolon §1).

> There are, among others, an actor out of a job, a murderer, a Mexican dipsomaniac, a man obsessed with a philosophical concept of time, an Indian oil millionaire who prefers waffles to any other food, and assorted females, mostly tough.—*The New Yorker,* Nov. 26, 1938

Commas are not used when conjunctions stand between the units of the series:

> A bit of tarnish on the brass work [ ] or untidy life preservers [ ] or matches on the decks seem to be of little concern to him.

Usage is divided on the comma before the last member of a series: *celery, onions, and olives,* or *celery, onions and olives.* Traditional formal usage is with the comma, but newspaper and business writing quite generally omit it and so does much informal writing. As a rule no real difference in meaning is felt, though there may be a difference in tempo. The omission might be awkward when the last unit of the series itself has an *and* (*Series):

> The menu was the same old line—roast beef, ham, chili, and pork and beans.

b) *Adjectives in series.* In the sentence

> When the long, cold, lonesome evenings would come, we gathered about the old wood stove and ate the chestnuts.

there are commas between *long—cold—lonesome* because each stands in the same relation to the noun *evenings.* There is no comma between *old* and *wood* because *old* modifies *wood stove* rather than just *stove.* A comma following *old* would throw more emphasis upon *wood* and might sometimes be wanted. Compare these two versions:

> The room presents a colonial effect with its old-fashioned, cross-beamed ceiling and gray, brick fireplace.
> The room presents a colonial effect with its old-fashioned cross-beamed ceiling and gray brick fireplace.

Either version is correct but in the first, *cross-beamed* and *brick* stand out as separate modifiers of their nouns.

Informal writing, especially in rapid narrative, tends to omit commas when the preceding adjective can sensibly be regarded as modifying the noun as it is modified by the other adjectives:

> a large round cast iron stove
> ten old broken down straight-back chairs

(*Large* modifies *round cast iron stove, round* modifies *cast iron stove; ten* can modify the complete phrase, *old* can modify *broken down straight-back chairs,* and so on.) But when the meaning is not cumulative, commas are used:

an atmosphere of chill, gray death
a new, more liberal Republican party

c) Two items connected by and *are not usually punctuated:*

In high school the student is paid six dollars a month for helping the teachers in their work [ ] and for doing odd jobs about the school building.

3. WITH NON-RESTRICTIVE MODIFIERS. Modifiers which do not limit the meaning of a noun or verb but add a descriptive detail are non-restrictive and are set off by a comma or commas. The expressions in italics are non-restrictive:

They had on old tattered overalls, *over which they were wearing a variety of differently colored sweaters.*
From where I was standing, *almost directly above the treasure,* I could see many articles that had been lost. [The clause *that had been lost* is restrictive and so not set off by a comma.]
Pigeons breed in the spring and the hen lays two eggs, *one of which usually hatches into a cock and one into a hen.*

A restrictive modifier, which is essential to a correct understanding of the word it modifies, is not set off by punctuation. The expressions in italics are restrictive:

Wouldn't it be as just to remove from his suffering a person *who has committed no crime* as to make suffer one *who has committed a crime?*
Great tracts were left, eaten bare of the grass *which had kept the soil in place.*

Many clauses may be considered either restrictive or non-restrictive, and their punctuation should follow the writer's sense of the closeness with which they limit the word they modify. The expressions in italics in these sentences might be set off by commas, depending on the writer's intention:

A winding road *that seemed to lead nowhere in particular* passed through the village.
It was quite a satisfaction *after working a difficult logarithm problem* to know that something had been accomplished.

Further examples of restrictive and non-restrictive expressions will be found in *Restrictive and non-restrictive.

4. WITH INTERRUPTING AND PARENTHETICAL WORDS AND PHRASES.
(*a*) *Interrupting constructions.* A phrase or clause that interrupts the direct movement of the sentence should be set off by commas, *two* commas:

> This last semester, *if it has done nothing else,* has given me confidence in myself.
> Over in the corner, *beside the dark and broken window where a newspaper was stuffed to keep out the rain,* sat Verona.
> Did intelligent people, *he asked himself,* do things like that?

Usage is divided over setting off short parenthetical words and phrases like *incidentally, of course.* Setting them off with commas is more characteristic of formal than of informal writing, though there is often a difference in emphasis according to whether or not they are used:

> These early attempts, of course, brought no results.
> These early attempts of course brought no results.
> For months after that, naturally, he made no attempt to see her.
> For months after that naturally he made no attempt to see her.
> The famous artist, oddly enough, preferred the company of common laborers to that of his own kind.

When a short clause or phrase interrupts a construction immediately after a conjunction that is preceded by a comma, usage varies:

> It hardly seems possible, but, [ ] *if I heard him right,* it is going to be done.
> In the first hour I found six references, and, [ ] *although they came slower after that,* I found ten before leaving the library.

Logic calls for two commas here, since the *but* and the *and* are parts of the constructions that are interrupted, and they would be found in formal writing. In informal writing the first of the two commas is' frequently omitted.

Adverbs that modify the verb or the statement closely should not be set off by commas when they are in their natural position:

> Perhaps [ ] they had never intended to come.
> They had never intended to come, perhaps.

b) *Connectives.* When a *conjunctive adverb stands after the first phrase of its clause, as it often does, it is usually set off by commas, and often it is set off when it stands first in the clause:

> The next morning, however, they all set out as though nothing had happened.
> The second plan, therefore, was the one determined upon for the holiday.

438

However, the next morning they all set out as though nothing had happened.

Because of setting off these heavy connectives some writers are tempted to put a comma after *but* and other more informal conjunctions. These are a part of the clauses in which they appear and should not be set off:

I was positive that if someone would just give me some guidance I could do much better. But [ ] the semester continued the same as before.

The ordinary American family could all ride comfortably in a low-priced car. Yet [ ] there is something about the larger cars that attracts buyers.

5. COMMAS WITH MAIN SENTENCE ELEMENTS. (*a*) *Comma following a long subject.* When the subject of a sentence is a long phrase or a noun followed by modifiers, that is, when it is a locution of five or six words or more, formal usage often puts a comma between it and the verb, but informal usage does not. In the following sentences a comma might or might not be used, depending upon the formality of the context:

Whether a program is appealing or not, [ ] is quickly reflected in the sale of the sponsor's product.

Everything that I had picked out as a flaw to be pounced upon and criticized, [ ] assumed a different meaning and became a vital part of the work.

b) *No commas following a short subject.* Care should be taken not to separate shorter subjects from their verbs:

The first family to come [ ] sends word back to those left in the Old Country.

The six boys [ ] all came on the run.

c) *Comma not used between verb and object.* There is some temptation to put a comma after a verb, separating it from its object or complement. This is especially true after verbs of saying. Such commas should be taken out in revision:

Since they knew nothing whatsoever about their future occupation, they must start what might be termed [ ] a second schooling.

It seems inevitable [ ] that the person who is hardworking and willing has a good deal put over on him.

d) *Commas in compound predicates.* Usage is divided over separating the two verbs of a compound predicate. Probably the better and more common usage is not to use a comma between the verbs unless the predicates are long or contrasted:

439

Thus in fifteen years rabbit raising has ceased to be a hobby [ ] and has taken a definite place among the industries of the world.

Pop could talk himself out of trouble [ ] and also talk himself into a lot of trouble.

6. For emphasis and contrast. The pause indicated by a comma tends to keep distinct the constructions it separates and to emphasize slightly the construction that follows the mark:

Temporarily the wine industry was all but ruined, and farmers turned to dairying, and to cooperation to give them a market.

This is especially true when a connective is omitted:

And afterwards I told her how I felt, how I kept feeling about her.

In the idiom *the more . . . the greater,* formal usage tends to have a comma, informal not:

. . . And the more meaning the Grammarian finds crowded into the verb [,] the happier he is.—P. B. Ballard, *Thought and Language,* p. 87

7. For clearness. Often a comma can guide a reader in interpreting a sentence and make it unnecessary for him to go back over it for meaning. In material that is likely to be read aloud, the writer should give special heed to this device. Two such constructions are especially helped by commas:

a) When a word has two possible functions. For or *but* may be either a conjunction or a preposition, and confusion may be avoided by using a comma before either when it is used as a conjunction:

The surgeon's face showed no emotion, but anxiety and a little nervousness must be seething behind that impassive mask. [To avoid reading "no emotion but anxiety"]

b) When a noun might be mistaken for the object of a verb.

When the boll weevil struck, the credit system collapsed and ruined a great part of the landowners and tenants. [Not: When the boll weevil struck the credit system . . .]

It is not necessary to have a session like this very often, but when you do, get everything off your mind that is disturbing you. [Not: but when you do get everything off your mind . . .]

After the parents had left, the children were introduced to the others in the class. [Not: After the parents had left the children . . .]

c) Sometimes a faulty interpretation of word grouping can be prevented:

The only way that you can develop honestly is to discover how you write now, and then write naturally in everything you hand in. [Avoiding: *now and then*] *d*) *Ordinarily when the same word occurs twice consecutively a comma should be used:*

What the trouble really is, is of no interest to him.

8. ROUTINE, CONVENTIONAL USES. (*a*) *In dates,* to separate the day of the month from the year: *May 26, 1939.* When the day of the month is not given, a comma may or may not be used: *In May 1939* or *In May, 1939.* The neater use is without the comma.
b) *In addresses,* to separate town from state or country when they are written on the same line: *Chicago, Illinois; Washington, D. C.; Hamilton, Madison County, New York; Berne, Switzerland*
c) *After salutations in informal letters: Dear Dot, Dear Len,*
d) *In figures, to separate thousands, millions, etc:* 4,672,342
e) *To separate degrees and titles from names:*

Elihu Root, Esq.	Charles Evans Hughes, Jr.
Wallace W. Emmett, A.B.	Wallace W. Emmett, A.B. '36
	Ronald C. MacKenzie, Ph.D.

f) After a weak exclamation like *well, why, oh* when it does not carry much stress
g) *A comma is not now commonly used to show the omission of a word* that is required to fill out a grammatical construction:

He must have taken the right-hand turn and I [,] the left.

9. COMMA COMBINED WITH OTHER MARKS. (*a*) *A comma is now rarely used with a dash.* *Dash §6
b) *When a parenthesis comes within a construction that would be followed by a comma,* the comma stands after the parenthesis. *Parentheses §5
c) *With quotation marks.* *Quotation marks §4, *b* and *c*

References: The most realistic and thorough study of punctuation is George Summey, Jr., *Modern Punctuation* (New York, 1919), but it is now somewhat out of date and needs to be done over again. Moe, "Teaching the Use of the Comma," *English Journal,* 1913, ii, 104-108, contains a schematic grammatical grouping of uses of commas. *Current English Usage* takes up several particular constructions.

Comma fault (CORRECTION: Revise the sentence marked, either *CF* changing the comma to a semicolon or a period, inserting an appropriate conjunction, or rephrasing to make it a more effective sentence. You should do more than merely remove the "comma fault"; you should make an effective statement. Your instructor's mark means that in his judgment it is not an effective run-on sentence and should be revised.)

A comma fault (or comma blunder or comma splice) is two or more statements in the form of independent sentences that are punctuated as a single sentence—that is, with a comma between them (or even run together with no mark at all). A few sentences of this sort are effective (see "Run-on sentences," p. 136), but here we are considering only those that by their form and by the lack of thought relation between the clauses are not.

There are various remedies for a comma fault:

1. The easiest, that satisfies the minimum requirements of conventional grammar, is to repunctuate, using a semicolon or a period instead of the comma. This often leaves two weak sentences instead of one good one.

2. If the statements really belong together in one sentence, the clauses may be joined by a conjunction that shows the relationship, probably retaining the comma.

3. Often the sentence needs to be rephrased—perhaps a relative pronoun used instead of a *this* or *these*, or a complete rewriting. Remember that the aim is to make an effective sentence.

The following examples show some common types with possible improvements:

The comma fault	Suggested revision
He had taken a couple of steps, stopped, reached out and turned a valve, as he did that he pointed out that all the valves were right-hand valves.	He had taken a couple of steps, stopped, reached out and turned a valve. As he did that he pointed out that all the valves were right-hand valves.
Two volumes of his great work are now completed, the first will be published next year.	Two volumes of his great work are now completed, the first of which will be published next year. Also possible: Two volumes of his great work are now completed, and the first will be published next year. Two volumes of his great work are now completed. The first will be published next year.
Charley then crossed the room and threw a switch which started a motor, returning he wiped the perspiration from his forehead with the back of his hand.	Charley then crossed the room and threw a switch which started a motor. When he returned he wiped the perspiration . . .
They still produce aluminum tips for broken skis, these are very successful as a temporary device.	They still produce aluminum tips for broken skis, which are very successful as a temporary device.

Carelessly run together sentences are one of the most serious faults in elementary writing and anyone who has not learned to avoid them must take extra pains to remove them from his writing.

For a more complete discussion and more examples of comma faults and of successful run-on sentences, see "Run-on sentences," p. 136. See also *Contact clauses, *Conjunctions.

Commands and requests Simple commands are expressed by the imperative form of the verb, which is the same as the infinitive:

Hurry up!   *Shut* the door, please.
Fill out the coupon and *mail* it today.
"Always *do* right. This will gratify some people and astonish the rest."—MARK TWAIN

In speech the force of the command or request is shown by the stress and tone of voice, which are hard to represent on paper. Emphatic commands are punctuated with an exclamation mark, less emphatic with a period. The form with *do* is often emphatic (*Do* come!) and in speech various auxiliaries are added. Negative commands are expressed with *not* and the *do* form of the verb: Don't go yet.

Softened or more polite commands and requests depend on phrasing and usually involve auxiliaries or adverbs of courtesy. Often these commands and requests are in the pattern of a question.

Try and [or *to*] get them in on time.
You will write at least six pages.
Please think no more of it.
Would you be willing to take part in this program?
Would you please close the window.
Let's go around and see what we can do with him.
Suppose we say nothing more about it.

In indirect discourse an imperative becomes an infinitive or, more formally, a clause with *should*:

He told us to write a 5000 word paper [or]
He said that we should write a 5000 word paper [Direct form: "Write a 5000 word paper"].
He wired me to come at once [Direct: "Come at once"].

For further discussion of forms of commands see Curme, *Syntax*, pp. 419, 430-36.

Commercial usage *Business English

committee is a *collective noun, to be construed as singular or plural according as the group or the individuals are meant. The singular would usually be the form desired.

The committee meets today at four.
The committee get together with difficulty.

common ("a common friend") *mutual

Common noun *Noun §1

compare—contrast *Compare* is used in two senses: 1. To point out likenesses (used with *to*); 2. To examine two or more objects to find likenesses or differences (used with *with*). *Comparing* in the second sense may discover or describe *differences* as well as *likenesses*. *Contrast* always means *difference*.

> He compared my stories to Maupassant's [said they were like his].
> He compared my stories *with* Maupassant's [pointed out like and unlike traits].

In the common construction with the past participle, either *to* or *with* is used:

> Compared *with* [or *to*] Maupassant's, mine are pretty feeble.
> In comparison *with* [not *to*] Maupassant's, mine are pretty feeble.

Idioms with *contrast:*

> He contrasted my work *with* [sometimes *to*] Maupassant's.
> In contrast *to* [rarely *with*] Maupassant's, my stories are pretty feeble.

Stress: the noun *contrast* (kon′trast); the verb *contrast* (kən-trast′, kən trast′əd, kən trast′ing).

Comparisons For comparisons as figures of speech see "The most common figures, Metaphors, similes, analogies," p. 235; for comparison as a method of paragraph development see "Contrast and comparison," p. 102.

Comp **Comparison of adjectives and adverbs** (CORRECTION: Change the form of the adjective or adverb marked in your paper in accordance with §§1-4 below or change the construction with a comparative or superlative in line with §5.)

1. FORMS. English adjectives and adverbs are compared, that is, they change their forms to show a greater degree of the quality or whatever they name, in two ways: (*a*) *Synthetic form*. The change of degree may be shown by adding *-er* or *-est* to the positive form:

	POSITIVE	COMPARATIVE	SUPERLATIVE
ADJECTIVE:	early	earlier	earliest
	hoarse	hoarser	hoarsest
	hot	hotter	hottest
ADVERB:	fast	faster	fastest
	soon	sooner	soonest

b) *Analytic form.* The change in degree may be shown by prefixing *more* and *most* to the positive form. This form is used for all adjectives and adverbs of three syllables or more. For many of two syllables it is the only form, and it may be used with any. It may also be used with those of one syllable, so that for many comparatives and superlatives there are two forms:

ADJECTIVE:	exquisite	more exquisite	most exquisite
	empty	emptier, more empty	emptiest, most empty
	able	abler, more able	ablest, most able
ADVERB:	comfortably	more comfortably	most comfortably
	often	oftener, more often	oftenest, most often
	hotly	more hotly	most hotly

Words with a short vowel followed by a single consonant double the consonant to indicate the short sound (*thin, thinner, thinnest*). Words ending in *y* change the *y* to *i* before the synthetic endings: *dry, drier, driest, shy, shier, shiest* (sometimes *shyer, shyest*).

2. CHOICE BETWEEN FORMS. The meanings of the analytic and synthetic forms are the same, so that the one can be used that better fits the form of the phrase or the rhythm of the expression, that sounds better. But the synthetic form places the stress on the root part of the form and so tends to emphasize the quality (kind'er), and the analytic form allows the stress to fall on the sign of the degree (more' kind, You are most' kind) so that there is some difference in the suggestion value of the two.

3. MEANING OF THE DEGREES. The comparative degree is used to express a greater degree (It is *warmer* now) or to make specific comparison between two units: "He was *kinder* [*more kind*] than his wife."

The superlative is used to indicate the greatest degree of a quality among three or more people or things (He was the *jolliest* of the whole group; This is the *brightest* tie in the showcase). The form with *most* is also used as an intensive to indicate an extreme degree: "You are *most kind*"; "She is *most clever*," in which no specific comparison is intended. This absolute superlative is not so common in formal English as in informal and colloquial English.

4. COMPARISON OF ABSOLUTES. In their central meaning such adjectives as *black, dead, excellent, fatal, final, impossible, *unique* are not compared, since their meaning is absolute: There are no degrees of *deadness* or *blackness* or *impossibility*. But in common use the meaning of these words is not absolute so that in informal and vulgate English they are frequently compared: "This was even *more impossible*." Many are used figuratively with less absolute

meanings ("This is the *deadest* town I was ever in"), which naturally admit comparison.

5. IDIOMS WITH COMPARATIVES AND SUPERLATIVES. (*a*) *as much as if not more than.* Colloquially people are likely to say "the styles vary as much if not more than the colors" but in writing both comparative constructions should be completed:

> The styles vary as much *as* if not more *than* the colors.
> Germany is as strong *as* if not stronger *than* she was in 1914. [or]
> Germany is as strong as she was in 1914, if not stronger.

Similarly, superlative constructions should be completed:

> INCOMPLETE CONSTRUCTION: It is one of the largest if not the best department store on the Pacific Coast.
> COMPLETE CONSTRUCTION: It is one of the largest department stores on the Pacific Coast, if not the best.

b) *as . . . as.* Sometimes *than* is carelessly used for the second *as* in a sentence like this:

> I pay almost ten times as much for it *as* [not *than*] for the bigger bus ticket.

See *as . . . as.

c) Comparatives with *other.* With a comparative, idiom calls for *other* when the comparison is with something in the same class of things but not when the comparison is with things of a different class:

> She is a better dancer than the other girls.
> She is a better dancer than the boys [than any of the boys].
> It is hard to find more beautiful scenery in any part of the world.

d) Superlatives are not completed by *other:*

> Jerry was the best cook of all the [not *other*] cooks in the surrounding camps.
> The Egyptians had obtained the highest degree of cultivation in medicine that had up to that time been obtained by any [not *other*] nation.

e) Superlative of two objects. In colloquial and familiar English a superlative is often a form of emphasis: "We saw the loveliest flowers when we visited her garden.—Hasn't she the sweetest voice?" This often leads to statements like "His new novel is the best of the two," in which the *best* is really an emphatic word for *better.* These expressions are usually avoided in formal writing but are regularly found in informal and familiar usage. Fries says (p. 101):

The use of the superlative rather than the comparative for two, thus ignoring a dual as distinct from a plural, is a fact of Standard English usage and not a characteristic limited to Vulgar English.

f) The two terms of a comparison should be comparable:

Not: His salary was lower than a shoe clerk.
Comparable: His salary was lower than a shoe clerk's [Or: than that of a shoe clerk].
Not: His face was round and healthy looking, like a recent college graduate.
Comparable: His face was round and healthy looking, like a recent college graduate's.

Reference: Curme, *Parts of Speech*, Chs. 11, 13; *Syntax*, Ch. 25; Fries, pp. 96-101

complement—compliment *Complement* means a number or amount that makes a whole, or an allotment (related to *complete*):

He had his full *complement* of good looks.   *Complementary* angles

Compliment has to do with politeness and praise:

He *complimented* them on their progress.
Their progress deserved his *compliment*.
"the *complimentary* close" of a letter

Complement A complement is the noun or adjective completing the meaning of a linking verb and modifying the subject:

He was *busy*.   He became *the real head* of the concern.

See *Linking verbs, *Predicate adjective and predicate nominative.

Complex sentences are made up of one principal clause and one or more dependent (subordinate) clauses. So many combinations are possible that detailed classification would be tedious. Instead a passage of fairly typical expository prose is given in which half the sentences are complex. The subordinate clauses are in italics.

(1) The glamorous F. B. I. remains the favorite of young men *who are ambitious to tilt a lance in the crusade against crime.* (2) Thousands of applications are on file for the next batch of appointments. (3) Those *who get appointments* undergo a training course of fourteen weeks and graduate into a salary of $3,200 a year. (4) An agent's progress depends solely upon the skill *he shows* in handling his assignments. (5) The highest salary *he can get* is $5,400. (6) Salaries for agents in charge of field offices, the next grade, range from $5,600 to $6,400. (7) Above agents-in-charge come inspectors and assistant directors, *whose salaries run from $6,500 to $7,500.* (8) All the higher jobs are filled from the ranks.

(9) An agent's life is a helter-skelter one, hard to blend with ordinary family life. (10) Most of his time is likely to be spent away from home, travelling on assignments about the area *of which his field office is headquarters*. (11) Transfers from one office to another are frequent, *because much of the Bureau's effectiveness depends upon the mobility of its personnel*. (12) The transfers usually come suddenly. (13) An agent of the New York office looking forward to dinner with his family may be ordered during the afternoon to leave immediately for El Paso or San Francisco by plane. (14) Or he may get such an order in the middle of the night. (15) His family follows along later, at his expense. (16) Ownership of a home is out of the question. (17) Even an agent's choice of apartments is limited, for he must negotiate an arrangement for voiding his lease upon short notice, and most landlords shy from this. (18) Seven out of ten agents are married.

(19) *When an agent is travelling*, the government allows him railroad fare and $5 a day for such expenses as meals, lodging, taxicab fares, tips, and entertainment of prospective informants. (20) The result of this parsimony is *that he spends from $50 to $150 a month of his own money to make up the difference*. (21) Agents are entitled to an annual leave of twenty-six days, but rarely get more than two weeks, *because the Bureau is perpetually short-handed*. (22) Many forego vacations entirely. (23) Agents are supposed to love their work more than play, and a surprising number of them do. (24) *When a married agent dies or is killed*, each of his fellow-agents contributes $10 to a fund for the widow. (25) Besides upward of $6,000 realized in this way, the widow receives a $5,000 award from Congress, and a pension of from $45 to $50 a month. (26) She may also have a clerical job at F. B. I. headquarters, *if she wants it*. (27) All of this helps to make up for the fact *that an agent cannot obtain life insurance / because his work is rated as hazardous*. (28) Eleven agents have been killed *since Hoover became Director in 1924*.— JACK ALEXANDER, *The New Yorker*, Oct. 9, 1937

Twelve of these sentences are simple: 2, 6, 8, 9, 12, 13, 14, 15, 16, 18, 22, 25. Two are compound (17, 23).

There are no compound-complex sentences, though 21 has a *compound predicate.

Exactly one half of the twenty-eight sentences are complex. The functions of italicized subordinate clauses are as follows:

Adjective clause modifying *men* [1]
Adjective clause modifying *Those* [3]
Adjective clause modifying *skill* (introductory *that* not written) [4]
Adjective clause modifying *salary* [5]
Adjective clause modifying *assistant directors* [7]
Adjective clause modifying *area* [10]
Adverbial clause of cause [11]

Adverbial clause of time   [19]
Noun clause, complement of *is*   [20]
Adverbial clause of cause   [21]
Adverbial clause of time   [24]
Adverbial clause of condition   [26]
Noun clause in apposition with *fact* / Adverbial clause of cause   [27]
Adverbial clause of time   [28]

See *Clauses, and for some of the effects and possibilities of complex sentences "Subordination and sentence movement," p. 125; see also *Compound sentences §4 for compound-complex sentences.

complexioned (complected) *Complected* in such phrases as "He is a dark-complected man" is vulgate or local for "a dark-complexioned man." *Complected* is a formal word meaning "woven together"; *complexion* and *complexioned* refer to facial coloring.

Composition of words *Origin of words §3

Compound-complex sentences *Compound sentences §4

Compound predicate Two or more verbs having the same subject are known as a compound predicate: "The youngster *bawled* and *stamped* his feet"; "Ruth *wrote* and *mailed* three letters."

Compound predicates are one of the chief devices of economy in writing. Note how far removed these sentences are from the one-small-idea-to-a-sentence type so frequently used by immature writers:

They (1) accepted the quinine and, in their gratitude, often (2) kissed the hygienists' hands. Heeding their advice, they (1) graveled the village roads, (2) began to drain their lands, (3) enlarged the windows of their dwellings, (4) built sidewalks, sanitary backhouses, and concrete platforms for manure, and so on.—Louis Adamic, *The Native's Return*, p. 318

For further discussion see *Subject and verb.

Compound sentences are sentences containing two or more complete statements (that is, each with a subject and complete verb) of coordinate grammatical value, without a subordinate clause.

1. Usually the clauses of a compound sentence are connected by one of the coordinating conjunctions, most commonly by *and, but, for, or*, and the combinations *either . . . or, neither . . . nor*:

What a fool he was to be thus startled *but* always he had hated cats from childhood.—Walter Duranty, *Babies Without Tails*, p. 11

Either you learned these simple things in high school *or* you will have to learn them in college.

2. A compound sentence may stand without a connective (*Contact clauses). Such sentences are usually punctuated with a semicolon:

> We need not bother here to decide the constant argument as to whether history is art or science; let us say that it is like architecture in being a science out of which art can grow.—BONAMY DOBRÉE, *Modern Prose Style*, p. 142

> They are generous-minded; they hate shams and enjoy being indignant about them; they are valuable social reformers; they have no notion of confining books to a library shelf.—E. M. FORSTER, *Aspects of the Novel*, p. 33

> No child would ever begin wasting its time by composing second-hand fairy tales if he were not encouraged to do it by sentimental mothers; he would much prefer to discourse upon his guinea pigs or his first railway journey.—W. E. WILLIAMS, *Plain Prose*, p. 15

Compare "Run-on sentences," p. 136.

3. The clauses of a compound sentence may be connected by a conjunctive adverb (*however, moreover, whereas, consequently, therefore . . .*):

> It put the G-men's coup of the previous day distinctly in the shade, for it dealt with tony crooks, *whereas* the fugitives the G-men had caught were hoodlums, most of whom did not even wear neckties.— JACK ALEXANDER, *The New Yorker*, Oct. 9, 1937

See *Conjunctive adverbs.

4. Since one or more of the principal clauses of a compound sentence can be modified by subordinate clauses, we have the category of *compound-complex sentences:*

> He was an old man with a long beard, whose clothes were rags; but Mr. Kiddle had all the way wished to tell someone how proud he was of Ada, who did the running, so he was glad to have even a tinker to talk to.—T. F. POWYS, *Mr. Weston's Good Wine*, p. 66

This sentence has three main clauses (making it compound): *He was an old man . . . but Mr. Kiddle had all the way wished . . . so he was glad to have . . .;* and three subordinate clauses (making it compound-complex): *whose clothes were rags, how proud he was of Ada, who did all the running.*

In current style there are relatively few compound sentences made up of two unmodified coordinate clauses, and relatively more compound-complex sentences. This type of sentence (of the *aggregating sort, at least) as contrasted with either simple or unmodified compound sentences, marks a mature style.

Compound subject Two or more nouns or pronouns standing as the subject of a verb are called a *compound subject*:

Capitalists, militarists, and ecclesiastics co-operate in education, because all depend for their power upon the prevalence of emotionalism and the rarity of critical judgment.—BERTRAND RUSSELL, *What I Believe,* p. 53

The verb following a compound subject is plural:

Christianity and humanity *have* gone hand in hand throughout history.

Some special cases will be found described under *Subject and verb § 2b.

Compound words Compound words are combinations of two or more words or word-like elements: *doorknob, notwithstanding, quarter-hour, father-in-law, drugstore.*

Questions about the use of the hyphen in compound words are discussed in *Hyphen, and questions about their plurals in *Plurals §5. See also *Group words, *book.

Concession *although

Concluding paragraphs (CORRECTION: Revise the very end of your paper so that it rounds out the discussion of your subject and so that it ends strongly.) *Concl*

For discussion of concluding paragraphs and examples, see "Concluding paragraphs," p. 70.

Concord is the agreement of words in case, person, gender, and number. In this book questions of concord are treated under the various parts of speech. See especially *Reference of pronouns, *Subject and verb.

Concrete words (CORRECTION: Replace the abstract word or words by concrete ones.) *Concr*

Concrete words name persons and things that can be seen and touched (*bus, waitress, filing case*), in contrast to abstract words for acts, ideas, qualities, relationships (*flowing, theory, cleanliness*).

For discussion see "Concrete words," p. 187, and "Abstract and concrete words," p. 223; see also *Imagery.

Conditions Conditional clauses state a condition or action necessary for the truth or occurrence of the main statement of a sentence. *If* is by far the most common conjunction for conditional clauses, with its negatives *if not* and *unless* (= *if not*), and *whether* (= *if . . . if, if . . . or if*). In formal writing *in case, provided, provided that, on condition that, in the event that,* and other phrases are used.

1. SIMPLE CONDITIONS. Simple (or practical) conditions are statements of actual or reasonable conditions under which the main statement will hold. The indicative (ordinary) verb forms are used:

> If the semaphore arm is horizontal, you know that a train is in that block of track.
> He will be there unless something happens to his car.
> Whether he comes or not, I shall go just the same.

An older type of condition survives in some proverbs:

> Spare the rod and spoil the child. [If you spare the rod, you will spoil the child.]

2. LESS VIVID CONDITIONS. Less vivid (theoretical or hypothetical but still possible) conditions are usually made with *should . . . would*:

> If he should raise his offer another $100, I would take it. [or] If he raised his offer, I would take it.
> If you revised your papers carefully, your writing would improve and would receive a higher grade.

3. CONTRARY TO FACT CONDITIONS. Conditions that cannot be met, contrary to fact conditions, formerly were stated with the subjunctive and still are in formal writing (sometimes even with a rather archaic inversion). The indicative is also used in this type of condition, especially in informal writing:

> FORMAL: If I were you, I would charge at least that.
> INFORMAL: If I was going to be there, I'd be glad to help.
> FORMAL: Had I known what I now know, I should never have let him go.
> INFORMAL: If I had known what I do [or know] now, I should [I'd] never have let him go.
> FORMAL: If he were only here, to . . .
> INFORMAL: If he was only here, he . . .

See also *if, *Subjunctives.
Reference: Curme, *Syntax*, pp. 317-32, 421-29; Fries, pp. 104-107

Congruence of tenses *Tenses of verbs §2

Conjugation The inflectional changes of a verb or a group of verbs of the same type to show person, number, voice, mood, and tense. See *Verbs, *Tenses of verbs, *Principal parts of verbs.

Conjunctions Conjunctions introduce and tie clauses together and join series of words and phrases.

In this *Guide-Index* conjunctions are discussed according to their conventional types:

*Coordinating (*and, but, for* . . .)
*Correlative (*either* . . . *or, not only* . . . *but* . . .)
*Conjunctive adverbs (*however, therefore, consequently* . . .)
*Subordinating (*as, because, since, so that, when* . . .)

There are also articles on many of the particular conjunctions: *although, *and, *as, *because, *but, and so on. The article *Contact clauses discusses joining clauses without connectives; §7 of Chapter 5, p. 136, discusses in detail contact clauses and *Comma faults.

In these articles we are following the traditional grouping of conjunctions, although obviously the difference between certain coordinating conjunctions and the conjunctive adverbs is slight, and often in use the difference between subordinating and coordinating conjunctions cannot be reasonably seen. The meaning of these words is more important than their type. After considerable study, Professor Fries says:

> The difficulty of finding a reasonable set of criteria by which to separate coördinate from subordinate clauses and thus coördinating function words from those that are subordinating, argues that, in English, this distinction is really of practically no importance. Each of these function words signals a particular set of relationships between the clauses which it joins and the precise nature of the relationship is vitally important. Whether we further classify that relationship as a "coördinate" or a "subordinate" one makes no difference whatever.—*American English Grammar*, p. 211

But until a thorough study has been made of the matter, we have to follow the conventional groupings for purposes of reference.

Reference: Fries, pp. 206-40; all grammars have discussions.

Conjunctions, Use (CORRECTION: Make the conjunction marked more accurate [§ 1] or more appropriate to the style of the passage [§ 2].)

1. ACCURATE CONJUNCTIONS. The fitting together of clauses marked by an exact use of conjunctions is a sign of mature, practiced writing. In everyday speech we get along with a relatively small number—*and, as, but, so, when,* and a few others. We don't bother to emphasize shades of meaning and exact relationships, which are suggested by pauses, tones of voice, gestures. In writing, accurate connectives go a long way toward making up for the loss of these oral means of holding ideas together.

Accurate use of conjunctions needs to be stressed. There are some easy temptations, like using *but* when there is no contrast between the statements (*but §2). Some conjunctions vary in

453

definiteness of meaning: *As* means *because*, but means it very weakly (*as §4); **while* may mean *although* or *whereas*, but the core of its meaning relates to time, and careful writers restrict it to that. Such niceties in the use of these words are discussed in the articles on the particular conjunctions.

2. WEIGHT. It is important for the conjunctions to be appropriate to other traits of style. Their weight should fit with the weight of other words and with the formality or informality of constructions.

The chief fault in weight of conjunctions has to do with the **conjunctive adverbs (however, therefore, consequently . . .)* in ordinary, informal writing. These words are heavy and fit best in rather formal style. *But* and *however*, for example, both connect statements in opposition, but one cannot always be substituted for the other. *But* fits in all levels, but *however* is often too formal or too heavy for informal writing.

> The entrance and registration desk didn't strike me as beautiful. From here, however, I went upstairs and then I could see what they meant. [But from here . . .]

The English language has a number of long connecting phrases that are often used in place of shorter, more compact conjunctions:

> At this time football was distinctively a military pastime in Rome *in the same manner in which* [as] polo is among the soldiers today.

The use of many long connections will weaken a written style.

See *Conjunctive adverbs and *Function words.

3. REPETITION OF CONJUNCTIONS. Repeating a conjunction at the beginning of each element of a series of two or more in the same construction gives distinctness to each element, avoids possible confusion, and gives the advantages of clearcut *parallelism. This is more appropriate in formal writing and often gives a definite rhythm:

> . . . designs of spears and shields and bastions and all the pomp of heraldry. . . .—NORMAN DOUGLAS, *Siren Land*, p. 152

> For those five days and nights the Australians lived and ate and slept in that gallery of the mine of death, . . .—JOHN MASEFIELD, *Gallipoli*, p. 165

Note that in such series no commas are used between the items.

In opposition to this, omitting *and* before the last member of a short series results in a crisp emphasis:

> High vacuums are essential not only to the distillation of vitamins but also in the manufacture of thermos bottles, radio tubes, X-ray apparatus, [∧] electric lamps.—*Time*, Nov. 28, 1938

See *Series, *Telegraphic style.

4. COORDINATION VS. SUBORDINATION. For discussion of this phase of the use of conjunctions see *Subordination and "Coordination and subordination," p. 124.

References: Kennedy, § § 56 and 110; Curme, *Parts of Speech*, Chapter 7, *Syntax*, § § 19 and 21, and index references

Conjunctive adverbs 1. A number of words primarily adverbs are used also as connectives. They are called *conjunctive adverbs* (or *relative adverbs*, or *illative conjunctions*). Their adverbial meaning remains rather prominent, so that they are relatively weak connectives and need special discussion. Except *when* and *where* and *so* they are coordinating conjunctions and make compound sentences. The most common are:

accordingly	furthermore	*namely
*also	*hence	nevertheless
anyhow	*however	(*so)
anyway (colloquial)	indeed	still
*besides	likewise	*then
consequently	*moreover	*therefore

However [adverb] the election goes, the public will lose.

The results were disappointing; however [conjunction] we were not surprised.

The lights were not yet [adverb] turned on.

He had been appointed by the governor, yet [conjunction] he did not support the party's policies.

2. WEIGHT AND USE. The important fact about the conjunctive adverbs is that most of them are relatively heavy connectives. Except *so* they are most appropriate in formal writing and in rather routine, stiff exposition, but are not so appropriate in easy, informal writing. A few of them can weigh down a passage and make it decidedly uncomfortable reading. They are now more used to connect the thought of separate sentences than the thought of clauses within the same sentence.

One of the duties of theme-readers is to remove these stilted connectives from the ordinarily simple and straightforward writing of students. Note these appropriate and inappropriate uses:

It is, *therefore,* unfortunate that at a time like the present, which plainly calls for a Socrates, we should instead have got a Mencken. [Appropriate, as is suggested by the formal sentence structure; connects with thought of preceding sentence]—IRVING BABBITT, *On Being Creative*, p. 205

Herr Zweig has gone to quite a bit of trouble to pad out his story, which is hardly rich or complex enough to bear the weight of a full-

dress biography. *Also,* he talks a great deal about "Destiny," that convenient item of verbal idiocy by the use of which Teutonic biographers live and have their very being. [*And* would do at least as well as *also*.]
—CLIFTON FADIMAN, *The New Yorker,* Dec. 5, 1938

Courtesy demands that they be attentive during the speech, *also* during the choir selection. [*And* would be a stronger connective here.]

When morning came, *however,* I was still sick, *yet,* when the bugle blew, I got up. *Consequently,* I looked very white at breakfast. [Connectives much too heavy for the material and context]

3. POSITION. Conjunctive adverbs are often placed within their clauses instead of at the beginning. This helps take the initial stress from them and gives it to more important words. When they are so placed, they are usually set off by commas as in the sentences in §§1 and 2 above.

4. PUNCTUATION. The conventional rule of editors is that a clause introduced by a conjunctive adverb is preceded by a semicolon. This is generally true (see the examples above) but the semicolon is used not because of the conjunctive adverb but because the clauses are rather heavy and the connecting force of the conjunctive adverb relatively weak. With the lighter conjunctive adverbs, especially with *so, then,* and *yet,* a comma is often sufficient:

The whole forenoon had been a complete bore, *so* we wanted to make sure that we had a good time after lunch.

The advice sometimes given to strengthen *so* and *then* by adding *and* ("*and so* we wanted to make sure . . .") is usually wrong, since *and* adds nothing to the meaning of the connective. If the illustrative sentence above was to be really improved, it could have been written:

The whole forenoon had been such a complete bore that we wanted to make sure we had a good time after lunch.

See *however, *namely, *so, *then, *therefore.

connected with, in connection with Wordy locutions, usually for *in* or *with*:

The environment in connection with a fraternity [in a fraternity] will be something you have never experienced before.

Connectives See *Conjunctions and *Prepositions and the articles there referred to.

Connotation The connotation of words—their overtones, the meanings and values that are suggested rather than definitely expressed in their dictionary meanings—is discussed under "Connotation," p. 189, and in Chapter 8.

consequently *Conjunctive adverbs

considerable—considerably In speech there is a tendency not to distinguish the adverb *considerably* from the adjective *considerable*. The following are correct:

> The night crew came on and that helped considerably. [Adverb modifying *helped*]
> The night crew was considerable help. [Adjective modifying *help*]

Consistency Although consistency in itself is not an ideal (writing may be consistently bad), and although writing, like other activities, must vary somewhat with circumstances and with states of mind and body, we have reason to expect a person's writing to be generally consistent with itself. Most people tend toward either formality or informality. We should expect some to punctuate fully, spell conservatively, use somewhat literary words and full constructions; others will tend to be less formal, use more open punctuation, the simpler spelling forms, more colloquial words and turns of expression. This tendency may extend to attitudes and opinions, though formal writing does not always mean conservative ideas, nor informal writing liberal ideas.

It is rather important that a writer should keep fairly consistent with his general trend, departing from it only consciously and for good reason. A formal writer may have to step down somewhat to meet his readers; an informal writer may have to tighten up his expression in academic papers or on a subject of more dignity than he usually treats. It is important in such cases that the writer pay very careful attention to making his paper consistent in tone throughout. In most writing, however, consistency can be gained by the use of English that is in harmony with the writer's general habits and quality of mind.

See Chapter 2, especially "Appropriateness to speaker or writer," p. 47.

Consonants In a consonant sound the breath is either restricted or stopped—as contrasted with vowel sounds, which are made without friction and with fuller resonance. The letters representing consonant sounds are called *consonants*: b, c, d, f, g, h, j, k, l, m, n, p, q, r, s, t, v, w, x, y, z.

This *Index* has a brief article on each of these letters and on some consonant combinations (*sh, th, wh* . . .). See also *Pronunciation, *Doubling final consonants, *Division of words.

Const **Construction** (CORRECTION: An obvious fault or inconsistency in grammatical construction. Revise it. [For some of the commonest grammatical slips see "Shifted constructions," p. 129 and Chapter 9, "Minimum Essentials," p. 250.])

Construction means the grammatical setting of a word in a sentence or, more concretely, a group of words in grammatical relationship to each other. In *the black cat, the* is an article, and *black* an adjective, both modifying the noun *cat*; the phrase as a whole is a construction. A grammatical pattern may be spoken of as a construction, as in the phrases *sentence constructions, parallel constructions*.

contact At present *contact* as a verb meaning to "get in touch with a person" is a problem child. Webster has the noun *contact* "a coming or being in touch physically or mentally." (He made the most of his fraternity contacts.) The *conversion of the noun in this sense to a verb is no more extreme than other conversions we use readily.

The objections to "Will you contact Mr. Hubble?" and so on, rest on the fact that the use came out of salesmanship—and many people have unpleasant associations with being "contacted" or with brokers' "contact men." Others object to using business terms in other contexts. The boy who wrote on an examination that he was "glad to have contacted Dostoievsky in the course" was using a word inappropriately.

The word is primarily commercial and familiar and should be used in other circumstances only when you are pretty sure your audience will not shy at your borrowing a business term.

Contact clauses Two or more clauses of a sentence that stand together without a specific connective between them are known as *contact clauses*. (This is Professor Jespersen's name for them; the relationship is also called *parataxis*, and the omission of a conjunction usually expressed is called *asyndeton*.)

Many coordinate sentences are in the form of contact clauses, as in the famous "I came, I saw, I conquered" or in "But in him the pretence is justified: he has enjoyed thinking out his subject, he will delight in his work when it is done" (Max Beerbohm, *Yet Again*, p. 77). A subordinate clause may also be set beside the main clause without connective:

. . . and Soames lowered his eyes, he did not want to embarrass the girl.—JOHN GALSWORTHY, *Swan Song*, p. 103

Give your decision, it will probably be right. But do not give your reasons, they will most certainly be wrong.—BERNARD HART, *The Psychology of Insanity*

This very old type of sentence has been outlawed in the past by prescriptive grammar, though never quite abandoned by writers. In recent years it has re-emerged into literature from speech, where it is and always has been a natural and common form of expression.

Contact clauses have a definite bearing upon one of the perennial problems of writing, the "comma fault," since many clauses put together without expressed connectives are really expressive as they stand and need none. They are especially common and effective in rapid narrative where specific labeling of causes and results would slow up the movement, as in the sentence just quoted from Galsworthy. They are less common in straight exposition but occasionally occur. Many, of course, are the result of carelessness but many also, as these examples suggest, are a symptom of a rapid and natural style. Deciding on the effectiveness of contact clauses is one of the more difficult problems of students and teachers.

Successful and unsuccessful contact clauses are discussed fully in Chapter 5, "Run-on sentences," p. 136.

References: Curme, *Syntax*, pp. 170-73; Jespersen, pp. 360-61

content, contents ADJECTIVES: The rather formal *content* (He would be content with less) and the more common *contented* (He would be contented with less) are stressed on the second syllable: kən tent′, kən ten′təd.

NOUNS: As a noun, *content* is used more as an abstract (the content of the course) and in amounts (the moisture content); *contents* is rather more concrete (the contents of the box, the contents of the book). The nouns are pronounced kon′tent, kon′tents; kən tent′ and kən tents′ are British.

Context The context is the discourse that surrounds a word or passage that is being separately discussed: "The word sounds insulting, but in its *context* it could not possibly give offense."

1. The context is tremendously important in giving actual meaning to words. What, for instance, does the word *check* mean? By itself no one can tell even whether it is noun or verb or adjective, much less which of the fifteen senses of the noun or fourteen senses of the combined transitive and intransitive verbs is meant. Yet in actual use, in definite contexts, the word gives no trouble:

They were able to *check* the fire at the highway.
The treasurer's books *check* with the vouchers.

He drew a *check* for the entire amount.
The tablecloth had a red and white *check*.
He moved his bishop and proclaimed "*Check!*"
With difficulty he held his temper in *check*.
He had the *check* list on the desk in front of him.

And so on. *Check* has more senses than most English words, but a very large proportion of words have more than one sense so that their exact meaning must be gathered from the context—and ordinarily it can be.

2. Statements of ideas depend for full understanding upon the context in which they stand, and in quoting or alluding to a writer's thought we should be careful to take the context into account. Cardinal Newman's definition of a gentleman as a man who never inflicts pain is often referred to as though it represented Newman's ideal—but in its context (*The Idea of a University,* Discourse viii) he was showing that this gentleman is all very well but without religious conviction he falls far short of being an ideal type. Taking care that allusions and quotations are true to the context in which they occurred, that they really represent the ideas of their authors, is one mark of a careful writer.

See "Meaning from context," p. 190.

continual, continuous *Continual* means "frequently or closely repeated":

Dancing requires continual practice.
Continual dropping will wear a stone.
He continually interrupted the lecture with foolish questions.

Continuous means "without interruption":

A continuous procession of cars passed during the hour.
He has been continuously in debt for ten years.
BUT: He is continually running in debt.

Cont **Contractions** (CORRECTION: The contraction marked is inappropriate to the style. Use the full form.)

Since contractions are words from which an unstressed syllable is dropped in speaking, they obviously belong to spoken English and to familiar and colloquial types of informal written English. Contractions are ordinarily out of place in treatments of dignified subjects and in a formal style whether in routine exposition (as in academic papers) or in more literary compositions.

Contractions are absolutely necessary in reporting most *conversation and in writing dialog for plays and stories:

"Your mother has the damnedest number of friends I ever heard of," said Father. "She's everlastingly meeting some old friend or

other wherever she goes. I never see people I know when I'm traveling. But there isn't a city in Europe where your mother wouldn't spot
a friend in five minutes."—CLARENCE DAY, *Life With Father*, p. 114

In informal English the fitness of a contraction is usually determined in part by the naturalness with which it falls into place, in
part by the rhythm:

> I didn't always appreciate French cooking myself. It tasted all right,
> but it was dainty and there wasn't much of it.—*Ibid.*, p. 11

Did not and *was not* would slow up the movement slightly.

The apostrophe ordinarily stands in the place of the omitted
letter or letters (*doesn't, can't, shouldn't, he's*), though only one
apostrophe is used in *shan't, won't,* and *ain't.* Some experimental
writers, like George Bernard Shaw, have dropped the apostrophe
from the common contractions. That seems a sensible practice in
the contractions of *not* (*shant, doesnt*). But a few contractions
would, without the apostrophe, look like other words (*I'll—ill,
he'll—hell*).

Contrary to fact conditions See *Conditions §3, *Subjunctives.

contrast For the word, see *compare—contrast. For contrast as
a paragraph relationship, see "Contrast and comparison," p. 102.

Conversation It is harder to write natural and convincing conversation than most people who haven't tried it will suppose. But
conversation is necessary, not only in stories and plays but in many
expository articles, to add interest and to keep the material in
close touch with actual experience by giving glimpses of people
and dramatizing facts. Popular exposition (magazine articles)
needs anecdotes or small scenes with people discussing or illustrating the ideas of the article; and in giving a portrait of a person it
is almost always necessary to let the reader hear him speak.

Most amateurs make conversation sound like their own writing,
in fact they merely put quotation marks around their own words.
A little observation of how people really talk will show that this is
useless. The speeches should, above all, show the words and constructions of *colloquial English, of the English spoken by the
kind of person represented, not the more formal turns of typical
written English. It should show the contractions, clipped expressions, and casual grammar of speech. The first step to writing
good conversation is to observe how you talk yourself, and how
others talk.

A speech or two may be worked into a paragraph, as in this anecdote, to give it life as well as to carry the point:

461

All the newspapers sent photographers to the Shinnecock reservation near Southampton to get pictures of the recent Indian powwow. One brisk little cameraman took a series of shots of a ceremonial dance, then approached one of the dancers with pad and pencil to get data for the captions. "That dance you was just doing," he said, "what do you call it?" "Do you mean the solo dance?" asked the brave. "Yeah," said the cameraman. "What's that in English?"— *The New Yorker*, Oct. 27, 1938

Though written conversation is based on real speech, it isn't a literal reproduction of it. Not even realistic novelists give all of their lustier characters' profanity and vulgarity. (See *Profanity.) It is not necessary to present completely the grammar of vulgate English if it is clearly suggested, if obvious literary and formal constructions are avoided, and if the general sentence movement is oral. Nor is it necessary to suggest the pronunciation exactly. A few g's dropped, a few local vowel sounds respelled are better than a page speckled with apostrophes and distorted spellings. The latter usually attract more attention to themselves than they deserve and hinder the reading. The point is to *suggest* rather than *reproduce* the effect of speech.

Most writers like to see, occasionally, how close they can come to reproducing speech, but this passage shows the cost in spellings that attract attention to themselves:

"Sure," I says. "It's out in Bensonhoist. Yuh take duh Fourt' Avenoo express, get off at Fifty-nint' Street, change to a Sea Beach local deh, get off at Eighteent' Avenoo an' Sixty-toid, an' den walk down foeh blocks. Dat's all yuh got to do," I says.

"G'wan!" some wise guy dat I neveh seen befoeh pipes up. "Whatcha talkin' about?" he says—oh, he was wise, y'know. "Duh guy is crazy! I tell yuh what yuh do," he says to duh big guy. "Yuh change to duh West End line at Toity-sixt'," he tells him. "Get off at Noo Utrecht an' Sixteent' Avenoo," he says. "Walk two blocks oveh, foeh blocks up," he says, "an you'll be right deh." Oh, a *wise* guy, y'know.

"Oh, yeah?" I says. "Who told *you* so much?" He got me sore because he was so wise about it. "How long you been livin' heah?" I says.

"All my life," he says. "I was bawn in Williamsboig," he says. "An' I can tell you t'ings about dis town you neveh hoid of," he says.

"Yeah?" I says.

"Yeah," he says.

"Well, den, you can tell me t'ings about dis town dat nobody else has eveh hoid of, either. Maybe you make it up yoehself at night," I says, "befoeh you go to sleep—like cuttin' out papeh dolls, or somp'n."

"Oh, yeah?" he says. "You're pretty wise, ain't yuh?"

"Oh, I don't know," I says. "Duh boids ain't usin' my head for Lincoln's statue yet," I says. "But I'm wise enough to know a phoney when I see one."

"Yeah?" he says. "A wise guy, huh? Well, you're so wise dat some one's goin' t'bust yuh one right on duh snoot some day," he says. "Dat's how wise *you* are."—THOMAS WOLFE, *From Death to Morning,* pp. 92-93

Stage directions can help the reader visualize the scene, sometimes catch tones of voice, and feel the emotions of the speakers; but it is not necessary to label the speakers if it is clear from the words spoken who says them. This fragment of a scene is self-explanatory:

"I've been thinking, Reuben, about what is best for you."
"You needn't. I'm all right."
"I don't like to leave you here alone."
"I'm not alone. Susan will stay with me. She told my grandmother so."
With a glance at the open door Deborah lowered her voice, but Susan caught the words.
"Are you happy with Susan?"
"Of course. I'm—I'm used to her."
"And you're not used to me. Is that it?"
"I suppose so."
Deborah gathered herself together as one gathers himself for a first daring plunge into deep water.
"You must know that I want to do all I can for you, Reuben. I'm your mother after all. You're always welcome to come to Boston to stay with me. Your stepfather told me to tell you. The schools are better there, and it might be best for you."
Emboldened by his mother's temerity, Reuben found his own voice. Susan, listening, understood the cost of his words. She could hear him drawing himself slowly up on the cane seat and against the back of his grandmother's chair where he sat.
"Thank you, mother, and my stepfather, too. But I'd rather stay here in my own house where I belong."—MARY ELLEN CHASE, *Silas Crockett,* pp. 279-80

The examples given in this article show the conventions of paragraphing and punctuating conversation. There are further details of these mechanics in *Quotation marks. Books on the writing of fiction have discussions of writing conversation.

Conversion The use of a word generally found as one part of speech in the function of a different part of speech is called *conversion:* a *must* book; a *commercial* (adjective as noun in sense of the advertising part of a radio program); in the *know.*

For discussion see *Parts of speech §2.

Coordinating conjunctions 1. The coordinating conjunctions are:

　　*and　　*but　　*for　　nor (= and not)　　*or　　*yet

Colloquially *only* (I'd come only I have a class) and *while* (He's an expert, while I don't know anything about the game) are used as coordinating conjunctions. The *conjunctive adverbs (therefore, however, and so on) are coordinating connectives, as are the *correlative conjunctions (either . . . or, not only . . . but, and so on).

　　2. These conjunctions are used between words, phrases, clauses, or sentences. It is important that the elements they connect should be equal in grammatical rank, parallel in form, and substantially equivalent in thought:

　　WORDS: books and papers; books, pamphlets, and magazines; sugar or salt

　　PHRASES: in one ear and out the other

　　CLAUSES: I would venture to say *that his description is perfect*, but *that there are some who would not agree with that verdict.*—BONAMY DOBRÉE, *Modern Prose Style*, p. 69

　　INDEPENDENT CLAUSES: What they talk of was in the books, but there was the stimulus of personality.—ARTHUR E. HERTZLER, *The Horse and Buggy Doctor*, p. 181

　　SENTENCES: It may be granted in many industries and trades that the substitution of collective bargaining for individual bargaining will properly result in higher wages and better conditions of work. But will the results of sound collective bargaining generally prove to be satisfactory to employees?—GEORGE W. TAYLOR, *The Atlantic Monthly*, Sept. 1938

　　3. For different effects of repeating or omitting conjunctions in a series see *Conjunctions §3 and *Series.

　　4. For coordination vs. subordination see "Coordination and subordination," p. 124 and *Subordination. For various uses of coordinating conjunctions see *Conjunctions, *Clauses § 1, and articles on individual conjunctions.

Coordination The relationship between two or more elements of the same grammatical rank. See *Coordinating conjunctions § 2.

Copula See *Linking verb.

Copy Manuscript before printing is *copy*. For points of form see *Typewritten copy, "Preparing the manuscript," p. 303.

Corrections in copy For suggestions about making corrections in manuscript see "Corrections in copy," p. 305.

Correlative conjunctions. 1. Some coordinating conjunctions are used in pairs:

both . . . and either . . . or neither . . . nor so . . . as
not only . . . but [but also] whether . . . or

2. Except *either . . . or* and *both . . . and*, these correlative conjunctions are slightly formal, showing a more conscious sentence
planning than is common in familiar or informal English:

> Not only was the water muddy, but it had dark greenish tadpoles
> swimming in it.

3. Since these correlatives are coordinating conjunctions, the
elements they connect should be of equal grammatical value and
in parallel form:

NOUNS: He said that both *the novel* and *the play* were badly written.
ADJECTIVES: He must have been either *drunk* or *crazy*.
PHRASES: They can be had not only *in the usual sizes* but also *in the
outsizes*.
CLAUSES: Whether *the sale was for cash* or *a mortgage was given*,
it seemed too much to pay.

For number of verb in constructions with *either . . . or*, see
*Subject and verb § 2*b*, and as a reference, Dorothy J. Hughes,
College English, 1941, ii, 697-99.

could See *can, may (could, might).

Counter words Words that are used more freely than their exact
meanings warrant have been called *counter words*. They are especially words of general approval or disapproval. Their use is a
matter of fashion and is related to slang, except that they are ordinary English words and lack the element of surprise that good
slang has. In Elizabethan times *fair* was such a word; recently
keen, delicious, definitely have had such currency. In ordinary
speech *cute, fierce, fine, grand, lousy, lovely, gorgeous, poor* are
samples, and in more reputable circles words like *creative, dynamic,
vital*, and often epithets like *red, radical, fascist, conservative, reactionary* are used as vague expressions of like or dislike without
regard to their actual meaning.

In advertising and other more or less forced writing *super-,
-conscious* (we are *air-conscious, flower-conscious, defense-conscious*
by turns), *-conditioned*, and at the moment *streamlined, bottle-
neck, propaganda* are all counter words. They are appropriate in
colloquial English (in which *certainly* has the sense of *yes* and
preceded *definitely* as counter word for *very*) but seem out of
place in serious writing:

> Today, the halfway spot in the two-week streamlined fair . . .
> Again, their spirit may be irrevocably broken, their lives turned into
> a streamlined hell.

Countries See *Proper names.

couple 1. *Couple* means strictly two persons or things associated in some way, typically as in "a married couple." Colloquially it is equivalent to the numeral *two*: a couple of pencils.

2. This colloquial usage has resulted in frequent omission of the following *of:*

He'd had a couple drinks.   I'll be gone only a couple days.
A couple boys were throwing stones at a dog.

This clipped idiom is finding its way into print in informal or adventurous writing:

At seven the next morning, a couple [$_\wedge$] members of the cast, which had sat up to get the reviews, broke into his room screaming "It's historic!"—*The New Yorker,* Dec. 30, 1933

See *Prepositions § 3c.

Course names In general discussions the names of college subjects that are proper adjectives (the languages, that is) are capitalized, and the others not:

He studies algebra, history, chemistry, German, English literature, and the rest without seeing that these are really just the pieces in a great picture puzzle which, if assembled, will reveal the image of the whole world.

In writing a list of courses including one or more of these proper adjectives, it is usual to capitalize them all, though it is not necessary:

My program is Biology, Chemistry, European History, English Composition, and French 105.
My program is biology, chemistry, European history, English composition, and French 105.

In referring to the various departments of an institution, all names would be capitalized:

the Department of Applied Psychology   the School of Commerce
the English Department   the Chemistry Department
the School of Biological Sciences   the Department of History

Current English See "Current English," p. 5.

curriculum *Curriculum* still has the Latin plural *curricula,* though educational writers are beginning to use *curriculums.* The adjective is *curricular,* and the compound with *extra* is written with or without a hyphen: *extra-curricular* or *extracurricular. Curriculum* is coming to be used as an adjective:

. . . and his extra-curriculum influence on their morals and manners.—R. M. Hutchins, *Harper's Magazine*, Oct. 1936

Curves A name for the punctuation marks (). See *Parentheses.

D Besides its typical sound as in *die, do, addict, pod, addle, d* is pronounced *t* when it follows the sound of *f, k, p,* or *s* in the same syllable: *asked* (askt), *blessed* (blest, but bles'ed), *kicked* (kikt), *raced* (rāst), *telegraphed* (tel'ə graft).

Before an unstressed *i-* or *y-*sound, *d* sometimes becomes *j*: *grandeur* (gran'jür), *soldier* (sōl'jər). This pronunciation is especially common in vulgate English and explains in'jən (*Indian*), i mē'jit (*immediate*—generally so pronounced in British English), and local extensions of the sound to stressed *u-*syllables: jü'ti (*duty*).

D is a strong sound and besides being the opening sound of a number of words of mild profanity begins many words of a negative meaning: *defeated, dejected, dilapidated, disappointed, disaster, distressed.*

Compare *T.

Dangling modifiers (CORRECTION: Revise the sentence so that the *DM* expression marked clearly modifies the word it should.)

A construction which from its position in a sentence seems to modify a word which it cannot sensibly modify "is misrelated" or "dangles" and should be avoided in writing.

1. DANGLING PARTICIPLES. A participle which is used as an adjective should modify accurately either a noun or pronoun:

Looking further to the left, we saw the spire of a church. [*Looking* clearly modifies *we*.]

Defined in psychological terms, a fanatic is a man who consciously overcompensates a secret doubt. [*Defined* clearly modifies *fanatic*.]— ALDOUS HUXLEY, *Proper Studies*, p. 220

A participle that precedes the main clause should modify the subject of that clause, and one that follows should refer clearly to a noun or pronoun in the clause.

Motoring down Route 17 toward New York City, numerous signs read "Visit Our Snake Farm." [For: *Motoring* down Route 17 toward New York City, *we* saw numerous signs . . .]

What if, forced to climb over this solid cloud bank, ice should form on the wings and force them down into the wild country? [The ice isn't forced to climb.]

Born in England in 1853, John MacDowell's seafaring activities began after he had emigrated to this country. [His seafaring activities were not born in England.]

467

Dangling participles should be avoided simply because educated readers do not expect to find them. As a rule there is no real question of the proper meaning of the sentence, though sometimes the faulty reference of a participle is ludicrous as in Professor Kennedy's gem:

Having swelled because of the rains, the workman was unable to remove the timber.

This dangling construction should not be confused with the *absolute construction, in which the participial phrase is equivalent to a subordinate clause and is properly used:

Remembering always that the weather and Dizzy Dean are subject to change without notice, everything else is set and in place for the big baseball festivities in Washington today. [If we remember . . .] —JOHN KIERAN, *The New York Times*, July 7, 1937

See *Participles for further examples of these constructions.

References: Curme, *Syntax*, pp. 158-60; Reuben Steinbach, "The Misrelated Constructions," *American Speech*, 1930, v, 181-97

2. DANGLING INFINITIVES. Infinitive phrases may be misrelated:

To get the most out of a sport, the equipment must be in perfect condition. [The equipment does not profit from the sport.]

To get the most out of a sport, you must have your equipment in perfect condition.

This construction should not be confused with an absolute infinitive phrase which is quite correct:

To judge from his looks, he can't be more than forty-five.

See *Infinitives §4.

3. DANGLING CLAUSES AND PHRASES. Subordinate clauses without a subject may be said to dangle if the subject to be supplied is not the same as the expressed subject of the main clause:

While [I was] taking a walk, the Joneses called.

If convicted [If he is convicted], the law may sentence him to death.

Phrases are sometimes similarly misrelated:

At eleven, our family moved to Kansas City. [When I was eleven, our family moved to Kansas City.]

*Gerund §3

For exercises dealing with dangling modifiers see p. 263.

Dash (–, —, ——) Three dashes of varying lengths are used in printing: – (en dash), — (em dash, the usual mark), and —— (2-em dash). On the typewriter use a hyphen for the first, two hyphens not spaced away from the neighboring words for the usual dash, and four hyphens for the long dash.

The em dash, the one we have in mind when we say just *dash*, has aroused more discussion and more violent feeling than punctuation seems to deserve. Some textbooks and some publishers forbid its use generally, while others specify minute shades of meaning which they believe it indicates. Some writers rarely use it. Others, especially in matter not intended for publication, use it at the expense of other marks.

A dash is roughly equivalent to a comma, that is, it separates small units within a sentence, but if used sparingly it suggests a definite tone, usually a note of surprise, an emotional emphasis. From a strictly logical point of view some other mark could always be substituted for a dash, but there would be a difference in movement and suggestiveness in the sentence. At its best it is a rather abrupt and emphatic mark.

1. The most typical use of the dash is to mark a sharp turn in the thought or construction of a sentence:

Of course, there is one place safe from lawyers—in heaven.—ARTHUR E. HERTZLER, *The Horse and Buggy Doctor*, p. 134

The danger of using terms like "romantic" and "classic"—this does not however give us permission to avoid them altogether—does not spring so much from the confusion caused by those who use these terms about their own work, as from inevitable shifts of meaning in context.—T. S. ELIOT, *After Strange Gods*, p. 27

2. A dash is often used before an inserted or added phrase, usually one that summarizes what has just been said or that gives contrasting or emphasizing details of what has been said, or often a striking apposition. This dash has the force of a vigorous comma.

The waiting, the watching, the hundreds of small necessary acts about the sickroom—all this was past.

The elements of every story are these five: character, incident, nature, fate, and milieu—the social, historical, vital background.—D. H. PARKER, *Principles of Aesthetics*, p. 236

. . . but they initiated a process that has culminated in the one indisputable achievement of post-War poetry—its catholicity of diction.—F. W. BATESON, *Poetry and Language*, p. 120

In the organic world, Darwin sought to grasp living things in their relationships—struggle and existence, natural selection, and survival of the fittest.—C. A. BEARD, *The Discussion of Human Affairs*, p. 62

He [the Englishman of the 1870's and 80's] was strongly in favor of peace—that is to say, he liked his wars to be fought at a distance and, if possible, in the name of God.—GEORGE DANGERFIELD, *The Death of Liberal England*, p. 7

469

3. A dash is often used between two compound clauses of a sentence, for abrupt separation:

The "womanly" woman became as obsolete as the buggy. The nurse must tend the children, the cook must order the meals—life must be spectacular, not frittered away in little household dullnesses.—Irene and Allen Cleaton, *Books and Battles*, p. 92

4. A dash is sometimes used to enclose parenthetical statements that are more informal than a parenthesis would be, separating the expression from the context more than a comma but less definitely than parentheses would:

The general effect upon readers—most of them quite uneducated— is quite different from what the serious messiah intends.—T. S. Eliot, *After Strange Gods*, p. 36

While books were being stricken from the lists with such alarming inclusiveness—so that Mencken was provoked to remark, "It is possible for anyone to have a book suppressed in Boston merely by advancing the idea. I wager I could suppress four books in as many minutes if I should go to Boston and make the effort"—while this deplorable state of affairs existed, the "art" magazines that were being chased out of many less Puritan cities remained unmolested on Boston newsstands.—Irene and Allen Cleaton, *Books and Battles*, p. 77

5. Overuse of dashes naturally takes away from their special quality and proves that they are, as Mr. Dobrée calls them, "a sandy joint."

She [Marlene Dietrich] was turned into a static image of lorelei charm, frozen in a lovely pose—and to bring that image again to life, there seems to be no proposal except to point again to its over-publicized legs, and its—by this time—rubber-stamp "allure."

See also *Schoolgirl style.

6. Formerly a dash was often combined with other marks, especially with a comma or a colon, but recently this use has declined. The dash adds nothing in the salutation of a letter (*Dear Sir:—* means no more than *Dear Sir:*) and adds a displeasing mark to the page. Within sentences the old comma-dash combination has very generally disappeared also, so that now we find either a comma, or if emphasis makes it useful, a dash alone.

7. Double dash. Besides being used in some arbitrary places prescribed by particular publishing houses, the 2-em dash is used chiefly as an end stop in dialog when a speech is interrupted:

". . . I can't say, of course, whether or not my layman's logic adds lustre to the gladsome light of jurisprudence——"

"Your reasoning is consistent as far as it goes," cut in Markham tartly. "But it is hardly complete enough to have led you directly to the linen-closet this morning."—S. S. VAN DINE, *The Greene Murder Case*, p. 220

"Harvard Club. You——" The sap, the hopeless sap.—SALLY BENSON, *People Are Fascinating*, p. 30

8. EN DASH. A writer does not need to worry about the en dash, but printers use it, slightly longer than a hyphen, between inclusive figures (*1837–1901*) and instead of a hyphen when one or both elements of an expression ordinarily requiring a hyphen is made up of two words: *the New York–Bar Harbor express.*

data Pronounced dā′tə or sometimes dat′ə or (affecting Latin) dä′tə.

Strictly *data* is a plural, with a little used singular *datum*. Its meaning is actually collective and may sometimes stress a group of facts as a unit and so be used with a singular verb. When it refers to the individual facts, *data* is used with a plural:

SINGULAR IDEA: The actual data of history *consists* of contemporary facts in the form of remains and documents.—MORRIS R. COHEN, *Reason and Nature*, p. 381

SINGULAR IDEA: Data concerning measurement of social attitudes *has* been included in the next chapter . . .—LUELLA COLE, *Psychology of Adolescence*, p. 102

PLURAL IDEA: When the data *have* been secured the task is to analyze, to sift, to select and to arrange those data which *bear* upon each particular phase of the object or event examined until at the end the scientist has what one might call a logical construct.— G. D. HIGGINSON, *Fields of Psychology*, p. 10

EITHER POSSIBLE: These data are [This data is] unpublished.

The singular verb can be safely used in any but the most formal writing.

date Informal and colloquial for "appointment, engagement" ("I had a date for that evening"); slang and familiar in the sense of "person with whom one has an engagement" ("After all, she was his date"). *Blind date* is one of the more useful and economical slang expressions, expressing in two syllables something that would take several words to express in formal English.

Dates Unless you have good reason for some other form, write dates in the common method:

November 27, 1942   June 16, 1941

Never write the year out in words except in formal social announcements, invitations, etc. Expressions like "January in the year 1885" are wasteful. *January 1885* is enough.

If saving space is important, or in business or reference writing, months having more than four letters should be abbreviated:

Jan. Feb. Mar. Apr. Aug. Sept. Oct. Nov. Dec.

In familiar and informal writing, figures are convenient: 11/27/42, 6/16/41. In England and other countries the day of the month is usually put first, but that is confusing in the United States, unless Roman numerals are used for the month: 7-X-41 (October 7, 1941). The form *7 October 1941* is more common British than American usage. It has a small advantage in that it makes a comma unnecessary.

Better style now usually omits the *st, nd, th* from the day of the month: May 1 rather than May 1st, September 17 rather than September 17th.

In rather formal style the day of the month may be written in words when the year is not given (September seventeen or September seventeenth).

Roman numerals are rarely used for the year except for decoration, as on the title page of a book.

See *Numbers §1*a*; *Letters; *Social correspondence.

Dative case English has no form for the dative case.

A noun in a construction that in another language might have a dative is in the common case form and a pronoun is in the accusative case form. Usually we have a phrase made with *to, for,* or *on*.

The dative indicates that the action is for the advantage or disadvantage of the person or object it names or that the act in some way refers to the person or object. Such a noun or pronoun is called an "indirect object." *Objects §2.

If both an indirect and a direct object are used with the same verb, the indirect usually precedes if it is the simple form and follows if it is the prepositional form:

They gave *him* three dollars.   They gave *the man* three dollars.
They gave three dollars *to him* [*to the man*].
They set aside three dollars *for him*.
She wasn't wasting any time *on him*.

References: Curme, *Parts of Speech*, pp. 131-33, *Syntax*, pp. 103-109

Dead **Deadwood** (Correction: Remove the meaningless word or words, revising the sentence if necessary.)

Deadwood is a convenient label for a type of *wordiness in which a word or phrase adds nothing at all to the meaning of the statement.

In many *cases* students [Many students] have profited by this.
He was a handsome [looking] man.
The book is divided into various sections, all dealing with [the matter of] unemployment.

Many phrases of this sort make writing flabby and are a mark of amateur or careless writing.

For further examples and discussion, see "Removing deadwood," p. 161.
For an exercise dealing with deadwood, see p. 179, Exercise 6.

Declarative sentences A declarative sentence makes a statement:

The day that war was declared saw a complete overturn in many people's opinions.
Considerably over nine tenths of the sentences that we speak and write are declarative.

See "Sentences classed according to their clauses," p. 127, and articles *Simple, *Compound, and *Complex sentences.

Declension Change of form of nouns (and in many languages the form of adjectives and participles also) to show number (singular or plural) and case (nominative, genitive, dative, accusative). Declension plays a relatively small part in English grammar.

See *Case, the articles on the various cases, *Plurals, and the articles referred to there.

Definite article See *the.

definitely *Definitely* is one of the most frequently misspelled words. Remember there is no *a* in it and associate def i *ni* tion with def i *nite* and def i *nite* ly.

At present *definitely* is overused as a *counter word to give emphasis or in the sense of "certainly, quite" (I will not do it, definitely; He was definitely worse than usual; She definitely disapproves of those methods) instead of in its exact sense of "clearcut, in a definite manner."

Definitions For paragraphs of definition see "Definition," p. 95.

Degree (of adjectives and adverbs) See *Comparison of adjectives and adverbs.

Degrees Ordinarily a person's academic degrees are not given with his name except in college publications, reference works, etc. When used, they are separated from the name by a comma, and in campus publications are often followed by the year of granting:

Harvey J. Preble, A.B.   Harvey J. Preble, A.B. '08
James T. Thomson, M.A.   James T. Thomson, A.B. '21, A.M. '24
James T. Thomson, Ph.D., M.D.

As a rule, except in reference lists, only a person's highest degree in each academic or professional field need be mentioned.

If the institution granting the degree is named, the following forms are usual:

George H. Cook, A.B. (Grinnell), A.M. (Indiana), Ph.D. (Chicago)

The common degrees given "in course," that is, at the completion of a required amount of college or university work are:

A.B. (or B.A.)—Bachelor of Arts
A.M. (or M.A.)—Master of Arts
B.S.—Bachelor of Science
B. Arch.—Bachelor of Architecture
B.D.—Bachelor of Divinity
M.E.—Master of Engineering
M. Ped.—Master of Pedagogy
(*or*, Ed. M.—Master of Education)
M.B.A.—Master of Business Administration

B.E.—Bachelor of Engineering
LL.B.—Bachelor of Laws
B. Mus.—Bachelor of Music
Ph.B—Bachelor of Philosophy
M.S.—Master of Science
Ph.D.—Doctor of Philosophy
S.T.D.—Doctor of Sacred Theology
M.D.—Doctor of Medicine
D.D.S.—Doctor of Dental Surgery

The common honorary degrees, given by institutions as a sign of respect ("pro honoris causa"), are:

D.C.L.—Doctor of Civil Law
D.D.—Doctor of Divinity
D.Sc.—Doctor of Science

D. Litt. (D. Lit., Lit.D.)—Doctor of Literature
L.H.D.—Doctor of Humanities

Delete means "take out, erase, remove." It is a direction to printers made by putting a Greek small *d* (δ—delta) in the margin and drawing a line through the matter to be removed.

To delete material in your manuscripts, simply draw a line through it (don't use parentheses or black it out completely).

Demonstrative adjectives and pronouns. *This, that, these, those* are called demonstrative adjectives or demonstrative pronouns, according to their use in a sentence:

ADJECTIVES: *This* car we bought in May.
                Those fellows never think of anyone else.

PRONOUNS: *This* cost a good bit more than *those*.
                That's a good idea.

See *that, *this, *kind, sort.

Denotation is the exact, literal meaning of a word, contrasted with its *connotation* or *suggestion*. *Fire* denotes the chemical and physical process of combustion, or a particular burning. It suggests uncontrolled power, destruction. See "Denotation," p. 186.

Dependent clause A dependent clause modifies or supports in some way a word or sentence element or the whole sentence:

The house *that stood on the other side* was even more dilapidated. [Clause modifies *house*.]
Since Truman had gone to the same school, they got on famously for a time. [Adverbial clause modifying the following statement]

Ordinarily a dependent clause does not stand by itself but is part of a complex sentence.

See *Clauses, "Coordination and Subordination," p. 124, and "Incomplete Sentences," p. 131.

depot An "Americanism," but a perfectly good Americanism, for "railroad station." *Depot* also has a more general meaning of "a place for storing things, especially merchandise or war supplies." Pronounced dē′pō; often (especially British) dep′ō.

Derivation of words *Origin of words

descendant *Descendant* is used both as adjective and noun; *descendent*, only as adjective. Obviously, to be on the safe side, use descend*ant*.

NOUN: He claims to be a descendant of Benjamin Franklin.
ADJECTIVE: Nearly all the people of the town are descendant from [more usual, *descended from*] these first settlers.

Description, Descriptive order See "Impressionistic paragraphs," p. 88.

detail Formal pronunciation dē tāl′; informal and vulgate usage divided but likely to be dē′tāl, especially in situations where the word is used a great deal (army life, architecture, composition, etc.).

Details (CORRECTION: Develop this topic more fully by giving *Det* pertinent details.)

The development of a topic in writing usually comes from the use of details, small bits of observation, particular facts, and so on. They not only make the reader see clearly what you are discussing but are one of the chief sources of interest.

For discussion and illustration of various uses of details see the types of paragraphs in Ch. 4, p. 81. See also "Abstract and concrete words," p. 223.

Development of ideas, development of paragraphs See The Forms and Uses of Paragraphs, p. 53, and Kinds of Paragraphs, p. 81.

devil no longer receives the courtesy of a capital except for stylistic emphasis.

Diagramming sentences See "Sentence elements," p. 119, "Order of sentence elements," p. 122, and Exercises p. 144.

Diagrams, graphs, etc. The function of diagrams, charts, graphs, and illustrations is to make a writer's meaning more clear and more concrete than his words alone could. They cannot be a substitute for a discussion in words, but they can make it easier for readers to grasp figures, to understand relationships, and especially to make comparisons between facts that can be graphically portrayed. They have also an incidental value for an article in that diagrams and charts attract attention and interest. It is part of a writer's work to prepare appropriate diagrams to accompany his text where they can be useful.

1. GENERAL POINTS IN HANDLING DIAGRAMS AND CHARTS. (*a*) The first step toward a diagram or chart is compiling the data. Guesses, opinions, and so on should not be graphically represented; only definite facts and especially facts that can be measured mathematically. The nature of the material will usually determine which sort of graphic device is appropriate.

b) A graphic device should be accompanied by the exact data it represents, either in the text of the paper or in a table or explanation placed with the graph. A reader needs to know the exact figures upon which the graph is based.

c) The graph should be made intelligible by clearly indicating the years, amounts, per cents, the scale it is drawn on, and so on. This is usually done at the bottom and along the sides.

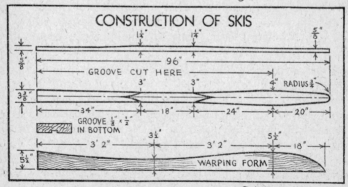

Science and Mechanics,
February 1939

2. Types of graphic devices. Some of the commonest and most useful graphic devices are illustrated on pp. 476-78.

a) Diagram. A schematic representation of the structure of something, a plan showing dimensions, directions for work, etc., as in the diagram at the bottom of the opposite page.

b) Chart. Showing organization and relationship:

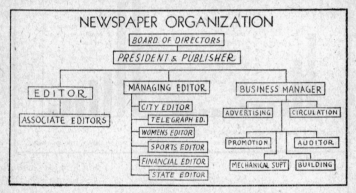

D. J. Hornberger and Douglass W. Miller,
Newspaper Organization, Appendix B,
August 1930

c) Graphs. Showing two or more variable facts, typically amounts that vary in time:

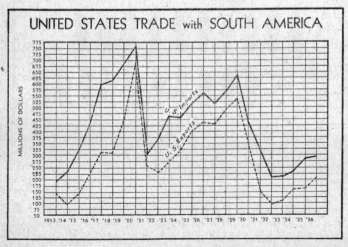

Fortune, December 1937

d) *Bars.* To make comparison of amounts, etc.:

WHY PEOPLE LEAVE HOME—
AND WHERE THEY GO

Calendar Year 1937
THOUSANDS OF PERSONS RECEIVING PASSPORTS OR RENEWALS

OBJECT OF TRAVEL
1. Fun
2. Family Affairs
3. Educational
4. Commercial Business
5. Professional Business
6. Employment
7. Missionary
8. Personal Business
9. Scientific
10. Official Business
11. Health

DESTINATION
1. Western Europe
2. West Indies
3. Northern Europe
4. Mediterranean Area
5. Far East
6. Central America
7. South America

SOURCES: OBJECT OF TRAVEL—PASSPORT DIVISION, DEPT. OF STATE
DESTINATION—IMMIGRATION & NATURALIZATION SERVICE, DEPT. OF LABOR

The Chicago Tribune,
October 26, 1938

e) *Pictorial statistics.* Pictorial symbols to dramatize the material about which figures are given:

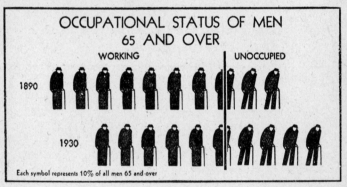

OCCUPATIONAL STATUS OF MEN
65 AND OVER

WORKING   UNOCCUPIED

1890

1930

Each symbol represents 10% of all men 65 and over

RUDOLF MODLEY, *How to Use
Pictorial Statistics*

f) *Maps.* A simple map will be found on pages 8 and 9.

Compare *Illustration (Pictorial).

References: Secrist, Horace, *Statistics in Business* (New York, 1920), Ch. 5, and chapters on graphic methods in other introductions to statistics.

Dialects (CORRECTION: Change the word marked to one that is *Dial*
in general use in the United States.)

A dialect is the speech (words, sounds, stress, phrasing, grammatical habits) characteristic of a fairly definite region, or more accurately still, it is speech that does not attract attention to itself among the residents of a region.

Conspicuous dialectical words are usually out of place in formal writing unless they are used to give a definitely local flavor. They are more effective in speech, in fiction, and in rather informal writing.

For description of dialects in the United States, see "Dialects and localisms," p. 6, and for their appropriateness in speaking and writing, see p. 10.

Dialog See *Conversation and *Quotation marks.

Diction (CORRECTION: Replace the word marked by one that is *D*
more exact, more effective, or more appropriate.)

Diction means primarily the choice of words to use in speaking or writing. Good diction means that the words seem to the reader or listener well chosen to convey the meanings or attitudes of the writer or speaker; faulty diction, that the words either fail to convey the meaning fully or accurately or do not satisfy the reader's expectation in some other way.

Chapter 7, The Meaning of Words (p. 182) discusses exactness in the use of words, the use of dictionaries and increasing your vocabulary; Chapter 8, Qualities of Words (p. 213) discusses traits of effective and ineffective words. Chapter 1, Varieties of English (p. 1) describes localisms and variations due to levels of usage. Many specific words have articles of their own (*contact, *drunk, *hope, *however, *notorious, *try and—try to, *ye—the . . .). Very often the solution to a question of diction will be found by referring to a good dictionary.

For exercises see pages 30, 50, 208, 247.

Dictionaries For description of various dictionaries and suggestions for their use, see "The usefulness of dictionaries," p. 196, and for dictionary exercises, p. 208.

dieresis (dī er'ə sis) Two dots placed over the second of two consecutive vowels to show they are to be pronounced separately: *reëxamine, coöperation, zoölogy.* A hyphen is often used to indicate that the vowels are to be kept separate, especially in words with *re-* (*re-enlist*). There is a tendency not to use either dieresis or hyphen in the more commonly used words, so that *cooperation, zoology* are now the more usual forms.

different The standard American idiom with *different* is *from:*

His second book was entirely different from his first.
He was so different from his sister that we were all surprised.

Different from should ordinarily be written.

Colloquial and vulgate usage is divided, using *from* occasionally, sometimes *to* (which is common British idiom), and more often *than:*

. . . as smart and vain and sweet a girl as Clyde had ever laid his eyes upon—so different to any he had ever known and so superior.— THEODORE DREISER, *An American Tragedy*, p. 225

Different than is becoming more common when the object is a clause:

The house was a good deal different than he remembered it. (This idiom is neater than "different from what he remembered.")

Different is colloquially used as a synonym for *original:*

This book is original [not: *different*] and interesting.

Reference: D. L. Bolinger, *The English Journal*, 1939, xxviii, 480

Digraph Two letters used together to spell a single sound are known as a *digraph*. English uses many digraphs:

ea as in *head* or *heat*	*ee* as in *seed*
ei as in *either* or *neighbor*	*oa* as in *coat*
oo as in *book* or *food*	*ph* as in *physics*
sh as in *shall*	*th* as in *then* or *thin*

dining *Dine, dined, dining, dining room* all have to do with eating —as does *dinner* with two *n*'s and a short *i*; *dinning* (short *i*) has to do with *din*, "noise."

Dine and *dining* are formal words. *Dinner* is used in all levels.

Diphthong A diphthong is a vowel sound made up of two identifiable sounds gliding from one to the other. The commonest English diphthongs are:

$\bar{\text{i}}$ (ä + i)   oi (ô + i)   ou (ä + u̇)   ū (i [y] + ü)

For others and for further details of variations in the pronunciations of these, see Kennedy, pp. 186-90, and the pronunciation sections of dictionaries.

Direct address The name or descriptive term by which a person or persons are addressed in speaking, reading, or writing:

My friends, I wish you would forget this night.
That's all right, *Mrs. Shephardson.*
What do you think, *doctor*, about his going home now?

As these examples show, words in direct address are separated from the rest of the sentence by a comma, or if they are in the midst of the sentence, by two commas.

Direct discourse See *Conversation, *Quotation marks.

Direct object See *Objects, *Accusative case.

Display Matter that is not written consecutively, that in the written or printed copy is set off by itself instead of being run in with the text, is called display matter. Typical display lines are titles on books and articles, newspaper headlines and subheads, large type lines in advertisements, headings and inside addresses of letters. The type is usually larger and blacker than the body type. Ordinarily no punctuation is needed after display lines.

Ditto marks (") Ditto marks are used with lists and tabulations in reference works instead of repeating words that fall directly underneath. In typewritten manuscript, use the same character for ditto marks as for quotation marks:

```
m, as in man, men, mine, hum, hammer
n, "   " no, man, manner
```

Ditto marks are not used in consecutive writing, nor are they used now in footnotes or bibliographies. In general they are much less used than formerly.

As a word *ditto* (for "I think the same," and so on) is slang.

Divided usage Usage is said to be *divided* when two or more forms exist in the language, both in reputable use in the same dialect or level. *Divided usage* is not applied, for example, to *localisms, like *sack—bag—poke*, or to differences like *ain't* and *isn't* which belong to separate levels of the language. It applies to spellings, pronunciations, or constructions on which speakers and writers of similar education might differ.

There are many more of these divided usages than most people are aware of. For instance, both *Webster's* and the *Standard* dictionaries record these and hundreds of other instances of divided usage:

IN PRONUNCIATION:
  abdo'men—ab'domen
  adver'tisement—advertise'ment
  ēther—īther

  lē'ver—lev'er
  ī'solate—is'olate

IN SPELLING:
  gray—grey
  traveler—traveller
  catalog—catalogue

  drought—drouth
  millionaire—millionnaire

481

IN VERB FORMS:
   Past tense of *sing: sang* or *sung*
                  ring: rang or *rung*
   Past participle of *show: shown* or *showed*
                      prove: proved or *proven*

There are differing conventions in punctuation, as some people always use a comma before the last member of a series (to love, honor, and obey) and many do not (to love, honor and obey).

Divided meanings of words of course are generally recognized, as *craft* may mean "cunning, skill, a trade, those engaged in a trade, a vessel or a group of vessels"; *nice* means "pleasant" as well as "making or showing fine distinctions."

It is hard for some careful speakers to realize that others may speak somewhat differently from them and still be in good standing. Obviously we should all make sure before trying to call a person to account, seriously or playfully, for a differing usage that it is not equally reputable. Furthermore, we might well give up a desire for uniformity in small matters which make no great difference and in which the experience of the language obviously shows that divergence is possible.

If your style is rather free, take the simpler spelling, the more open punctuation, the more colloquial form; if you are rather conservative, you will often choose the longer spelling, the heavier punctuation, the more formal expression. When you have opportunity to choose between variants, choose the one more appropriate to your general tendency or that is more common among the audience you are to reach—or probably better still, take the one that comes most naturally to your own speech.

Many of the specific entries in this handbook treat questions of divided usage, as *but that—but what, *due to, *either, *gladiolus, *hanged—hung, *proved—proven.

References: Besides the divided usages recorded in the dictionaries and in Curme and other large grammars, two books treat them exclusively: Hall, J. Lesslie, *English Usage* (Chicago, 1917), and Leonard, S. A., *Current English Usage* (Chicago, 1932, 1935). Hall discusses usage of earlier English writers; Leonard, contemporary usage.

Div **Division of words** (CORRECTION: Break the word at the end of this line between syllables [and note paragraphs 2 and 4 below].)

Whenever it is necessary in manuscript or in print, a word is divided at the end of a line by a hyphen ("division hyphen"). In preparing manuscript if you will leave a reasonable right hand margin, you will not be forced to divide so many words as you will if you crowd to the end of the line. A good habit is not to divide words unless the lines will be conspicuously uneven if the last one is completely written or completely carried over to the next line. In manuscript for publication most publishers prefer an uneven right margin to divided words.

When it is necessary to divide a word, break it between syllables. Both the divided parts should be pronounceable; that is, words of one syllable, like *matched, said, thought* should not be divided at all. English syllables are difficult to determine but in general they follow pronunciation groups: *autocratic* would be divided into syllables *au to crat ic,* but *autocracy* is *au toc ra cy.*

The following words are divided to show typical syllables:

| mar gin | hy phen | long ing |
| hi lar i ous | ac com plished | pitch er |

Double consonants are usually separable:

| ef fi cient | com mit tee | daz zling | bat ted |

A single letter is not allowed to stand by itself, that is, do not divide at the end of lines words like *enough* (which would leave a lone *e* at the end of a line) or *many* (which would put a lone *y* at the beginning of a line).

Words spelled with a hyphen (*half-brother, well-disposed*) should be divided only at the point of the hyphen to avoid the awkwardness of two hyphens in the same word.

Division of words is primarily a printer's problem and fuller directions than this handbook gives will be found in the stylebooks of publishing houses (like the *Manual of Style* of the University of Chicago Press). Note the divisions made by the compositors at the ends of lines in this and other books. It will often be necessary to refer to a dictionary to find the proper syllabication of words.

do Present forms: I, you *do*; he, she, it *does*; we, you, they *do.* Past, *did*: They *did* as well as they could. Past participle, *done*: He knew he had *done* wrong. It was well *done*.

1. Do as an auxiliary. All verbs except *be* and the auxiliaries (*can, may, shall* . . .) may be conjugated with *do,* as follows:

Present	Past
I do wish	I, you, he, she did wish
you do wish	we, you, they did wish
he, she does wish	
we, you, they do wish	

The *do* forms are used:

a) For emphasis:

I do′ wish he'd come. (Contrast "I wish he'd come.")
He did′ have his lunch, because I saw him go into Carter's.

b) In questions:

Do you think I was right?
Did you like the show as well as you expected to?

c) With *not* (Colloquially contracted to *don't, doesn't, didn't*):

He did not feel well enough to go out.
I don't expect to go.

2. Do as a pro-verb. *Do* is used to avoid repetition of a simple verb that has just been used:

I like him better than you do [i.e., than you like him].
That's what you used to do. [meaning completed in the context]

3. Do in idioms. *Do* has many idiomatic meanings and is part of many idiomatic phrases in informal and vulgate usage: A girl *does* her hair; a steak is well *done*; we *do away* with things; *do for* (which may mean "be enough"—That will do for you—or "put the finishing touches on"—That did for him—or, in some localities, "work for, serve"—She does for Mrs. Lawrence); *done for; do in; do over* (redecorate); *do up* (wrap up, launder, or in past, be used up).

Reference: Fries, pp. 146-49

doff, don These words, archaic or formal for "take off" and "put on" (especially clothes), are used only by writers who are self-consciously or habitually somewhat affected in their speech.

Dollar sign See *Money.

don't Contraction of *do not*, universally used in conversation and often in informal writing when *do not* would seem too emphatic or when rhythm seems more comfortable with the shorter form.

In vulgate usage *don't* = *doesn't*, and the usage often finds its way into familiar speech and even into casual writing: "He don't look as well as he used to." Educated speakers and writers avoid it. *Current English Usage* (p. 121) marked "It don't make any difference what you think" disputable, because it was approved by 40% of the judges.

Double negative 1. In formal and informal english. Two negative words in the same statement are not used in formal and informal English (Not "He couldn't find it nowhere" but "He couldn't find it anywhere").

In informal English one negative statement modifying another negative statement often gives a qualified meaning or a meaning with some special emphasis: "He is not sure he won't slip in at the last minute" does not mean "He will slip in at the last minute" but "He may possibly slip in . . ." "And don't you think he isn't clever" stands for something more complex than "He is clever"— for "I've found out he's clever" or "You'd better believe he's clever [though I know you don't yet]."

2. IN VULGATE ENGLISH. Although double negatives are probably not so common in vulgate English as comic writers suggest in their cartoons and stories, two negatives are very often used to make an emphatic negative in this level. "I don't have nothing to lose" makes negative two parts of the idea and in many speech situations is the vulgate way of emphasizing the negative; if the *nothing* isn't stressed, it is a simple negative in two parts, as French uses *ne . . . pas*. Such a double negative is not a backsliding from the idiom of more formal English but a direct descendant of early English in which two negatives were used in all levels of the language. Chaucer wrote:

> In al this world *ne* was ther *noon* him lyk.
> A bettre preest, I trowe that *nowher noon* is.

This construction, now lost to written English, survives in vulgate usage. The objection to it is not that "two negatives make an affirmative," for they do not—only a person being perverse would misunderstand a double negative. The objection is simply that the construction is not now in fashion among educated people.

3. HARDLY, SCARCELY. In college writing there is danger of falling into a concealed double negative when using *hardly* or *scarcely*. *Hardly* means "not probably" and *scarcely* means the same a little more emphatically. Consequently in formal and informal English a sentence like "For the most part our college paper contains hardly nothing" should read "For the most part our college paper contains *hardly anything*" and "For a while we couldn't scarcely see a thing" should read "For a while we *could scarcely* see a thing."

Compare *but §3, *can't hardly.

Double prepositions (*off of, in back of* . . .) *Prepositions §3*b

Doubling final consonants **1.** Words of one syllable ending in a single consonant following a single vowel (*brag, fat, win*) double the consonant before adding a syllable beginning with a vowel (*-able, -ed, -er, -ing, -y* . . .):

485

brag: bragged, bragging
fat: fatted, fatter, fatting, fatty
win: winner, winning

The consonant is not doubled:

In words with two vowel letters before the final consonant (*daub, daubed; seed, seeded*)
In words with two consonants (*help, helped; hold, holding*)

In *quit*, the *qu* is a substitute for *kw*, so that it comes in the class with one vowel (*quitting*).

2. In words of more than one syllable ending in one vowel and one consonant, the final consonant is traditionally doubled if the word is accented on the last syllable (but see §3 below). A few words so accented are very common:

con trol': controlled, controller, controlling
re fer': referred, referring
Also: confer' equip' excel' infer'
occur' prefer'

If the accent of the lengthened word shifts to an earlier syllable, the consonant is not doubled:

infer'—in'ference prefer'—pref'erence
refer'—ref'erence

If the word is not accented on the last syllable, the consonant need not be doubled, and in American usage preferably is not doubled, though usage is divided on many words:

ben'e fit: benefited, benefiting
com'bat (or com bat'): combated or combatted, combating or combatting, but always com'ba tant
o'pen: opened, opening par'allel: paralleled, paralleling

Usage on *bias, diagram, kidnap, quarrel, travel, worship* is divided, but usually one consonant is preferred.

3. The rules given above regarding words of more than one syllable are really unnecessary. *Controled* and *benefitted* spell their respective words as accurately as the traditional *controlled* and *benefited*—really more accurately. In fact, *The Chicago Tribune* and other periodicals practicing simple spelling regularly use *controled, patroled*, and so on. But writers must realize the weight of tradition and should not use such forms as *controled* and *benefitted* if their reader or readers will be surprised or offended by them.

But the part of the rule for doubling final consonants that applies to words of one syllable is useful, because it keeps distinct a number of pairs of words similar in appearance:

bat: batted, batting—bate: bated, bating
din: dinned, dinning—dine: dined, dining (but dinner)
grip: gripped, gripping—gripe: griped, griping
plan: planned, planning—plane: planed, planing
scrap: scrapped, scrapping—scrape: scraped, scraping

The boy who wrote "The scene in which she almost kills her husband is griping" did not say what he intended.

Outmoded institutions should be scrapped, not scraped.

4. Words already ending in two consonants keep them before suffixes beginning with a vowel but are likely to lose one consonant before suffixes beginning with another consonant:

enroll: enrolled, enrolling, but enrolment (or enrollment)
install: installed, installing, installation; instalment or installment
fulfill   skilfull or skillfull   welfare   [but] stillness

Reference: Kennedy, pp. 231, 238-39

doubt Idioms with *doubt*:
NEGATIVE (when there is no real doubt), *doubt that*:

FORMAL: I do not doubt that he meant well.
INFORMAL: I don't doubt but that [vulgate: but what] he will come.

POSITIVE (when doubt exists), *that, whether, if*:

FORMAL: I doubt whether he meant it that way.
          I doubt that he meant it that way (indicating unbelief really more than doubt).
INFORMAL: I doubt if he meant it that way.

dove—dived The past tense of *dive* is *dived* or *dove*.

draft, draught The spelling of *draught* (from the Old English *dragan*, to draw) has gradually come to represent its pronunciation (draft). *Draft* is always the spelling for a *bank draft*, the *military draft*, a *draft of a composition*, a *draft of air*; usage is divided on the word in the sense of a maker of drawings—*draftsman* or *draughtsman*; *draught* is more common for a *ship's draught*, a *draught of fish*, and for a *draught of ale* or *beer on draught*—though *draft* is rapidly gaining in this last sense.

drought—drouth Both forms are in good use, *drought* probably more common in formal English, *drouth* in informal and colloquial.

It is true the longest drouth will end in rain.—ROBERT FROST

Newspaper accounts of the unusually dry seasons of the mid-1930s did much to give *drouth* increased currency. Compare *height—heighth.

487

drunk It seems to take courage to use this natural word. We either go formal—*intoxicated;* or grasp at respectability through euphemisms—*under the influence of liquor* or *indulged to excess;* or make a weak attempt at humor with one of the dozens of slang phrases like *get plastered.* But *drunk* is the word.

Drunk is also the past participle of *drink:* drink, drank, drunk.

due to The preposition *due to* is especially interesting as an illustration of the difficulties a locution has in rising from vulgate and familiar usage to the informal and formal levels. *Due to* as in

> The Mediterranean has its share of minority problems and they have become more prominent *due to* Italo-British tension in that area.— *Kaltenborn Edits the News,* p. 99

has long been used popularly, especially by magazine writers, and occasionally in more formal literature by Galsworthy and others of undisputed respectability. Advocates of strict usage have set themselves sternly against it, forgetting perhaps that *owing to,* which they have usually suggested should be substituted for it, has come from a participle to a preposition in exactly the same way.

Due was originally an adjective and is still most strictly used as one: "The epidemic was *due* to the brown rat," in which *due* modifies *epidemic.* But the prepositional use is convenient and has been increasingly common in print:

> *Due to* world conditions with which we are all familiar, England will, within ten years, have a protective tariff.—A. EDWARD NEWTON, *The Atlantic Monthly,* Sept. 1924

Opinion of *due to* as a preposition is then divided. A writer should consider whether or not it is appropriate to his style: if he is rather formal, he should not use *due to* as a preposition; if he is less formal he doesn't need to worry—except perhaps when writing for readers who are known to be formal.

An excellent example of a linguist's approach to a matter of divided and debatable usage is Professor John S. Kenyon's treatment of *due to* in *American Speech* (1930), vi, 61-70. He presents an imposing number of quotations from current writers, discusses the history of the phrase, and concludes:

> Strong as is my own prejudice against the prepositional use of *due to,* I greatly fear it has staked its claim and squatted in our midst alongside of and in exact imitation of *owing to,* its aristocratic neighbor and respected fellow citizen.

A person may not care to use *due to* himself, but in view of actual usage today he hardly has the right to deny it to others.

dynasty Pronounced dī′nəs ti in the United States, more often din′əs ti in England.

E 1. The "long *e*" sound (ē) is found variously spelled in stressed syllables: s*ee*d, rec*ei*ve, sh*ie*ld, l*ea*d (lēd), p*eo*ple, k*ey*, qu*ay*, *ae*gis, Ph*oe*be, mach*i*ne.

An unstressed or lightly stressed long *e* may vary in pronunciation from long *e* in platform delivery (dē send'—*descend*) to a slurred vowel in rapid speech (də send'). Since the sound is a natural consequence of the light stress, no special symbol is used to represent it: krē āt' (*create*), ē'kō nom'iks (*economics*).

Before *r*, the sound of long *e* is altered, as in *beer*, *bier*, *weird*, *dear*, *sere* (but not always in *hero* and *zero*). These words are respelled with the long *e* symbol (bēr, wērd, and so on) in indicating pronunciation.

2. "Short *e*" sound (e) is also variously spelled, as in f*e*d, l*ea*ther, b*u*ry, m*a*ny, s*ai*d, and so on.

Before final *r* or *r* plus a consonant, short *e* represents the sound in *learn*, *fern*, *err*, marked ė (lėrn, fėrn, ėr).

3. "Unstressed *e*" (as in *kindness*, *difference*) represents a slight and sometimes indefinite sound in speech. It may be represented in phonetic transcription by *e* when slowly and rather formally spoken (kīnd'nes), or a sound close to short *i* (kīnd'nis), or the slurred vowel sound represented in this book by ə (kīnd'nəs).

Before *l*, *m*, *n*, and *r* unstressed *e* becomes really a part of the consonant ("vocalic" *l*, *m* . . .). In this book this *e* is also represented by ə: set'əl (*settle*), wúd'ən (*wooden*), but'ər (*butter*), and so on. How much *e* quality such syllables have depends on the speaker's speech habits and upon the slowness and emphasis of the particular utterance.

4. Miscellaneous sounds represented by *e*: E may represent long *a* before *r*, as in *there* (ᴛʜār); ä as in *sergeant* and many words in British usage which in the United States have ė (*Derby*, *Berkeley*, *clerk*).

An *e* following certain consonants may modify the sounds they represent: *ocean* (ō'shən), *grandeur* (gran'jür), *righteous* (rī'chəs).

5. Silent or mute *e*: In general words spelled with a final silent *e* drop the *-e* before additions beginning with a vowel and keep it before additions beginning with a consonant:

change: changed, changing; changeless (but changeable)
grease: greased, greaser; greasewood
like: likable, liking; likeness
pursue: pursuant, pursued, pursuing
use: usable, used, using; useful, useless
EXCEPTIONS: awful, duly, ninth; judgment (or judgement)

A few other exceptions keep -e to indicate pronunciation, chiefly after c and g before suffixes beginning with a, o, or u:

change: changeable   courage: courageous   notice: noticeable
See *-ce, -ge.

In a few words the -e is retained to avoid confusion with other words or to keep the connection with the root word obvious:

lineage (lin′ē ij) vs. linage (līn′ij)
singe-ing (sin′jing), dye-ing (dī′ing)

References: Fowler, "Mute -e"; Kennedy, pp. 243-45

each 1. As a pronoun, *each* is singular:

Each of the three has a different instructor.
Each ran as fast as his [her] legs could carry him [her].

2. As an adjective, *each* does not affect the number of a verb; when the subject modified by *each* is plural, the verb is plural:

Each applicant has to fill out the blank in full.
Three students, also from this county, each receive a scholarship.
They each feel keenly about it.

3. Colloquially, and increasingly in writing, *each* is regarded as a collective (Compare *every):

Each of these peoples undoubtedly modified Latin in accordance with *their* own speech habits.—BAUGH, p. 35

Reference: Russell Thomas, "Concord Based on *Meaning* versus Concord Based on *Form*," *College English*, 1939, i, 38-45

each other is in good use for more than two, although formal usage frequently has *one another*.

GENERAL: The men from farms on both sides of the river were shouting to each other.
FORMAL: The men from farms on both sides of the river were shouting to one another.

eat The principal parts of *eat* are:

IN FORMAL AND INFORMAL USAGE: eat (ēt), ate, eaten
IN LOCAL AND VULGATE USAGE: eat, eat (et or ēt), eat (ēt or et).

Eat is more common as the past tense in British than in American writing and is pronounced et.

Echo phrases Sometimes it is convenient to form a phrase on the pattern of one well known, or to echo one less known but apt. This is a type of allusion, though it is by no means necessary that the allusion be recognized. It pleases the writer to use it, it should of course convey his idea, and it will be recognized by some readers. The echo phrase may be either serious or light.

I have seen American textbooks in which lesson after lesson is devoted to the lofty purpose of eliminating *got*. As though the fear of *got* were the beginning of wisdom. ["The fear of God is the beginning of wisdom."]—P. B. BALLARD, *Thought and Language*, p. 205

. . . and in general she [Kay Boyle] is so determined to be sensitive to scenery and mood at every turn that the god's truth is you can't see the forest for the prose. [He couldn't see the forest for the trees.] —OTIS FERGUSON, *The New Republic*, Oct. 21, 1936

. . . one man's humor is another man's poison.—*New York Times Book Review*, March 13, 1938

. . . but democracy means simply the bludgeoning of the people by the people for the people.—OSCAR WILDE, *The Soul of Man Under Socialism*

In informal writing, echoes of common phrases usually fit, and in more formal writing there is certainly no harm in a writer showing that he has read a bit—but a parade of echo phrases is a nuisance.

See "Allusion," p. 241.

economic Pronounced ē′kō nom′ik or ek′ō nom′ik; and so also *economical, economics, economist.*

Economical means saving, thrifty; *economic* means having to do with business or economics.

Economy Economy in writing means leading a reader to the writer's exact meaning without unnecessary handicaps to understanding. Few, simple, exact words are its basis. But the fewest words and the simplest constructions are not always the most economical, for they may oversimplify the message, or they may limit its readers to those who are practiced in following such a style. Unnecessary words and needlessly complicated expressions are not economical. Exact words in idiomatic constructions, figures of speech that really illuminate the subject, direct development of materials are the means to true economy.

See "Sentence economy," p. 161; "Words that weaken," p. 214; "Appropriateness to reader or listener," p. 45.

ed 1. *-ed* or *-t.* In the past tense and past participles of verbs in which the *-ed* is (or may be) pronounced as *t*, simpler spelling has *-t*. A few words have been rather generally adopted with this sound and spelling:

crept   dreamt   leapt   slept
past (as the participle but not as the past tense: We *passed* the house vs. Once *past* the house.)

A number of other possibilities are not generally spelled with the *t*: *askt, jumpt, shipt, spelt.*

2. -ed or 'd. When *-ed* is added to words that have endings not common in English, *'d* is sometimes used instead, as in *un-idea'd, shanghai'd.*

3. -ed in adjectives. There is a tendency, especially in informal style, to drop the *-ed* ending from participles commonly used as adjectives, if the form that remains is that of a noun:

bake goods　　ice tea　　an old fashion manner　　a good size town
grade school [now the regular form]　　the same color hat

This tendency is characteristic of familiar and informal style and is rare in formal writing.

Editorial we　See *we § 2.

Editorial standards　See *Stylebooks; *Newspaper English, "Foundation of good English," p. 37, and general notations on Formal English.

-ee　An ending denoting the one who receives or is directly affected by an act or grant of power, the opposite of nouns in *-er* (*payer*, one who pays; *payee*, one who is paid):

assignee　　　grantee　　　mortgagee

It takes two people to say a thing—a sayee as well as a sayer. The one is as essential to any true saying as the other.—SAMUEL BUTLER, "Thought and Language"

effect　See *affect, effect.

e.g.　Abbreviation of Latin *exempli gratia*, "for example." E.g. is not usually italicized. See *namely for punctuation and use.

-ei-, -ie-　Words with *-ie-* are much more common than words with *-ei-* and on the whole give less spelling trouble. The most common sound represented by *-ie-* is ē.

Some common words with *ie* are:

achieve	cashier	fiend	grievous	pier
belief	chief	financier	hygiene	priest
believe	clothier	frieze	niece	shriek
bier	field	grieve	piece	siege

PLURAL OF NOUNS ENDING IN *-y*: academies　　companies　　lies lotteries

THIRD PERSON SINGULAR PRESENT OF VERBS IN *-y*: dies　　fortifies fries　　lies　　shies　　ties

OTHER WORDS IN *-ie-*: mischief　　sieve　　view

-ie- is not used after *c*.

There are fewer words with *ei* but their spelling needs careful watching.

The most common sound spelled *ei* is ā:

deign	feint	neigh	rein	sleigh
eight	freight	neighbor	seine	veil
feign	heinous	reign	skein	weigh

A number of words spell the sound ē with *ei*, especially after *c*:

ceiling	perceive	either	neither	weir
conceive	receive	leisure	seize	weird

And a few words spell other sounds with *ei*:

counterfeit	forfeit	heir	height	their

In some words *i* and *e* stand together but are parts of different syllables:

fi ery   headi er   si esta

either 1. *Either* means primarily "one or the other of two," as adjective (either way you look at it), or pronoun (bring me either). For emphasis the pronoun is usually supported by *one* (bring me either one). Used of three or more objects (either of the corners) it is loose and rare; "any one of the corners" is the more usual idiom.

Either is usually construed as singular, though its use as a plural is increasing (Fries, p. 56):

Either is good enough for me.

Either Grace or Phyllis will come, but *she* won't be able to stay long.

2. *Either* with the meaning "each" is rare in present English and definitely formal: "broil the fish on either side, with one turning"—"on either side of the river." *Each* or *both* would be more common in such expressions.

3. The pronunciation ī′ᴛʜər has not made so much progress in the United States as in England, and outside some communities in New England and a few families or circles that radiate from New England it is usually an affectation. Say ē′ᴛʜər, unless your family or social group generally says ī′ᴛʜər. Similarly, *neither* is usually nē′ᴛʜər, occasionally nī′ᴛʜər. The use of ī′ᴛʜər and nī′ᴛʜər by a public speaker affects an audience unfavorably in a large part of the country.

either . . . or *Correlative conjunctions

elder, eldest These archaic forms of *old* survive in formal English and they are used only of members of the same family: "the elder brother," "our eldest daughter," and in some phrases like "the elder statesmen."

Elegant variation is a name applied to the use of synonyms to avoid use of pronouns or repetition of nouns.

See *Reference of pronouns § 5.

Ellipsis (. . .) 1. A punctuation mark of three or sometimes four periods spaced is called an ellipsis (plural *ellipses*). Formerly asterisks (* * *) were used but they have been generally discontinued because they are too conspicuous. When an ellipsis comes at the end of a statement marked with a period, that period is added, as in the first and third instances in this passage:

> As Beret drank in these words the tenseness all left her; the weapon she had seized dropped from her hand; her body straightened up; she looked about in wide-eyed wonder. . . . Were those church bells she heard? . . . But the voices were beginning again on the other side of the wall. . .*. Hush! Hush!—O. E. Rölvaag, *Giants in the Earth*, p. 416

2. (*a*) The ellipsis is an editorial mark showing where a word or more, which is not needed for the purpose of a writer making the quotation, has been left out. In the following quotation the ellipsis marks the omission of two lines not essential for the meaning of the statement:

> After long delays caused by the presentation of a list of Italian and German provisos which constitutional governments could not accept . . ., a diplomatic conference assembled in London to map a program for maintaining neutrality.—H. F. Armstrong, *We or They*, p. 32

Any omission in quoted matter should be indicated by such ellipses.

b) An ellipsis is also used to show that a series of enumeration continues beyond the units named; it is equivalent to *et cetera*:

> the coordinating conjunctions (and, but, for . . .)

3. In narrative an ellipsis is used to mark hesitation in the action, suggesting passage of time, as in the quotation above from *Giants in the Earth*, and in the one from Conrad Aiken below:

> "Well—I can see this much. You *are* in love with her. Or you couldn't possibly be such a fool. But it's precisely when you're in love that you need to keep your wits about you. Or the wits of your friends. . . . You *mustn't* marry her, Harry."
> "Well—I don't know."
> "No! . . . It would be ruinous."—Conrad Aiken, "Spider! Spider!"

It is also used to mark a statement that is unfinished or is let die away:

I go away to a town, a big strange town, and try to hammer out a good book. The days come, the days go, and big ships sail into the harbor. . . .—ALBERT HALPER, "Young Writer Remembering Chicago"

Elliptical constructions *Ellipsis* and *elliptical* refer to a construction in which a word or words can be supplied from a neighboring construction:

I work a good deal harder than you [Supply: *work*].

In an elliptical construction the word to be supplied should be in the same form as it stands in the construction from which it is understood:

NOT: We sold everything that they could not.
RIGHT: We could sell everything that they could.

(Of course colloquial English is not so precise as this.)

The notion of ellipsis has often been misused to apply to the shorter of two possible ways of expressing a notion. A person may write either:

We went through the same experience that you did [or]
We went through the same experience you did.

The second form is not actually elliptical but a shorter idiom; a *that* is not "omitted," it just isn't thought or spoken or written. The choice between the longer and shorter constructions is a matter of style rather than grammar. Formal English uses the longer ones, tends to fill out all constructions. Informal and colloquial English uses the shorter constructions freely. In revising a paper it is usually possible for a writer to tell from the movement of a passage whether he should use the longer or shorter of two standard forms.

See "Long and short constructions," p. 163.
References: Curme, Syntax, p. 2 and index references; Jespersen, *The Philosophy of Grammar*, p. 306 and index references; for a more traditional treatment of ellipsis, see Kennedy, pp. 508-12.

else 1. Because *else* follows the word (usually a pronoun) it modifies, it takes the sign of the possessive (an *idiom):

I hated wearing somebody else's clothes.
At first he thought the book was his, but finally decided it was somebody else's.

2. *Else* is used as a colloquial *intensive and sometimes appears in writing where it adds nothing to the meaning and should be removed:

Finally I started talking, just to hear something [else] besides the roar of the motor.

3. *Nothing else but* is a vulgate phrase, not used in written English:

VULGATE: There was nothing else but wheat as far as you could see.

WRITTEN ENGLISH: There was nothing but wheat as far as you could see.

embarrassed Spell with two *r*'s and two *s*'s.

emigrate—immigrate *Emigrate* means to move out of a country or region, *immigrate* to move into a country. An *emigrant* from Norway would be an *immigrant* to the United States.

Emph **Emphasis** (CORRECTION: Strengthen the emphasis of this passage by one or more of the methods suggested below.)

The ideal of emphasis is to lead your reader to see your ideas in the same relative importance in which you regard them—the most important as most important, the less important as less important, the incidental as incidental. Emphasis does not necessarily mean force, but rather the accurate conveying of your view of your subject.

There are several ways in which emphasis can be conveyed, one or more of which will help you in controlling the reader's mind. Most of these are discussed more fully in other articles of the *Guide-Index*, referred to in this summary.

1. POSITION. In most types of writing, except news stories and reference works, the most emphatic position is the last, and the second most emphatic position is the first. The point you most want the reader to carry away should ordinarily be put last in a paper, and an important one that will immediately interest him should stand first. Paragraphs follow a similar plan. Sentences should "end with words that deserve distinction," and not many should begin with locutions that postpone meaning, "There was," "It is."

See "Beginning paragraphs," p. 67; "Concluding paragraphs," p. 70; "Position," p. 172.

2. MASS OR PROPORTION. Position is supported by the amount of space given to a particular point. It is necessary to watch the last topics in a paper, which are likely to be hurried over and so

underdeveloped that they do not seem as important as their writer intends.

3. DISTINCTION OF EXPRESSION. The words used have a good deal to do with emphasis. In general, big words and long *function phrases weaken a statement, as do general and indefinite words. Fresh, concrete, simple words in direct and economical constructions make for a clearcut emphasis. See Chapter 8, p. 213, Qualities of Words.

4. SEPARATION, DISTINCTNESS. Marking the stages of thought in a paper by extra spacing or by numbers makes separate ideas stand out more strongly. Careful paragraphing, even occasionally putting a single sentence in a paragraph by itself if it deserves special emphasis, makes units that help clarify the relationship between topics. Putting ideas in separate sentences keeps them distinct, and making the important statements main clauses and the contributing statements subordinate clauses shows their relative importance. Punctuation in part represents the pauses of speech, which usually come *after* important locutions.

See "Transitions between paragraphs," p. 65; "Coordination and subordination," p. 124; "Separation of elements," p. 171.

5. REPETITION. Repetition of valuable words drives them home, and repetition of statements either in similar words or in different, perhaps figurative expressions, is a useful form of emphasis if it is not overdone.

See "Repetition in sentences," p. 168; "Restatement," p. 94.

6. INTENSIVES. Words added to intensify meaning are generally used in speaking, but they are less useful in writing. See *Intensives, *very; "Intensives," p. 166. *Exaggeration is a legitimate form of intensifying. Labeling a statement "It is interesting to note," "This is an important phase of the subject" is not usually convincing. Such phrases can be done away with in revision by making the fact or opinion stand out in other ways.

7. MECHANICAL DEVICES. Writing and printing have various mechanical means—*underlining (italics), *capitals, emphatic punctuation—for stressing words and passages. These devices are used by amateur writers often in an attempt to make up for deficiencies in style or content.

See *Schoolgirl style; "Mechanical devices," p. 166.

Emphasis is to be tested in revision, when the writer takes the role of reader and tries to see if his paper really represents his view of the subject. There is no better guide for this critical reading than to watch for convincing emphasis.

en-, in- *In-* is either a native English prefix or a prefix of Latin origin; *en-* is the same Latin prefix modified in French. (*Em-* and *im-* are variant forms.) In several common words, usage is divided, though usually one form is more common. This is a type of problem for which Fowler and other British-made dictionaries are not safe guides to American usage, for we tend to use *in-* more than the English do. The safest way is to consult a recent American dictionary.

Here are a few samples with Webster preferences put first when there is a choice:

embark	encourage
embed—imbed	endorse—indorse
embellish	endure
enable	endeavor
enchant	enforce

enclose—inclose (gaining)
engrain—ingrain (usually *ingrained* in the past participle and adjective: an ingrained habit)
ensure—insure (*insure* in the financial sense, *insurance*, etc.)
entwine—intwine

incase—encase	
incrust—encrust	infold—enfold
	inquire—enquire

The *en-* forms often suggest a slightly more formal style than *in-*.

Endorsing papers See "Endorsing manuscript," p. 304.

End-stop A mark of punctuation used at the end of a sentence, usually a period, exclamation mark, or question mark. The double or two-em dash (——; *Dash §7) is used as an end-stop in conversation *when a speech is interrupted*:

> "Continuing?" Von Blon brought himself up straight in his chair. "I don't understand. You said a moment ago——"
> "That Ada had been poisoned," finished Vance. "Quite. But d'ye see, she didn't die."—S. S. VAN DINE, *The Greene Murder Case*, p. 280

The *ellipsis (. . .) is often used as an end-stop for a sentence that is intentionally left unfinished or that is let die away:

> He put his elbows on his knees and his head in his hands. "I can't stop his girding at me, and I can't make him hear. . . ."— MARY JOHNSTON, "The Two Business Men," *Harper's Magazine*, Sept. 1928

When two end-stops would fall together at the end of a sentence, as when a question stands within a sentence, only one mark, the more emphatic or more necessary for meaning, is used:

When we say, for example, that Miss A. *plays* well, only an irredeemable outsider would reply "Plays what?" So, too, . . .—C. Alphonso Smith, *Studies in English Syntax*, p. 8

For further comment on end-stops see the articles on the individual marks.

English language English is a member of the Indo-European family of languages, which includes most of the languages of Europe, a large number of the languages of India, the languages of Persia, and certain adjoining regions. The Indo-European family is divided into eight branches. One of these, the Germanic, to which English belongs, comprises the following:

Germanic
- North (Scandinavian)
  - Swedish
  - Danish
  - Norwegian
  - Icelandic
- East (Gothic—extinct)
- West
  - German
  - Dutch-Flemish
  - Frisian
  - English

A brief selection of facts about the different periods of our language will show some of the roots of the richness—and confusion—of modern English.

1. Old English, 450-1100. The Angles, Saxons, and Jutes brought to England from their old homes in northeastern Europe somewhat differing Germanic dialects. They pushed back the native Celts from the parts of the island they conquered, so that Celtic speech contributed almost nothing to English, but survived in Welsh, Cornish, and Highland Scotch. The conquerors' languages developed into several main dialects—Northumbrian, Mercian, Kentish, West Saxon—which together are known as Old English (or Anglo-Saxon). These dialects still leave their marks in the vulgate speech of various parts of England. They had many points in common, and were gradually brought together, each making some contribution, but East Midland, a descendant of Mercian, contributed the most to what now after seven or eight hundred years we know as English.

Somewhat less than a quarter of the present English vocabulary goes back to the words of Old English. The modern descendants of Old English words are often changed in meaning and almost always in pronunciation—according to regular processes: Old English *stan* becomes Modern English *stone*, *ban* becomes *bone*, etc. Our common verbs—*go, sit, eat, fight, whistle,* many of our most common nouns—*meat, house, breakfast, land, water,* and adjectives like *fast, slow, high* go back to Old English words, so that though less than a fourth of the dictionary words are of this "native" origin, they play a part in our speech out of proportion to their number.

Furthermore, most of the machinery of our language is from Old English: the articles *a, an, the,* most of the connecting words— *around, at, by, for, from, in, into, out, under . . . as, like, since, when;* most of the pronouns (*I, we, us, . . .*); the inflectional endings of nouns (*house—houses, boy—boys—boy's*) and of adjectives and adverbs: *merry—merrier—merriest* or *more merry—most merry;* harsh*ly,* kind*ly;* the forms of verbs: pass, pass*es,* pass*ed,* pass*ing.* These endings are applied to words borrowed from other languages (*indict-ed, political-ly*), so that although three quarters of the vocabulary may come from Romance or other languages the borrowed words are built into an English pattern. And when we consider word order we see that the texture of English is Germanic and it must be regarded as a Germanic language.

Within the Old English period the practice of absorbing words from other languages was already strong. A number of Latin words, some of them originally Greek, were taken in, most of them pertaining to the church (*abbot, priest, school, . . .*), though there was still a tendency to translate the elements of the Latin words into Old English elements, so that we have *gospel* from *god spell,* "good news," which is a translation of the Greek-Latin *evangelium.*

In the ninth century the east and north of England was conquered by the Danes, whose language left a large number of words and forms, partly because it was a closely related language, partly because of the intimacy between the two peoples. The *sk* words are likely to date from this mixture—*sky, skin, scream, skirt* (a cousin of the Old English *shirt,* both related to *short*), place names ending in *-by* and *-thorp,* and a number of common words like *odd, anger, egg.* Nearly five per cent of our words are Scandinavian.

A number of the most conspicuous irregularities of Modern English existed already in Old English: *be, is, are, was, were, been* as forms of the verb "to be"; *may, might, shall, should, ought,* and the other "auxiliaries"; our pronouns—*I, my, me, we, our, us, he, she, it, . . .* These words are in such common use that they have never been brought into any consistent grammatical pattern. Here and there we have remnants of Old English forms that lost out in the development of the language, like the plurals *children, oxen, men, geese,* instead of the regular plural in *-s.*

There is a considerable body of writing from the Old English period. It includes poems, sermons, riddles, history, translations from Latin, and most conspicuously the *Anglo-Saxon Chronicles*, *Beowulf*, and the large group of writings and translations in West Saxon made by or at the court of Alfred the Great, King of the West Saxons 871-901. Some 30,000 different words are found in this literature.

2. MIDDLE ENGLISH, 1100-1500. The conquest of England by the Norman-French in 1066 was the most far-reaching single historical event influencing our language. The speakers of Old English in the main became serfs, servants, everything but leaders in affairs. Their language was seldom used in official proceedings and rarely written. One result was the loss of the more elevated Old English words that had been used in poetry and that would correspond to the rather archaic vocabulary of our formal literature.

A far-reaching development of this period was the decline and in some instances complete loss of the inflectional endings that Old English had used. The definite article was no longer declined (our *the* is the sole descendant of eight forms in Old English); *-n* disappeared from the infinitive of most verbs, and other endings, since they were in unstressed syllables and did not receive full pronunciation, dropped away. This process went far to make English one of the least inflected languages.

On the other hand the language of the invaders was making its way. The words for the acts of the ruling class—war, government, law, social activity—were Norman French and they have generally come down to modern English: *siege, soldier, judge, jury, suit, dinner, servant, obey*. Over a fourth of our current English words are from Norman French. The majority of the Norman French words were ultimately from Latin, though considerably changed in form. For many notions Modern English has two roughly synonymous words, one Norman French, one Old English: *dress—clothes, aid—help, cottage—hut, solitary—lonely*. Some French spellings made their way into English, like *gu* for hard *g—guest, guess; qu* for *cw, queen* for Old English *cwen*.

In 1362 English was restored as the language of the law courts, an official recognition that it was reasserting itself again after conquest. The speech of the region around London was now the basis for future development, not only of a spoken language but of a literary language. How far the fusion of Old English and Norman French resources had gone can be seen from a few lines by Chaucer, written in the 1380's. The Norman French words are in italics:

> "What folk ben ye, that at myn hoomcominge
> *Perturben* so my *feste* with *crynge?*"
> Quod Theseus, "have ye so greet *envye*
> Of myn *honour*, that thus *compleyne* and *crye?*
> Or who hath yow misboden, or *offended?*
> And telleth me if it may been *amended;*
> And why that ye ben clothed thus in blak?"
>
> GEOFFREY CHAUCER, "The Knightes Tale"

Except for the Old English *misboden* ("insulted"), all of these words, both native and French, are in use today, though *quod* (quoth) is archaic, and in spite of some differences in spelling, the passage can be read by anyone. Many of the words show inflectional endings that have since been dropped or changed: *ben* for *are* or *be*, perturb*en*, tell*eth,* and the final *e* of nouns.

3. EARLY MODERN ENGLISH, 1500-1700. In this period we have the beginnings of conscious concern for the language and actual or attempted "improvement" by manipulation of words and constructions, "schoolmastering the speech." The early printers, from 1476 on, felt the need for uniformity, especially in spelling and choice of word forms, and began the domination of these traits that ever since in the written language has been exercised by publishers. Translators and writers believed the language was rough, unpolished, incapable of doing what Latin and Greek had done and what Italian could do. They set about enlarging the vocabulary, chiefly by transliterating words from Greek and Latin. More than twenty-five per cent of modern English words are pretty directly from classical languages and very often we have two words that go back to the same Latin original, one brought in by the Norman French and one taken in directly later: *paint—picture, certainty—certitude.* Latin was the language of the Church at the beginning of this period, though after the Reformation the Book of Common Prayer and the King James translation of the Bible became tremendous forces for elevated English. Most books of the learned world were in Latin—and college classes were conducted in Latin, even in America, until a century and a half ago.

The spoken language was vigorous and was written down in some popular literature but most literature that has survived was from the hands of university men and conscious stylists. Shakespeare shows the complete range, from formal, Latinized lines to rough and tumble lines, often combining the elevated and the simple in a single speech:

> No, this my hand will rather
> The multitudinous seas incarnadine
> Making the green one red.

Prose style lagged behind poetic, especially in sentence sense, producing "sentence heaps" running to hundreds of words. In the sixteen hundreds the wealth of experiment of the preceding century was analyzed and many words and phrases were disposed of. The less useful and more ponderous of the Latin importations were dropped, and interest in native words increased the proportion of Saxon words in use. Prose style especially developed in directness and sureness until in Dryden modern English prose is usually said to be established. In spite of small differences in idiom and word order, this paragraph does not seem nearly 300 years old:

To begin, then, with Shakespeare. He was the man who of all modern, and perhaps ancient poets, had the largest and most comprehensive soul. All the images of nature were still present to him, and he drew them, not laboriously, but luckily; when he describes anything, you more than see it, you feel it too. Those who accuse him to have wanted learning, give him the greater commendation: he was naturally learned; he needed not the spectacles of books to read nature; he looked inwards, and found her there. I cannot say he is everywhere alike; were he so, I should do him injury to compare him with the greatest of mankind. He is many times flat, insipid; his comic wit degenerating into clenches, his serious swelling into bombast. But he is always great, when some great occasion is presented to him; no man can say he ever had a fit subject for his wit, and did not then raise himself as high above the rest of the poets,

Quantum lenta solent inter viburna cupressi.

The consideration of this made Mr. Hales of Eaton say, that there was no subject of which any poet ever writ, but he would produce it much better done in Shakespeare; and however others are now generally preferred before him, yet the age wherein he lived, which had contemporaries with him Fletcher and Jonson, never equalled them to him in their esteem: and in the last king's court, when Ben's reputation was at highest, Sir John Suckling, and with him the greater part of the courtiers, set our Shakespeare far above him.—JOHN DRYDEN, *An Essay of Dramatic Poesy* (1668)

4. MODERN ENGLISH 1700- This *Index* gives a partial picture of current English and suggests in some of its specific articles changes that have taken place in the last few generations. Such articles may be taken as continuations of this brief historical sketch, for by 1700 English had become substantially the language we now know and use. The vocabulary has been enlarged in the last two centuries chiefly from two sources: borrowings from India and America and from all peoples touched by British and American traders; and through scientific coinages, chiefly from Greek and Latin roots. There has been, especially in recent years, a tendency toward shorter and more direct sentences. The paragraph has become a more distinct unit in written expression. The most important point for study in this period has probably been the different levels of usage, and different traditions of style, especially formal and informal style and the relations between them.

Today the language of England and the British Empire and of the United States is spoken by considerably over 200,000,000 people—perhaps the largest group of people who can easily understand each other.

The result of this varied history is a language full of anomalies, with exceptions to every rule, but of unusual range, combining something of the rapidity and smoothness of the Romance languages with the strength of the Germanic.

References: Baugh, Robertson, McKnight; Kennedy, Chs. 4, 5. Otto Jespersen, *Growth and Structure of the English Language* (various editions), describes the accumulation of the English vocabulary, and his *Language* (New York, 1923), Part iv, discusses language change especially apropos of English.

Enlarging vocabulary See "Increasing your vocabulary," p. 205.

en route Pronounced, formal än rüt; informal, more completely Englished, on rüt, and locally, in rout.

On the way often fits a sentence more naturally:

They were en route [on the way] to Philadelphia.

enthuse A back formation (*Origin of words §3*d*) from *enthusiasm*. Many people object to it, and the dictionaries label it "colloquial." But *enthuse* seems to be an improvement over the only locution we have for the idea, the clumsy *be enthusiastic over* or *about*. It is now in fairly general use.

envelop, envelope The verb *envelop* is pronounced en vel'əp; the noun *envelope*, en'və lōp; less commonly—reflecting the word's French origin—on'və lōp; and locally en vel'up.

Envelope See *Letters §§1, 3.

Epigrams An epigram is a short, pithy statement, usually with a touch of wit, in either verse or prose. In prose this means really a detached or detachable and "quotable" sentence. Epigrams are the chief stock in trade of columnists and newspaper "paragraphers" (writers of the one- or two-sentence remarks that come at the end of the editorial columns in some dailies). In consecutive prose, epigrams sometimes become too prominent, attract too much attention to themselves, or suggest straining for effect. But they can be really useful for focusing attention or for putting a fact or opinion so that a reader can remember (and perhaps repeat) it.

> One test of musical comedy, we have always felt, is whether it breaks out into song or breaks down into it.—FRANK S. NUGENT, *The New York Times*, Dec. 3, 1937

> It's no disgrace to be poor, but it might as well be.

> Bees are not as busy as we think they are. They jest can't buzz any slower.—KIN HUBBARD, *The Sayings of Abe Martin*.

Closely related to epigrams are *aphorisms*—pithy statements but more likely to be abstract and not necessarily witty. The essays of Francis Bacon are packed with aphorisms, and some modern essayists use them too:

> To spend too much time in studies is sloth; to use them too much for ornament, is affectation; to make judgment wholly by their rules, is the humour of a scholar. . . . Read not to contradict and confute; nor to believe and take for granted; not to find talk and discourse; but to weigh and consider. . . . Reading maketh a full man; conference a ready man; and writing an exact man.—FRANCIS BACON, "Of Studies"

Proverbs are the often quoted, concrete expressions of popular wisdom. They are likely to make observations on character or conduct. As a rule their authors are unknown.

> Still waters run deep.
> It's hard for an empty sack (bag) to stand upright.
> Red sky at night, sailors delight;
> Red sky at morning, sailors take warning.
> It never rains but it pours.
> Alcohol and gasoline don't mix.

A good many proverbs are very old and contain words or constructions not now in use that sometimes give wrong impressions. In "The exception proves the rule," for example, *prove* does not mean what it does today but has its old meaning of "test," which makes the saying intelligible.

Writers about people, especially about "common people," should remember the vast store of popular oral literature in the form of proverbs and the pithy remarks thrown off (true epigrams) in the midst of everyday scenes. A farmer said, pitching wet clover hay onto a hayrack, "It only takes a thousand pounds of this to make a ton," or as Sinclair Lewis has Sam Clarke say in *Main Street* "I never read anything I can't check against."

A special type of epigram is *paradox*, which makes a statement that as it stands contradicts fact or common sense or itself, and yet suggests a truth or at least a half truth:

All generalizations are false, including this one.

Dr. Richards is no mystic; he is a behaviourist, a behaviourist being a psychologist who does not believe in psychology.—P. B. BALLARD, *Thought and Language*, p. 265

Reference: *The Oxford Dictionary of Proverbs,* compiled by William G. Smith (Oxford, 1936)

-er, -or Names of persons or things performing an act (nouns of agent) and some other nouns are formed in English by adding *-er* to a verb (*doer, killer, painter, thinker*), but many, chiefly nouns taken in from Latin or French (*assessor, prevaricator*), end in *-or*.

Since the two endings are pronounced the same (ər), it is hard to tell whether *-er* or *-or* should be written. Here are a few as samples; a dictionary will have to settle most questions.

WITH -ER:

advertiser	consumer	mixer
*adviser (now shift-	debater	peddler (pedlar)
ing to advisor)	engraver	propeller
better (bettor)	manufacturer	subscriber
condenser		

WITH -OR:

accelerator	detector	proprietor
administrator	distributor	rotor
ancestor	editor	spectator
bachelor	governor	sponsor
benefactor	inventor	supervisor
carburetor	(or inventer)	transgressor
competitor	legislator	ventilator
conductor	motor	warrior
conqueror	objector	

There are a few nouns of agent ending in *-ar*: beggar, burglar, liar.

-er, -re Many words formerly ending in *-re* are now spelled *-er* in American usage. This group includes:

caliber	maneuver	niter	sepulcher
center	meager	ocher	somber
fiber	meter	saber	specter
luster	miter	scepter	theater

British usage tends to *-re* in most of these words, though Fowler says they are being changed to *-er* one by one, because "we prefer in England to break with our illogicalities slowly."

An American writer who wishes a slightly archaic flavor will tend to use the *-re* forms; most will naturally use the *-er* forms.

Theater is divided in spelling, partly because it is found in a good many proper names of buildings and companies which were set up when *theatre* was the more common spelling, partly because of the leisure class associations of the word. Keep the form actually used in proper names and ordinarily use *theater* elsewhere.

Acre, lucre, mediocre keep the *-re* to make sure the *c* is pronounced *k* (contrast *soccer*), and *ogre* is the current form, though some words with *g*, like *meager*, have changed.

err Usually pronounced ėr; but there is some, and perhaps a growing tendency to pronounce it er, from *analogy with *error* (er'ər).

erstwhile Archaic (or affected) for *former*

Esq., Esquire Written following a man's name in the inside and outside address of a letter, *Esq.* or *Esquire* is formal, with archaic or British suggestion, and in the United States is not often used except to professional men, chiefly to lawyers. No other title (such as *Mr., Dr., Hon.*) should be used with the word: Harry A. Kinne, Esq.

Essential modifier See *Restrictive and non-restrictive.

etc., et cetera *Etc.*, usually read *and so forth*, is sometimes a convenient way to end a series that samples rather than completes an enumeration, but it belongs primarily to reference and business usage:

> The case is suitable for prints, maps, blueprints, etc.

Its inappropriateness can be seen in a sentence like this:

> A student's professors can be of immense aid to him because of their knowledge of boys and their habits, customs, needs, ideals, etc.

Writing out *et cetera* now seems an affectation. In consecutive writing most people would probably use the English "and so forth." It is better to avoid these end tags (which really take away from emphasis by putting a catch all at the end of a clause or sentence) by rephrasing the list, preceding it by *such as* or some other warning that the list you have given is not exhaustive:

> The case is suitable for such large sheets as prints, maps, and blueprints.

An *ellipsis (. . .) can be used to show that a series could be continued:

> The common prepositions (*by, for, in, with* . . .) are followed by the accusative case.

507

And etc. shows the writer doesn't realize that the *et* of *etc.* means *and,* so that he is really writing *and and so forth.*

Etymology *Origin of words

Euphemisms A euphemism is a softened word used in place of one that names more vigorously some suffering, or something unpleasant, or something regarded as not quite nice: *pass away* for *die, natural son* for *illegitimate son* or *bastard, expectorate* for *spit, separate from the college* for *expel* or *fire* or *flunk out.*

Occasionally euphemisms are warranted to avoid hurting someone's feelings. But in general it is safer—and better style—to call things by their right names, even if they are somewhat unpleasant.

For further discussion and examples see "Euphemisms," p. 218.

Euphony means harmonious or pleasing sounds. For discussion of euphony as a quality of style, see "Euphony," p. 174.

every and its compounds 1. *Every, everybody, everyone* are grammatically singular:

Every man on the team did his best.
Everybody likes the new minister.
Everyone took his purchases home with him.

Colloquially these words are treated as collectives. A verb immediately following *everyone* or *everybody* is usually singular, but a pronoun referring back to it from a little distance is likely to be plural:

Everybody took off their hats.

This is reasonable, since the reference is to a number of people. To make these expressions conform to formal written usage, it is often better to change the *everybody* to a more accurate plural or collective than to change the later pronoun:

They all did their best. The crowd took off their hats.

Reference: Fries, p. 50

2. *Everybody* is always written as one word; *everyone* is usually written as one word, but when the *one* is stressed, as two:

Everybody knew what the end would be.
Everyone knew what the end would be.
Every one of the family knew what the end would be.

3. *Every so often, every bit as* (*happy,* etc.) are useful informal and colloquial idioms:

Every so often someone in the crowd would give a terrific shout.
They are every bit as happy as they expected to be.

4. *Every place* is a colloquial and vulgate adverbial phrase, somewhat more reputable than *any place* (*any §4):

Every place I looked the people said the same thing.

ex Prefixed to words describing former positions, offices, relationships; hyphened:

ex-husband   ex-errand-boy   ex-president

Exact connective *Conjunctions §1 and articles on particular connectives, *as, *but, *so, *while . . .

Exact use of words See "The responsible use of words," p. 194.

Exaggeration The figure of speech (hyperbole) in which a statement is enlarged or overstated. See "Exaggeration and understatement," p. 239.

Examples See "Illustration," p. 100.

except, accept *Except*, as a verb, means to "leave out, exclude": "He excepted those who had done the assignment from the extra reading." It is decidedly formal, and *excused* or even *exempted* would be more natural in the sentence given.

Accept means to *get* or *receive* and is slightly formal: "I accept with pleasure"—"He accepted the position."

Confusing the two words in writing, practically always due to carelessness rather than to ignorance, comes from the fact that we see and write the preposition *except* ("Everyone except you") so much oftener than we do either of the verbs.

exception "And this was no exception" is a colorless and often wordy way of combining a particular and a general statement:

Practically every science class makes field trips an integral part of its activities, and we were no exception.
[Revised] As in almost every science class, field trips were an integral part of our activities.
Most young actors experience numerous difficulties in their early appearances. I was no exception. [Like most young actors, I experienced . . .]

Exclamation mark (!) An exclamation mark (or point) is used after an emphatic interjection and after a phrase, clause, or sentence that is genuinely exclamatory, and after forceful commands. Clearcut exclamations offer no problem:

Oh! Ouch! No, no, no!
"But," he protested, "it's the chance of a lifetime!
A number of children playing on the quay saw him, and with a wild cry of "Squirrel! Squirrel!" went after him.—W. H. HUDSON, *The Book of a Naturalist*, p. 61

He stumbled up to the fireman.

"Not that wall! Not that! That wall's all right. You'll spoil my pictures! Shoot at the centre!"—JOHN GALSWORTHY, *Swan Song*, p. 325

But many interjections are weak and deserve no more than a comma:

Well, well, so you're in college now.

Often sentences cast in exclamatory pattern are really statements put that way for variety (*Exclamations) and the exclamation mark is optional. Its use would depend chiefly on appropriateness and the emphasis intended and on whether the writer tends to close punctuation (which is likely to show a number of exclamation marks) or open (which is more likely to rely on commas).

The country! [Or, a period] Why anybody ever went to the country. . . . He might be in New York with the gang. Playing ball in the streets, dodging the trucks, the cars, the cabs! [Or, a period]

Exclamation marks are more characteristic of imaginative writing, especially of fiction, than of factual writing. In factual writing it is well to remember that in some newspaper offices the exclamation mark is known as a screamer—and that its overuse is a mark of nervousness or of *schoolgirl style.

Exclamations are expressions of feeling or emphatic statements of fact or opinion. They range from the simple and often involuntary *Oh!* or *Ouch!* to fully developed sentences.

One-word exclamations may be regarded as full sentences if they deserve that much emphasis:

Oh! You nearly upset my plate.

or as parts of sentences if they seem to belong with other sentence elements:

Oh! you're here at last!   [or]   Oh, you're here at last!

Many exclamations begin with *what* or *how*:

What a view!   How could you!
How lucky you are!

An exclamation expressing an emphatic opinion gives not only emphasis but variety in a passage:

But the methods chosen for the transition must always bear those human values in mind, for a whole new social order must inevitably result from a new kind of economic system, and in the process of slow nurture and growth initial trends may be all-important. Compulsion is a bad way to make men free!—ALFRED M. BINGHAM, *Insurgent America*, p. 6

510

But used just for variety or to give emphasis to what are really commonplaces, exclamations are usually ineffective and give the effect of a strained or schoolgirlish style:

Think how often you have judged a person by the way in which he speaks! Think of a salesman who is a poor talker! It sounds like the height of unreality, but what a situation in this highly competitive world! Think of a college professor who could not intelligently lecture to his classes because he had not learned the art of elocution!

excuse, pardon Small slips are *excused*, more considerable faults (and crimes) are *pardoned*. "Pardon me" is sometimes incorrectly considered more elegant than "Excuse me" in upper-class social situations. *Excuse* has also the special meaning of "giving permission to leave."

expect means "to look forward to" and also "to look for with confidence." In formal English it is usually kept close to some meaning involving anticipation, but in colloquial usage its meaning is extended and weakened to "suppose"—"I expect you'd better be going."

Experiment in English Language and literary style tend to become stereotyped; the same kinds of words are used over and over in the same kinds of constructions; their effectiveness in conveying individual impressions decreases. The more important writers escape monotony by the force of their message or the individuality of their expression, and most of them more or less consciously either ignore conventions of language or experiment with words or constructions.

Almost anyone with an interest in writing will experiment in his own familiar writing, trying out spellings, unusual words or combinations of words, unorthodox sentence patterns. Some writers in their published work experiment also. We might call any departure from the commonly written and printed English an experiment —if it is not just the result of carelessness or ignorance. Advertisers are active experimenters, using shortened spellings, created words, and free sentence forms. At the other extreme purists may also be regarded as experimenters, trying to limit speaking and writing to the formal vocabulary and formal constructions, as it never has been in all its history. *Basic English is an experiment, aiming to communicate with a vocabulary of 850 words.

Writers like Damon Runyon and P. G. Wodehouse are really experimenters, since they create a lingo for their stories by taking ordinary traits of speech and pushing them further than natural usage would. This bit from Mr. Wodehouse shows his potpourri of colloquialisms, slang, literary phrases (and allusions), and created words (*bonhomous*):

> From his earliest years the Biscuit had nourished an unwavering conviction that Providence was saving up something particularly juicy in the way of rewards for him and that it was only a question of time before it came across and delivered the goods. He based this belief on the fact that he had always tried to be a reasonably bonhomous sort of bird and was one who, like Abou Ben Adhem, loved his fellow men. Abou had clicked, and Lord Biskerton expected to click. But not in his most sanguine moments, not even after a Bump Supper at Oxford or the celebration of somebody's birthday at the Drones, had he ever expected to click on this colossal scale. It just showed that, when Providence knew it had got hold of a good man, the sky was the limit.—P. G. WODEHOUSE, *Big Money*, p. 286

In the last few years a good deal of experiment in English has gone on in formal, not to say highbrow, literature, especially on the part of James Joyce, Gertrude Stein, and E. E. Cummings. One of the chief interests of these writers, aside from freshening the nature of English prose, has been to carry expression closer to thought, creating, especially, sentence patterns that follow or at least suggest the actual thought of a character or of the writer himself.

Miss Stein's explanation of why she does not use commas conventionally both describes and illustrates an individualist's approach to these problems of language. She holds that because most writers use commas in certain ways is not sufficient reason for her doing it. She asks if commas really convey her sense of her meaning or if they are just lazy props, keeping the reader from a properly active participation in understanding?

What does a comma do.
I have refused them so often and left them out so much and did without them so continually that I have come finally to be indifferent to them. I do not now care whether you put them in or not but for a long time I felt very definitely about them and would have nothing to do with them.
As I say commas are servile and they have no life of their own, and their use is not a use, it is a way of replacing one's own interest and I do decidedly like to like my own interest my own interest in what I am doing. A comma by helping you along holding your coat for you and putting on your shoes keeps you from living your life as actively as you should lead it and to me for many years and I still do feel that way about it only now I do not pay as much attention to them, the use of them was positively degrading. Let me tell you what I felt and what I meant.

. . . .

When it gets really difficult you want to disentangle rather than to cut the knot, at least so anybody feels who is working with any thread, so anybody feels who is working with any tool so anybody feels who is writing any sentence or reading it after it has been written. And what does a comma do, a comma does nothing but make easy a thing that if you like it enough is easy enough without the comma. A long complicated sentence should force itself upon you, make you know yourself knowing it and the comma, well at the most a comma is a poor period that it lets you stop and take a breath but if you want to take a breath you ought to know yourself that you want to take a breath. It is not like stopping altogether which is what a period does stopping altogether has something to do with going on, but taking a breath well you are always taking a breath and why emphasize one breath rather than another breath. Anyway that is the way I felt about it and I felt that about it very strongly. And so I almost never used a comma. The longer, the more complicated the sentence the greater the number of the same kind of words I had following one after another, the more the very many more I had of them the more I felt the passionate need of their taking care of themselves by themselves and not helping them, and thereby enfeebling them by putting in a comma.—GERTRUDE STEIN, *Lectures in America*, pp. 219-21

More recently, in *Finnegans Wake*, Mr. Joyce has gone on to experiment with words, breaking up familiar words, changing sounds slightly, combining elements:

Yet he made leave to many a door beside of Finglas wold for so witness his chambered cairns silent that are at browse up hill and down coombe and on eolithostroton, at Howth or at Coolock or at Enniskerry. Olivers lambs we do call them and they shall be gathered unto him, their herd and paladin, in that day when he skall wake from earthsleep in his valle of briers and o'er dun and dale the Wulverulverlord (protect us!) his mighty horn skall roll, orland, roll.

Liverpoor? Sot a bit of it! His braynes coolt parritch, his pelt nassy, his heart's adrone, his bluidstreams acrawl, his puff but a piff, his extremities extremely so. Humph is in his doge. Words weigh no more to him than raindrops to Rethfernhim. Which we all like. Rain. When we sleep. Drops. But wait until our sleeping. Drain. Sdops.

For most readers this is carrying experiment to the point of ridiculousness. Certainly it is paying little attention to a reader or to demands of communication. A writer of course can write merely to please himself, or for the fun of it (and there is much sheer fun back of most of this experimentation), but he cannot blame readers if they do not feel like bothering to decipher his cryptograms. Joyce was doing this quite voluntarily (or wilfully), for in *The Portrait of the Artist as a Young Man* and in the volume of short stories *Dubliners* he wrote a flexible and effective English. Similarly E. E. Cummings, whose *Eimi* is the story of a visit to Russia written in experimental prose, wrote one of the classics of the war in *The Enormous Room*—in a conventional but thoroughly individual prose. These experiments are not the work of writers who can't write English but of talented writers who are trying to make English prose more expressive, to make it come closer to representing their individual view of things.

Though these writers have pushed their experiments to the point of eccentricity, their work is useful. Because of the work of Joyce and Miss Stein, for instance, others, like John Dos Passos, Evelyn Scott, and Ernest Hemingway, have written with greater freedom. These, together with the vigorous if more conventional writers like George Bernard Shaw in his *Prefaces* and H. L. Mencken in his *Prejudices*, have gone a long way toward breaking up stereotypes of prose and toward making possible the notable vigor and flexibility of current writing.

These experimenters are worth reading and study—but not direct imitation. They are individualists who have tried to find expression for their individual needs. Imitating the external traits of the style of Damon Runyon or of Gertrude Stein will usually mean failure because the imitator's needs are not the same as those of the pioneers. But reading such writers should give a writer courage to try to find a method of presenting his material as he sees it, even if that means departing from some of the conventions of writing. This is part of the spirit of modern literature.

References: Dobrée, Part iv, §2, "Experiments"; Gertrude Stein, *Lectures in America* (New York, 1935), "Poetry and Grammar"

Expletives *it, *there is, there are

Expository paragraphs For examples and discussion see "Logical paragraphs," p. 93.

Expository writing Writing that is intended primarily to inform its readers—by presenting facts, giving directions, recording events, interpreting facts, developing opinions—is expository. People do not sit down to write "exposition"; the word is convenient for grouping various articles that convey information.

Expository articles differ in their emphasis from arguments, which are intended to influence the reader's beliefs or to lead him to some action. Imaginative writing is not primarily expository (although novels have been written to explain their author's point of view on something) but aims directly at pleasing or moving a reader. There may be subordinate expository movements, as when in a novel a character's situation or his past is explained.

The bulk of college writing, probably all except imaginative writing done in some composition courses, is expository. The articles in this *Guide-Index* are expository.

extra is either an adjective (He has an extra pair of shoes), an informal adverb (It was an extra hot day), or a noun (a newspaper, an actor, something added).

extracurricular means "outside the course of study" (extracurricular activities); sometimes hyphened but usually not. *Extracurriculum* seems to be gaining as an alternate adjective form.

F
The sound of *f* occurs spelled *f*, *ff*, *ph*, and *gh* (See *-ough). The words with *ph* go back to Greek words with *phi* (φ): *philosophy, telephone*; a few have been simplified to *f*: *fantasy, sulfur*. Nouns ending in *f* usually have the corresponding voiced sound (*v*) in the plural: *leaf—leaves, loaf—loaves, wife—wives; beef* has either *beeves* or *beefs*. In *of* the *f* is pronounced as *v* (ov).

fact (the fact that) *The fact that* is very often a circumlocution for which *that* alone would do as well:

> He was quite conscious [of the fact] that his visitor had some other reason for coming.

See "Removing deadwood," p. 161.

Factual and imaginative writing The fundamental distinction underlying types of writing is that in some types the writer's first responsibility is confining himself to facts (in so far as they can be found) or to reasoning based on facts; in others he has the liberty of fabricating any action or picture or idea that may serve his purpose.

The principal types of factual writing are: news stories, interviews, characterizations of people, biography, history, informational articles of all kinds; and, involving reasoning upon facts, reviews, editorials, critical articles on all sorts of subjects, personal essays, and discussions of more general ideas such as demonstrations of hypotheses, theories, ideals, philosophical concepts. Whatever other qualities these articles may have, whatever their virtues or faults, they are fundamentally good or bad according as they approach the truth and correspond to some strand of human observation or experience.

515

The imaginative types, in which the writer's conception is the controlling factor, are poems, plays, short stories, novels.

falls, woods These words give trouble because though plural in form they are really singular (or collective) in meaning. In informal and colloquial usage people speak of *a falls* or *a woods*. Formal usage keeps them strictly plural or uses *a waterfall, a wood.*

famed When *famed* is used for *famous* or *well known*, it usually suggests a journalese style, or a staccato one (as in *Time*):

> famed eating place   famed Nobel prize winner
> At seven thirty we anchored off the famed yachting center.

It is often a sign of amateur writing to label as *famed* (or as *famous*, for that matter) really well known people.

Fam **Familiar English** (CORRECTION: This passage is too familiar to stand in this paper. Make it somewhat more formal.)

Familiar English is the way we speak and write for ourselves— as in diaries and notes for future work—and with or for our friends. We know that we are not going to be judged by our language, as in part we are when we speak or write for strangers, and we can use our natural, easy speech—with contractions, clipped words and abbreviated sentences, allusions to our common background that might puzzle an outsider. For others we have to approach the standards set by editors and others for the language used in carrying on public affairs, but for our friends we can use what is really a sort of shirtsleeve—but not necessarily slovenly—English, an especially informal informal sort of usage.

See "Familiar English," p. 19

farther—further In formal English some people make a distinction between *farther* and *further*, confining the first to expressions of physical distance and the second to abstract relationships of degree or quantity:

> We went on twenty miles *farther*.
> He went *farther* than I but neither of us reached the town.
> He carries that sort of thing *further* than I would.
> He went *further* into his family history.
> He got *further* and *further* into debt.

In colloquial and informal English the distinction is not kept and there seems to be a rather definite tendency for *further* to be used in all senses.

Fascism—fascist Pronounced fash′iz əm, fash′ist; rarely fas′iz əm. *Fascism, Fascist* are capitalized when they refer to Italian politics as we capitalize *Republican* and *Democrat* in this country. When the word refers to a movement in another country in which the party has a different name, it need not be capitalized but often is. When it refers to the general idea of fascist politics, or an unorganized tendency, as in the United States, it is not capitalized.

Fascisti (singular, *Fascista*) has also been anglicized in pronunciation: fə shis'ti; Italian pronunciation fä shē'stē. *Fascismo* (fä shēz'mō) is rarely used in English, *Fascism* being the translation. Compare *Nazi.

faze A word which has worked its way from dialect (*feeze*, to disturb) to good American colloquial and informal usage. It means "to daunt or disconcert" and is almost always used negatively (The rebuke did not faze him). Do not confuse this word with *phase*, meaning "aspect."

feel *Linking verbs

fellow Colloquial and informal when used to mean "person"; formal in sense of "associate." Most commonly used in writing as adjective: his fellow sufferers; a fellow feeling ("a similar feeling," or "sympathy").

female Usage now restricts *female* to designations of sex, usually in scientific contexts. This leaves English without a single word for female-human-being-regardless-of-age.

fewer *less, fewer

fiancé, fiancée About a century ago the simple English *betrothed* was replaced by the French word (probably by "society" journalists), and now we are cursed not only with accent marks but with separate forms for the man (fiancé) and the woman (fiancée). Pronunciation for both is fē'än sä', with a strong informal tendency to fē'ən sä. The plurals are fiancés, fiancées. In newspapers and much informal writing the accent mark is dropped and probably it will soon disappear generally.

field Often deadwood, as in: I plan to work in [the field of] French.

Figures of speech (CORRECTION: This figure of speech is inappropriate, inconsistent, or threadbare. Revise the passage.)

Words can be used in their usual meaning or they can be borrowed to apply to other things. We can talk of music in terms of color, or moral problems in terms of a game, and so on. Fresh and appropriate figures can help a reader see and understand what you are talking about but careless or tasteless figures detract. They may be threadbare, used as often as "a ribbon of concrete" or "old man Winter." This sentence has one trite and one fresh figure:

> The strident shriek of a siren [Trite:] split the silence and [Fresh:] two searching fingers of light swung around the corner as if feeling for the scene of the disturbance.

They may be strained and unnatural, as in this mistaken description of morning:

> Over yonder hill Apollo thrust the blade of his golden sword, severing the filmy mist that blanketed the paths of old Onondaga.

Or they may be inconsistent ("mixed") as in this mélange:

> The personnel is subject to a further boiling down to the tune that each man should be selected for the qualities that fit him for the special role he has to play.

Such figures stamp a person as an immature writer.

The effective use of figures of speech is discussed in Chapter 8, "The figurative use of words," p. 229. The most commonly used figures are described in that chapter:

Metaphors, similes, analogies, p. 235
Metonymy and synecdoche, p. 238
Irony, p. 238
Exaggeration and understatement, p. 239

The less important figures are discussed in articles:

*Alliteration
*Climax
*Epigrams (and proverbs, para-
   doxes)
*Imitative words and phrases

*Incongruous details
   (oxymoron)
*Negatives
*Personification
*Puns

Figures (1, 2, 47) *Numbers

Final consonants *Doubling final consonants

finance, financier Pronunciation of these words is divided. Take your choice among:

VERB: fi nans′, fī nans′, with a strong tendency to shift the stress to fī′nans
NOUN: fi nans′, fī nans′, fī′nans (the last conforming to the English *noun and verb stress)
NOUN: fin′ən sēr′, fī′nan sēr′; occasionally fi nan′si ər

fine A *counter word of general approval, slightly more vigorous than *nice*, but of little value in writing and better omitted:

> Spring football practice has one aim, to weld eleven men into a [fine,] coordinated team.

Fine writing   "Fine writing" is generally a term of dispraise, applied to writing that is too pretentious to be appropriate. See "Words that weaken," p. 214, and "Qualities of figures of speech," p. 231. For legitimate elevation of style see *Heightened style.

Finite verbs   A finite verb form is one that is limited (Latin *finis,* "end, limit"), that is, that can be limited in *person* (by one of the pronouns or by a subject), or in *time* (by a tense form: *had gone*), or in *number* (singular or plural). These are contrasted with the "infinite" parts, the infinitives (*go, to go, to have gone*), participles (*going, gone*), and verbal nouns (*going*) which are not limited in person or number.

   Finite verbs can be main verbs in clauses and sentences (I *had gone* before he *came*); infinite parts ordinarily cannot (Before *coming, Gone* with the wind), but see *Infinitives §4 and *Participles §4.

first   *former—first, latter—last

First draft   The preliminary version of a paper. See "Writing the first draft," p. 298 and "Paragraphs in the first draft," p. 61.

first rate—first-rate   Written with or without a hyphen. An informal and colloquial word.

fish   The plural is also *fish* (We got only six fish in the whole day's fishing), except in speaking definitely of various species of fish, as in "Most of the income of the island is from these fishes: cod, halibut, and sword."

fix   In formal usage *fix* means to "fasten in place"; in informal usage it means to "repair" or to "put in shape." *Fix* as a noun meaning "predicament" (to be in a fix) is colloquial.

flaunt—flout   *Flaunt* (flônt) to "wave, display boastfully," and *flout* (flout), to "insult, treat with contempt," are sometimes confused.

Flowery language   originally meant too figurative language, but it is now loosely used for any highflown writing.

folk—folks   Formal English, and some local speech, uses *folk* as the plural; informal and colloquial usually has *folks*, especially in the sense of "members of a family."

   Folklore and *folkway* are written as one word, *folk dance, folk music, folk tale* usually as two; and *folk song* and *folksong* are both used.

Footnotes   For the use of footnotes in research papers and for their form, see "Footnote form," p. 338.

for For distinction between *because* and *for*, see *because.

A comma is usually needed between two coordinate clauses joined by *for;* without it the *for* might be read as a preposition:

He was glad to go, for Mrs. Crane had been especially good to him. [Not: He was glad to go for Mrs. Crane . . .]

for example The conventional abbreviation for *for example* is *e. g.* (Latin *exempli gratia*). For punctuation see *namely.

Foreign words in English 1. ANGLICIZING FOREIGN WORDS. English has always borrowed words and roots freely from other languages and is still borrowing, especially from Greek and French. Most borrowed words that have been used for a long time cannot be told from native English words, but those taken in recently often raise questions. They usually cross the threshold of English with their foreign pronunciation and spelling and perhaps with un-English plurals or other forms. The process of anglicizing brings them more or less in line with English usage, but, if they are used commonly, they may keep some of their foreign quality, like the *i* of *machine*, the silent *s* in *debris*, the *t* where English is tempted to put a *d* in *kindergarten*.

Many loan words are in a transition stage, showing two spellings (*maneuver—manoeuvre, role—rôle, fiancee—fiancée*); with others we are experimenting with pronunciations, the winner not yet clearly seen (*melee:* mā lā′, mā′lā, mel′ā, and even mē′lē; *zwieback:* tsvē′bäk, tswē′bäk, swī′bak, zwī′bak). Some words that have been in English a considerable time are still changing, especially in stress (*de brē′—deb′rē, am ə tėr′—am′ə tər*) and in consonant sounds (*massage:* mə säzh′—mə säj′). These words show how a rough compromise is worked out between English practice and the original form.

The speed and degree of anglicizing depends on the frequency of use of the word, the circumstances in which it is used, and the people who use it. The attitude of linguists is that if a word proves useful it will assume a natural English form. *Hors d'oeuvre* is a useful word and not difficult to say, but its looks are conspicuously un-English. If menu makers would spell it *orderve*, we could all be happy with it.

Formal writers and conservative editors tend to keep the foreign spellings longer than informal writers and popular editors. If the words come in through the spoken language, like those of the automobile vocabulary, they usually become English or near-English sooner than if they come in by way of literature: we have *chassis* (shas′i or shas′is, sometimes chas′is), *chauffeur* (shō′fər—the spelling lagging), *garage* (gə räzh'—in England gar'ij), *detour* (dē'tür). Words that come in through and remain in literary or "polite" circles change more slowly, in both spelling and pronunciation: *tête-à-tête, faux pas, nouveau riche.*

2. USE OF BORROWED WORDS. The best reason for using an unnaturalized or partly-naturalized word is that it supplies a real lack in English, perhaps says in one word what English would have to use a phrase or sentence to express. *Entrepreneur,* "one who undertakes business, especially assumes commercial risk" is useful since the English *undertaker* has a special meaning of its own. *Beige,* "the color of unbleached wool or cotton," *suède, tableau, protégé* are useful. We have also taken in a number of words and phrases of doubtful usefulness: *entre nous,* when we have *between ourselves,* or *in confidence; affaire du coeur* for *love affair, raison d'être,* for *reason for being,* and so on. Most of the words given in the list in §4 (p. 522) are a definite convenience to users of English, but the general use of foreign words needs to be watched.

Sometimes the gain in force or tone or suggestion, as *ersatz* is stronger than *substitute,* and *liaison* brings with it either a connotation of social unconventionality or of military activity, depending on the context. *Nouveau riche* brings its suggestion of dispraise, replacing an earlier borrowing, *parvenu,* which in turn displaced the more blunt *upstart.* French words are often used for tone, especially in discussing (and more especially in advertising) women's fashions: *chic, svelte, lapin (rabbit* in other places)—and even *sacque,* which doesn't exist in French. A couple of generations ago French was used a good deal for polite social euphemisms, to avoid plain English: *demimonde, fille de joie, femme de chambre, enceinte, accouchement, double entendre.* Now these have generally gone out of use except with the falsely modest, their place once more taken by straight English. Parade of foreign words, a temptation to some who are learning a language or have just returned from abroad, is usually in bad taste, and their use even by people wholly at home with the languages is likely to be inappropriate. Fitness to material, to readers, and to the writer himself (at his natural best) will usually decide whether a foreign word should be used.

3. HANDLING BORROWED WORDS IN COPY. (*a*) *Italics.* Words which have not been completely anglicized are printed in italics in magazines and books and should be underlined in copy. Newspapers do not use italics for such purposes, and their practice of course has tended to lessen the use of italics by others. There are always many words on the borderline which will be found some-

times in italics, sometimes not. Formal writers tend to use more italics; informal, fewer. Consult a recent dictionary for doubtful words—remembering that it will represent conservative usage.

b) Accent and other marks. Words recently taken in from French are usually written with accent marks if they were so written in French. Newspapers do not use accent marks except in some departments like the editorial, art, music, and fashion pages. After they have been used for a time in English, the accents are usually dropped unless they are necessary to indicate pronunciation. *Matinee, melee, role* do not need marks; *café* does. Similarly *cañon* is now usually spelled *canyon*, but: *piñon*. A cedilla shows that a *c* before *a* or *o* is pronounced *s: façade, soupçon.*

In German all nouns are capitalized, and recent or infrequent borrowings from German are capitalized in English, usually if they are still printed in italics. *Anschluss, Realpolitik, Weltanschauung,* but *hinterland, kindergarten, blitzkrieg.*

c) Plurals. English usually brings borrowed words into its own system of conjugation and declension, though some words change slowly, especially words used most in formal writing (**formulae— formulas,* and so on). *Beaus* is now more common than *beaux,* and *tableaus* is gaining on *tableaux.* See *Plurals §4.

A few French adjectives are kept in both masculine and feminine forms: **blond—blonde, *naive—naïve* (the form *naif* is relatively rare).

d) Pronunciation. For pronunciation of borrowed words, see the examples given in the list below or consult a dictionary.

4. List of borrowed words. This list contains a small selection of loan words in fairly common use. Those in italics would ordinarily be italicized in print. When two forms are separated by a dash, they are both common. A form in square brackets is less common than the other. Pronunciations are indicated for words which might offer difficulty. A word marked with an asterisk (*) is separately discussed in an article of its own. For words not given here consult a recent dictionary. See *Pronunciation §3 for key to symbols.

agenda (ə jen′də)
aid-de-camp—aide-de-camp
  (ād′də kamp′—ād′də kän′)
*à la
à la carte
*alamode
amateur (am ə tėr′—am′ə tər)
*beau: plu. beaus [beaux]
beige (bāzh)

blitzkrieg′
*blond (masc.), blonde (fem.)
*bourgeois (būr′zhwä—
  būr zhwä′)
brassiere [brassière]
  (brə zėr′—bräs′i är′)
buffet (bù fā′)
bushido (bü′shē dō)
cadet (kə det′)

café (ka fá′)

canyon [cañon]

chassis (shas′i, shas′is [chas′is])

chic (shĕk—shik; often chik)

cliché (klē shä′—kli shä′)

coiffure (kwä fūr′)—
  coiffeur (kwä fėr′)

communiqué (kə mū′nə kā′—
  kə mū′nə kā)

connoisseur (kon′i sėr′—
  kon′i sür′)

corps, plu. corps (kōr; plu. kōrz)

coup, plu. coups (kü; plu. küz)

coup d'état (kü dä tä′)

crèche [creche] (krāsh—kresh)

crepe—crêpe (krăp)

crescendo (krə shen′dō—
  krə sen′dō)

crochet, crocheting
  (krō shā′, krō shā′ing)

curé (kü rā′)

debonair, (fem.) debonaire

debris (de brē′—deb′rē)

debut (dā′bū—dā bū′)

debutante (deb′ū tänt)

detour (dē tūr′—dē′tūr)

dirndl

Don Juan (don jü′ən—
  don hwän′)

Don Quixote (don kwik′sōt—
  don kē hō′tä)

dramatis personae
  (dram′ə tis pər sō′nē)

éclair—eclair (ā klãr′—ē′klãr)

*e. g.

ennui (än′wē)

entrepreneur

entree—entrée

ersatz

et al.

faux pas, plu. *faux pas* (fō′pä′)

fete [fête] (fāt)

*fiancé, fiancée (fē′än sā′
  [fē′ən sā])

garage (gə räzh′—gə räj′)

hari-kari (hä′ri kä′ri)

hinterland (hin′tər land′)

hors d'oeuvres (ôr dėrv′)

ibid.

*i. e.

*kindergarten

liaison (lē ä zôɴ′—lē ä′zən—
  lē′ə zən)

lingerie (lan′zhə rē—laɴ zhə rē′)

liqueur (li kėr′—li kūr′)

maneuver [manoeuvre]

massage (mə säzh′—mə säj′)

matériel—materiel

matinee (mat i nā′—mat′i nā)

mayonnaise

melee (mā lā′—mā′lā, mel′ā;
  mē′lē)

menu (men′ū—mā′nū; French
  pronunciation not current)

milieu (mē lyē′)

monsieur (mə syē′) plu. messieurs—messrs. (mes′ərz—mā-
  syē′)

moujik—muzhik (mü′zhik)

*naive [naïve]—naif sometimes
  used

negligee [négligé] (neg′li zhā—
  neg li zhā′)

nouveau riche—nouveau riche
  (nü vō rēsh′) plural: nouveaux
  riches

obbligato—obligato

papier mâché (pā′pər mə shā′)

passé (pa sā′—pas′ā)

première—premiere (prə myãr′—
  pri mēr′)

précis (prā sē′—prā′sē)

protégé, fem. protégée
  (prō′tə zhā)

pronto

quasi (kwä′sī [kwä′si])

questionnaire [questionary]
  (kwes′chən ãr′)

ragout (ra gü′)

rapport (ra pōrt′)
  en rapport (äɴ rä pōr′—
  än rä pōr′)

Realpolitik (rā äl′pō li tēk′)

rendezvous (rän′də vü—
  ren′də vü) plural: rendezvous
  (rän′də vüz—ren′də vüz)

repertoire (rep′ər twär
  [rep′ər twôr])—repertory

résumé (rā zū mā′—rez′ū mā)

revue (ri vū′)

ricochet (rik ō shā′—rik ō shet′)

*role [rôle]

salon—*salon* (sä lôɴ′)

slalom (slä′lōm)

status quo (stā′təs kwō—stat′əs-
  kwō)

523

stein (stīn)
svelte (svelt)
tableau (tab′lō—tab lō′), plural
  tableaux—tableaus (tab′lōz)
tête-à-tête (tāt′ə tāt′); accents being dropped in informal usage
via (vī′ə)

viz. (that is)
vs.—vs (versus)
Weltanschauung
  (velt′än′shou′ung)
Weltschmertz (velt′shmerts′)
zwieback (tsvē′bäk—tswē′bäk—
  [swi′bak—zwi′bak])

See *English language, *Latin and English, *Origin of words, *Plurals §4.

Matthews, Brander, "The Englishing of French Words," Society for Pure English *Tracts*, 1920, v, 3-20; Palfrey, T. R., "The Contribution of Foreign Language Study to Mastery of the Vernacular," *Modern Language Journal*, 1941, pp. 550-57.

Formal correspondence *Social correspondence

Form **Formal English** (CORRECTION: The word or passage marked is too formal for the subject or for the style of the rest of the paper. Revise, making it more informal.)

Formal English is the level of usage characteristic of people who work a good deal with books, in general of members of the various professions. It is appropriate for discussions of ideas, for scientific and scholarly writing, for addresses to audiences of some education, for literary works that are intended for a somewhat restricted reading public. Formal English is not so appropriate for day-to-day speaking and writing, for accounts of personal experience, casual comment, and other sorts of writing intended for the general reading public.

For discussion and examples, see "Formal English," p. 25, and for its appropriateness, see Ch. 2. See also *Heightened style.

Form of manuscript See "Preparing the manuscript," p. 303.

former—first, latter—last *Former* and *latter* refer to a group of only two units:

> The mountain and the squirrel
> Had a quarrel,
> And the former called the latter, "little prig";
> > RALPH WALDO EMERSON, *Fable*

First, last refer to items in a series, usually of more than two:

> The first president had set up a very informal organization.
> His last act was to advise his family on their future.

Latest refers to a series that is still continuing (the latest fashions). *Last* refers either to the final item of a completed series (their last attempt was successful) or to the most recent item of a continuing series (the last election).

Forms of discourse For the last hundred years or so it has been conventional to divide writing into "four forms of discourse"— Narration, Description, Exposition, and Argument. This division allows concentration on certain traits of material, organization, and style peculiar to each type. It is now less used than formerly because the types are rarely found in a pure state—description contributes to all, notably to narration, and so on—and a person does not think of himself as writing one of these forms but rather a particular sort of article or type of literature.

This book divides writing into two broad types, Factual Writing (biography, history, informational and critical articles and books of all sorts) and Imaginative Writing (poems, plays, short stories, novels).

*Factual and imaginative writing

formula Plural *formulas* or *formulae*, the former now the more common

Formulas Every language has some phrases that have become fixed by long usage in certain situations: *once upon a time, Ladies and gentlemen, Good morning, How are you? Yours truly*. Occasionally fresh substitutes can be found for these but more often the attempt merely calls attention to itself. Such phrases, though stereotyped, are too useful to be called trite, and they are not, as most trite expressions are, substitutes for some simpler locution. They should be used without apology and without embarrassment whenever they are needed.

Fractions Fractions are written in figures when they are attached to other figures (72¾), or are in a series that is being written in figures (½, ⅔, 1, 2, 4 . . .), or are in tables or reference matter. Usually in consecutive writing they are written in words. Hyphens may be used between the numerator and denominator if neither part itself contains a hyphen, but they are less used than formerly and are not used at all when the numerator has the value of an adjective (as in "He sold one half and kept the other").

seven tenths, or seven-tenths
eight twenty-sevenths   twenty-nine fortieths

Decimals are increasingly used in place of fractions in expository writing, since they are more flexible and may be more accurate. They are always written in figures:

.7   .42   3.14159

*Numbers

Frag **Fragmentary sentence** (CORRECTION: The construction marked is not a complete sentence. Revise by completing its form, by joining to a neighboring sentence, or by rewriting the passage.)

A fragmentary sentence is a sentence part carelessly or ineffectively punctuated as a whole sentence. By their form phrases and subordinate clauses suggest dependence on another construction and usually they require the independent statement to complete their meaning. Ordinarily one should be joined to the preceding or following sentence or made into an independent sentence. Since they are almost always careless in college writing, they are one of the most serious errors and should be avoided.

Three common types with suggested revision follow:

FRAGMENTARY SENTENCE	REVISED
Since 1939 we had been walking slowly in the direction of war. [Phrase:] Step by step until finally there was no other alternative but to declare war.	Since 1939 we had been walking slowly in the direction of war, step by step, until there was no other alternative but to declare war.
He talked the whole fifty minutes without taking his eyes off his notes. [Participial phrase:] Apparently not noticing that half the class was asleep.	He talked the whole fifty minutes without taking his eyes off his notes. Apparently he did not notice that half the class was asleep.
The first six books I looked for couldn't be taken out of the library. [Subordinate clause:] Because they were on reserve for an advanced history course.	The first six books I looked for couldn't be taken out of the library because they were on reserve for an advanced history course.

For further discussion and other examples of fragmentary sentences, see "Fragmentary sentences," p. 134. See also *Dependent clause, *Phrases. For exercises on "Fragmentary sentences," see p. 252. See also *Contact clauses.

French words See *Foreign words in English.

freshman, freshmen These words are pronounced alike (fresh′-mən), so that their spelling is often confused, not so often when they are used as nouns (a freshman, forty freshmen) as when *freshman* is used as an adjective (freshman class, freshman spirit). *Freshmen* should never stand before a noun in this construction.

It is not usually necessary to capitalize *freshman* (or *sophomore, junior, senior*) but courtesy or emphasis often makes a capital appropriate, and very often one is used when speaking of the Freshman Class, the Junior Class, as a definite organization.

Friendly letters *Letters §2

-ful, full When the adjective *full* is used as a suffix to nouns of measure (*basketful, spoonful*) or of feeling or quality (*peaceful, sorrowful, soulful*) it has only one *l*.

The plural of nouns made with *-ful* is usually made with *-s*: *spoonfuls, basketfuls* (or *basketsful*). *spoonful, spoonfuls

Function words **1.** Some words contribute relatively little to the meaning of a statement, serving rather to indicate relationships, to point out grammatical functions. Some such words are:

a) *Prepositions*, which join nouns to other words in a construction; the *of* in the phrase form of the genitive (of the man) is conspicuously a functional word.

b) *Conjunctions*, which show the relation between clauses

c) *Auxiliary verbs* (*shall* go, *has* gone, *did* go) and *linking verbs (He *is* smart, She *looks* well.)

d) *Pronouns*, which besides identifying persons or things refer from one statement to a preceding

e) *Some adverbs and adjectives*, most conspicuously *more* and *most* in comparisons of adjectives and adverbs (more handsome, most handsome)

2. STYLISTIC QUALITIES OF FUNCTION WORDS. Different levels of usage have some characteristic habits in the use of function words. Formal style, for instance, tends to keep relative pronouns, while colloquial and informal style is likely to omit them:

INFORMAL: Is there such a thing as *modern* prose, with characteristics the older prose does not possess?—BONAMY DOBRÉE, *Modern Prose Style*, p. 210

FORMAL: Is there such a thing as *modern* prose, with characteristics [which] the older prose does not possess?

The more elaborate sentences of formal English tend to make appropriate heavier connectives, such as *conjunctive adverbs (*however, accordingly* . . .); informal style tends to rely more on coordinating conjunctions (*but, for, and* . . .) and subordinating conjunctions (*although, because, since* . . .).

Colloquial English shows a good many compound or group prepositions, for many of which formal English would use a single preposition: *in back of* (*behind*); *in regard to* (*about*). Too many of these long connectives tend to give a rather weak movement to a sentence and a rhythm without many strong stresses. In rapid speech they are passed over easily but they sometimes become conspicuous in writing (See *Rhythm).

Functional words change a good deal from time to time. Consider this passage from the King James Version of the Bible (1611):

> Who comforteth us in all our tribulation, that [so that] we may be able to comfort them which [who] are in any trouble, by the comfort wherewith [with or by which] we ourselves are comforted of [by] God.—2 Corinthians 1:4

Particular points about the use of function words are made in various articles dealing with specific words or types of words; this article merely suggests that they are worth watching for both linguistic and stylistic reasons.

Reference: Fries, Chapters 7-9

Fundamentals The selection of what are to be regarded as fundamentals in estimating a piece of writing depends on judgment, and judgments vary. In this book the fundamentals are taken to be the following, the most important first:

The material presented is the most fundamental factor and deserves most consideration in the process of writing and most weight in criticizing and evaluating a piece of writing. Nothing can take the place of important and interesting material, though its values can be increased or diminished by the treatment.

The method and attitude of the writer is of next importance. He may use too few details or too many, he may select them according to an intelligent or an unwise or biased principle, he may have an exaggerated idea of the importance of his subject, or approach it with too much or too little sentiment, reverence, humor, realism.

The plan of an article, *the plot* of a story are important, since in part through them the writer guides the reader to see his sense of the matter. Too slow a beginning, too trivial an end are serious faults, as is lack of relation shown between parts.

Finally a piece of writing is affected by the *mechanics and style* of the writer, which may either hinder the reader or increase his satisfaction. Poor material presentably written has no future, but worth-while material even if poorly written can with sufficient work be made presentable.

We consciously or unconsciously make some such balancing of qualities in deciding what we think of what we read. Realizing the relative worth of these qualities makes it easier for student and teacher to understand each other's judgments.

Fundamental sentence errors See *Comma fault, "Incomplete sentences," p. 131; *Fragmentary sentences, p. 134, "Run-on sentences," p. 136, and Exercises, p. 252.

funny In formal English *funny* means only "comical," "laughable"; in informal, colloquial, and vulgate English it means also (and almost instead) "odd": "That's funny. I thought he did."

further See *farther—further.

Future tense, future perfect tense *shall—will; *Tenses of verbs

G G, like *c*, spells a "hard" and a "soft" sound. The hard sound, in words chiefly of Old English and Germanic origin, is more common than the soft, which is found chiefly in words from Latin and French.

1. *Hard g* (g). G is hard before *a, o*, and *u* (except in the British *gaol* [*jail*]): *garrulous, gong, gutter;* when doubled: *doggerel, noggin, toboggan;* at the ends of words: *beg, dig, fig;* it is hard, exceptionally, in *get*, and frequently before *i: begin, gill* (of a fish), *gig;* and it is hard before another consonant in the same syllable: *togs.*

Gh spells hard *g*, properly in *ghetto*, uselessly in *aghast* and *ghost.* The *g* would be hard anyway before the *a* and *o.*

Gu, taken from French, spells hard *g: guard, guess, guide, guernsey.*

2. *Soft g* (j) is found typically before *e* and *i: gem, gentleman, genus, gill* (the measure), *gibbet, gin.* It is often spelled *ge* or *dge: age* (āj), *edge* (ej), *fudge* (fuj).

3. G is sometimes pronounced *zh*, chiefly in partly anglicized words from French: *garage, massage, mirage.* These words tend to have soft *g* after they have been in English a long time (*carriage, marriage*): *garage* is often gə räj′ (in England, gar′ij); *massage* is tending toward mə säj′.

4. *Silent g.* Initial *g* is silent in *gnaw, gnat, gnome, gnu* . . . and *g* is often silent before *m* or *n: diaphragm, sign.* It becomes sounded in some derivatives of this latter type of word: *signal.*

5. "*Dropping g's.*" In formal usage the present participle ends in the consonant sound that is spelled *ng;* in vulgate and in much colloquial English present participles are ended in *n: singin', laughin'.* This is usually referred to as "dropping g's," though actually there is no *g* sound involved but two different nasal consonants. The form in *n* is the older. Originally the present participle ended in *-and* and later in *-en* or *-in*, and this has always been the form for the majority of speakers of English. In the speech of London and vicinity, which became the basis of written English, the present participle was confused with the verbal noun, ending

in *-ung*. Now everyone *writes* the participle with *-ing* but many continue the old pronunciation with *-in*. (See Milton Ellis, *English Journal*, 1937, xxvi, 753.) Compare **ng*.

Gathering material See "Gathering material," p. 294, and for gathering material for a research paper, Ch. 13, §§ 3-5, p. 324.

geisha is a noun, so that *geisha girl* is redundant, but commonly used. Pronounced gā′shə. Plural, *geisha* or *geishas*.

Gender Gender is the indication in language of sex or sexlessness. Many languages have special endings for masculine, feminine, and neuter nouns and for adjectives modifying them, but English abandoned this system several hundred years ago. Now, except in pronouns and a few nouns with endings such as *-ess, -us, -a, -or, -ix, -e, -eus, -euse* (*actress, mistress, alumnus, alumna, actor, aviator, aviatrix, administratrix, blonde, commedienne, masseur, masseuse*) gender is indicated only by the meaning of a word: *man—woman, nephew—niece, rooster—hen*. . . . Compounds, partly to show gender, partly for emphasis, are common and expressive: *she-witch, he-bear, boy friend, girl friend*. Nouns referring to inanimate objects are neuter. Often gender is indicated only when a singular pronoun is used:

> The speaker hesitated, choosing *his* next words deliberately.
> The novelist has presented *her* chief character effectively.

In formal, literary English there is a sort of personification (or animation) in which the sun or moon or a ship or almost any object may be referred to as *he* ("The sun sent forth his cheering beams") or more often as *she* ("The brig made her way sturdily through the mountainous waves"). In colloquial and vulgate usage this plays a still greater part. Pronouns are frequently used, especially if intimacy or affection is involved: a car or a college or a country or any object may be a *she*.

We need a pronoun to represent either-he-or-she. Referring to a baby or an animal of unknown sex, *it* is the usual solution; otherwise *he*. See **he-or-she*, **blond, blonde*, **naive—naïve*.

Genitive case (CORRECTION: Correct the form of the genitive case marked. [Usually this means using an apostrophe.])

   1. The genitive (or possessive) case in English is formed in three ways:

   a) *The s-genitive.* *'s* is the spelling of the genitive case of all nouns in which the case is pronounced with an added sound (s or z) and of all pronouns except the personal (*I, you, he* . . .) and relatives (*who, which, that*):

boy's horse's   one's somebody's
men's brother-in-law's   King of England's

An apostrophe alone may be added to words that already end in an *s- sh-* or *z-* sound, as in regularly made plurals:

horses'   Moses' *Jones' (singular)
Joneses' (plural) coaches' conscience' (for conscience' sake)

Words of one syllable ending in these sounds seem increasingly to have *'s*, pronounced as an added syllable:

Charles' (chärlz)—Charles's (chärl′zəz) coach's (kōch əz)
fish's (fish′əz) Zeus' (zūs) or Zeus's (zūs′əz)

The *s*-genitive stands before the noun it limits (the doctor's first case), but it may be in the predicate position with no noun expressed (The criticism is Smith's).

When two coordinate nouns are in the genitive, the sign of the case is added only to the last one in informal usage:

Fred and Bert's first attempt. [FORMAL: Fred's and Bert's]
He had never thought of his wife and children's future.

b) *The of-genitive:* He had never known the love of a child (= a child's love); the plays of Shakespeare.

The *of*-genitive always stands after the noun it limits: the leaves of the tree (vs. the tree's leaves).

The *of*-genitive is rather more common with names of inanimate objects than the *s*-genitive is, but both are used; the *s*-genitive is the more common form with names of people, though both are used:

the car's rattles the rattles of the car
a stone's throw the flowers of the field
a day's work the work of a lifetime
Doctor Clark's house the house of Doctor Clark

In most instances sound—euphony and rhythm—of the phrase decides whether the *s*- or *of*-genitive is used. The *of*-form is longer, often fits into sonorous and emotional phrases (at the home of Doctor Clark), and allows a more characteristic English rhythm than the compact *s*-genitive.

There is also a possible difference of meaning between the two forms. "Miss Rutherford's picture" would usually mean a picture belonging to Miss R., though it might mean a picture of Miss R. "A picture of Miss Rutherford" can mean only that Miss R. is represented in the picture.

c) *Double genitive.* Using both the *s*- and *of*-genitives together is an English idiom of long and respectable standing. It is especially common in locutions beginning with *that* or *this* and usually has a colloquial flavor:

that boy of Henry's   these hobbies of Miss Filene's
friends of my father's   no friend of ours

An older genitive made with *his* following the noun (the doctor his reasons = the doctor's reasons) is now obsolete though it is sometimes used in bookplates: John Oates—His Book.

d) *Genitive of the personal pronouns.* The personal and relative pronouns have genitive forms without an apostrophe:

| my | your | his | her | its | our | your | their | whose |

It is as important not to put apostrophes in these pronouns as it is to put one in a noun in the genitive. See *Pronouns §1, *its, *which, *who.

2. Uses of the genitive. The most common function of the genitive is to indicate possession:

the professor's house   my son   Bert's wife

The genitive also indicates a number of other relationships:

Description: a man's job children's toys suit of wool
Doer of an act ("Subjective Genitive"): the wind's force
    the force of the wind Sinclair Lewis' second novel with the dean's
    permission with the permission of the dean
[The subjective genitive is usual with gerunds:] The doctor's coming
    relieved the strain. *Gerund
Recipient of an act ("Objective Genitive"): the policeman's
    murderer the murderer of the policeman the bill's defeat
Adverb: He drops in of an evening.

More details of these and other genitive relations will be found in the large grammars.

References: Curme, *Parts of Speech*, pp. 133-36, *Syntax*, pp. 70-88; Fries, pp. 72-88

Genteelism See *Euphemisms.

gentleman *man, woman

German words *Foreign words in English

Ger **Gerund** (Correction: Make the construction with this gerund correct and idiomatic.)

1. Form and use. A *gerund*, or *verbal noun*, is the form of the verb ending in *-ing* when used as a noun. It has the same form as the present participle but differs in use.

Gerund: *Running* a hotel appealed to him.

PARTICIPLE: *Running* around the corner, he bumped into a cop. (*Running* modifies *he*.)

Broncho Bill Schindler started the ball *rolling* [participle, modifying *ball*] by *crashing* [gerund] into the heavy guard rail.

A gerund may take an object (as in *running a hotel*) or a complement (*being a hero*), and it may serve any of the functions of a noun:

SUBJECT: ·*Looking* for an apartment always fascinated her.
OBJECT: He taught *dancing*.
PREDICATE NOUN: Seeing is *believing*.
ADJECTIVE USE: a *fishing* boat (a boat for fishing, not a boat that fishes)

When not in one of these constructions a gerund is related to the rest of the sentence by a preposition (§3).

Gerunds may be modified by adjectives when the noun function is uppermost, or by adverbs when the verb function is more emphasized:

ADJECTIVE: *Good boxing* is first-rate entertainment.
ADVERB: *Boxing well* was his great pride. ·

2. SUBJECT OF A GERUND. The subject of a gerund is sometimes in the genitive and sometimes in the accusative case. In formal writing the genitive is more common, in informal writing, the accusative.

a) When the subject is a personal pronoun or a word standing for a person, it is usually in the genitive:

His coming was all that she looked forward to.
She looked forward to *Bob's coming*.

b) If the subject is a plural noun, it is likely to be in the accusative:

I don't approve of *men drinking*.
I don't approve of *students coming and going* as they like.
WITH A PRONOUN: I don't approve of *them drinking*, or I don't approve of *their drinking*.

c) If the subject is abstract or the name of an inanimate object, it is usually accusative:

It was a case of *imagination getting* out of control.
The *roof* [or *roof's*] *falling in* was only the first disaster.

d) When the subject is modified by other words, it is accusative:

In spite of the *plan* of the committee *being voted down* no one could offer a better one.
The principal's *contract running out* gave them an excuse for letting him go.

e) When the subject is stressed, it is usually in the accusative, even if it is a pronoun:

> Who would have thought of *him* [stressed] *getting* the prize?
> Have you heard about *Gertrude* [stressed] *getting* a job?

3. PHRASES WITH GERUNDS. Gerunds are frequently used in phrases:

> *In coming to an agreement,* they had compromised on all points.
> It's the best thing *for coughing at night.*

The gerund phrase should modify the word the writer intends it to:

MISRELATED: *In coming to an agreement,* a compromise had to be voted. (The compromise did not come to the agreement, but *they* or some other word meaning the voters.)

MISRELATED: *After reading sixteen books,* the subject is still a blank to me.

ACCURATE: *After reading sixteen books,* I am still blank about the subject.

4. THE AND GERUNDS. In current style there is a tendency to use gerunds without *the* and with a direct object rather than an *of*-phrase. This emphasizes the verbal phase of the word and makes for economy and force.

> His chief amusement is *telling jokes* on Roosevelt.
> [Rather than: His chief amusement is *the telling of jokes* on Roosevelt.]
> In *revising the first draft,* a writer can check all the spellings.
> [Rather than: In *the revising of the first draft.*]

5. IDIOMS WITH GERUNDS. Many words are followed by gerunds, others with infinitives. For example:

GERUNDS	INFINITIVES
cannot help *doing*	compelled *to do*
capable *of painting*	able *to paint*
the duty *of paying*	obligation *to pay*
the habit *of giving*	the tendency *to give*
an idea *of selling*	a wish *to sell*
his object *in doing*	his design *to do*

Compare *Participles, *Infinitives.
Reference: Curme, *Syntax,* Chapter 24

get, got 1. PRINCIPAL PARTS: *get, got, got* or *get, got, gotten:*

> I am getting a new racket.
> I got six inside of an hour.
> I had already got [gotten] mine.

Rebel though I was, I had got the religion of scholarship and science.—LINCOLN STEFFENS, *Autobiography*, p. 127

Gotten was brought to America by the colonists of the seventeenth century, when it was the usual English form, and has remained in general American usage ever since, while in England the form has given way to *got*. Today both forms are used by Americans as the past participle, the choice between them depending largely on the emphasis and rhythm of the particular sentence.

2. GET AS A LINKING VERB. *Get* is one of the most popular verbs in idiomatic phrases, in most of which it doesn't have its original meaning shown in the sentences under §1, but is a relatively colorless linking verb. Most of these idioms are colloquial or vulgate, and some are slang:

get cold	get sick	get tired	get scared
get going	get to go	get in touch with	
get left	get on my nerves	get away with	
get me?	get it across	get together	

"But I got to," she cried. "I just have to talk to somebody. I didn't go home. I got worried, awful scared. . . ."—ARTHUR SOMERS ROCHE, *Shadow of Doubt*, p. 93

Got is also redundant—and so generally confined to colloquial and vulgate usage—in expressions like "Have you got a pencil?" "I've got to study now." "Have you a pencil?" and "I have to study now" mean just as much and sound more formal—but in free and easy speech the *got* adds a little emphasis, being more vigorous than *have*. Ordinarily in writing these constructions are confined to dialog.

3. GET AS AN AUXILIARY. *Get* is increasingly used as an informal emphatic passive auxiliary:

He got thrown out inside of an hour.
Our house is getting painted.
We all got punished on Friday.

See Curme, *Parts of Speech*, p. 218.

ghost writer A person who writes for another, the latter usually signing and taking the credit.

Given names Ordinarily either spell out or use the initial of given names (rather than such abbreviations as *Chas.*, *Thos.*, *Wm.*):

F. T. Graves	or	Frederick T. Graves
T. W. Lane	or	Thomas W. Lane

gladiolus A revealing example of *divided usage. The singular is pronounced glə dī′o ləs or glad i ō′ləs, and commonly, especially among florists, glad i ō′lə, the plural glə dī′o lī, gla di ō′lī, glad i ō′-ləs iz, and (of *gladiola*), glad i ō′ləz. Gla dī′o lus is the closest to the word's Latin origin and is usual with botanists for the name of the genus. The *clips *glad* or *glads* are a way out of the confusion.

glamor, glamour *Glamor* is probably the more usual spelling, though *glamour* was one of few *-our* words to survive in the United States and will still be found. (Compare *savior.*) The adjective would always be *glamorous.*

go 1. *Go* is a useful little word, especially as a *linking verb in a number of idioms, most of them colloquial:

go blind	go on! (= I don't believe you!)
go back on	go in for

2. *Go and* is a colloquial form of emphasis: Go and try it your-self (no actual movement meant); She went and shot the bear her-self. These are primarily oral expressions but they would be appro-priate in some informal writing.

3. *Going on* in stating ages (seven, going on eight) is a colloquial and familiar idiom—more vigorous than the formal "between seven and eight."

good—well *Good* is an adjective, *well* is either an adjective or an adverb: I feel *good* and I feel *well* (adjectives) are both usual but have different connotations (*good* implying actual bodily sensa-tion, *well* referring merely to a state, "not ill").

In vulgate usage *well* is rarely used, *good* taking its place ("He rowed good" for "He rowed well"). Avoid this usage.

good-by—good-bye Both are in use—and the hyphen is dropping out in informal use: *goodbye, goodby.*

Good English Good English is language that is effective for a par-ticular communication, that is appropriate to the subject and situa-tion, to the listener or reader, and to the speaker or writer. When the g is capitalized in this book (Good English), this more or less technical meaning is intended (otherwise, good English).

See Chapter 2, p. 35.

grade school—graded school *Graded school* is the formal word but *grade school* is much more common, and always appropriate.

graduate The idiom *to be graduated from* an institution has gen-erally gone out of use except in formal and somewhat archaic writ-ing, replaced by *graduated from:*

He graduated from Yale in 1902.

Grammar *Grammar* is a word of various applications. It is used to mean the actual form of a language, "the English way of saying things." It is also used to apply to a systematic description of the ways of language or of a language. Sometimes it is used to mean practically the whole of linguistic science; sometimes it includes only a few arbitrarily selected topics in language. Usually it includes at least the study of *the forms of words, the parts of speech, syntax* (constructions), and frequently *the derivation of words* and *pronunciation*. A particular "grammar" is a selection of the facts of language that suits the writer's purpose. Only the grammars in several volumes, like those of Jespersen and of Curme, approach anything like a complete description of English.

1. SCIENTIFIC GRAMMAR. There are three types of scientific grammatical study:

a) *Descriptive grammar* aims to present the facts of a particular language, gathered from systematic observation of speaking and writing, describing the forms of words, spellings, pronunciations, constructions in actual use, without attempting to guide the language habits of speakers and writers—though obviously serving as the basis for such guidance.

b) *Comparative grammar* studies the forms and constructions of a set of related languages, as Greek, Latin, German, English, and the other Indo-European languages, to show their earlier history.

c) *Historical grammar* studies the evolution of the words and syntax of a language, usually explaining present forms and usage in the light of the past.

Sometimes *philosophical grammar* is spoken of, as in Jespersen's title *The Philosophy of Grammar*. It means a presentation of general principles, equivalent to *linguistic theory*.

2. PRESCRIPTIVE GRAMMAR. Besides these types of scientific grammar we also speak of *prescriptive grammar*, called also *normative grammar*. A prescriptive grammar is a body of rules presented as guides to expression, statements of how, in the belief of the writer, people should speak and write. Many English grammars of this type, represented principally by textbooks prepared for the use of students, are now in disrepute because they are far out of touch with scientific grammar and with actual usage. Too many school grammars represent either older usage or traditional rules that are not consistently followed and some that have never been followed by users of English. Typically they present formal English as though it was the only English and definitely discourage informal and colloquial usage, which occupy the center stage in the scientific grammars.

537

One unfortunate result of prescriptive grammar is that the teaching of formal English has seemed so unreal to students, who, unable to separate the useful from the useless advice they receive, have paid almost no attention at all to their teaching. If they talked as their textbooks said they should, they would be laughed at; consequently they have usually continued their natural colloquial or even vulgate speech.

Although the usage recommended in schools will probably always be a little behind that being practiced by actual writers, school grammar is now gradually getting away from traditional prescriptive grammar and is coming closer in line with the picture of actual usage presented by scientific grammars.

3. GRAMMATICAL TERMS. Many people steadfastly refuse to learn the technical terms of grammar. Students who gaily toss about *schizophrenic, marginal utility, Hanseatic League, dicotyledonous,* or *trinitrotoluene* will not learn the pronunciation and meaning of *parataxis, predicate adjective, subjunctive, metonymy,* or even *apostrophe* or *agreement*—and some teachers of the subject try to work without naming exactly what they are talking about. Many of the words are a bit difficult—Greek or Latin names that have been taken into the language—but they are not nearly so difficult as the vocabulary of psychology or chemistry. It is true that grammatical nomenclature has been in a sorry way and that commissions in both England and the United States have not been able to standardize names for many of the facts of our language, but there is a large and useful vocabulary for discussing language and style, a vocabulary that is absolutely necessary if we are to discuss in any detail our own and others' writing.

This book uses a good many of these terms, without apology, though when there is a choice of name usually the simpler and more suggestive has been taken. It is only good sense to gain control of the words that name common facts of usage and style.

See p. 38; *Linguistics; *Latin and English § 4.

References: The works in the bibliography at the beginning of this *Guide-Index,* specifically Fries and Pooley, discuss many of the particular rules of prescriptive grammar besides offering their own observation of usage; see especially Fries, Chs. 1, 2, 11, and Ballard, who shows a similar attack on traditional grammar in England.

grand *Counter words

gray is much more common spelling than *grey,* but both are used.

Greek alphabet The first college societies, usually for both social and intellectual aims, were formed when Greek was a prominent subject in the course of study. Many of them had Greek names or Greek mottoes and referred to themselves by the abbreviations for these words: Phi Beta Kappa (ΦΒΚ) for Φιλοσοφία Βίου Κυβερνήτης, ("Philosophy is the guide of life"). Their descendant societies, although very few of their members know the Greek language, are still "Greek letter societies."

Recent scientists have sometimes used Greek letters to name members of a series, as *alpha- beta-, gamma-rays.*

Neither the classical nor the English names of these letters are used consistently in fraternity names or other uses of Greek letters in English. Even in the pronunciation of *Phi Beta Kappa* the two systems are mixed: fī (English) bātə (classical) kapə (English). This worries a few purists, but usage is the guide in language and the prevalent pronunciation should be followed. The accompanying table may be helpful.

THE GREEK ALPHABET

GREEK LETTERS CAPITAL	SMALL	ENGLISH EQUIVALENT	NAME OF THE LETTER	CLASSICAL	ENGLISH (†Marks One More Used)
A	α	a	alpha	älfa (alfa)	†al′fə
B	β	b	beta	†bātə	bē′tə
Γ	γ	g	gamma	gäma (gama)	†gam′ə
Δ	δ	d	delta	delta	del′tə
E	ε	e	epsilon	epsilon	ep′si lon
Z	ζ	z (dz)	zeta	†zātə	zē′tə
H	η	a (ä)	eta	†ātə	ē′tə
Θ	θ	th (thin)	theta	†thātə	thē′tə
I	ι	ē	iota	ēōta	†ī ō′tə
K	κ	k	kappa	käpa	†kap′ə
Λ	λ	l	lambda	lämda	†lam′də
M	μ	m	mu	mü	†mū
N	ν	n	nu	nü	†nū
Ξ	ξ	x (ks)	xi	†ksē	zī
O	ο	o	omicron	omikron	om′i kron
Π	π	p	pi	pē	†pī
P	ρ	r	rho	rō	rō
Σ	σ s[1]	s	sigma	sigma	sig′mə
T	τ	t	tau	tou	†tô

[1] s is used at the end of a word, elsewhere σ.

Υ	υ	y (u)	upsilon	üpsilon	†ŭp′si lon
Φ	φ	f (ph)	phi	fē	†fī
Χ	χ	ch	chi	chē (Ger. ch)	†kī
Ψ	ψ	ps	psi	psē	†sī
Ω	ω	ō	omega	†ōmāga	ō mĕg′ə

grill—grille The cooking device and the eating place are spelled *grill* (*grille* only in attempts at a fancy name). The decorative iron work is spelled either *grille* or *grill*.

Group words In English many groups of two or more words (that is, phrases) function as though they were single words. *High school* is not the noun *school* modified by the adjective *high* so much as a noun in its own right; it might well be spelled as a single word (and sometimes is). Many of our verbs are made up of a verb plus an adverb: *close up, hold off, look into* (*Verb-adverb combinations); many prepositions are phrases: *according to, in opposition to, by means of.*

Other typical group words are:

NOUNS: hay fever back door holding company home run
safety razor baby blue school year sacrifice hit express train
VERBS: dig in back water back step (military) flare up
follow through follow up show up blow up
PREPOSITIONS: in spite of in consequence of previous to due to

"In such cases," Professor Krapp says, "it is contrary to the idiom of the language to try to analyze the groups into their constituent parts so as to give every word, standing alone, a clearly defined structural value" (*Modern English*, p. 315). Consequently in this book we ignore the superficial difference between a part of speech that is one word and one that is a group of words. "Noun" or "verb" or "preposition" refers to both the single words and to a *group word* functioning as noun or verb or preposition.

References: Curme, *Syntax*, Ch. 30; Krapp, pp. 313-16 (where he calls such phrases "function groups")

guarantee—guaranty *Guarantee* is the usual spelling, and is right in all senses.

guess *calculate, guess, reckon

gymnasium *Gym* is the common colloquial *clip.

gypsy—gipsy Spelling is divided, partly because the odd appearance of the two *y*'s is shifting the spelling to *gipsy*. Capitalize as the name of a specific people and use lower case for the sense merely of "wanderer." Compare *pigmy—pygmy*.

H **1.** The *h* (h) sound always occurs at the beginning of sylla-bles: *harsh, heel, high, horrible, ahead.*

2. *H* is likely to be silent at the beginning of unstressed syllables: *forehead* (for'əd), *behind* (when spoken rapidly in unstressed part of phrase, bē ĭnd'), *he, his, her,* etc., when lightly spoken (Give it to *him'* vs. *Give'* it to [h]im).

H is silent in *rh* words—*rhetoric, rhyme, rhythm.*

In many words from French the *h* was formerly not pronounced: *habit, history, hotel* . . . but now is except in *heir, honest, honor, hour.* So long as the *h* was not pronounced, *an* was used before these words and it is still by some people in the forms in which the stress is not on the first syllable: *an historical work, an habitual error,* though *a* is now much more common. See **a, an.*

3. In words like *huge* and *humor* many people drop the *h,* leav-ing ūj and ū'mər.

4. W*h* spells the sound of *hw except in whole, who, whoop: when* (hwen). See **wh.*

Habitual action W*ould* is the typical auxiliary for habitual action in the past, especially in formal English:

He would always go by the longer way.

Habitual action is also expressed by *used to* or by an adverb:

He used to go by the longer way.
He usually went by the longer way.

Hackneyed A term describing an overused word or phrase. See "Trite words," p. 214.

had better, had rather *Had better* is the usual idiom for giving advice or making an indirect command:

You had better take care of that cold.   You'd better go.

Had rather and *would rather* are both used to express preference:

He would rather ski than eat. He had rather ski than eat. Since the *had* or *would* is unstressed in speech (and the contraction *he'd* often used), it is hard to tell which is being said. Informally a shorter form without *had* is common ("If he asks you to do it, you [ ] better do it"). This would be written only in a definitely light style (as in *The New Yorker*).

half The more formal idiom is *a half,* the informal *half a:*

INFORMAL: He ran half a mile; half an hour.
FORMAL: He ran a half mile; a half hour.

541

A *half a* (a half an hour) is a redundancy, characteristic of careless colloquial or vulgate usage.

hangar So spelled. Pronounced usually hang′ər, sometimes hang′-gär.

hanged—hung In formal English the principal parts of *hang* when referring to the death penalty are *hang, hanged, hanged,* the archaic forms kept alive by legal phrases such as "hanged by the neck until dead"; in other senses they are *hang, hung, hung*: Murderers are *hanged,* pictures are *hung.*

Informal usage does not keep this distinction, using *hang, hung, hung* in all senses:

> They hung the Turk that invented work
> In the Big Rock Candy Mountain.

In the passive *hang* may mean "to have a picture hung in an exhibition":

> If you frittered your good daylight away chaffing with sparrows, how could you ever get hung anywhere?

happen At present an overworked qualifying verb:

> When I finally got off in Oakland it happened to be raining.
> As it happened, I passed the physics test but flunked the history.
> One of the most interesting plays I have read in a long time was assigned in my English course; the play happened to be *Justice* by John Galsworthy.

All these *happen*'s are *deadwood and could be dropped with gain in neatness and no loss in meaning.

hardly *Double negative §3

have 1. As a verb of independent meaning *have* means to "own, possess," in a literal (have a car) or transferred sense (have the measles). There are many idioms with *have,* such as:

> to have a look   the book (or gossip . . .) has it that
> have it your own way   to have it out (in a fight)
> to have the ocean in view (or in front)

INFORMAL: He had his arm broken. He had a broken arm.
FORMAL: He suffered a broken arm.

2. As an auxiliary *have* plus a past participle makes the perfect tense (They have come); *shall* or *will have* plus a past participle makes the future perfect tense (They will have gone by then); *had* plus a past participle makes the past perfect (They had gone to the beach before we arrived). See *Tenses of verbs.

3. CONTRACTIONS. In speech, *he, she, it has* are contracted to *he's, she's, it's* (He's not tried to in years; It's rained for over a

week.), and *I, you, we, they have* are contracted to *I've, you've, we've, they've.*

Would have, wouldn't have are sometimes written *would of, wouldn't of,* an erroneous attempt to represent what is spoken as *would've, wouldn't've.* Compare *could have, might have.*

In vulgate usage the redundant "If he'd have tried" (If he would have tried) is a common idiom for "If he'd tried," but it would not be written except in reproducing conversation.

4. *Had ought* and *hadn't ought* are vulgate idioms, redundant but emphatic:

VULGATE: He had ought to take better care of himself.
MORE FORMAL: He ought to take better care of himself.
VULGATE: He hadn't ought to lie like that.
MORE FORMAL: He ought not to [shouldn't] lie like that.

5. *Have got.* For the redundant colloquial and vulgate *have got* see *get §2.

6. *Had better.* See *had better.

healthful, healthy *Healthful* means "giving health"; *healthy* means "having health." Persons, animals are *healthy;* places, food are *healthful.*

height—heighth Vulgate English usually has *heighth,* like *width* and *breadth* (and the original Old English form had *th*), but *height* is the only form current in formal and informal English. Contrast *drought-drouth.

Heightened style Typically a heightened style makes conspicuous use of the connotation of words, especially their overtones of sentiment and emotion, it tends to use the more literary and less colloquial parts of the language, it uses figures of speech, sentences with definite patterns, as of parallelism, balance, and climax, and it makes considerable use of sound, euphony, and rhythm.

In fiction such a heightening of style is often appropriate for passages of elevated feeling, portraying the emotions of a character, as in Conrad's famous description of young Marlow's first experience of the East:

"I need not tell you what it is to be knocking about in an open boat. I remember nights and days of calm, when we pulled, we pulled, and the boat seemed to stand still, as if bewitched within the circle of the sea horizon. I remember the heat, the deluge of rain-squalls that kept us bailing for dear life (but filled our water-cask), and I remember sixteen hours on end with a mouth dry as a cinder and a steering-oar over the stern to keep my first command head on to a breaking sea. I did not know how good a man I was till then. I remember the drawn faces, the dejected figures of my two men, and I remember my youth and the feeling that will never come back any more—the feeling that I could last for ever, outlast the sea, the earth, and all men; the deceitful feeling that lures us on to joys, to perils, to love, to vain effort—to death; the triumphant conviction of strength, the heat of life in the handful of dust, the glow in the heart that with every year grows dim, grows cold, grows small, and expires—and expires, too soon, too soon—before life itself.

"And this is how I see the East. I have seen its secret places and have looked into its very soul; but now I see it always from a small boat, a high outline of mountains, blue and afar in the morning; like faint mist at noon; a jagged wall of purple at sunset. I have the feel of the oar in my hand, the vision of a scorching blue sea in my eyes. And I see a bay, a wide bay, smooth as glass and polished like ice, shimmering in the dark. A red light burns far off upon the gloom of the land, and the night is soft and warm. We drag at the oars with aching arms, and suddenly a puff of wind, a puff faint and tepid and laden with strange odours of blossoms, of aromatic wood, comes out of the still night—the first sigh of the East on my face. That I can never forget. It was impalpable and enslaving, like a charm, like a whispered promise of mysterious delight."—JOSEPH CONRAD, *Youth*, pp. 36-37

In factual writing a heightened style is also appropriate in passages with feeling, as when a writer is presenting a course of action or an opinion, especially of full praise or blame, or some ideals about which he feels deeply and about which he wishes his reader not only to think but to feel. (See the paragraph by Bertrand Russell, p. 177.)

Although this emotional heightening of style is more usual in formal writing, a more informal and "plain" style may show similar traits:

The people came out of their houses and smelled the hot stinging air and covered their noses from it. And the children came out of the houses, but they did not run or shout as they would have done after a rain. Men stood by their fences and looked at the ruined corn, drying fast now, only a little green showing through the film of dust. The men were silent and they did not move often. And the women came out of the houses to stand beside their men—to feel whether this time the men would break. The women studied the men's faces secretly, for the corn could go, as long as something else remained. The children sent exploring senses out to see whether men and women would break. The children peeked at the faces of the men and women, and then drew careful lines in the dust with their toes. Horses came to the watering troughs and nuzzled the water to clear the surface dust. After a while the faces of the watching men lost their bemused perplexity and became hard and angry and resistant. Then the women knew that they were safe and that there was no break. Then they asked, What'll we do? And the men replied, I don't know. But it was all right. The women knew it was all right, and the watching children knew it was all right. Women and children knew deep in themselves that no misfortune was too great to bear if their men were whole. The women went into the houses to their work, and the children began to play, but cautiously at first. As the day went forward the sun became less red. It flared down on the dust-blanketed land. The men sat in the doorways of their houses; their hands were busy with sticks and little rocks. The men sat still—thinking—figuring.—JOHN STEINBECK, *The Grapes of Wrath*, pp. 6-7.

There has been a good deal of argument among critics about this heightening of style. Some appear to feel that prose is better the more it has characteristics usually associated with poetry. Those who prefer the plain style seem to feel that any departure from simple direct statement is somehow dishonest. But the question is not of the qualities of poetry (or verse) and prose. There are several kinds of style, all with long and honorable traditions in English literature. (The heightened style owes much to the Oriental and more poetic passages in the King James Version of the Bible.) All good styles have their uses and the real question is of their appropriateness to the subjects and situations in which they are used. The two special dangers of the heightened style are that it may be used for an ordinary statement that would make its mark better if it was simply told, and that writers believing this style better than others may attempt it even when they have no aptitude for it or when the immediate subject does not call for it.

In a plea for "fine writing," Logan Pearsall Smith tells that seeing a large map of the United States in a consular office abroad suggested to him that American writers are not interested in style— and to most readers his putting of this relatively simple idea will seem overwritten:

Youth has its dreams, its longings for distinction; among all the eager young men and women of that vast country, nowhere on those prairies or among those mountains, by the side of no lake or river or of either ocean, in not one of those resounding cities or multitudinous universities, does the thought no longer come to any one, I asked myself, that the instrument of speech which they make use of all day long has resonance sleeping within it of unimaginable beauty? Never to any one of them does it now occur to try to master, as others have mastered, the ironic echoes which are latent in English Prose? The golden sceptre of style gilds everything it touches, and can make immortal those who grasp it: to no one of those aspiring

545

youths does the thought ever suggest itself that it might be an adventure among adventures to try to wield that wand?—LOGAN PEARSALL SMITH, "Fine Writing," *Reperusals and Re-collections*, p. 332

At present a heightened style is out of fashion. Our fiction writers especially seem to avoid it, using instead a plain, and sometimes too plain, telling of their tales. In factual writing it is perhaps more common, because of the interest in and feeling for their ideas that our more earnest writers show. It is so out of fashion that some writers with real depth of feeling probably avoid it intentionally. For a writer to repress a genuine tendency to an appropriate heightening of style is as dangerous as forcing it when a writer does not have sufficient feeling to warrant it. There are various reasons for the vogue of the plain style—the dominance of realistic fiction, the supposedly scientific temper of thought, the journalistic quality of much writing. Virginia Woolf, in a paragraph itself somewhat heightened, blames education—which can be only one of the several reasons—and by implication pleads for more heightened style in writing:

If this is true, if there is now a uniformity and a drill and a discretion unknown before, what do you think can be the reason? In one word, and I have room for one only and that is murmured in your private ear—education. Some years since, for reasons, unknown but presumably of value, it must have occurred to someone that the arts of reading and writing can be taught. Degrees were given at the universities to those who showed proficiency in their native tongue. And the teachers of the living language were not old and hoary; as fitted their subject they were young and supple. Persuasion sat on their tongues, and the taught, instead of mocking, loved their teachers. And the teachers took the manuscripts of the young and drew circles of blue chalk around this adjective and circles of red chalk around that adverb. They added in purple ink what Pope would have thought and what Wordsworth would have said. And the young, since they loved their teachers, believed them. Hence it came about that instead of knowing that the sun was in the sky and the bird on the branch the young knew the whole course of English literature from one end to another; how one age follows another; and one influence cancels another; and one style is derived from another; and one phrase is better than another. They took service under their teachers instead of riding into battle alone. All their marriages —and what are the five years between twenty and twenty-five in the life of a writer but years of courtship and wedding, of falling in love with words and learning their nature and how to mate them by one's own decree in sentences of one's own framing?—all their marriages were arranged in public; tutors introduced the couples; lecturers supervised the amours; and examiners finally pronounced whether the fruit of the union was blessed or the reverse. Such methods, of course, produced an erudite and eugenic offspring. But, one asks, turning over the honest, the admirable, the entirely sensible and unsentimental pages, where is love? meaning by that where is the sound of the sea and the red of the rose, music, imagery and a voice speaking from the heart?—VIRGINIA WOOLF, "All About Books," *The New Republic*, April 15, 1931

References: Logan Pearsall Smith, "Fine Writing," *Reperusals and Re-collections* (New York, 1937) and his anthology, *A Treasury of English Prose* (Boston, 1920). The opposite point of view is presented in a review of the *Treasury* by Arthur Clutton-Brock, included in *More Essays on Books* (New York, 1921). Dobrée, Part iii, Emotive Prose. John Livingston Lowes, "The Noblest Monument of English Prose," *Essays in Appreciation* (Boston, 1936).

hello is the common American greeting. Variants, mostly British, are *hallo, halloo, hollo*. Plural *hello*'s.

The verb ("to shout in greeting or to attract attention") is generally given in dictionaries as *hollo* or *hollow*, but this is an archaic form not heard in the United States. We all say *holler*.

help but   *can't help (but)

hence A formal word for the less formal *consequently, therefore*; rare in current informal writing. *Conjunctive adverbs

he-or-she (his-or-her) English has no third person pronoun to refer to individuals of either or both sexes. Since we must often refer to nouns that name either or both male and female, the language has developed three ways of making up for the lack of an accurate pronoun:

1. The most usual and most satisfactory way is to use *he* or *his* alone even when some of the persons meant are female, since *he* can be regarded as referring to *person* as much as to *man:*

Mr. Brown and Miss Trevor led the discussion, each giving his opinion of the poem.

There is considerable discussion whether a man or a woman will be appointed to the vacant cabinet post. Whoever receives the appointment will find his task a difficult one.

Sometimes when the typical individuals or the majority of the group referred to would be women, use *her* in the same way:

Each one of the teachers in this school is required to submit her report to the principal in person.

2. Sometimes both *he* and *she* are used:

A teacher gives his or her own opinions on matters of politics and religion and often influences a pupil to think as he or she does. [Either of the two pronouns would be better in this sentence than both of them.]

Every student wishes to participate in some activity authorized by his or her college. [*His or her* sounds pedantic here; *his* alone would be better.]

The two pronouns are almost always clumsy and really no more accurate, since the meaning is determined by the antecedent. The use of *he and/or she* has been called "correct but not commendable."

3. The third way is to resort to a plural pronoun. This is the usual informal colloquial solution, and it is frequently written:

Neither [a man and a woman] tasted what they ate.—KATHERINE ANNE PORTER, *Flowering Judas*, p. 26

he said In writing conversation, "he said," "she said" are the safest labels for a speech unless a more specific word (*whispered, asked, faltered . . .*) really applies. See *Conversation, *Quotation marks.

highbrow After a period of slang overuse, *highbrow* has settled down as a useful informal word, and *lowbrow* has too:

Crotchety highbrow critics hemmed and hawed about his playing, but they had to admit that his mimicry was extraordinary.—*Time*, Feb. 13, 1939

The cult of the lowbrow and the technique of showmanship have unquestionably invaded every field of literary and intellectual activity.—*The Saturday Review of Literature*

high school Capitalize only when referring to a particular school (some newspaper styles do not use capitals even then):

I graduated from high school at seventeen.
I graduated from Bismarck High School in 1934.
These two high schools will now play for the championship.
Working on a high school paper is good training.

Some periodicals are now printing the word as a compound: *highschool*.

himself, herself *Himself* and *herself* are used in two ways:

1. As reflexive pronouns, referring to the subject of the sentence:

He took it upon himself to see that it was done.
George has always taken himself pretty seriously.
She looked at herself in the window and gave her hat a little pull.

2. As emphatic tags, intensives:

He told me himself.
I looked up and there was Mrs. Goodenow herself.

Compare *myself, *yourself, yourselves.

his-or-her *he-or-she

Historical present Using the present tense in a narrative of past events. See "The time relation," p. 82.

holdup Informal and colloquial. No hyphen in the noun. The verb is written in two words:

There was a holdup in the block last night.
They had planned to hold up the messenger as he left the bank.

holler *hello

home, homely, homey 1. *Home* is used as a noun, verb, adjective, and adverb—an example of the English habit of making one form serve several functions (*Parts of speech §2):

NOUN: His home was now in Cleveland.
VERB: The bird homed in an hour and twenty minutes.
ADVERB: He came home unexpectedly. Ram the shell home.
His remark went home.
ADJECTIVE: home duties, home manufactures, home run

In "They are home," "They are not home," *home* is a colloquial clip for *at home*. *To home* in these phrases is vulgate.

2. *Home—house*. Writers careful of their words use *house* for a building, *home* for a house looked at as the seat of a person's living. Real estate men (realtors) use *home* for *house* to capitalize on sentiment in their business.

3. *Homely*. In formal English *homely* means "informal, unassuming, characteristic of home life." In colloquial and vulgate English *homely* usually means "coarse, ugly in appearance."

4. *Homey* is a good informal word: The lodge had a cheerful, homey atmosphere.

Homonyms Two words of different meanings that are pronounced alike (*bear, bare*; *plain, plane*) are called *homonyms* (or *homophones*).

English has a great many such pairs of words, most of them in common use. They exist for different reasons. Some Old English words once different have fallen together because of changes in form through the centuries: *bear* (the animal) from *bera*, *bear* (the verb) from *beran*; *plain* and *plane* both go back to Latin *planus*, but the spelling of the first was altered in coming through

549

Old French. Many words are from different languages, having fallen into similar forms by accident: *rest* meaning "peace" is from Old English, *rest* meaning "*remainder*" is from French; and *bark* of a tree is from Scandinavian, *bark* of a dog from Old English, and *bark*, the vessel, a more recent borrowing from French-Italian.

There is very little chance of misunderstanding these words because their context will tell which is which—though their similarity is often capitalized in *puns. But homophones like *plain—plane* make a good deal of trouble in spelling. Much of this confusion is really carelessness, for the words are common. Try to visualize the ones that bother you, in phrases that show their meaning, something like these:

priest at the *altar*—Who can *alter* human nature?
Father gave his *assent* to the marriage.—the *ascent* of Mount Everest
bearing pain—*baring* his arm
a lower *berth*—his tenth *birth*day
born in June 1922—"*borne* by the wind"
bow (bou) of the boat—*bow* (bō) of a violin—*bow* (bou) of the head—*bough* (bou) of a tree
the *bridal* party, *bridal* suite—a horse's *bridle*, the *bridle* path
a house-to-house *canvass*—with *canvas* spread
The *capital* of Illinois is Springfield.—The *capitol* has a gilded dome.
A woman despises insincere *compliments*.—the *complement* of the angle
There are five members of the *council*.—*counsel* for the defense, *counsel* is advice
a *dual* personality—a pistol *duel*
the trophy cups on the *mantel*—a *mantle* covered her
a *piece* of paper—*peace* or war
air*plane*, *plane* geometry—the Great *Plains*, a *plain* statement
He *rode* horseback.—The *road* was macadam.—He *rowed* a dory.
a box of *stationery*—a *stationary* engine, *stationary* desks
tea to drink—*tee* on a golf course

Reference: Kennedy, §82

Honorable As a title of respect, for persons in political office of some prestige, this word is capitalized and is usually preceded by *the*; it may be abbreviated in addresses when initials or first name is used.

the Honorable Robert M. LaFollette   the Hon. Robert M. LaFollette
the Honorable Member from South Carolina

hope "In hopes of a better day to come" is colloquial and vulgate for *in the hope of*.

After leaving Montreal, we drove on in the hope [not: in hopes] of reaching Quebec as soon as possible. (or: in hope of reaching)

In informal writing *hoping* is more usual:

After leaving Montreal, we drove on, hoping to reach Quebec as soon as possible.

Hours In consecutive writing, especially if it is formal, hours are written in words: at four o'clock.

In newspapers and in much informal writing, figures are used, especially if several times are mentioned:

at 4 p. m.   just after 9 a. m.   from 10 to 12   *a. m. and p. m.

however 1. As a connective, *however* is more appropriate to the fully developed sentences of formal style, and is especially useful as a connective between sentences:

Occasionally the beat man writes his own story in the press room of the public building in which he is stationed, and sends it to the office by messenger. This, however, is unusual as it involves loss of time.—C. D. MacDougall, *Reporting for Beginners*, p. 65

That, as prose, is simple, easy, fluent, and flexible; what is important, however, is that it is written, apparently, in the *tones* of every day, though here and there we can detect traces of literary forms— 'only that which' instead of 'only what'; 'How to act' instead of 'what to do'; it is extraordinarily difficult to rid one's self of terms of that kind.—Bonamy Dobrée, *Modern Prose Style*, p. 219

We can read many pages of informal English without encountering *however*, its place being taken by the lighter *but*, even as a connective between sentences:

Both the psychology of the artist and the history of the arts are interesting, and may be valuable, topics of investigation. But it should be clearly recognised that the history of the forms of the arts has no direct connection with the arts as they are.—Rupert Brooke, *John Webster and the Elizabethan Drama*, p. 24

Amateur writers are likely to overuse *however*; *but* would usually be more appropriate to the simple directness of their statements:

During the eight weeks I was in the hospital, Al visited me twice, assuring me that as soon as I was able, I could have my old job. But [better than *however*] after four weeks of convalescing at home, it was time for me to go to college.

Many people think that Model T's are always getting out of order. This is not always the case, however. Ours has . . .   [Better]

Many people think that Model T's are always getting out of order, but that is not always true. Ours has . . .

When *however* is used, it is usually placed after the first word or phrase of its clause, as in the first two quotations in this article. Clauses of one sentence connected by *however* are usually substantial enough to be separated by a semicolon, as in the Dobrée quotation. *Conjunctive adverbs, *but

2. As a simple adverb, *however* modifies an adjective or other adverb:

> He'll have to go with the others, however little he may want to do it.
> However hard we tried, the current swept us back.

human, once a noun in good standing, fell to the level of humorous and undignified usage, and now seems slowly being brought back into good standing.

> With all his heart he wants to come close to some other human, touch someone with his hands, be touched by the hand of another.— SHERWOOD ANDERSON, *Winesburg, Ohio*, p. 287

Humor Humor is primarily a matter of material, rather than of words, coming from shrewd observation of the amusing doings of people, from the ironical contrasts in life, from seeing likenesses or observing incongruous situations that escape the average person, from parodying or farcing ideas, from elaborating the trivial instead of the important strand of a thought, from plain exaggeration or understatement.

A humorous writer is usually an informal writer, using the resources of the language with freedom—old words in new senses, new words, misformed words, colloquial words, words with double connotation (*Puns), and constructions that suit his immediate fancy. An enumeration of the qualities of humor is not very useful, but a few specimens may remind you of some of the possibilities:

> The notion that such persons ["writers of light pieces running from a thousand to two thousand words"] are gay of heart and carefree is curiously untrue. They lead, as a matter of fact, an existence of jumpiness and apprehension. They sit on the edge of the chair of Literature. In the house of Life they have the feeling that they have never taken off their overcoats. Afraid of losing themselves in the larger flight of the two-volume novel, or even of the one-volume novel, they stick to short accounts of their misadventures because they never get so deep into them but that they feel they can get out. This type of writing is not a joyous form of self-expression but the manifestation of a twitchiness at once cosmic and mundane. Authors of such pieces have, nobody knows why, a genius for getting into minor difficulties: they walk into the wrong apartments, they drink furniture polish for stomach bitters, they drive their cars into the prize tulip beds of haughty neighbors, they playfully slap gangsters, mis-

taking them for old school friends. To call such persons humorous, a loose-fitting and ugly word, is to miss the nature of their dilemma and the dilemma of their nature. The little wheels of their invention are set in motion by the damp hand of melancholy.

Such a writer moves about restlessly wherever he goes, ready to get the hell out at the drop of a pie-pan or the lift of a skirt. His gestures are the ludicrous reflexes of the maladjusted; his repose is the momentary inertia of the nonplussed. He pulls the blinds against the morning and creeps into smokey corners at night. He talks largely about small matters and smally about great affairs. His ears are shut to the ominous rumblings of the dynasties of the world moving toward a cloudier chaos than ever before, but he hears with acute perception the startling sounds that rabbits make twisting in the bushes along a country road at night and a cold chill comes upon him when the comic supplement of a Sunday newspaper blows unexpectedly out of an areaway and envelopes his knees. He can sleep while the commonwealth crumbles but a strange sound in the pantry at three in the morning will strike terror into his stomach. He is not afraid, or much aware, of the menaces of empire but he keeps looking behind him as he walks along the darkening streets out of the fear that he is being softly followed by little men padding along in single file, about a foot and a half high, large-eyed, and whiskered.—JAMES THURBER, *My Life and Hard Times*, Preface

Always fair game for a humorist are things taken at their face value or things taken more seriously than they really deserve. Applying the judgment of common sense to inflated reputations often results in humor by sheer contrast with the usual opinions. In the following passages two different methods and different styles are shown in this sort of attack, one on a sentimental poem that has been taken too seriously, the other on Shakespeare-worship.

The boy who stood on the burning deck has been played up as an example of youthful heroism for the benefit of the young of our race ever since Mrs. Felicia Dorothea Hemans set him down in black and white. I deny that he was heroic. I insist that he merely was feeble-minded. Let us give this youth the careful once-over: The scene is the Battle of the Nile. The time is August, 1798. When the action of the piece begins the boy stands on the burning deck whence all but him had fled. You see, everyone else on board had had sense enough to beat it, but he stuck because his father had posted him there. There was no good purpose he might serve by sticking, except to furnish added material for the poetess, but like the leather-headed young imbecile that he was he stood there with his feet getting warmer all the time, while the flame that lit the battle's wreck shone round him o'er the dead. After which:

> There came a burst of thunder sound;
> The boy—oh! where was he?

> Ask of the winds, that far around
> With fragments strewed the sea—

Ask the waves. Ask the fragments. Ask Mrs. Hemans. Or, to save time, inquire of me.

He has become totally extinct. He is no more and he never was very much. Still we need not worry. Mentally he must have been from the very outset a liability rather than an asset. Had he lived, undoubtedly he would have wound up in a home for the feeble-minded. It is better so, as it is—better that he should be spread about over the surface of the ocean in a broad general way, thus saving all the expense and trouble of gathering him up and burying him and putting a tombstone over him. He was one of the incurables.—IRVIN S. COBB, A *Plea for Old Cap Collier*, pp. 40-41

It costs a shilling to cross any doorstep in Stratford, and once inside, the visitor finds himself on the very spot where Shakespeare signed his will or wrote *The Tempest* or did something or other which makes it necessary to charge an additional sixpence for the extra sanctity involved. Through all the shrines surge English and American tourists, either people who have read too much Shakespeare at the expense of good, healthy detective stories or people who have never read him at all and hope to get the same results by bumping their heads on low beams. Both categories try heroically to appear deeply moved, an effort which gives their faces a draped look. Were it not for the countryside round about, I would not stay an hour in Stratford—I keep expecting that somebody all dressed up as the immortal bard will come rushing out with a jingle of bells and a jovial shout, and I will have to confess apologetically that I am a big girl now and too old to believe in Shakespeare.—MARGARET HALSEY, *With Malice Toward Some*, pp. 65-66

Amateurs need to be reminded that a good deal of light writing has already been done and that no amount of word juggling and no number of stale quips emphasized by a question mark (?) can conceal a lack of really humorous insight. A glance at the college comics will show in what a groove "humor" runs—though at the same time it can show the occasional flash of illuminating humor that makes life more genial.

Compare *Irony, *Sarcasm.

Reference: Max Eastman, *The Enjoyment of Laughter* (New York, 1936); E. B. and Katherine B. White, A *Subtreasury of American Humor* (New York, 1941), especially the preface

Hyperbole *Exaggeration

Hyphen (-) 1. A hyphen is used to mark the division of a word at the end of a line of manuscript or print. The problem in this

use is to divide the word between syllables. This is discussed in
*Division of words.

2. In certain types of compounds of a preposition and a root
word a hyphen is necessary to avoid confusion, or for emphasis or
appearance:

a) Between a prefix ending with a vowel and a root word beginning with the same vowel:

   re-elected   re-enter   pre-eminent   pre-existent

(See *pre-, *re-; See also *dieresis.)

   Usage is divided on words made with *co-*, the more common ones
now generally being written solid:

   co-operate or cooperate   co-ordinate or coordinate

b) To avoid confusion with another word:

   re-collect—recollect   re-cover—recover

c) Between a prefix and a proper name:

   anti-Nazi   ex-President Hoover   pro-Roosevelt

d) When the prefix is stressed:

   ex-husband   ex-wife   anti-vivisection (or antivivisection)

3. With modifiers preceding a noun:

a) Occasionally some pairs of modifiers might be ambiguous without a hyphen: *a light yellow scarf* might be either a light scarf that
was yellow or a scarf that was light yellow, so that *light-yellow* is
safest for the latter meaning, and conservative writers would put
light, yellow scarf for the first. There is a distinction between a
great-grandfather (indicating relationship only) and a *great grandfather* (indicating quality of a grandfather). When an adverb has
the same form as an adjective, many people use a hyphen if the
adverb modifies a participle: a *late-flowering iris* (an iris that
flowers late), *slow-moving goods*. But ordinarily such expressions
would not be mistaken however they were written, except by people
perversely analyzing the phrases.

b) Usage is divided on hyphening noun phrases when used as
modifiers, as in *seventeenth century philosophy*. Formal writers
would usually write *seventeenth-century*, informal *seventeenth
century*. This division applies to such expressions as the following:

   a Seventh Avenue shop   a college professor attitude
   the drugstore clerk manner   summer vacation freedom
   two-hundred-pound, six-foot-two halfbacks

c) Other modifying phrases, especially long humorous coinages,
are usually hyphened:

Aside from its practical uses, this appeals to what might be termed the "I-know-a-guy-who" streak in human nature.—JACK ALEXANDER, *The New Yorker*, Aug. 1, 1936

That kind of tail-between-the-legs philosophy has no place in America.—*Country Gentleman*, Jan. 1939 .

Shorter phrases will be found written variously. *Onshore* is usually one word; *first rate* is found as two words or hyphened; *dirt cheap* would usually be two words. A dictionary will give the commoner form of this type of phrase.

d) A hyphen is used to carry the force of a modifier over to a later noun ("suspension hyphen"):

The third-, fourth-, and fifth-grade rooms have been redecorated.
In both thirteenth- and fourteenth-century texts

4. A hyphen is conventionally used in certain group words:
a) In the compound numerals from twenty-one to ninety-nine, and in fractions, though this use is decreasing.

one hundred sixty-two   one thirty-second   three-sixteenths
forty-seven   ninety-ninth

b) In names of family relationships:

HYPHENED: father-in-law, daughter-in-law, etc.
ONE WORD: stepson, stepdaughter, stepmother
TWO WORDS: half brother, half sister (sometimes hyphened)

c) In compounds with *self-*, which are usually hyphened in dictionaries but are often found in print as two words:

self-contained   self-government—self government
self-help—self help   self-importance   self-pity—self pity

Selfhood, selfless are written as one word.

If words of this sort raise any question, consult a recent dictionary—but note the comments on the general use of hyphens made in the next section.

5. The question of compound and occasionally compounded words is more complex. Many compound words will be found written in three ways, as two words, hyphened, or as one word. As a rule the form does not affect meaning: *tax payers, tax-payers,* and *taxpayers* all pay taxes; *a red headed roommate, a red-headed roommate,* and a *redheaded roommate* all have red hair. We find *fire escape* and *fire-escape,* (but not *fireescape* because of the two *e*'s); *golf links* and *golf-links; sugar beet* and *sugar-beet.*

In the past, words that were becoming fused into compounds were required to pass through a probationary period with hyphens before being admitted as single words. *Baseball*, for instance, was hyphened for a time, and *football* and *basketball* until quite recently. There is less tendency to use hyphens now, except in quite formal writing, and compounds are now made immediately without hyphens if the word is really needed. A hyphen is more likely to be used when one of the elements has two or more syllables:

> . . . and we have even seen their guilty simulacra in tenement-house and shopfronts.—LEWIS MUMFORD, *Sticks and Stones*, p. 180

Schoolbook is usually written solid, *pocket-book* often hyphened or as two words; *reference book* would almost always be found as two separate words.

The only consolation is that hyphening is more a publisher's worry than a writer's. A publisher may wish for uniformity in principle and may struggle to get it in printing particular words, though absolute consistency is impossible. The University of Chicago Press *Manual of Style*, for instance, devotes nine pages to rules for hyphening, and stylebooks of newspaper and other publications have numerous rules, many of them arbitrary choices of form made simply to insure consistency. But in a person's ordinary writing, he does not need to be too particular. For words in common use he can consult a dictionary or do as he finds reputable publications doing.

It is obvious that use of hyphens should be appropriate to other traits of style, especially to punctuation. In general, formal and conservative writers tend to use more hyphens, informal writers tend to use fewer, and those who follow an open punctuation often get along with almost no hyphens. The present style is to use rather few, writing the word pairs as two separate words or joined as one.

Contrast these passages from contemporary writers:

> And the face was also surly, hang-dog, petulant, and servile—the face of one of those little men—a door-man at a theater, a janitor in a shabby warehouse, office building, or cheap apartment house, the father-in-law of a policeman, the fifth cousin of a desk sergeant, the uncle of a ward heeler's wife, a pensioned door-opener, office-guard, messenger, or question-evader for some Irish politician . . .—THOMAS WOLFE, "Death the Proud Brother," *From Death to Morning*, p. 43

> At the broker's office there was the usual welldressed elderly crowd in sportsclothes filling up the benches, men with panamahats held on knees of Palm Beach suits and linen plusfours, women in pinks and greens and light tan and white crisp dresses.—JOHN DOS PASSOS, *The Big Money*, p. 382

Thomas Wolfe, consistent with his rather conservative usage, has more hyphens than most people would use; Dos Passos, in keeping with other traits of his venturesome style, runs as single words several which are conventionally hyphened or written as two words. Such word joinings are a matter of style rather than of correctness, and appropriateness is more important than rules.

The conclusion one comes to after a serious consideration of current habits in the use of hyphens is well put by John Benbow in *Manuscript & Proof*, the stylebook of the Oxford University Press of New York: "If you take hyphens seriously you will surely go mad."

I 1. Long *i* (ī). The sound of long *i* is a diphthong, sliding from *a* or *ä* to short *i* or short *e: ice, wild, find, guide, night, tiny*. It is variously spelled as in *aye, eye, by, buy, bye, lie*.

In unstressed syllables ī has the same sound but is somewhat shorter: dī am′ə tər.

2. Short *i* (i̇). As in *bit, city*. Before *r* it spells the sound represented by ė: *bird* (bėrd), *third* (thėrd).

3. Continental *i* (ē). In a few words the Continental (European) value of *i* is preserved: *machine* (mə shēn′), *police* (pō lēs′), *visa* (vē′zə), and in recent unanglicized borrowings, *chic* (shēk).

4. As a consonant (y). *I* may represent a *y* sound before a vowel, especially in rapid pronunciation: *opinion* (ō pin′yən), *Indian* (ind′yən).

For the plural *-ies* see *Plurals §1*b* and *Y. See also *-ile.

I 1. The pronoun *I* is written with a capital simply because in the old manuscript hands a small *i* was likely to be lost or to get attached to a neighboring word, and a capital helped keep it a distinct word. There is no conceit implied.

2. The widely circulated rumor that *I* should not be the first word in a letter (sometimes even that it should not be the first word of a sentence) is unfounded. *I* can be used wherever it is needed. People with only average concern for themselves need not worry; the conceited will give themselves away anyway. Circumlocutions to get around the natural use of *I* are usually awkward and likely to attract attention to themselves:

There is a feeling in me [I feel] that relief projects have had a disastrous effect on morale.

The best way to avoid conspicuous use of *I* (or of any other word) is to keep it out of emphatic sentence positions, especially from the stressed beginning of a sentence. A subordinate clause or longish phrase put first will throw the stress off the *I*:

> After a long struggle I decided to go.   [instead of]
> I decided to go, after a long struggle.

3. Omission of *I*. In clipped personal writing—diaries, casual and informal letters—*I* is often appropriately omitted if the style is also clipped in other respects:

> A drive to Nahant yesterday afternoon. Stopped at Rice's, and afterwards walked down to the steamboat wharf to see the passengers land.—Nathaniel Hawthorne, *American Note-Books*, Aug. 31, 1835

*It's me, *myself, *we §2 ("editorial we"), *Impersonal style

ibid. *Ibid.*, the abbreviation of the Latin *ibidem*, "the same," is used in a footnote to refer to the work mentioned in the immediately preceding footnote. See "Form of footnotes," p. 341.

idea strictly means a "concept," something thought about something. It is frequently used as a substitute for *intention* and similar words in constructions that are usually wordy:

> I got the idea that [I thought] every policeman was my enemy.
> We started out with the idea in mind of going to a dance. [We started out intending to go to a dance . . . or some such direct statement of purpose.]

The idiom with *idea* is *of . . . ing*, not *to . . .*:

> Early in the flood I got the brilliant idea of joining [not: to join] the Red Cross.

Idiom and idioms (Correction: The expression marked is not the *Id* idiomatic English construction. Revise it, referring to an article in this *Index* or to a dictionary if you are not sure what it should be.)

The word *idiom* is used in two different, almost opposed, senses:

1. It may mean *the usual forms of expression of a particular language*, as we may compare German idiom with English idiom, meaning the ways in which words are characteristically put together in the two languages. German has been fond of suspended constructions, the separable prefixes (*Wo gehst du hin?*) and participial constructions, but English tends to complete its constructions immediately. In French, adjectives come after the nouns they modify (*une maison blanche*), in English they come before (*a white house*); in French the adjectives have different forms for singular and plural and for masculine and feminine, but in English we have only one adjective form for all uses. In learning a foreign language we must acquire a certain vocabulary, but perhaps even more important, we must be able to put those words to work in patterns that are genuinely French, German, or Italian.

"Idiomatic English" connotes *natural, meaningful* English rather than *correct* English. It ordinarily is contrasted with stilted or formal English and suggests then not a mastery of academic English but of the great common language.

2. The word *idiom* may also mean an *accepted phrase that violates the usual construction of the language,* either departing from the typical grammar (like *somebody else's,* in which the sign of the possessive is added to the adjective rather than to the noun) or from normal logical meaning (like *to center round,* which is ridiculous when analyzed). These idioms are usually particular phrases which we learn separately—easily in our own language, with difficulty in another—differing from the idioms discussed in the preceding section, which are patterns for large numbers of locutions.

Collecting English idioms is a good sport and trying to analyze them is better. Considering them grammatically and literally, what can you make of these?

to come in handy	let's don't
two weeks ago tomorrow	be your age
to catch fire	strike a bargain
catch a cold	to be taken in (deceived)
a living wage	look up an old friend
many is the time	getting on in years

The point to remember about these expressions is that though they are exceptional in some way, they are thoroughly respectable members of the language. No one needs to apologize for using them, for they are part of the general stock in trade of the informal language and most of them are just as appropriate to the formal language.

The dictionaries of course give a great many idioms, usually listed under the most important word in the phrase. The *Oxford English Dictionary* is especially rich in idiomatic expressions. See *Phrases, *Prepositions.

-ie- in spelling See *-ei-, -ie-.

i. e. is the abbreviation for Latin *id est,* "that is." It is not common now outside rather routine reference exposition, *that is* being ordinarily written. For punctuation with *i. e.,* see *namely.

if 1. *If* is a subordinating conjunction introducing a condition:

If the weather holds good, we shall stay another week.
If they had known the beacon was out, they would have come in before sunset.

See *Conditions. Reference: Fries, pp. 224-25

2. *If* and *whether*. In formal usage, *if* is used for conditions, and *whether*, usually with *or*, is used, though not consistently, in indirect questions, in conditions, and in expressions of doubt:

SIMPLE CONDITION: If the weather holds, we will come.
INDIRECT QUESTION: He asked whether the mail had come in.
He asked whether they were all going or only some of them.
DOUBT: They had all been wondering whether the doctor would get there in time.
From the first returns they could not be sure whether the state was Republican or Democratic.

In formal English *if* is not used with *or*:

No matter whether [Not *if*] the boy goes to preparatory school or high school, his father has to pay local school taxes.

In informal and vulgate English *whether* is rarely used, so that the indirect questions above would go:

He asked if they were all going or only some of them.
He asked if the mail had come in.
He was so old, and so shrunken, that it was difficult to tell, at first, if he was a man or woman.—WILLIAM MARCH, *The Little Wife*, p. 101

3. Colloquially *if* is used for *although* or *but* in certain expressions:

She was a good dog if she did bark at strangers.

*when, as, and if

-ile Usage is divided on the pronunciation of words ending in -*ile*. Some of the more common are:

agile	aj′il [aj′il]	infantile	in′fən til, in′fən til
fertile	fer′til	juvenile	jü′və nil, jü′və nil
futile	fū′til	reptile	rep′til
gentile	jen′til	textile	teks′til, teks′til
hostile	hos′til	versatile	ver′sə til

British pronunciation more commonly has -il: fer′til, hos′til, rep′til, ver′sə til.

ilk *Ilk* is an archaic Scotch expression which turns up in some English essays or in would-be humorous writing for *sort:* "more of that ilk."

ill *sick

Illative conjunctions (*Accordingly, however, moreover, nevertheless . . .*) *Conjunctive adverbs

illiterate Strictly *illiterate* means "not able to read or write"; from weakening it means "uncultivated." Usage that is loosely referred to as *illiterate* in this *Index* is called *vulgate*. See "Vulgate English," p. 20.

illusion *Illusion*—"a deceptive appearance," as *an optical illusion, an illusion of wealth*—is sometimes confused with *allusion*, "a reference to something written or to someone or something": He alluded to recent events without recounting them.

Illustration (Literary) For paragraphs developed by giving illustrations, see "Illustration," p. 100.

Illustration (Pictorial) Pictorial illustration greatly helps the interest and understandability of an article—though it cannot (in spite of the great picture magazines) take the place of text. Illustrations for articles and books are often arranged for by the publisher, but the writer can suggest possibilities or he can submit drawings or photographs. Many feature articles are accepted by newspapers and magazines largely because of their illustrations.

A student can often add considerably to the value of a paper by drawings or by snapshots. These can be inserted by tucking the corners into slits cut in the manuscript pages, so that they can be taken off after they have served their purpose. Travel papers, narratives of experience, and explanations of processes profit especially from illustration.

Compare *Diagrams, graphs, etc.

Imagery An image is a word or group of words that makes an appeal to one of the "senses": sight (*bright, yellow, thick brown hair*), hearing (*rumble, far away shouts, three loud booms*), taste (*sweet, sour, a pickled pear*), smell (*jasmine, a blown out candle*), touch (*smooth, glassy, a tweed coat*), and the muscular tension known as the kinesthetic sense (*squirm, jogging heavily along*). Obviously a word may appeal to more than one sense (*tweed, glassy, jasmine . . .*), though in a specific context one would usually be dominant. Whether a reader's senses are actually "aroused" depends chiefly on his suggestibility. Some are easily stimulated by words; some are more sensitive to one sense than to another. For the study of imagery in writing, it is enough that words *capable* of suggesting sensory images are present; we cannot be sure of the response of anyone but ourselves. But images—actually sensed or

potential—are the foundation of most writing, of all in fact that
is not dealing principally with ideas.

Imagery is especially characteristic of poetry, in which ideas,
states of mind, and feelings are often represented by images and
what they suggest:

> Jack Ellyat felt that turning of the year
> Stir in his blood like drowsy fiddle-music
> And knew he was glad to be Connecticut-born
> And young enough to find Connecticut winter
> Was a black pond to cut with silver skates
> And not a scalping-knife against the throat.
> STEPHEN VINCENT BENÉT, *John Brown's Body*, p. 22

Fiction, too, since it must present pictures of people and places
and actions, has much imagery:

> The sun came in warm in long streaks across the floor, and the giant
> geranium plants made a pattern across its gold. When we touched our
> glasses, white circles of light would move on the walls and ceiling,
> and the cut-glass dish with the peaches in it made a rainbow-bar on
> the cloth.—JOSEPHINE JOHNSON, *Now in November*, p. 83

In expository prose images are the basis of discussions of people,
of experience and situations, of things and processes. Even in
expressions of opinion and discussions of ideas, most writers keep
in close touch with the visible and touchable world. Current writing is conspicuously concrete and imageal.

Studying the images in a writer's work will usually show what
has impressed him in his experience, what appeals to him—colors,
lines, odors, what not—and your writing also should show images
drawn from your experience. If you are interested in dogs or sailing
or fabrics or foods, words from those fields should crop up, not
only in papers in which they are the main subject but to add to
the interest and detail of other papers, too. Images that come
from your own experience and that definitely appeal to you will
carry over clearly to a reader and are infinitely better than the trite
roses and violets of accumulated literature. Don't take out of your
writing an image that really appeals to you, unless it would mislead
a reader.

References: Rickert, Ch. 3, gives a detailed classification of images and suggestions on their use; George G. Williams, *Creative
Writing* (New York, 1935), Ch. 7.

There are a number of studies of the imagery of particular
writers, for example: Caroline F. E. Spurgeon, *Shakespeare's Imagery and What It Tells Us* (New York, 1936).

See discussion of concrete and abstract words, p. 223, and the suggestions for use of details in various sorts of paragraphs in Ch. 4, p. 81, especially "Analysis," p. 98 and "Figurative words," p. 229.

Imaginative writing *Factual and imaginative writing

Imitative words and phrases **1.** A number of words imitate, or suggest in their pronunciation, particular "sounds of nature": *bang, buzz, clank, swish, splash, whirr, pop, clatter, cuckoo, ping pong.* These words have become definite members of the English vocabulary and will be found in dictionaries. It is possible to make new ones to fit specific sounds, and they are often necessary, especially in fiction. Sometimes it is better to use the conventional forms even when they are not very exact (*humph, uh huh*) rather than make new ones, which may puzzle a reader.

2. When such words are used for special effect in writing they form a trait of style known as *onomatopoeia* (on′ə mat′ə pē′ə). Imitative words or sounds in a series that suggest the action or idea or tone of the subject matter are a useful form of intensification of meaning, as in Pope's famous lines:

> 'Tis not enough no harshness gives offense,
> The sound must seem an Echo to the sense:
> Soft is the strain when Zephyr gently blows,
> And the smooth stream in smoother numbers flows;
> But when the loud surges lash the sounding shore,
> The hoarse, rough verse should like the torrent roar:
> When Ajax strives some rock's vast weight to throw,
> The line too labours, and the words move slow;
>
> ALEXANDER POPE, *An Essay on Criticism*, lines 364-71

Often a picture or a narrative can be sharpened by using an imitative word instead of a general or colorless word like *said* or *walked*: *barked, droned, snarled, whined; clattered, stamped, strutted.* Conspicuous striving for such words will make a passage seem melodramatic, but accurate words that come naturally will add to its effectiveness.

In *The Red Badge of Courage* Stephen Crane frequently uses imitative words to good effect:

> The regiment snorted and blew. . . . The song of the bullets was in the air and shells snarled among the tree-tops. . . . Near where they stood shells were flip-flapping and hooting. . . . Occasional bullets buzzed in the air and spanged into tree trunks. . . .

immigrate *emigrate—immigrate

Imperative mood The imperative has the form of the infinitive: *Go!* Please *shut* the door. *Verbs

Imperative sentences *Commands and requests

Impersonal constructions *there is, there are, *it

Impersonal style See "Choice between personal and impersonal styles," p. 43.

imply—infer Strictly a writer or speaker *implies* something in his words or manner; a reader or listener *infers* something from what he reads or hears.

> The dean implied, by the way he tilted his head and half closed his eyes, that he doubted my story.
> One might infer from his opening words that the speaker was hostile to all social change.

Infer has been used so much with the meaning of "imply" that that is given as a secondary sense of the word.

in 1. Uses:

PREPOSITION: in the box   in town   in the rain   in a circle   in training   in words   in bronze
ADVERB: mix in   They are not in.   Put in the butter.
ADJECTIVE: an in train
NOUN: the ins and the outs
VERB: (local) to in the beets, to in the car

2. IN COMBINATIONS: *In* is often found in colloquial doubling of prepositions:

in back of   in behind   in between

In most writing these would be simply:

back of   behind   between

See *Prepositions § 3b.

in—into—in to *In* generally shows location (literal or figurative); *into* generally shows direction:

He was in the house.   He came into the house.
He was in a stupor.   He fell into a deep sleep.
He walked in the street.   He walked into the street.

Colloquially *in* is often used for *into*:

He fell in the brook.

In to is the adverb *in* followed by the preposition *to*:

They went into the dining room.
They went in to dinner.

in-, en- *en-, in-

565

in-, un- *In-* or *un-* (variants *im-*, *il-*) prefixed to many words gives them a negative meaning: *inconsiderate, incapable, uneven, unlovable, unlovely, unloved.* If you are not sure whether a word takes *in-* or *un-*, you will have to consult a dictionary—an American dictionary, since British usage differs in many words. *Un-* is likely to be used with words from Old English and *in-* with words from Latin, but this is not a safe guide (witness *indigestible, undigested, inequality, unequal, inadvisable, unadvised*). A sample list follows:

inadequate	indecipherable (also	immoral	undistinguished
inadvisable	undecipherable)	impractical	unedited
inartistic	indistinguishable	unacceptable	unescapable
inaudible	inept	unadvised	unessential
incapable	inexperienced	unalterable	unnamed
incapacitate	infallible	unbelievable	unnatural
incommunicable	infrequent	uncertain	unnecessary
incompatible	insubstantial	uncollected	unnoticeable
incomplete	(unsubstantial)	uncommu-	unrecognizable
incomprehensible	insupportable	nicative	unresponsive
inconclusive	illiberal	uncompleted	unsung
inconsequential	illiterate	uncontrollable	unsustained
inconsolable	immoderate	uncontrolled	unversed

in our midst Country journalese for "in town," "with us":

A distinguished visitor from Chicago spent the day in our midst.

incidental, incidentally The adverb should be spelled in full: incidenta*lly.* *-al ly

Incoherence Writing is incoherent when it lacks connection within itself or when the relationship between parts (of a sentence, of a paragraph, of a whole paper) is not evident. Various examples of incoherence are discussed in *Dangling modifiers, *Participles, and in Chapters 4 and 5.

Incomplete comparisons *Comparison of adjectives, adverbs §5

Incomplete sentences See "Incomplete sentences," p. 131; *Fragmentary sentences

Incongruous details One minor trait of modern style is the use of contrasting or inconsistent words or details, especially in a series. Used unintentionally, incongruous details may be awkward, but when controlled they have various advantages.

1. A series of incongruous details is often used instead of an abstract noun, to suggest a variety of objects or experiences. Such a series may be either light or serious:

The earth, just as she stands, has a lot of qualities which we cherish:

we like the climate, we like the food, and we like the view from the porch.—*The New Yorker*, June 30, 1934

In a single-minded attempt of that kind, if one be deserving and fortunate, one may perchance attain to such clearness of sincerity that at last the presented vision *of regret or pity, of terror or mirth,* shall awaken in the hearts of the beholders that feeling of unavoidable solidarity; of the solidarity in *mysterious origin, in toil, in joy, in hope, in uncertain fate,* which binds men to each other and all mankind to the visible world.—JOSEPH CONRAD, *The Nigger of the Narcissus*, Preface

The first group of italicized words in this sentence is a more exact and more vivid substitute for *emotion* and the second is a colorful and impressive substitute for *human experience* or some such generality.

2. A combination of a concrete and an abstract word is sometimes used as a source of humor, as in Washington Irving's "brimfull of wrath and cabbage."

When an abstract and a concrete word are attached to the same construction they need to be watched. "At the expense of democratic people and ideals" would be better if the last phrase was made separate: "At the expense of democratic people and of democratic ideals."

3. A vigorously contrasting detail may heighten the effect of a statement or drive home a point, often with a note of severe irony.

Among those who have much to be thankful for this week are the football players. From now on they do not have to have their faces stepped on and their character molded.—HOWARD BRUBAKER, *The New Yorker*, Nov. 26, 1938

When my generation of country-raised folks were kids, we shure had a lot of hardships to put up with. We had to walk to school, for instance. There were no nice, comfortable school busses for us to ride back and forth and get killed in.—CAL TINNEY, *The Philadelphia Record*, Dec. 6, 1938

Increasing vocabulary See "Increasing your vocabulary," p. 205.

incredible—incredulous A story or situation is *incredible* (unbelievable); a person is *incredulous* (unbelieving).

Indefinite article *a, an

Indefinite it, they, you *it, *they, *you

Indefinite pronouns (*any, some . . .*) See *Pronouns §8 and the separate articles referred to there.

Indefinite reference of pronouns *Reference of pronouns §2

Indention *Indenting* in manuscript or printed copy is beginning a line in from the left-hand margin. In longhand copy, paragraphs are indented about an inch, in typewritten copy from five to eight spaces.

Hanging indention is setting in lines below the first line, as in many newspaper headlines, *outlines, headings, and addresses of *letters. If a line of verse is too long to stand on one line, the part brought over to the second line should be indented:

> Why do they prate of the blessings of Peace? we have
>   made them a curse,
> Pickpockets, each hand lusting for all that is not its
>   own;
>
> ALFRED TENNYSON, "Maud"

For indenting quotations, see *Quotation marks § 1*d*.

Independent clause A clause grammatically complete and capable of "standing alone" but forming part of a compound sentence. This sentence has three independent clauses (which would still be "independent," but in this instance clumsy, if they were connected by *and*):

> In actual life events rarely reach a conclusion as definite and complete as the short story demands; there are always loose threads somewhere; not even death itself ends a career.—DAVID LAMBUTH AND KENNETH A. ROBINSON, *Art and Craft in the Short Story*, p. 3

Indicative mood The usual form of the verb in sentences and clauses

> They *sat* on the porch even though it *was* late October.
> *Will* you *come* if you *are invited?*

See *Verbs; compare *Subjunctives, *Imperative mood.

Indirect discourse (**Indirect quotation**) Quotations that are paraphrased or summarized in the writer's words instead of being quoted exactly as originally spoken or written are in indirect discourse:

> INDIRECT: He said he wouldn't take it if they gave it to him.
> DIRECT: He said, "I won't take it if they give it to me."

*Quotation marks § 2*b*, *Tenses of verbs § 2

Indirect object *Objects § 2

Indirect question A question restated at second hand:

> INDIRECT: He asked if everyone was all right.
> DIRECT: He asked, "Is everyone all right?"

See *Questions § 3.

individual *person

infer *imply, infer

Infinitives 1. TENSES OF INFINITIVE. The forms of the English infinitive are:

ACTIVE	PASSIVE
PRESENT: ask, to ask	be asked, to be asked
PERFECT: have asked, to have asked	have been asked, to have been asked

The present infinitive indicates action occurring at the same time as that of the main verb or in a time future to that of the main verb:

> He is here now *to ask* you . . .
> They had come *to ask* you . . .
> He is coming (future) *to ask* you . . .

The perfect infinitive primarily indicates action previous to the time of the main verb:

> I am glad *to have been* one of his boys.

2. *To* AND THE INFINITIVE. *To* is the "sign of the infinitive" when the infinitive is used as a noun. (Just *to hear* him talk is an inspiration) and usually when it is used to complete the meaning of a verb:

> They all tried *to get* in first.   He set out *to get* Phi Beta Kappa.

After some verbs no *to* is used: *can, may, shall, will, do, dare, make, help, need* . . . :

> Do make him *stop*.   It would help us *finish* the job.

In short, clear, unemphatic series of infinitives in parallel constructions, the *to* is not repeated:

> *To sit* and *smoke* and *think* and *dream* was his idea of pleasure.

In more formal series of infinitives, when the actions are not part of one general process, or when the separate verbs deserve emphasis, the *to* is repeated:

> *To walk* around among these exhibits, *to see* the horse races where runners, trotters, and pacers with Kentucky and Tennessee pedigrees compete on a mile track, and then *to listen* to the political speakers discussing "purr-ins-a-pulls" and "the Const-ti-too-shun"—this made a holiday for the farmers and city people who came.—CARL SANDBURG, *Abraham Lincoln: The Prairie Years*, II, 6

3. TYPICAL USES OF INFINITIVES.

SUBJECT: *To err* is human, *to forgive*, divine.
OBJECT: He wanted *to go* fishing.
> He tries *to do* every one at least twice.

ADJECTIVE MODIFIER: wool *to spin*, money *to burn*
    They have plenty of fresh fish *to eat*.
ADVERBIAL MODIFIER (purpose, result, etc.): He bought *to sell* again.
    They came *to play*.   Reporters are constantly on the move from
    one place to another *to cover* important happenings.
WITH AUXILIARIES: He will *pass* this time.
    They didn't dare *go* over the fence.

4. SUBJECT OF INFINITIVES. The infinitive is coming more and
more to serve as a verb in a subordinate construction, so that
grammarians now speak of a *to* clause or an infinitive clause.
The subject is in the accusative case.

Supposing them to be new men [= that they were new men], we
all shouted, "Get off the grass!"

Often these constructions are absolute:

To judge by the appearances [= If you judge by the appearances],
the party must have been pretty rough.   To make a long story short,
they didn't go.

After the infinitive of a *linking verb that has no expressed
subject, formal English would often have a nominative complement, informal an accusative:

FORMAL: I always wanted to be *he*.
INFORMAL: I always wanted to be *him*.

Compare *Participles § § 3, 4; *Gerund.
5. SPLIT INFINITIVE. See *Split infinitive.

Compare *Gerund.
Reference: Curme, *Syntax*, Chapter 23

Inflection   Inflection is the change of form by which some words
indicate certain grammatical relationships, as the plural of nouns
or the past tense of verbs. For English inflections see *Case, and
the articles referred to there; *Plurals; *Pronouns; *Verbs; *Comparison of adjectives and adverbs; *Analytic and synthetic forms.

References: Curme, *Parts of Speech*; Kennedy, Chapter 11

Inf   **Informal English**   (CORRECTION: The word or passage marked is too
informal for the subject or for the style of the rest of the paper.
Revise, making it more formal.)

Informal English is the typical language of an educated person
going about his everyday affairs. It shows more effect of education and social standing than Vulgate, but not so much of the
more precise usage of Formal English. It is appropriate to all the
needs of communication except some discussions of ideas and of

some elevated subjects intended for a rather restricted audience or for occasions in which a formal style is expected.

For discussion and examples, see "Informal English," p. 12.

inquiry Pronunciation divided: in kwīr′i, in′kwir i

inside (of) *Inside*, usually with the doubling of the preposition to *inside of*, is colloquially used in expressions of time:

> The snow will all be gone *inside of a week*.

Informal, without distinctly colloquial flavor:

> The snow will be gone *in a week*.

The more formal idiom is *within*:

> The snow will be gone *within a week*.

inst., ult. Abbreviations such as *inst*. (of the current month: "Yours of the 18th inst. duly rec'd and contents noted") and *ult*. (of last month) are not now used by businessmen who pay attention to their correspondence. *Business English

instance Frequently deadwood. *In many instances* = *often*.

institutions of higher learning is a clumsy phrase, and more abstract than *colleges and universities*. It would be a convenience if we had one word for the notion, or a group word as economical even as *secondary schools* for "high and preparatory schools." Either *colleges* or *universities* is often used to apply to both.

intelligentsia (in tel ə jent′si ə) a plural or collective word, means intellectual or educated people as a group, often with a suggestion of too great preoccupation with intellectual matters.

Intensive pronouns *Pronouns § 4 (Reflexive pronouns), and *himself, herself, *myself, *yourself, yourselves

Intensives Adverbs like *very, too, much*, and some constructions, like the superlative of adjectives and adverbs, are used to emphasize meaning. See "Intensives," p. 166 for discussion, and *very, *Comparison of adjectives and adverbs § 5, *himself, *myself.

References: Fries, pp. 200-206; Curme, *Parts of Speech*, pp. 48-50

interest, interested, and their opposites The adjective *interested* has two opposites: *uninterested*, which is merely its negative, and *disinterested*, which means "not motivated by personal interest, impartial," though informally the latter is sometimes used in the sense of *uninterested*. The noun *interest* has no antonym made from itself (*disinterest* not being a word in general use). It is necessary to resort to specific words like *boredom* or phrases like *lack of interest*.

> The interest of the audience was sustained at a high pitch.
> We were all interested in reading Hardy.
> The students were uninterested in the conflict between science and religion.
> Osborne was wholly disinterested when he suggested an increase in salary for all county officials.

Interjections *Exclamations

Interrogation point *Question mark

Interrogative pronouns *Pronouns § 3

Interrogative sentence *Questions

Interrupted sentence movement See "Interrupted movement," p. 157.

into, in to *in—into—in to

intramural No hyphen. It means "within the walls," specifically college activities carried on by groups from the same college; the opposite of *intercollegiate*.

Intransitive verbs *Transitive and intransitive verbs

Introductions See "Beginning paragraphs," p. 67, and *Outline form § 2*j*.

Introductory words For handling words like *namely, that is, for example*, see *namely and other introductory words.

Inversion (Placing the verb before its subject—"Came the first clap of thunder, and we all struck out for the house.") See "Inverted order," p. 123, and "Inverted movement," p. 156.

Invitations *Social correspondence

invite is ordinarily a verb. Its use as a noun (in'vīt) is colloquial or would-be humorous: "Did you get an invite?"

Irony Irony is implying something markedly different, sometimes even the opposite, from what is actually said. See "Irony," p. 238.

-ise *-ize, -ise

isolate Pronunciation divided: ī'sō lāt, is'ō lāt, with the first more common; also ī'sō lā'shən, is'ō lā'shən.

it is the neuter third person singular pronoun, used to refer to an object, a situation, or an idea. *It* is also used to refer to a baby or an animal whose sex is unknown or unimportant for the statement

(The dog wagged *its* tail). *It* is used further in certain impersonal statements about the weather, events in general (impersonal *it*):

It rained all night.   It's the way things go.

It is also used to refer to the idea of a preceding statement, though this is not done in formal English (*this):

We changed two tires in record time. It [Formal: *This*] is not easy to do on a dark and rainy night.

In general, sentences beginning "It is . . ." or "It was . . ." ("anticipatory subject") are wordy and weakening, since they have put a colorless phrase in the emphatic beginning of the sentence:

[It was] then [that] his wife had taken to going with other men.

See *there is, there are, *its, *it's, *it's me.

Italics In manuscript, both longhand and typewritten, italics are shown by underlining. Specific uses of italics are listed in *Underlining. See also *Foreign words in English, *Titles of articles, books, etc., *Type.

its The possessive pronoun does not have an apostrophe:

The dog wagged *its* tail.   A car is judged by *its* performance.
But we were deceived about *its* real value.

Associate *its* with *his* and *hers*.

it's The contraction of *it is* or *it has*:

It's going to rain.   *It's* rained for over a week now.

It's me The argument over "it's me" is a case of theory vs. practice. The theory is that after the verb *be* the nominative form should always be used, but this theory is consistently contradicted by the actual usage of good speakers.

We tend to use the nominative form of a pronoun (the question cannot arise with a noun) when it is the subject and stands before a verb and to use the accusative in most other positions, especially when it is in "object territory," as Professor Fries calls it. (Compare *who, whom.) The French have met a similar situation with "C'est moi."

All the large grammars of English regard *it's me* as acceptable colloquial usage—and since the expression is not likely to occur except in familiar speech, that gives it full standing. Fowler approves it, and one of the "judges" in *Current English Usage* (p. 108) wrote:

I sounds quite mad in certain cases; e.g., pointing to a photo: "Which is I?"!!! "Oh, I see, that's I"!!! Absolutely non-English, hang all the grammarians on earth.

573

Us and *him* after *be* are less common, but usage is divided. *Current English Usage* found "If it had been *us*, we would admit it" uncertainty established and "I'll swear that was *him*" and "I suppose that's *him*" disputable. Very often speakers who try to be correct resort to some circumlocution, saying instead of "It was *she* (or *her*)" "That's who it was."

The upshot of the discussion is that in their natural colloquial settings "It's me," "It was him all right," "Something was wrong —was it him or the crowd?" are appropriate.

References: *Current English Usage*, pp. 108-109; Wallace Rice, "Who's there? Me," *American Speech*, 1933, No. 3, 58-63; Robertson, pp. 492-503; Fries, p. 91

-ize, -ise English has many words ending in the sound of īz, some of which are spelled *-ise* and some *-ize*, and on many usage is divided. American usage, differing somewhat from British, prefers *-ize*, as in the following common verbs of this class:

anesthetize	dramatize	revolutionize	sympathize
apologize	memorize	sensitize	visualize
characterize	realize	standardize	

-ise is the usual spelling in the following:

advertise	despise	franchise	surmise
advise	devise	merchandise	surprise
arise	disguise	revise	
chastise	exercise	supervise	

Both *-ize* and *-ise* are commonly found in:

> baptize—baptise criticize—criticise
> Compare: analyze—analyse

In general, follow American usage, and when that is divided, use whichever you are accustomed to.

Some readers object to recent extension of the verbs in *-ize*, such as *concertize, picturize*, but there seems little reason for the objection except when one duplicates in meaning a verb already in common use.

J is a common spelling for the soft *g* sound at the beginning of syllables: *jam, jet, jibe, journey, jury*. At the end of syllables the sound is variously spelled, often by *-dge*: *edge* (ej), *judge* (juj). Some foreign sounds of *j* are kept in particular words: Latin (y),

Hallelujah; French (zh) *bijou* (bē′zhü), jabot (zhä bō′); Spanish (h): *marijuana* (mä′ri hwä′nä).

Jargon 1. APPLIED TO STYLE. Sir Arthur Quiller-Couch popularized *jargon* as the name for verbal fuzziness of various sorts—wordiness, abstract for concrete words, big words, and the use of words that add nothing to the meaning of a statement. See "Removing deadwood," p. 161, "Words that weaken," p. 214, and "Abstract and Concrete Words," p. 223.

Reference: Sir Arthur Quiller-Couch: *On the Art of Writing* (New York, 1916), pp. 100-126

2. LINGUISTIC SENSE. *Jargon* is a word used among linguists to mean a dialect composed of the mixture of two or more languages. Jargons involving English are used by non-English-speaking peoples in doing business with the English. The best known are the Chinook jargon of the Pacific Northwest, Beach-la-Mar (or Bêche-de-mer) of the Pacific islands, and the Chinese-English jargon, pidgin-English.

References: Kennedy §17; Otto Jespersen, *Language* (New York, 1922), pp. 216-36; and the sources referred to in these references

3. POPULAR SENSE. *Jargon* is used popularly as a label for any speech that a person feels to be inferior to his own. It may be applied to *gibberish* (speech with nonsense or meaningless words), or more often to speech with specialized or peculiar words or grammar, like "the jargon of a fraternal order," "the jargon of psychoanalysis."

job Informal and colloquial for the formal *position:* He got a job at Baker's. The word *position* has more dignity and is usually thought of as better paid. *Job* is shoptalk for something made, as an automobile, refrigerator . . . ("a nice little job there").

Jones—Plural and possessive forms The plural of *Jones* and of most nouns ending in an *s-* or *z*-sound is formed by adding *-es*, pronounced as a separate syllable: *Joneses* (jōn′zəz), *consciences* (kon′shən səz), *Jameses*. When two syllables ending in an *s-* or *z*-sound are in the root word, usage is divided: *the Moses* seems more euphonious than *the Moseses*.

In the possessive, usage is divided. We may say and write *Dr. Jones'* (jōnz) *office* or *Dr. Jones's* (jōn′zəz) *office*. Probably the first form is the more common. Also: For *goodness'* sake, *Charles'* collection, though *Charles's* (chärl′zəz) collection is equally possible.

The possessive plural is pronounced the same as the plural and written by adding (') to the plural form: *Joneses', Moses'* or *Moseses'*.

Journalistic, journalese *Newspaper English

judgment—judgement *Judgment* is the preferred spelling, though both forms are used.

just For position of *just* see *only §2.

K as in *kill, kick, park*. The *k* sound is spelled *c* in many words (*call, actual, cute* . . .), *ck* (*back, track* . . .), and also with other letters, as in *queen, chord, cheque*. *K* before *n* is silent in a number of Germanic words (*knave, kneel, knife*).

Business changes many words with the *k* sound spelled as *c* to *k* (*Kwik Kleaners*), either to make the alliteration more obvious or to make a trademark. See Louise Pound, "The Kraze for 'K,'" *American Speech*, 1925, i, 43-44.

K *K* is used by many teachers as the theme-correction symbol for *awkward*. (CORRECTION: The expression marked is awkward. Revise to make it read more smoothly.)

kid *Kid* is colloquial and familiar for *child, youngster*.

kind, sort *Kind* and *sort* are both singular nouns in form:

> This kind of person is a menace at any party.
> This sort of thing shouldn't be allowed.

But *kind* and *sort* are so closely associated with the noun they stand before that they seem like adjectives, and colloquially the demonstrative adjectives used with them usually agree with the principal noun of the construction:

> Those sort of ideas in his head and that sort of life with his wife . . .—A. S. M. HUTCHINSON, *If Winter Comes*, p. 324

> You next reach the conclusion that, as these kind of marks have not been left by any other animal than man . . .—T. H. HUXLEY, "The Method of Scientific Investigation"

The *Oxford English Dictionary* has examples of *these kind of* and *these sort of* from the fourteenth century to the present, many of them from the "best authors." Fries found the plural regularly used with *kind* and *sort* by his Group I (Standard English) writers (p. 58). Vulgate uses *them kind*. Only the vigilance of editorial copy readers keeps the construction from being as general in writing as in speech. (Jespersen, *Essentials of English*

Grammar, p. 202, even suggests that *kind* and *sort* be regarded as unchanged plurals and therefore correct.) But the construction still has only colloquial and vulgate standing.

kind of, sort of In vulgate speech *kind of* and *sort of* are used as adverbs, equivalent to *rather, somewhat* of more formal usage:

I feel kind of logy today. It was sort of dull, but he said a lot.

In formal and informal English these would be:

I was rather [somewhat, a little, very, pretty] tired. It was pretty [very, rather] dull, but he said a good deal.

kind of [a], sort of [a] Strictly you have a *kind* or *sort* of a class of objects, not of one object: *a kind of story*, not *a kind of a story*. But in informal English *kind of a* and *sort of a* are very common, and they are fairly common among respected writers:

I want to find someone on the earth so intelligent that he welcomes opinions which he condemns—I want to be this kind of a man and I want to have known this kind of a man.—JOHN JAY CHAPMAN, *Letters*, p. 124

And now, Catchuman arriving to inquire where he was likely to find a local lawyer of real ability who could be trusted to erect some sort of a defense for Clyde.—THEODORE DREISER, *An American Tragedy*, II, 182

Now, suppose the battle of Salamis had been fought, not in the full light of Greek history, but in the misty dawn of the Epos, what sort of a story should we have had?—GILBERT MURRAY, *The Rise of the Greek Epic*, p. 200

These two sentences from the same short story show the two idioms in differing degrees of formality, in different tempos:

. . . he had never once brought her a comical, stuffed animal or any sort of an object with a picture of a Scottie on it.

Bob McEwen wasn't the sort of man to do a sentimental thing like that unless he meant it.—SALLY BENSON, *People Are Fascinating*, pp. 30, 31

In formal writing *kind of a* and *sort of a* should be avoided.

kindergarten preserves the sound and spelling of its German origin and is pronounced and spelled with *t* and not *d* in the final syllable.

L is a "liquid" consonant that varies considerably in the actual pronunciation of different people and with its position in a word: *land, leaf, almost, silly, fill*. L is silent in a few common words:

almond (usually), *folk, half, salmon, talk, walk, would, yolk.* It is often not sounded in other words as in *golf course* (gôf′kôrs′).

Labeling material It should usually be unnecessary to label a statement as *interesting, amusing,* or *important,* or to point out a joke or a dig by (?) or (!). A good story teller doesn't need to begin "You'll laugh at this," and a good writer can usually *show* that what he is saying is interesting or important without labeling it. Instead of beginning "Let me relate an amusing incident from my summer experience," just tell it well and the reader will see that it is amusing.

Labeling an emotion that is clearly suggested in a narrative weakens the effect.

> "What was it, conductor, did we blow a fuse?"
> "No," he said, "we just killed three people back at a crossing."
> [The effect of this sentence was electrifying.] "We just killed three people . . ." Maybe they were college boys driving home to spend Christmas with their folks. . . .

lady *man, woman

laissez faire The spelling is still French, and the pronunciation (le sā fār′) still near French, but it is not italicized except in conspicuously formal writing.

Language study See Chapter 1 and *Linguistics.

last *former—first, latter—last

last (at long last) An archaic idiom recently revived. It is slightly more emphatic than *at last,* at least when it is spoken, but usually the phrase has a British or formal connotation as in this:

> An economic power born of the travail of men at long last asserts its title to political dominance.—HAROLD J. LASKI, *The Rise of Liberalism,* p. 268

last, latest *Last* means the final item of a series; *latest,* the most recent in time of a series which may or may not be continued:

> Allan Nevins' latest (we hope it won't be his last) biography is of Grover Cleveland but also tells the story of Peter Cooper.

Latin and English 1. LATIN WORDS. Many Latin words came into English in early periods of the language, either direct or through French, and cannot now be told from other English words: *patience, candle, receive* . . . (See *English language). Most borrowings from Latin are subject to the same process of anglicizing as other *foreign words in English, and in general they are pronounced like English words—*agenda* (ə jen′də), *erratum* (i rā′təm or i rä′təm)—instead of according to the system of sounds now taught in Latin classes.

Since no people now speaks Latin, new borrowings come in through written rather than spoken use and belong to the formal dialects, used chiefly in science, law, religion, medicine, and academic work. Since practically all college work was carried on in Latin—by both teachers and students—until about 1750, and a good deal of it later than that, considerable Latin is preserved in college use. Many diplomas are in Latin, and at some institutions the commencement formulas are in Latin. At a more routine level, several Latin words and abbreviations are used in the *footnotes of academic research (*ibid., passim, supra, infra, loc. cit.* . .), though there is a definite tendency to use English words for many of these.

Prefixes of Latin origin (*ante-, ex-, in-, pre-, re-, sub-* . . .) and other compounding elements, such as *uni-* (*unilateral*), *bi-* (*biweekly*), are active in forming new English words. At present scientific words are being formed more from Greek than from Latin elements.

2. LATIN FORMS. English continues to use the Latin forms for some words that are used principally in the formal dialects (*alumnus—alumna, bacillus—bacilli*), but those commonly used have either English plurals or both (*formula, formulas* or *formulae; focus, focuses* or *foci; stadium, stadiums* or *stadia*).

See *Plurals § 4, *data.

3. LATIN CONSTRUCTIONS. The general reading of Latin literature by educated English and Americans, especially between 1750 and 1850, had a considerable effect on English style, tending to rather long and involved sentences. The decline of this reading of Latin is one of several causes of the current direct sentence movement.

A less advantageous and more particular effect of Latin on English has been through the crude translations of elementary Latin classes in which constructions such as the ablative absolute have been set over into un-English idioms: "The baggage wagons having been arranged in a circle, the Romans were prepared to defend the camp" when English would more naturally have "After the baggage wagons had been arranged in a circle, the Romans . . ."

4. LATIN AND ENGLISH GRAMMAR. The first and a number of other English grammars were composed by men thoroughly familiar with Latin, who believed that English was or at any rate

should be a language like Latin. As a result, English, which was a Germanic language in structure, was described in terms of Latin grammar, and rules were devised for making the language fit the picture. This may be one reason for the conventional taboo of the *split infinitive (which would be impossible in Latin because the infinitive is one word, as in *laborare* where English has *to work*) and of putting a preposition at the end of a sentence (*Prepositions § 3d), which is impossible in Latin but is a characteristic English idiom.

Only recently has English grammar been based squarely on a study of the English language and freed from the categories and some of the rules of Latin grammar.

latter, later *Latter* (lat'ər) and *later* (lā'tər) are often carelessly confused. The habit of reading your copy aloud to yourself should catch this type of error. See *former—first, latter—last.

lay—lie In vulgate English the work of these two verbs is generally done by one (*lay, lay* or *laid, laid*). Formal and careful informal writing use them as follows:

> lie ("to recline," intransitive), lay, lain
> lay ("to place," transitive), laid, laid

You *lie* down for a rest or *lie* down on the job; a farm *lies* in a valley. You *lay* a floor, *lay* a book on the table, *lay* a bet, *lay* out clothes. Yesterday you *lay* down to rest (colloquially often *laid*), you *laid* a book on the table.

Egg laying is *lay, laid, laid.*

-le words A large and interesting group of English verbs ends in *-le—fiddle, giggle, meddle, tickle, waddle, whistle, whittle*—in which the ending usually suggests an action continued or habitually repeated.

Lab*el* (verb and noun), mant*el* (the shelf), and nick*el* give some spelling trouble because they are exceptions to the usual English spelling of this final syllable.

lead, led *Lead* and *led* show the confusion that English suffers because of representing one sound by different symbols. *Lead* [lēd], the present tense of the verb, gives no trouble; but *led*, the past tense, is often confused with *lead* (led), the metal, and misspelled.

> Please lead the horse away.
> The culprit was led into the office.
> Lead is known as a base metal.

Leaders Leaders, or "period leaders," are a line of spaced periods used to guide the reader's eye across a page to some item, word, or number that completes the sense. They are often used in statistical tables and the table of contents of a book:

In typed copy, hyphens are often used instead of periods.

learn—teach Vulgate English often uses *learn* in the sense of *teach* (He learned me how to tie six kinds of knots). Educated usage keeps the distinction:

He *taught* me how to tie six kinds of knot.
I *learned* how to tie knots from him.

leave *let (leave)

-ledge, -lege Two common words are spelled with the ending *-ledge*:

acknowledge (acknowledging, acknowledgment)   knowledge

Words spelled with *-lege* should not be confused with them:

allege (alleged, alleging)   college   sacrilege (sacrilegious)

Legal language Most legal matters are carried on in a jargon bristling with long series of synonyms (do hereby give, grant, bargain, sell and convey), archaic or foreign (French, Latin) words for everyday things and situations, abbreviations and stereotyped phrases that puzzle laymen and sometimes lawyers themselves. The need for precision and of certain technical words is of course great, but the reason for much of the jargon is unconsidered tradition. Perhaps this jargon must be tolerated in legal business, but lawyers and others who have much to do with law should realize that it is a trade jargon (shoptalk). When they are off duty they should try to speak and write appropriately to non-professional situations.

There are many lawyers and judges whose speeches, briefs, and decisions are written with distinction and with only as many technical terms as the subject demands. The style is properly formal, the allusions must be to cases that give precedents, but room may be found for allusion also to general experience, without any loss of exactness.

A brief dissenting opinion of Mr. Justice Holmes illustrates a compact but readable judicial style. A majority of the Supreme

Court had decided that the State of Ohio could tax a membership in the New York Stock Exchange owned by a resident of Ohio, on the ground that it was personal property, not like real estate, which would be taxed by the state in which it lay.

The question whether a seat in the New York Stock Exchange is taxable in Ohio consistently with the principles established by this Court seems to me more difficult than it does to my brethren. All rights are intangible personal relations between the subject and the object of them created by law. But it is established that it is not enough that the subject, the owner of the right, is within the power of the taxing State. He cannot be taxed for land situated elsewhere, and the same is true of personal property permanently out of the jurisdiction. It does not matter, I take it, whether the interest is legal or equitable, or what the machinery by which it is reached, but the question is whether the object of the right is so local in its foundation and prime meaning that it should stand like an interest in land. If left to myself I should have thought that the foundation and substance of the plaintiff's right was the right of himself and his associates personally to enter the New York Stock Exchange building and to do business there. I should have thought that all the rest was incidental to that and that that on its face was localized in New York. If so, it does not matter whether it is real or personal property or that it adds to the owner's credit and facilities in Ohio. The same would be true of a great estate in New York land.—*Representative Opinions of Mr. Justice Holmes,* edited by Alfred Lief, pp. 265-66

Reference: Benjamin N. Cardozo, "Law and Literature" (pp. 3-40 in the volume of the same title—New York, 1931)

leisure Usual American pronunciation, lē′zhər; sometimes lezh′ər.

less, fewer *Fewer* refers only to number and things that are *counted*:

> Fewer cars were on the road.
> There were fewer than sixty present.

In formal usage *less* refers only to amount or quantity and things measured:

> There was a good deal less tardiness in the second term [amount].
> There was even less hay than the summer before.

In general usage it refers also to number:

> In the making of the present work no less than 513,000 terms of all kinds were critically examined, revised, or defined.—Preface to *New Standard Dictionary*

less, lesser Both are used as comparatives (of *little*), *less* more usually referring to size, or quantity (less time, less food), *lesser* a formal word, referring to value or importance (a lesser writer).

let (leave) A very common vulgate idiom is the use of *leave* where formal and informal English use *let*. Both idioms are shown in this sentence by a student who was obviously making a transition between the two levels:

By the time I got to high school, I was cured of the practice of leaving [vulgate] notebooks go, but I fell immediately into the habit of letting [informal] homework slide.

College people should use *let—let it go, let it lie where it is* . . .

let's Contraction of *let us*. Needs an apostrophe.

Letters 1. GENERAL OBSERVATIONS ON CORRESPONDENCE. (*a*) *Materials*. The stationery stores are full of novelties, which may appeal to one's taste, but the standard sizes and styles of paper are never outmoded and are usually cheaper and of better quality:

Note paper—A four-page sheet to be folded once across the middle for the envelope.

Club paper—A sheet about 7¼ by 11 inches, with two folds fitting an envelope 3¾ by 7½.

Business letter paper—8½ by 11 inches, to be folded twice across for a long envelope or folded across the middle and then twice more for the ordinary envelope about six inches long.

A fairly good quality of stationery is worth its cost in the good impression it helps make on the reader.

Typewritten copy is of course the norm in business correspondence. In personal letters there is some question, though in the United States so many people do their own typing that among acquaintances typewritten copy is quite good form—and usually welcome. In the earlier stages of a friendship longhand is perhaps preferable, and it should almost always be used for invitations and acknowledgments and in any letters conveying unusual sentiment or feeling. (*Typewritten copy)

b) *Styles*. Professional stenographers have set a high standard of mechanical excellence in business letters, and an amateur should follow their example in making the pages appeal to the reader's eye. This means leaving good margins, centering the body of the letter on the page so that the whole may present a neatly balanced and proportioned appearance, spacing the parts of the letter so that they are kept distinct but still form a unit, and so on. The paragraphs are usually short, perhaps only three or four sentences, and spaced so that they stand out distinctly.

Ingenuity can usually find a way of subduing even long addresses that must sometimes be used in headings. Find an arrangement of the lines that looks well in your typing or longhand. The items may be centered:

315 South Massachusetts Hall
Hanover, New Hampshire
February 8, 1942

Long firm names should usually be written in two lines:

The Commercial Travelers Mutual
Accident Association of America
Utica   New York

TAYLOR BOOKSHOP
80 WINCHESTER STREET
NEW YORK CITY

June 16, 1942

Mr. James T. Foster
2645 Grantham Terrace
Kew Gardens, L.I., N.Y.

Dear Sir:

Several weeks ago you asked us to let you know when the new Fischer edition of Shakespeare would be on sale. It is obtainable now, and we think you will like it very much. The volumes are three by four inches in size, bound in red and gold.

There are 25 books in the complete set, which costs $15.75, but separate volumes may be bought for 65¢ each. We are enclosing a list of the works included in the Fischer edition.

If you wish to place an order, we shall be glad to take care of it for you.

Yours truly,

Elizabeth Reagan

Form for Business Letter

Style in indenting and in punctuation at the end of display lines is divided. In typed letters a straight lining at the left of the heading and inside address is more usual now than a hanging *indention:

STRAIGHT FORM—MORE COMMON	INDENTED FORM—LESS COMMON
Graham, Sutton and Company 1007 E. Newgate Street Chicago, Illinois	Graham, Sutton and Company 1007 E. Newgate Street Chicago, Illinois

In longhand letters the indented form is more common.

The form used for the address on the envelope should be consistent with that used for the heading and the address on the first page of the letter; that is, either the straight or the indented form should be used throughout.

Punctuation marks may be used at the end of display lines but they have now been generally dropped because they serve no useful purpose and the page looks tidier without them:

CURRENT STYLE	OLD-FASHIONED STYLE
Graham, Sutton and Company 1007 E. Newgate Street Chicago, Illinois	Graham, Sutton and Company, 1007 E. Newgate Street, Chicago, Illinois.

c) *Envelopes.* The first requirements of the address on the envelope are completeness and clearness, for the sake of the post office people who must handle the letter. "Address your mail to street and number."

The best way to see how letters should be folded is to examine the practice of reputable business houses in the folding and placing in envelopes of letters using your size of stationery.

2. PERSONAL LETTERS. (*a*) *Form.* The form of personal letters varies with the intimacy between the writer and recipient. No heading except the date is needed between regular correspondents, but the writer's address in the heading is a convenience and often a necessity in letters to occasional correspondents. They may not keep address books and aren't likely to remember exact addresses.

The salutation varies:

Dear Bob,   Dear Miss Breckenridge,
Dear Miss Breckenridge: (The colon is more formal.)
FORMAL: My dear Miss Breckenridge:

Formal personal letters, especially between professional men who are not intimate, may have the salutation "Dear Sir": and the recipient's name at the bottom, flush with the left margin.

The complimentary close ranges from "Yours" or any other expression of sentiment to "Yours sincerely," "Cordially yours,"

"Yours very truly," between people little acquainted. When there is any doubt, rely on one of the regular formulas for the close, "Yours truly," "Yours very truly." Sentence conclusions ("Assuring you of our continued interest, I beg to remain, Yours very truly") are now out of fashion.

b) *Tone and style.* It would be useless to lay down rules to govern letters to relatives and friends. They should represent your own sense of what the reader will like and what will sound like yourself. They are like conversation, and the style will ordinarily be *familiar or whatever you would use when face to face with the recipient. But, as in so much conversation, we often sink to our laziest in letters to the people we write the oftenest. It is worth while occasionally to read over a letter to see if *we* would enjoy receiving it, to see if we have told enough to make the incidents interesting, to see if we have written with reasonable care, if we are paying our readers the courtesy they deserve in neatness and appropriate expression. Revising an occasional letter will perhaps raise the average of them all, if we can do that without losing a natural tone.

It is conventional to say that the art of letter writing is dead. Perhaps not so many Contributor's Club essays are sent through the mail as formerly, but an occasional letter we receive and an occasional published volume show that letter writers can still describe events racily, can still hit off the people they meet in apt characterizations, and can occasionally discuss ideas with some insight and gusto. These letters are a challenge to us when we have material that deserves special attention.

For formal invitations and so on, see *Social correspondence.

3. BUSINESS LETTERS. Since business letters usually pass between people who are not acquainted or who at least are not writing for reasons of friendship at the moment, certain matters of form are important in handling routine information.

The writer's complete address is necessary, either in a printed letterhead or in a written heading, to serve as an address for the reply. An inside address is conventional (and useful when the letter is dictated or when several are being written at the same time or when it is to be filed). In addressing a firm, *Messrs.* is not often used in the United States. The salutations are:

Dear Sir: Gentlemen: Dear Sirs:
Dear Madam: Ladies: (Formal or showy, Mesdames:)

When a letter is intended for a particular member of a firm, this form is sometimes used:

Graham, Sutton and Company
1007 E. Newgate Street
Chicago, Illinois
Gentlemen:
Attention Mr. Stephen Lange

A less formal and more direct form of address is perhaps more commonly used.

Mr. Stephen Lange
Graham, Sutton and Company
1007 E. Newgate Street
Chicago, Illinois
Dear Mr. Lange:

When a man's position is made part of the inside address, arrange it so that no one line becomes conspicuously longer than the others. In general the title should be joined to the individual's rather than to the firm's name:

Professor R. S. Crane, Chairman
Department of English
The University of Chicago
Chicago, Illinois

Mr. Leonard T. Hosic
Personnel Director
Allen, Swift and Company
4826 Commercial Street
Allentown, Ohio

The body of a business letter should be clear, direct, and as brief as is consistent with clearness. A separate paragraph is used for each item or for each sub-division of the message. The tone may be curt in routine matters—amateurs are apt to indulge in unnecessary explanation—or it may be full and persuasive. In all letters, especially those asking questions or outlining plans, all relevant information should be given.

The desire for brevity should not lead to a telegraphic style or short-cuts in expression. The old tags like "Yours received and contents noted," "In reply to your favor of the 12th inst.," and "Would say" have disappeared from the correspondence of careful business houses.

The best way to become informed on business letters is to study the practice of reputable companies. If you are specially interested in business correspondence, start a collection of the best examples that come your way.

The close of a business letter is:

Yours truly,   Yours very truly,   Very truly yours,

or some such formula. Only the first word is capitalized and the phrase is followed by a comma (though some writers are dropping the comma, since it is as unnecessary as those once standing after the display lines).

*Business English. Any recent manual of business writing will give further details of form and suggestions for content.

Letters of the alphabet The plural of letters of the alphabet is usually formed by 's, sometimes, especially of capitals, by the *s* alone:

Taboo is spelled with two o's or a *u*.   two *F*s

Levels of usage Usage varies according to the education and social class of the writer and reader, speaker and listener, and according to the usual circumstances in which particular words and constructions are found. This is one of the fundamental facts of language, and one that causes many problems in speaking and writing. This *Guide-Index* distinguishes three main levels, Formal, Informal, and Vulgate English, and various subdivisions of these. It is necessary to understand the distinctions between them to be able to apply the specific suggestions made in the various particular articles. They are described in full in "Levels of usage," p. 11. See especially the table of levels on p. 13.

lever Both lev′ər and lē′vər are in good use, the second felt by many to be more stylish.

liable *likely—apt—liable

Library work See Chapter 13, p. 319, The Research Paper.

lie *lay—lie

lighted—lit Both forms are in good use as the past tense and past participle of *light*. *Lighted* is probably more common as the adjective and past participle:

a lighted lamp   He had lighted a fire.

Lit is perhaps more common as the past tense:

He lit a cigaret. [or] He lighted a cigaret.

Use whichever fits the rhythm of the sentence better.

lightning, lightening The flash is *lightning*; making lighter (a load) is *lightening*.

like—as 1. In written English *as* and *as if* are used to introduce clauses of comparison:

People try to get to college as they used to try to get to heaven.
Habit grips a person as an octopus does.
He dives so that it looks as if he would land flat, but he enters the water perfectly.

2. In colloquial English *like* is often heard in such constructions, instead of *as* or *as if*. *Like* is less common in the East than in the West and South, but it is used more or less throughout the United States and in England also.

He dives so it looks like he would land flat.

"I get around the country a good bit, gentlemen, and I can tell you as a fact that he's slipping. Like you just said, people are waking up to the fact that somebody's got to pay for all this spending."— Gluyas Williams, "Raconteurs," *The New Yorker*, Oct. 8, 1938

He treated her like a child, joking with her like she was a two year old. (Report of oral testimony in court)

In all regions and in all dialects *like* is used when the clause is verbless:

Habit grips a person like an octopus.
She took to selling like a duck to water.
That description fits him like a glove.

3. In the last few years the colloquial use of *like* as a conjunction has greatly increased. The vogue of fiction, in which it often stands appropriately in the conversation and sometimes in the informal prose surrounding the conversation, as well as the popular radio programs in colloquial or vulgate English are doubtless in part responsible for this increased currency. In fact, if editors and publishers did not enforce the use of *as* instead of *like* according to the rules in their stylebooks, it is possible that *like* would become the dominant form, and it increasingly appears in print:

Eleanor was alone like in her dreams.—John Dos Passos, *The 42nd Parallel*, p. 217

You used to go in there and find Henry not at the middle of his desk, but sitting at one end, nervously, like he was afraid of the job.— Cal Tinney, *The Philadelphia Record*, Nov. 17, 1938

This use of *like* in public address is quite common, even among careful people. One of our most fastidious radio announcers said:

You can play Information Please in your home just like the experts do here in the studio.

Historically both forms are good, since both are parts of the older *like as* ("Like as a father pitieth his children . . ."). Some speakers have taken *as*, others *like*. *Like* is preferable from the standpoint of meaning, because *as* has several different meanings and several functions in the language and so is relatively weak. *Like* is more exact and more emphatic in a comparison than *as* can be.

This construction is worth careful observation to see if *like* gains sufficient reputability so that it can be safely used in writing. Meanwhile, be on your guard.

References: Curme, *Syntax*, pp. 281-82; Pooley, pp. 134-36

likely—apt—liable The principal meanings of these words are:

likely: expected, probably
liable: possible [of an unpleasant event]; responsible [as for damages]
apt: tending toward, naturally fit

Likely is the most commonly needed of the three, and colloquially both *apt* and (in some localities) *liable* are used in the ordinary sense of *likely*:

It is likely to rain when the wind is southwest. [Or, if the rain is viewed with disfavor], It is liable to rain when the wind is southwest. [Or, colloquially], It is apt to rain when the wind is southwest.

line is business English (What's your line?—a line of goods) or slang (He handed her a line). As a counter word it is usually deadwood and could better be left out:

My own experience along business lines [that is, *in business*] has been slight.
Another book along the same lines as "Microbe Hunters" [similar to "Microbe Hunters"], but with a fine story, is "Arrowsmith."

Linguistics 1. THE SCIENCE OF LINGUISTICS. The science dealing with language is called *linguistics* (sometimes *philology*, its older name) and a scientific student of language is a *linguist* or *philologist*. Linguistics is a complex science, with numerous subdivisions, each with its technique for observing and considering its material, its hypotheses, laws, and theories, and often forecasts of future trends. The principal subdivisions of linguistics are:

a) *Phonetics*, the study of sounds, how they are made by the vocal organs and how they are manipulated in various languages, types of pronunciation, and sound changes. See *Pronunciation.

b) *Accidence* (or *morphology*), the forms of words, especially their inflections, as in the conjugations of verbs, declensions of nouns and pronouns, comparison of adjectives and adverbs. These forms are discussed under the heads of the various parts of speech: *Adjectives, types and forms, *Nouns §2, *Verbs, and in other articles like *Accusative case, *Plurals, *Subjunctives.

c) *Orthography*, which means merely spelling. See Ch. 10, p. 267.

d) *Etymology*, the derivation of words and the steps by which they have moved from their early to their current forms. See *Origin of words.

e) *Semantics* (or *semasiology*), a newly enlarged branch of linguistics, studies the meanings of words and the ways in which these meanings change. See Chapter 7, p. 182, The meaning of words.

f) *Syntax* is the study of the use of words in phrases, clauses, sentences. See *Grammar, *Idiom and idioms, *Phrases, *Clauses, Chapters 5 and 6 (Sentences), and many particular entries.

g) *Philosophical grammar* (or *linguistic theory*) is an especially live branch of the study at present; it deals with general laws of language and speculates on its possible origins, functions, underlying tendencies.

There are various applications of these sciences, such as *Lexicography*, the art of dictionary making. See "The usefulness of dictionaries," p. 196.

The various types of *Grammar* (a general term for a selection of linguistic facts) are described under that head.

Since language is an activity of people, a phase of conduct, linguists cannot work entirely by themselves but are helped by other scientists, especially psychologists, ethnologists, and sociologists, and in turn give materials to them. And on the other hand, the study of language runs into artistic considerations, contributing to literary criticism and the art of composition, where language is not only described but its effectiveness must be considered, and taste and judgment count as well as scientific principles.

The outstanding trait of a linguist's approach to language is detachment—contrasting with the emotion often shown by nonprofessional users in defending or disapproving matters of speech. A linguist accepts "He ain't got none," "You're all wet" as facts of language—as well as words like *hemolysis* and *sternutation*. This does not mean that he uses all of these locutions himself or recommends them to others, but he notices that certain people use them and he observes and defines their place in the language. See the articles on *due to, *like—as, and other debated locutions.

2. RECORDING EXAMPLES OF USAGE. If we are going to study our language in college, we should study it scientifically as far as that is possible and so put our effort on a par with other college subjects. This means that first we should observe carefully the spoken and written language of others, especially of those whose language we should like our own to resemble. We should get rid of preferences and prejudices that are not supported by good usage, so far as that is humanly possible. We should investigate and even experiment with particular usage so far as we can and come to some conclusion as to its fitness for our own expression. In short, we should become amateur linguists—students of our language.

Anyone who is seriously interested in such an approach to his language will do everything possible to sharpen his observation of actual usage, so that he won't have to be completely dependent on dictionaries and handbooks. Especially if he is interested in some particular trend, in sentences, perhaps, or in some idioms, such as the prepositions used with *different*, he might keep track of what he finds in actual listening and reading.

The easiest way to do this is to have a file of observations on 3x5 or 4x6 slips or cards. The 4x6 are probably the more useful, since they have space for recording more than one example and for discussion. The slips should be labeled at the top with the name of the particular point dealt with, under which it will be filed. Exact reference should be made to the source of the quotation, or to the speaker and place and circumstances of speaking.

1. EXAMPLE OF USAGE

Sub-class of the topic

Label—the topic illustrated

The example

Exact source— If from speech put down time, place, and identify speaker

```
Verbless sentence---Answers to questions
    When an editor does the work and you still
    have to make corrections on the proof be-
    cause his work was not perfect, can you make
 #  him pay for them?  Not likely.  If the printer
    does the preparation and you have to make
    the corrections in the type to get a satis-
    factory result, will the printer make the
 #  corrections gratis?  Hardly, unless you have
    a very clear agreement with him in writing.
            John Benbow Manuscript & Proof
            N. Y.  Oxford  1937  p. 22
```

2. TOPIC WITH RECORD OF INVESTIGATION

Label "Authorities"

Special source

Reasoning

Conclusion

```
    drought--drouth
Web.Coll.5th ed:  drought.  Also drouth
Not in Fowler
Coll. Standard '36  drought
                    drouth
Sylvanus Kingsley, editorial writer Portland
Oregonian, in Words Sept. 1936: prefers drouth
as 'the more practical and popular etymology'--
but 6 of 1 and half dozen of the other
OE drugath. th puts it in group with abstracts
width, breadth.  See height-heighth.  Get quotes
of actual use.  Shows influence of events on
language, since notable dryness of recent years
has given the word currency and brought into
prominence the colloquial form
Usage divided.  Drought probably more common in
formal use, but drouth gaining esp. in news-
papers.
```

The first slip reproduced on page 592 shows a quotation taken down to illustrate the use of *verbless sentences. The second slip contains the data that stands back of the entry *drought— drouth in Part 2 of this *Guide-Index.*

Keep the slips in alphabetical order, unless you have a great many of them and want to make some topical groupings. You don't need to worry about your file getting unwieldy, for you won't gather many unless you are really interested, and if you are interested they will form a hobby—and will help you make accurate statements about English usage instead of just guessing.

References: The works given in the Bibliography at the beginning of this book. Of these the best for a beginner are probably Ballard, Kennedy, Krapp, and McKnight.

Linking verbs (Correction: The verb marked is used as a linking verb and should be followed by an adjective or noun construction.) *Link*

1. A verb may be used so that it has little or no meaning of its own but functions chiefly in connecting a subject with a predicate adjective or noun. In such a construction it is called a *linking verb* or *copula. Be* is most commonly used as a linking verb, since in its ordinary use it has little specific meaning and performs chiefly the verb functions of tense, person, number:

The man *is* a carpenter.   This bottle *was* full.

Many other verbs are used as linking verbs—Curme counts about sixty in current English and says, "Their wide and varied use is the most prominent feature of our language" (*Parts of Speech,* p. 67). Instead of having a verb of full meaning like *colden,* English uses the nearly meaningless verb *turn* or *get* and the adjective *cold,* which carries the chief part of the meaning, in such a sentence as *The weather turned cold.* Many verbs are used with full meaning of their own (as *fell* in "The tree *fell* in the water") or as linking verbs (as *fell* in "She *fell* silent" or "He *fell* ill"). Some typical linking verbs are:

He *became* a doctor.   The butter *tastes* rancid.   She *felt* sad. He *acts* old.   The ground *sounds* hollow.   He *grew* more and more distant.   He *appeared* to be gaining ground.   This *looks* first rate.   The conductor *looked* miserable.

His features *had become* sharper; his eyes, with their black-blue glitter of chilled steel, *had become* harder and more impenetrable. His flaxen hair, still profuse, and his little bi-forked beard, *had turned* darker. His nose *had grown* thinner, reminding one of the beak of a bird of prey.—Dmitri Merejkowski, *The Romance of Leonardo da Vinci,* p. 403

2. *Be* and other linking verbs are followed not by adverbs but by adjectives or nouns in single words or phrases or clauses, known as *predicate adjectives* and *predicate nominatives* respectively.

*be §2, *Predicate adjectives
References: Kennedy, pp. 476-77; Curme, *Parts of Speech*, pp. 66-69, *Syntax*, pp. 26-28 (list on p. 27)

Literal use of words See "Figurative use of words," p. 229.

literary *Literary*, as applied to style, usually means possessing traits that are characteristic of the more conservative tradition of English literature. Its connotation may be "distinguished" or it may be "bookish." See "Formal English," p. 25.

Litotes (lī′tō tēz, lit′ō tēz) *Negatives, *Understatement

little *Little* is an informal word, overused by sentimentalists ("little dear" and so on). *Small* is the more formal word for size.

loan as a verb In spite of attempts to keep *loan* only as a noun and to make *lend* the corresponding verb, *loan* is still properly a verb, at least in American usage:

I loaned [or lent] him $2.
He got a loan of two dollars.

Loan words Words that have been taken into English from other languages (*khaki, intelligentsia*) and have become English words. *Foreign words in English, *Origin of words §2*b*

Local **Localisms** (CORRECTION: The expression marked is in local use only. Replace it by a word or construction in general English use.)

A *localism*, or *provincialism*, is a word or other expression in regular use in a certain region but not in others in which the same language is used. The southern, western, and northeastern sections of the United States differ somewhat in sounds, in words, and in constructions. Localisms are appropriate to conversation, familiar writing, stories, and to much other informal writing, but are often out of place in impersonal and formal writing.

For discussion see "Dialects and localisms," p. 6.

locate is colloquially used for *settle* (The family located near the present town of Nashua) and for *find* (I can't locate the letter now). It is wordy in defining the location of specific places:

Zermatt is [located] right near the Italian border, just to the west of the Italian Lake District.

Locution is a handy term for referring to a word or a unified group of words; that is, it may be applied to a single word or to a phrase or clause considered as a meaning group. *Phrase, a meaning group, that is* are three locutions.

Long variants Some amateur writers are tempted to add an extra prefix or suffix to a word that already carries the meaning they intend. They write *ir*regard*less*, though *regardless* already means "without regard to." Some like to add sonorous suffixes that are quite useless, like the *-ation* in *origination*, which means no more than *origin*.

Some other tempting long variants to be avoided are:

confliction for *conflict*   *analyzation* for *analysis*
emotionality when only *emotion* is meant
commercialistic for *commercial*
ruination for *ruin* (*ruination* is a colloquial emphatic form of *ruin*)
hotness for *heat*
intermingle for *mingle*   *subsidization* for *subsidizing*
repay when simple *pay* is meant, as in paying dividends
Unnecessary *-al* endings, as *transportation*[al] system, *government*[al] policy
utilize when only *use* is meant

Some of these words are not in good use at all (*irregardless, analyzation*) and show lack of observation of language in anyone who uses them. Others are in use but show poor judgment in the writer who chooses them when more compact forms exist. If any number are used they will weigh down a piece of writing and make it flabby.

See *Origin of words §3 and compare "Big words," p. 220.
Reference: Fowler, Long variants

look When used as a verb of complete meaning, equivalent to *seem, look* is modified by an adverb:

look searchingly   look sharp

As a linking verb, equivalent to *appear, look* is followed by an adjective which modifies the subject:

He looks well, or healthy, or tired . . .

Loose sentences Sentences in which the grammatical form and the essential meaning are complete before the end. See "Loose and periodic sentences," p. 157.

lose, loose Associate the spelling with the pronunciation:

lose (lüz)—lose a bet, lose sleep, lose money
loose (lüs)—loose a knot, a loose screw
loosed (lüst)—untied, freed
lost (lôst)—a lost road, a lost soul, lost his way

lot, lots of The colloquial uses of these words, appropriate in speech and in some informal writing, are avoided in formal writing:

Colloquial:	We tried a lot of different kinds.
Formal:	We tried a good many different kinds.
Colloquial:	He has lots of friends . . . a lot of money.
Formal:	He has many friends . . . a good deal of money.

Do not join the article *a* to lot: *a lot*, not *alot*.

lousy Except when meaning "infested with lice" *lousy* is a more or less violent slang word of abuse, just now weakened to a counter word of disapproval, expressive if not used too often, but offensive to most ears.

lovely is a colloquial *counter word of approval, useful chiefly because its pronunciation can (by some people) be drawn out indefinitely and practically sung (a lovely time).

lowbrow *highbrow

lc **Lower case** (Correction: Use a lower case ["small"] letter instead of a capital in this word. See *Type, *Capital Letters.)

-ly A few adjectives end in -*ly* (*comely, kindly, lovely*), but -*ly* is more distinctively an ending for adverbs, representing the Old English adverbial ending -*lice* of adjectives and participles:

brightly	formerly	graciously	frankly

---

*Adverbs, types and forms § 3

M The sound represented by the letter *m* is a nasal consonant, made with lips closed: *man, music, diamond, drummer, sum, lamp*.

M may represent a syllable by itself ("vocalic *m*"): *spasm* (spaz′əm), *tell 'em* (tel′əm). Some people tend to make *m* vocalic in words like *elm, film* (el′əm, fil′əm) instead of pronouncing single syllables (elm, film).

madam As a formula of address *Madam* or *Dear Madam* is used to both married and unmarried women.

Magazine indexes See "Periodical indexes," p. 328.

majority, plurality Strictly *majority* means "more than half of" a certain number; *plurality* means "more than the next highest." *Plurality* is not much used now in the United States, the meaning of *majority* being extended to "an excess of votes over all others cast"—and even often used in the exact sense of *plurality*, simply the excess of votes over the next highest. In an election with three candidates and 12,000 votes cast, one received 7000, one 3000, and one 2000; the winner would have a *plurality* of 4000 (in loose usage, a majority of 4000); he would have a *majority* of 2000.

Colloquially *majority* is often used of amounts or quantities as well as of numbers:

COLLOQUIAL: We spent the majority of the day there.
WRITTEN: We spent most of the day there.
WORDY: The majority of students are interested in football.
BETTER: Most students are interested in football.

Malapropism A malapropism is a confusion of two words somewhat similar in sound but different in meaning, as *arduous* love for *ardent* love. Malapropisms are the cause of many *boners but are often intentionally used for humorous effect, as they were by Sheridan in creating the part of Mrs. Malaprop in *The Rivals*, whose speeches gave the name to these confusions in language:

"I would by no means wish a daughter of mine to be a progeny of learning. . . . Then, sir, she should have a supercilious knowledge in accounts;—and as she grew up, I would have her instructed in geometry, that she might know something of the contagious countries. . . ."—RICHARD BRINSLEY SHERIDAN, *The Rivals*, Act I, Scene ii

Malapropisms are more effective in speech than in writing.

man, woman These are preferred to the more pretentious *gentleman* or *lady*, except when *man* or *woman* would sound conspicuously blunt.

In business English the original social distinctions between *woman—lady*, and *man—gentleman* have been almost reversed. A salesman faced with a customer who wanted to exchange a purchase, turned to his fellow salesmen and said, "Did any of you gentlemen wait on this man?" And a woman looking for work asked, "Are you the woman who wanted a lady to wash for her?"

Ladies and gentlemen is a *formula in addressing an audience. The singular form alone is used as an adjective:

manpower   manholes   woman hater

manner *In a . . . manner* is very often *deadwood. "He did it clumsily" has a more definite emphasis than "He did it in a clumsy manner."

Manner Adverbs of manner answer the question *How? Barely, brightly, gracefully, nicely, quick* or *quickly, swimmingly* are adverbs of manner. They are formed now by adding *-ly* to adjectives and participles, though a number of older adverbs of manner do not have the -ly: *sharp* or *sharply*, *slow* or *slowly*, etc. (*Adverbs, types and forms §3)

As, as if, as though (formal) and colloquially *like* are conjunctions introducing adverbial clauses of manner:

He looked as if he'd seen a ghost.   They left as noisily as they came.
They went as though there was a fire.

MS Manuscript form (CORRECTION: Your manuscript is not acceptable. Revise or rewrite as directed.)

See "Preparing the manuscript," p. 303, for details of good manuscript practice. See also *Typewritten copy.

Margins See "The page," p. 304.

Material Some suggestions on gathering and handling material will be found in "Gathering material," p. 294, and Ch. 13, pp. 324-35.

matinee Spelled without an accent mark. Pronounced mat ə nā', but tending toward mat'ə nā (as in England).

may *can—may (could—might)

may be, maybe *Maybe* is a colloquial adverb meaning "perhaps," a cutting down of *it may be*; *may be* is a verb form:

Maybe you'll have better luck next time. He may be the next mayor.

me *Pronouns §1, *between you and me, *It's me

Mean Meaning of words (CORRECTION: The word marked is inexactly used. Replace it by one that represents your meaning.)

For discussion of meaning of words, see Chapter 7, p. 182.

Mechanics of writing includes punctuation, spelling, forms of words, word order, and sometimes sentence movement.

For discussion of some points of "mechanics" and exercises, see Chapters 9-11, p. 250 ff.

medieval Some years ago the American Historical Association decided to change the spelling from *mediaeval* to *medieval*, now the usual form. Pronunciation mē'di ē'vəl, sometimes med'i ē'vəl.

medium Plural usually *mediums*, always in the spiritualistic sense, practically always in the general sense, and usually now as applied to the different advertising *mediums* (newspapers, magazines, radio, billboards, etc.). *Media* is most used in scientific contexts.

messrs. is the abbreviation of French *messieurs* but pronounced as English, mes'ərz. It is used as the plural of *Mr.* (Messrs. Roosevelt and Wallace) and sometimes, though rarely now in

American usage, used in addressing firms (Messrs. Brown, Hubbell and Company).

Metaphor A figure of speech in which a comparison is implied rather than stated: a *finger* of light, a slender *thread* of sense. See "Metaphors, similes, analogies," p. 235.

meter is now more common spelling than *metre*. The second *e* drops out in derivatives: *metrical, metrics, metric system.*

For a description of English meters see *Verse form.

Metonymy (me ton′i mi) A figure of speech in which the name of something closely associated with a thing is substituted for its name: *paper* for financial assets, in *Dickens* for in Dickens' works. See "Metonymy and synecdoche," p. 238.

midst A rather formal word except in the preposition *in the midst of. In our midst* and so on are country journalese for "with us," "in our town."

might *can—may (could—might)

might of *have §3

Minimum essentials See Chapter 9, p. 250.

Mispronounced words A list of words offering difficulty in pronunciation is in *Pronunciation §5.

Misrelated construction *Participles §2, *Dangling modifiers

miss Plural *misses,* sometimes pronounced mis ēz to distinguish from missis (Mrs.): "the Misses Angel and Joyce." When the misses are from the same family the plural could be, formally, the Misses Smith; colloquially, the Miss Smiths.

Miss is used only with a person's name—except in humor or sales talk. *Missy* is the diminutive, often disparaging.

Misspelled words See Chapter 10, p. 267 and *Spelling.

mix, mixer *Mix* is informal and colloquial for *associate with; mixer* for *sociable* person or for the person who develops new acquaintances readily. Though slang in their origin, they seem excusable because of the colorlessness of the more reputable words. The objection often made to *good mixer* is not so much linguistic as that college students seem to overvalue "mixing."

Mixed figures of speech See "Consistency," p. 233.

Mixed usage Many errors in writing spring from the unintentional mixture of different levels of usage. Colloquial or conspicuously informal words or idioms may stray into formal writing; vulgate locutions may appear in informal writing, or so may a word usually confined to law or business. Distinctly formal words and idioms are equally inappropriate in informal writing—and often appear because the writer is trying to avoid some natural expression. The principal way to develop in language is to cultivate feeling for different styles and their fitness for a given job. See Chs. 1 and 2.

Modal auxiliaries *Auxiliary verbs and entries on *be, *can—may, *have, *shall—will, and other auxiliaries

Modifiers Modifiers are words or groups of words that restrict, limit, make more exact the meaning of other words. In these examples the words in italics modify the words in small caps:

a *cold, windy* DAY He FAILED *miserably.* a *truly* GREAT . . . a *truly great* MAN *Coming around the corner,* WE met him head on. *As we came around the corner,* we SAW him boarding a trolley.

In general the modifiers of nouns and pronouns are adjectives, participles, adjective phrases, adjective clauses; the modifiers of verbs, adjectives, and adverbs are adverbs, adverbial phrases or clauses.

*Adjectives, use; *Adverbs, use; *Clauses; *Participles; *Dangling modifiers; *Phrases; *Restrictive and non-restrictive

Money **1.** Exact sums of money are usually written in figures:

72¢ $4.98 $5 $168.75 $42,810

Round sums are more likely to be written in words:

two hundred dollars   a million and a half dollars

In factual books or articles involving frequent references to sums of money, however, figures are often used throughout.

2. In consecutive writing, amounts are usually written out when used adjectively:

A Million Dollar Baby in the Five and Ten Cent Store.

Informally, figures are often used: an 85¢ seat.

3. Commas and periods, $ and ¢ signs are used as in the examples in §1 above.

For an example of writing sums of money in text, see the paragraphs of illustration in *Numbers §2.

Months In reference matter and informal writing, the names of months with more than four letters are abbreviated in dates:

Jan. 21, 1939   Aug. 16, 1940   Dec. 25, 1941
But: May 1, 1939   June 30, 1940   July 4, 1941

When only the month or month and year are given, abbreviation would be rare:

January 1939   Every January he tries again.

In formal writing the names of the months would not be abbreviated at all.

*Numbers §1*a*; *Dates

Monosyllables A monosyllable is a word of one syllable:

asked   bright   feel   fill   longed   word

Monosyllables should not be divided at the end of lines, not even words like *asked, longed.* *Division of words

A *polysyllable* strictly has three or more syllables, but since we use *dissyllable* (having two syllables) rather rarely, *polysyllable* usually means a word having two or more syllables.

Monotony *Variety in writing, and the articles there referred to

Mood By the forms of mood, a verb may distinguish the way in which the statement it makes is regarded by the writer:

INDICATIVE: as a fact, a statement
SUBJUNCTIVE: as a wish, possibility, doubt
IMPERATIVE: as a command

See the articles *Indicative mood, *Subjunctives, *Commands and requests, *Verbs.

moral, morale Although the *e* is not in the French noun we borrowed during the War as mō räl′ ("a confident mental state"), it is a convenient and natural English way of showing there is something peculiar in the pronunciation. It also distinguishes this *morale* from *moral* (concerning right conduct).

morale: mə ral′ or mə räl′ (*A 4)
moral: mor′əl, or môr′əl

moreover is a heavy connective (= *besides*), rarely needed in informal writing. *Conjunctive adverbs

most (almost) *Most* is the common colloquial clip (*Clipped words) of *almost:* "A reduction in prices will appeal to most everybody." It would be used in writing conversation and in informal style, but is ordinarily out of place in written English. Reference: Pooley, pp. 136-37

Mostly is colloquial and vulgate.

Mr. is not written out with names but is when it is used, colloquially, without a name:

Mr. Schlesser   Mr. John T. Flynn   "They're only two for five, mister."

It is one of the class of abbreviations from which a period is being increasingly omitted. *Abbreviations, §3

Mrs. is written out only in representing colloquial or vulgate usage and is then spelled *missis* (or *missus*):

Mrs. Dorothy M. Adams   Mrs. Adams   "Where's the missis?"

Mrs. is not combined with a husband's title except in small town *journalese. Write *Mrs. Dodd*, not *Mrs. Prof. Dodd*.

A man and wife register at hotels as *Mr. and Mrs. Alex T. Schofield* rather than as *Alex T. Schofield and wife*.

MS. MS., usually in caps, is the conventional abbreviation for *manuscript*; plural MSS. The colloquial and shoptalk word for manuscript intended for publication is *copy*.

must has recently become an (informal) adjective:

the President's must legislation
This is a must article for every intelligent American.

It has long been a noun in newspaper shoptalk, a *B. O. M.* being a *Business Office Must*, a story that has to be run because of some advertising tieup. See *Auxiliary verbs.

mustache Spelling divided: *mustache—moustache*. Pronunciation also divided, the more informal mus′tash gaining over məs tash′.

Mute e *E §5

mutual An effect of connotation in the use of a word is shown in the phrase a *mutual friend*. *Common* would be the natural word for the phrase, since it applies to something shared alike by two or more; but *common* has other, unsavory, senses—"notorious" (*a common scold*) and "vulgar" (*common manners*)—which handicap *a common friend* and probably even *a friend we have in common*. A *mutual friend* is also helped by the phrase *a mutual friendship*, in which *mutual* has its usual meaning of "reciprocal," and of course by the currency of Dickens' title, *Our Mutual Friend*.

myself A reflexive pronoun, referring back to *I* when used as an object or as an intensive:

OBJECT: I shave myself.
INTENSIVE: I saw the whole thing myself.

In vulgate and much colloquial English *myself* is used as subject but not in good written style.

VULGATE AND COLLOQUIAL: Another fellow and myself saw the whole thing.

INFORMAL: Another fellow and I saw the whole thing.

*Pronouns §4, *self, *himself

N (n), as in *now, gnaw, inning, been.* N may be a syllable by itself ("vocalic *n*"), as in *often, listen, garden.*

N is generally silent in *kiln* and in a number of words after *m*: *autumn, damn, hymn, solemn.* In derivatives of such words usage is divided on sounding the *n*. It is not sounded in *hymned* (himd) and in *damned* only in archaic or ultra poetic contexts (dam′ned). It is sounded in *autumnal, solemnity,* and in general before a suffix when the suffix begins with a vowel.

An ñ (the wavy line called a *tilde*) is found in some words from Spanish. If the word is commonly used, the spelling is usually changed to *ny* (*canyon* instead of *cañon*).

The symbol N is used in this book to indicate French pronunciation, in which no *n* is sounded, but the preceding vowel is nasalized: *en route* (äN rüt′).

naive—naïve The form without the dieresis (*naive*) gaining over naïve. It is unnecessary to keep the French masculine form *naif* in English. *Naive* can do all the work. Pronounced nä ēv′.

naivete—naïveté Pronounced nä ēv′tā′ (not nä ēv′i tā′).

namely and other introductory words 1. The beginning of wisdom in handling "introductory words" like *namely, that is, for example, such as* is to use them as seldom as possible. *Namely, viz., i. e., e. g.,* and some others belong chiefly in routine expository prose. *For example, for instance, such as* are more adaptable to readable prose. Very often such words can be omitted altogether in compact, informal writing:

> He instructed us in the mysteries of punctuation: [such as] semicolons between clauses of a compound sentence, position of quotation marks with other marks, commas with non-restrictive clauses.

2. In formal style or in a long, rather complicated sentence, an introductory word would usually be preceded by a semicolon:

> The interview is of value, then, because it aids in discovering certain traits; e. g., emotional and temperamental attitudes—which do not submit so readily to other modes of attack.—G. D. HIGGINSON, *Fields of Psychology,* p. 395

When one of these words introduces a series of short items, it is more often followed by a comma than by a colon:

The boys in training are thoroughly grounded in the fundamental processes of the work: the planning, the building, and the launching.

The boys in training are thoroughly grounded in the fundamental processes of the work, for example, planning, building, and launching.

No comma should follow *such as:*

Large animals, such as bears, moose, and elk, are often found here.

Names In factual writing all names used should be complete and accurate. In current writing, handmade names and other dodges are not used much except in humor. In the following they stamp the paper as amateur:

Across the table sat Cornelius Van Stuck-up between two feminine admirers whose names I will not mention but will call Miss X and Miss Y. Miss X said to Miss Y . . .

Use the real names of people and places unless there are serious reasons for avoiding them, and if there are, invent convincing names or use pronouns or "a man" or some inconspicuous device. This use of actual names is one trait of the specificness and immediacy of current style.

In imaginative writing judgment and ingenuity are needed to choose satisfactory names for characters. They should suggest real names of people of the right social stratum, but not be the names of actual people (except by accident). They should not be the commonest names nor should they be eccentric ones either; ordinarily they should be somewhere between *John* and *Mary* and *Ichabod* and *Jacquinetta*. Studying names and collecting them and watching those used in stories will furnish raw materials for naming your own creations. *Proper names

Narrative paragraphs See "Chronological paragraphs," p. 82.

nature For expressions like *of a violent nature* (= *violent*), see *Deadwood, and "Removing deadwood," p. 161.

Nazi Pronounced nä'tsi; sometimes nat'si, and rarely nä'zi. Plural *Nazis* (nä'tsiz). *Nazi* is a political nickname for the National Socialist party of Germany and is capitalized like *Republican* or *Democrat*. The type of party represented by National Socialists is usually referred to as *fascist* or *totalitarian*. Compare *Fascism, fascist.

necessary Spelled with one *c* and two *s*'s.

Very often a verb is more direct and emphatic, less polite than a construction with *necessary:*

You *must* [or *have to*, rather than *It is necessary that you*] pay your tuition before receiving your class cards.

necessity The idiom is *necessity of doing* something (not *to do* or *for doing* something):

I don't see *the necessity of reading* so many pages to get so few facts.

Often *need* will be more concise:

I don't see *the need of reading* so many pages . . .

need—needs Both are third person singular of the verb *need*, but used in different idioms. *Needs* is the form in affirmative statements, *need* or *does not need* in negative statements, *need* or *does . . . need* in questions:

	He needs a haircut.
	He needs to have a haircut. (Infinitive with *to*)
	Does he need a haircut?
FORMAL:	He need not have a haircut. (Infinitive without *to*)
INFORMAL:	He doesn't need a haircut.
FORMAL:	Need she come?
INFORMAL:	Does she need to come?

Negatives 1. For use of two negatives see *Double negative.

2. A statement may sometimes be made more emphatic or striking by being put negatively (in a figure of speech known as *litotes* or *understatement*):

He was . . . extremely the antithesis of coarse which "refined" somehow does not imply . . .—E. E. CUMMINGS, *The Enormous Room*, p. 150

[Referring to Neville Chamberlain] . . . this far from subtle man. —H. N. BRAILSFORD, *The New Republic*, Oct. 26, 1938

The assimilating power of the English language is not less remarkable than the complexity of its sources.—J. B. GREENOUGH and G. L. KITTREDGE, *Words and Their Ways in English Speech*, p. 147

Tell us, doctors of philosophy, what are the needs of a man. At least a man needs to be notjailed notafraid nothungry notcold not without love not a worker for a person he has never seen,
that cares nothing for the uses and needs of a man or a woman or a child.—JOHN DOS PASSOS, *The New Republic*, June 3, 1936

3. Sometimes a word of negative meaning is combined with one of positive meaning. Usually they must be separated:

I have learned through this practice to overcome stage fright and have gained in vividness of speech. [Not: I have learned to overcome stage fright and vividness of speech . . .]

Negro Capitalize, like *Caucasian, Indian.* Plural, N*egroes*

neither For pronunciation and use see *either §3.

neither . . . nor *either . . . or, *Correlative conjunctions

Neologism is the name for a newly made word. See *Origin of words and "New words and constructions," p. 6.

nephew Usual American pronunciation, nef′ū; more characteristic of British English, nev′ū.

Newspaper English 1. Its virtues. Joseph Pulitzer's famous motto for workers on the old *New York World* still stands as the ideal for the material and style of newswriting—*Accuracy, Terseness, Accuracy.* Complete accuracy is not easy for a reporter who has perhaps only a few minutes in which to get the facts of a complicated event, and terseness is not easy either for a man who writes habitually, often of very similar happenings, without any personal interest in his material. The result is that newspapers contain some of our worst writing, but a reporter who tells of events simply, in words that are appropriate to them and to his readers, may produce some of our best writing.

There is of course no special dialect for newswriting. Papers have some conventions for giving ages, names, places of residence, and other routine matters, but good newspaper English is simply informal English applied to the daily recording of affairs. It is a style written to be read rapidly and by the eye—tricks of sound outside the headlines are out of place.

There has been a good deal of argument about college preparation for newspaper work. Courses and schools of journalism give practice in the form of news stories and in editing copy. But the fundamental traits of a good newspaper man are ability to get information and to see the values of the facts he gets—qualities which can be developed but can't be taught unless they are latent in the person to begin with. A prospective journalist needs an introduction to as many fields as possible, the reading of the best literature of the past, and as a direct influence on his writing, the best of the present. He can sharpen his writing by practice, and by acquiring skill in formal and informal English can lay a foundation for writing that can easily be specialized to the practices of a particular paper in a couple of weeks of actual work on it.

2. Journalese. The two most common sins of newswriting are inflation (*Big words) and *triteness, which we can lump as symptoms of *journalese.* Granting that "our fair city," "ample outlet for her histrionic ability," and scores of such trite phrases belonging to

paleo-journalism are not found now outside small town papers, there is still a vast amount of wordy and lazy writing in newspapers. Every *stylebook contains a list of journalese expressions to be avoided. Here are a few collected (and translated) by George Olds, of the Springfield, Mo., *News:*

According to the report issued this morning by City Auditor Ernest Jared	City Auditor Ernest Jared reported today
Shields denied he made a statement he was alleged to have made to police officers admitting he knew—	Shields denied admitting to police he knew
Affirming the assumption that he was resentful of the meeting	Admitting he resented
But Judge Holly dismissed the charges against her. Although he dismissed the charges against Mrs. Coates, Judge Holly commented that her conduct had been "suspicious."	But Judge Holly dismissed the charges against her, although he termed her conduct "suspicious."

Editor and Publisher, Feb. 2, 1935

Such wordiness and ponderous phraseology is likely to be found in newspaper stories of all kinds. Some are italicized in these quotations:

The *process* of eliminating Jews from *participating* in German commerce, finance and business entered its final stage today with the announcement of a series of decrees and ordinances, which were at once put into effect. They *virtually spell attrition* for Jewish *economic and business activities* of every sort.

Mrs. . . . told the police her husband had been out of work for three years and was despondent. She had just *obtained a position* in a bookbindery. She *arose* at 7:30 a. m. and went into the kitchen to *prepare* breakfast. She *remarked* to her husband she was glad she would not have to *remain* at home *during the day*, because it was getting on her nerves.

Then he hit her. . . .

Triteness is the next worst offense in journalese. In *The New Yorker*, Frank Sullivan had his cliché expert, Mr. Arbuthnot, testify to journalistic triteness, including such special topics as these:

Q—Mr. Arbuthnot, what happens at railroad stations on holidays?
A—Well, there is what our Society of Cliché Experts likes to refer to as a holiday exodus. I mean to say, fully 1,500,000 pleasure-seekers leave the city, railroad officials estimate. Every means of transportation is taxed to its utmost capacity. . . .

Q—Mr. Arbuthnot, what kind of hopes do you have?

A—High hopes, and I don't have them; I entertain them. I express concern. I discard precedent. When I am in earnest, I am in deadly earnest. When I am devoted, I am devoted solely. When a task comes along, it confronts me. When I stop, I stop short. I take but one kind of steps—those in the right direction. I am a force to be reckoned with. Oh, ask me anything, Mr. Dewey, anything.

Q—All right. How about the weather? Where does weather occur?

A—You think you can stump me with that? Well, you can't. Weather occurs over widespread areas. Winter holds the entire Eastern seaboard in its icy grip. Snow blankets the city, disrupting train schedules and marooning thousands of commuters. Traffic is at a standstill—

Q—Hold on a minute, my friend. You've left out something.

A—I have not. What?

Q—Traffic is virtually at a standstill.

A—Oh, a detail, Mr. Dewey. All right, I concede you that. Ten thousand unemployed are placed at work removing the record fall as cold wave spells suffering to thousands. Old residents declare blizzard worst since '88—. —FRANK SULLIVAN, "The Cliché Expert Tells All," *The New Yorker*, June 20, 1936

3. HEADLINES AND HEADLINESE. While writers of news stories have to write with an eye on inches of space, headline writers have to watch every letter. A given style of head has a "count" of so many letters, and, as the compositor says, "there ain't no rubber type." This necessity for compression and—above the fold on the front page at least—a desire to "sell the papers" gives rise to the punch of headlines. As the Waterbury, Conn., *Republican* style sheet puts it:

PUT PUNCH IN HEADS
SAYS OLD SLOT MAN

———

Wants Accurate, Terse, Positive
and Pungent Guides to
News

———

BEGS FOR ACTIVE VERBS

———

Bald-Domed Editor Wants Blue
Pencil Novices to Lay Off
Fuzzy Words

This leads to the omission of *function words (*a, an, the,* connectives) and to the use of short words and *clipped forms:

Fly ocean; tell fight with gale 3 miles in air—12 Navy planes battered

To save space, short words are used, nouns are used as verbs, verbs as nouns, and any words or even long phrases as adjectives:

> Poland Denies *Tie-up* with Reich
>
> Superintendent and Supervisor Refute
> Charge of Spying on *Traction Company*
> *Bus Drivers' Union Enrollment* Meeting

Worrying that headline style will ruin our language is useless. Usage in headlines, in spite of abuses, is in line with good informal English—and the requirements of communication will prevent it from becoming too common. Though headlinese style should be kept in its place, the feeble circumlocution of the stories that often stand below the heads is a greater menace to our language than the clipped and punchy heads.

References: Kennedy, §14. There are many textbooks on newspaper writing. Two of the most useful are: C. D. MacDougall, *Interpretative Reporting* (New York, 1938) and George C. Bastian, *Editing the Day's News* (New York, 1932). The stylebooks of newspapers are important. Some, like that of *The Detroit News*, are for sale. The University of Missouri School of Journalism publishes a *Deskbook*, frequently revised. The magazine *Editor and Publisher* is the best source on current American journalism.

Newspaper titles For writing names of newspapers see *Titles §3.

New words *Origin of words, and "New words and constructions," p. 6

Nexus Jespersen introduced *junction* and *nexus* as names for two types of word relationship. He called the relationship in which two or more words are joined to form a single name (*a warm day, a first class speech*) *junction*. The relationship in which the two terms are joined by a verb but are kept distinct (*The day is warm. The speech sounded first rate*) he called *nexus*. Under nexus he included locutions that were similar in pattern but did not have a verb, such as He left *the window open* (which obviously is quite different from the junction *the open window*) and *Happy the man* (which is different from the happy man), and various others.

The doctrine of nexus is not making so much headway among grammarians as its usefulness suggests. It is elaborated in Jespersen's *The Philosophy of Grammar*, Chapters 8 and 9, and in *Essentials of English Grammar*, Chapter 9.

ng is the pronunciation symbol for the nasal sound most frequently spelled *ng* (*long, bringing*) but also spelled *n: anchor* (ang′kər), *angry* (ang′gri), *sink* (singk), *uncle,* (ung′kəl).

Pronunciation is divided when a syllable ending in *n* is followed by one beginning with *g* or *k: congress* (kong′gres) but *congressional* (kən gresh′ən əl or kong gresh′ən əl).

nice is a *counter word indicating mild approval, so general in meaning that it is of little use in writing. The word's former meaning of "exact, precise," as in *a nice distinction*, is confined to formal writing. (See Charles C. Fries, *The English Journal*, 1927, xvi, 602-604.)

nickel Most words with this last syllable (əl) are spelled *-le*, but *nickel* has not been in the language so long as most of them and keeps the *-el* of its German or Scandinavian origin.

Nicknames Nicknames are rarely appropriate in formal writing. In familiar and informal writing they are appropriate and should be used naturally, without apology. Some writers will put a nickname in quotes the first time it is used, but not when it is repeated, because the quotes call unnecessary attention to it.

no For use as a sentence adverb and as a complete sentence *yes.

No. The abbreviation *No.* for *number* (from the Latin *numero*, "by number") is written with a capital. It is appropriate chiefly in business and technical English. In the United States *No.* is not written with street numbers.

no account, no good, nohow . . . There are a number of colloquial and vulgate phrases made with *no* whose fitness in writing needs to be watched:

no account COLLOQUIAL: a no account cousin
 INFORMAL, FORMAL: a worthless cousin
no good COLLOQUIAL AND INFORMAL: The boat is no good now.
 INFORMAL, FORMAL: The boat is useless now.
nohow VULGATE: We couldn't get there, nohow.
 INFORMAL, FORMAL: We couldn't get there by any means
 (or, any way we tried, and so on).
no place VULGATE: Where you going? No place.
 COLLOQUIAL AND INFORMAL: Where are you going? Nowhere.
 Compare *any and compounds with any.
no use COLLOQUIAL AND INFORMAL: It's no use trying that road.
 She's no use in a crisis.
 FORMAL: It is of no use to try that road.

nobody, nothing, nowhere are written as single words. *Nobody* and *nothing* are singular:

Nobody thinks that way any more.
Nothing is further from the truth.
The dog could be found nowhere.

Nominative absolute *Participles §4

Nominative case A noun or pronoun that is the subject of a finite verb is in the nominative (or subjective) case. The form of the nominative singular is the common form of the noun, to which, typically, the endings for the genitive and for the plural are added. *I, you, he, she, it, we, you, they* are the nominative forms of the personal pronouns; *who, which,* and *that* are the nominative forms of the relative pronouns.

Besides serving as the subject of a verb, words in the nominative case are used in the predicate as "predicate nominatives" after *linking verbs: He was a *carpenter*; They all became *generals*. *Predicate adjectives

The same form is also used in direct address (for which some languages have a separate vocative case): *Polly,* put the kettle on. *Subject and verb

Nonce-word Strictly, a word used but once so far as existing writing shows; a word coined for the occasion and not attaining general use. *Un-black* in the following sentence would be called a nonce-word:

> She liked black coffee, black cigarettes, black Italian shawls, which was interesting, since she was so distinctly un-black herself, but all creamy and pale gold in the white Capri sun.—WILBUR DANIEL STEELE, "Bubbles," p. 95

*Origin of words §2a

none, no one *None* is a single word, but *no one* is often used instead of *none,* for emphasis.

None may be either singular or plural, and now is more common with the plural:

> As only ten jurors have been chosen so far, none of the witnesses was required. [or: were required]
> She tried on ten hats, but none of them were attractive.
> I read three books on the subject, no one of which was helpful.

Reference: Fries, pp. 50, 56

No paragraph (CORRECTION: Join these two paragraphs, if necessary revising the expression to relate the ideas.) *No P*

No punctuation (CORRECTION: Remove the punctuation mark indicated [See especially "Commas to avoid," p. 281].) *No Pn*

Non-parallel structure *Shifted construction

Non-restrictive clauses, modifiers *Restrictive and non-restrictive

not hardly, not scarcely *Double negative §3

not only . . . but also *Correlative conjunctions

not to exceed Business and legal; in other contexts *not more than* is usual:

> The undersigned will be liable for property damages, not to exceed $500 for one accident.
> The enrollment in the course was to be not more than fifty.
> Not more than two people could live on that pay.

Note taking See "Gathering material: note taking," p. 294.

notorious means well known for unsavory reasons—"a notorious cheat"; *famous* is well known for accomplishment or excellence—"a famous writer, aviator." *Noted* is journalistic for *famous* or *well known.*

Noun and verb stress A number of nouns and verbs are differentiated in speaking by stressing the first syllable in the noun and the last in the verb although the spelling is identical. Some of these are listed below.

Noun	Verb
com'pound	com pound'
com'press	com press'
con'duct	con duct'
con'flict	con flict' (often con'flict)
con'trast	con trast'
con'vict	con vict'
de'crease	de crease'
di'gest	di gest'
es'cort	es cort'
ex'tract	ex tract'
in'cline	in cline'
in'crease	in crease' (often in'crease)
in'sult	in sult'
prod'uce	pro duce'
re'cess (or re cess')	re cess'
rec'ord	re cord'

Several of these that are in common use show the natural English tendency to shift the stress back to the first syllable. The following words are both nouns and verbs with the same stress:

> ac'cent   cos'tume   dis'count   im'port

De'tail is both noun and verb where it is commonly used, as in the Army.

Noun clauses A noun clause is a construction having a subject and finite verb that functions in a sentence as a noun. Most noun clauses are introduced by *that*, some by *what, who, whoever, whatever*. They are usually subjects or objects:

SUBJECT: *That anyone could raise his grade by studying* had never occurred to him.
Whether or not he should go had bothered him for days.
OBJECT: He assured me *that it would never happen again*.
     or: He assured me *it would never happen again*.
PREDICATE NOMINATIVE: His guests were *whomever he met on the way home*.
OBJECT OF PREPOSITION: Sam is always sure of *what he does*.
APPOSITIVE: The doctrine *that we must avoid entangling alliances* was first stated by Washington.

The clauses italicized below are noun clauses in the constructions named:

People who live in earthquake countries know *that a bad shock is usually followed for days or weeks by others of gradually lessening severity* [object of *know*]. That is *what is happening after the "peace" of Munich* [predicate nominative]. A dozen fundamental changes are taking place, any one of which would normally make headlines for many months.
What is left of Czechoslovakia [subject] is now completely under German tutelage. Hitler has announced, in the curious Nazi terminology, *that the Czechs will henceforth be "loyal" to the German Reich* [object of *announced*]. The Masonic orders are being disbanded; communism will probably be made illegal; compulsory labor camps, German style, have been started. When the Hungarians massed their troops on the Czech border, it was to Berlin and Rome *that Prague appealed* [predicate nominative], ignoring Paris and London. The Hungarians will get a fat slice of Slovak territory, but not a continuous border with Poland, which would cut Czechoslovakia in two.—*The New Republic*, Oct. 26, 1938

*Clauses, *Reason is because

Nouns 1. TYPES. A noun is the name of a person, place, thing, quality, action, or idea: *George Washington, hunter, Washington, D. C., home, automobile, goodness, hunting, immortality*.
Nouns are classified as follows:
a) *Proper nouns*, names of particular people and places, written with a capital and usually without *the* or *a*: *Anne, George W. Loomis, London, Georgia, France, the Bay of Naples*. See *Proper names. In contrast with these proper nouns, all the other groups are *common nouns*.

b) *Concrete nouns,* names of particular objects: *leaf, leaves, road, panda, manufacturer.* *Abstract and concrete

c) *Mass nouns,* names of materials in general rather than materials in particular forms: *water, coffee, cement, steel, corn.*

d) *Collective nouns,* names of a group of things regarded as a unit: *fleet, army, company, committee, trio, bevy.* *Collective nouns

e) *Abstract nouns,* names of qualities, actions, ideas: *kindness, hate, manufacture, idealism, fantasy, concept.* Many of them are *gerunds: *fishing, drinking, manufacturing.*

2. Forms. Nouns may be single words or compound words (*bathroom, bookcase, log-rolling*) or they may be *group words: *high school, hub cap, go getter, motor car.*

Nouns change their forms to make the plural, most of them adding *-s: boys, kindnesses, manufacturers.* *Plurals

Nouns change their form for case only in the genitive, typically by adding *'s: boy's, Harriet's.* *Genitive case

A very few nouns in English have different forms for masculine and feminine gender: *confidant—confidante, executor—executrix, actor—actress.* *Gender

3. Functions. The principal functions of nouns are:

Subject of a sentence: The *wind* blew for three days. (*Subject and verb)

Object of a verb: The wind blew the *silo* over. (*Objects)

Object of a preposition: in the *night,* behind the *house,* after *breakfast,* of the *president* (*Prepositions)

Predicate nominative: He became *president* of the firm. (*Predicate adjective, Predicate nominative)

Possession: The *woman's* first dress for two years (*Genitive case § 2)

Apposition: The first settler, *Thomas Sanborn,* came in 1780. (*Apposition)

Adjectival modifier: The *horse's* tail was braided; a *baby* hippopotamus; the best *high school basket ball* team in years. *Genitive case, *Parts of speech § 2, *Adjectives, types and forms § 6

Adverbial modifier: He came two *months ago. Mornings* he would work a little. *Adverbs, types and forms § 5

References: Kennedy §§ 50, 103; Curme, *Parts of Speech,* Chs. 1, 9, *Syntax,* Chs. 2, 4, 26, and other references

nowhere near Colloquial and informal:

It was a good score but nowhere near as large as we'd hoped for [Formal: "not so large as" or "not nearly so large as"]

nowheres Vulgate for *nowhere.*

614

Number *Number* is the singular and plural aspect of nouns and verbs. See *Plurals, *Subject and verb, *Reference of pronouns.

number is a collective noun, requiring a singular or plural verb according as the total or the individual units are meant:

> A number of tickets have already been sold.
> The number of tickets sold is astonishing.
> A number of the pages were torn.
> The number of pages assigned for translation was gradually increased to eight.

See also *amount, number.

Numbers (CORRECTION: Revise the figure or figures in this passage in the light of the suggestions below.) *Numb*

1. FIGURES ARE USED FOR (*a*) *Dates.* Only in formal *social notes are dates written out in words. *1st, 2nd* (*2d*), and so on may be used when a date is given without the year, but not ordinarily with the year:

> Oct. 4, 1938   October 4, 1938   October 4   October 4th

Years are always written in figures.

b) *Hours* when a.m. or p.m. is used:

> 5 p. m., but five o'clock

c) *Street numbers* (with no comma between thousands):

> 2841 Washington Avenue   Apartment 3C, 781 Grand Street

d) *Pages and other references:*

> page 642   pp. 431-82   chapter 14 (or chapter xiv)
> Act III, scene iv, line 28

e) *Sums of money,* except sums in round numbers or, in formal style, sums that can be written in two or three words:

> $4.98   75¢   a million dollars (or, informal, $1,000,000)

f) *Statistics* and series of more than one or two numbers:

> In the last election the Republicans gained 81 seats in the House of Representatives, 8 seats in the Senate, and 13 new governorships.

2. FIGURES OR WORDS. Usage varies in writing numbers that are parts of consecutive sentences. In general, newspapers and informal writing have figures for numbers over ten, words for smaller numbers; rather conservative magazine and book styles have figures for numbers over 100 except when they can be written in two words:

615

Informal (newspaper): four, ten, 15, 92, 114
Formal (book): four, ten, fifteen, ninety-two, 114. But practice is not consistent.

This passage illustrates a typical book style in use of figures and sums of money:

With a well-integrated, rapidly growing organization, Swedish coöperators were ready to go forward to new triumphs—over galoshes this time. It sounds funny but it is not at all; the victory over the galosh trust—really the rubber trust—was a very tangible achievement. Galoshes are a necessity in the Swedish winter, to say nothing of the Swedish spring and the Swedish fall. And four manufacturing firms, formed into an air-tight trust, exploited this necessity for years. Annual profits of 60 per cent, 62 per cent and even, in one exceptional year, 77 per cent were recorded. On a capital of less than a million dollars the four factories realized in fourteen years more than twelve and a half million dollars and voted many stock dividends besides. As in the case of the milling trust, the public yelled long and loud but with no visible results.

At the annual coöperative congress in 1926 it was decided that K. F. [Kooperativa Förbundet, the Coöperative Union] should declare war on the galosh trust. This was the unanimous and enthusiastic opinion of the Congress. Within a few weeks, merely on the basis of this announcement, the trust reduced the price of a man's galoshes more than fifty cents, with corresponding reductions all down the line. K. F. informed the trust that this was not enough, and when there were no further reductions the war was begun in earnest.

The trust was obviously not going to sell one of its factories at anything like a reasonable price but when K. F. threatened to build a plant of its own, the enemy heeded the warning, recalling what had happened to other cartels that had remained adamant. In a remarkably short time K. F. had negotiated the purchase of a factory at Gislaved, and by January 1, 1927, after complete modernization, it took over operation of this plant. The result, within a year, was another seventy cents sliced off the price of a pair of galoshes. Having achieved this, K. F. began the manufacture of automobile tires at the Gislaved plant and by 1932 was producing 50,000 tires a year.
—Marquis W. Childs, *Sweden—The Middle Way*, pp. 12-13

When most writing was longhand it was conventional to express numbers in words and then repeat them in figures in parenthesis. In clear copy, especially in typewritten copy, this is no longer necessary and is not done except in legal or important business documents.

Except in dates and street numbers, a comma stands between each group of three digits counting from the right:

1939 (the year)   1,938 bushels   4,682,921 $14,672.

Numbers in two words between 21 and 99 are usually hyphened, though the practice is declining: *forty-two* or *forty two*.

3. In consecutive writing a number at the very beginning of a sentence is written in words rather than in figures:

Two to 3% of loading and up to 10% is common and 20 to 30% is specially surfaced papers.—"Paper Manufacture," *Encyclopaedia Britannica*, p. 234

4. ARABIC AND ROMAN NUMERALS. Arabic numerals (1, 2, 88 . . .) are used in almost all places where numbers are not expressed in words. Roman numerals (i, ii, cxlvi . . .) are occasionally used to number units in rather short series, as in outlines, chapters of a book, acts of a play, though now less often than formerly. The preliminary pages of books are almost always numbered with Roman numerals. Sometimes they are used on title pages for the date, and on very formal inscriptions.

In Roman numerals a small number preceding a larger is to be subtracted from the larger (ix = 9, xc = 90). The following table shows the common Roman numerals:

1	i	12	xii	40	xl	101	ci
2	ii	13	xiii	41	xli	110	cx
3	iii	14	xiv	49	xlix	199	cxcix
4	iv	15	xv	50	l	200	cc
5	v	19	xix	51	li	400	cd
6	vi	20	xx	60	lx	500	d
7	vii	21	xxi	70	lxx	600	dc
8	viii	25	xxv	80	lxxx	900	cm
9	ix	27	xxvii	90	xc	1000	m
10	x	29	xxix	99	xcix	1500	md
11	xi	30	xxx	100	c	1940	mcmxl

5. PLURAL OF FIGURES. The plural of a figure is written either with *s* or *'s*:

SIX FIVES: six 5s, six 5's   BY TENS: by 10s, by 10's

6. CARDINAL AND ORDINAL NUMBERS. The numbers in simple counting, indicating number only, are *cardinal numbers*: 68, 129 . . . The numbers indicating order, *first, second, third* . . . are *ordinal numbers*. Except in numbering items in a rather routine enumeration, ordinals should be spelled out rather than abbreviated to *1st, 2nd, 3d*. . .

Since the simple forms *sixth, ninth*, and so on can be either adjective or adverb, the forms in *-ly* (*sixthly, ninthly*) are unnecessary.

See also *Fractions, *Money.

O Speakers of English vary in their pronunciation of the *o* sounds as they do of the *a* sounds. Pronunciation of particular words, especially with short *o*, can be indicated only roughly because of this widespread variation. Four general types of *o* can be distinguished:

1. LONG o (ō), the sound in *oh, oats, note, soldier, sew, trousseau* (trü′sō or trü sō′).

Before an *r* the sound of long *o* is somewhat modified, as in *door* (dōr), and may approach open *o*, as in some pronunciations of *horse, born,* and so on.

In unstressed and rapidly spoken words the sound of long *o* is shorter but has much the same quality: *obey* (ō bā′), *hotel* (hō tel′).

2. SHORT o (o) as in *not, stop, wander.* A clearcut short *o* is not very often pronounced, and is more characteristic of New England than of other parts of the country. The more common American pronunciation is the open *o* (sôft, and so on). And in Western English it approaches broad *a* (säft).

3. OPEN o (ô), most clearly identified in its spelling *aw* (*law, lawn, spawn*) but also the vowel sound in *lord, all, fault, fought, taught* (lôrd, ôl, fôlt, fôt, tôt).

4. SLURRED o (ə). In slighted syllables *o* may spell the slurred vowel ə: *actor* (ak′tər), *nation* (nā′shən), *button* (but′ən), or it may entirely disappear as in most people's pronunciation of *chocolate* (chôk′lit) or *sophomore* (sof′mōr).

O represents several other vowel sounds: ü as in *move*; u̇ as in *wolf,* and represented by *oo,* as in *room* (rūm), *broom* (brūm); u as in *son, money*; ė as in *work.*

See also *ou.

O, oh O is always capitalized, and in conventional writing it is so closely related to some other word, often a name in direct address, that it is not followed by a mark of punctuation:

O dear, I suppose so. O yes. O God, unseen, but ever near. O Billy, come here.

Oh is an exclamation, followed by a comma if the force is weak, by an exclamation mark if the stress is strong. It is capitalized at the beginning of a sentence, but generally not in the middle of a sentence.

Oh! Don't do that! Oh, I wish he would.

In informal writing the distinction between O and *oh* is not always kept, and O is often found where traditional usage would have *oh.*

Objective case *Accusative case, *Objects, *who—whom, *It's me

Objects 1. An *object of a verb* is the noun or pronoun or clause that names the person or thing or idea or quality that is affected by the action of the verb: "The four men pushed *the car* out of the mudhole—He took *her* to the three formals of the year— I didn't believe *that he told the truth*." *Accusative case

An object usually comes after the verb or preposition of which it is the object:

They made the *boat* themselves.
Terry chased the *cat* up a tree.
at his *house*   between the *devil* and the deep blue *sea*
in the *paper*   between *you* and *me*

When an object comes before the subject and verb, only the meaning can identify it: "This *boat* the boys made themselves." When the meaning would not certainly identify the object, English uses the passive:

The rest of the boys *were chased* across the street by the tougher two or three [instead of: The rest of the boys the tougher two or three chased across the street].

2. An *indirect object* names something indirectly affected by the action of the verb: "In desperation she showed *him* the snapshot album—He gave *the church* a memorial window." The indirect object comes before the direct object unless it is the form with a preposition: "He gave a memorial window *to the church*."

3. The *object of a preposition* is the word or phrase or clause whose relation to some other part of the sentence is shown by the preposition, as *some other part of the sentence* and *the preposition* in this definition and the clause in "Your grade will depend chiefly on *what you do on the examination*." *Prepositions

Obsolete *Obsolete* means a word no longer used (like *eft*— "again") or a meaning of a word no longer used (like *can* in the sense of "know," *dole* in the sense of "grief"). See "Obsolete expressions," p. 4.

occasion, occasional, occasionally If you realize that *occassion* would be pronounced o kash'ən (like *passion*) and that *occasion* is pronounced okā'zhən, you may not be so likely to misspell these words. Two *c*'s and one *s*.

-oe- (œ) *-ae-, -oe-

of, off Besides its use as a preposition of numerous meanings, *of* is used to make the phrasal (analytic) genitive: *of a man* = *a man's*, and so on.

Of is frequently used in colloquial and vulgate doubling of prepositions—*inside of, off of, outside of. Inside of* and *outside of* are also used in informal writing, but not *off of*, which should be reduced to *off*: "He stepped off [of] the sidewalk."

The colloquial contraction *'ve* for *have* is often carelessly written *of*:

I could have [or, *could've*, not could *of*] gone if I'd wanted to.
I ought to have [not *to of*] gone then.

often Pronouncing the *t* is usually a localism, but it is sometimes sounded in singing to make a more emphatic second syllable. *Oft* is archaic, used by amateur poets who have to count their syllables, and *oftentimes* is a colloquial expansion.

Oh *O, oh

OK, O.K. Business and colloquial English for "correct, all right, approved": "The foreman put his OK on the shipment." Occasionally spelled *okay, okeh*. As a verb the forms are OK, OK'ed or OK'd, OK'ing. *Oke* and *okeydoke* are slang.

The origin of *OK* is uncertain. Webster says "probably from Choctaw *oke, hoke*, yes, it is"; Standard says "Error due to misreading of *O. R.*, 'Ordered recorded.' "

Omission in a quotation is indicated by ellipses (. . .). See *Ellipsis.

Omissions The omission of certain words that is typical of colloquial and vulgate speech raises questions of appropriateness in writing. Some of these are discussed in *telegraphic style and in the following articles: articles, *a, an, *the; *be* as an auxiliary, *be §3; prepositions, *Prepositions §3c; pronouns, *Relative pronouns; *that, *very; *Elliptical constructions; *Clauses §2.

one 1. The use of the impersonal pronoun *one* is characteristically formal, especially if it must be repeated:

FORMAL: One can't be too careful, can one?
INFORMAL: You can't be too careful, can you?

It is difficult, too, I find, to be as frank in talking with women as with men; because I think that women tend more than men to hold a preconceived idea of one's character and tastes; and it is difficult to talk simply and naturally to any one who has formed a mental picture of one, especially if one is aware that it is not correct. But men are slower to form impressions, and thus talk is more experimental; moreover, in talking with men, one encounters more opposition, and opposition puts one more on one's mettle.—A. C. BENSON, *From a College Window*, p. 75

This repetition of *one*, often to avoid *I*, often when *you* would be more natural, is deadly. American usage stands firmly by older English usage in referring back to *one* by *he, his, him* (or *she, her*):

One is warned to be cautious if he would avoid offending his friends and bringing their displeasure down upon his head.

*they, *you

2. *One* is used to hold a second adjective to a noun that precedes it with another adjective:

Fred took the new copy and I took the old one.

The plural *ones* is often used:

She has two velvet dresses and three silk ones.

3. *One* is very often *deadwood, taking emphasis from the adjective which carries the real meaning:

The plan was certainly [an] original [one].

Reference: Fries, pp. 245-46

-one *One* is written solid with *any-, every-, some-* in making an indefinite pronoun; but when the *one* is stressed they are written as two words:

Anyone can do that.   Any one of the four will be all right.
Everyone preaches better than he practices.
Every one in the class was surprised.
Someone ought to tell her.   Some one of the plans will work.

*any §2, *every and its compounds, *some and compounds

one of those who In written English the clause following *one of those who* and similar locutions is plural:

He is one of those people who believe in the perfectibility of man. [*Who* refers to *people*.]
That's one of the books that make you change your ideas. [*That* refers to *books*.]

Colloquially the singular is often heard:

He is one of those people who believes in the perfectibility of man.

only 1. The importance of the position of *only* has been greatly exaggerated. Logically it should stand immediately before the element modified:

I need only six more to have a full hundred.

But usage is not always logical, and in this construction it is conspicuously in favor of placing the *only* before the verb of the statement. There is no possible misunderstanding in the meaning of:

I only need six more to have a full hundred.

There are instances in which the placing of *only* can make a foolish or a funny statement:

with only a face that a mother could love

And when the restricted phrase is emphatic, crucial for the meaning of the statement, *only* should be placed next to it:

When he was fighting in the bantam class he weighed only 118 pounds.

is more exact and emphatic than

When he was fighting in the bantam class he only weighed 118 pounds.

But placing *only* with the verb is a characteristic and reputable English idiom:

In reality we only have succession and coexistence, and the "force" is something that we imagine.—HAVELOCK ELLIS, *The Dance of Life*, p. 91

They only opened one bag and took the passports in and looked at them.—ERNEST HEMINGWAY, *The Sun Also Rises*, p. 94

The knowledge required can only exist where governments of millionaires devote themselves to its discovery and diffusion.—BERTRAND RUSSELL, *What I Believe*, p. 66

2. The same is true of *even, ever, nearly, just, exactly,* and such limiting adverbs, though they are used much less than *only,* and some of them only in formal English, so that the idiom is not so common. Like *only* they can be so placed that they spoil the emphasis:

The way I can stand in front of a store window and persuade myself that I need some novel and unnecessary article even surprises me [better, surprises even me].

But they often stand quite idiomatically before the verb.

3. As a coordinating conjunction, meaning *but, only* is chiefly colloquial:

I'd love to come, only I have to study for an exam.

Onomatopoeia *Imitative words and phrases

onto—on to When *on* is an adverb and *to* a preposition in a separate locution, they should of course be written as two words:

The rest of us drove on / to the city.

When the words make a definite preposition, they are usually written solid:

The team trotted onto the floor.   They looked out onto the park.

Onto is frequently used as a colloquial double preposition when *on* or *to* by itself would be used in writing:

They finally got on [Colloquial: onto] the bus.
The crowd got to [Colloquial: onto] James Street.

or is a coordinating conjunction and should connect words or phrases or clauses of equal value, like *and, but,* or *for.* *Coordinating conjunctions, *Compound sentences

WORDS: He must be drunk or crazy.
CLAUSES: We could go by car or we could go by train.

Two subjects joined by *or* take a singular verb if each is singular, a plural verb if both are plural or if the one nearest the verb is plural:

Cod liver oil or halibut oil is often prescribed.
Cod liver oil or codliver oil capsules have the same effect.
Cod liver oil capsules or cod liver oil has the same effect.

This last type of construction would usually be avoided in favor of the second.

Or correlates with *either* and sometimes in informal English with *neither:*

Either ē'ᴛʜᴧr or ī'ᴛʜᴧr is correct.
INFORMAL: Neither ā'ᴛʜᴧr or ī'ᴛʜᴧr is widely used in America.
FORMAL: Neither ā'ᴛʜᴧr nor ī'ᴛʜᴧr is widely used in America.

*Correlative conjunctions

-or, (-our) American spelling prefers *-or* in such words as *color, governor, honor.* When referring to Jesus Christ, *Saviour* is usually spelled with the *u* but in other senses without it. *Glamour* still survives, but the *u* is rapidly being dropped from this word.

British usage is divided on this point, though of course to an American reader the words in *-our* are conspicuous. Fowler said that the American change to *-or* has actually hindered the simplification that was going on in England:

Those who are willing to put national prejudice aside & examine the facts quickly realize, first, that the British *-our* words are much fewer in proportion to the *-or* words than they supposed, &, secondly, that there seems to be no discoverable line between the two sets so based on principle as to serve any useful purpose. By the side of *favour* there is *horror,* beside *ardour pallor,* beside *odour tremor,* & so forth. Of agent-nouns *saviour* (with its echo *paviour*) is perhaps the only one that now retains *-our, governor* being the latest to shed its *-u-.*—H. W. FOWLER, *Modern English Usage,* p. 415

He looked for a continued shedding of the *-u.*

In quoting directly from British writings and in referring to British institutions, like the Labour party, their spelling should be exactly followed; otherwise use -*or*.

References: Fowler, "-our & -or"; *Oxford English Dictionary*, "-or"; John Benbow, *Manuscript & Proof* (New York, 1937), pp. 75-77, discusses spelling in American books that are to be circulated in England.

oral, verbal Strictly, *oral* means "spoken," and *verbal* means "in words"; but *verbal* has been so long used in the sense of *oral* that the sense is recognized in dictionaries:

He delivered an oral message.   He had only a verbal agreement.

Ordinal numerals *Cardinal numerals, *Numbers §6

Organization of papers *Outline form, and "Planning the paper," p. 297

Origin of words 1. THE STUDY OF WORD ORIGINS. The words that we use all have histories. Some, like *chauffeur, mores, television, parapsychology,* are relatively new in English; some have been in the language for centuries, like *home, candle, go, kitchen;* others have recently added new meanings, as *antenna,* a biological term for the "feelers" of insects, probably now means for most people a piece of radio equipment. *Etymology,* the study of word origins, traces the changes in spellings, and combinations of word elements (as in *dis/service, wild/ness, bath/room, room/mate*) and pursues the word or its component parts to Old English and beyond or to a foreign language from which it came into English, and so on back to the earliest discoverable forms. Of some words, especially colloquial words like *dude, stooge, rumpus,* the origin is unknown; for others, like *OK* or *blizzard,* it is debated. But the efforts of generations of scholars have discovered pretty full histories for most words. These are given briefly in most dictionaries and more fully in the *Oxford English Dictionary* and in special works.

Most people working with words have some curiosity about where they come from and about how new ones can be made. They find that our everyday words in general come down directly from Old English (*get, go, house, sister*), or if they are of foreign origin, that they were borrowed many centuries ago (*candle, debt, pay, travel*). The vocabulary of high society has many French words, of both early and recent borrowing (*debutante, gallant, fiancée*). The vocabulary of philosophy and abstract thought has a large Latin element (*concept, fallacy, rational, idealism*), and the vocabulary of science has many Greek words (*atom, hemoglobin, seismograph*).

The sources of words will often reveal something about our history, as the many Norman French and Latin words in law (*fine, tort, certiorari, subpoena*) remind us of the time when the government of England was in the hands of the Norman French, following 1066. But it is more important to discover what meanings the words have had, in their earlier career in English, and in the foreign languages from which they have come. These early meanings have often left traces in the suggestive value of the words, and often even abstract words, which once had specific, concrete meanings, may become more vivid when their histories are known. *Supercilium* in Latin meant "eyebrow," so that our *supercilious* suggests a scornful lifting of the eyebrow. *Rehearse* is from a French word meaning to "harrow again." *Sarcophagus* is, according to its Greek originals, "a flesh eater," referring to the limestone coffins that hastened the disintegration of bodies. *Profane* (Latin) meant "outside the temple" and gathered the meaning of "against religion, the opposite of sacred." *Alcohol* goes back to an Arabic word for a finely ground powder, used for painting eyelids, and from its fineness the word became applied, in Spanish, to specially distilled spirits, and so to our alcohol.

Following up the biographies of words is interesting—it makes a good hobby—and it very often will sharpen a writer's sense for the exact meaning and for the suggestion carried by a given word. Such results are personal and depend on finding bits about a word's past that appeal to you. This article chiefly presents the various ways in which words have arrived and are still arriving in English. There are two general processes—the coming of new words, either created or borrowed, and the compounding or clipping of the words and parts of words that are already in the language. Then this stock of words is increased in usefulness by changes in meanings of the already established forms.

2. New words. (*a*) *Creation of words.* Outright creation of words is rare. Even *gas*, first used by Von Helmst, a Belgian scientist, probably had the Greek *chaos* or some Dutch or Flemish word behind it. *Kodak* is probably an actual creation, as are some other trade names. Popular words like *dud, burble* were also creations, good sounding words someone made up. *Imitative words like *buzz, honk, swish, whiz* are attempts to translate the sounds of nature into the sounds of language. Various exclamations of surprise, pain, scorn started unconsciously—*ow, ouch, fie, phooey*

—but they became regular words, used by anyone. But most words now used by English-speaking people have a background in already existing words or elements of words.

Occasionally a person coins a word for a particular place, known as a *nonce-word* (used but once). One might write that a certain person "was the acme of hasbeenivity" and *hasbeenivity* would be a nonce-word, and would probably remain one. As a rule arbitrary coinages do not stick. Of the large group suggested by Gelett Burgess (in *Burgess Unabridged*) not many are used, and only two have made the serious dictionaries (*blurb, goop*). Many similar words used in localities or in particular families, perhaps originated by children, never become part of the language.

b) *Borrowed words.* English has always borrowed words freely, from Latin, German, French, and from less dominant languages with which English-speaking people have come in contact. It has assimilated words of quite un-English form: *khaki* (Hindustani), *seersucker* (Persian, Hindustani), *tycoon* (Japanese), *ski* (Norwegian), *hors d'oeuvres* (French), *intelligentsia* (Russian). The various words for *porch*, itself Norman French but the oldest and most English-seeming of the group, come from various languages: *piazza* (Italian), *portico* (Italian), *stoop* (Dutch), *veranda* (Anglo-Indian).

Dictionaries, histories of English, and books on language detail the story of past English borrowings. The process is still going on, though perhaps more slowly than at some periods. Some words come into English at the formal level and remain formal words: *intelligentsia, bourgeois, chef-d'oeuvre, objet d'art, Zeitgeist, Anschluss,* and many others of political, philosophical, scientific, or literary bearing. *Sphygmograph* and many other scientific words are recent compoundings of Latin and especially of Greek words which are not otherwise in English usage—so that they may be regarded as borrowings as well as compounds. Other words come in at the informal level, especially when large numbers of people go abroad, as during a war (*boche, camouflage, poilu, ersatz*) or when a foreign invention becomes suddenly popular, as in *chauffeur, garage, chassis, tonneau* of the automobile vocabulary. Some words brought by immigrants have stuck: *sauerkraut, kohlrabi, pronto, piñon, kosher, shillalah* (*shillaly*), *goulash*.

Many are dropped before they gain any general currency. The useful words are more or less adapted to English spelling and pronunciation and become true English words: See *English language, and for suggestions about the use of recently borrowed words, *Foreign words in English.

3. CHANGES IN FORM OF WORDS. (*a*) *Word composition.* Most new words are made by putting together two or more word elements to make a new word of different meaning or function, as *un-* added to *interesting* gives a word of the opposite meaning, *uninteresting,* or *-ize* added to the noun *canal* gives a verb, *canalize.* The elements may be a prefix placed before the root word (*mis-related*), or a suffix added (*foolish-ness*), or a compounding element like *mono-* (*mono-syllable, mono-rail*), or two independent words built together (*book-case, basket-ball, gentle-man*). *Group words like *high school, out of town,* though not written as single words, could be included as a type of word composition.

A list of prefixes and suffixes that are still active in English would take several pages. A few of the more common prefixes are:

*a- (not): asymmetrical, amoral, atypical
ante- (before): anteprohibition era
anti- (against): antiprohibition
bi- (two): bivalve, biplane, bicycle
dis- (not): disinterested, dispraise
eu- (well): eugenics, eulogy, euphony
in- (in): income, impart, instill
in- (not): inelegant, impractical
mis- (wrong): mistake, misnomer
*pre- (before): preview, prenatal, pre-empt
*re- (again): revise, redecorate
up- (up): upend (verb), upswirl (noun)

A few suffixes are:

-en (to make a verb): heighten, lighten, weaken
-ful (full): playful, spoonful
-fy (to make): electrify, horrify
-ish (to make an adjective): dryish, foolish, smallish
-ize (to supply with): circularize

Compounding elements include a number of words or roots, many of them Greek:

-graph- (writing): biography, photograph
micro- (small): microcosm, micrometer, microphone
mono- (one): monotone, monorail
-phil- (loving): philanthropy, philately, Anglophile
-side-: sidewall, sideswipe, ringside
-smith: locksmith, silversmith, gunsmith
-trop (turning): geotropic, heliotropic

For more complete lists of prefixes, suffixes, and compounding elements see Kennedy, pp. 335-51.

Sometimes unnecessary and unused elements are added to words, as in [ir]regardless, origin[ation]. For such words see *Long variants.

Several pairs of prefixes and suffixes have the same meaning, so that two words of the same meaning but somewhat different in form exist side by side, especially words with in- (not) and un- and nouns with -ness, -ity, or -tion:

aridness, aridity
completeness, completion
corruption, corruptness
ferociousness, ferocity
humbleness, humility

indistinguishable, undistinguishable
torridness, torridity
unobliging, disobliging
unrobe, disrobe

When such a pair exists, take the one that is more familiar to you or that fits best in the rhythm of the sentence. But try not to make your style conspicuous by coining a form when there is already a good similar word in use. The only sure way to know is to consult a good dictionary.

b) *Blends.* Informal and colloquial English have a number of words that show the liberties that the users of language have always taken with their words and always will take. Some of their experiments have proved useful and have become a part of the main English vocabulary.

One common type is *blends*, or portmanteau words, made by telescoping two words into one, often making a letter or syllable do double duty. *Squish* is probably a blend of *squirt* and *swish; electrocute* of *electro-* and *execute, avigation* of *aviation* and *navigation.* Many "Timewords" are blends: *cinemactress, socialite,* P W *Administrator;* and they are common in business: *servicenter, corrasable* (a paper—*correct* plus *erasable*), the names of many firms and products, like *Socony, Nabisco, Richlube.* In colloquial humor they abound: *posilutely, absotively, solemncholly, absogoshdarnlutely* and also in more serious conversation, often presenting two ideas at once: *snoopervize* (*snoop—supervize*), *politricks, happenstance, anecdotage, slanguage.* They are specially useful in a humorous context or in one of suggested dispraise.

c) *Clipped words.* One of the commonest types of word change is clipping, dropping one or more syllables to make a shorter and more speakable form: *ad* from *advertisement, bus* from *omnibus, taxi* from *taxicab* (or ultimately from *taximeter cab*), *quote* from *quotation, mob*—an eighteenth-century clip from *mobile vulgus*—*auto, movie, plane, phone, Frisco,* and so on. *Shoptalk has many clips—*mike* for *microphone* or *micrometer,* depending on the shop, and so on. The speech of any closely related group is full of clips; campus vocabulary shows a full line: *ec, home ec, poly sci, grad, prom, dorm, ad building, varsity, lab, exam, gym, prof, pre-med,* and scores more.

Clipped words are written (when they are appropriate to the context) without apostrophe or period, as they stand in the paragraph above.

d) Back formations. A back formation differs from clips like *exam* and *auto* chiefly in that it is formed on analogy with other words and is usually needed to serve as a different part of speech. *Beg* was formed from *beggar,* corresponding to *hunt, hunter.* A number of back formations have made their way, like *diagnose* from *diagnosis, edit* from *editor;* some, like **enthuse,* are slowly making their way into the common vocabulary; but most are formed in fun, like *burgle,* and are used either in humor or in a derogatory sense, like *orate. Donate* seems unnecessary, since we have *give,* but *enthuse* is more justifiable, since it takes the place of the clumsy *be enthusiastic over.*

e) Common nouns from proper names. A number of words have come into general use because of some association with a person or place: *boycott,* from the name of an Irish land agent who was "boycotted"; *macadam,* from the name of the inventor of the road surface, John L. MacAdam; *sandwich,* from an Earl of Sandwich; *jersey,* from the island of Jersey; *madras* from Madras, India.

f) Playful formations. Blends and back formations are likely to have a playful note and so do some other word shifts that can't be classified, except that they often represent a popular pronunciation, like *nooz* or *colyumist. Colyum* and *colyumist* are making their way, since they make it possible to point out a particular kind of *column.* Some, like *hire education,* are either nonce-words or convenient puns. Some become quite generally used: *dingus, doodad, beanery, sockdolager. Jalopy* seems a perfect word for its meaning.

Watching these recent and familiar formations may lead to a study of the earlier and less obvious origins of words in the general English vocabulary.

References: The great authority on the origin of English words is the *Oxford English Dictionary,* and now the *Dictionary of American English* is supplementing it for words peculiar to the United States.

Besides general books on English, the following pay special attention to origin of words: Otto Jespersen, *Growth and Structure of the English Language* (various editions); George H. McKnight,

English Words and Their Backgrounds, New York, 1923; *Picturesque Word Origins,* Springfield, Mass., 1936; H. F. Scott, W. L. Carr, G. T. Wilkinson, *Language and Its Growth,* Chicago, 1935; Kennedy, Chapter 9.

Originality is applied to writing in two somewhat different senses:
1. The first refers to material. Material is "original" when it is gathered by the writer from his experience, from his observation of people, events, or places, or from documents like letters, newspapers, and other sources that have not been worked over. Secondary or secondhand material has been worked over by someone else, as in textbooks, encyclopedias, most magazine articles and books. This material has been organized and given form in words. Original material has to be sorted, selected, and laid out by the writer. Obviously one can learn more and find more profitable practice in handling original than in handling secondary material.

Most student papers should contain some original material. The content may come entirely from the writer's experience. At least the central idea, the purpose can come from his present desires, some of the examples, details, or applications can come from his observation, and the opinions and the point of view can represent the way he thinks. Merely rewriting a magazine article is not a profitable exercise in composition. Putting together material from several such secondary sources is more useful, since it requires selection and comparison of material. But the most useful work for growth in writing is in composing papers in which a good deal of the material is original. The writing is a little harder, but it is more fun, and the gain is much greater than in simply working over what others have done. Compare *Plagiarism.

2. Originality in expression, in style, is a different matter. The English language has been used a long time, and absolutely new words and phrases are rare. The most threadbare figures and phrases can be avoided, and an honest attempt to tell exactly what the writer sees and believes will ordinarily result in straightforward, readable writing, which is more valuable than mere novelty. The one sure fact is that striving too hard for originality is almost certain to result in strained writing, uncomfortable to writer and reader alike. When a style deserving the label "original" appears, it is usually the byproduct of an active and independent mind, not the result of trying to be different.

Orthography means spelling. See Chapter 10, p. 267 and *Spelling.

other in *Comparison of adjectives and adverbs §5, *c* and *d*

ou represents the sound of *ou* in *bout, out, house,* of *ow* in *cow* (kou), of *ough* in *bough* (bou).

Words spelled with *ou* are variously pronounced: trouble (trub′əl), soul (sōl), soup (süp), trousseau (trü sō′).

-ough (-augh) A handful of words containing *-ough* and *-augh* are one of the minor scandals of English spelling. They are common words so that children learn most of them well enough— but it is hard to believe they should be asked to do so.

The objection to these forms is not so much that they are cumbersome, as that they "spell" such different sounds—*although, bough, cough, thorough, through, bought.* This can be explained by the history of the pronunciation of the individual words, chiefly by the fact that the pronunciations now generally current have come from different localities of early English speech—but that does not defend them. See "Inconsistencies in English spelling," p. 267.

At present *altho* and *tho* and to a less extent *thru* and *thoro* are widely used in familiar writing and are commonly used in business writing, especially in advertising. They are used in a number of periodicals and in some books, though most publishers still go by traditional stylebooks. They are given as alternative spellings in the recent dictionaries. In a questionnaire answered by over a hundred college and university English teachers, nearly one half allowed or encouraged the use of these forms in themes. They are still out of place in formal writing, and their use in informal writing should depend chiefly on their appropriateness to other traits of style and to the expectations of readers.

ought See *have §4 for *had ought* and *hadn't ought.*

-ous, -us *-ous* is an adjective ending: *fictitious, ominous; -us* is a noun ending: *cactus, campus, impetus.*

Outline form (CORRECTION: Revise the form of your outline according to the directions given in this article.) *Outl*

An outline is a schematic statement of the material that has been or that is to be presented in an article, showing *the order of topics* and *the general relationship between them.* An outline can test the organization of a paper that has been written. But the chief purpose of outlines is to make writing both easier and more effective. Once the material has been laid out, writing is relatively easy. You can focus on one stage at a time. You can see how the whole will shape and won't have to worry whether to put *this* in *here* or wait until later—you can write with confidence. Short, simple papers do not need formal outlines, though often some scratch notes will be handy. But the longer the paper and the more complicated the material, the more necessary and important a plan, represented by some sort of outline, becomes.

The way an outline grows out of the material you have decided to present in your paper is described as step five of The Writing Process, "Planning the paper," p. 297. This article takes up questions of form of outlines.

1. TYPES OF OUTLINES. There are various standard types of outlines.

a) Scratch outline. Most writing is done from very casual notes jotted down with due attention to meaning but without regard to form. The points are grouped according to some system of the writer's own devising. This is proper, and more themes should be written from such informal notes than are. Since this outline is an entirely personal document, not to be shown to anyone else, there is no point in making suggestions for it. Every writer should work out some method by which he can help himself sort out and organize his material and make it easier for him to write an orderly paper.

b) Topical outline. The most common type of formal outline is the topical outline. The subjects are noted in brief phrases or single words, numbered consistently as in this example:

I Have Learned to Work   [Title]

The keynote of this autobiographic sketch is the part played in the development of my character by habits of work. [Sentence statement]

I. The work habit formed early [Main head]
   A. The evils of idling taught by my parents [Subhead]
   B. Chores required regularly of all children in my family
   C. A newspaper route for fun and profit
II. Working in summer vacations during my high-school years
   A. Necessity of earning money
     1. For various school activities
     2. To save for my future college expenses
   B. Ways and means
     1. Selling popcorn and candy at baseball games
     2. Selling magazines and subscriptions
     3. Acting as lifeguard at seashore resort
III. Beneficial results of this work
   A. Practical results
     1. Many additional clothes and social activities
     2. A bank account for my college expenses
     3. Skill acquired and contacts made, valuable for getting jobs during college vacations

B. More permanent results
1. Strengthening of character—avoiding mischief—habit of industry
2. Realization of value of money
3. Carry-over into academic life of work habits
4. Above all, self-reliance developed

c) *Sentence outline.* A sentence outline differs from a topic outline only in that each head and subhead is a complete sentence. It is more formal, requires more effort to draw up. Its chief advantage is that it forces the outliner to think through his ideas more thoroughly in order to give them more complete and elaborate statement.

The Transformation of Henry Fleming

The purpose of this paper is to trace the growth of the character Henry Fleming in Stephen Crane's *The Red Badge of Courage.*

I. Henry's boyish idea of war underwent a change on the eve of battle.
   A. He had enlisted because he thought of war romantically and pictured himself performing heroic feats.
   B. A few days before his regiment was to have its first engagement, his idea of the glory of war was modified.
      1. He observed his fellow soldiers, listened to their boastful remarks.
      2. He began to doubt his own courage, feared he might run from danger.

II. He failed in the first test.
   A. As the regiment went into the firing line, he wished he had never enlisted.
   B. For a time he remained in the line and did his duty.
      1. He was bewildered.
      2. Feeling himself to be in a "moving box," he did as the others did about him.
   C. Overcome by fear, he finally turned and ran to the rear.
   D. As a skulker, he had a miserable experience.
      1. Discovering that his regiment had unexpectedly held its ground, he felt cheated.
      2. Joining a column of the wounded, he was shamed when asked about his own wound.

III. He regained his self-confidence.
   A. Dealt a blow on the head by a deserter, Henry rejoined his regiment, expecting to be ridiculed.
   B. When his fellow-soldiers assumed that he had been wounded in action, Henry saw that his cowardice had passed unnoticed.

C. In the next day's battle he acted creditably.
   1. Enraged at the enemy, he fought furiously and desperately.
   2. Praised by his lieutenant, he saw himself in a new light.
   3. He became color-bearer and urged his fellows on to the charge.

IV. After this first engagement, Henry was no longer his old self.
  A. He had had a chance to see himself in a new perspective.
  B. For a time he was tortured by thoughts of his cowardly conduct of the first day.
  C. Then he rejoiced at having become a man and overcome fear.

d) *Paragraph summaries.* It is sometimes helpful to prepare for writing a short paper by jotting down in advance the topic of each paragraph. This method would not work well for long papers, because it does not distinguish subheads. *This is the only type of outline in which the entries correspond exactly to the paragraphs of the paper.*

2. OUTLINE TECHNIQUE. Most of the conventions of outline form are shown in the examples just given, but they may be worth isolating for comment.

a) *The title.* The title of the paper should stand over the outline, but it is not a part of the outline and should not be numbered. The heads should carry their full meaning and not refer back to the title by pronouns.

b) *Sentence statement.* It is a good idea to put between the title and the first main head a sentence stating the subject and scope of the whole paper. If this is done it should be a full, meaningful sentence, not a mere announcement of the topic.

c) *Numbering systems.* The most widely used numbering system alternates letters and figures, as shown in the examples in this article. Avoid intricate or confusing schemes of numbering.

d) *Indention.* Write the main heads flush with the left margin and indent subheads two or three spaces—enough to make them clearly in a different line—from the left, as shown in the examples.

e) *Punctuation and capitalizing.* No punctuation is needed at the end of lines in a topic outline. In the sentence outline the punctuation should follow regular sentence practice as shown in the example. Only the first word of a head and proper names are capitalized. An outline head is not a title.

f) *Meaningful heads.* Each head should be complete, understandable by itself. This outline is useless:

My Vocation
I. The work I am interested in
II. Why I prefer this type of work
III. What my responsibilities would be
IV. Some of the attractions of this position.
V. The chances for success
VI. Why I want this particular position

A more exact statement of topics would show that II and IV belong together, and very likely V and VI as well.

Subheads should carry full meaning. General labels like "Causes" or "Results" are useless, as are these from an outline for "The House of Morgan":

A. Started by Junius Spencer Morgan
   1. What he did
B. Succeeded by J. P. Morgan I
   1. What he did
C. Succeeded by the present J. P. Morgan
   1. What he is doing

Meaningful heads are especially important in outlines made part of a finished paper or to be shown to someone for criticism.

g) Heads of equal importance. The main heads of an outline, those usually marked by Roman numerals, should be of equal importance to the subject: they show the several main divisions of the material. Similarly, the first line of subdivisions of these heads, those usually marked by capital letters, should designate logical and equally important divisions of one phase of the subject. The same principle applies to further subdivisions under any subhead.

EQUAL HEADINGS:	UNEQUAL HEADINGS:
Books I Have Enjoyed	Books I Have Enjoyed
I. Adventure stories	I. Adventure stories
II. Character studies	II. *Treasure Island*
III. Autobiographies	III. Autobiographies
IV. Books on ethics and religion	IV. What I like most

h) Headings in parallel form. Parallel heads or subheads are expressed in parallel grammatical form. A sentence outline should use complete sentences throughout, not lapse into topical heads; a topic outline should use topic heads, not sentences. Topic heads or subheads should use phrasing parallel to that of other heads of the same rank, that is, the heads in a particular series should be all nouns or all adjectives or all phrases, or whatever is the most appropriate form.

PARALLEL HEADS:	HEADS NOT PARALLEL:
The Art of Putting	The Art of Putting
I. The stance	I. The stance is fundamental
II. The grip	II. The grip
III. The back-swing	III. Importance of the back-swing
IV. The contact with the ball	IV. Stroking the ball
V. The follow-through	V. Follow through with care

i) Division of topics. Since a topic is not "divided" unless there are at least two parts, an outline should have at least two subheads under any main head. For every heading marked *I* there should be at least a *II*, for every *A* there should be a *B*, and so on.

PROPER SUBDIVISION	ILLOGICAL SINGLE HEADS:
The Tripartite System of Government	The Tripartite System of Government
I. The executive branch	I. The executive branch
A. President	A. President and Cabinet
B. Cabinet	
II. The legislative branch	II. The legislative branch
A. The House of Representatives	A. The House
B. The Senate	B. The Senate
1. Special functions	1. Functions
2. Special privileges	
III. The judicial branch	III. The judicial branch
A. The Supreme Court	A. The Supreme Court
B. Lower courts	

A single detail may be included in the statement of heading, as, for an organization in which the whole executive power lay in the president:

I. The executive branch (The President)

Sometimes an exception is made for an outstanding illustrative example, which may be put in an outline as a single subhead:

   B. Injustice of grades in figures
      1. Example: My almost-Phi Bete roommate

j) Introductions and conclusions. Dividing a paper into "I. Introduction—II. Body—III. Conclusion" is not necessary. The introduction and conclusion to a paper are usually too short to need a special heading—the paper is all body. The first and last topics are from the main body of material, chosen with a special view to their fitness for meeting and for leaving a reader. See "Beginning paragraphs," p. 67 and "Concluding paragraphs," p. 70.

3. POSITION OF OUTLINES. An outline of less than half a page may stand on the first page of a paper, and the text can begin below it. A fuller outline should stand on a page by itself and be placed before the first page of text.

out loud Informal and colloquial for *aloud:*

INFORMAL: He was reading the newspaper out loud to the family.
FORMAL: He was reading the newspaper aloud to the family.

out of date *Out of date, out of doors, out of town* are hyphened in formal writing when they stand before a noun but not necessarily in informal writing:

FORMAL: He has an out-of-date model.
INFORMAL: He has an out of date model.
IN PREDICATE: His model is out of date. (Not usually hyphened)

over Compounds with *over* are not usually hyphened:

overanxious   overalls   overdraft   overseas

owing to *due to

P is characteristically pronounced as in *purr, tip, puppy.* It is silent in a few common words (*raspberry, cupboard, receipt*) and in a number of words from Greek—*pneumonia, psalm, psychology.*

After *m, p* is often silent in such words as empty (em'ti), generally in vulgate and often in informal usage. A *p* is often inserted after *m* in words such as *dreamt* (drempt) and *warmth* (wôrmpth). In *pumpkin,* two levels of pronunciation are recognized: formal, pump'kin; informal, pung'kən.

Paging manuscript Pages of copy should be put in their right order and numbered, preferably in the upper right corner and in ordinary figures (1, 2, 3 . . . , not in Roman numerals). The only way to make sure of numbering them is to do it as the page is begun.

paid (payed) *Paid* is the spelling of the past tense and past participle of *pay* (He *paid* his bills) in all senses except *payed out a line, rope, etc.,* and occasionally in that sense also.

pair In business usage and in much informal usage the plural of *pair* is *pair* when it comes after a number: six pair of socks. In other positions *pairs* is the usual plural.

Pair of stairs is an idiom now usually considered archaic or local, but is still occasionally found:

The building must have been walled and roofed and at least one pair [flight] of stairs built by the summer of 1676, . . .—S. E. MORISON, *Harvard College in the Seventeenth Century,* p. 425

pamphlet The common misspelling of this word is careless. Test it by pronouncing, *pam phl*et.

pants—trousers In formal usage the word for men's breeches is *trousers*; in the other levels and in colloquial usage the word is *pants*.

Paradox *Epigrams

Par **Paragraphs** (CORRECTION: This paragraph is unsatisfactory. Revise or rewrite it.) The most common faults in paragraphs are:

1. *Underdevelopment*—Lack of details to establish the picture or statement intended.

2. *Lack of connection*—Either actually unrelated statements put together, or the existing relation between statements not made clear to a reader.

Paragraphs are fully discussed in Ch. 3, p. 53, The Forms and Uses of Paragraphs, and Ch. 4, Kinds of Paragraphs, p. 81. These two chapters include the following topics:

CHAPTER 3: "The purpose of paragraphs," p. 53; "Length of paragraphs," p. 56; "Writing paragraphs," p. 58; "Connections between statements in a paragraph," p. 63; "Transitions between paragraphs," p. 65; "Beginning paragraphs," p. 67; "Concluding paragraphs," p. 70

CHAPTER 4: "Chronological paragraphs," p. 82; "Impressionistic paragraphs," p. 88; "Logical paragraphs," p. 93

Paral **Parallel constructions** (CORRECTION: Make the two or more elements in this series parallel in form.) Typical shifted (unparallel) constructions are these:

SHIFTED:	MADE PARALLEL:
To me orientation week seems both [noun:] a necessity and [adjective:] worth while.	To me orientation week seems both [two adjectives:] necessary and worth while.
Jack has received offers from Hollywood not only [phrase:] for his fishing experiences but [clause:] because he resembles the late Will Rogers.	Jack has received offers from Hollywood not only [two phrases:] for his fishing experiences but for his resemblance to the late Will Rogers.

For other examples and suggested remedies see *Shifted constructions and "Failure in parallelism," p. 129, and for successful parallelism as a means of effective sentences, see "Successful parallelism," p. 128, and "Parallelism and balance," p. 159.

Paraphrase A paraphrase is a restatement of a writer's ideas in different words. It is now usually applied to digesting the contents of a passage in one's own words, as in note taking.

Parataxis See *Contact clauses.

Parentheses ( ) **1.** Parentheses (often called *curves* and by printers called *parens*) are sometimes used in writing, chiefly to inclose words, phrases, or whole sentences that add to the clearness of a statement without altering its meaning and that are allowed to stand outside the construction of the sentence. These additions are likely to be (1) illustrations, (2) definitions, or (3) added information thrown in for good measure, as in the first sentence of this paragraph.

> This bill, commonly called the Lockport plan, has been the basis of all later city-manager charters (there are now 438).

> Of all such emotions religious earnestness is the most fatal to pure biography. Not only does it carry with it all the vices of hagiography (the desire to prove a case, to depict an example—the sheer perversion, for such purposes, of fact), but it disinterests the biographer in his subject.—HAROLD NICOLSON, *The Development of English Biography*, p. 111

> Sondelius even brought in the negro doctor, Oliver Marchand, not on the ground he was the most intelligent person in the island (which happened to be Sondelius's reason) but because he "represented the plantation hands."—SINCLAIR LEWIS, *Arrowsmith*, p. 376

These uses are slightly stiff and belong most appropriately to rather formal exposition, and should be used sparingly.

2. Sometimes parentheses are used to mark an apologetic aside, as much as to say "You know this, but let me remind you"—though this use is less common today than formerly.

> James Madison (the fifth President) enunciated the doctrine in 1823.

3. Parentheses are often used to inclose the letters or figures used to mark items in an enumeration, as in the second sentence (above) of this article, though this tends to make the numbers or letters more conspicuous than they deserve to be.

4. Recent fiction has developed another convenient use of parentheses. When the action is carried on in two different planes—one in the present, another in the past; one in a character's mind, the other in physical action—the one which receives less space, that is, is less emphatic, may be put in parentheses.

> . . . ears are still in outside world, peeping Toms sticking out on both sides of my head, why can't I take them in like snails, but you can't, you can close your eyes but you can't make your ears stop thinking. ("Thirty love! Net ball!" float in from that other world.) Voices outside losing their separateness, merging, sweet distant song,

like shell held to ear, going round and round in Natalie's brain, ears going to sleep at last. . . .—Tess Slesinger, *Time: The Present*, p. 341

5. Parentheses and other marks. When the parenthetical unit is a complete sentence, the period comes *inside* the curves, though it may be omitted. Punctuation marks belonging to the sentence including the parenthesis come *after* the second curve:

> There is a sort of glum morality about the scene in which we are shown what would have happened if the inventor had married for money instead of love (Mr. Anderson's gifted mechanism is equipped not only to recall the past but also to mix it up a little), and in the end, the suggestion that the device might be manufactured in quantity and sold on the installment plan seemed ominous to me.—*The New Yorker*, Oct. 9, 1937

> Misbehaviors which meant disqualification: "babbling" (barking to the extent of interfering with the chase); "loafing" (showing no inclination to hunt); "running cunning" (failing to work fairly on a trail).—*Time*, Nov. 28, 1938

parliament Pronounced pär′lə mənt. Capitalized when referring to the British Parliament or any other specific body.

Parse Parsing is describing the grammatical forms and functions of the words in a sentence. The sentence *A hermit lived in the ruined abbey* might be parsed: *Hermit* is a noun in the nominative case, subject of the verb *lived*; *in the ruined abbey* is an adverbial phrase of place; *abbey* is a noun in the accusative case, object of the preposition *in*, modified by the adjective *ruined*.

part (**on the part of**) is often a rather clumsy way of saying *by*, *among*, *for*, and the like:

> In the past ten years there has been a definite move on the part of [*by* or *among*] our religious leaders to unite all Protestant denominations in one church.

> It resulted in less wild driving on the part of [*by*] young people.

Part **Participles** (Correction: The participial construction marked is not good English. Revise it in the light of §2 [making it modify a particular noun as an adjective] or §5 [stating the idea in a subordinate clause].)

1. Forms of participles

	ACTIVE	PASSIVE
Present	asking, speaking	being asked, being spoken
Past	having asked, having spoken	asked, having been asked spoken, having been spoken

The simple participle forms (*asking, asked, speaking, spoken*) are used in various tenses of the verb:

I am asking   I am being asked   I have asked   I have been asked

Although the participles are referred to as present and past, they do not indicate definite time themselves but time in relation to the context in which they are used.

2. As ADJECTIVES. When not a part of a phrasal verb form, the participles are most commonly verbal adjectives. They have qualities of adjectives in that they modify nouns and pronouns (The pen *used* in signing the treaty . . . a *coming* man . . . the leaves *falling* in the street). They have qualities of verbs in that they may take an object (*Following these clues*, he soon found them) and be modified by adverbs (The car, *rolling crazily* . . .).

Sometimes in analyzing a sentence it is difficult to tell a participle used as an adjective from a passive voice. The decision rests on whether the participle modifies the subject, as a predicate adjective with a linking verb, or whether it describes an action.

PASSIVE VOICE: The candidate of the Republican party was defeated.
PREDICATE ADJECTIVE: The candidate was defeated but happy.

When used as an adjective, a participle should refer clearly to some particular noun or pronoun:

Opening his shirt at the neck, he went back to his chopping [*Opening* modifies *he*]
Looked at from this point of view, a college education may be a liability. [*Looked* modifies *college education*]

There should be no reasonable doubt of what is modified. A modifying participle "dangles" or is "misrelated" when it seems to refer to a word the writer does not mean it to refer to:

MISRELATED: Walking on the campus, several of my class usually pass by.
PROPER: Walking on the campus, I usually meet . . .
MISRELATED: Combined with his scientific understanding, Dr. Hertzler is a man who would have made his name for wisdom in any profession.
PROPER: Dr. Hertzler's scientific understanding would have made him a name in any profession.

Because the reader expects these participles to refer to the subject of the following clause, he is disappointed. It is not so much a matter of meaning, for the sentence with a dangling participle is rarely ambiguous (though it may be amusing). It is rather a matter

641

of accurate expression: Participles used as adjectives should modify definite words. *Dangling modifiers § 1

3. As coordinate verbs. Participles often have the value of a second verb, especially in colloquial and informal usage. In "He had been in the city two weeks, taking in all the night clubs and in general having a high old time" the *taking* and *having* are not adjectives modifying *he* but have the value of verbs: "He had been in the city two weeks and [or a separate sentence] he had been taking in all the night clubs . . ." This construction is not so common in formal English as it once was but occasionally is a way of making the verb less conspicuous and the movement more rapid.

4. In absolute constructions. The participle-as-adjective should not be confused with the participle in a phrase which relates to the whole sentence (to the situation) rather than to a particular word. Some such phrases are very common, perhaps even *formulas.

> Generally speaking, we expect snow before December.
> Judging from her looks, she isn't under fifty.
> Judged by any absolute standard, he should fail the course.
> Putting two and two together, we decided they had never intended to come.
> Beginning with the class of 1943, the tuition was raised $50.

Such participial phrases are equivalent to subordinate clauses (If you put two and two together . . . and so on).

5. Unidiomatic participles. The use of participles and verbal nouns in English seems to be increasing, but there is a tendency for amateur writers to use participles in constructions in which they would never use them in speaking in which a subordinate clause would be more natural:

> Uncle Joe was prompt, *necessitating our hurrying* [so that we had to hurry].
> The sea was running heavily, *being boosted* by a strong southeast wind. [Omit the *being*]

Especially conspicuous are unidiomatic "Nominative absolutes," made like Latin ablative absolutes:

> He being right there, I let him do the work. [Since he was right there . . .]

> Then, *the feature being ended*, the ship came down the hill, and the cadets marched by to show us in what a volcanic world we were living. [Then, after the feature was ended . . . or, perhaps, The feature ended, the ship . . .]

642

6. V*ery* WITH PARTICIPLES. *very § 1

Compare *Gerunds.

References: Curme, *Syntax*, pp. 158-60; C. A. Smith, *Interpretative Syntax* (Boston, 1906), pp. 55-59; Reuben Steinbach, "The Misrelated Constructions," *American Speech*, 1930, v, 181-97; H. C. Wyld, *A Short History of English*, pp. 237-58

Parts of speech Although in our speaking and writing we are not conscious of using nouns or verbs or adjectives, we need to be able to identify the parts of speech if we are going to describe and discuss grammatically what we have written. For analysis we have to know whether we are using nouns or verbs, pronouns, prepositions.

1. There are three criteria for placing a word in a certain part of speech: the grammatical function it serves or generally serves in speech—subject, object, modifier, and so on; its type of meaning—the name of something, description of a quality, a connecting relationship, and so on; and the forms it may assume—like the *'s* of the noun genitive or *-er* of the comparative of an adjective or adverb. The part of speech to which a word belongs often cannot be definitely decided by looking at the word by itself; we need to know how it is used. These qualities are all discussed in the articles on each part of speech. Here the traditional eight parts are identified by their type of meaning, an imperfect but the simplest criterion.

NOUNS—Names of people, places, things, qualities, acts, ideas, relationships: *President Roosevelt, Key West, gearshift, confusion, gambling, relativity.*

PRONOUNS—Words which refer indirectly to people, places, things, etc.: *he, it, someone, which.*

ADJECTIVES—Words which point out or indicate a quality of people, places, things, etc.: *both, the highest, warm, thorough, Hanoverian.*

VERBS—Words that specify actions, states, feelings, existence of people, places, things, etc.: *fall, fall into, dislike, become.*

ADVERBS—Words which, typically, tell how, where, when, to what degree acts were performed or that indicate a degree of quality, etc.: *severely, there, yesterday, much.*

PREPOSITIONS—Words that link nouns and pronouns to other words by showing the relationship between them: *to, about, behind.*

CONJUNCTIONS—Words that connect words (the horse *and* carriage), phrases (in the house *and* in the garden) and clauses (The rain was over *and* we started again, or *After* the rain was over we started again).

EXCLAMATIONS—Words that are expressions of strong feeling (*Ouch!*).

References: Jespersen, *The Philosophy of Grammar*, Chapters 4-6; Curme, *Parts of Speech*, pp. 1-105; Kennedy, Chapter 8

2. CONVERSION OF PARTS OF SPEECH. English uses one part of speech to perform the function of another part of speech with great freedom. *Hurry* may be a verb (I'll hurry right over), or a noun (I'm in a great hurry), or an adjective (a hurry call); *better* is the comparative of the adjective *good* or of the adverb *well* ("I could have better [adverb] spared a better [adjective] man"); it is a verb (to better your condition); or a noun (our elders and betters); *home* is used as a noun, a verb, an adjective, or an adverb; and so on through a long list of words. This change of function from one part of speech to another is called *conversion*. It is a sign of the economy of our language in forms of words, and is made possible because in English we have so few particular endings belonging specifically to various parts of speech. These shifts are not confusing because the word's position or context in a sentence shows what its function is.

The use of adjectives as nouns is particularly characteristic of informal English: *wets* and *drys* were the two factions in the prohibition argument; an *empty* may be a bottle or a freight car. Many of the semi-technical words of trade and business are of this type: "The regular driver handles the ordinary orders, but I must take the *rushes* [adjective to noun] out in the *pickup* [verb to adjective] truck."

One of the most convenient forms of conversion is the use of a noun in the adjective function: the art room; a baseball game; the high school gymnasium; a basement tenement. Most of these do not attain to full conversion, that is they do not become complete adjectives so that they can be compared, yet they serve as adjectives and have to be construed as adjectives. Nouns are especially common as adjectives in newspaper headlines, in which they often replace longer adjectives ("Let *U. S.* Citizens Alone, Italy Told") or replace phrases with *of* ("Madison *Oil Trial* Prosecutor to Head *Medical Trust* Quiz"). See *Newspaper English § 3.

The use of a noun or some other part of speech as a verb is likely to increase vividness: She jumped into the roadster and *nosed* her down the street; *Power* your car with reliable gas. "Don't you *she* me!" (as a Russian princess said to an American girl who was not following the courtly locutions in talking about her). The opposite change, from verb to noun, is less spectacular but very convenient: He had five *tries*; a friendly *get together*; I have taken a five room *rent* in Springfield, Illinois.

Conversion is an outstanding trait of colloquial and informal English, though less used in formal English. Need and appropriateness can be your guides. When an equally expressive verb or noun exists, there is no reason for running the risk of attracting attention to your words by a borrowing from some other part of speech—but freedom in handling the parts of speech is in the best tradition of our language. Convert a noun into an adjective or into a verb whenever it seems the natural form of expression.

Reference: Kennedy, *Current English* § 58

party *person

passed, past The past tense and past participle of *pass* are *passed* (He *passed* the first post; He had *passed* . . .), though *past* is fairly common as the participle. *Past* is the adjective (*past* favors), preposition (*past* the crisis), and adverb (*past* due, They went *past*). Pronunciation: past or päst (*A § 4).

passer-by Usually hyphened, to avoid suggesting the pronunciation pas′ər bi. Plural *passers-by*.

passé Pronunciation divided: pa sā′ or pas′ā.

Passive voice (CORRECTION: Change the passive verb or verbs to *Pass* active.)

Amateur writers tend to use passive statements ("The music *was enjoyed* by us" instead of "We *enjoyed* the music") when active verbs would be more natural, and so add to other traits of wordiness they are likely to show. Passives are sometimes used to avoid *I*:

PASSIVE: The situation *was taken in* by me with great amusement.
ACTIVE: I took in the situation with great amusement.

This passage shows both effective and ineffective passives:

1941 is here. With it comes a host of '41 model automobiles. Most of these cars *were heralded in* during the closing months of 1940. They *were awaited* in anxious curiosity by the buying public. In many instances, they *were looked forward to* with too much anticipation. For the owners of '39 and '40 model cars, it meant that theirs were worth just so much less.

Were heralded in is a legitimate passive, although an awkward phrase, because the "heralders" need not be named; and *were awaited* throws *the buying public* to the end of the sentence for emphasis and the passive would not be noticeable if it was not followed by *were looked forward to*, which clearly shows that the writer is not paying attention to his work. Those two sentences might better stand:

The buyers awaited them in anxious curiosity, many of them with too much anticipation.

The use of passive verbs is often objectionable because it involves a thoughtless shift from the active voice and adds to the wordiness of what is usually already wordy and fuzzy writing.

For profitable use of the passive voice see *Voice § 3.

Past tense, Past perfect tense *Tenses of verbs

Pathetic fallacy Crediting places and things with human emotions is known as the pathetic fallacy. A certain amount of such metaphor is natural and often successful. But the sea and clouds and winds and mountains have too often been given human emotions, or at least emotional adjectives, by amateur and professional melodramatists, so that now such figures are usually ineffective.

Huge waves bared white jagged crests of *angry* froth as they roared across the shallows to crash high upon the sandy beach. The tide as it approached flood pushed *grasping* tongues of *angry* sea water up to the breakwater and the frail dinghies, rowboats, and canoes moored in the safety of its lee. Out beyond Salt Island the clouds seemed to be resting on the sea *as if their tremendous weight had at last borne them down to rest.*

patriot, patriotic Pā′tri ət and pā′tri ot′ik are the dominant American pronunciations. Pat′ri ot′ik is more common than pat′ri ət.

peeve Informal and colloquial for *annoy.* As a noun *peeve* (and *pet peeve*) is probably still slang. *Peeve* is a back formation from *peevish* (*Origin of words § 3d).

per *Per* (Latin, "through, by, by the, among," etc.) is most appropriate when used in phrases that are still close to their Latin originals—*per capita, per cent*—or in a definitely commercial setting—*$18 per week, $2.60 per yard, forty-four hours per week,* or in certain standardized technical phrases—*revolutions per minute.*

Because of its commercial and technical connotation, *per* is less appropriate in general prose, where the English equivalent phrase usually fits more naturally: *$18 a week, 20¢ a quart, four times a year.*

As *per* is in business use only: "as per the attached schedule."

per cent is not followed by a period, and may be written as one word. It is informally used instead of *percentage* or even of *proportion:*

Only a small percent of the class was [or, were—collective agreement] there.

per-, pre- Many English words begin with these two prefixes. Do not spell the *per*-words with *pre*-: write *per*form, *per*spire, and so on.

Perfect infinitive *Infinitives §1

Perfect tense *Tenses of verbs

Period (.) **1.** The principal function of the period is to mark the end of a statement, that is, the end of every completed sentence not definitely a question or exclamation. This gives us no trouble, though sometimes in hasty writing we carelessly omit the period.

Sometimes sentences in the form of exclamations or questions are really to be regarded as statements. After such a sentence a writer may use the exclamation mark or question mark, but he will usually have a period if the tone is lacking in emotion or if he wishes to minimize the emotion of the sentence form he has chosen (*Rhetorical questions).

2. MISCELLANEOUS CONVENTIONAL USES:

a) After abbreviations: Oct. n.b. Mr. Wm. Fraser (*Abbreviations § 3)

b) In sums of money, between dollars and cents: $5.66. The period is not used unless the dollar sign is used: 66 cents or 66¢; $0.66. (*Money § 3)

c) Before decimals, or between the whole number and the decimal: .6, 3.14159, 44.6%

d) A period is sometimes used between hours and minutes represented in figures (2.36 p.m.) though a colon is most usual 2:36 p.m.). (*Colon §3*a*)

e) Three spaced periods (. . .) are used as *ellipses, to mark the omission of words.

3. PERIOD IN COMBINATION WITH OTHER MARKS. Most American publishers place a period coming at the end of a quotation inside the quotation marks: "The longer you put it off," he said, "the harder it's going to be." (*Quotation marks § 4*b*)

Period fault See "Fragmentary sentences," p. 134 and *Fragmentary sentence.

Periodic and loose sentences See "Loose and periodic sentences," p. 157.

Periodical indexes See "Periodical indexes," p. 328.

Person Pronouns are classified in three *persons:*

FIRST PERSON, THE ONE SPEAKING: *I, me, we, us*
SECOND PERSON, THE ONE SPOKEN TO: *you*
THIRD PERSON, THE ONE SPOKEN OF: *he, she, it, one, they, him, his, her, them,* and so on

Nouns are regarded as third personal.

Except in the verb *be* (*I am, you are, he is* . . .) English verbs have only one form to distinguish person, the third singular: I have, you have, he *has*; we, you, they have.

person is the ordinary word for referring to a human being without making any particular distinction. *Individual* has the same meaning (though it is applied also to single objects and animals as well) but emphasizes the person's singleness, aloneness, and is slightly heavy or pretentious unless that emphasis is needed. *Party* is legal, or vulgate.

In person and *personally* are current intensives in business and colloquial usage (Ronald Colman in person; I personally think). These expressions are usually not appropriate in writing.

Personal pronouns *Pronouns, types and forms § 1

Personification Personification is a figure of speech in which an object or animal or quality or ideal is given some attributes of a human being:

> Deal gently, *Love*, with him and her
> who live together now!
>
> Rex Warner, *Poems*, p. 71

It is less common today than formerly, and less common in prose than in verse. Flat and unessential personification is likely to have an amateur sound:

> No steam engine can brag of half the efficiency of this.

Compare *Pathetic fallacy.

ph is a *digraph for the *f* sound in words of Greek origin: *photography, photograph.* . . . In *Stephen, ph* represents *v*, as it is in the British pronunciation of *nephew* (nev′ū).

Most words with *ph* belong to the formal vocabulary, so that the natural and expected simplification to *f* is rather slow. A few, like *fantasy* and *sulfur* are already changed. Advertisers and humorists are experimenting with *telegraf, foto*, and so on.

phase means "aspect," "side" (as of a question). It is overused for *part, kind*, and so on: "a phase of college that I dislike."

phenomenon, phenomena The plural of *phenomenon* is *phenomena* (phenomena of the mind).

Since *phenomenon* means "any observable fact or event," care should be taken to see if some more exact word would be more effective.

Phenomenal colloquially means "remarkable," as in "his phenomenal rise to power."

Phi Beta Kappa *Greek alphabet

phone is the normal informal and colloquial clip for *telephone* (on the phone; Phone me later). No apostrophe.

Phonetics is the division of language study that deals with the sounds of language, their formation, changes, and the exact representation of pronunciation by phonetic symbols. *Pronunciation

photo as a clip from *photograph* is in colloquial use, but is not so widely current as, say, *phone* for *telephone*, because of the convenient substitute *picture*.

Phrasal verb A verb formed by an auxiliary and an infinitive or past participle: *will go, must go, has gone, had gone*. Even in the tenses which have simple forms (*goes, went*), we get slightly different shades of meaning by using phrasal forms (*am going, did go, was going, etc.*). *Verbs

Reference: Kennedy, pp. 522-29

Phrases 1. As a UNIT OF EXPRESSION. A phrase is a group of words which functions as a unit in a clause or sentence:

up the steep hill   had gone   coming along the bridle path
in regard to   fore and aft   The New Deal

A phrase does not have a subject or predicate, though the subject, object, and verb of a clause or sentence are often phrases:

The poor old beast [subject] could hardly stand up [verb modified by adverb *hardly*].

Most words by themselves, as they stand in a dictionary, cannot fit into sentences until they are set in phrases. They need modifiers to make their meaning more exact; they need connectives to tie them to other words. Out of such phrases, clauses and sentences are built. Unless the phrases are natural and accurate expressions of idea or feeling, the sentence will fail in communication. In fact, a good case could be made for regarding phrases as the central feature of writing and speaking, more fundamental than sentences, rivaled only by paragraphs in importance for study and practice.

Phrases are not only units of meaning; they are the physical units of reading, since we read by meaningful groups of words rather than by single words. Most phrases fall within the limits of the typical eye span (what an eye grasps at one fixation)—six words or thirty letters. Phrases that are easy to grasp with the eye and easy to comprehend with the mind are fundamental to good writing.

2. PHRASE FORMS. Phrases are classified according to their composition:

PREPOSITIONAL: in the morning   before the war   in the room
PARTICIPIAL: coming into the room   pasted on the wall
GERUNDIAL: before his learning French
INFINITIVE: to live in peace   Contrast an "infinitive clause" with subject (in the accusative) and object or complement: "They wanted him to be elected."
VERB: have gone   am going

3. PHRASE FUNCTIONS. Phrases function as single parts of speech:

NOUNS: (Subject) *The first four games* were lost. (Object) He lost *the first four games.*   (Genitive) the works *of the masters* (Indirect object) He left his fortune *to the University.*
VERBS: They *will go* in the morning.
ADJECTIVES: a heart *of gold*   *Crossing the street,* he nearly was hit by a car.
ADVERB: beyond the town   in the morning   He did it *in the Dutch manner.*
PREPOSITIONS: in regard to   in order to   alongside of

For the use of phrases see *Idiom and idioms, *Participles, *Prepositions.

pianist, piano Pronunciation divided: pi an′ist, pē′ə nist, the first the more common by a great deal. The word applies to men and women players, so that *pianiste* is unnecessary as a feminine form.
Piano is pronounced pi an′ō; rarely pi ä′nō. Plural *pianos.*

picnic Now usually spelled *picnic;* before endings beginning with a vowel, *k* is added to the second *c* to keep the *k* sound: *picnicker, picnicked, picnicking.*

Place names *Proper names; for punctuation, *Comma §8*b*

Plagiarism *Plagiarism* means offering, as one's own, material as it has been written by another. The copied matter may range from a few sentences to a whole paper copied from another student or from a book or magazine. (We are not considering here the more complicated problem of plots taken from stories or movies, and so on.) There are various reasons for copied papers in a composition course. A very few students are dishonest, trying to get a credit without any mental effort. Once in a while one is playing the ancient game of putting-something-over-on-the-instructor, in part at least to see if it can be done. More often, at least in beginning courses, the motives are more complex. A student who plagiarizes may be scared or so befogged in what is for him a difficult or puzzling course that he resorts to the only way he sees of getting a good grade. And sometimes a student doesn't clearly understand what rights he has in using the materials of others or in receiving help.

In English compositions obviously the work should be done independently, not in "collaboration" with another student.

The first two sorts of copying need no consideration. The student must take the consequences if the source of his paper is recognized, or even if the instructor is sure by comparing it with his other papers that it is not his own work. The other two sorts deserve consideration, and help. Whatever the motive, the penalty —failing the paper or perhaps, if it is an important one, failing the course—is not an instance of vengeance, but a sign of failure, failure in the fundamental purpose of a composition course, which is to increase students' skill in communicating their information, ideas, and fictions to others. Copying others' work is the most complete failure possible.

The student who is scared or puzzled should go at once to his instructor and discuss his situation frankly, the reasons for his difficulties, the present faults in his work, and ways to overcome them. Serious effort intelligently directed will always bring improvement. And a student who feels he is moving in the right direction, even if slowly, is doing something important, and work in the long run is more satisfying and less wearing than worry.

The student who has not learned how to handle material got from reading and study needs guidance in the fundamentals of study and scholarship. A writer expects that what he has published will be read and will be used; but he has a right to expect that his exact words will not be used without his permission and that his facts and ideas will not be used without his receiving credit.

Anyone using published material, then, has a twofold responsibility: first, of absorbing the ideas into his own thought, and second of giving credit to important sources. A student—or anyone else—is not *composing* when he is merely copying. He should read and digest the material, get it into his own words (except for brief, important quotations that are shown to be quotations). He should be able to *talk* about the subject before he *writes* about it. Then he should refer to any sources he has used. This is not only courtesy, but a sign of good workmanship, part of the morality of writing. In an informal paper the credit can be given informally, perhaps a note on the cover saying "This paper is based on . . ."; or it may be in the body of the paper: "Professor Keane said in a lecture . . . ," "Walter Lippmann wrote recently . . . ," or "So-and-so said . . ." Or credit may be given more formally in footnotes at the bottom of the page (as described in §9 of Chapter 13 [p. 338]). Footnotes must be used in a research paper, but one or two would be in order in any paper for which a student has found material in print. The greatest temptation to plagiarism is in a research paper, in which the material is supposed to be digested from reading various sources. But a research paper offers also the best opportunity for learning how to gather, digest, and give credit for material from published sources. At any rate it is necessary for college students to learn how to use such material accurately and honestly—by getting it into their own words and giving appropriate credit to sources used.

plenty *Plenty* as an adverb (I was plenty worried—the car is plenty large) is marked colloquial by the dictionaries. It is in good informal use but would rarely be found in formal writing.

The colloquial omission of *of* after *plenty* (plenty of time—plenty time) results in an adjectival use. This idiom is sometimes found in print:

> Out into darkness, out to night,
> My flaming heart gave plenty light, . . .
> JOHN MASEFIELD, *The Everlasting Mercy*

Pleonasm Pleonasm is repetition, especially using two words for the same grammatical function (My Uncle Fred, *he* said he would give me twenty-five cents for every bird I could find and name). It is quite common in children's speech and in colloquial English but not often used in written prose.

Plurals The plural of the great majority of English nouns is made by adding -*s* to the singular form of the noun. This -*s* is pronounced as part of the syllable to which it is added.

buckets   days   rooms   trees

There are five *Romes* in the United States.

But several groups of words form their plurals in other ways:

    1. Special groups in -*s* or -*es*.

a) Nouns ending in the *sound* of ch, j (*edge*), s, sh, x, or z, in which the -*s* could not be pronounced as part of the final syllable, add -*es*, or if they end in silent -*e*, pronounce this *e* and the added *s* as a syllable:

birches   churches   bridges   ledges   buses (or busses)
kisses   bushes   *Joneses   axes   fixes   buzzes   quizzes

    A number of words ending in -*s* have the same form in both singular and plural:

billiards   headquarters   means   morals
athletics   civics   mathematics   politics (and all words in -*ics*)

b) Nouns ending in -*y* preceded by a consonant change the *y* to *i* and add -*es*:

beauties   bodies   caddies   cherries   cities   cries

Drys, standbys are exceptions to this rule (speaking of a prohibitionist as a *dry*).

These plural forms should not be confused in writing with the genitive singular in '*s*: *beauty*'s, *body*'s, *caddy*'s, and so on.

Words ending in *y* preceded by a vowel merely add -*s*:

bays   boys   moneys [sometimes monies]   monkeys   toys

c) Words ending in -*o* preceded by a vowel make a regular plural with -*s*:

cameos   folios   studios

Words ending in -*o* preceded by a consonant vary and have to be remembered or looked up in a dictionary. Some of the commoner of these are:

WITH -*s* ONLY:
banjos   cantos   dynamos   Eskimos   Filipinos
mementos   pianos   silos   solos   sopranos   zeros
WITH -*es* ONLY:
echoes   heroes   Negroes   tornadoes
noes   potatoes   tomatoes   torpedoes   vetoes

Several words in -*o* are used with either -*s* or -*es*. The -*es* form is usually the more common, but the increasing number of -*os* forms suggests that English is gradually reducing these irregular words to the regular plural form:

cargoes, cargos   desperadoes, desperados   dominoes, dominos
hoboes, hobos   mottoes, mottos   tornadoes, tornados

d) Some words ending in an *f* sound have their plural in -*ves*:

calf, calves   half, halves   knife, knives   leaf, leaves
loaf, loaves   self, selves   shelf, shelves   thief, thieves

Many words ending in *f*-sounds are regular:

beliefs   chiefs   dwarfs   fifes   gulfs   proofs   roofs

Some have two forms:

elf, elves—elfs   hoof, hoofs—hooves   scarf, scarfs—scarves
staff, staffs—staves   wharf, wharfs—wharves

Calf and others of this type have colloquial plurals in -*fs* (*calfs*).

2. SAME FORM FOR BOTH SINGULAR AND PLURAL:

NAMES OF ANIMALS: fowl, sheep   fish [*fishes* for varieties of fish]
ALL WORDS IN -*ics*: athletics, civics, politics

A NUMBER OF WORDS RARELY, IF EVER, USED IN THE SINGULAR:

barracks	means	pains	smallpox
bellows	measles	pants	species
gallows	mumps	scissors	tactics
goods	odds [in betting]	slacks	trousers

foot, *pair colloquially in measurements and so on

3. SURVIVALS OF OLDER ENGLISH PLURAL FORMS:

IN -en: child, children   ox, oxen
         brother, brethren [Archaic or church use]

CHANGE OF VOWEL: foot, feet   goose, geese   louse, lice
man, men   mouse, mice   tooth, teeth   woman, women

4. FOREIGN LANGUAGE PLURALS. English keeps the foreign form of many words that have been borrowed from other languages. As they become more commonly used, the plural is usually formed regularly in -s; words used chiefly in scientific or formal writing tend to keep the foreign form longer. *Antenna,* for instance, makes *antennae* in biology but *antennas* for the more popular radio use. When the word is in transition, both forms will be found.

A few borrowed words that now regularly have plurals in -s or -es will suggest the extent of the change to English forms:

area	census	encyclopedia	museum
arena	circus	era	panacea
asylum	cupola	forum	panorama
bonus	dilemma	ignoramus	plateau
bureau	diploma	metropolis	quota
campus	dogma	minus	

Some common words that still have the foreign form or sometimes are found with the foreign plural (as in academic, formal, or scientific writing) are:

addendum -da	*beau beaus, beaux	*formula -las, -lae
alumna -nae	cactus -ti, -tuses	focus -ci (scientific),
*alumnus -ni	chateau -teaus,	-cuses (general)
ameba -bae, -bas	-teaux	fungus -gi, -guses
analysis -ses	cherub cherubs,	*gladiolus -luses, -li
apparatus -tus,	cherubim	hiatus hiatus, -tuses
-tuses	(scriptural)	hypothesis -ses
appendix -dixes,	crisis crises	index indexes, indices
-dices	criterion -teria	larva -vae
automaton -ta,	curriculum	libretto -tos, -ti
-tons	-lums, -la	locus loci
axis axes	datum *data	madame mesdames
bacillus -li	diagnosis -ses	matrix -trixes,
basis bases	erratum -ta	-trices

*medium -dia, -diums
memorandum -da, -dums
momentum -tums, -ta
moratorium -iums, -ia
monsieur messieurs
minutia (rare) minutiae
nautilus -luses, -li
nebula -las, -lae
neurosis -ses

nucleus -clei, -cleuses
oasis oases
opus opera (humorous, opuses)
ovum ova
parenthesis -ses
*phenomenon -na, -nons
psychosis -ses
radius radii, radiuses
rostrum -trums, -tra
series series
species species
stadium -diums, -dia

stimulus -li
stratum -ta, -tums
syllabus -bi, buses
synopsis -ses
synthesis -ses
tableau -bleaus, -bleaux
terminus -nuses, -ni
thesis -ses
trousseau -seaus, -seaux
vertebra -brae, -bras
vortex -tices, -texes

5. COMPOUND AND GROUP WORDS. Most compound words and group words add -s to the end of the group, whether written as one word or several:

attorney generals (or attorneys general) bookcases high schools
cross examinations postmaster generals (or postmasters general)

In a few compounds in which the more important element stands first, the plural sign is added to that:

daughters-in-law kings of England mothers-in-law passers-by
poets laureate (also, poet laureates) sons-in-law

6. PLURALS OF FIGURES, WORDS, LETTERS. Usually the plural of a letter of the alphabet, of a word discussed as a word, or of a figure is written with -'s:

There are two *c*'s and two *m*'s in *accommodate*.
Three 2's six 8's
Don't use several *that*'s in a row.

But usage is divided and the plural of figures and capital letters especially is often made with -s:

three 2s six 8s two Cs and two Fs
And there are few more useful practical suggestions in composition than this: Use no more *ands* or *buts* than you can help.—BARRETT WENDELL, *English Composition*, p. 145

7. PLURAL SUBSTITUTES. A plural notion is expressed often by a phrase that remains grammatically singular:

College after college has gone in for intramural sports.
The coach, with the captain and manager, makes up the schedule.
The coach, together with the captain and manager, makes [often *make*] up the schedule.

Singular and plural constructions are treated in *Subject and verb, *Reference of pronouns.

References: Curme, *Parts of Speech*, pp. 112-27, *Syntax*, pp. 539-48; Kennedy, pp. 438-45; Fries, p. 40 ff.

p.m. *a.m. and p.m.

Poetic diction refers to the formal and often archaic words that occur in verse, usually of second-rate or immature poets—*aught, beauteous, e'er, ere, eerie, wight*.

The language of poetry often tends to be elevated, to use words that through long use have become symbols for human sentiments, but the better poets have used the language of their times, have expressed their reaction to experience in natural words. Anyone beginning to write in verse should avoid words that will seem merely odd to his readers, that will seem to be words as words rather than immediate relation of experience.

Poetry When a full line or more of verse is quoted, it should be lined off as it was written, somewhat indented, enough so that it is nearly centered if the line is short. The first word of each line should be capitalized if it was capitalized in the original. Quotation marks are not needed around lines of verse quoted in prose when so spaced. See *Verse form for English meters.

politics is construed as either a singular or plural word but should not be both in the same passage.

In almost any group, politics is a subject which will arouse controversy.

Republican politics were offensive to the Federalists.

Polysyllables *Monosyllables

Positive degree of adjectives and adverbs is the simple adjective form (*poor, high, golden*) or adverb form (*slow, slowly, bitterly*). See *Comparison of adjectives and adverbs.

Possessive adjective *My, your, his, her, its, our, your, their* (the genitive case forms of the personal pronouns) are called possessive adjectives when they modify a noun:

my car   his first lecture   their experiences

Possessive case *Genitive case. Use of the possessive with verbal nouns in *-ing* is discussed in *Gerunds.

Possessive pronouns *Pronouns

Potential mood The expression of ability or possibility (usually involving *can, may, might, could*) is sometimes referred to as the potential mood or as a potential subjunctive. *can—may (could—might)

practical *Practical* and its derivatives give some trouble in spelling, partly because we slur syllables in pronunciation—*practically* becoming prak′ti kli or even prak′t′li, *practicability* becoming prak′ti bil′i ti—and it is a temptation to spell the word as it is spoken rather than the recognized written form.

> *practical*, adjective: a practical scheme, He has a practical mind.
> *practically*, adverb: They were practically minded; colloquial in phrases like "practically all there"
> *practicable*, adjective: a practicable method
> *practicability*, noun: They questioned the practicability of the idea.

pre- The prefix *pre-* meaning *before* in time (*pre-exist, pre-Victorian*), or in place (*precerebral*), or rank (*pre-eminent*), is separated by a hyphen from the root to which it is joined: (1) when the root begins with *e: pre-election, pre-eminent, pre-empt, pre-engaged, pre-existence*; and (2) when the root is a proper name: *pre-American, pre-Elizabethan.*

To other words it is joined directly: *prearrange, preheat, preoccupied, preprint, preview, prewar.*

Précis A *précis* is a concise summary of facts, or, more often, of an article or other written document, giving in a brief space the essential content, the attitudes, and emphasis of the original.

Precious, preciosity Applied to style, *precious* and *preciosity* (rarely *preciousness*) mean "excessive attention to, fastidiousness in the use of words," or, less often, "too great care in pronunciation."

Predicate A predicate is the verb and its dependent words that complete the meaning of the subject of a subordinate or independent clause. It may be a verb of complete meaning (The big bell *tolled*), a verb and adverbial modifier (The sun *went behind the cloud*), a transitive verb and its object (He *finally landed the big fish*), a *linking verb and complement (The oldest member of a family *is usually the first to go*).

Two verbs depending upon one subject are known as a *compound predicate:

The three of them *washed* and *wiped* the whole lot in fifteen minutes.

*Subject and verb, *Compound sentences, *Complex sentences

Predicate adjectives, Predicate nouns Adjectives and nouns that complete the meaning of linking verbs are called predicate adjectives and predicate nouns (or nominatives):

PREDICATE ADJECTIVE: The horse is *fast*.　I feel *bad*.　It is going to turn *warm*.

PREDICATE NOUN: The horse is *a chestnut*.　Jackson became *a doctor*.

See *Linking verbs.

predominant is the adjective: "a predominant sentiment," "a sentiment predominant in the village." *Predominate* is the verb: "This sentiment predominated in the village." These words are heavy for *prevailing, prevail,* or some such word.

prefer The better idiom is with *to*:

I prefer *Babbitt* to *Main Street*.
He preferred going by train to going in their car.

*Had [or Would] rather . . . than is less formal and more used:

He *had* [or *would* or *He'd*] rather go by train than in their car.

Prefix A prefix is a word or syllable that can be placed before a word or root to make another word of different meaning or function: *anti-* (*antiprohibition*), *bi-* (*biweekly*), *mis-* (*misfit*). *Origin of words §3a

prejudice Remember the spelling of *prejudice* by associating it with *pre judge* or the adjective *pre ju di cial*.

Prepositional phrase A phrase made up of a preposition and its object: *without hope, in a hurry, toward a more abundant life, in the old stone house.*

Prepositional phrases are construed as adverbs or adjectives:

They came *at just the right time*. [Adverb of time]
He lives *in the white house*. [Adverb of place]
The woman *in the black dress*. [Adjective]

To suggest the importance of prepositional phrases in English, here is a sentence of forty-two words in which twenty-seven stand in prepositional phrases (in italics), fifteen in other constructions:

The settings *of the novels* ranged *from the fjords of Norway to the coasts of Tasmania*, and every page betrayed that intimate knowledge *of a foreign country* which can only be acquired *by a thorough study of the chattier sort of guide-books*.—STEPHEN VINCENT BENÉT, *Thirteen O'Clock*, p. 71

Prep **Prepositions** (CORRECTION: Change the preposition in the phrase marked in line with suggestion in §3 below, making it more exact or idiomatic (§3a), less conspicuous (§3b), or making the construction less colloquial (§3c, d).)

Prepositions 1. DEFINITIONS. A preposition is a word which relates a noun or phrase to some other element of the sentence: to a verb (He showed her *to* her room), to a noun (the click *of* flying wheels), or to an adjective (old *in* experience). A noun following a preposition is called its object (*room, wheels, experience* in the examples just given). Many words used as prepositions are also used as adverbs or conjunctions, and some, like *after, but, since,* serve as the three parts of speech, depending on their function in a sentence, as *since:* (Preposition) The wettest summer *since* the Flood; (Conjunction) *Since* the price was so low, we took three; (Adverb) He hasn't been around *since.* For this reason some grammarians group all prepositions as *particles* with varying functions. In this article and the ones on conjunctions and adverbs we shall not draw the lines very closely.

2. LIST OF PREPOSITIONS. The list on pages 659-61 shows characteristic uses of the commoner prepositions. Many of them show both a concrete and an abstract meaning. Fries estimates that nine of them (*at, by, for, from, in, of, on, to, with*) account for over 92% of prepositions used.

ABOARD   aboard the airliner (Formal: on board)
*ABOUT   about the town, about her, about his work
*ABOVE   above the clouds, above the average, above suspicion
ACCORDING TO   according to the reports, according to Hoyle
ACROSS   across the bow, across the street (Colloquial: cross, I'm going cross lots)
AFTER   after dark, we all ran after him (Technical: of a drawing based on another's drawing, after Newcourt)
AGAINST   against the door, against the grain
AHEAD OF   ahead of his generation, ahead of time
ALONG   along the shore, along the route
ALONGSIDE   alongside the dock (Colloquial: alongside of)
AMID (AMIDST)   Formal: amid the smoke, amidst the ruins
AMONG   among the lucky ones (used of three or more)
APART FROM   apart from the others, apart from his own earnings (rather formal)
APROPOS   (apropō; rather formal) apropos our discussion
    also: apropos of our discussion
AROUND   around the edge, around the town (Colloquial: around five o'clock)
AS FAR AS   as far as the door, as far as New Orleans
*AS TO   as to the objection, as to your interest
AT   at home, at Johnstown, at his suggestion, at midnight
BACK OF   back of the screen, back of the house, back of the proposal
BECAUSE OF   because of the war, because of his need
BEFORE   before the flood, before an audience, before replying

BEHIND   behind the door, behind the pretense
BELOW   below the surface, below our level
BENEATH   beneath the surface, beneath contempt (more formal than *below*)
BESIDE   beside the sea, beside the point, beside oneself
BESIDES   besides those named, no other besides this
*BETWEEN   between New York and Philadelphia, between life and death, between two mountains
BEYOND   beyond the river, beyond reach, beyond my understanding
BY   by the house, by an inch, by force, by himself, by night
CONCERNING   concerning my friend, concerning our interests
CONTRARY TO   contrary to orders, contrary to our expectation
DESPITE   (Formal) despite hostile criticism
DOWN   down the chute, down the slope, down the list
*DUE TO   due to an error, due to carelessness
DURING   during the last ten years, during the services
FOR   for you, for profit, for the community
FROM   from the attic, from the Far East, from fear
IN   in the country, in the house, in the Bible, in trouble
IN PLACE OF   in place of the old regulations
*INSIDE   inside the house, inside ten minutes (Colloquial: inside of ten minutes)
IN SPITE OF   in spite of the law, in spite of his prejudices
IN VIEW OF   in view of these concessions
INTO   into the mountains, into the street, into the subject (*in—into—in to)
LIKE   like a horse, like a tornado
NEAR   near the window, near the top, near exhaustion
*OF   of Wisconsin, of the same color, of my opinion, of the king
*OFF   off the path, off the platform (Colloquial: off of the path)
ON ACCOUNT OF   on account of the weather, on account of his belief
*ONTO   onto the train, onto the beach (Formal: on to the beach)
OUT OF   out of the auditorium, out of sight
OVER   over the fence, over the plains, over her head
OWING TO   owing to the emergency, owing to our inability
PAST   past the stores, past the mark, past the hour
*PER   per day, per pound
ROUND   round the Maypole, round the town
SINCE   since his election, since Victorian days
THROUGH   through the first barrier, through accident
THROUGHOUT   throughout the day, throughout his speech
*TILL   till morning, till the intermission
TO   to Los Angeles, to the ocean, to Governor Smith, to the point
*TOWARD   toward Fort Worth, toward dinner time, toward the truth
UNDER   under the awning, under cover, under the arch
UNTIL   until dusk, until two o'clock (*till, until, 'til)
UNTO   (Archaic) unto death, unto the last drop
UP   up the slope, up the scale

UPON   upon a sure foundation, upon further investigation
UP TO   up to this point
VIA   via the Nickel Plate
WITH   with his fellows, with caution, with the affirmative
WITHIN   within bounds, within the city, within a year

3. USE OF PREPOSITIONS. (*a*) *Exact or idiomatic prepositions.*
A number of words are accompanied by certain prepositions, as contented *with* conditions, *in* my estimation. Some words have various meanings with different prepositions, as agree *with* (a person), agree *to* (a suggestion), agree *in* (principles, qualities).

You can add indefinitely to this list:

deprive *of* pleasure	hindrance *to* advancement
eligible *for* membership	impressed *by* (or *with*) his
fascinated *by* this glamor	ability
This glamor had fascination *for*	means *of* winning
him.	pride *in* his college
fear *of* fire, fear *for* his safety	unconscious *of* their stares

The right preposition does not give much trouble with words that we use commonly, because we learn the words by hearing or seeing them in their usual constructions. Obviously it is safer to learn words as they are actually used, to learn *acquiesce in* (acquiesce in a decision) rather than just *acquiesce*. If a person uses an unidiomatic preposition, it is probably because he is not at home with the word or is confused because usage is divided on that particular locution (as *different *from* or *than* or *to*). Dictionaries give the appropriate preposition used with particular words. This book treats a few idioms that are likely to raise questions: *ability (to); *agree to, agree with; *all (of); *compare—contrast; *different.

A special reminder is needed that when two words are used which are completed by different prepositions *both* prepositions should be used:

The first lesson learned by the sturdy Italian boy just over from the "old country" was *obedience to* and *respect for* others besides his parents. [Not: obedience and respect *for* others . . .]
Most people find it difficult to reconcile their *interest in* and their *fear of* snakes.
The committee acknowledged its *interest in*, but denied its *responsibility for*, housing conditions.
A real *knowledge of* and *interest in* national affairs is the aim of this class.

When both words call for the same preposition, it need not be repeated:

Observers from the North were astonished to find the slaves both *obedient* and *submissive to* their masters.

The box office refused to make any *allowance* or *refund for* tickets purchased from an agent.

b) Prepositions bulking too large. English has a number of group prepositions (*according to, in regard to, by means of . . .*) that sometimes become conspicuous because they bulk too large for their purely functional work of showing relationship. They are not grammatically wrong of course, but used in any noticeable numbers tend to make a flatfooted style. For many of them a simple preposition can be substituted with real gain.

In these examples, sometimes one of the words can be omitted (the word in brackets) or a simple preposition (in brackets) substituted:

We made supper [*consisting*] *of* beans, fried potatoes, and steak.

Consumers Research attempts to furnish reliable information *in regard to* [*about*] all sorts of goods and services.

For politeness' sake the pronoun of the first person stands last when used [*in connection*] *with* other pronouns: "*He, you,* and I had better do it."

It has been said that in six months after graduation from college a man can pick up as much practical knowledge *connected with* [of] business administration as a non-graduate can in ten years.

. . . recent demonstrations *on the part of* [*by*] certain students in Columbia University . . .

Prepositions sometimes bulk too large in writing because we carry over to paper our colloquial tendency to use double prepositions when single prepositions would do the work: *in back of* for *back of, outside of* for *outside, off of* for *off. . . .*

These are not appropriate in formal English, which at its best makes one word do its exact duty, but may be in order in informal English if they help give an easy tone and if they do not become too noticeable. The writer should decide whether these colloquial idioms are appropriate to other traits of his style.

Even when they entered college, they had various views *as to* [more formally: *of*] just what their goal was.

Each launch is dotted with men successfully combating the fish [*in*] *between* equally successful combats with the bottle.

For further examples and discussion see the articles *as to, *of, off, *onto, and so on; *Function words.

The general advice is that prepositions should not attract particular attention or be allowed to weigh down a statement, since

662

they are function words, but that at the same time a style should not be stiffened by trying to avoid natural phrases.

c) Colloquial omission of prepositions. Informal and colloquial English show not only a frequent piling up of prepositions but the opposite tendency too—dropping a preposition that would be used in formal English. Prepositions, especially *of*, receive so little stress that they naturally drop out entirely in rapid speech and this same trait is now increasingly found in writers whose style is conspicuously colloquial. A few examples (with the omitted preposition of formal English in brackets) will suggest the tendency:

. . . of permitting forward passing [at] any place behind the line of scrimmage.—JOHN KIERAN, *The New York Times*, Dec. 30, 1937

Malcolm Cowley . . . pointed out that the color [of] cloth we were using for the Giants faded too easily; . . .—BENNETT A. CERF, *The New Republic*, Apr. 21, 1937

The most notable piece of equipment was an apparatus which made it possible to run the presses [at] almost twice their former speed.

Just as I got my last shirt out [of] the drawer . . .—VINCENT MC-HUGH, *Caleb Catlum's America*, p. 85

A *couple [of] days later . . .

d) Preposition at end of sentence. It was once fashionable for textbooks to put a stigma upon prepositions standing at the end of their constructions (What did you do it *for?*). But postponing the preposition is a characteristic English idiom, even though it runs contrary to our usual tendency to keep words of a construction close together. In fact it is so generally the normal word order that the real danger is in clumsiness from trying to avoid a preposition at the end of a clause or sentence:

Tell me what it is to which you object [what you object to].

To whatever authority we may appeal, he will quibble over the method to be adopted [Whatever authority we may appeal to . . .]

Extreme cases are possible (like the boy's "What did you bring that book for me to be read to out of for?"); but there is no reason for hesitating to let a preposition fall at the end if natural idiom and rhythm place it there. (Compare *Verb-adverb combinations.)

Placing the preposition at the end is such a firmly fixed habit that sometimes we use one at the beginning and at the end:

. . . in the lives of different individuals *with* whom he had come in contact *with*.

Obviously such a sentence shows lack of revision.

References: Curme, *Syntax*, pp. 566-69; Fowler, pp. 457-59 and other index entries; Fries, Chapter 7; Hall, pp. 213-17

Present tense *Tenses of verbs; for the "historical present" see pp. 83-84.

preventive Preferred by most people to *preventative*.

principal—principle Associate *principal* as an adjective (the *principal* reason—the *principal* man of the town—the *principal* force involved) with other adjectives ending in *-al*: historical, political, musical.

Principal as a noun is probably an abbreviation of a phrase in which it was originally an adjective: the *principal* that draws interest was once *the principal sum*; the *principal* of a school, *the principal teacher*; the *principal* in a legal action, the *principal party*; the *principals* in the cast of a play or movie, the *principal actors*. These are the only common uses of *principal* as a noun.

The noun meaning a general truth (the *principles* of science) or a rule of conduct (a man of high *principles*) is *principle*.

Prin **Principal clause** The main or independent clause of a complex sentence. *Clauses, *Complex sentences

Principal parts of verbs (CORRECTION: Change the verb form to the one in good use, as given in the list below or in a dictionary.)

The principal parts of a verb are the infinitive (*ask*), the past tense form (*asked*), and the past participle (*asked*). Most English verbs are "regular"; that is, their past tense and past participle are formed by adding *-ed* to the infinitive. A number, most of them descended from Old English strong verbs (compare the strong verbs in modern German), make these past parts by a change in vowel (*strike, struck, struck*). Some of these are becoming regular (*shined, weaved*), and many are made regular in colloquial and vulgate usage (*blowed, growed*). Reference: Fries, pp. 59-71

The following list includes a number of verbs with these irregular parts or with some other question of form. A form in parenthesis is decidedly less common in writing, and those labeled *vulg.* (vulgate) would not ordinarily occur in current writing. A recent dictionary should be consulted for other verbs. Those marked * are discussed further in separate entries in Part 2 of this book.

INFINITIVE	PAST TENSE	PAST PARTICIPLE
arise	arose	arisen
bear	bore	borne
		*born (given birth to)
begin	began (vulg. begun)	begun (vulg. began)
bid (to buy)	bid	bid

INFINITIVE	PAST TENSE	PAST PARTICIPLE
bid (order)	bade	bidden
bite	bit	bitten, bit
blow	blew (vulg. blowed)	blown (vulg. blowed)
break	broke	broken (colloq: broke)
*burst	burst	burst
catch	caught	caught
choose	chose	chosen
come	came (vulg. come)	come
dig	dug (digged)	dug
*do	did	done
dive	*dove, dived	dived, dove
draw	drew	drawn (vulg. drawed)
drink	drank (archaic and vulg. drunk)	*drunk (drank—drunken)
*eat	ate	eaten (eat)
fall	fell	fallen
find	found	found
flee	fled	fled
fly	flew	flown
forget	forgot	forgotten, forgot
freeze	froze	frozen (froze)
*get	got	got, gotten
give	gave (vulg. give)	given
go	went	gone
grow	grew (vulg. growed)	grown
hang	hung, *hanged	hung, hanged
hear	heard	heard
know	knew (vulg. knowed)	known
*lay	laid	laid
lead	led	led
lend (*loan)	lent	lent
let	let	let
lie (see *lay)	*lay	lain
light	*lighted, lit	lighted, lit
lose	lost	lost
pay	*paid (of ropes: payed)	paid
plead	pleaded, plead	pleaded, plead
prove	proved	*proved, proven
ride	rode	ridden
ring	rang, rung	rung
run	ran (vulg. run)	run
say	said	said
see	saw	seen

665

INFINITIVE	PAST TENSE	PAST PARTICIPLE
set	set	set
shine	shone, shined	shone, shined
show	showed	showed, shown
shrink	shrank, shrunk	shrunk
sing	sang, sung	sung
sink	sank, sunk	sunk
sit	sat (vulg. set)	sat (vulg. set)
slide	slid	slid (slidden)
sow	sowed	sown, sowed
speak	spoke	spoken
spit	spit, spat	spit, spat
spring	sprang, sprung	sprung
stand	stood	stood
steal	stole	stolen
swim	swam, swum	swum
take	took	taken
tear	tore	torn
throw	threw (vulg. throwed)	thrown
wake	waked, woke	waked, woke
wear	wore	worn
weave	wove (weaved)	woven, wove
win	won	won
wind	wound (nautical: winded)	wound
wring	wrung	wrung
write	wrote	written

prior to Heavy (often journalese) for *before*

Prior to [Before] coming here he had been at Stanford.

privilege So spelled (but often misspelled)

process, procedure, proceed We naturally spell *process* with one *e*, and *proceed* with two *e*'s; but only memory can make us spell *procedure* with one *e*. The verb is proceed and the two nouns are process and procedure. The pronunciation prō′ses is British rather than American; say pros′es. Pros′ə sēz is usually an affectation for the plural; say pros′es əz.

Proceed means "to go," strictly in a rather formal fashion, and is best kept for movement (We proceeded at a decent rate of speed). "We proceeded to unpack" usually means no more than "We unpacked" or "Then we unpacked."

Profanity Styles change in the handling of "cuss" words and profanity. At present most writers, most editors, and most publishers are liberal, much more liberal than formerly. In fiction, where the words pass through a character, simply be sure they are fitting and called for. Both cussing and cursing are primarily oral, matters of muscular release rather than of meaning, and they often attract more attention to themselves in print than they deserve. That is, you can't put on paper all the vulgarity proper to a vulgar person's speech; the effect will be suggested by an occasional bit of cussing. In biography, criticism, and miscellaneous informational articles you have less freedom. There double dashes and euphemistic blankety-blanks are more likely to be found. Such devices ordinarily give the impression of a writer who is playing at being tough or who hasn't the courage to use language he believes is really appropriate. Use the expressions the subject seriously calls for, compromising as little or as much as your temperament and circumstance demand. In matter submitted to magazines, editors will make whatever alterations their policies demand.

Professor Write:

Professor Tewksbury [or] Prof. E. W. Tewksbury [or]
E. W. Tewksbury, professor of electrical engineering.

The colloquial *prof* is a clipped word, not an abbreviation, and if it is written should not have a period:

He said all profs were a little crazy anyway.

Strictly speaking *professor* should be confined to names of assistant professors, associate professors, and professors. Applying it to instructors is sometimes a well-meant courtesy but more often carelessness. Teachers who are doctors of philosophy ("Ph.D.'s") are often addressed as *doctor*, though now that most teachers have the degree, the title has lost its distinction. In official and business usage an *instructor* who has a doctor's degree is often addressed as *doctor*. It would be better to address all teachers as *Mr.* or *Miss* or *Mrs.*—as many professors would prefer. Students should follow the conventions of their own campus.

Progressive verb forms Those made with *to be* and the present participle:

I am asking   he was asking   they have been asking

_____
*Tenses of verbs, *Verbs

Pronominal adjectives Several types of pronouns, used also as adjectives, are called pronominal adjectives:

INTERROGATIVE:	*Which* way did he go?
DEMONSTRATIVE:	*that* way *this* book *those* boys
POSSESSIVE:	*my* hat *his* idea *your* dog *their* seats
INDEFINITE:	*some* people *each* person *all* men

667

Pron **Pronouns, types and forms** (CORRECTION: Change the form of the pronoun marked to the one expected in the grammatical construction in which it stands.)

A pronoun is a word that represents ("means") a person or thing or idea without naming it. Usually the meaning of a pronoun is completed by referring to a noun that names the person or thing or idea and that has been recently used in the discussion, called its *antecedent* (as the two *that*'s in this sentence refer to *noun* and *its* refers to *pronoun*). For some pronouns, the "indefinites" *all, anybody, few . . .* (§8), the reference is either directly to the persons or things meant or it is made clear by the context in which it stands.

Pronouns are used in all the grammatical functions of nouns, as subjects, objects, appositives, and so on (*Nouns §3). Their uses are described in *Reference of pronouns. This article lists the various types of pronouns and their case and plural forms.

1. THE PERSONAL PRONOUNS

			NOMINA-TIVE	GENITIVE	ACCUSA-TIVE
1ST PERSON	SINGULAR:		*I	my, mine	me
	PLURAL:		we	our, ours	us
2D PERSON	SINGULAR:		you	your, yours	you
	PLURAL:		you	your, yours	you
3D PERSON	SINGULAR:				
		MASCULINE:	he	his	him
		FEMININE:	she	her, hers	her
		NEUTER:	*it	its (of it)	it
		EITHER GENDER:	*one	one's	one
	PLURAL:		they	their, theirs	them

Archaic forms of the second person singular, *thou, thy* or *thine, thee,* are used only in religious services, by the Society of Friends, and occasionally in poetry.

Mine, formerly used before words beginning with a vowel or *h* (*mine eyes, mine help*) is no longer so used: *my eyes, my help.* The emphatic form of the genitive is used without a noun:

The money is *mine* (*ours, yours, hers, theirs*).
Yours came a whole week before *mine.*

Some of the most common grammatical problems come from the fact that the personal and relative pronouns have separate forms for the nominative and accusative cases and our nouns do not. (*between you and me, *It's me, *who, whom §§2, 3)

2. Relative pronouns

*who	whose	whom
*that	of that	that
*which	of which, whose	whom
what = that which		

Whoever, whichever, whatever (and archaic: whosoever, whichsoever, whatsoever) usually have an accent of surprise, irritation, or playfulness.

As is archaic or vulgate as a relative pronoun (*as §2):

Handsome is as handsome does.
Them as has gits.

3. Interrogative pronouns. *who, *which, what; occasionally whoever, whatever

4. Reflexive pronouns. Reflexive or intensive pronouns are made of the personal pronouns plus the suffix -self or -selves. They are called reflexive because the action of the verb is directed toward the subject of the construction (He shaves himself; She bought herself two hats). *himself, *myself

When used as intensives, these words are usually construed as adjectives:

The president himself delivered the address.
I can finish the job myself.

5. Reciprocal pronouns. *each other   one another (formal)

6. Numeral pronouns. The *cardinal numerals (one, two, three . . .) and the ordinals (first, second, third . . .) are used as pronouns: Three were there; The eighth won.

7. Demonstrative pronouns

*this, these   *that, those   (Compare *kind, sort)
the *former, the latter, the first, the second . . .
*such, *so (I told you so)
*same

8. Indefinite pronouns. A large number of words, of greater or less indefiniteness, often function as pronouns:

all	each one	neither
another	*either	*nobody
*any	everybody (*every §2)	*none
anybody	everyone	no one
anyone	everything	nothing
anything	few	*one, oneself
*both	many	other
*each	much	several

*some	someone	*such
somebody	something	

Questions on the uses of pronouns are discussed in *Reference of pronouns.

References: Curme, *Parts of Speech*, Ch. 10; *Syntax*, index references; Fries, index references; Kennedy, §51 and index references

Pronunciation The greater part of anyone's use of language is spoken; consequently his pronunciation—the tone, the stress, the quality of particular sounds—is extremely important. A book cannot help much in this, since pronunciation is learned almost entirely by conscious or unconscious imitation of other speakers, but it can perhaps suggest an attitude toward a few of the major questions in spoken English. As with words, constructions, and other traits of language, pronunciation varies according to the level of the speech used and varies in different regions. Some principles of selection from among the various forms of divided usage is a help to satisfactory pronunciation wherever a question arises.

1. LEVELS OF PRONUNCIATION. From the point of view of their social standing, various types of pronunciation can be grouped under the general headings of vulgate, informal, and formal usage, each of which will differ somewhat between regions.

a) Vulgate pronunciation is the speech of people with relatively little education, used appropriately in their daily occupations but out of place in public affairs or in social groups using some other level of speech. Vulgate pronunciation is usually somewhat slower than informal speech, often being a "drawl." The local qualities of sounds that are characteristic of the educated usage of a region are more conspicuous in the vulgate. Short *a* may be conspicuously flat, as in *calf* or *laugh*; the characteristic Western *r* may be more conspicuous, and the Southern *r* may disappear altogether (as mō for *more*, where educated speakers would often have mōə), or a New Englander may add an *r* to a word ending with a vowel (He had no idear of how to run a farm). In a good deal of New England and Western speech there is a nasal quality. Unstressed syllables may be completely lost, as kump′ni for *company*. Final consonants are often slighted and words run together. There are many individual words or groups of words that have vulgate pronunciations more or less widely current in a dialect area or throughout the whole country: rīl for *roil* (once in good use); ū′mən for *human*; dipthēr′i ə for *diphtheria*; woild for *world*; wunst for *once*. One of the results of an effective education is a dropping of the more conspicuous traits of vulgate pronunciation. This is an important social matter, since dress and speech are the principal superficial marks of class distinction.

b) At the other extreme is formal pronunciation, found chiefly in the platform speaking of ministers, teachers, and of others who make public appearances, in the stage pronunciation of actors and the more consciously trained radio announcers, and sometimes in an exaggerated form in concert singing. This speech is somewhat slower than usual conversational speech, without the relaxed quality of a drawl, though it may slur certain syllables rather consciously (as the *-ary* words noted in §4*c*). It is likely to give a fuller and more distinct value to individual vowel sounds, tends to use broad or intermediate *a* (*a §4); its *r*'s are neither omitted nor fully sounded, and so on. The stresses are somewhat heavier than in informal speech and tend to stress individual words rather than phrase units. Dictionaries for the most part record this rather conscious platform enunciation in indicating the pronunciation of words, though more recent dictionaries tend to give more attention to informal speech.

c) Between these two extremes is informal pronunciation, usual in the conversation of educated people, and, spoken somewhat more slowly than in conversation, now quite usual in platform appearances. It shows more regional flavor than formal pronunciation but not so much as the vulgate. Its stresses are lighter than in formal speech and it is more rapid than either formal or vulgate. The stress is more a phrase or sentence stress than a presenting of individual words: *Saturday* by itself might be pronounced sat'ər dā, but in "I shan't be here Saturday" it would become sat'ər di and in rapid speech would be sat'ə di or sa'ə di (and in vulgate even sa'di). Function words (*the, and, that, there, to,* the pronouns) rarely get their full values in typical speech and rarely need them. Vowels tend to become shorter, many become slurred (ə), and consonants that are hard to sound in their position are slighted or dropped or assimilated with other sounds as *t* in *often* (ôf'ən) or in *sit down* (si doun'), or *th* in *clothes* (klōz). This represents the process by which *cupboard* has become kub'ərd and *Christmas* has become kris'məs. In words that are not in common use, however, such slighting of consonants is usually felt as vulgate rather than informal: *strictly* (formal and informal, strikt'li; vulgate, strik'li) or *Arctic* (formal and informal, ärk'tik; vulgate, är'tik).

A person's pronunciation should be appropriate to the situation in which he is speaking and also should represent his own standards. Ordinarily the exactness of formal pronunciation is out of place in conversation, even in "cultivated" conversation, as are the laxities of vulgate. Too conscious attention to pronunciation in informal situations will handicap the speaker and irritate the listener. Pronunciation in appearances before groups must necessarily be somewhat slower, more distinct, but fundamentally it is a refinement of the speaker's better conversational style.

2. REGIONAL DIFFERENCES IN PRONUNCIATION. A single standard of English pronunciation is even more impossible than a single standard in the use of words or in grammatical constructions, which are stabilized somewhat by written literature. Since pronunciation necessarily is learned from personal associations, it naturally and unavoidably shows variety between regions. An educated Londoner, Scotsman, Bostonian, Chicagoan, Atlantan will show traits of their native speech but not enough to handicap them in talking with each other. British-made dictionaries are not satisfactory guides for pronunciation in the United States. American-made dictionaries have tended to represent New England and eastern pronunciation, partly because many words would have to be respelled two or three times if all parts of the country were to be considered.

The best that a person can do in checking his pronunciation when a real question comes up is to consult a *recent, carefully edited American* dictionary and compare its recommendations with the usage of the group with which he lives. For a person who is likely to consult a dictionary at all, this will mean the more or less educated people in his community. If the dictionary offers a choice, he should take the word he hears around him unless another is more natural to him and he wants to keep that, risking being a little different. If the one he hears consistently from fairly well educated people is not recorded in the dictionary, he is still safe in using that.

The problem of a person going to live in a different part of the country is more complex. Should he drop his native speech and do as the Romans do? If he makes a specific and hasty effort to pick up the new speech, he will be almost sure to make mistakes, that is, he will confuse the two. If he can stand off the first attacks on his speechways, he will soon find that he will attract less attention. Then he will naturally acquire, bit by bit and without forcing, many of the new ways. He need not be ashamed of honest traces remaining of his native speech. (See "Variations due to place," p. 6)

In fact, the words to worry about are not the ordinary colloquial words so much as the new ones acquired in taking up new work or a new social status or new ideas or, in college, new subjects of study. Care should be taken to get a conventional pronunciation of these new words (*acclimate, desultory, schizophrenic . . .*) as they are learned, to be at home with them from the beginning.

As Fowler puts it (p. 466); "The broad principles are: Pronounce as your neighbours do, not better." For the majority of words your neighbors are the general public. For words in more restricted use, your neighbors are the group that uses them. Consequently there will be more local flavor in informal and familiar speech, less in speaking to limited and special audiences. It is more important to avoid vulgate pronunciations than the regional pronunciations of educated people.

3. PRONUNCIATION KEY. In this book the pronunciation of words is indicated by respelling them in the following letters and symbols given below.

Further details of the sounds represented by each letter of the alphabet, with examples, will be found in the articles on the separate letters, *a, *b, *c, and so on in Part 2 of this book.

The stress of syllables is represented by a ′ for a main stress and a′ for a lighter stress, placed after the stressed syllable: ag′ri-kul′chər.

A long vowel in a lightly stressed syllable is shorter than in a fully stressed syllable: contrast the o of *obey* (ō bā′) and of *below* (bə lō′).

a	apple (ap′əl), fact (fakt)
ā	age (āj), obey (ō bā′)
ä	far (fär), father (fä′ᴛʜər)
b	back (bak), robber (rob′ər)
ch	child (chīld), church (chėrch)
d	do (dü), did (did)
e	bet (bet), effect (e fekt′)
ē	equal (ē′kwəl), see (sē), police (pō lēs′)
ė	term (tėrm), burnt (bėrnt)
f	fat (fat), stuff (stuf)
g	go (gō), baggage (bag′ij)
h	hotel (hō tel′)
hw	wheel (hwēl), whether (hweᴛʜ′ər)
i	if (if), pithy (pith′i)
ī	ice (īs), buy (bī)
j	jam (jam), edge (ej), age (āj)
k	king (king), back (bak), cocoa (kō′kō)
l	life (līf), silly (sil′i), fill (fil)
m	am (am), meet (mēt), sample (sam′pəl)
n	note (nōt), inner (in′ər)
ng	sing (sing), song (sông)
o	rock (rok), stop (stop)

ō open (ō′pən), hope (hōp), go (gō)
ô bought (bôt), ball (bôl), caught (kôt)
oi voice (vois), boil (boil)
ou house (hous), out (out), cow (kou)
p paper (pā′pər), cap (kap)
r reach (rēch), try (trī), tired (tīrd), door (dōr)
s say (sā), listen (lis′ən), yes (yes)
sh she (shē), rush (rush), cushion (kush′ən)
t tie (tī), sit (sit), kitten (kit′ən)
th thin (thin), both (bōth), bath (bath)
TH that (THat), bother (boTH′ər), bathe (bāTH)
u cup (kup), butter (but′ər)
u̇ full (fu̇l), put (pu̇t)
ü rule (rül), tool (tül), move (müv)
ū useful (ūs′fu̇l), music (mū′zik)
v very (ver′i), salve (säv or sav), save (sāv)
w will (wil), with (wiTH or with), won't (wōnt)
y young (yung), yellow (yel′ō)
z zero (zēr′ō), breeze (brēz), trees (trēz)
zh measure (mezh′ər), rouge (rüzh)
ə, called *schwa* (shvä), represents the slurred or indefinite vowel
sound of many unstressed syllables. It is variously spelled:
a in *sofa* (sō′fə), *e* in *secretary* (sek′rə ter′i), and by the other
vowels and combinations of vowels.

An *r* following a vowel changes the vowel's sound, as in *care, sere, core, sure,* but a separate symbol is not used to represent the change: kār, sēr, kōr, shür.

French *u* and German *ü* are represented by ʏ, and French *n,* which gives a nasal value to a vowel preceding in the same syllable, by ɴ: en route (än rüt′).

4. SPECIAL POINTS IN PRONUNCIATION. (*a*) *Slurred vowels.* The naturalness of slurred vowels (the italicized vowels in *again, academy, dormitory, laboratory, circus*) has been explained in the discussion of informal pronunciation (§1*c*). For suggestions on spelling these words see *Slurred vowels.

b) *Stress.* In general, English is a rather strongly stressed (accented) language. The force of the stress varies a good deal among individual speakers. The stress of particular words (*detail, *address) varies with their meaning or with the frequency of their use. Some of the effects of a writer's stress that show in his writing are discussed in the article *Rhythm. See also *Noun and verb stress.

c) *Secondary stress.* A word of three or especially of four syllables is likely to have a main and a secondary stress: *secondary* sek′ən der′i, *incidental* in′si den′təl. One of the differences between British and American pronunciation is that we tend to keep secondary stresses in many words in which the British have but one:

necessary: American nes′ə ser′i; British nes′əs ri
dictionary: American dik′shən er′i; British dik′shən ri
laboratory: American lab′rə tō′ri; British lab′ə rə tri [or la bor′ə tri]

A few Americans attempt to follow the British shortening of such words, in the belief that the shorter pronunciation is the more genteel. But we are not as a rule very skillful in skipping over the syllables of long words and such pronunciations do not fit our speech rhythms. Most people's reactions to the attempt are those of this rhyme:

> She who lisps with manner airy
> "*Diction-ry*" for "diction*ary*,"
> "*Culin-ry*" for "culin*ary*,"
> "*Semin-ry*" for "semin*ary*,"—
> Cart her to a cemetery!
>   A. S. PHILLIPS, *Word Study*, Nov. 1937

d) Pronunciation and spelling. Words really live in their oral forms, and any guide to pronunciation must start with the spoken words, not the written. But our spelling represents, roughly at least, the sounds of words, or often it represents the sounds they once had. (See Chapter 10, p. 267.)

When words are acquired from reading rather than from hearing, they are very often over-pronounced, in what are known as spelling pronunciations. *Sophomore* on most campuses is two syllables, sof′mōr, but people who see it more than they hear it are likely to sound the middle o slightly (sof′ə mōr); *yearling* is yĕr′ling where it is regularly used, yēr′ling as a spelling pronunciation. Genuine familiarity with words is usually shown by using the oral rather than the spelling pronunciation.

5. PRONUNCIATION LIST. This list is in part to raise questions of pronunciation. The pronunciations suggested should be tested by comparing them with those you hear. For most words that raise questions of pronunciation, consult a good recent dictionary, as suggested in § 1 of this article.

Pronunciations of other words will be found in the articles on each letter of the alphabet, *Foreign words in English, *Spelling, *Proper names, and in various articles on particular words.

When two forms are given, no choice is implied; a distinctly less common form stands in brackets. A large number of words are spoken in two or more ways in good usage.

An * means that there is a separate entry on that word.

abdomen ab dō′ mən, ab′dō mən

absorb ab sôrb′, ab zôrb′

absurd əb sėrd′ [əb zėrd′]

acclimate ə klī′mit, ak′lə māt

*adult ad′ult, ə dult′

advertisement əd vėr′tiz mənt,
ad′vər tīz′mənt

aerial âr′i əl, ā ēr′i əl

ally (noun) al′ī, ə lī′; plural
more often ə līz′; verb ə lī′

alma mater al′mə mā′ter
[äl′mə mä′tər]

alternate (verb) ôl′tər nāt, al′tər-
nāt; (adjective) ôl′tər nit, al′-
tər nit, ôl tėr′nit, al tėr′nit

amateur am′ə tėr′, am′ə tūr,
am′ə chər

amenable ə men′ə bəl,
ə mē′nə bəl

apparatus ap′ə rā′təs, ap′ə rat′əs

applicable ap′li kə bəl

Aryan är yən, ar i ən

atypical ə tip′i kəl, ā tip′i kəl
(See *a-)

aviation ā′vi ā′shən

aye (yes) ī

bade bad

*biography bī og′rə fi, bi og′rə fi

*bureaucracy bū rok′rə si
[bū rō′krə si]

business biz′nis

chauffeur shō′fər, shō fėr′
(*Foreign words in English § 1)

chic shēk, shik [chik]

combatant kom′bə tənt

company kum′pə ni; vulgate
kump′ni

*contents kon′tents [kən tents′]

coup kü [küp]

coupon kü′pon, kū′pon

coyote kī′ōt, kī ō′ti

*data dā′tə, dat′ə, dä′tə

debut də bū′ [dā′bū]

debutant deb′ū tänt, deb′ū tänt′,
deb′ū tant

decade, dek′ād, de kād′, dek′əd

desperado des′pər ä′dō,
des′pər ā′dō

diphtheria dif thēr′i ə; vulgate
dip thēr′i ə

diphthong dif′thong

disputable dis pūt′ə bəl,
dis′pū tə bəl

drama drä′mə, dram′ə

*economics ē′kə nom′iks,
ek′ə nom′iks

*either ē′ŦHər, ī′ŦHər

electricity ə lek′tris′ə ti

Elizabethan i liz′ə bē′thən,
i liz′ə beth′ən

err ėr [er]

exquisite eks′kwi zit, eks kwiz′it

finance fi nans′, fī′nans

formidable fôr′mi də bəl

fortnight fôrt′nit, fôrt′nīt

gibbous gib′əs

*gladiolus glad′i ō′ləs,
glə dī′ō ləs

gunwale gun′əl

harass har′əs, hə ras′

height hīt [vulgate hīth]

heinous hā′nəs

*human hū′mən

idea ī dē′ə

impious im′pi əs

indict in dīt′

isolate ī′sō lāt, is′ō lāt

juvenile jü′və nil, jü′və nīl

kimono ki mō′nə, ki mō′nō

laugh läf, laf (*a § 4)

launch lônch, länch

*leisure lē′zhər, lezh′ər

lever lev′ər, lē′vər

lilacs lī′ləks

matrix mat′riks, mā′triks

menu men′ū, mā′nü

mischievous mis′chə vəs
[mis chē′vəs]

news nūz, nüz

oasis ō ā′sis, ō′ə sis

orgy ôr′ji

*parliament pär′li mənt

patriot pā′tri ət [pat′ri ət]

penalize pē′nəl īz, pen′əl īz

percolator pėr′kə lā′tər

*Phi Beta Kappa fī bā′tə kap′ə

*pianist pi an′ist, pē′ə nist

pleasure plezh′ər

premier prē′mi ər [prem′yər] =
prime minister, prē′mi ər,
prə mēr′

presentation prez′ən tā′shən,
prē′zen tā′shən

process pros′es, prō′ses

pronunciation prō nun′si ā′shən

quay kē

ratio rā′shō, rā′shi ō
real rē′əl
reel rēl
research ri sėrch′, rē′sėrch
rodeo rō′di ō, rō dā′ō
rotogravure rō′tō grə vūr′,
  rō′tō grā′vŭr
*route rüt, rout
sociology sō′shi ol′ə ji, sō′si ol′ə ji
strictly strikt′li, vulgate strik′li
sumac shü′mak, sü′mak

swastika swos′ti kə swäs′ti kə
  (*A § 4)
the ᴛнə, ᴛн̄ē
tomato tō mā′tō,tō mä′tō,
  tō mat′ō
usage ū′sij, ū′zij
vaudeville vôd′vil, vôd′ə vil,
  vôd′vil
white hwīt, [wīt]
worsted wüs′təd

*Colloquial and written English, *Foreign words in English,
*Proper names, *Rhythm, *Spelling

References: Kenyon; Robertson, Chapter 7; "A Guide to Pronunciation," *Webster's New International Dictionary*, second edition, especially Part I, "Standard Pronunciation." For the International Phonetic Alphabet, used in scientific transcription of
speech, see any issue of *American Speech* and most books on
linguistics.

Proofreading After copy has been set in type it must be checked
for typographical and other mistakes before it is ready to be
printed. A tentative print is made on long sheets known as *galley
proof*. After the type has been corrected and made up into the
pages which are to be finally printed, *page proofs* are taken and
read for a last check.

Corrections are indicated in proof by abbreviations and symbols
placed at one side of the line to be changeα, with a *caret (∧)
inserted at the exact point in the line where the change is to be
made. Proofreader's marks are illustrated on page 678. See publishers' stylebooks for further details.

Proper adjectives Proper nouns used as adjectives and adjectives
directly derived from proper names and still referring to the place
or person are capitalized. After proper adjectives lose the reference to their origins, they become simple adjectives and are not
capitalized.

  the French language   American interests
  the Indian service, but india ink
  a Paris (or Parisian) café, but paris green

Proper names Considerable care needs to be taken to spell and pronounce the names of people, places, companies, institutions as the
people most concerned with them wish to have them spelled and
pronounced. Many are rare or in some way unusual—*Thames*
(temz), *Worcester* (wüs tər), *San Joaquin* (san′wä kēn′). Analogy
cannot be relied on: it is Waco (wā′kō), Texas, but Saco (saw′kō),
Maine.

PROOFREADER'S MARKS

℈	Delete and close up		en⎮	En dash
℈	Reverse		;⎮	Insert semicolon
⌒	Close up		⊙	Insert colon and en quad
#	Insert space		⊙	Insert period and en quad
¶	Paragraph		?⎮	Insert interrogation point
□	Indent one em		?	Query to author
⊏	Move to left		⌒	Use ligature
⊐	Move to right		⑤⑰	Spell out
⊔	Lower		tr	Transpose
⊓	Elevate		wf	Wrong font
⋀	Insert marginal addition		bf	Set in **bold face** type
⋁⋀	Even space		rom	Set in (roman) type
⨯	Broken letter		ital	Set in *italic* type
↓	Push down space		caps	Set in CAPITALS
⚊	Straighten line		sc	Set in SMALL CAPITALS
‖	Align type		lc	Set in lower case
⋀	Insert comma		⟋	Lower-case letter
⋁	Insert apostrophe		stet	Let it stand
⋁	Insert quotes		no¶	Run in same paragraph
=⎮	Hyphen		ld⟩	Insert lead between lines
em⎮	Em dash		hr #	Hair space between letters

From *A Manual of Style*, The University of Chicago Press

In place names the recommendation to use the pronunciation current in the place is complicated because the inhabitants often do not agree. *Chicago* is pronounced both shi kaw′gō and shi cä′go. English has tended to anglicize or even to rename many foreign places: *Paris* (pa′ris instead of pä rē′); *Prague* (präg instead of the continental präg or the Czech prä′hä). One cemetery monument has *Loyd* on one side and *Lloyd* on the other, to represent the husband's and the wife's preferred spellings.

Many fairly common names occur in various forms: *How—Howe, Harvey—Hervey, Cohen—Cohn—Kohen, Mac-Mc-M′,* and so on. Special care is needed with names having silent letters or some peculiarity of spelling or phrasing: Pittsburg*h*, Lindberg*h*, the Johns Hopkins University, the State University of Iowa, the Ohio State University.

Dictionaries and encyclopedias give the pronunciation and spelling of the best known people and places. For foreign names in current news, we can try to follow the national newscasters. They will show some variation, but they have made an effort to find a reasonable pronunciation.

Getting proper names in the right form is courtesy as well as accuracy. This is especially important in all published work.

References: Holt, Alfred H., *American Place Names* (New York, 1938); Read, Allen W., "The Basis of Correctness in the Pronunciation of Place-Names," *American Speech*, 1933, viii, 42-46; Recent dictionaries. *Course names

Proportion *Emphasis §2

proposition is originally a business word for *offer, plan, proposal,* which is inappropriate in general usage. "I have a proposition for you" = "I have a plan . . ."

Prosody *Verse form

proved—proven As the past participle of *prove, proved* (He had proved . . .) is much more common than *proven* and is always right. But *proven* is often used (It had proven quite satisfactory; of proven worth).

Proverb *Epigrams

Pro-verb *do §2

Provincialisms *Localisms

psychology, psychiatry Watch the spelling of these words:

psychology   psychologist   psychoanalyze   psychoanalysis
psychiatric (sī′ki at′rik)   psychiatry (sī kī′ə tri, rarely sī′ki at′ri)
psychiatrist (sī kī′ə trist, rarely sī′ki at′rist)

public is a *collective noun and takes either a singular or plural construction according as the writer wishes to stress the whole group or the individuals:

The *public is* invited.   The *public are* invited.
His *public is made up* of the very young and the fairly old.
    Consult the libraries and you will find that the ordinary public do not read poetry.—P. B. BALLARD, *Thought and Language*, p. 250

Punctuation (CORRECTION: Correct the obvious error in punctuation. If the change to be made is not clear to you, consult the *Index* article on the particular mark.) **P**

A discussion of the function and general uses of the punctuation marks, and of differing styles of punctuation ("open" and "close") will be found in Chapter 11, p. 276.

Details of the uses of the individual marks will be found in the *Index* articles on each:

’	*Apostrophe	!	*Exclamation mark
*	*Asterisk	-	*Hyphen
{ }	*Brace	....	*Leaders
[ ]	*Brackets	( )	*Parentheses
∧	*Caret	.	*Period
:	*Colon	?	*Question mark
,	*Comma	" "	*Quotation marks
—	*Dash (including the	;	*Semicolon
	long dash ——) (2M)	——	*Underlining (for
...	*Ellipsis		italic type)

See also: *Division of words; *Letters; *Quotations; *Restrictive and non-restrictive; *Series.

Puns A *pun* is a figure of speech in which a word is used in two senses at once (the nut that holds the wheel = automobile driver) or in which a word is substituted for another of similar sound but different meaning (hire education). Reasonable punning is a healthy use of language, which may be funny or serious. The objection often made to puns is to their overuse or to puns which involve sound and not meaning. Good puns are appropriate to colloquial and informal usage, usually giving an accent of ironic humor (as in Dorothy Parker's "a girl's best friend is her mutter") or of light dispraise:

Europe will feel greatly relieved if it can get through this month without disaster. There is nothing madder than a March Herr Hitler.
—HOWARD BRUBAKER, *The New Yorker*, March 18, 1939

Compare *Homonyms.

Purist A purist is a person who is overcareful in the use of language, especially one who wishes everyone to follow the rules of prescriptive grammar (*Grammar §2) and who tries to hold words to their strictest meanings. Dictionaries and scientific grammars are more liberal.

Purpose Adverbial clauses of purpose are most commonly introduced by *so that*:

He is packing tonight *so that* he can start early in the morning.

More formally, *that* is used; and more wordily, *in order to, for the purpose of, with a view to.* Colloquially *so is used alone:

He is packing tonight *so* he can start early in the morning.

put in, over ... *Put in* is good informal usage for *spend* (put in time, put in money). *Put over* (a plan, a sale), *put across* (a scheme, an idea) are colloquial and are often objected to because they are too frequently used.

Q is an unnecessary letter in English. It was brought into English use in words borrowed from French, originally derived from Latin (*question, quarter, quiet*), and later borrowings directly from Latin added to the number (*quorum, quota*). Some Old English words with *kw* sound (spelled *cw*) were respelled with *qu*: *quick* (from *cwic*), *queen* (from *cwen*), *quench* (from *cwencan*).

Q is always followed by *u* in English. *Qu* is ordinarily pronounced *kw* (*quite, quill, quadrilateral*) though in a few words the French value, *k*, is kept: *coquette* (kō ket′), *quatorze* (kə tôrz′). Final *-que* is *k*: *antique* (an tēk′), *unique* (ū nēk′). It is not necessary to keep the French pronunciation in words that have been anglicized: *Quebec* (kwi bek′—French kā bek), *questionnaire.

Question mark (?) (CORRECTION: Punctuate this sentence as a question.)

1. The principal use of the question mark is as the end-stop to a question (What was the real reason?).

2. A question mark may or may not be used after a request that is phrased as a question, depending on the formality of the style:

> FORMAL: Will you please return this at your earliest convenience?
> INFORMAL: Will you please return this at your earliest convenience.

3. A question mark is no longer used after an indirect question (He wanted to know what the real reason was).

4. A question mark is used to show that a statement is approximate or questionable, as with uncertain dates:

Geoffrey Chaucer 1340?-1400 [or] Geoffrey Chaucer 1340(?)-1400

5. A question mark in parentheses as a mildly sarcastic comment or to label would-be witticisms is now out of fashion and is better omitted:

> No fashionable woman would think of going to a football game unless she looked like a giant squirrel or some other innocent(?) fur-bearing animal.

6. When a question mark and quotation marks fall together, the question mark is outside if the quoting sentence is the question, inside if the quoted sentence is the question:

He asked, "Did you really say that?"
Did you really say "I thought you were older than that"?

After a double question only one question mark is used.

Did she ask, "How many are coming?"

See *Quotation marks §4.

questionnaire keeps the French spelling, with two *n*'s. The English form *questionary* does not make much progress.

Pronounced as an English word: kwes′chǝn är′.

Questions 1. In speaking, a rising inflection usually marks a question, and in writing, a question mark at the end. But usually a question is more accurately indicated by the form of the sentence. It may be introduced by an interrogative word:

PRONOUN: *Who* was that? *What* would you do in his place?
ADJECTIVE: *Which* way did he go? *What* book shall I read next?
ADVERB: *Where* shall we eat? *When* will you be coming back? *How much* is that one? *Why* didn't you say so in the first place?

A question may be indicated by inverted word order, the verb coming before its subject. In older English any verb could stand first (*Came* he yesterday?), but now this order is found only with *be, have, shall, will, can, may, must, need,* and *ought* (*Was* he there?) and in colloquial subjectless sentences (*Want* this one?). Ordinarily a phrasal verb is used and the auxiliary comes before the subject (*Do you think* he would go if he was asked?). A statement is turned into a question by an inverted clause at the end (He didn't try, did he?).

A direct question that is parenthetically part of another sentence sometimes begins with a capital and sometimes not:

He felt a strong urge—as indeed who doesn't?—to write a really good modern novel.—NOEL COWARD, *To Step Aside,* p. 9

2. Questions are useful, if sparingly used, to focus the reader's attention, either to introduce a change in subject, as in the first of the two quotations that follow, or to emphasize by the change in sentence movement an important point, as in the second:

Will it ever be possible for the middle classes to gain real individualism? To achieve the goal, they must undergo a "radical" change. The old picture of the original Babbitt, symbolized by Louis Philippe, with his cumbersome form, his pear-shaped head, his thick neck swallowing up his chin, his prominent belly, and ridiculous frock-coat tightened at the waist, must disappear. In its place must be substituted the portrait of a young man, possessing the trim build of an athlete; the eager willingness to work, produce, and share; and the sharp mentality of a scholar.—F. C. PALM, *The Middle Classes, Then and Now,* p. 409

We are beginning to see that the ideal of a liberal education is too large to be put into four years of a college course. It is the growth of a lifetime spent in contact with the actual world. But it is not too much to ask that in a university the student should be brought into contact with different types of the intellectual life, and that each type should be kept distinct. He should learn that the human mind is a marvelous instrument and that it may be used in more than one way.

Variety in courses of study is less important than variety and individuality of mental action. How does a man of science use his mind? How does an artist feel? What makes a man a jurist, a man of business, a politician, a teacher? How does ethical passion manifest itself? What is the historical sense?

These are not questions to be answered on examination papers. But it is a reasonable hope that a young man in the formative period of his life may learn the answers through personal contacts.—SAMUEL McCHORD CROTHERS, *The Pleasures of an Absentee Landlord,* pp. 48-49

Occasionally a question makes an effective opening for a paper, but it should be a genuine question, leading to the subject, and not a general one concocted just "to get attention."

3. An indirect question is a question that is not quoted directly but is made a subordinate member of another sentence. An indirect question is not marked with either a question mark or with quotation marks, and the tense of the verb is changed, if necessary, to fit the sentence in which it stands:

DIRECT: "What are our plans for tomorrow?"
DIRECT: He asked what our plans for tomorrow were.
INDIRECT: He asked, "Do you really understand what you have read?"
INDIRECT: He asked us if we really understood what we had read.
He always asks us whether we understand what we have read.

4. For a statement cast in the form of a question see *Rhetorical question.

quite In formal English *quite* means "entirely, wholly," as in "quite gone." In informal and colloquial English, it is reduced in meaning to "somewhat, very, rather": "I am quite tired"; "We went quite a long way."

This meaning passes over into a number of convenient colloquial phrases: *quite a few, quite a little, quite a lot. Quite some time* is colloquial.

Quotation marks (" ") (CORRECTION: Make the quotation marks conform to conventional usage. [The most frequent slips are: forgetting the end quotation marks; punctuation with interrupted quotations, §4c; quotation marks combined with other marks, §4a, b.])

1. METHODS OF INDICATING QUOTATIONS. (*a*) Double quotes (" ") are the usual marks. The mark before the quoted matter is the *open-quote,* and the one after is the *close-quote.*

b) The use of single quotes (' ') is common in England and is increasing in the United States. They are used by *The Atlantic Monthly* and by many publishers in some of their books. The single quotes are as accurate as the double and are much less spotty on the page.

c) For quotations within quotations, double and single quotes are alternated. If you begin with the double marks: " '. . .' "; if you begin with the single: ' ". . ." '. If there are quotations within two such quotations, continue to alternate the double and single quotes as needed.

d) Indenting is used to indicate quotations, especially in factual writing involving numerous quotations of some length, as in this book. No quotation marks are used, and in print the size of type is usually reduced. Publishing houses have rules about how long a quotation must be to be reduced and indented—that it should run to at least five lines, for example, or consist of more than one complete sentence. In double spaced typewritten manuscript, such quotations are usually indented and single spaced; in longhand copy they are simply indented.

2. PRINCIPAL USES OF QUOTATION MARKS. (*a*) Quotation marks are used to indicate all passages taken from another writer, whether a phrase or a page or more. The quoted matter may be worked into the constructions of the quoter's sentence, or it may stand by itself:

> From the enormous mass of material put at his disposal, Mr. Garnett chose those letters that would make "a book in which Lawrence's career, his intellectual development and the details of his life should be recorded, traced and documented almost entirely in his own words."—CHARLES POORE, *The New York Times,* March 10, 1939

When speeches or a short conversation are not given for their own sake but to illustrate a point, they are usually put in the body of the paragraph:

> Do these instances of the beginnings of new words give us any hints in the search for those new words for which every passing month shows the urgent need? I think they do. First, simplicity and euphony —though not simplicity at all costs. Many years ago, I was chaffing an old friend about the deficiency of his native Welsh. "It's very lacking in the most ordinary scientific terms," I remarked. "For example?" "Well, what's the Welsh for *galvanometer?*" I asked. "And if it comes to that, what's the English for it?" A very proper rejoinder which, correctly interpreted, means that *gas* is preferable to

aeriform fluid, and *drop-counter* to *stalagmometer*. All within reason, of course: does it follow, for example, that *foreword* is better than *preface?*—ALLAN FERGUSON, "The Scientist's Need for New Words," *The Listener*, April 21, 1937

b) There are no half quotes. A sentence is either an exact quotation, in quotation marks, or else it isn't and so is not quoted. A speech summarized or quoted "indirectly" is not marked:

DIRECT QUOTATION: The manager told me, "I work harder in one day keeping the girls busy than they work all week."
INDIRECT QUOTATION: The manager told me that he worked harder in one day keeping the girls busy than they worked all week. [Not: The manager told me "that he worked harder in one day keeping the girls busy than they worked all week."]

c) Some adventurous writers of fiction—William Saroyan, William Carlos Williams (in *Life Along the Passaic River*), and a few others—do not use quotation marks in the dialog of their stories, but the practice is not common, and dropping them is somewhat confusing. See *Conversation for their use in dialog.

3. MISCELLANEOUS USES OF QUOTATION MARKS. (*a*) Newspapers and many magazines use quotes around titles of books and periodicals, for which formal writing uses italics:

Down on Boston's historic waterfront, a yachting-supply firm has in its window a display of books intended for the practical use of mariners. Standing between Bowditch's "New American Practical Navigator" and Dutton's "Navigation and Nautical Astronomy" is Mitchell's "Gone with the Wind."—*The New Yorker*, Dec. 4, 1937

In academic style, which uses italics for titles of books and the names of periodicals, quotes are used for titles of written works shorter than volume length, for single poems, short stories, magazine articles, but not ordinarily for chapter titles. See "Form of bibliographical entries," p. 325, and *Titles of articles, books, etc.

b) In formal writing words that are used as words rather than for their meaning, like the examples in this book, are put in italics (underlined in manuscript); in informal writing they would often be put in quotes:

"Capitalism" is thus a shape, a form, which speaks, commands, fights, runs away. Asked to define it, the debater on the left introduces more abstractions: "Absentee ownership," "surplus value," "class struggle," "private ownership of the means of production," "exploitation of the masses," "imperialism," "vested interests," "proletariat," "bourgeoisie," the "profit system," and many more. The great words roll.—STUART CHASE, *The Tyranny of Words*, p. 275

c) In formal writing a word from a conspicuously different level of speech may be put in quotation marks, but this practice is less common than formerly. In informal writing there is less need for these apologetic quotes, because there is greater latitude in choice of words. If the word is appropriate, use it without apology, and if it isn't appropriate, ordinarily don't use it.

> Everybody told Bib what a sucker [not "sucker"] he was, but he still had confidence in the designer of the plane.
> After the Yale man had said his piece, the Dartmouth frosh started to blow his horn again. [The question here is whether the *said his piece, frosh,* and *blow his horn* are appropriate; if they are not, quotes will not make the sentence respectable.]

Colloquial figures of speech do not need to be quoted:

> A dirt path would be easier to walk on and at the same time wouldn't wear out so much cowhide. [Not "cowhide"]

d) Practice differs in writing single words that are spoken or thought:

> Stephen said "Yes," so we went to work at once.
> Stephen said *Yes,* so we went to work at once.
> Stephen said Yes, so we went to work at once.

Probably the first form is the most common.

4. QUOTATION MARKS AND OTHER MARKS. (*a*) When a question mark or an exclamation mark ends a quotation, it is placed inside the quotes:

> "Don't go near that wire!" he shouted.
> Then in a calm voice she asked, "Why couldn't you have said so in the first place?"

When a question mark or exclamation mark belongs to a sentence that includes a quotation, it is placed after the quotes:

> What kind of work can a man put into "the cheapest building that will last fifteen years"?—LEWIS MUMFORD, *Sticks and Stones,* p. 172

b) Most American publishers put commas and periods inside the close-quotes, whether they belong with the quotation or not. The reason for this is that the quotes help fill the small spot of white that would be left if the comma or period came outside. Some writers follow the conventions that apply to the exclamation and question marks, putting comma or period inside the quotes if it belongs with the quotation, outside if it belongs with the quoting sentence, but this usage is much less common.

Semicolons usually stand after the quotation mark.

c) Introductory words and stage directions are set off by a comma, or by two commas if they interrupt the quotation:

Robert said, "I should think that by this time you would have learned what he expects of you."

"History," it has been said, "does not repeat itself. The historians repeat one another."—Max Beerbohm, *Works*, p. 43

(Note that *does* is not capitalized after the interruption, because it does not begin a sentence.)

The comma after a short informal introductory phrase is really unnecessary, since the quotes keep the two elements distinct, and there is noticeable tendency to do without it:

The OED says "The stress conte'nt is historical, & still common among the educated."—H. W. Fowler, p. 93

"Poetry gives most pleasure" said Coleridge "when only generally and not perfectly understood"; . . .—A. E. Housman, *The Name and Nature of Poetry*, p. 36

When quoted phrases are closely built into the construction of a sentence, they are not set off by commas:

I hurried past the zero case with its cream molds, just barely saying "Hi!" to Danny and the girls behind it.

"I give him the book" has two equally correct passives: "He is given the book" and "The book is given to him."—E. H. Sturtevant, *Linguistic Change*, p. 138

A formal introduction to a quotation is usually followed by a colon, as in the statements introducing the examples in this article.

See "Suggestions for taking notes," p. 334, and "The first draft," p. 337; *Conversation; *Plagiarism.

q. v. means "which see" (from Latin *quod vide*). Is is used as a cross reference label in some reference works, though now more generally replaced by the English *see*.

R (r) as in *ready, arch, arrears, car*.

The *r*-sound shows wide variation, more than that of any other consonant. It varies in different English-speaking regions, from Scotch and North of England "burrs" to a slight vowel sound (as in dōə for *door*) or even to complete omission. In American speech, *r* is strongest in Western pronunciation, less conspicuous in New England and Southern.

The *r*-sound also varies according to its position in a word. It is strongest, in all regions, before a vowel: *real, rob, children, fairy*.

Before a consonant sound it varies: as in *bark* from bäk to bärk or in *burn* from bén to bérn. At the end of a word *r* is likely to be slighted, especially if the following word begins with a consonant sound: *are* (ä or är), *fare* (fāə or fār); if the following word begins with a vowel, the *r*-sound is usually full as in *far away*. In vulgate and sometimes in educated informal pronunciation *r* is intruded where none belongs to the word, as in "an idear of what's right," or it is transposed ("metathesis"), as in mod'rən for *modern*, ad'ri on'daks for *Adirondacks*.

In this *Guide and Index* the *r* symbol indicates the pronunciation of words with the expectation that the speaker will render the sort of *r* that he is accustomed to.

For further details of *r* in American pronunciation see Kenyon, pp. 156-61.

racket The spelling *racquet* is British. Write *tennis racket*.

Racket in the sense of an illegitimate way of making money, usually involving threats or violence, has made its way from slang into the informal language. Used to mean any business or particular way of making money (the baseball racket, the lumber racket), it is still slang unless used to imply illegitimate means.

radio takes the regular verb and noun endings: *radioed, radioing, radios, radio's*.

raise—rear *Rear* is now formal in the sense of *rearing* a child or of being *reared*. *Bring up* in this sense is current in all levels of usage. *Raised* is good informal and colloquial usage: "I was born and raised in Kentucky."

rarely means "seldom" (or in archaic and formal English, "with rare skill," as "a rarely carved panel").

Rarely ever (I rarely ever go) is an established colloquial idiom.

ration (rations) *Ration* is pronounced rā'shən or rash'ən, the latter especially in the Army and wherever rations are handled in large quantities (or numbers).

re- The prefix *re-*, meaning "again," is hyphened: (1) when the word to which it is joined begins with *e*: *re-enact, re-enlist, re-enter, re-examine*, and (2) when the form with hyphen can have a slightly different meaning from the form without:

reform, to change, improve—*re-form*, to shape again
recover, to regain—*re-cover*, to cover again

and (3) (rarely) for emphasis, as in "now *re-seated* in fair comfort," or in informal or humorous compounds, *re-re-married*.

Ordinarily there is no hyphen: *rearrange, refine, remit*.

reaction has escaped from chemistry and the biological sciences to become a *counter word for any response of feeling or idea:

> Let me have your reaction to [often *on*] this.
> She reacted violently when he appeared.
> My reaction to this poem was on the whole favorable.

The objection to *reaction* in such use is the objection to all counter words. It tends to crowd out more appropriate or more exact words—*opinion, attitude, feeling, response, impression,* and any number of words for exact feelings and opinions.

Reading and writing We naturally read for entertainment and for instruction; our inclinations lead us to the first type and either inclination or class assignments to the latter. But besides these fundamental motives to reading anyone interested in writing has another—reading to set a goal for his own writing. This does not mean consciously imitating *Time* or *The New Yorker* or Charles A. Beard or Aldous Huxley or Pearl Buck. It means rather reading with attention and occasional analysis the writers who genuinely appeal to us and allowing what does appeal genuinely to influence casually and naturally our own way of writing.

This sort of reading influence is especially necessary in college because a student must read so much in textbooks and routine reference books and in the literature of earlier periods. This earlier literature furnishes material for thought and feeling—but very often an English major loses touch with the idiom of his own time. To counteract the effect of this college reading, a student interested in writing needs to read as widely as he can in the better current magazines and books, fiction and non-fiction, especially of the type that he hopes to write. It is not likely that he will write papers that will be better than what he reads and he has no very sure background for judging his own work except a sensitive and critical reading of the somewhat similar work of the more important writers of his time.

real—really *Real* is not used in formal writing except as an adjective: "a real experience, a real chore." In vulgate and familiar use, *real* is an adverb, a more emphatic *very* (Write real soon; It's real pretty; It went off real well).

Really is both an informal and a formal adverb (a really successful party. It really went off well).

realtor This business coinage has an advantage not possessed by most of its class, since it is much more economical than *real estate agent*. Pronounced rē'əl tər, rē'əl tôr.

reason is because In formal English the construction beginning "The reason is . . ." is completed by a noun or a noun clause, to balance the noun *reason:*

The reason for my poor work in French was [noun:] my intense dislike of the subject.

The reason for my poor work in French was [noun clause:] that I disliked the subject intensely.

But in speech not many noun clauses introduced by *that* are used and the connective that most obviously stresses the notion of reason is *because,* so that in colloquial English we should probably find:

The reason for my poor work in French was because I didn't like the subject.

"The reason is because . . ." is frequently found in writing:

In general it may be said that the reason why scholasticism was held to be an obstacle to truth was because it seemed to discourage further enquiry along experimental lines.—BASIL WILLEY, *The Seventeenth Century Background,* p. 7

Current English Usage calls this construction "Acceptable colloquially" (p. 145). See Pooley, pp. 119-20; F. N. Cherry, "Some Evidence in the Case of 'is because,'" *American Speech,* 1933, viii, 55-60.

Reasons For paragraphs developed by giving reasons for the idea stated in the topic sentence, see "Reasons," p. 106.

receipt—recipe (ri sēt′—res′i pi) Both words mean "a formula, directions for making something." Locally one or the other may be preferred by cooks, but they are interchangeable in actual meaning. *Receipt* also means "a written acknowledgment for something received."

Reciprocal pronouns *Each other, one another* are called reciprocal pronouns. They are used only as objects of verbs or prepositions. In formal usage some writers keep *each other* to refer to two, *one another* for more than two. General usage has *each other* for all senses.

They had hated each other for years.
FORMAL: For the first time all the members really saw one another.
INFORMAL: For the first time all the members really saw each other.

reckon *calculate, guess, reckon

Redundancy, Redundant See "Repetition," p. 168, *Repetition, *Wordiness.

Reference of pronouns (CORRECTION: Change the pronoun marked *Ref* [or revise the sentence] so that its reference will be exact and obvious and the pronoun itself will be in the conventional form.)

A pronoun refers to something without naming it, so that its meaning (except of an indefinite pronoun) is completed by its reference to some other word or group of words, called its *antecedent*. This fact makes using pronouns accurately more complicated than the use of other words, which name and so refer directly to persons or things or actions or qualities. The personal and relative pronouns are further complicated by having a separate case form for the accusative, as nouns do not. And in writing, the form and reference of pronouns can be seen clearly, so that their casual use, which does not attract attention in speech, should be made more exact and the conventions of published usage should be followed. For these reasons a writer needs to watch his pronouns especially, and in revising a paper he should make sure that they are accurate in form and in reference. Since a college student almost always knows the form that is appropriate in a given sentence, an exact use of pronouns is simply a matter of care. Testing the reference of pronouns is one of the specific jobs of revision.

This article runs over the principal points in the use of pronouns in formal and informal English.

1. EXACT AND CLEAR REFERENCE. (*a*) If the meaning of a pronoun is completed by reference to a particular noun, the reference to this antecedent should be exact and obvious.

The first hundred miles, which we covered before lunch, were rough, but they seemed to go faster than the sixty we did in the afternoon. [The noun *miles* is the antecedent of *which* and of *they*.]

All purchases for the University pass through a central purchasing office. These include books, trucks, building materials, food, and hundreds of other items. [*These* refers to *purchases*.]

Swimming may be more fun than calisthenics, but it can't give such a general development. [*It* refers to *swimming*.]

On July 3 Mr. Havermeyer asked Mr. Paige to come to his house. [*His* refers to *Mr. Havermeyer*. Although another name has been mentioned, only a perverse reading would fail to understand the statement. *The former's* instead of *his* would be pedantic here.]

Professor Frank thought that McKinly was grateful to *him* for allowing *him* to graduate. [The first *him* refers to *Professor Frank*, the second to *McKinly*. Actually no ambiguity is possible here and the sentence would be all right in speech and informal writing.]

691

Confusion may arise when the pronoun seems to refer to a nearby noun to which it cannot sensibly refer o. when there is no noun nearby; when it refers to a noun used subordinately in the preceding construction, perhaps to one used as a possessive or as an adjective; and when two or more pronouns are crossed so that the exact reference isn't readily clear. Usually to improve such a reference the sentence must be revised.

He isn't married and doesn't plan on *it*. [. . . and doesn't *plan to marry*.]

The next year he had an attack of acute appendicitis. *It* broke before the doctors had a chance to operate. [*It* cannot refer to *appendicitis* in the statement made. The second sentence should begin *His appendix broke*. . . . Slips in reference are common when the pronoun refers back to a noun in the preceding sentence.]

A legislator should be a man who knows a little about law and government and he should know how to apply *them* to the best interests of his people. [For *them* put *his knowledge*.]

Bill provided more excitement one afternoon when he was skipping rocks across the swimming hole and cut open *a young girl's head who* was swimming under water. [. . . and cut open *the head of a young girl who* was swimming under water.]

To many of us the word *geology* means little in our everyday lives. Yet *it* deals with materials in use for making our homes and factories, metals of which our cars are made, and the fuel which enables us to drive them. [*It* should refer to *geology* (the science), not to *the word*. To revise, drop *the word* in the first line.]

Businessmen without regard for anyone else have exploited the mass of workers at every point, not caring whether *they* were earning a decent living wage, but only whether *they* were getting a lot of money. [The first *they* refers to *workers*, the second to *businessmen*. The sentence needs complete rewriting, but the second part could be improved somewhat by saying: . . . not caring whether they paid a decent living wage, but only whether they were getting a lot of money.]

Remember that clear reference is a matter of *meaning*, not just of the presence or position of certain words.

b) Formal and informal usage differ somewhat in the use of pronouns to refer to the idea of a phrase or clause. Formal usage avoids such a construction, but informal and general usage has it freely.

INFORMAL: Her friend was jealous of her clothes and money and had taken this way of showing it. [*It* refers to the idea in *was jealous*.]

FORMAL: Her friend was jealous of her clothes and money and had taken this way of showing her jealousy.

INFORMAL: He never seemed to realize when academic tempests were brewing, which was probably a good thing.—J. R. PARKER, *Academic Procession*, p. 86. [*Which* refers to the idea of the first clause.]

FORMAL: He never seemed to realize when academic tempests were brewing. This was probably a good thing.

INFORMAL: From his firm grip, piercing eyes, and stern mouth I could see that he was not to be trifled with, which was well proved a few weeks later. [*Which* refers to the *that*-clause.]

FORMAL: From his firm grip, piercing eyes, and stern mouth I could see that he was not to be trifled with. This was well proved a few weeks later.

c) In conversation the reference of pronouns is freer than in writing. The following colloquial examples, which would probably pass unnoticed in a conversation, show one reason why in writing we sometimes find pronouns that seem inexact or that do not conform to editorial standards.

COLLOQUIAL	WRITTEN
Gordon's mother asked me to take him fishing because he was so interested in *it* but had never caught *one*.	Gordon's mother asked me to take him fishing because he was so interested in *it* but had never caught *a fish*.
Everyone likes to dance and knew he would get plenty of *it* during the party weekend.	Everyone likes to dance and knew he would get plenty of *dancing* during the party weekend.
In aquaplaning the ropes should never be wound around the wrists, because if thrown *he* would be dragged along and injured.	The ropes should never be wound around *the planer's* wrists, because if thrown *he* would be dragged along and injured.

2. AGREEMENT OF PRONOUN WITH ANTECEDENT. Pronouns referring to specific antecedents agree with the antecedents in number, gender, and person.

a) *Agreement in number.* A pronoun agrees with its antecedent in number: singular antecedent, singular pronoun; plural antecedent, plural pronoun.

SINGULAR: *Jimmy* tried to go quietly, but *he* couldn't keep from whistling.

PLURAL: *The boys* had tried to go quietly, but *they* couldn't keep from whistling.

In formal English, *each, every, everyone* are referred to by singular pronouns (*every and its compounds § 1):

Almost everyone has some little superstitions which *he* would not violate for love or money.

693

In colloquial English these words are treated as collectives
(*every § 1) and are found usually with a plural pronoun:

Almost everyone has some little superstitions which *they* would not
violate for love or money.

Maugham takes anyone from a gigolo to a lord and develops
them [Formal: *him*] with equal ease and finesse.

This colloquial agreement is sometimes found in print, but editors
usually bring it in line with formal usage before publication.
Reference: Russell Thomas, "Concord Based on *Meaning* versus
Concord Based on *Form*: The Indefinites," *College English*, 1939,
i, 38-45

A collective noun is referred to by either a singular or a plural
pronoun, depending upon its meaning in the sentence (*Collective nouns):

Singular: When a *gang* of rabbit hunters spreads out over a field,
it doesn't lose any time.

Plural: When a *gang* of rabbit hunters spread out over a field, *they*
don't lose any time.

Often when a pronoun does not agree with its antecedent, the
antecedent could be changed rather than the pronoun:

Putting himself in the shoes of the slave owner, Lincoln realized
that they had a right to feel as they did toward emancipation. [This
could be made consistent by making *slave owner* plural better than by
changing *they* to *he*.]

Labor's third and major contention is that they do not receive an
adequate return for the services they render. [Here changing *Labor's*
to *The workers'* would be more accurate than changing the pronouns
to the singular.]

b) *Agreement in person.* Except in indefinite pronouns (§ 3 of
this article), there is little difficulty with agreement.

First person: I wish Mr. Patterson had told *me* before.
Second person: You should have thought of that *yourself.*
Third person: The woman had said *she* was over twenty-one.

A relative pronoun agrees with its antecedent:

[Formal:] I, *who am* your nearest relative, would help you.
He is one of those people who do just what they want to. [*They*
refers to *who* which refers to *people*.]

c) *Case of pronouns.* The case of a pronoun depends upon the
construction in which it stands, not upon its antecedent. See
*Case and the articles there referred to; *be § 2, *who, whom.

3. Indefinite reference. Often pronouns are used to refer to
the writer's group or to the readers or to people in general instead

of to specifically mentioned people. English has no such convenient pronoun as the German *man* or the French *on*. Our *one* has a definitely formal and stiffish connotation. We and *you* seem to be slightly more personal, more expressive, and are very generally used, as in various articles in this book. This is a question of style rather than of grammar, and whether *you* or *they* ("They say . . .") or *we* or *one* or *people* or some other noun is used depends on their fitness in the particular passage.

Care should be taken to keep indefinite pronouns consistent, not shifting from *one* to *you*, for example:

When *you* have worked a day here *you* have really earned your money.

[Or] When *one* has worked a day here *he* has really earned his money.

[Not] When *one* has worked a day here *you* have really earned your money.

An indefinite pronoun should not be substituted for a definite personal pronoun:

For *me* there is no fun in reading unless *I* can put myself in the position of the characters and feel that *I* am really in the scene. [Not: For *me* there is no fun in reading unless *you* can put yourself in the position of the characters and feel that *you* are really in the scene.]

The indefinite pronouns (*all, any, each, everybody, few, nobody, somebody,* and so on [*Pronouns §8]) have no expressed antecedent, so that their use involves consistency but not agreement.

Since English has no single pronoun to mean he-or-she, the masculine *he* is conventionally used instead (*he-or-she):

The time comes to every senior when *he* [Not: *he or she*] anxiously looks forward to that eventful day.

4. Unnecessary pronouns. Sometimes a possessive pronoun is used where *the* would be more idiomatic:

We stopped to see the [rather than *our*] first unusual sight.

5. Avoiding pronouns. Pronouns are necessary and convenient but because they do lead sometimes to inconsistent uses (that are marked by teachers and editors), some writers tend to avoid them, using a noun instead. The result is usually unidiomatic or clumsy English:

That's the reason I hesitate to picture the owner of *a grip* from the appearance of *the bag*. [Better: That's the reason I hesitate to picture the owner of *the bag* from *its* appearance.]

Arrest of *the woman* yesterday followed several days of observation of *the woman's* [*her*] activities by agents of the Stores Mutual Protective Association.

Pronouns are especially useful to bind together clauses and sentences. In the following paragraph each sentence seems to be a new beginning, but with pronouns instead of *Mr. Frothingham*, the paragraph would be closely connected:

Roland W. Frothingham died at his home on Commonwealth avenue on Tuesday. Mr. Frothingham [He] was born in Boston in 1846 and had lived here ever since. Mr. Frothingham's [His] ancestors came from Ipswich. Mr. Frothingham [He] was educated at Chauncy Hall School and at Harvard College.

6. OMISSION OF PRONOUNS. In familiar writing and in conversation, pronouns, especially *I*, are often omitted (*I § 3, *Subjectless sentences) and in colloquial and informal writing the relative pronoun is often omitted from relative clauses (*Relative clauses).

The first man [*that*] I met had never heard of such a street.

For the classes and forms of pronouns, see *Pronouns; for further instances of their use, see the articles on particular pronouns, *I, *we, *who, whom, *himself, *myself, and so on.

References: All grammars treat the use of pronouns. The discussions in the large grammars (Curme, Jespersen . . .) are extended and discuss many special uses.

For exercises on pronouns see "Cases of pronouns," p. 257.

References See "The working bibliography," p. 324 and "Footnote form," p. 338.

Referent (ref′ ər ənt) is the object, class of objects, act, situation, quality, or fancy which a word means. The referent of *book* is either a particular book being discussed or a generalized notion based on our observation of various books. For discussion see "Denotation," p. 186.

Reflexive pronouns *Pronouns § 4, *himself, *myself

regard (**regards**) Good English uses the preposition phrase *in regard to*; vulgate and low colloquial uses more often *in regards to*.

regardless *-less* is a negative ending and makes the word mean "without regard to"; prefixing an *ir-* (*irregardless*) doubles the negative and makes a word without standing.

Relative clauses A relative clause is an adjective clause introduced by a relative pronoun, *that*, *which*, or *who*:

The rain *that began in the morning* kept on all night.

The coach was now abused by the alumni *who two years before had worshiped him.*

The road to the left, *which looked almost impassable*, was ours.

A relative clause stands immediately after the noun it modifies. In the first sentence above, the clause modifies *rain*, in the second *alumni*, and in the third *road*.

In colloquial and informal English relative clauses often have no pronoun:

The man I met that afternoon has been my friend ever since. [Formal: The man *whom* I met . . .]

The ideas we held in common were few indeed. [Formal: The ideas *that* we held . . .]

In informal English a relative pronoun is often used to refer to the idea of a clause, but this is rare in formal English (*Reference of pronouns § 1*b*):

INFORMAL: These planes can climb very fast, *which* is their greatest value.

FORMAL: These planes can climb very fast, *a fact which* is their greatest value.

---

*that, *who, whom, *which, *Restrictive and non-restrictive

Several relative clauses in succession make for an awkward, or at least conspicuous, house-that-Jack-built sentence that should be avoided:

People *who* buy houses *that* have been built in times *which* had conspicuous traits of architecture *which* have been since abandoned often have to remodel their purchases completely.

Relative pronouns The relative pronouns are *as, that, what, whatever, which* (*of which, whose*), *who* (*whose, whom*), *whoever*.

Somebody, *who* [or *whom*] I don't know, shouted, "Put 'em out."

The Senator, *whose* term expires next year, is already worrying.

I haven't read the same book *that* [as] you have.

That refers to persons or things, *who* to persons. *Which* refers to animals or objects or situations, and also to collective nouns even if they refer to persons:

The army which mobilizes first has the advantage.

The Board of Directors, which met on Saturday . . .

The Board of Directors, who are all bankers, . . .

Particular points in the use of each of these relatives will be found in separate entries on each, especially those on *that, *which, *who, whom. See also *Restrictive and non-restrictive.

remember In vulgate English *remember* is supported by *of* (I don't remember of doing that) and colloquially by *about* (I don't remember about that at all). In most written English the unsupported verb is used:

I don't remember doing it.   I don't remember that at all.

Renaissance—Renascence The long spelling is the more common. *Renaissance* is pronounced ren′ə säns′, or, less commonly, ri nā′səns; *Renascence* is usually pronounced ri nas′əns. The word is capitalized when it refers to the period of history, not when referring to a revival, as "the pre-war renaissance in American poetry."

Rep **Repetition** (CORRECTION: Revise so as to remove the ineffective repetition of word, meaning, or sound.)

Repetition of word, thought, or sound may be an effective trait of style, contributing especially to emphasis. Successful repetition is discussed in Chapter 4, "Restatement," p. 94 (repetition of idea as a method of paragraph development); Chapter 6, "Repetition," p. 168 (repetition of words); Chapter 6, "Sound and rhythm," p. 174 (repetition of sounds). This article reviews only some unsuccessful sorts of repetition (also discussed in Chapter 6, p. 168).

1. WORDS AND PHRASES. A word that is the name of the subject of a paper or of one of its important parts must occur frequently, though pronouns and economical sentences can keep down the repetition. Unnecessary, ineffective repetition is usually a mark of carelessness or insensitiveness. An attentive reading over would have led the writers of the following to revise their sentences, removing the obvious repetitions and other deadwood too:

The administration of the Incan government was *based* on a decimal *basis*. [. . . was on a decimal basis]

The Indian's culture was so different from the white man's [culture] that he has done very well to change as much as he has in such a short [period of] time.

From here on there was no trail and if there had been it would have been snowed under [by the snow of] the night before.

Especially conspicuous is repetition of a word used in a different sense:

Our club is as much a fraternity as any house along the row. Our unity and fraternity [Substitute: *brotherhood*] have brought us real satisfaction and much success.

2. MEANING. Meaning of single words or of longer groups is often repeated in near synonyms:

. . . *where* he did very successful work *there*. [Drop the *there*]

In *many* books the setting [*very often*] is in some foreign country.

At eight thirty [in the morning] you punch the time clock for the start of the day.

Here comes an elderly woman whose feet and legs are harnessed into a pair of the [antiquated and] almost obsolete high-button shoes.

New leg kicks are shown him, new arm stretches are demonstrated, and different ways of breathing illustrated. [He is shown new leg kicks, new arm stretches, and different ways of breathing.]

3. SOUND. Jingles and rhyming words are out of place in prose and do not occur so often as repetitions of unstressed syllables, especially the -*ly* of adverbs:

practical*ly*   unanimous*ly*   real*ly*   extreme*ly*   time*ly*

Reports Business and technical reports are a form of presentation of material for easy and immediate reference. A report may contain the results of laboratory or field research, of any type of investigation, as in business and advertising surveys; it may be a more or less routine report of activity, processes, progress; or it may carry principally a recommendation for action or decision with the evidence upon which the recommendation is based. It is essentially an orderly presentation of data arranged for a specific purpose.

The parts of a typical report are:

1. Title page, carrying the title, name of the maker of the report, the person or group to whom it is made, place and date, and any other necessary preliminary information.

2. Letter of transmittal, usually a formal presentation of the report in the form of a letter from the maker to the recipient. The letter may contain special acknowledgments and other preface matter.

3. Table of contents, listing the main heads and usually at least one level of subheads, with page references.

4. Often a brief preliminary summary of the most important ideas developed in the body.

5. The body of the report, presenting the data, the apparatus or methods used in compiling it, necessary discussion, or recommendations.

6. An appendix, if necessary, containing tables of figures, documents, bibliographies, or any matter that would be hard to work into the body of the text.

7. Index, if the report is of more than a few pages.

In style the outstanding features of a report are clarity and ease of reference. Usually the margins are wide, the spacing generous, the headings and directions to a reader many and revealing. Data is often thrown into the form of tables of statistics, diagrams, graphs, illustration. A report is usually compactly technical, in the vocabulary and idiom of the people to receive it, who are usually trained in the field.

The clarity, compactness, and adjustment to particular readers make a report a specialized but highly effective form of communication. Since its sole aim is presentation of data gathered for a specific purpose, it does not lend itself to amateur practice, but a student would do well to familiarize himself with the type of report likely to be used in the field in which he expects to work, and if possible to make a collection of reports for future guidance.

Fuller discussion of the method and form of reports will be found in books on business, scientific, and technical writing, such as the following:

Agg, Thomas R. and Foster, Walter L., *The Preparation of Engineering Reports* (New York, 1935)

Baker, R. P. and Howell, A. C., *The Preparation of Reports*, (New York) rev. ed., 1938 (The most comprehensive treatment)

Richardson, H. C., and others, *Practical Forms of Exposition* (New York, 1934), Chapter 9

Sypherd, W. O. and Brown, Sharon, *Engineer's Manual of English* (Chicago, 1933)

Requests *Commands and requests

researcher has been added to the English vocabulary as a needed shortening for *research worker*:

Private collections of newspapers have never been many, though at least two men have earned the gratitude of generations of researchers —Burney . . . and Hope. . . .—London *Times Literary Supplement* Feb. 6, 1930

Research paper A research paper is a record of study in some special field, scientific, social, historical, literary. Actual research involves the finding and discussion of new material; undergraduate research papers are usually based on secondary sources and represent rather a selection and arrangement of material that has been first gathered by others. They are primarily a record of intelligent reading in several sources on a particular subject.

The research paper is a good college exercise not only because a student learns something from his study but because it is training for further exact work. The research paper in English courses often is focused on method and form and so prepares for later papers. In a paper of this sort the stages of the writing process become especially clear and especially important, from choosing the subject to preparing a careful manuscript with footnotes and bibliography.

The methods and forms of an academic research paper are presented in detail in Chapter 13, p. 319.

Resolutions A resolution is a formal record of action taken by a meeting or an organization to be sent to someone. It is used typically in expression of sympathy or in recording of sentiment or in recommendation of action. The style is formal and the expression arranged in a standardized formula:

WHEREAS, The experiences of the past few weeks have shown . . .; and

WHEREAS, Our expectations of a more favorable attitude on the part of . . .; therefore be it

Resolved, That this body feels it its duty to inform . . .; and be it further

Resolved, That a copy of these resolutions be sent . . .

John W. Appel, Secretary

rest There are two *rest*'s in English, both in good standing. *Rest*, repose, is from Old English *rest*; *rest*, remainder, is from French *reste*.

Restrictive and non-restrictive (CORRECTION: Decide whether the *Rest* modifier marked is restrictive or non-restrictive. If it is restrictive, it should not be separated from the word it modifies by a comma; if it is non-restrictive, it should be set off by a comma or by two commas.)

1. RESTRICTIVE MODIFIERS. A restrictive modifier defines, limits, identifies the word it refers to, that is, it gives a fact that sets it off from other things of the same class. If the restrictive modifier is omitted, the statement either becomes meaningless, as in the first sentence below, or else it has a quite different meaning, as in the second:

It was a quite different looking person *who walked out into the cold frosty air a few minutes later.*

The right of the dictatorships *to decide how long this wholesale killing goes on* is unquestioned.

The italicized elements in the following sentences are restrictive and should stand as they are here, not set off by commas:

His opponent appeared at one of the really important rallies *with a drink too much in him.*

Every young man *who wished a successful career* tried to get a place in the Gay-Pay-Oo.

Reform should be an application *to wider fields* of methods *with which people are already familiar* and *of which they approve.*

These records are reproduced through a recording device *that will automatically play two hours before stopping.*

A piece of swing music reached my ears from a room down the hall *before I heard the tramping feet that seemed to go with it.*

In many states parole boards still persist in turning loose prisoners *who should remain behind bars.*

Mr. Colman proves his versatility as an actor *when he philosophizes one minute and punches his brother on the nose the next.* He portrays a man of action *if the occasion requires* and at the same time a mild-mannered, soft-spoken individual *who gives the impression of being able to think.* He has to make important decisions *when his brother and Margo tell him that this Utopia is a lot of hooey.* Mr. Colman is the only actor I have ever seen *who can show that he is thinking.*

2. NON-RESTRICTIVE MODIFIERS. Modifiers which do not limit the meaning of a noun but add a descriptive detail are non-restrictive and are set off by a comma or commas. As a rule a non-restrictive modifier can be omitted without altering the fundamental meaning of the statement.

A modifier that follows a proper noun is usually non-restrictive, since the name itself identifies exactly the person or place mentioned:

Josie, *aged 16,* told Ma and Pa Pansky a thing or two.

Just below Poughkeepsie, *which we reached in a little over two hours,* we had another breakfast in a roadside lunch wagon.

The modifiers italicized in the following sentences are non-restrictive and are properly set off by commas:

One miner, *who felt that the great beyond held better opportunities,* held a stick of dynamite between his teeth and hit the detonating cap with a hammer.

Cantaloupes are moving in considerable volume from California, *with an indicated crop somewhat larger than in 1936.* Western shipments will be supplemented the latter part of June and throughout July by supplies, *which are reported slightly below 1936,* from the second early states.

That extravagant behavior of the post-war decade, *which most of us thought to be the effect of war,* had really begun before the War. The War hastened everything—*in politics, in economics, in behavior*—but it started nothing.—GEORGE DANGERFIELD, *The Strange Death of Liberal England,* p. viii

The mystic on the other hand, *especially as pictured by the common man,* is all inchoate raptures, half-articulated moonshine.—IRWIN EDMAN, *Four Ways of Philosophy,* p. 165

A little practice should make a writer able to recognize restrictive and non-restrictive modifiers and so use the conventional punctuation.

Result Adverbial clauses of result are introduced typically by *so that, so, so . . . that, such . . . that,* and *that. So* is rather informal and colloquial, *such . . . that* and *that* likely to be formal. The most common is *so that.*

> He had been taught always to expect the worst, so that [so] he wasn't surprised.
> He was so used to suffering that one more disaster made little difference.
> The house was such an expense that they were giving it up.

Reverend is not used without the first name or initials of the person to whom it refers; the abbreviation is used in newspaper and more or less informal writing:

Reverend James Shaw   Rev. James Shaw
Reverend J. T. Shaw   Rev. J. T. Shaw
NOT: Rev. Shaw

The Reverend before a name is rather more formal:

the Reverend James T. Shaw   the Reverend Mr. Shaw

The reverend used instead of a clergyman's name (The reverend wasn't there) is colloquial and vulgate.

Revision Most people, amateurs and professionals, do better work if they write a first draft rather rapidly and then revise it. In revision a writer checks his material, to see if it is sufficient for his purpose; looks at the plan, the paragraphs, the sentences from a reader's point of view, so far as he can; and he looks at the small matters, spelling, punctuation, the words, and the grammatical constructions. Most of the points taken up in this *Guide-Index* are to be applied in revision.

For further discussion see Ch. 12, "Revising," p. 299, and Ch. 9 ("Minimum Essentials"), Ch. 10 (Spelling), Ch. 11 (Punctuation), and the alphabetical articles in this book you may need.

Rhetoric Rhetoric is the study of the theory and practice of composition, both oral and written.

The principles of rhetoric are so liable to abuse that the terms *rhetoric* and *rhetorical* are often used in a derogatory sense to imply excessive elaborateness in style, a show of words rather than a show of meaning. Partly because of this degradation of the word *rhetoric, composition* is often used in its place.

Rhetorical questions are really statements in the form of questions, since no direct answer is expected and the writer does not intend to give one. In conversation they often carry some special accent, of accusation, for example: "Could you have done any better?" =

703

"You couldn't have done any better." "What made you do that?" = "You didn't have any good reason for doing that."

In some writing rhetorical questions are used to suggest opinions, insinuating instead of stating. In the following series of questions Mr. Thompson is really giving his own opinion of war:

Is it not about time that our publicists, and likewise our statesmen, cease worrying and crying out on the matter of poison gas? How much longer will sensible people talk of the greater humanity of one mode of warfare as compared to another? How much longer will it be considered quite all right, or at least not worthy of especial comment, for a soldier to be shot through the head, neck, chest, abdomen or legs with bullets of all kinds and calibers, but thoroughly dishonest and uncivilized for him to be sprayed with deadly gas or liquid? Wherein is one sort of torture preferable to the other? What difference does it make to the soldier whether he dies from painful burns or from painful disemboweling?—RALPH THOMPSON, *The New York Times*, Feb. 5, 1937

And Professor Wiggam's Questions are suggested arguments:

(QUESTIONS FOR THE STATESMAN)

Since nearly three-fourths of your efforts are directed toward reversing this natural order of things, may I ask Your Excellency a few random questions? Why is it that of two brothers under my observation in the same environment, one entered the United States Senate, while the other all his life has conducted a fourth class, small town restaurant? Why has one of our greatest publicists an imbecile brother and a wayward sister? Why, of two brothers, reared under the same roof, with the same parental influence, does one become a village loafer and the other a philosopher? Why, out of the first fifty-one names in the Hall of Fame, are ten of them the sons and daughters of preachers? Why is one out of twelve of all the names in *Who's Who*, our most democratic roster of fame, the child of a minister? Is it necessary for me to present proof to you that ministers are on the average men of character and intelligence? Why out of the first forty-six names in the Hall of Fame, have twenty-six of them from one to three relatives of national renown? Does it not argue that they probably belong to great breeds, truly noble strains of blood? Why is it, that if you are born from certain strains of blood you have one chance in five of having a celebrated relative, and if from other strains your chance in this respect is hardly one in a thousand? Why has the Edwards family, living in thirty-three different countries, under differing environments, out of one thousand four hundred members given us one thousand four hundred social servants, many of world distinction, while the Ishmael family, studied by Eastbrook, out of approximately fifteen thousand members has given us nearly fifteen thousand social scourges?—ALBERT EDWARD WIGGAM, *The New Decalogue of Science*, p. 46

rhyme, rime The simpler spelling seems to be gaining slowly on *rhyme*. It is not only simpler but was the original spelling in English.

Rhyme is a characteristic of verse but is out of place and an unnecessary distraction in prose (As I lay in bed, I heard the *rain* in the *drain*).

Rhythm A detailed study of the rhythm of prose would belong to the study of literature, but a writer needs to remember that part of the effect even of written language comes from rhythm, from the frequency and intensity and arrangement of the stresses of his words. In reference works and news stories rhythm counts for little, but in writing that can be read aloud with pleasure it is a considerable factor and even in reading silently most people get some impression of the sound of a passage.

A rhythmical analysis of a short passage of formal and of informal prose will show some characteristic qualities of rhythm and can serve as a basis for further discussion of rhythm in prose.

Ånd só, | whĕn théir dáy | ĭs óvĕr, | whĕn théir góod | ănd théir évĭl | hăve bécŏme | ĕtérnăl | bў thĕ ímmŏrtálĭtў | ŏf thĕ pást, | bĕ ĭt óurs | tŏ féel | thăt, | whĕre thĕy súffĕred, | whĕre thĕy fáiled, | nó déed | ŏf óurs | wăs thĕ cáuse; | bŭt whĕrévĕr | ă spárk | ŏf thĕ dívĭne | fíre | kíndlĕd | ĭn thĕir héarts, | wĕ wĕre | réadў | wĭth ĕncóurăge- mĕnt, | wĭth sýmpăthў, | wĭth bráve wórds | ĭn whích | hĭgh cóurăge | glówĕd.

—BERTRAND RUSSELL, *Mysticism and Logic*, p. 56

Mŏthĕr | usĕd tŏ gó | tŏ thĕ cémetĕrý | ĭn Wóodláwn | wĭth hĕr árms | fúll ŏf | flówĕrs, | ănd láy | thĕ prĕttў thíngs | bў sŏme | héad- stóne, | ăs ă sígn | ŏf rĕmémbrănce. | Áftĕr ă whíle | shĕ bóught | ă cást-irŏn | cháir | ănd léft ĭt | óut thére, | ínsĭde | thĕ squáre | fámĭlў plót, | sŏ thăt whĕn | ĭt tóok hĕr | ă lóng tíme | tŏ árrănge | hĕr flówĕrs | shĕ cóuld sĭt dówn | ănd rést.

—CLARENCE DAY, *Life With Father*, p. 257

1. ANALYSIS OF RHYTHM. A sensitive reading aloud is the real test of rhythm, but occasional analysis will emphasize certain traits of rhythm and perhaps of other points of style. It is best to read the passage to be analyzed aloud naturally and then to go over it again, noting and marking the stresses. Although readers will vary somewhat in their reading of certain sentences, as they do in reading lines of verse, there will be a surprising agreement among readers after a little practice. Elaborate schemes for analysis of prose have been worked out, but a simpler scheme is given here that will be sufficient to indicate the principal qualities.

(*a*) *Stress.* The stress that syllables receive varies considerably in force, but usually it is sufficient to indicate three levels, lack of stress (x), full stress ('), and an intermediate, or secondary stress ('):

an intermediate or secondary stress

Care needs to be taken not to exaggerate the stress in reading for analysis.

b) Feet. In prose rhythm the "feet" do not cut across words as they do in analyses of verse, but follow sense units. Feet may range from one syllable to seven or eight syllables. They are arranged and named according to the position of the main stress:

RISING, beginning with unstressed or lightly stressed syllable and ending with a fully stressed syllable:

and so   with her arms   when their day

FALLING, beginning with a stressed syllable and ending with one of little or no stress:

mother   high courage   stressed syllables

WAVED, the foot beginning and ending with syllables of the same stress. This type may be subdivided into

CREST, in which the stressed syllables are in the middle:

eternal   and left it   to the cemetery

TROUGH, in which the stressed syllables are at the ends:

after a while   family plot

LEVEL, one stressed syllable or two or more stressed syllables:

glowed   no deed

Some readers tend to make shorter feet, representing slower reading and fuller stresses, and others make longer feet with fewer full stresses:

of the divine | fire   or   of the divine fire

in which | high courage   or   in which high courage

For practice work probably the first method is the better and it has been followed in the passages above.

c) Summarizing the feet. If a summary of the analysis would be useful, it can be made on some such plan as this:

		RUSSELL		DAY	
Rising feet					
	x ′	5		5	
	x x ′ (x ′ ′, etc.)	9		5	
	Longer	1		2	
	Total		15		12
Falling feet					
	′ x (′ ′)	3		6	
	′ x x	0		0	
	′ ′ x	1		0	
	Longer	0		0	
	Total		4		6
Crest					
	x ′ x	2		4	
	x ′ x x	1		0	
	x x ′ x	3		1	
	Longer	2		2	
	Total		8		7
Trough					
	′ x ′	0		1	
	′ x x ′	0		2	
	Longer	0		0	
	Total		0		3
Level					
	′	3		1	
	′ ′	1		0	
	Total		4		1

2. COMMENTS ON PROSE RHYTHM. (*a*) In contrast to verse, the rhythm of prose is marked by variety of movement; passages cannot be defined in two words like "iambic pentameter" (though the importance and actual descriptiveness of such metrical labels of verse have been exaggerated). Certain contrasts, such as a series of long feet broken by a short one and vice versa, are characteristic of good prose.

b) It is generally regarded that the movement of the end of a sentence and to a less extent of the end of subordinate elements, such as clauses, are the most important feature of rhythm. The ending will either be rising, with the heavy stress last, which usually gives a vigorous conclusion, or falling, with the unstressed syllable last. The beginnings of a series of sentences usually show variety in stress.

c) Usually a sentence should not be continued after a pleasing final rhythm. This explains in part why "tacked-on" expressions often seem ineffective.

d) Although beginning and ending are the most important elements in rhythm, good English prose does not sag in the middle of sentences. Wordiness or long functional phrases contribute to weak rhythm. For instance:

> The wheels that are made here vary greatly in size, becaúse óf the fact thất they aˇre máde fór áll types ŏf mắchínĕrý. Contrast: because they are made for all types of machinery.

e) The stresses of prose as of poetry (contrast lines in the same meter by Browning and by Robert Frost) vary considerably in their intensity. The stresses in the passage from Bertrand Russell are heavier than those in the one from Clarence Day.

f) Rising and waved rhythms are most characteristic of English prose. Falling and level rhythms are less common and are often useful for gaining variety. English sentences seem rarely to begin with a strong stress. The most common opening is the x ′ foot.

These suggestions can lead to detailed observation of prose rhythm that will point out some of the characteristic differences between writers. Sometimes such an analysis can suggest some changes in revising a manuscript to improve the rhythm of the sentences.

References: Norton R. Tempest, *The Rhythm of English Prose* (Cambridge, 1930), is probably the best discussion of the subject; Oliver Elton, *English Prose Numbers* ("Essays and Studies by Members of the English Association," iv., 29-54); Dobrée, pp. 22, 27; Rickert, Chapter 5; George Saintsbury, *A History of English Prose Rhythm* (London, 1922).

right In the sense of "very," *right* is a localism (We'll be right glad to see you).

Right along, right away, right off are colloquial and informal idioms.

rise In referring to people, *arise* is formal and poetic; *rise* is rather formal; *get up* is informal and colloquial.

role *Role* (a role in a play) is still conservatively spelled with the circumflex (rôle), but in common usage the accent has been dropped:

> Any *role* that seemed heroic attracted me.—Clarence Day, *Life With Father*, p. 82

Roman numerals For the forms and uses of Roman numerals (i, ii, iii, cxlvi . . .) see *Numbers §4.

round—around In colloquial and informal usage *round* and *around* are used interchangeably, with a definite tendency to use *round* (or to clip the *a* of *around* so short that it would be taken for *round*).

In formal English there is some tendency to keep *around* to mean "here and there" or "in every direction" and *round* for "in a circular motion" or "in a reverse motion":

I have looked all around.   There aren't any around here.
He is going round the world.   Everyone turned round.

Around is colloquial and informal in the sense of "about, near": He had around $200 in bills; Is anybody around [that is, around here]?

All-round is an informal adjective (an all-round flour, an all-round athlete), which is often *all-around* in colloquial usage.

Round has no apostrophe.

route The pronunciation rüt is general, but rout is in common use, especially in the Army and colloquially as of newspaper and delivery routes.

run In good informal use in the sense of "manage, operate" (He runs a hotel in Florida).

Run-on sentences A run-on sentence is made up of two or more grammatically complete sentences written as one, without a connective between the statements and punctuated with a comma or with no mark at all:

The average age of a college freshman is 18 or 19, some may be a year or two younger.
You may say, "Look at Switzerland, she is still neutral."

Ineffective run-on sentences are discussed in *Comma fault and effective ones in *Contact clauses. Both types are discussed more fully in "Run-on sentences," p. 136.

S represents principally two sounds, s and z: s as in *so, sorry, biscuit, crops*; z as in *easy, was, Jones*. In a few words s spells *sh*: *tension, sure, sugar*; and in some *zh*: *leisure, pleasure, measure*.

S is silent in several words, most of them from French: *aisle, debris, rendezvous, *island, Arkansas, Louisville*, often in *Saint Louis*, and usually in *Illinois*.

*sh For plurals in *-s* see *Plurals §1, *Jones, for the genitive of words ending in *-s*, *Genitive case § 1*a*.

said As an adjective *said* (the said person, the said idea) is legal and is not used in general writing. Compare *above.

saint The abbreviation *St.* is used with names (*St. John, St. Louis*); plural SS. (*SS. Peter and Paul*). Occasionally the French feminine form, *Sainte*, is used (*Sault Sainte Marie*); abbreviation *Ste.*

saith *Saith* is the obsolete third person singular of *say*, now *says*. Pronounced seth.

same *Same* is used as an adjective (the same color) and as a pronoun in such expressions as "The same happened to me once" and popularly in "I'll take the same," "more of the same." In these the reference is to something in the context or situation.

Same as a pronoun is also characteristic of legal and outmoded business use: "and enclose check for same" where better style would have *it* or *them* instead of *same*.

Sarcasm Sarcasm is a quality of some statements, a note of bitterness or reproach. The statement may be ironical (that is, to be interpreted differently depending on one's point of view), or it may be direct. The sarcasm lies in its harshness. *Humor, *Irony

say *Say* is the general word for speaking. *Talk* implies a continued "saying." *State* implies a formal "saying" (compare *statement*) and is better kept for this meaning (Not: "Mr. Owen stated that he was ready if we were").

In labeling the speeches of characters in a story, *said* is the best word to use, since it attracts least attention, unless there is reason for using a more specific word. *Conversation

Say in informal English also means "order, request" (He said to go back or we'd get in trouble).

Say in the sense of "suppose," "perhaps," "for instance" (Say they went sixteen miles) is colloquial and informal.

scarcely *Double negative § 3

scenario Pronounced si när′i ō; less often, si nä′ri ō; rarely now (except in England) shi nä′ri ō.

Schoolgirl style The "schoolgirl style" is characterized by sentimental counter words (*lovely, divine*), by exaggeration, and by reliance on all sorts of mechanical forms of emphasis—exclamation marks, dashes, capitals, one, two, and even three underlinings. These serve as satisfying muscular release to the writer and may add a sort of glow to a letter, but they should not be transferred to the printed page, and any suggestion of the style, except of course to help portray a character, should be avoided.

Scientific and technical writing The ideal of scientific writing was expressed very early in the modern scientific movement in Thomas Sprat's *History of the Royal Society* (1667). The members of the Society, he said, tried

to return back to the primitive purity, and shortness, when men delivered so many things, almost in an equal number of words. They have exacted from all their members a close, naked, natural way of speaking; positive expressions; clear senses; a native easiness: bringing all things as near the mathematical plainness as they can; and preferring the language of artizans, countrymen, and merchants, before that of wits or scholars.

Exactness rather than grace or variety, or even emphasis, is the goal of most scientific and scholarly writing, of most writing that is done by members of a profession to be read by other members. Occasionally it attains the ideal of "delivering so many things, almost in an equal number of words":

A stable, stainless, organic mercury compound solution of high germicidal value, particularly in serum and other protein media.

But if Thomas Sprat could read much current scientific writing, he would find that it had departed far from "the language of artizans, countrymen, and merchants."

The chief reason for the "big words" that seem to a layman the most conspicuous trait of scientific writing is that scientists have discovered and named qualities and things of which the average person is quite unaware. Their descriptions are more detailed than people in general need. Here, for instance, is a scientific description of the *n* sound:

§ 66. *n* as in *none, knit, canny, inn,* etc., is the voiced tongue-point alveolar nasal continuant corresponding to the voiced tongue-point stop *d* and the voiceless tongue-point stop *t*. All three sounds are made with the tongue point on the alveolar ridge (teethridge), and are hence sometimes called alveolar consonants, or, less accurately, dentals.—*Webster's Collegiate Dictionary,* Fifth edition, p. xiv

In contrast to the rather loose meanings of words in general usage, scientific writers try to confine their words to a single specific meaning. Ordinary people speak of *biliousness* and *eyestrain,* though those words have no definite meaning for doctors or oculists. Some scientific words are taken from the general vocabulary and given special meanings, like *magnitude* in astronomy, *force* in physics, *complex* in psychoanalysis, *dip* and *incline* in geology. But the tendency now is to build words from Latin or more often from Greek roots that are self-explanatory (to anyone who knows their elements): *photo-micrography, beta-methyl-amido-croton-anilide.*

The sentence structure and other traits of style in scientific writing are formal, appropriately formal because its audience is specialized. The style is impersonal, completely impersonal in monographs, textbooks, and articles in the scientific journals, less impersonal in popular treatments of scientific subjects. Three levels of scientific writing are illustrated in the following quotations. The first paragraph is a simple statement of fact:

The nature of the force exerted by a wave upon any obstacle, such as a cliff or beach, depends in part upon the type of wave and its condition at the moment of collision with the obstacle. If an unbroken oscillatory wave strikes a vertical wall or cliff the base of which reaches down to deep water, the wave is reflected back. At the instant of contact the crest of the wave rises to twice its normal height and the cliff is subjected to the hydrostatic pressure of this unusually high water column. The absence of any forward thrust of the water mass under these conditions is shown by the behavior of boats which have been observed to rise and fall with successive waves without touching the vertical wall only a few feet distant. Hagen concludes that under such circumstances débris must accumulate at the base of the wall and that therefore the prejudice against vertical sea walls and harbor walls, based on the fear of undermining by wave action, is ill-founded.
—DOUGLAS W. JOHNSON, *Shore Processes and Shoreline Development*, p. 57

That is part of an informative treatment of wave action, accurate and compact. It would be read, however, only by someone who was consciously looking for knowledge of the subject. The following passage is intended for a more general audience, though one limited to people of some intelligence and with a definite interest in more than the superficial appearance of their world. The facts are presented with a minimum of technical language and made more vivid by familiar comparisons ("rather like relays of messengers . . .").

These molecules move with very high speeds; in the ordinary air of an ordinary room, the average molecular speed is about 500 yards a second. This is roughly the speed of a rifle-bullet, and is rather more than the ordinary speed of sound. As we are familiar with this latter speed from everyday experience, it is easy to form some conception of molecular speeds in a gas. It is not a mere accident that molecular speeds are comparable with the speed of sound. Sound is a disturbance which one molecule passes on to another when it collides with it, rather like relays of messengers passing a message on to one another, or Greek torch-bearers handing on their lights. Between collisions the message is carried forward at exactly the speed at which the molecules travel. If these all traveled with precisely the same speed and in precisely the same direction, the sound would of course travel with just the speed of molecules. But many of them travel on oblique courses, so that although the average speed of individual molecules in ordinary air is about 500 yards a second, the net forward velocity of the sound is only about 370 yards a second.—SIR JAMES JEANS, *The Universe Around Us*, p. 90

For a still more popular audience the subject matter must be further simplified and the facts made dramatic, if possible, by being presented in action. Some technical words are used, but they seem to be incidental, even decorative, rather than fundamental as in formal scientific writing. The beginning of a discussion of coal-tar dyes illustrates this popular approach to scientific discussion:

If you put a bit of soft coal into a test tube (or, if you haven't a test tube, into a clay tobacco pipe and lute it over with clay) and heat it you will find a gas coming out of the end of the tube that will burn with a yellow smoky flame. After all the gas comes off you will find in the bottom of the test tube a chunk of dry, porous coke. These, then, are the two main products of the destructive distillation of coal. But if you are an unusually observant person, that is, if you are a born chemist with an eye to by-products, you will notice along in the middle of the tube where it is neither too hot nor too cold some dirty drops of water and some black sticky stuff. If you are just an ordinary person, you won't pay any attention to this because there is only a little of it and because what you are after is the coke and gas. You regard the nasty, smelly mess that comes in between as merely a nuisance because it clogs up and spoils your nice, clean tube.

Now that is the way the gas-makers and coke-makers—being for the most part ordinary persons and not born chemists—used to regard the water and tar that got into their pipes. They washed it out so as to have the gas clean and then ran it into the creek. But the neighbors—especially those who fished in the stream below the gas-works—made a fuss about spoiling the water, so the gas-men gave away the tar to the boys for use in celebrating the Fourth of July and election night or sold it for roofing.—EDWIN E. SLOSSON, *Creative Chemistry*, p. 60

Beyond such popularizations are the sensational treatments of scientific subjects which we associate with the magazine sections of some Sunday papers. Because of the cheapness and the inaccuracy of many of these articles, scientists and scholars have tended to scorn all popularizing of their materials. But in recent years there has been an increase of reliable and interesting scientific writing for general readers as more specialists have found a challenge in seeing how much of their subject matter they can find a way of conveying to a general reader. They are now leaving less of the work of popularizing to writers not sufficiently trained to do it well.

Until a person can write with authority about a specialized subject, he will most likely be doing popular or semi-popular articles. Students in college can try their hand at preparing material for a somewhat limited but non-professional group of readers. The style of such papers would be rather formal, and it has one real danger. The necessity for using genuine scientific words often leads to using *unnecessary* *big words. Writers in the social sciences especially have substituted unfamiliar words or *long variants for words of the general English vocabulary, as in "It is necessary to structure into a complex culture like ours a congruent hospitality to change in all institutional areas." If such writers would only visualize their readers, they would make more use of the general English vocabulary. Professor Ballard (p. 199) puts the general principle from the reader's point of view: "and when the common language fails in clearness, in dignity, or in freedom from ambiguity, it should be eked out by the language of the laboratory and of the study. Technical jargon is an evil, but a necessary evil. And necessary evils should be kept to a minimum." It is worth trying to see how much of your specialized information you can make available to an intelligent general reader.

An increasing number of jobs now depend on some ability to write adequately scientific or technical letters, reports, or articles. The director of research in a large corporation says:

> If you can't tell in written or oral English what your results are, it is impossible to get along in any industry. For instance, the laboratory worker must submit a condensed report of his experiments to his laboratory head. This man must in turn condense the reports of many workers and send a new report on to his superior. And so on, all the way up the line. If you can't put your thoughts and figures on paper in concise readable language, you're sunk.

See "Formal English," p. 25; "Big words," p. 220; "Abstract and concrete words," p. 223; "Shoptalk," p. 24.

References: Dobrée, pp. 85-94; Trelease, S. F. and Yule, Emma S., *Preparation of Scientific and Technical Papers* (3rd edition; Baltimore, 1936). Trelease and Yule has a useful Bibliography, pp. 116-18.

Seasons *Spring, summer, fall, autumn, midsummer,* and so on are not capitalized except for stylistic emphasis, as sometimes in poetry or nature essays.

seem *Seem* is often used as a counter verb, making a statement needlessly qualified or distant:

> Today in the newspapers we read a great deal about the German and Italian governments, the heads of which seem to be holding [that is, *are holding*] a series of meetings in Rome and Nuremberg.

In such a use *seem* is *deadwood. Compare *happen.

Can't seem is an illogical but useful informal and colloquial idiom for "be unable."

I can't seem to learn physics.

Segregating sentences Rather short sentences, carrying typically one principal statement and its modifiers, are called *segregating*, as contrasted with longer, more elaborate *aggregating* sentences. See "Sentence weight," p. 151.

self *Self* as a suffix forms the reflexive and intensive pronouns: *myself, yourself, himself, herself, itself, oneself, ourselves, yourselves, themselves*. These are used chiefly for emphasis (I can do that myself) or as a reflexive object (I couldn't help myself). *himself, herself, *myself

Self as a prefix is usually hyphened to the root word:

self-control   self-explanatory   self-made   self-respect

When *self* is the root word there is no hyphen:

selfhood   selfish   selfless   selfsame

Semantics The study of the meaning and changes in meaning of words. See Chapter 7, p. 182.

semi *Semi-* is a prefix meaning "half or approximately half" (*semicylindrical*), "twice within a certain period" (*semiweekly, semiannual*) or "partially, imperfectly" (*semicivilized, semiprofessional*). It is not usually hyphened except before proper names (*semi-Christian*) or words beginning with *i* (*semi-invalid*).

Semicolon (;) (CORRECTION: Use a semicolon as the mark of separation between these sentence elements.)   *Semi*

A semicolon is used to mark a degree of separation between sentence elements considerably greater than that marked by a comma, nearly as great as that marked by a period. There are a few situations in which a semicolon is usually found, but the chief question regarding its use is of appropriateness to traits of style (§4):

1. To SEPARATE UNITS THAT CONTAIN SMALLER ELEMENTS SEPARATED BY COMMAS. These may be items in a series, enumerations, figures, scores, or clauses with commas within them:

Other periodicals not entirely dissimilar were John Harris's *The English Lucian*, 1698; Ward's *Weekly Comedy*, 1699; "Sylvester Partridge's" *The Infallible Astrologer*, 1700; and the *Merry Mercury*, 1700.—GEORGE CARVER, *Periodical Essays of the Eighteenth Century*, p. xviii

Three things which a social system can provide or withhold are helpful to mental creation: first, technical training; second, liberty to follow the creative impulse; third, at least the possibility of ultimate appreciation by some public, whether large or small.—BERTRAND RUSSELL, *Proposed Roads to Freedom*, p. 169

It is two very simple things one would ask of the general reader— merely to be discontented with short cuts to literature; stories that are told just to fill out ingenious plots, poems that rephrase platitudes, essays that are smart but get nowhere—all writing that is machine-made, insincere, sloppy, meretricious, flat, stale, and unprofitable; and next, to ask for beauty in the right sense, to ask that a story or a poem be beautiful as a cathedral, a sword, a steel building, a race horse, an automobile, a carved gem can be beautiful.—H. S. CANBY, *Saturday Papers*, pp. 41-42

His [the Englishman's] character is like his climate, gentle and passing readily from dull to glorious, and back again; variable on the surface, yet perpetually self-restored and invincibly the same.— GEORGE SANTAYANA, *Soliloquies*, p. 38

2. TO SEPARATE COORDINATE CLAUSES NOT CLOSELY RELATED. *a*) Between contact clauses. A semicolon is used, especially in somewhat formal writing, between two *contact clauses (clauses with no expressed connective) if the separation in thought and structure is conspicuous. Usually the two statements could stand as separate sentences but the writer wishes to have them considered part of one idea. Contrasting statements are often punctuated with semicolons, as in the first of these examples:

Words and sentences are subjects of revision; paragraphs and whole compositions are subjects of prevision.—BARRETT WENDELL, *English Composition*, p. 117

Your religion does not promise you a perfect life on earth, nor free-dom from suffering; it does guarantee you the strength to bear suffer-ing. Your religion does not expect you to be free from sin or mis-takes in judgment; it does promise you forgiveness for your mistakes. Your religion expects you to continue making the best efforts you can on behalf of others; it does not guarantee that you or anyone can arrange the lives of people as he pleases.—HENRY C. LINK, *The Return to Religion*, pp. 68-69

The campus Nietzsche, at thirty, begins to feel the suction of Rotary; at forty he is a sound Mellon man; at fifty he is fit for Congress.—H. L. MENCKEN, *Prejudices: Sixth Series*, p. 66

See "Contact clauses," p. 136 and "Comma faults," p. 138. *b*) With heavy connectives. A semicolon is used between clauses connected by the weightier conjunctive adverbs (*however, more-over, nevertheless, consequently, . . .*). These are heavy connectives and usually link rather long clauses in a formal style.

This program implies better orientation of individuals to the manifold problems of adjustment; therefore, certain character traits, as well as specific abilities, should show positive change.—*The English Journal*, June 1937

In order to act properly he needs to view his act as others view it; namely, as a manifestation of a character or will which is good or bad according as it is bent upon specific things which are desirable or obnoxious.—JOHN DEWEY, *Human Nature and Conduct*, p. 121

A comma is now usually more common between clauses connected by the lighter conjunctive adverbs (*so, then, yet*). *Conjunctive adverbs

c) With coordinating conjunctions. A semicolon is used between clauses connected by coordinating conjunctions (*and, but, for, or,* . . .) if the clauses are long or if the connection is not close, or if for some reason (often for contrast) the writer wishes to show an emphatic separation between them.

History as actuality includes all that has been said, felt, done, and thought by human beings on this planet since humanity began its long career; and, if Darwin is right, since the evolution of the human organism began in the primeval dawn.—C. A. BEARD, *The Discussion of Human Affairs*, p. 69

She already had some furniture of her own, including what she could take from Truda; and Louis could let her have some of his—yes?—G. B. STERN, *The Matriarch*, p. 199

Therefore those teachers who cannot admit that they may be wrong should not teach English composition; nor should those who never suspect that their pupils may be abler than they.—L. R. BRIGGS, *To College Teachers of English Composition*, p. 19

The semicolon is used to separate parts of the sentence which are of more importance, or which show a division more distinct, than those separated by commas; or to separate sections already separated by commas.—JOHN BENBOW, *Manuscript & Proof*, p. 89

3. Semicolon and colon. Do not use a semicolon, which is a mark of *separation* as the examples in this article show, for a colon (:), which looks ahead, is a mark of *anticipation*:

There are two principal considerations in the use of semicolons: the degree of separation to be indicated between statements and the formality of the style of the passage.

4. SEMICOLONS AND OTHER TRAITS OF STYLE. Except for the specific situations described in §1, the use of semicolons is in part a stylistic matter. They are more appropriate, more necessary, in rather formal styles and in long, aggregating sentences. They tend to slow up the reading and are consequently fewer in narrative than in exposition. In informal styles commas would be used in preference, or if the distinction between the clauses is considerable two sentences would be written. In the following paragraph Mr. Cowley has chosen to rely on semicolons. In brackets are put commas and periods that might have been used in a more informal writing of the same passage.

College students inhabit an easy world of their own; [.] except for very rich people and certain types of childless wives they form the only American class that takes leisure for granted. Many, of course, earn their board and tuition tending furnaces, waiting on table or running back kick-offs for a touchdown; what I am about to say does not apply to them. The others—almost always the ruling clique of a big university, the students who set the tone for the rest—are supported practically without efforts of their own. They write a few begging letters; [,] perhaps they study a littler harder in order to win a scholarship; [,] but usually they don't stop to think where the money comes from. Above them, the president knows the source of the hard cash that runs this great educational factory; [.] he knows that the stream of donations can be stopped by a crash in the stock market or reduced in volume by newspaper reports of a professor gone bolshevik; [.] he knows what he has to tell his trustees or the state legislators when he goes to them begging for funds. The scrub-women in the library, the chambermaids and janitors, know how they earn their food; but the students themselves, and many of their professors, are blind to economic forces; [.] society, as the source of food and football fields and professors' salaries, is a remote abstraction.— MALCOLM COWLEY, *Exile's Return*, pp. 36-37

Students tend to use more semicolons than would be used by professional writers today in informal writing. They should consider the weight of the mark in view of the general movement of their writing and make sure that the movement of the particular sentence needs the degree of separation marked by the semicolon.

Compare *Comma, *Colon.

S Sentences (CORRECTION: Correct or improve the obvious fault in the sentence marked.)

The characteristics and problems of sentences are discussed in Chapters 5 and 6 under the following heads:

CHAPTER 5, Sentence Form: (1) "Definition," p. 115; (2) "Sentence elements," p. 119; (3) "Order of sentence elements," p. 122; (4) "Coordination and subordination," p. 124; (5) "Parallelism in sentence form," p. 128; (6) "Incomplete sentences," p. 131; (7) "Run-on sentences," p. 136; (8) "Writing and revising sentences," p. 141; "Exercises," p. 142.

CHAPTER 6, Qualities of Sentences: (1) "Sentence weight," p. 151; (2) "Variety in sentence movement," p. 155; (3) "Sentence economy," p. 161; (4) "Sentence emphasis," p. 165; (5) "Sound and rhythm," p. 174; (6) "Good sentences," p. 177; "Exercises," p. 178.

Many articles in the index discuss specific traits of sentences, such as *Conjunctions, *Dangling modifiers, *Participles, *Subject and verb.

Sentence outline   *Outline form §1c

Sequence of tense   *Tenses of verbs §2, *Questions §3

Separation for emphasis   *Emphasis §4; *Semicolon §2; "Separation of elements," p. 171

Series   Commas are used between the items of a series of three or more short items:

> The reason Odets has gained and held a public that by & large, does not share his Leftish ideas is obviously not the ideas themselves but his [three parallel adjectives:] *rich, compassionate, angry* [three nouns:] *feeling for people, his tremendous dramatic punch, his dialogue,* bracing as ozone.—*Time,* Dec. 5, 1938

> The supposed contents of the physical world are *prima facie* very different from these: [four short clauses:] *molecules have no colour, atoms make no noise, electrons have no taste, and corpuscles do not even smell.*—BERTRAND RUSSELL, *Mysticism and Logic,* p. 145

Usage is divided over the use of a comma before the last item of such a series. Many writers, especially in an informal style, do not use one:

> The danger of war did not loom as it loomed in 1915, but press, pulpit [,] and meeting house were the scenes of spontaneous outbursts.—*Time,* Nov. 28, 1938

If the members of the series are long, or not closely connected, or if the members have commas within them, they are separated by semicolons:

> Why, I am asked, do we read history and biography; what is the secret of their perennial charm; why is it that since almost the beginning of recorded time they have been the most permanent and most popular of all forms of literature?—W. C. ABBOTT, *The Bookbuyer,* Christmas 1935

For further examples and details see *Comma §2, *Semicolon §1.

Reference: R. J. McCutcheon, "The Serial Comma Before 'and' and 'or,'" *American Speech,* 1940, xv, 250-54

service The verb *service* (to service a car, a refrigerator) is commercial but needed and appropriate in business English. It means more than *repair* and has a different connotation from *maintain* or *keep up.*

set, sit People and things *sit* (past, *sat*) or they are *set* (past *set*), that is, "placed":

> I like to sit in a hotel lobby.
> I have sat in this same seat for three semesters.
> She set the soup down with a flourish.
> The post was set three feet in the ground.

A hen, however, *sets* [on her eggs]. In vulgate usage *set* is generally used for both verbs.

sh *Sh* is a digraph for a sound which has nothing to do with either *s* or *h*: *shall, shove, ash.* The *sh*-sound is represented by various spellings: *machine* (mə shēn'), *tissue* (tish'ū or tish'ü), *conscientious* (kon'shi en'shəs). Compare *zh.

shall—will, should—would The usage of *shall* and *will, should* and *would* has never been uniform in English, although some grammarians have attempted to insist on uniformity. The general practices in the more common situations needing these words are as follows:

1. INFORMAL AND COLLOQUIAL USAGE. (*a*) *Simple future.* In speech and informal writing the prevailing use in the United States, and in many other parts of the English-speaking world, is to use *will* in all persons:

FIRST PERSON:	I will ask	we will ask
SECOND PERSON:	you will ask	you will ask
THIRD PERSON:	he, she will ask	they will ask

This informal usage would appear in more printed matter if editors did not revise the copy to bring it in line with their stylebooks.
b) *Emphatic future.* In expressing determination in the future or for some special emphasis, informal and colloquial usage is divided. In speech the determination is expressed by stress, which may be used on either word: I shall' go, I will' go. There is some tendency to use *shall* in all persons as the emphatic form: I, you, he, she, we, you, they *shall* ask. Other words (I have to go . . .) are also used.
c) *Contractions.* In speaking and in informal writing where contractions are used, the future becomes *I'll, you'll, he'll,* and so on. *Won't* is used for *will not* (formed from an obsolete *woll* and *not*) and *shan't* for *shall not.*

d) In questions. *Shall* is likely to be used in the first and third persons, and *will* in the second in asking questions, but practice is not consistent:

> Shall I go?   Will you go?
> What shall we do now?   What will you do now?
> What shall he do?   What will he do with it?

In the negative, *won't* is the more common:

> Won't I look funny in that?   What won't he think of next?

2. Formal usage. In formal English some writers and editors use *shall* in the first person, *will* in the second and third persons in making the future tense, following handbook "rules" rather than actual usage.

First person:	I shall ask	we shall ask
Second person:	you will ask	you will ask
Third person:	he, she will ask	they will ask

In the emphatic future, expressing determination on the part of the speaker, formal English theoretically reverses this use of *shall* and *will*:

First person:	I will ask	we will ask
Second person:	you shall ask	you shall ask
Third person:	he, she shall ask	they shall ask

In asking questions a few people use the form of *shall* or *will* in a question that the answerer would use in his reply. This usage is distinctly formal and usually sounds unnatural.

> Shall you go? Answer: I shall (shall not) go.

3. Other forms of the future. The present tense is sometimes used to express future time, especially the progressive form:

> I am asking for a raise tomorrow.   I go next week.

Idioms with *go* and *be* are also used for the future:

> I am going to ask for a raise.   There is to be a dance Friday.

These various forms are used in all levels.
Shall is usual in laws, resolutions, etc.:

> A permanent organization shall be set up within a year.
> No singer shall receive more than $700 a performance.

4. Future expressing doubt. *Should* and *would* are used in statements that carry some doubt or uncertainty about the statement made. They are also used in polite or unemphatic requests:

> They should be there by Monday. [Contrast: They will be there by Monday.]

721

Would you please shut the door on your way out? [Contrast: Will you please . . .]

In the first person both *should* and *would* are used:

I would be much obliged if you could do this.
I should be much obliged if you could do this.

Usage is so much divided on the choice between these forms that one's feeling is probably the safest guide.

5. OTHER USES OF SHOULD AND WOULD. *Should* as an auxiliary used with all persons expresses a mild sense of obligation, weaker than *ought*:

I should pay this bill. [Contrast: I ought to pay this bill.]

In indirect discourse *should* and *would* represent the future tense of the direct speech:

DIRECT: "I will be ready at three," Mildred said.
INDIRECT: Mildred said that she would be ready at three.

Would has some currency in a colloquial or half-humorous idiom "that would be her picture," meaning "That is her picture, isn't it?"

References: Much has been written about the use of these words. As a beginning: Curme, *Syntax*, pp. 362-71; Fries, pp. 150-68 (a good short summary of actual usage); C. C. Fries, "The Expression of the Future," *Language*, iii, 87-95; Jespersen, Chs. 25, 26; Amos L. Herold, *The English Journal*, 1936, xxv, 670-76; Robertson, pp. 516-20.

shape Colloquial and informal in the sense of "manner, condition": They were in good shape for the trip.

Shift **Shifted constructions** (CORRECTION: Make the constructions marked consistent [parallel] in form.)

Elements of a sentence that have the same relationship to the statement being made should be expressed by words in the same grammatical construction; that is, the constructions should be parallel. (The two *should be* constructions in the preceding sentence are parallel.) Adjectives should be paralleled by adjectives, nouns by nouns; a specific verb form should be continued in a similar construction; active or passive voice should be kept consistently in a sentence or passage; and so on. Shifting from one form to another may confuse a reader and anyway it is a failure to follow conventional patterns of writing. Shifts can be removed in revision.

Some commonly shifted constructions are:

SHIFT IN SUBJECT: Once the car is started, you will get along all right.

CONSISTENT: Once you get the car started, you will get along all right.

ADJECTIVE TO NOUN: This book seems interesting and an informative piece of work.

CONSISTENT: This book seems interesting and informative.

SHIFT IN NUMBER: Japan [singular] had no desire to meet an equal force of the Allies, but as long as they [plural] hold numerical superiority they will fight daringly.

CONSISTENT: The Japanese [plural] have no desire . . .

PERSONAL TO IMPERSONAL: In fact going to summer school is worse than no vacation at all, for when you have no vacation you do not think about all the things a person could do if he had one.

CONSISTENT: . . . for when you have no vacation you do not think about all the things you could do if you had one.

PERSONAL TO IMPERSONAL: He immediately told his companions of the vast amount of water power these falls represented, and as they were a thrifty lot, it was decided to import a herd of sheep and manufacture woolen blankets.

CONSISTENT: . . . and since they were a thrifty lot, they decided to import a herd of sheep and manufacture woolen blankets.

ADVERB TO ADJECTIVE: Along these walks are the cottages, many of which have stood since the founding [adverbial phrase], and others more recent [adjective].

CONSISTENT: . . . many of which have stood since the founding, and others of which have been built more recently.

NOUN TO ADVERB: The association with these fellows [noun] and how to adapt myself to live with them [adverbial phrase] in itself will help me when I am through college.

CONSISTENT: Association with these fellows and adapting myself to live with them in itself will help me when I am through college.

NOUN TO ADJECTIVE: Anyone who has persistence [noun] or who is desperate enough [adjective] can get a job on a ship.

CONSISTENT: Anyone who is persistent or who is desperate enough . . .

NOUNS TO A CLAUSE: The most important factors are time and temperature, careful control at every point, and the mechanical equipment must be in perfect operating condition at any time of the day or night.

CONSISTENT: . . . and mechanical equipment in perfect operating condition at any time of the day or night.

PARTICIPLE TO CLAUSE: How many times have you seen a fisherman trying to get to his favorite fishing spot without scaring all the fish away but instead he sends out messages with his rhythmical squak-splash, squeak-splash.

CONSISTENT: . . . but instead sending out messages . . .

PARTICIPLE TO CLAUSE: I have heard complaints about the plot being weak and that the setting was played up too much.

CONSISTENT: . . . and the setting being played up too much.

For other examples see "Parallelism in sentence form," p. 128.

Ships' names The names of ships are indicated in three ways. In most books and generally in formal writing they are italicized (underlined in the manuscript):

> The *Caryatid*, in ballast, was steaming down the river at half-speed . . .—William McFee, *Casuals of the Sea*, p. 317

> Three vessels will carry on the popular "around South America" fad—the *Columbus*, the *Rotterdam*, and the *Gripsholm*.—*Business Week*, Nov. 6, 1937

In newspapers and personal writing there is a growing tendency to regard the names of ships simply as proper names, capitalizing them but not otherwise setting them off:

> The Columbus, before the advent of the Bremen and Europa, was the largest vessel in the German merchant marine.—*New York Herald Tribune*, Nov. 7, 1937

> The Queen Mary has three more round trips to make this year . . . —*The New York Times*, Nov. 7, 1937

Occasionally ships' names are found in quotation marks:

> The summer of 1926 David spent as a junior member of the American Museum Greenland Expedition, . . . on the stout little schooner "Morrissey." [Jacket of *David Goes to Greenland*. In the book *Morrissey* is italicized.]

Shoptalk *Shoptalk* is the colloquial language of people used in, or in talking about, their particular occupations. For discussion see "Shoptalk," p. 24.

should—would *shall—will §§4, 5, *Subjunctives §1*b*

show Colloquial, or theatrical shoptalk, in the sense of "a play" and usually humorous or vulgate for a dignified public performance, as of a concert; informal when applied to the movies (short for *picture show*). Informal and colloquial for "chance" (They didn't have a show of winning).

show up Colloquial for *appear* (He didn't show up for two hours) and for *expose* (I showed him up, all right).

sic *Sic* (Latin for *thus, so*; pronounced sik) in brackets is sometimes used to mark an error in quoted matter: The letter was headed "Danbury, Conneticut [*sic*], Jan. 2."

sick *Ill* is the more formal word. The two words mean the same, except that colloquially and in British usage *sick* is often specialized to mean "nauseated."

significant Spelled with one *g* and one *c*.

Silent letters Written English is particularly rich in silent letters, that is, letters which do not represent any speech sound. A few of them are the result of mistaken analogies, like the *s* of *island*, which is there from confusion with the French *isle*, though it comes from Old English *iglond* and has never had a pronounced *s*. Renaissance scholars inserted a number of letters that had been in the Greek and Latin words from which the English words were descended but which had never been sounded in English: Chaucer could write *det*, but we must write *debt* because the scholars recognized the word's descent from *debitum*.

But most of our silent letters act, as Professor Lounsbury put it, "as a sort of tombstone to mark the place where lie the unsightly remains of a dead and forgotten pronunciation": the pronunciation has changed but the spelling hasn't or hasn't changed exactly. There they stand, those final *b*'s in *bomb, comb, climb*, the initial *g*'s and *k*'s in *gnarl, gnash, knack, knave, knee, knife, knuckle*, the *p*'s in Greekish words like *pneumonia* and *psychology*, the *gh*'s in *through* and *night* and *caught* that mark former pronounced gutterals.

Silent letters are sometimes defended because they tend to keep a word in touch with its ancestry, but that fact is of use only to scholars, and there are not enough scholars to pay to spell the language for them. Some people think these spellings have an esthetic value, that *night* has a beauty not in *nite* or that the superfluous *h* gives *ghost* a special weirdness. But this reason doesn't seem very substantial, since we learn these words from hearing them, and whatever quality *ghost* has as a word comes more likely from the tone in which we heard it spoken.

These silent letters are gradually being dropped, quietly, surreptitiously almost. *Apophthegm* has recently lost its *ph*—it may sometime lose its *g* too. In familiar writing *altho* is quite common; business and familiar English use *nite* and other shortened forms. But most of the silent letters hold firm, making spelling difficult. Sometimes people who are not familiar with the sound of a word are led to pronounce a silent letter, giving a "spelling pronunciation," as pronouncing *indict* in dikt′ instead of in dīt′.

See "Inconsistencies in English spelling," p. 267; *Pronunciation §4d.

Reference: For groupings of silent letter words see W. A. Craigie, *English Spelling*, pp. 36-39, 67-73; Kennedy, pp. 241-47.

similar The last syllable is *-lar*. Do not confuse in spelling with *familiar*. Note the pronunciations: sim′ i lər, fə mil′yər.

similar to A wordy way of saying *like*: It was my first wreck and I hope I may never have another similar to that one [like it].

Similes See "Metaphors, similes, analogies," p. 235.

Simple sentences A simple sentence contains one grammatically independent statement (The man went across the street).

Simple sentences do not need to be bare, like those in a first reader. The subject or the verb may be compound, and either or both may be modified. Here are some sentences that from a grammatical point of view are equally "simple," though they vary in the amount of meaning they carry:

There are two or three large chests, a bedstead, the inevitable cradle occupied by the latest addition to the family. The small windows are seldom curtained. There are shelves for pots and pans, spoons and forks (often wooden), jars of gherkins, bottles of this and that, loaves of bread, sacks of flour, baskets of dried fruit.—Louis Adamic, *The Native's Return*, p. 271

(In the first sentence *occupied* is not a principal verb but a participle, modifying *cradle*.)

Italy and Germany rather than France and England took the lead in the Spanish Revolution. The narrow-minded attitude of the Baldwin Government toward the Duke of Windsor stirred increasing resentment abroad and in the dominions. Recovery had slowed down and was accompanied by labor difficulties.—*Kaltenborn Edits the News*, p. 123

See *Compound predicate, *Compound subject, "Segregating sentences," p. 151.

since *because

Singular number *Plurals, *Reference of pronouns, *Subject and verb, *Collective nouns, *Verbs

situated is often deadwood:

I was staying with friends in a little town in Canada called Picton, [situated] in the Province of Ontario.

It was a biplane and the front cockpit was [situated] right over the lower wing.

size As an adjective, *size* (a small size hat) is colloquial, typical of shoptalk. *Sized* would usually be the written form (a small sized hat).

ski Plural *skis*, sometimes *ski*. Verb: *ski, skied, skiing*. Pronunciation skē, or sometimes, following the Scandinavian, shē.

Slang Slang includes new words used principally for their novelty or force or color. They are natural and appropriate in rather light speech and writing, especially of sports, informal social activities, and the doings of young people. They are out of place in formal writing and should not be used in informal writing unless they add a quality that is appropriate and that the writer wishes. For further discussion, see p. 23.

slow, slowly Both *slow* and *slowly* are adverbs, each going back to an Old English adverb form (*slaewe* and *slaewlice* respectively). Use whichever sounds better in the sentence. *Slow* is rather more vigorous: *Go slow.* See *Adverbs, types and forms § 3.

Slurred vowels A good many words give spelling trouble because they contain various spellings for the vowel sound represented in this book by ə: ə kad′ə mi (*academy*). These are standard pronunciations, so that no drill in sounding the syllable can help. A number of these words are related to others in which this syllable has a stress, so that the vowel stands out. Such pairs as the following may help you to spell accurately the vowel italicized in the first word:

academy—academic	affirmative—affirmation
angel—angelic	apology—apologia
comparable—compare	competition—compete
definitely—definition	degradation—degrade
democracy—democratic	despair, desperation—desperado
dormitory—dormir (French)	extravagance, extravagant—
fertile—fertility	extravaganza
hypocrisy—hypocritical	laboratory—laborious
medicine—medicinal	preparation—prepare
ridicule—ridiculous	repetition—repeat
vigilance—vigilantes	

But for the great majority of words with slurred vowels either a good memory or a good dictionary is essential.

smart *Smart* is in general use in such idioms as *a smart child, a smart pace, the smart set, a smart thing to do.* It is a localism for "large, considerable": *a smart (or, right smart) crop.*

so *So* is not much used as a conjunction in formal English for two reasons: It is a word of many uses and consequently not very exact or emphatic in any one; it is overworked in colloquial English, often as a substitute for more definite words.

So is used colloquially as a subordinating conjunction to introduce clauses of purpose:

COLLOQUIAL: He started early so he could get good seats.
FORMAL AND INFORMAL: He started early so that he could get good seats; . . . in order to get good seats; . . . to get good seats.

So is more common in clauses of result, in which written English would usually have *so that* or change to a *since* construction:

COLLOQUIAL: I wondered what they would do with the logs, so I followed them through the woods.
INFORMAL AND FORMAL: Since [Because] I wondered what they would do with the logs, I followed them through the woods.
COLLOQUIAL: He is a fast reader, so he got through before I did.
INFORMAL: Since he is a fast reader, he got through before I did.
He is a fast reader, so that he got through before I did.
FORMAL: Since [Because] he is a rapid reader, he finished before I did.

As a coordinating conjunction, *so* is used in garrulous narrative, in colloquial and vulgate speech:

So we went out the Burlington road and pretty soon we got hungry. So we stopped and got some hot dogs . . .

This overuse of *so* is known as the "so-habit." In tightening up such narrative most of the *so*'s can be dropped; usually the sentences need to be completely reworded.

As an intensive ("feminine *so*"), *so* is also colloquial and often suggests schoolgirl style:

The poetry of Morris and Swinburne reads so much faster than most of Arnold's does. [. . . reads much faster (or: can be read much faster than most of Arnold's)]
We were so tired. [Contrast the informal: We were so tired that we didn't know what to do, or, We were so tired we didn't know what to do.]

Reference: Fries, pp. 226-27

so-called If you have to use *so-called*, don't duplicate the idea by putting the name of the so-called object in quotes: Not *the so-called "champion,"* but *the so-called champion.* The word is rather stiff, and in informal writing quotation marks would often be used instead (the "champion").

So-called is usually hyphened when it precedes its principal word but not when it follows:

Their so-called liberal views were merely an echo of the conservative attitude. [Their "liberal" views were . . .]
Their justice, so called, smacked of partiality.

so . . . that When several words come between *so* and *that* no comma should precede *that*:

All strands of the story are so interwoven [ ] that anything but the author's desired effect is impossible.

Social correspondence 1. INFORMAL NOTES. The form and tone of informal social notes—invitations, answers to invitations, thank-you letters—are those of familiar letters. (*Letters §§1 and 2) Giving all the necessary information of time, place, and so on, promptness in answering notes, and a tone of courtesy are more important than mechanical form. If the people concerned are not intimately acquainted, a somewhat formal tone and more details of address may be needed than when they are intimates. The first note below is written to an intimate acquaintance; the other two passed between teacher and student.

Dear Helen,

My sister will be home this weekend, and I am planning a little tea for her on Saturday afternoon at four o'clock. I should be very glad if you could join us at that time and help celebrate the homecoming. Please let me know if you can come.

Affectionately yours,
Dorothy

Dear Helen,

I am having a little supper-party for my voice students next Sunday evening, and I hope that you will be able to come. We shall eat at six o'clock and later listen to a special broadcast of fine voices that should give us some helpful pointers. The program won't be long; so if you have an engagement later in the evening this should not interfere.

Cordially yours,
Marian Hall

Dear Miss Hall,

Thank you for your invitation for Sunday evening. As luck would have it, though, our sorority is giving a Pledge Banquet that same evening and it is obligatory that I attend. Consequently I'm afraid I cannot be at your home then. I am sorry to have to miss it, for home cooking is such a treat and I wanted so much to hear the broadcast.

Very sincerely yours,
Helen James

2. FORMAL NOTES. Formal social correspondence—announcements, invitations, answers to invitations—is impersonal and standardized. It is used for social events indicating, usually, formal dress or a gathering with distinguished guests. The illustration shows the characteristic form of a printed or engraved invitation. Names are given in full, dates and other numbers are written in words, no punctuation is used at the ends of lines. Usually a reply is requested, either by *R.S.V.P.* ("répondez, s'il vous plait") or by *The favor of a reply is requested*. The engraver will help with the style of the note.

Delta Kappa Epsilon

requests the pleasure of your company

at a reception

in honor of

John Hughes Hunter

on Friday, the twenty-sixth of May

at eight o'clock in the evening

The favor of a reply
is requested

If the note is in longhand, the form of engraved notes is still followed.

Miss Jeanette Ames
Miss Eva Loy
request the pleasure of
Mrs. Henry Jackson's
company at a Breakfast Bridge
on June twenty-eighth
at the Kingston Club. Ten o'clock

In answering an invitation the form of the invitation is adopted, and the exact words are followed so far as possible. The names, dates, and place are repeated.

730

Mrs. Henry Jackson accepts with pleasure the kind invitation of Miss Jeanette Ames and Miss Eva Loy to a Breakfast Bridge on June twenty-eighth at the Kingston Club.

Solecism An error in use of words or constructions

some, and compounds with some 1. In formal and informal written English, *some* is usually a pronoun (Some buy ink indifferently) or an adjective (some people, some ideas).

2. As an adverb, *some* is in good informal use with comparatives (It was some better than I expected), for the more formal *somewhat*. It is informal and colloquial when used with verbs (We traded some that afternoon). It is slang as a heavily stressed adverb (We were going some', I was some' tired).

3. The compounds *somebody, someway, somewhat, somewhere* are written as one word. *Someone* (Someone is coming) is usually one word but may be two if the *one* is stressed (Some one of them). Someday is written as one word or as two.

4. *Some place* is colloquial and vulgate for *somewhere*. *Someway* and *someways* are colloquial, and *somewheres*, vulgate.

Compare *any, and compounds with any.

sooner (than) After *no sooner* the connective used is *than*, not *when*:

The fly had no sooner hit the water than [not *when*] a huge trout snapped at it.

sophomore In spite of the dictionaries, *sophomore* is generally pronounced as two syllables, sof'mōr. The word is both noun and adjective. The adjective *sophomoric* refers to supposed undesirable traits of sophomores, as in *a sophomoric style* or *sophomoric conduct*.

sort *kind, sort

sort of *kind of, sort of

sort of [a] *kind of [a], sort of [a]

species *Species* has the same form in both singular and plural, though some distinguish in pronunciation: singular, spē'shiz; plural, spē'shiz or spē'shēz.

Specie (spē'shi), meaning money in coin, is a different word, a collective noun without plural form.

Spelling (CORRECTION: Correct the spelling of the word marked, *Sp* referring to a dictionary if necessary.)

731

Chapter 10, p. 267, describes some of the general characteristics of English spelling and makes some specific suggestions for improving spelling habits. It is useful also to study groups of words that have some trait in common. The following index articles treat such groups. Those marked † give the most useful rules or suggestions for mastering large groups of words.

-able, -ible (desirable, legible)

Accent marks in spelling (as in words from French, like *café*): See Foreign words in English §§ 3*b*, 4.

-ae-, -oe- (ameba, esthetic)

† al ly (fatal, politically)

American and British usage (color, colour; theater, theatre)

-ance, -ence (attendance, existence)

Apostrophe (Bob's picture, the companies' charter)

-cal, -cial (musical, judicial)

Capital letters

† -ce, -ge (peaceable, courageous)

Contractions (didn't, he'll)

Dieresis (reëxamine)

† Doubling final consonants (refer—referred)

† E § 5 (silent or mute *e*) (changeable, likeness)

ed (exceptions to rule)

† -ei-, -ie- (achieve, feign, receive)

en-, in- (encourage, inquire)

-er, -or (debater, objector)

-er, -re (luster, scepter)

Foreign words in English (chauffeur, ersatz)

† Homonyms (words pronounced alike but spelled differently: plain, plane; altar, alter)

Hyphen (re-enter, father-in-law, forty-seven)

in-, un- (incapable, unedited)

-ize, -ise (apologize, advertise)

-le words (meddle, nickel)

-or (-our) (honor, Saviour)

-ough (-augh) (although, cough)

Plurals (beauties, birches, heroes, knives)

re- (reform, re-form)

Silent letters (debt, night)

† Slurred vowels (comparable, repetition)

Besides these general articles there are a number of brief comments on particular words, such as *all right, *fiancé, *glamor, *species.

The following list contains many words that give difficulty in spelling. It is not exhaustive and is by no means a substitute for a dictionary, but it can be used as the basis for a discussion of spelling. Perhaps it can be most useful if you check the particular words in it that you are not sure of and occasionally skim through those to fix them better in mind. In the margins add others that have troubled you—in every way possible make it *your* list.

* means that there is a separate article in Part 2 of this book, discussing that word.

A dash separating two words (*adviser—advisor*) means that the two forms are about equally common.

A second form in brackets (*encyclopedia* [*encyclopaedia*]) means that the form in brackets is now less common than the other.

A few words are identified by pronunciation or definition in parentheses.

absence
accessible
accidentally
accept (receive)
access (admittance)
accommodate
accustom
ache
acquainted
across
adaptation
*address
advice (noun)
advise (verb)
*adviser—advisor
*affect (to influence)
aggravate
aggression
aggressor
*airplane [aeroplane]
aisle (of a theater)
alcohol
allege
all ready
already
*all right
allusion
alma mater
altar (of a church)
alter (to change)
*although—altho
altogether
*alumnus, alumni,
  alumna, alumnae
amateur

analogous
analogy
analysis
analyze [analyse]
anesthetic [anaes-
  thetic]
angel (ān'jəl)
angle (ang'gəl)
announcer
annual
answer
antecedent
antiknock
anxiety
apology
apparatus
apparent
appearances
appreciate
arctic
argue
argument
aroused
article
ascent (going up)
ascertain
asinine
assassin
assent (agreement)
association
*athlete
athletics
attacked
attendance
attendant

attorney
attractive
audience
autobiography
auxiliary

bachelor
balance
baritone [barytone]
believe
benefited
berth (a bed)
better [bettor] (noun)
bibliography
birth (being born)
breath (breth)
breathe (brēŦH)
bridal (of a bride)
bridle (of a horse)
brilliant
Britain (Great
  Britain)
Briton (a Britisher)
bureau
*bureaucracy
*bus, buses—busses
business

café
cafeteria
calendar (of days)
can't
çanvas (sailcloth)
canvass (to go about)
capital (city)

733

capitol (building)
captain
carburetor [carburettor]
carriage
casualties
ceiling
center [centre]
challenger
champagne
chieftain
changeable
*chaperon
characteristic
characterize
chauffeur
choose, choosing
(present)
chose, chosen (past)
cigaret—cigarette
cocoa
coercion
collar
collegiate
*colonel
color
colossal
*column
comedy
commit
committee
comparative
compel
compelled
competitor
complaint
complement (to
fill out)
compliment (to
praise)
concede
conceive
concerto (kon cher′tō)
connoisseur
conqueror
conscience
conscientious
consciousness
consistent

contemptible
control, controlled
cooperative—
co-operative
[coöperative]
corps (kōr)
corpse (kōrps)
corrugated
costume
council (a group)
councillor—councilor
counsel (advice)
counselor—counsellor
courteous
courtesy
crept
curricular (adjective)
*curriculum (noun)
curtain
custom
cylinder
cylindrical

dairy (dār′i)
damned
debater
deceased (də sēst′)
deceive
decent (dē′sənt)
decide, decision
defendants
*definite
definition
dependent (adj. or
noun)
descent (də sent′)
*descendant
describe, description
desert (dez′ərt, waste)
desert (də zėrt′,
leave)
despair, desperate
dessert (də zėrt′, of a
meal)
develop [rare:
develope]
dexterous—dextrous
diagrammatic

diaphragm
diary (dī′ə ri)
die, dies, dying
dietitian [dietician]
dilapidated
*dining room
dinning (noise)
diphtheria [diftheria]
dirigible
disappearance
disappointment
disastrous
disciplinary
discretion
diseased (di zēzd′)
disgusted
dispatch [despatch]
dissipate
distributor
disturbance
divine
doctor
dominant
don't
dormitory
dry, drier, driest
dual (two)
duel (fight)
dye, dyed, dyeing

echo, echoes
ecstasies
effect (*affect)
eligible
eligibility
embarrass
emphasize, emphatic,
emphatically
employee, employees
[employé, em-
ployés]
encyclopedia [ency-
clopaedia]
energetic
enforce
engraved
environment
equipment

equipped
especially
esthetic—aesthetic
exaggerate
examine, examining,
    examination
exceed, excessive
excel, excellence
except (to omit)
exhausted
exhilarating
existence
expeditionary
*extracurricular
extravagant
extremely
exuberance

facile, facility
fairway (golf)
fallacy
familiar
fascination
February
*fiancé, fiancée
fiery
financier
flier—flyer
fogy [fogey] (fō′gi)
forehead (for′ed)
foreign
forfeit
formally
formerly
forty four—forty-four
fracas
frame house
frantically [franticly]
fraternities
*freshman
fulfill—fulfil
fundamental
furniture
futurity

gage—gauge
gelatine—gelatin
ghost

ghostlike
*grade school—
    graded school
grammar, gram-
    matical
*gray [grey]
grandeur
grief, grievous
gruesome [grew-
    some]
*guarantee
guardian
guerilla (fighting)
guidance

handicap, handi-
    capped, handi-
    capping
handkerchief
    (hang′kər chif)
handsome (han′səm)
*hangar
harassed (har′əst or
    hə rast′)
*height
heinous (hā′nəs)
hindrance
hoard
hoarse (in throat)
horde
hors d'oeuvre
horizontal
huge
human (hū′mən)
humane (hū mān′)
hurriedly
hygiene
hypnosis, hypnotic,
    hypnotize [hypno-
    tise]
hypocrisy, hypocrite,
    hypocritical
hysterical

illiterate
illogical
imaginary
imagination

immediately
implement
impromptu, im-
    promptus
inadequate
incessantly
incidentally
incredible
independence
indictment
indispensable
ingenious
ingenuous
initiation
innuendo, innuendoes
inoculate
intellectual
intelligent
intern [interne]
interpretive [inter-
    pretative]
intolerance
inventor—inventer
irrelevant
irreligious
irresistible
irreverent
itself

jalopy—jaloppy
johnnycake
jollity
judgment
    [judgement]

khaki
kidnap, kidnaped—
    kidnapped, kidnap-
    ing—kidnapping
kimono, kimonos
*kindergarten
kitchenette
    [kitchenet]
knowledge
knuckles

laboratory
ladle (lā′dəl)
later (lā′tər)

735

latter (lat'ər)
laurel
laxative
*lead
led
legacy
legitimate
leisurely
liable
liar
librarian
lightening (a load)
*lightning (a flash)
likable [likeable]
liqueur
liquor
livelihood
loneliness
loose (lüs)
*lose (lüz)
lunatic

mackerel
magazine
magnificent
maintain, mainte-
    nance
maneuver
    [maneuvre]
mantel (the shelf)
mantle (the cloak)
manual
manufacturer
mean, meant
medieval [mediaeval]
mediocre
Mediterranean
metal
mettle
millionaire
miniature
minute
mischievous
misspelled
mold [mould]
moral (mor'əl)
*morale (mō ral' or
    mō räl')

mortgage
motto, mottoes—
    mottos
mountainous
murmur
muscle
musical (adj.)
musicale (noun)
mustache—moustache
mysterious

*naive—naïve
naphtha [naftha]
necessarily
*Negro, Negroes
neither
*nickel
niece
ninety ninth—ninety-
    ninth
noticeable
notoriety

obbligato—obligato
obedience
obey
obliged
obstacle
*occasion, occasion-
    ally
occur, occurred,
    occurring
official
oily
omit, omitted,
    omission
oneself
opportunity
optimism
organization [organ-
    isation]
organize [organise]
origin, original
outrageous

*paid
pajama [pyjama]
pamphlet

pantomime
parallel, paralleled
*parliament
paroled
participate
particularly
*passed, past
pastime
pedestal
perform
permissible
perseverance
persistent
personal
personnel
perspiration
persuade, persuasion
Philippines
physician
piano, pianos
pickle
picnic, picnicked
pique (pēk)
piqué (pē kā')
plaguey
plain
plane
playwright
pneumatic
pneumonia
politics
possibility
potato, potatoes
preparation
*practical
practicability
practice [practise]
preceding
preference
prejudice
presence
prevalent
primitive
*principal
principle
privilege
probable, probably
professor

program [pro-
gramme]
pronounce
pronunciation
propaganda
propeller
protein
psychoanalysis
psychoanalyze
psychology
publicly
pumpkin
pursue, pursuit

quantity
quantum
quarantine
quay [quai] (kē)
quiet
quite
quixotic
quiz, quizzes

realize
really
*receipt, recipe
receive
recipient
reclamation
recognition
recommend
re-enter
refer, referred,
reference
reforestation
regional
relevant
religious
reminisce
*Renaissance—
Renascence
rendezvous
repellent
repetitious
reservoir
resistance
reverent
respectfully

respectively
restaurant
rhetoric
*rhyme, rime
rhythmical
ridiculous

sacrilegious
salary
sandwich
saxophone
scandalous
scar (skär)
scare (skār)
scenario
scenic
schedule
secretarial
seize
semester
senator
sensible, sensibility
separate
sergeant (sär'jənt)
severely, severity
shear
sheer
sieve
*significance
*similar
sincerely, sincerity
sirup—syrup
site (of a city)
*ski, skis [ski]
skeptical [sceptical]
slimy
sluggish
soccer
soluble
sophistication
*sophomore
speak, speech
specifically
specimen, specimens
specter [spectre]
spicy, spiciness
sponsor
staccato

stationary (fixed)
stationery (paper)
statue
stature
statute
stomach-ache
story [storey] (of a
building)
stretched
studying
subsidize, subsidization,
subsidy
subtle [subtile]
succeed, success
*suit (sūt)
suite (swēt—sūt)
sulfur—sulphur
superintendent
supersede
suppose
suppress
surprise
susceptible
syllable
symbol
symmetry, sym-
metrical
syphilis

taboo [tabu]
tariff
technique [technic]
temperamental
*theater [theatre]
their
there
therefore
they're
thorough [thoro]
though—tho
thousandths
through—thru [thro]
to, too, two
today [to-day]
together
traffic, trafficking
tragedy, tragic
tremendously

737

truly
Tuesday
typical
tyranny

undoubtedly
unprecedented
until (*till)
usually
utensil

vacuum
vegetables
vengeance
ventilate, ventilation
vertical

vice (evil)
vigilance
vigilantes
vilify
villain
*vise [vice] (the tool)
visibility
*vitamin [vitamine]
volume

warfare
warring
warrior
weather
weight, weighty
weird

whether
whoop
whose
who's (who is)
woolen [woollen]
woolly—wooly
write, writing,
written
wrought

yacht
you're (you are)

zoology [zoölogy],
zoological

Besides the articles listed on p. 732, the following articles have lists that may be used to supplement this spelling list:
*Foreign words in English §4
*Principal parts of verbs
*Pronunciation §5

Spelling pronunciation *Pronunciation §4d

Split infinitive The word order in which an adverb comes between the *to* and the verb in an infinitive (She asked them *to please sit down*) is called a split infinitive. Awkward split infinitives are avoided:

AWKWARD: After awhile I was able to, although not very accurately, distinguish the good customers from the sulky ones.
IMPROVED: After awhile I was able to distinguish—though not very accurately—the good customers from the sulky ones.

Since the adverb modifies the verb, its natural position seems to be next to the verb. Changing the position of *eventually* in this sentence would result in awkwardness:

He requested the Ministry of Forests to reforest the barren mountains in Macedonia in order to eventually eliminate the mosquito-breeding swamps.—LOUIS ADAMIC, *The Native's Return*, p. 321

References: Curme, *Syntax*, pp. 458-65; Fowler, "Split Infinitive" (for overprecise distinctions); Fries, p. 132

spoonful, spoonfuls The standard plural of *spoonful, tablespoonful, teaspoonful,* is *spoonfuls, tablespoonfuls, teaspoonfuls.* Similarly, *basketfuls, carfuls, cupfuls, shovelfuls, tubfuls*

Colloquially *cupsful, carsful, shovelsful* and so on are often heard.

Squinting modifier *Ambiguity §2

Staccato style A staccato style has—as its principal characteristic —short, emphatic sentences, often exclamations or questions, usually without expressed connectives between the statements. The words, especially verbs, are likely to be vigorous. It is effective in short passages that deserve sharp stressing but is likely to be tiresome and to lose its emphasis if it is long continued.

> Hindenburg was shortening his lines. He was quitting northern France and Belgium. But he was holding the Argonne. Day by day the representatives of our G. H. Q. had shown us the map with every enemy division and reserve force marked. Hindenburg had thirty-two reserve divisions at the beginning of our Argonne drive. When November began two or three remained. What had become of an army of German reserves?—GEORGE SELDES, *You Can't Print That!* p. 35

Compare *Telegraphic style.

Standard English In so far as *Standard English* is a useful term it applies to the language that is used in the conduct of public affairs, that is used in the various types of literature, in periodicals and books, in speeches, in letters and documents. In this sense it corresponds roughly to the combined Formal and Informal levels of usage and excludes Vulgate. See p. 38 for further discussion.

still *Still* is an adverb in the sentence "It's still raining" and a conjunction (*conjunctive adverb) in "I can see your point of view; still I don't agree with you."

stomach No final -*e*. But *stomach-ache*

stop *Stop* is colloquial in the United States in the sense of "stay" (We stopped two days in Los Angeles). It is the normal British usage.

story A *story* is a narrative of either real or imaginary happenings. Typically we think of a story as an imaginary tale, a short story or novel, though a newspaper account of actual events is a news story.

A discussion of ideas may be an editorial, an article, a critical article, a review, a treatise, but it is not a story. A poem would be referred to as a story only if it was a narrative, and though plays are stories, their special form calls for reference to them by their proper name. Try to keep *story* for its real meaning.

strata *Stratum* is the singular, *strata* its plural.

street In many newspapers and in some informal writing, *street* is not capitalized as part of an address (41 High street). In formal writing it would be capitalized.

The abbreviation *st.* is not much used except to save space in lists or reference works.

Stress *Pronunciation § 4, *b, c*; *Rhythm; *Noun and verb stress

Strong verbs See *Principal parts of verbs.

Structural words *Function words

Style Style has been defined in a number of well-known aphorisms: "Proper words in proper places make the true definition of a style" (Jonathan Swift); "Style is the dress of thoughts" (Lord Chesterfield); "Style is this: to add to a given thought all the circumstances fitted to produce the whole effect that the thought ought to produce" (Stendhal); "Style is the ultimate morality of mind" (A. N. Whitehead); and the most often quoted of all, "The style is the man" (Comte de Buffon).

Such definitions are good starting-points for discussion, and they suggest ideals that may guide a person's thought and perhaps his practice. But whatever *style* may mean to critics and philosophers, for a student or writer it is most helpfully taken, in a more concrete sense, to mean a speaker's or writer's use of language, the sources of the listener's or reader's impressions of his manner of thought and expression. The connotation of *style* is of the effectiveness of the expression (rather than of description of usage or questions of correctness). An analysis of style takes into account the qualities of words, phrases, idioms, sentences, and arrangement of material.

The following adjectives are often used in describing qualities of style. Some of them are words of general meaning that are applied to style (*flat, mature*); others are technical words for qualities of language (*allusive, archaic, precious, trite*); several of them are practically synonymous (*verbose—wordy, local—provincial*). With many of the words you will be already acquainted; the meaning of the others you can find from class discussion, from referring to a good dictionary, or from the pages given to treatments in this *Guide and Index.*

*abstract, pp. 188, 223
*academic
affected
*alliterative
allusive, p. 241
amateur
Anglo-Saxon
archaic, p. 4
awkward
careless

*clear
climactic, p. 173
*colloquial
complex
concise, p. 161
concrete, pp. 187, 223
difficult
dignified, p. 25
direct
easy

economical, p. 161
elementary
*emphatic, p. 165
*epigrammatic
euphonious, p. 174
exact, p. 194
*experimental
figurative, p. 229
flabby, p. 214
flashy, p. 23

flat	loose	riming
fluent	mannered	*schoolgirl
formal, p. 25	mature	*scientific
graceful, p. 174	metaphorical, p. 235	self-conscious
*heightened	*monotonous, p. 155	simple
highflown	natural, p. 47	slangy, p. 23
*humorous	nervous	smart
*idiomatic	old-fashioned, p. 4	smart-Aleck
*imagistic	*onomatopoetic, p. 564	smooth
*imitative	overloaded	solid
immature	overmodified, p. 361	sophisticated
impersonal, p. 43	pedantic	*staccato
informal, p. 12	pithy	stiff
interrupted, p. 157	poetic	*suggestive
involved, p. 157	pompous	*technical
ironical, p. 238	precious	*telegraphic
*journalese, p. 606 §2	precise	trite, p. 214
*journalistic, p. 606 §1	prosaic	varied, p. 155
juvenile	provincial, p. 6	verbose
*Latinized	purple	vulgate, p. 20
literal, p. 186	repetitious, p. 168	weak
local, p. 6	*rhythmical, p. 166	*wordy

To discuss the style of a passage, read it attentively for a general impression. Then read it once or more slowly to note the qualities of words, phrases, sentences, perhaps marking some that attract particular attention or that are good illustrations of the qualities you find. Test your original impression in the light of this analysis. Try not to let an interest in details blind you to general qualities of style.

References: Dobrée (the best introduction); Rickert; many articles in Fowler; works on literary criticism.

Stylebooks For editors and printers *style* means the method of handling various mechanical matters such as capital letters, punctuation, forms of plurals, division of words, details of typography. Since usage is divided on many of these points, a publisher chooses what form will be used in his publications. Most newspapers, magazines, and publishing houses have stylebooks—documents ranging from a single page to elaborate volumes containing the particular rules to be followed in preparing copy for specific publications. They often show arbitrary choices, to attain a consistency that most publishers feel is desirable. One factor in recent changes in practices in writing and printing has been the decision of some of the newer publishers to let authors' copy stand nearly as written, so long as it is consistent.

Most newspaper stylebooks are not generally available, though that of *The Detroit News* is for sale, and a *Deskbook* is published by the University of Missouri School of Journalism. The University of Chicago Press *Manual of Style* (frequently revised) is the most influential stylebook among book publishers. John Benbow, *Manuscript & Proof* (New York, 1937), representing the style used by the American Oxford University Press, is a briefer and more modern stylebook.

S&V Subject and verb (CORRECTION: Make the subject and verb of this clause or sentence agree according to the principles given in §2 below.)

1. SUBJECT AND VERB AS SENTENCE ELEMENTS. The backbone of the typical English sentence is a subject and a verb. (For exceptions see p. 131, "Verbless sentences," and p. 133, "Subjectless sentences.") The subject names the starting point of the action or statement, and the verb advances the statement by specifying an action, state, feeling, or the existence of whatever the subject names. Except in inverted sentence order (pp. 123, 156) the subject stands before the verb and we identify it as the subject because of this position, as the *object follows the verb. In the sentence

> The submarine sank the cruiser

we know that the submarine and not the cruiser did the sinking because *submarine* is in the subject position in the sentence.

Simple sentences have one subject and one verb, though either or both may be compound, that is, the subject may consist of more than one noun word, or there may be more than one verb to one subject:

ONE SUBJECT AND ONE VERB: (s) *Six cars* (v) *passed* in the next fifteen minutes.
    (s) *Two of the men,* unfortunately, (v) *had* never *played.*
COMPOUND SUBJECT: (s1) *Freshmen* and (s2) *sophomores* take military training.
COMPOUND PREDICATE: All freshmen (v1) *room* in dormitories and (v2) *eat* at the Commons.
COMPOUND SUBJECT AND COMPOUND PREDICATE: (s1) The *fleet* and (s2) the *air force* together (v1) *sank* or (v2) *damaged* twenty-one Japanese ships.

Compound sentences have more than one independent subject-verb element, joined in some way to show their grammatical equality:

    (s1) *The first two drafts* of the article (v1) *were* impossible, but (s2) *the third* (v2) *showed* some promise.

Complex sentences have one or more independent clauses and one or more subordinate clauses. In the following sentence the subjects and verbs of the independent clause and of five subordinate clauses are marked:

(s of independent clause) Such *knowledge* of my own countrymen as (s1) I (v1) *have acquired* while reaching a ripe middle age (v of independent clause) *convinces* me that (s2) *one of the most cogent reasons* against the imposition of harsh measures of repression on the German people as a whole (v2) *is* that (s3) *the British people* (v3) *will* after a very short period *refuse* to enforce them, and that (s4) *the counter-reaction* (v4) *may* again, as in the few years preceding the present conflict, *lead* to an attitude of leniency (s5) *which* (v5) *is* almost indistinguishable from careless indifference to consequences— SIR ANDREW MCFADYEAN, "Don't Do It Again!" *The Atlantic Monthly*, Nov. 1941, p. 575

In some statements *there* stands as an *anticipatory subject*, the real subject following the verb:

There are (real subject:) men of all schools of opinion.

For further discussion see Chapter 5, Sentence Form, p. 115, and Part 2 articles such as *Compound predicate, *Compound sentences, *Compound subject, *Complex sentences, *there is, there are.

2. AGREEMENT OF SUBJECT AND VERB. A verb agrees with its subject in number and person. This usually means with the grammatical number of the subject. Since, except for the verb *be*, our verbs have one form for both numbers and for all persons except the third singular present, relatively few problems in agreement can arise.

SINGULAR: *I am* more tired than usual. A *chair was placed* in the corner. *This job takes* four weeks. *The job took* four weeks.

PLURAL: *We are* more tired than usual. *Three chairs were placed* along the wall. *These jobs take* four weeks. *The jobs took* four weeks.

The problems that arise in agreement of the subject and verb are either from a sentence form in which the grammatical number of the subject is uncertain or is blurred by the presence of other words, or from agreement with the meaning of the subject rather than with its grammatical form.

a) *Collective nouns.* Agreement according to meaning is seen most clearly in collective nouns, which take either a singular or plural verb, depending upon whether the speaker or writer is emphasizing the group as a whole or the individuals of which it is composed. Obviously the verbs and pronouns of a given sentence should be all plural or all singular in referring back to a collective subject.

EMPHASIZING THE UNIT: The class *is* the largest in six years.

EMPHASIZING THE INDIVIDUALS: The class *are* by no means all intellectual giants.

For further examples and discussion see *Collective nouns.

b) *Compound subjects*. Ordinarily a compound subject has a plural verb:

Alice and Francis *were* the first to arrive.

The text of the poem and the commentary *make* quite a sizable volume.

When the two elements of a compound subject refer to the same person or thing, the verb is singular:

The best teacher and the best scholar here *is* Professor Babcock.

The spirit and accomplishment of these men *speaks* for itself.

The verb is often singular when the compound subject follows:

There *is* both health and wealth in this way of life.

For the winner there *was* a large cash prize and weeks of glory.

When a second part of the subject is connected with the first by *with, together with, as well as,* the agreement varies. In formal English such a construction is kept singular. In informal English a plural is often found if the expression is equivalent to a compound subject:

The rudder is the only essential control in taxiing, and this together with a regulative speed *keeps* the plane going in a relatively straight line.

The winner with the four runners-up *were* given a reception. (To make this more formal, the *with* should be changed to *and*, rather than the *were* to *was*.)

He is not an impressive speaker, since his hesitating manner with long "uh's" interspersed in the address *make* [FORMAL: *makes*] him rather difficult to listen to.

Subjects connected by *or* take a singular verb if both are singular, a plural verb if both are plural or if the one nearest the verb is plural:

A novel or a biography *is* to be read outside of class.

Novels or biographies *were* the same to him.

A novel or five short stories *were* to be read.

In questions in colloquial usage the plural is common:

Are Fred or Harry in?

c) *Plural modifier of singular subject.* When a rather long plural modifier of a singular subject comes between it and the verb, formal English has a singular verb, but informal and colloquial has often a plural verb.

This *group* of essays *is* [not *are*] concerned with problems in sociology and philosophy as they are related to biology.

The *form* of your bibliography and footnotes *is* not standard.

To a beginner on the organ the array of stops and pistons, manuals, couplers, and pedals *seems* [colloquial: *seem*] at first quite bewildering.

Two thousand dollars *worth* of pictures *were* [FORMAL: *was*] destroyed.

In colloquial and vulgate English the plural is used with constructions with *kind* and *sort*:

This kind of shoes are a good deal more comfortable.

*kind, sort

d) *Relative pronouns.* A relative pronoun referring to a singular noun has a singular verb (The person *who takes* enough pains can do it) and one referring to a plural noun has a plural verb (The people *who take* pains win in the long run). In idioms like "This is one of the most discouraging things that has come out of the situation," formal usage has *that have come*, since the antecedent of *that* is *things*; informal and colloquial usage often has *that has come*, because the central idea (of *one*) is singular.

FORMAL: Jeffrey is one of those moderns *who are* making their money talk.

COLLOQUIAL: Jeffrey is one of those moderns *who is* making his money talk.

See *Synesis.

e) *Subject and complement or predicate of different number.* The verb agrees with the subject:

A day's work is four trips.   Four trips make a day's work.

f) *Plural subject with singular meaning.* When the idea conveyed by a plural subject is singular in intent, the verb is singular:

Late hours was getting them down. [Equivalent to: It was late hours that was getting them down.]

References: Curme, *Syntax*, Chapter 4; Fries, pp. 188-90, 249-50, and index references; Pooley, pp. 78-85

3. PUNCTUATION BETWEEN SUBJECT AND VERB. Since the subject and verb are part of one construction, they should not normally be separated by a comma:

Another example of what can happen [ ] is furnished by the experience of two young women who were staying at the hotel.

Occasionally in formal writing a comma is used after a long or complicated subject, but it is rarely, if ever, necessary:

The weekend which eight members of the club had been anticipating for months [,] had finally arrived.

See *Comma §5.

4. STYLISTIC COMMENTS. (*a*) *Decrease in number of verbs.* The number of verbs in typical English sentences has conspicuously decreased in recent years. The first two sentences of *Robinson Crusoe* (1719) contain eleven verbs, besides two participial phrases that are not counted:

I (1)was born in the year 1632, in the city of York, of a good family, though not of that country, my father being [participle] a foreigner of Bremen, who (2)settled first at Hull. He (1)got a good estate by merchandise, and leaving [participle] off his trade, (2)lived afterward at York, from whence he (3)had married my mother, whose relations (4)were named Robinson, a very good family in that country, and from whom I (5)was called Robinson Kreutznaer; but, by the usual corruption of words in England, we (6)are now called—nay, we (7)call ourselves, and (8)write our name Crusoe, and so my companions always (9)called me.

Nineteenth-century prose, in spite of conspicuous exceptions in writers like Macaulay, shows a general tendency to *aggregating sentences. Since the writers were fond of full grammatical constructions, they tended to use several verbs in a sentence. The following passage from Cardinal Newman's *The Idea of a University* (1852) has three sentences with six, five, and thirteen verbs respectively:

This then (1)is how I (2)should solve the fallacy, for so I (3)must call it, by which Locke and his disciples (4)would frighten us from cultivating the intellect, under the notion that no education (5)is useful which (6)does not teach us some temporal calling, or some mechanical art, or some physical secret. I (1)say that a cultivated intellect, because it (2)is a good in itself, (3)brings with it a power and a grace to every work and occupation which it (4)undertakes, and (5)enables us to be more useful, and to a greater number. There (1)is a duty we (2)owe to human society as such, to the state to which we (3)belong, to the sphere in which we (4)move, to the individuals towards whom we (5)are variously related, and whom we successively (6)encounter in life; and that philosophical or liberal education, as I (7)have called it, which (8)is the proper function of a University, if it (9)refuses the foremost place to professional interests, (10) does but postpone them to the information of the citizen, and, while it (11) subserves the larger interests of philanthropy, (12) prepares also for the successful prosecution of those merely personal objects, which at first sight it (13) seems to disparage.

Current prose will average a little over two verbs to a sentence. A fairly typical paragraph shows that the sentences are shorter, more compact, and that the number of verbs is smaller, in the following paragraph ranging from one to four with an average of two:

Imbeciles (1) are not different in kind from normal folk, only in degree. Between the idiot and the man of exceptional ability (1) stretches an unbroken series of graded types. The method of teaching which (1) is found suitable for the lowest type (2) will be suitable—with proper modifications—for the highest. If the best way of teaching deficients (1) is to interest them in what they (2) have to learn, then that (3) is also the best way of teaching the normally and abnormally intelligent. It (1) pays to treat the minds of idiots as though they (2) were delicate living organisms requiring careful nurture; it (3) does not pay to teach mechanically, even when such teaching (4) is backed by threats and flagellations. Imbeciles (1) cannot learn, even after countless repetitions, the things which (2) do not interest them. The same (1) applies to more intelligent children. True, they (1) are intelligent enough to learn something, even when the teaching (2) is dull, mechanically repetitive, and brutal. But they (1) would learn more if they (2) were taught by the same methods (*mutatis mutandis*) as have (3) proved successful in the training of imbeciles.—ALDOUS HUXLEY, *Proper Studies*, pp. 101-102

This paragraph suggests that many ideas are now expressed in phrases or single words that might formerly have been, or that today in a formal style might be expressed in clauses. Mr. Huxley's phrases in the left-hand column below might have been the clauses written in the right-hand column:

HUXLEY'S PHRASES	SYNONYMOUS CLAUSES
only in degree	they are different only in degree
with proper modification	if properly modified
the normally and abnormally intelligent	those who are normally and those who are abnormally intelligent
requiring careful nurture	that required careful nurture
True	It is true that

Some of these changes are economical, and some tend toward abstractness (as "with proper modification" instead of "if properly modified"), but whether effective or not, modern writers show a tendency to use relatively few clauses.

b) Unnecessary verbs. Verbs that add nothing to the meaning of a sentence are fairly common in amateur writing and like other specimens of deadwood, tend to make the style heavy. The verbs in brackets in the following sentences could well be omitted:

Let me make clear what I mean [when I mention] "democracy." (*When I mention = by*)

The cars with two-wheel brakes cannot stop so quickly as those [do] [which have] four-wheel brakes. [. . . as those with four-wheel brakes.]

In 1917 a drought [occurred that] brought a scarcity in wheat and sent prices sky-high. In the two succeeding years still more serious droughts [occurred which] wiped out many a winter-wheat farmer.

The central office of the organization [is] in New York [and] is in communication with all American and foreign branches of the company.

In revision such unnecessary verbs can be deleted.

c) Verbs that count. Verbs that contribute to the meaning tend to make a style more active and more concrete and may often replace abstract nouns (as *if properly modified* might replace *with proper modification*). *Constructions with verbs should ordinarily be kept for statements that are of major importance, since a clause gives somewhat more emphasis than a phrase.* The quotations in this *Guide and Index* from current writers are worth examination for their use of verbs.

References: Gardiner, Chapter 5; Otto Jespersen, *The Philosophy of Grammar* (New York, 1924), Chapter 10; L. A. Sherman, *Analytics of Literature* (Boston, 1893), Chapters 19-26

Subjective case *Nominative case, *Subject and verb

Subjectless sentences See "Subjectless sentences," p. 133.

Subjects of papers See "Focusing on a subject," p. 292, and "Subjects of research papers," p. 322.

Subjunctives Subjunctive verb forms have been used to show some attitude of feeling or doubt of the speaker toward the statement he is making.

1. FORM OF SUBJUNCTIVES. (*a*) *Simple subjunctive:* In current English the subjunctive form of a verb is identifiable only in certain forms of the verb *be* (If I, you, he . . . *be*, If I, he . . . *were*), and in forms, made with *to be* (If he *were asking*) and in the third person singular (If he *ask* instead of the indicative If he *asks*, If he *have* instead of If he *has*).

b) Subjunctive with auxiliaries: Some grammarians include as subjunctives all the locutions that can be used in expressing ideas

748

that may also be, or have at some time been, expressed by the subjunctive, or the forms that could be used in translating subjunctives found in other languages. Under this system several auxiliaries—*may, might, should, would, let, have to,* and others— become subjunctives. This broad interpretation makes consideration of the subjunctive more complicated than is necessary, since the meaning and connotation come from the meaning of the auxiliary or from adverbs. For that reason, in the following discussion only the simple subjunctive is considered.

References: For argument in favor of confining *subjunctive* to the simple forms, see Otto Jespersen, *The Philosophy of Grammar,* pp. 315-21, and for description of the subjunctive with auxiliaries, Curme, *Syntax,* Chapter 20.

2. Uses of the subjunctive. English makes much less use of the subjunctive mood than most of the modern European languages do. There are a number of idioms in which the subjunctive may be used in English, especially in formal English. It is common in wishes, conditions, qualified or doubtful statements, and in *that*-clauses and after expressions like *It is necessary.* The following examples illustrate typical uses of the subjunctive and give alternative idioms that would be more common in informal and colloquial usage.

a) *Formulas.* The subjunctive is found in numerous formulas, locutions surviving from a time when the subjunctive was used freely. Most of these are no longer general idioms; that is, we do not make other sentences on the pattern of *Far be it from me. . . .*

Far be it from me   Heaven forbid   If need be   Heaven help us
Be it said   Suffice it to say   God bless you

Many petty oaths have this form: *Confound it;* Grades *be hanged.*
   Some of these formulas are used in all levels of the language; some, like *Come what may,* are rather formal, and the oaths are chiefly colloquial.

b) *In that-clauses.* The subjunctive is used in many idioms for recommendations, resolutions, demands, and so on. These idioms are usually in a formal, often legal, context. Note the following examples:

FORMAL: We recommend that the Commissioner *designate* for this use the land formerly belonging to Mr. Brewster.
FORMAL: I suggest that he *watch* closely the movements of these troops.
FORMAL: I ask that the interested citizen *watch* closely the movements of these troops.

INFORMAL: I ask the interested citizen to watch the movements of these troops closely.

FORMAL: . . . the order that he *be* dropped.

INFORMAL: . . . the order to drop him.

FORMAL: It is necessary that every member *inform* himself of these rules.

INFORMAL: It is necessary for every member to inform himself of these rules—It is necessary that every member should inform himself of these rules—Every member must [should] inform himself of these rules.

c) In conditions. In formal English the subjunctive is used in *if*-clauses when there is doubt of fulfillment of the condition, or when the condition is "contrary-to-fact," that is, impossible (as in "If I *were* you . . .").

FORMAL: I had to do all this if I *were* to arrive in Hartwick by ten o'clock.

INFORMAL: I had to do all this if I *was* to arrive in Hartwick by ten o'clock.

FORMAL: The fellow who worked next to him in the plant had been turned off, and Jim could not help wondering if that *were* [Informal and more usual: *was*] a sign that some of the rest of them would be discharged, too.—ERSKINE CALDWELL, *Kneel to the Rising Sun,* p. 129

FORMAL: If correspondence *be* [More usual: *is*] necessary with this Bureau in regard to your Adjusted Compensation, you are respectfully requested to refer to A3380129.

FORMAL: If the subject of a verb *be* [More usual: *is*] impersonal, the verb itself may be called impersonal.—ARTHUR G. KENNEDY, *Current English,* p. 296

The subjunctive is most common in contrary-to-fact conditions.

If one good *were* really as good as another, no good would be any good.—IRWIN EDMAN, *Four Ways of Philosophy,* p. 80

There has recently been an increase in the use of the subjunctive in formal American writing, even in situations in which it has nothing to add to the meaning:

After the booker had collected his commission, if he *were* on a salary basis, he had to pay protection money to members of the combination.—ROBERT I. CENTER, *The Atlantic Monthly,* Oct. 1937

This usage has not been paralleled in recent British writing or in informal American usage. Many of these subjunctives have been inserted by editors and do not represent the usage of the writers of the articles in which they stand.

In all of these constructions a speaker or writer has a choice between the indicative (which may be an "auxiliary") or an infinitive and the subjunctive mood. In speech and in informal writing some idiom with the indicative would be more usual; in formal writing the subjunctive would probably be used. Professor Fries found that in both standard and vulgate English the subjunctive was found rather seldom, in considerably less than one fifth of the locutions in which it might be used. Students in foreign language courses should remember that very few French and German subjunctives can be satisfactorily translated by an English subjunctive form. They should try to find the natural, idiomatic English way of expressing the idea that is naturally and idiomatically expressed by the subjunctive in the language they are translating.

References: The point of view presented in this article will be found in general in Ballard, pp. 12-23; Fowler, article "Subjunctives"; Fries, pp. 103-107; Hall, pp. 311-14; Jespersen, Ch. 27; Leonard, p. 120; Pooley, pp. 61-64; Bevier, Thyra J., "American Use of the Subjunctive," *American Speech*, 1931, vi, 207-15. A different point of view will be found in Curme, *Syntax*, Ch. 20; Kennedy, §106; Lloyd, C. A., "Is the Subjunctive Dying?" *The English Journal*, 1937, xxvi, 369-73.

Submitting manuscript The conventions of submitting manuscript for publication are simple:

The manuscript should be carefully typed, double spaced, on good paper (*Typewritten copy). Generous margins should be left for editorial operations. Plenty of space should be left around the title, half a page or so. Keep a carbon copy for reference.

The writer's name and address stand in the upper left-hand corner. The approximate length in words may be put in the upper right-hand corner.

It is not necessary to inclose a letter with the manuscript, since its purpose is obvious, unless there are some useful facts to give, such as the sources of material or suggestions for illustration.

Mail in a comfortable-sized envelope. Short manuscripts can go in 9 inch envelopes, folded twice; those from 4 to 12 pages can go in envelopes about 6x9 inches, folded once; and longer ones in large envelopes, flat.

Photographs or drawings should be carefully packed between stiff cardboard, and clearly labeled.

Inclose an envelope large enough to hold the manuscript as it is folded, addressed to yourself, and carrying sufficient postage for its return. The editor will probably want to use it.

Subordinating conjunctions The most common subordinating conjunctions—words that connect subordinate clauses with the main clauses of sentences—are:

after	because	since	when
although	before	so that	where
as	how	though	while
as if	if	till	why
as long as	in order that	unless	

The relative pronouns (*who, which, that, what*) function also as subordinating conjunctions.

Sub **Subordination** (CORRECTION: Make the less important of these statements grammatically subordinate to the more important.)

Subordinate sentence elements modify the sentence as a whole, the subject, verb, object, or some other important element. They may be single words, or phrases, or clauses, but usually an important phrase (like a participial phrase) or subordinate clauses is meant. Subordinate clauses are introduced by the connectives listed in *subordinating conjunctions or by relative pronouns. They are used as nouns, adjectives, or adverbs.

The chief point to remember is that subordination should represent or correspond to a relationship between ideas. The more important should be in main clauses or principal words, the less important in subordinate constructions. The exact connective shows the thought relation to the rest of the sentence.

Problems of subordination are discussed specifically in "Coordination and subordination," p. 124, and in various articles including *Clauses, *Complex sentences, *Coordination, *Conjunctions, *and.

Substandard English See "Vulgate English," p. 20.

Substantive A substantive is a noun, or a word (pronoun, adjective, infinitive, . . .), or a group of words used as a noun. *Nouns, *Noun clauses

such As an intensive, *such* is colloquial and informal (It was such a hot day; such nice people). In formal writing the construction would be avoided or completed (Such nice people as they are). Accurate constructions with *such* are:

There was such a crowd that [not: so that] we couldn't even get to the door.

The invitation is extended to such non-members as are interested. (*As* is a relative pronoun. A more informal construction would be: The invitation is extended to all non-members who are interested.)

A good lecturer? There's no such thing. (*No such a thing* is colloquial and vulgate.)

Various possible constructions with *such* are rarely used and seem somewhat stiff and unidiomatic:

His condition was such that he could not be moved. [Better: His condition would not allow him to be moved.]

Psychologists could probably find various reasons why it is regarded as such. [. . . why it is regarded so.]

As a coordinating conjunction, introducing examples, *such as* has a comma before but not after:

He was interested in all sorts of outlandish subjects, such as palmistry, numerology, and phrenology.

Suffix A syllable that can be placed after a word or root to make a new word of different meaning or function: *-ize* (*criticize*), *-ish* (*foolish*), *-ful* (*playful*). *Origin of words § 3a

Suggestion Making use of the associations, the connotations of words, is called *suggestion*. The words *liberty, immemorial, mystical, butcher, homey,* and thousands of others have acquired associations from their past use that may call to a listener's or reader's mind some feeling or attitude that goes beyond their original core of meaning. Relying on suggestion may be misleading or at least may be a substitute for exactness, but a responsible use of suggestive words adds color and often pleasure and keeps writing from a dead flatness.

For discussion see "Connotation: The suggestion of words," p. 189, and especially p. 191. *Heightened style

suit, suite *Suit* is pronounced süt or sūt; *suite* (a group of attendants, a series of rooms, and so on) is swēt or süt, sūt. The latter pronunciation is more usual in commercial talk of a set of furniture.

Sunday school Capitalize only the *Sunday* except in names of particular Sunday schools:

Sunday school   the Methodist Sunday School

Superlative of adjectives and adverbs *Comparison of adjectives and adverbs. For the informal "absolute superlative" ("You are *most kind*") see that article § 3.

sure *Sure* is primarily an adjective: sure footing; Are you sure? As an adverb, *sure* instead of *surely* or equivalent to *certainly* or *yes*, is slangy colloquial (Sure, I'm coming; That sure is fine of you).

swim The principal parts are *swim, swam* or *swum, swum.* "He *swam* half a mile" is more common in writing than "He *swum* half a mile."

Syllabication *Division of words

Synecdoche See p. 238.

Synesis (sin'i sis) In vulgate English and to a less extent in informal English there is a tendency for constructions to follow the *meaning* rather than a custom of *grammar* that might apply. Following the meaning rather than grammatical convention is known as *synesis*. In earlier days, before so much stress had been put on correctness, this construction was pretty common and found in the best places: Then Philip went down to the city of Samaria and preached Christ unto *them* (Acts viii.5)—where the pronoun's grammatical antecedent is *city* (singular) but the meaning is plural, that is, he preached to the people of the city. A collective noun has a singular verb when the group is meant or a plural verb when the individuals are meant (The team leaves tonight—The team were completely worn out. All of his 160 pounds is bone and muscle). In *these kind of shoes,* the strict grammatical agreement would be *this kind,* but since we are talking about *shoes,* it seems natural to say *these.*

In formal English such locutions are out of place. In vulgate English they are the normal and proper expressions—and should be used in writing much dialog. Between the two extremes of style the problem of agreement is more complicated. The forces of the schools have been set firmly against some of the common idioms for so long that most educated readers will feel they are at least slipshod, even when difficult to spot (as in "one of the most important messages that *has* [for *have*] come out of Spain"). They cannot be objected to on the basis of meaning, because they make the meaning more sure than the more conventional construction. They are to be avoided in public writing because so many readers will object to them and because a writer ordinarily intends to follow the conventions of grammar as well as make his meaning clear. Sometimes in conspicuously informal writing they fit.

---

*Collective nouns, *kind, sort, *Reference of pronouns, *Subject and verb § 2

Synonym A synonym is a word that means almost the same as another word. For use of synonyms see "Synonyms," p. 192.

Syntax *Syntax* means the relationship between the words or other locutions in a sentence. Many articles in this *Index* discuss points of syntax, as, for example, *Adjectives, use; *Subject and verb; *Word order.

T (t) as in *type, quote, attach*.

D represents t after the sound of *f, k, p,* or *s* in the same syllable: *laughed, fixed, confessed, tipped, picked*. T is silent in *Christmas, often, listen, thistle, mustn't*, and many other words, and in ordinary speech in words like *sit down. Ti* is pronounced ch in such words as *question* and often sh (*nation, notion*). Compare *D.

taboo—tabu *Tabu* looks un-English and *taboo* is more generally used. Plural *taboos*; past tense of the verb, *tabooed*; pronounced tə bü′.

Tabulations Series of facts can often be more clearly presented in a table systematically arranged in convenient and meaningful columns. Any group of more than three or four numbers should be tabulated (See p. 154 for an example), and a series of short items, as below in *Tenses of verbs. Formal outlines are in tabular form, as at the head of the chapters in this book.

Occasionally in the body of a paper it is convenient to cast a series of parallel statements in a numbered tabulated form. The device should not be overworked, but it is a good way of securing emphasis by display:

> The English textbook of the future, to sum up, must recognize the social nature of language, and English in particular, by
>   1. acknowledging that language is the tool of the social group,
>   2. granting that utility is the only valid basis for the creation or perpetuity of a language form,
>   3. pointing out the part each individual speaker plays in the retardation or acceleration of change,
>   4. regarding the written language in its proper light as the secondary and partial representation of the real language.—ROBERT C. POOLEY, *Grammar and Usage in Textbooks on English*, p. 151

Tautology *Tautology* is unprofitable repetition of meaning (the *modern* college student *of today*). See "Repetition," p. 168.

taxi The plural of the noun *taxi* is *taxis*; as a verb, the principal parts are *taxi* (sometimes *taxy*), *taxied, taxiing* or *taxying*.

teach *learn—teach. The principal parts are *teach, taught, taught*.

Technical English *Scientific and technical writing, "Shoptalk," p. 24

technique—technic *Technic* (tek′nik) is a variant form of *technique*. It is also used, especially in the plural (*technics*), for *technology*.

Telegraphic style "Telegraphic style" refers to writing in which as many *function words are omitted as possible. It suggests also compact constructions and vigorous words. It is not appropriate in general writing but is used in some reference works to save space, for vigor in newspaper headlines ("U.S. Asks DuPont, Raskob Pay Taxes"), and occasionally in such styled writing as occurs in *Time*.

temperament In spelling get in the *a*.

Tense **Tenses of verbs** (CORRECTION: Make the tense of this verb conventional in form [§ 1] and consistent with others in the passage [§§ 2, 3].)

    1. FORMS OF ENGLISH. Except for the simple present and past tense forms, English verbs show distinctions of time by various phrase combinations, often supported by adverbs ("he is *about* to go" as a future). The following table presents the verb phrases most commonly associated with tense distinctions:

		ACTIVE	PASSIVE
PRESENT TENSE		he asks he is asking he does ask	he is asked he is being asked
PAST TENSES	*Past perfect* (Past of some time in the past)	he had asked he had been asking	he had been asked
	Past (A time in the past not extending to the present)	he asked he was asking he did ask	he was asked he was being asked
	Perfect (Past, extending to the present)	he has asked he has been asking	he has been asked
FUTURE TENSES	*Future* (Future, extending from the present)	he will ask he will be asking he is going to ask	he will be asked
	Future perfect (Past from some future time)	he will have asked he will have been asking	he will have been asked

A more complete conjugation of *ask* will be found in *Verbs §1.

The time of a verb is often made more exact by an adverb or by the context:

>He had come *Tuesday.*
>*When Harriet comes,* she will be asked to explain all this.

The present tense is used to make a statement that is generally true, without reference to time:

>Oil *floats* on water.
>The Captain reminded the ladies that the equator *is* an imaginary line.

With an adverb of time the present may refer to the future (He comes tomorrow) or to a statement without specified time: "He comes to us well recommended" may refer to one who has come already or who will come. For the "historical present," used in vivid narrative of past events, see pp. 83-84.

For further details of the future tense see *shall and will.

Participles and infinitives express time in relation to that of the main verb of the statement in which they stand. The present infinitive expresses the same time as the main verb or, often with an adverb, a time in the future:

>Our team is playing *to win.*
>I hope *to go abroad* next summer.

A past infinitive expresses action prior to that of the main verb:

>I am sorry *to have disappointed* you.

A present participle generally refers to the time of the main verb:

>*Rounding* a turn in the road, he came suddenly in full view of the lake.

2. SEQUENCE OF TENSES. When the verb of a main clause is in the past tense, the verb in a subordinate clause is also in the past tense:

>Frank knew that the Statlers were visiting us.
>Frank knew that the Statlers would visit us the following week.
>The old man wondered whether the train had arrived.
>I have never seen Slim when he hadn't [not: hasn't] a wad of tobacco in his mouth.

A present infinitive is, however, usual after a past verb:

>I thought you would have liked to ride [not: to have ridden] in their car.
>They intended to stop [not: to have stopped] only an hour in the village.

3. CONSISTENT USE OF TENSES. It is confusing to a reader to find tenses shifted without definite reason, as in this paragraph:

I *sit* down at my desk early with intentions of spending the next four hours studying. Before many minutes *passed*, I hear a great deal of noise down on the floor below me; a water fight *is* in progress. Study *was forgotten* for half an hour, for it *was* quite impossible to concentrate on Spanish in the midst of all this commotion. After things *quiet* down I *begin* studying again, but I *have* hardly *started* when a magazine salesman *comes* into the room, hoping to snare a large sale. After arguing with him for several minutes I finally *got* rid of him.

Shifts of this sort should be carefully avoided.

Reference: Curme, *Syntax*, Chapter 18; Fries, pp. 59-71, 128-98; Leah Dennis, "The Progressive Tense: Frequency of Its Use in English," *PMLA*, 1940, lv, 855-65

Term paper See Chapter 13, p. 319, The Research Paper.

textbook Now usually written as one word.

th *Th* spells a voiceless sound (th) as in *path* (path), *think* (thingk), and a voiced sound (ᴛʜ) as in *paths* (paᴛʜz), *the* (ᴛʜǝ, ᴛʜĭ, ᴛʜē), *bathe* (bāᴛʜ). *Th* is silent in *isthmus* and pronounced *t* in *Thomas* and *thyme*.

than *Than* is a conjunction introducing the second member of an unequal comparison:

Nobody was **better** aware of the need for action than he was.
You will get there earlier than I will.

Than is often a preposition. Since the clause with *than* is usually verbless (*than he, than I*), it appears rather as a preposition and in colloquial and informal usage is followed by an accusative:

COLLOQUIAL AND INFORMAL: You are certainly faster than him.

In *than whom*, used in all levels, it is a preposition:

We admire the precision and grace of Donald Budge, than whom there is no greater tennis player.

Reference: Jespersen, p. 133

Than is the idiom after *no sooner*:

He had no sooner opened the door than the flames flared up.

Then is often carelessly written for *than*.

For other comparative idioms with *than* see *Comparison of adjectives and adverbs §5, *a* and *b*.

that 1. CONJUNCTION. (*a*) *That* should usually be repeated with each of a series of parallel subordinate clauses:

> But he also sees *that* Lafayette was a rigorously honest and honorable man, *that* he had many of the essential talents of the political compromiser, the moderate, and *that* these very talents help explain his failure in the French Revolution.—CRANE BRINTON, *The Saturday Review of Literature*, Dec. 3, 1938

b) *That* should not be repeated within a single clause:

> Many people think *that* if an article is advertised by a good joker or a good band [that] it is a good product to buy.
>
> Mr. Van Paassen says *that* in comparison with the later bombardments of Barcelona and Valencia [that] Toledo may be considered mere child's play.

2. RELATIVE PRONOUN. *That* refers to persons or things, *who* usually to persons, *which* usually to things.

> The number of men *that* [or *who*] fall within the age limits of the draft is 3,500,000.
>
> He solved in five minutes a problem *that* [or *which*] I had struggled with for five hours.

That introduces clauses that are more often restrictive, *which* introduces clauses that are usually non-restrictive:

> The book that she selected for her report [restrictive] was the longest on the list.
>
> The privilege of free speech, which we hold so dear [non-restrictive], is now endangered.

3. CLAUSES WITHOUT THAT. Clauses are made without the introductory *that* (either as a conjunction or a relative pronoun). Such clauses are more characteristic of informal writing than of formal:

> He said he would go.   He said that he would go.
> I remembered my mother's birthday fell on March 10.
> I remembered that my mother's birthday fell on March 10.
> The first man he met turned out to be Alexander.
> The first man that he met turned out to be Alexander.

4. THAT WHICH. *That which* is formal and archaic for *what:*

> He had no clear idea of *what* [not: that which] he was trying to say.

5. DEMONSTRATIVE THAT. *That* (or *this*) is used to refer to the whole idea of a preceding statement when the reference is clear:

> While I was studying, he sometimes turned on the radio. That was annoying, but I didn't object.

If the *that* refers to an idea suggested but not contained in a particular word, the sentence should be revised to make the reference clear:

VAGUE REFERENCE: My uncle is a doctor, and that is the profession I intend to enter.

EXACT: My uncle's profession is medicine and that is going to be mine too.

6. THAT AS AN ADVERB: *That* is used colloquially or locally as an adverb:

I am that hungry I could eat shoe leather.

FORMAL: I am so hungry that I could eat shoe leather.

Reference: Curme, *Syntax*, index references; Fries, pp. 51, 228-51, and index references

that is *That is* introduces a statement the equivalent of, or the explanation of, what precedes. It is a formal connective and is best kept to introduce long series of complete statements. In such a use it is preceded by a semicolon and followed by a comma:

The men worked continuously for three whole weeks to complete the dam on time; that is, they worked twenty-four hours a day in three shifts, seven days a week.

In briefer constructions, a comma would be more usual, and in informal writing the *that is* would be omitted from the sentence:

They used the safest explosive for the purpose, that is, dynamite.

INFORMAL: They used the safest explosive for the purpose, dynamite.

Compare *namely and other introductory words.

the 1. The repetition of the article before the various nouns of a series emphasizes their distinctness:

The color, the fragrance, and the beautiful patterns of these flowers make them universal favorites.

The color, fragrance, and pattern of these flowers are distinctive.

2. In the idiom *the . . . the,* in which the *the* is an adverb rather than an article, usage is divided over the punctuation. In formal writing a comma is usual between the phrases, in informal not:

The greater one's economic insecurity the greater the tendency to sacrifice spiritual independence.—STUART CHASE, "The Luxury of Integrity," *The Nemesis of American Business*

FORMAL: The greater one's economic insecurity, the greater the tendency to sacrifice spiritual independence.

3. Keep *the* with the name of our country: *the* United States.

theater [theatre] See *-er, -re.

their *Their* is the genitive of *they*. *Theirs* is the emphatic or absolute form:

> This table is exactly like theirs.

Colloquially *their* is used to refer to the collective indefinite pronouns (*anybody, anyone, everybody, everyone*), though these are singular in form.

> COLLOQUIAL: Everybody finally found their hats and coats.
> FORMAL: Everybody finally found his hat and coat.

Themes Although one of the purposes of composition courses is to improve the expression of students, merely putting grammatical sentences end to end is not a sufficient task for college students. The aim of themes, as of other sorts of writing, should be to interest and inform readers. The papers should be of a sort that, well enough done, would be suitable for publication.

The chief difficulty with themes is that their writers forget their possible readers and affect a style that is unnatural to them. They write unnaturally:

> As the early morning sun is slowly breaking through the mist and the roosters are making their way out of hen houses to crow the early hours of day, one might hear the creaking of doors and the sound of padded feet while lying in bed waiting for breakfast. Upon getting out of bed into the chilly morning air and looking out of a window into the farmyard, one could see an elderly, stout gentleman busily working about.

Instead of such artificiality, the writers of themes would do well to write simply and directly, like the professional writers quoted in this book. Keeping a reader in mind is the best way to get over this "theme attitude."

themselves Compare *himself, *myself.

then *Then* is an adverb of time, often used as a connective (conjunctive adverb). Often the connection between clauses is made closer by using *and then*:

> The next three hours we spent in sightseeing; then we settled down to the business of being delegates to a convention.
> He ate a good meal, and then he took a nap before starting home again.

Then too is overused as a connective in amateur writing:

> A reader enjoys a fast moving story; then too he may enjoy finding something that will set him thinking.

BETTER: A reader enjoys a fast moving story, and he may also enjoy finding something that will set him thinking.

then—than These words are often carelessly confused in writing. *Then* is an adverb of time, *than* a conjunction in clauses of comparison:

Then the whole crowd went to Louie's.

I think *Rebecca* was better than any other novel I read last year.

therefore *Therefore* is a conjunctive adverb, a rather heavy connective, unnecessarily formal for ordinary writing:

FORMAL: My experiences in preparatory school had been very unpleasant; therefore I was surprised to find college students and college teachers so agreeable.

INFORMAL: My experiences in preparatory school had been so unpleasant that I was surprised to find college students and college teachers so agreeable.

there is, there are 1. *There* and *it* are used as anticipatory subjects, the real subject following the verb. *There is* is followed by a singular subject (often colloquially by a plural), *there are* by a plural:

There is a size for every need.

There are several ways in which this can be done.

Reference: Fries, p. 56

2. Frequent use of these impersonal constructions tends to give a lack of emphasis:

There was a vague feeling of discontent evident in everyone's manner.

DIRECT: A vague feeling of discontent was evident in everyone's manner.

It is said that college students are easily discouraged.

DIRECT: College students are said to be easily discouraged.

these kind, these sort *kind, sort

they *They* is colloquially used as an indefinite pronoun but generally it is not so used in writing:

COLLOQUIAL: They have had no serious accidents at that crossing for over two years.

WRITTEN: There have been no serious accidents . . .

COLLOQUIAL: They made the great reflector at Corning.

WRITTEN: The great reflector was made at Corning.

thing *Thing* is often deadwood:

Religion is a personal thing. [Religion is personal.]

The first thing you do is to [First you] get a few small twigs burning.

this *This*, like *that*, is often used to refer to the idea of a preceding clause or sentence:

He had always had his own way at home, and this made him a poor roommate.

The company train their salesmen in their own school. This [More formally: This practice] assures them a group of men with the same sales methods.

thou *Thou, thy, thine, thee* are archaic pronouns for the second person, used now only in the formal language of church services. Amateur poets should avoid them except in archaic contexts.

though *although

till, until, ['til] These three words are not distinguishable in meaning. Since *'til* in speech sounds the same as *till* and looks slightly odd on paper, it may well be abandoned. Use *till* or *until* according to the stress or the feel of the phrase you want. *Until* is most often used at the beginning of sentences or clauses:

Until he went to college, he never had thought of his speech.
He had never thought of his speech till [until] he went to college.

Time In subordinate clauses the various time relationships are indicated by the conjunctions *after, *as, as long as, as often as, as soon as, before, since, *till, until, when, whenever, *while.*

Titles of articles, books, etc. Titles should be given accurately and in an appropriate form.

1. FORMAL USAGE. In most college writing, in most books, and in some periodicals, the titles of books and the names of magazines and newspapers are put in italics; that is, they would be underlined once in the manuscript. Capitals are used for the first word, for all nouns, pronouns, verbs, adjectives, and adverbs, and for prepositions that stand last or that contain more than five letters:

Not for Just an Hour   *All This and Heaven Too*
Black Is My True Love's Hair   *Parts of Speech and Accidence*
The Atlantic Monthly   *The Kansas City Star*

Often the *the* of magazine and newspaper titles is not capitalized and in some periodicals the name of the city in a newspaper name is not italicized (the Milwaukee *Sentinel*).

Titles of short stories and magazine articles are put in quotation marks when they are used with or near titles of books or names of periodicals. They are often italicized when used without reference

763

to their means of publication, especially in discussion of them as works of literature. Usage is divided on the titles of poems, but academic writing tends to use italics though the titles of short poems are often in quotation marks.

The words *Preface* and *Introduction* and the titles of chapters in books are capitalized but not italicized or quoted.

2. INFORMAL USAGE. In many magazines (*The New Republic, The Saturday Evening Post,* for example) and in most newspapers, titles of books and names of periodicals are treated as proper names, capitalized but not quoted or italicized.

In formal papers for college courses and in theses formal usage should be followed; in informal college papers, like many themes, either style may be used, as the instructor prefers.

3. In typed copy it is simpler to write titles all in capitals (to save backing up and underlining). This is the common form in publishers' letters.

See "Form of bibliographical entries," p. 325.

Titles of themes Since titles help interest a reader in a paper, a striking and easily remembered title is an advantage. But strained titles are often ludicrous, and if no good title comes to mind, it is better just to name the subject of the paper as exactly as possible in a few words and let it go at that. Don't postpone writing a paper (or handing one in) to hunt for a clever title. In published work the title is sometimes made by the editor rather than by the writer.

The title stands outside the paper and the first sentence should not refer back to it by a pronoun.

today 1. *Today* (like *tonight* and *tomorrow*) is hyphened now only by formal writers and by conservative publishers, or by people who learned to spell when the hyphen was generally used. Recent dictionaries prefer *today*.

2. *Today, of today* are often deadwood, adding nothing to the meaning of a statement already placed in the present:

Economic conditions [of today] are more unsettled than they have been for two generations.

too When *too* in the sense of *also* comes within a construction it is usually set off by commas, but in informal writing it usually is not when it comes at the end:

"I, too, have become a philosopher," she said sadly.—IRWIN ED-MAN, *Philosopher's Holiday,* p. 74

I'm going too. [FORMAL]: I'm going, too.

Topical outline *Outline form § 1*b

Topic sentences See p. 59.

toward—towards These words are identical in meaning and use, except that *toward* is slightly more characteristic of formal usage, perhaps for reasons of euphony.

Transitions between paragraphs (CORRECTION: Make the relation *Trans* between the thought of these two paragraphs obvious to a reader.)
For discussion of transitions see p. 65.

Transpose (CORRECTION: Transpose, that is, reverse the order of *Tr* the elements marked for greater clearness or a more emphatic order.)

Transitive and intransitive verbs A verb is transitive when it is used with an object to complete its meaning (They fought the whole gang). A verb is intransitive when it does not have an object, when the recipient of the action is not named (The choir will sing; They hid in the tall grass). Many verbs are used in both constructions, usually with different meanings (He wrote two books [transitive]; She cannot write [intransitive]). Dictionaries note whether a verb is typically used transitively or intransitively, and in what senses. *Lie* and *sit* are intransitive; *lay and *set are transitive. *Linking verbs are regarded as intransitive.

Reference: Curme, *Parts of Speech*, Chapter 4

Triads Parallel series of three units are so common in writing, especially in formal writing, that they form a definite trait of style. Such a series is called a triad:

> To delight in war is a merit in the soldier, a dangerous quality in the captain, and a positive crime in the statesman.—GEORGE SANTAYANA, *Reason in Society*, p. 84

Trite (CORRECTION: Replace the trite expression with one that is *Trite* simpler and fresher.)
Trite words are usually figures of speech that have been overused or groups of words that are used too often and too easily together: *the picture of health, the order of the day* (outside an army post), *reign supreme, from the face of the earth, crack of dawn*. Such expressions weigh down a style and are a mark of amateur writing or of insensitiveness to words.
For fuller discussion and examples see "Trite words," p. 214.

trough Formal pronunciation trôf; colloquial and vulgate pronunciation divided between trôf and trôth. The two final sounds represent two developments of an Old English guttural (*trog*) in different English dialects.

try and—try to The formal idiom is *try to* (Try to get your work done before five o'clock). The informal and colloquial idiom is *try and* (try and do it; Try and get your work done before five o'clock). The idiom is old and its users include Thackeray and Matthew Arnold (See Hall, p. 309).

Type Typography is a complex technical field, but many people make a hobby of it, and most writers have some curiosity about it. A few of the fundamental facts about type are given here.

1. TYPE FACES. There are many different type faces, each with its characteristic appearance. Every type face is made in many standard sizes and style variations. Some popular faces for book and periodical use are:

Caslon, **Bodoni,** Garamond, Baskerville, Granjon, Gothic,

The above faces are all set in the ten point size.

This *Guide-Index* is set in the following type faces and sizes:

The text is set in 10 point Electra.

The quotations are set in 9 point Electra.

The entry words are set in 10 point **Metromedium.**

The titles of the chapters of
the book are in 14 point **Metroblack**

Additional information about the type used in this book can be found on the last printed page.

2. TYPE STYLE VARIATIONS. A given face and size of type is available in several standard variations of style. The most common are:

NAME AND EXAMPLE	ABBREVIATION	· INDICATED IN MANUSCRIPT BY
ROMAN CAPITALS	Caps.	Three lines underneath
roman lower case	l. c.	Unmarked manuscript
ROMAN SMALL CAPITALS	s. c.	Two lines underneath
ITALIC CAPITALS	Ital. Caps.	One line underneath and labeled "all caps"
italic lower case	ital.	One line underneath
BOLD FACE CAPITALS	b. f. caps.	Wavy line underneath and labeled "all caps"
bold face lower case	b. f.	Wavy line underneath

There are, of course, combinations of the above styles: Caps and lower case, CAPS AND SMALL CAPS, *Italic Caps and lower case,* **Bold Face Caps and lower case.**

3. TYPE MEASUREMENT. Type is measured in *points*, a point equalling 1/72 of an inch. A square unit of type of any size is an *em*. Space is usually measured in *pica* (12 point) *ems* (1/6 of an inch).

This line is set in six point type.

This line is set in ten point type.

This line is set in fourteen point type.

---

*Proofreading

References: The University of Chicago Press *Manual of Style* contains much information about type, as do other stylebooks and books on journalism and advertising and typography.

Typewritten copy In general, typewritten copy follows the customs of good manuscript but some points need special emphasis. Use only one side of the sheet, leave good margins (especially at the right side, since letters cannot be compressed as in longhand), and keep type clean and the ribbon in good ink. Ordinarily use a black ribbon.

Regular manuscript should be double spaced, though in personal writing it may be single spaced and for economy single space may be used in business writing. If it is single spaced, the line should be kept fairly short to make the reading easier. In writing first drafts on the typewriter, leave plenty of space for revision, perhaps using triple space between lines and extra space between paragraphs.

In single spaced typing, use double space between paragraphs, and in double space make a triple space between paragraphs if you wish an open appearance or special emphasis on the paragraphs. Indent paragraph first lines from five to eight spaces.

Long quotations may be indicated in double spaced copy by indenting the number of spaces being used for paragraphs and single spacing the quoted matter. No quotation marks are used with this style.

The standard typewriter keyboard has no symbol for the figure 1. Use the small l (not I). For a dash use two hyphens not spaced away from the words on each side. Space after all other punctuation marks.

Transposed letters should be erased and retyped or corrected by the proofreader's symbol. See *Proofreader's marks. Strikeovers are often hard to read. A few mistakes can be corrected in ink, but if there are so many that the page will look messy it should be retyped.

767

All manuscript for a printer, business letters and reports, and all impersonal writing should be typed. In the United States we are so accustomed to typescript (and our handwriting is on the whole so illegible) that it can be used in a good deal of personal correspondence. There is an added courtesy in longhand, and "social correspondence" should usually be handwritten. Students believe they receive better grades on course papers that are typed. The ease of reading typescript may have some such result when the instructor is reading principally for content, but in English compositions that advantage may be offset in part by the clearness with which the errors stand out.'

Anyone who expects to do much writing should be able to use a typewriter. Rebuilt machines are quite satisfactory and cost much less than new ones. A person can easily learn to type faster and more accurately than he can write with a pen.

See "Preparing the manuscript," p. 302.

U 1. There are two "long u" sounds: (ü) as in *rule* (rül), *move* (müv), *lose* (lüz), *booby* (bü′bi), *hoodoo* (hü′dü); and (ū), diphthong beginning with a *y*-sound and ending with ü, as in *use* (ūs or ūz), *few* (fū), *cute* (kūt), *beauty* (bū′ti), *you* (ū.) The latter sound varies among different speakers and is modified considerably by neighboring sounds.

2. There are two "short u" sounds: (u) as in *cup* (kup), *fun* (fun), *under* (un′dər), *son* (sun), *love* (luv), *come* (kum), *trouble* (trub′əl), *does* (duz), *other* (uᴛн′ər); and (ù) as in *full* (fùl), *pull* (pùl), *wood* (wùd), *woman* (wùm′ən).

3. *U* as in *burn* and *curl* is represented by ė (bėrn, kėrl). An unpronounced *u* is sometimes spelled after *g*, as in *guard*, *guess*.

un- (Negative prefix) See *in-, un-.

Underlining In longhand and typewritten copy we underline words and passages to correspond to the conventions of using *italic* type. In familiar writing, rules are not important but in formal manuscript and in material to be printed, the conventions are of great importance. Newspapers have generally abandoned italics but most magazines and books continue to use them, and in academic writing—course papers, articles in the learned journals, monographs, dissertations, reference books—rather strict conventions should still be followed.

Underlining is used:

1. To INDICATE TITLES OF BOOKS AND PERIODICALS. The complete title should be underlined:

I like Babbitt and Arrowsmith the best.
He took Time and The Reader's Digest.

For details of this use see *Titles of articles, books, etc. and "Form of bibliographical entries," p. 325. Compare *Ships' names.

2. FOR EMPHASIS. Words that would be heavily stressed if the sentence was spoken may be underlined:

He was the man that night.

Any word a writer wishes to emphasize may be underlined (italicized in print), but this is a rather mechanical form of emphasis and loses its force if overused. Whole sentences, except in textbooks and manuals, are better not underlined, since there are more intelligent ways of securing emphasis. As Fowler (p. 305) put it: "To italicize whole sentences or large parts of them as a guarantee that some portion of what one has written is really worth attending to is a miserable confession that the rest is negligible."

*Emphasis §7, *Schoolgirl style

3. To MARK WORDS AND LOCUTIONS BEING CONSIDERED NOT FOR THEIR MEANING BUT AS WORDS, a common use in this and all books on language:

If we take such a sentence as I am hungry, neither a grammarian nor a logician would have any difficulty in pointing out the predicate, though one would say that it was am hungry and the other that it was simply hungry.—P. B. BALLARD, Thought and Language, p. 88

4. To MARK FOREIGN WORDS:

But good clothes were a sine qua non.

*Foreign words in English

Understatement Understatement is a figure of speech, the opposite of exaggeration. See p. 240.

unique In strict formal usage unique means "single, sole, unequaled," and consequently cannot be compared. In informal usage, like so many words of absolute meaning, it has become somewhat generalized to mean an emphatic rare, and is sometimes found compared with more or most:

. . . the more unique his nature, the more peculiarly his own will be the coloring of his language.—OTTO JESPERSEN, Mankind, Nation and Individual from a Linguistic Point of View, p. 204

United States We live in *the* United States, and the article should be kept. *American

Unity Unity is a by-product of clear thinking. It is a relative quality. Gross disregard of unity, including material that is quite unrelated to a paragraph or to a paper, can be discovered by a reader. But genuine unity is to be judged in the light of the writer's purpose. Any statement that he can build into his discussion, that he can relate to his subject, will be appropriate. The test of unity is not in any general principles that can be applied in every situation but in appropriateness to the writer's view of his material and his consistent carrying out of his purpose.

Various matters related to unity are discussed in Chapter 3, The Forms and Uses of Paragraphs, and in Chapter 5, Sentence Form.

until *till, until, 'til

Usage Most of this book discusses matters of English usage. For general principles, see Chapters 1 and 2.

used to The spelling *use to* represents what we say, but should be written *used to*.

V (v) as in *very* (ver′i) *vivid* (viv′id), *save* (sāv), *Stephen* (stē′vən), *of* (ov).

Variety Variety in expression comes principally from an active and natural way of writing, and conscious effort can do little but remove the monotonous passages that sometimes occur in tired or inattentive composition. An unpleasant sameness can be attended to in revision. Just keep in mind that if a passage seems flat and monotonous to the one who wrote it, it will probably be even more displeasing to anyone else.

Phases of variety in writing are treated in the following places in this book:

In material and development: A fresh and convincing treatment of a subject will usually show variety in interest and in methods of development. See Chs. 3 and 4, pp. 53 and 81, especially the description of different sorts of paragraphs in Chapter 4.

In sentences: Sentences especially can be revised in the interest of variety by seeing that they vary in length, that they vary in movement, especially that there are not long series of simple or compound sentences of the same pattern and that they begin with differing first elements. See Chs. 5 and 6, pp. 115 and 150, especially p. 155, "Variety in sentence movement," and p. 124, "Coordination and subordination."

In words: Although exactness is more important than variety in words, sometimes conscious attention in revision can add to their variety and at the same time increase their accuracy. See Ch. 7, p. 182, and Ch. 8, p. 213, Qualities of Words, and "Repetition," p. 168.

Verb-adverb combinations In "I looked up at the top of the tree," the verb *look* is used in its ordinary sense and is modified by the adverb *up*. In "I looked up the word in the dictionary," *looked up* is a verb meaning "investigated," a meaning not explained by a literal use of the two words. Similarly a man may *break out* (literally) of jail, or *break out* with measles; he can *stand by* a certain tree, or *stand by* as a radio listener; he can *look after* a departing car, or *look after* the children. In each of these pairs of expressions, the first has a verb modified by an adverb in its ordinary meaning, and the second is really a different verb, with a meaning of its own, composed of the verb and the adverb combined.

Besides these few samples there are hundreds of such verb-adverb combinations in use, most of them one-syllabled verbs with adverbs, like *about, around, at, by, down, for, in, out, through, to, up, with.* They are used most naturally in the informal and colloquial level of the language, where they often give an emphatic rhythm differing from the more formal *investigate, sacrifice (give up), surrender (give up).* This pattern is now the most active way of forming new verbs in English.

Because of the colloquial tendency to use superfluous adverbs, a writer needs to watch out for adverbs that add nothing to his meaning:

We found [out] that what had looked like snow was a mound of quartz.
The college student meets [up with] a different type of instructor in English than he had in high school.

Compare *Prepositions § 3*b*.

Reference: Kennedy, pp. 297-303

verbal *oral, verbal

Verbal nouns *Gerund

Verbals The parts of a verb that function as nouns or adjectives are grouped as *verbals*. *Gerunds* (or verbal nouns) are used as nouns (though they may still have a subject or object), *participles* are used as adjectives, and *infinitives* are used as adjectives or nouns.

GERUNDS: *Swimming* is better exercise than *rowing*.
Having been invited pleased him enormously.

INFINITIVES: His only ambition was *to pass*.
It was too good *to last*.
To have asked for more would have wrecked the whole conference.
He had plenty of money *to spend*.

PARTICIPLES: He reached the float, *swimming* as easily as before he had been hurt.
Asked to take a part, he refused at first but finally accepted.
Having been invited, he began to make plans.

For forms of verbals see *Verbs and for their various uses see *Gerund, *Infinitives, and *Participles.

Verbless sentences See p. 131 and *Fragmentary sentences.

Verbs 1. CONJUGATION. The following synopsis of *ask* in the third person singular shows most common patterns of the conjugation of a verb in English:

PRINCIPAL PARTS: ask, asked, asked

INDICATIVE MOOD

	Active voice	Passive voice
PRESENT:	he asks he is asking he does ask	he is asked he is being asked
PAST:	he asked he was asking he did ask	he was asked he was being asked
PERFECT:	he has asked he has been asking	he has been asked
PAST PERFECT:	he had asked he had been asking	he had been asked
FUTURE:	he will ask he will be asking he is going to ask	he will be asked
FUTURE PERFECT:	he will have asked he will have been asking	he will have been asked

SUBJUNCTIVE MOOD

PRESENT:	(if) he ask	(if) he be asked
PAST:	(if) he were asking	(if) he were being asked (if) he were asked

IMPERATIVE MOOD

ask	be asked
be asking	
do ask	

INFINITIVES

PRESENT:	(to) ask	(to) be asked
PAST:	to have asked	to have been asked

GERUNDS

PRESENT:	asking	being asked
PAST:	having asked	having been asked

PARTICIPLES

PRESENT:	asking	being asked
PAST:		asked
PERFECT:	having asked	having been asked

Compare *Tenses of verbs.

2. SYNTAX OF VERBS. A number of *Index* articles treat in detail various constructions involving verbs. The principal articles are these:

Absolute constructions	Parts of speech
Collective nouns	Principal parts of verbs
Conditions	shall—will, should—would
Dangling modifiers	Split infinitives
Fragmentary sentences	Subject and verb
Gerunds	Subjunctives
Infinitives	Tenses of verbs
Linking verbs	Transitive and intransitive verbs
Objects	very
Participles	Voice

Vernacular *Vernacular* formerly referred to the native, spoken language—as opposed to the literary languages of Latin or Norman French or the language of other conquerors. It now means colloquial and vulgate English, the native homely, spoken language as contrasted with formal or literary English.

Verse A full line or more of verse quoted in a paper should be lined off and written exactly as it is in the original. It should be indented from the left margin and, if very short, far enough not to leave a conspicuous blank at its right.

Verse form The form of a line of verse is described by telling the arrangement of the stressed syllables (the kind of "foot"), the length of the line (the number of feet), and any other qualities of movement or variation from the typical movement that it shows. This article presents the vocabulary and an outline of the facts necessary for describing verse form.

THE FEET

Iambic ×′ (An iamb)
Trochaic ′× (A trochee)
Anapestic ××′ (An anapest)
Dactylic ′×× (A dactyl)
Spondaic ′′ (A spondee)

THE LENGTH OF LINES:

Dimeter: Two feet
Trimeter: Three feet
Tetrameter: Four feet
Pentameter: Five feet
Hexameter: Six feet
An Alexandrine

OTHER FACTS:

A line is *end-stopped* if its end corresponds with a distinct sense pause, either the end of a sentence or of a major sentence element; it is *run-on* when the construction is carried over the end of the line.

Anacrusis: An extra unstressed syllable at the beginning of a line
Catalexis: The dropping of the final unstressed syllable
Feminine ending: An extra unstressed syllable at the end
Refrain: A line repeated, typically at the end of each stanza of a poem

A *cesura* (*caesura*) is a rhythmic pause within a line.

Two successive lines rhyming are a *couplet.*

A four-line stanza is a *quatrain,* which may have any rhyme scheme: abab, abba; an iambic tetrameter quatrain rhyming abcb is the *ballad stanza.*

More complex stanza forms (sonnet, ode, ballade, and so on) are described in books on literature and poetry.

Blank verse is unrhymed iambic pentameter. *Free verse* is verse of varied length lines with a flexible movement, usually unrhymed.

EXAMPLES OF SCANSION:

Iambic pentameter (feminine ending):

×′ ×′ ×′× ×′ ×′×
A thing of beauty is a joy forever

Anapestic tetrameter:

×× ′ × × ′ ×× ′ ×× ′
There are brains, though they moulder, that dream in the tomb

Trochaic tetrameter (catalectic), a couplet:

′ ×′× ′ × ′
Souls of poets dead and gone,

′ ×′×′ ′ × ′
What Elysium have ye known,

These examples show that scansion tells the typical physical characteristic of verse but does not define the rhythm and should not precisely control the reading. (The *is* in the first line above is hardly stressed, or the last syllable of *Elysium.*)

Compare *Rhythm (of prose).

Reference: For the more important qualities of poetry, such as imagery, tone color, rhythm (not to mention meaning), see Earl Daniels, *The Art of Reading Poetry* (New York, 1941), and other books on poetry and literature.

vertebra The plural is either *vertebrae* (vẽr′tə brē) or *vertebras*, with *vertebrae* still the more common.

very 1. VERY AND PAST PARTICIPLES. In formal English many people will not use *very* with a past participle in a phrasal verb (He was very excited)—because by rights *very* is an intensive, supposedly marking a high degree of a *quality*, as in *very happy*, and the verb function of the participle denotes an action rather than a quality. The formal locution would be: "He was *very much* excited."

This distinction, since it is based purely on grammatical reasoning, is too subtle for users of colloquial and informal English, who use *very* to modify such participles without any qualms (I shall be very pleased to come; We shall be very delighted to have you).

When the President and the trustees finally decided to allow the Psychology Department to sponsor a clinic, Dr. Bonham was very elated.—JAMES REID PARKER, *Academic Procession*, p. 13

2. VERY AS AN INTENSIVE. *Very* has been overused and is still overused so that it is of doubtful value as an intensive. A writer should watch to make sure that it really adds to the meaning of his phrase.

The Emporia Gazette once described its war upon *very* this way:

"If you feel you must write 'very,' write 'damn.'" So when the urge for emphasis is on him, the reporter writes "It was a damn fine victory. I am damn tired but damn well—and damn excited." Then, because it is the Emporia (Kan.) Gazette, the copy desk deletes the profanity and the quotation reads: "It was a fine victory. I am tired but well—and excited." That's how the Gazette attains its restrained, simple, and forceful style. Very simple.

viewpoint A natural and economical substitute for the clumsy *point of view*. It is not stigmatized in the dictionaries.

Before we condemn him for affectation and distortion we must realize his viewpoint.—E. M. FORSTER, *Aspects of the Novel*, p. 182

vise—vice The name of the tool is more commonly spelled with s, but both *vise* and *vice* are used. *Vice*, the quality of evil in people, is always *vice*, and the adjective is *vicious*.

vitamin The preferred spelling is *vitamin* and pronunciation vī′tə min; vit′ə min and vit′ə mēn are variant pronunciations.

"... from Latin *vit-a* life + amine; named *vitamine* by Casimir Funk in the belief that an amino-acid was present, and later changed to *vitamin* to avoid suggesting this."—*Oxford English Dictionary.*

viz. Viz. is abbreviation of the Latin *videlicet* [vi del'ə set], to wit, namely. Viz. exists only in the language of rather formal documents or reference works. It is read "namely."

Vocabulary See Ch. 7, p. 182, especially "Supply of words," p. 183, and "Increasing your vocabulary," p. 205.

Vocative *Direct address

Voice 1. DEFINITION AND FORMS. When the subject of a verb is the doer of the action or is in the condition named by its verb, the verb is in the active voice:

The congregation *sang* "Abide with Me."
They *will go* swimming.   Our side *had won.*
Jimmy's father *gave* him a car.   We *rested* an hour.

When the subject of a verb receives the action, the verb is in the passive voice:

"Abide with Me" *was sung* by the congregation.
Jimmy *was given* a car by his father.
The pit *was dug* fully eight feet deep.
They *were caught.*

The passive form is usually a form of the verb *be* and a past participle:

	Active	*Passive*
PRESENT:	he asks (is asking)	he is asked (is being asked)
FUTURE:	he will ask	he will be asked
PERFECT:	he has asked	he has been asked
INFINITIVES:	to ask, to have asked	to be asked, to have been asked
PARTICIPLES:	asking	being asked, asked

For full conjugation see *Verbs § 1.

Get and *become* and other verbs are used to form a passive, especially in colloquial English:

If he should get elected, we'd be lost.
Our house is getting painted.

2. USE OF ACTIVE VERBS. Active verbs are more common than passive. They make the simple assertion that is the basis of the typical clause or sentence and allow objects and modifiers, which are usually important, to stand at the emphatic end of the sentence. In this paragraph of expository prose there are seventeen active verbs and one passive:

When one *approaches* Manhattan Island, for instance, from the Staten Island Ferry or the Brooklyn Bridge, the great towers on the tip of the island sometimes *look* like the fairy stalagmites of an opened grotto; and from an occasional vantage point on the twentieth floor of an office building one *may* now and again *recapture* this impression. But *need* I *point out* that one *can count* on one's fingers the number of buildings in New York or Chicago that one *can approach* from the street in similar fashion? For the millions who *fill* the pavements and *shuttle back and forth* in tubes, the skyscraper as a tall, cloudward building *does* not *exist*. Its esthetic features *are* the entrance, the elevator, and the window-pocked wall; and if there *has been* any unique efflorescence of a fresh style at these points, I *have been* unable to discover it.

What our critics *have learned* to admire in our great buildings *is* their photographs—and that *is* another story. In an article chiefly devoted to the praise of the skyscraper, in a number of The Arts, the majority of the illustrations *were taken* [passive] from a point that the man in the street never *reaches*. In short, it *is* an architecture, not for men, but for angels and aviators!—LEWIS MUMFORD, *Sticks and Stones*, pp. 173-74

3. USE OF PASSIVE VERBS. Passive verbs may be less frequent, but they have several important uses.

The recipient of the action may be more important, in the writer's mind, than the doer:

> The well *was drilled* in solid rock.
> Our house *was painted* last year.

In indefinite statements the passive is often used when the doers may not be known or are not to be named in the statement:

> Much *has been written* on both sides.
> . . . the majority of the illustrations *were taken* from a point . . . [in the Mumford paragraph]

The passive allows various degrees of emphasis by placing either the name of the act or of the doer at the end:

> Our house *is being painted* (vs They *are painting* our house, active).
> Our house *was painted* by Joe Mead and his brother (vs Joe Mead and his brother *painted* our house, active).
> "Abide with Me" was sung by the choir (that is, not by the congregation).

Sometimes the passive shows a change in the relation between subject and verb (though the shift should not be made within a sentence unless the action is continuous):

> We *drove* [active] there and *were taken out* [passive] in a dory.

4. OVERUSE OF THE PASSIVE. For the objectionable use of passive verbs when active would be more effective, see *Passive voice.

Reference: Curme, *Syntax*, pp. 102-103; Fries, pp. 188-93; Jespersen, Chapter 12

Vowels *Consonants and articles on the separate vowels, a, e, i, o, u

Vulg **Vulgate English** (CORRECTION: Change the vulgate word or form or idiom to one appropriate to educated usage.)

For discussion of uneducated or "substandard" English see p. 20.

W (w) as in *wild* (wīld), *twinkle* (twing′kəl), *quick* (kwik). W is silent in *write* (rīt), *two* (tü), *sword* (sōrd), and other words, and spoken though not spelled in *one* (wun), *once* (wuns).

wake English is oversupplied with verbs for waking from sleep (intransitive) and waking someone else from sleep (transitive). Each is used in both senses:

awake (*awaked, awaked*). Rather formal; more commonly used intransitively (I awoke).
awaken (*awakened, awakened*). Formal.
wake (*waked* or *woke, wake* or *woke* [*woken*]). More widely used than the preceding.
waken (*wakened, wakened*). Less common than *wake*.

The usual colloquial and informal solution is the verb-adverb combination *wake up* (*waked* or *woke up*):

She waked up at eleven. She waked me up at six.

want The formal and informal idiom with *want* is with an infinitive:

FORMAL, INFORMAL: I want you to get all you can from the year's work.
VULGATE: I want for you to get all you can from the year's work.
VULGATE: I want that you should get all you can from the year's work.

Want is colloquial for *ought, had better*:

COLLOQUIAL: You want to review all the notes if you're going to pass his exam.

In the sense of *lack* or *need, want* is formal and suggests British usage:

The letter, though clear, wants correcting.

way, ways W*ay* is colloquially and informally used for *away* (W*ay* over across the valley). W*ay* is used in a number of colloquial idioms (*in a bad way, out our way,* I don't see how she can act *the way* she does).

W*ays* is colloquially used for *way* in expressions like *a little ways* down the road.

we 1. INDEFINITE WE. *We* is used as an indefinite pronoun in expressions like W*e find,* W*e sometimes feel,* and to avoid passive and impersonal constructions. *Reference of pronouns § 3

2. EDITORIAL WE. In editorial columns and in some other regular departments of periodicals, like "The Talk of the Town" in *The New Yorker,* the writer refers to himself as *we.* In some instances the *we* refers to an editorial board that determines the opinions expressed but more often it is a convention. It is less used than formerly.

The usage has passed into familiar and informal writing, especially of a light tone. Used merely to avoid using I, *we* is usually conspicuous and to be avoided. *I §2

well *good—well

wh is the English spelling for *hw: what* (hwot or hwut), *when* (hwen), *wheel* (hwēl), *whether* (hweᴛʜ′ər), *why* (hwī). In *who* (hü), *whole* (hōl, hol), *whoop* (hüp), and the common pronunciation of *whether* (weᴛʜ′ər), *why* (wī), *when* (wen), and so on, *wh* represents h or w.

when W*hen*-clauses are used in colloquial and vulgate English as equivalent to nouns but not in good English:

> VULGATE: Welding is when two pieces of metal are heated and made into one.
> WRITTEN: Welding is heating two pieces of metal and making them one.

Reference: Fries, pp. 233-34

when, as, and if Securities are advertised "when, as, and if issued," and the phrase *when and if* or *if and when* is used in talking about goods whose future is uncertain. It should not be used when the matter is certain, or in non-business contexts except for barely possible humor.

where W*here*-clauses are used in colloquial English as the equivalent of nouns:

> COLLOQUIAL: Etching is where you cut lines in a copper plate and then print from them.

WRITTEN: Etching is cutting lines in a copper plate and printing from them.

Where is used to introduce a relative clause:

COLLOQUIAL: He wants a job where he will be with people.
MORE FORMAL: He wants a job in which he will be with people.
The interest is one where a wit may always win much . . .—BARRETT WENDELL, *English Composition*, p. 137
This is the place where most men stop.

whether *if § 2, *Conditions

which 1. *Which* refers to things and to groups of people regarded impersonally (The legislature which passed the act . . .).
Informally *which* refers to the idea of a preceding clause:

INFORMAL: He was growing gray, which bothered his wife a good deal.
FORMAL: He was growing gray; this bothered his wife a good deal.

Compare *this.

Whose is often used as the genitive of *which*, instead of the more cumbersome *of which*:

This story of the life of General Custer is *Boots and Saddles*, whose author is the General's wife.

2. AND WHICH. *And* and *but* are carelessly used to join a *which* clause, which is subordinate, to a main statement:

INACCURATE: He got the contract to install new copper work on the Post Office, and which will require 4500 pounds of lead-coated copper.
ACCURATE: He got the contract to install new copper work on the Post Office, which will require 4500 pounds of lead-coated copper.

while *While* most exactly is a connective of time:

While the rest were studying, he was playing cards.

While also means *though* or *but*, but rather weakly:

Haiti is probably the most primitive of all the islands, while [More exact: *but*, or *though*] Jamaica runs her a close second.
Magazines, newspapers, and scientific books became my chief interest, while [More exact: *but*] plays and poems were still a torture to me.

While is colloquially used for *and*:

The second number was an acrobatic exhibition, while [*and*] the third was a lady trapeze artist.

In England the House of Lords corresponds to our Senate, while [*and*] the House of Commons corresponds to our House of Representatives.

Awhile is an adverb, written as one word: *Awhile ago*. In phrases in which *while* is a noun, the *a* should be written separate: *In a while; After a while*.

Reference: Fries, pp. 236-37

Whitespace Whitespace has the function of a punctuation mark in display matter. It has now taken the place of commas and periods at the ends of lines and envelope addresses, in letter headings, in titles of books and articles, lines that are spaced off in advertisements, posters, etc., in matter set in tables or columns. No punctuation marks are used at the ends of lines in formal social notes. In indented quotations whitespace has displaced the quote marks. These various uses have helped relieve the spottiness of correspondence and many printed pages.

who, whom 1. *Who* refers to people, to personified objects (a ship, a country), and occasionally to animals:

Diogenes Checkpoints says what is needed is a list of horses who should be out of training.—AUDAX MINOR, *The New Yorker*, Aug. 27, 1938

Whose is often used as the genitive of *which*. *which § 1

2. In formal English *whom* is always used as the accusative form. In informal English when the *who* stands before a verb or preposition of which it is the object, *who* is the generally accepted form:

Who [object of *introduce*] do you introduce to whom [object of the immediately preceding *to*]?
No matter who [object of *meet*] you meet, the first thing you mention is the weather.

3. When *who* is the subject of a verb separated from it by other words, the nominative is used:

He made a list of all the writers who [subject of *were*] he thought were important in the period.

Whom sometimes occurs here, probably as the result of trying to keep the formal practice of using *whom* when it is a preceding object (§2):

. . . factory laborers and factory owners, young conscripts and seasoned army officers, folk whom [subject of *have disappeared*] I discover have disappeared for treason against National Socialism since they wrote . . .—NORA WALN, *The Atlantic Monthly*, Jan. 1939

4. A verb of which *who* is the subject has the number of the antecedent of the *who:*

> I'm one of the few people who don't [antecedent *people*] like to read many books.
> I'm one who doesn't [antecedent *one*] like to read books.

Reference: Fries, pp. 95, 237

will *shall—will

wire *Wire* is informal and colloquial for *telegram, telegraph. Live wire* (a person) is colloquial.

woods *falls, woods

Word composition *Origin of words §3

Wordy **Wordiness** (CORRECTION: Compress this passage by replacing the wordy expressions by more compact and exact ones.)

The use of more words than are needed to convey one's ideas accurately and fully results in flabby writing. Unprofitable words can be removed or replaced by more economical words in revision. The commonest types of wordiness are:

1. CIRCUMLOCUTION—the use of several words instead of one exact word:

> *destroyed by fire* means *burned*
> *come in contact with* usually means *meet* or *know*
> *the necessary funds* usually means no more than *the money*
> *in this day and age* means *today*
> *the sort of metal they use for plating the shiny parts of automobiles* might mean *chromium*

See "Direct phrasing," p. 163.

2. LONG FUNCTION WORDS—functional phrases that might be replaced by one or by fewer words:

WORDY: *During the time that* she was in Los Angeles she had at least six different jobs.
ECONOMICAL: *While* she was in Los Angeles she had at least six different jobs.

See *Function words §2.

3. DEADWOOD—words which add nothing to the meaning of the construction:

> The cars are neat and graceful [in appearance].
> In the majority of cases they do not.
> [for] The majority do not.

See "Removing deadwood," p. 161.

4. FORMLESS, FUZZY WRITING:

WORDY	REVISED
It has some of the best ski trails in the country and as far as the other cold weather sports are concerned, they have them too, along with one of the most fashionable hotels in the country.	They have a very fashionable hotel, all the cold weather sports, and some of the best ski trails in the country.

See also "Long and short constructions," p. 163, "Repetition," p. 168, and specific articles like *case, *exception, *happen, *Passive voice, *seem, *there is, there are.

Word order (CORRECTION: Revise the order of words or other elements so that the meaning will be more clear, or the sentence will be more natural, or more effective.) **WO**

The order of words and of other locutions in a sentence is a fundamental part of English grammar and in addition contributes to some effects of style, especially of emphasis. The work done in many languages by inflections (endings) is in English performed largely by *function words (prepositions, auxiliary verbs, and so on) and by the order in which the words stand. Since we pick up the standard word order as we learn to talk, it offers very little difficulty. We use naturally the subject-verb-object order of clauses and sentences (p. 122), we put adjectives before their nouns and relative clauses after their nouns, and in general put modifiers near the words to which they refer.

This article is intended to bring the fact of word order to your attention rather than to cover its large number of details. It emphasizes three instances in which the order is variable.

1. POSITION CHANGED FOR EMPHASIS. As a rule an element taken out of its usual position receives increased emphasis, as when the object is put before both subject and verb, or a predicate adjective put first:

OBJECT FIRST: That book I read when I was sixteen.
PREDICATE ADJECTIVE FIRST: Lucky are the ones who register early.

See "Position," p. 172.

2. INTERRUPTED CONSTRUCTIONS. When a word or words interrupt a construction, the effect is usually unhappy unless the interrupting word deserves special emphasis:

BETWEEN SUBJECT AND VERB: In fact, Japan, at the present time, is spending more each year than she did for the entire Russian war.

NATURAL ORDER: In fact at the present time Japan is spending more
. . .

BETWEEN VERB AND ADVERB: He played quietly, efficiently on.
He took a pack from his pocket and she took one thoughtfully out.
MORE NATURAL: He played on, quietly, efficiently.
He took a pack from his pocket and she took one out thoughtfully
[or, and she thoughtfully took one out].

In formal English some writers avoid placing an adverb between
the auxiliary *be* and a participle:

INFORMAL: The subject must be one that can be adequately treated
in four or five pages.
FORMAL: The subject must be one that can be treated adequately in
four or five pages.

See "Interrupted movement," p. 157, *Split infinitive.

3. MISLEADING WORD ORDER. English usually has a modifier close
to the word modified and care must be taken that modifiers separated from their main words are not misleading.

MISLEADING	IMPROVED
I wish to order one of the machines which I saw advertised in *The Saturday Evening Post* sent to the above address.	I wish to order sent to the above address one of the machines which I saw advertised in *The Saturday Evening Post*.
Her uncle, King Leopold, was even unable to influence her.	Even her uncle, King Leopold, was unable to influence her.
This success in villages will probably be duplicated in the cities as time goes on at an accelerated rate.	As time goes on, this success in villages will probably be duplicated at an accelerated rate in cities.
Until recently the chains have been able to get special prices on the goods they buy from producers with little opposition.	Until recently the chains have been able to get with little opposition special prices on the goods they buy from manufacturers.

*Ambiguity §2

References: Curme, *Syntax*, Ch. 17; Fries, Ch. 10; Kennedy, pp.
500-508; C. Alphonso Smith, *Studies in English Syntax* (Boston,
1906), Chapter 2, "The Short Circuit in English Syntax"

WW **Words** (CORRECTION: Replace the word marked by one that is
more exact, m re effective, or more appropriate.)

General questions of the use of words are treated in Ch. 7, p. 182,
The Meaning of Words, and Ch. 8, p. 213, Qualities of Words.
Many specific words that are likely to raise questions have articles
of their own (*contact, *drunk, *hope, *however, *notorious, *try

and—try to, *ye—the . . .). Very often the solution to a question of diction will be found by referring to a good dictionary.

Most of this book is about words. Some of the more general topics about words or their uses will be found under the following heads, in the alphabetical articles marked * or in the chapters at the page given.

world In expressions like "in the business world, in the educational world" *world* is deadwood. Say "in business, in education."

worth while Written as two words, or hyphened (especially when preceding its noun: a worth-while book), or (occasionally) as one word.

would *shall—will, should—would §§4, 5

would of *have §3

would rather *had better, had rather

Written English *Colloquial and written English

X is an unnecessary letter in English. It spells several sounds represented by different phonetic symbols (ks) as in *fox* (foks), *exclusive* (eks klü′siv), *exceed* (ek sēd′); (gz) as in *exist* (eg zist′), *exhibit* (eg zib′it); (ksh) as in *luxury* (luk′shủ ri); (gzh) as in *luxurious* (lug zhür′i əs—or luk shür′i əs); (z) in *xylophone*, *Xantippe*.

In British usage *ct* is sometimes spelled *x* as in *inflexion*.

Y (y) as in yes (yes), beyond (bi yond′). Y also spells *i*-sounds, as in *sky* (skī), *bloody* (blud′i).

A final *y* is often changed to *i* before a suffix beginning with a vowel: *duty—dutiable, try—tries, body—bodies, bodied;* but *play—played, playing, playable, fly—flying.*

ye = the In Old English *th* of *the* was represented by the letter thorn, Þ. In early printing the letter *y*, which looked most like the thorn, was used to represent it. Consequently we find *ye* (*the*), *yat* (*that*), *yem* (*them*) in early books and even oftener find the forms in manuscript down to about 1800.

The *y* then represents *th* and is pronounced *th*. Its use in recent faking of antiquity has not changed this fact: Ye Olde Coffee Shoppe is just The Old Coffee Shop and should be so pronounced.

ye = you Ye, originally the nominative plural and then the nominative singular of the second person pronoun (now *you*), survived for a long time in poetry and other literature with a tendency to be archaic (sermons, florid oratory) but is now obsolete.

yes Yes and *no* are adverbs. They may modify a sentence (Yes, you're right) or may have the value of a coordinate clause (No; but you should have told me) or they may stand as complete sentences. ("Do you really intend to go with him?" "Yes.")

yet Yet is an adverb (The books haven't come yet; [Archaic:] We shall yet win), and in formal English it is also used as a conjunction (*conjunctive adverb), equivalent to *but*:

His speech was almost unintelligible, yet for some unknown reason I enjoyed it.

you You is used as an indefinite pronoun (It's a good book, if you like detective stories; Then you must protect them from rats) in speech and informal writing. Formal English would more often use *one* or a different construction. *one, *they

When *you* is used in an informal approach to readers or to an audience, it sometimes may be unintentionally personal (or even insulting), or seem to indicate an invidious distinction between writer and reader.

Take, for instance, *your* [better: *our* or *one's*] family problems.

(The government radio program at first called This Is Your Enemy was wisely renamed This Is Our Enemy.)

In familiar English *was* is used with *you* referring to one person, and in vulgate *you was* is both singular and plural.

you all In Southern American *you all*, contracted to *y'all*, is frequently used as the plural of *you*, as in some other regions *you folks* is used. It is also used when addressing one person regarded as one of a group, usually a family, as in Benbow's speech to Popeye, "If it's whiskey, I don't care how much you all make or sell or buy" (WILLIAM FAULKNER, *Sanctuary*, p. 4), in which the *you all* refers to Popeye and his household.

It is sometimes asserted that *you all* is also used as a singular, addressing one. (See almost any volume of *American Speech*, especially ii and iv.) It apparently is occasionally used as a singular but this use is regarded by educated Southerners as an error.

yourself, yourselves Compare *himself, *myself.

Z (z) as in *Zion* (zī′ən), *buzz* (buz), *busy* (biz′i), *shoes* (shüz).

zh The phonetic symbol representing the sound in *rouge* (rüzh), *measure* (mezh′ər) and so on. See *G §3, *S.

& *Ampersand

Acknowledgments

THE AUTHOR GRATEFULLY acknowledges the kindness of authors and publishers in giving permission to reproduce material in this *Writer's Guide and Index to English* as follows:

The American Baptist Publication Society: the selection from *Your Money and Your Life* by S. K. Yeaple. Used by permission of The American Baptist Publication Society.

The American Mercury: the selection from "College Is No Place to Get an Education" by Albert Jay Nock from *The American Mercury*, February, 1939. Used by permission of *The American Mercury*.

Sherwood Anderson: the selection from *The Triumph of the Egg* by Sherwood Anderson. Used by permission of Mrs. Sherwood Anderson.

D. Appleton-Century Company: the selections from *Recovery—The Second Effort* by Sir Arthur Salter, *The Illiteracy of the Literate* by H. R. Huse, *The Red Badge of Courage* by Stephen Crane, *Vagabonding Down the Andes* by Harry A. Franck, *Creative Chemistry* by Edwin E. Slosson, *An Experience Curriculum in English*, *The Psychology of Language* by W. B. Pillsbury and C. L. Meader, and *American English Grammar* by C. C. Fries. Used by permission of D. Appleton-Century Company.

The Atlantic Monthly: the selections from "Newton on Blackstone" by A. Edward Newton, January, 1937, "Architecture and Geography" by Ramsay Traquair, August, 1938, "Rackets and Labor" by George E. Sokolsky, "Toward a National Labor Policy" by George W. Taylor, "Insight" by Archibald Rutledge, "Eduard Beneš" by Carl Joachim Friedrich, "Open 'er Up!" by William C. Rogers, "Daughters of Queen Victoria" by E. F. Benson, "Salute to Ireland" by W. Horsfall Carter, September, 1938. The selections by Robert I. Center, October, 1937, and Nora Waln, January, 1939. Used by permission of *The Atlantic Monthly*.

The Bobbs-Merrill Company: the selection from *The New Decalogue of Science* by Albert Edward Wiggam, copyright 1923. Used by special permission of the publishers, The Bobbs-Merrill Company.

Albert & Charles Boni, Inc.: the selections from *The Bridge of San Luis Rey* by Thornton Wilder. Used by permission of Albert and Charles Boni, Inc.

Brandt & Brandt: the selections from *Thirteen O'Clock*, published by Farrar & Rinehart, Inc. Copyright 1932, by the Butterick Company;

copyright 1925, 1928, 1930, 1932, 1935, 1936, 1937, by Stephen Vincent Benét. From *John Brown's Body*, published by Farrar & Rinehart, Inc. Copyright 1927, 1928, by Stephen Vincent Benét. From *The 42nd Parallel*, published by Harcourt, Brace & Company. Copyright 1930 by John Dos Passos. From *The Big Money*, published by Harcourt, Brace & Company. Copyright 1933, 1934, 1935, 1936, by John Dos Passos.

Gelett Burgess: the selection from *Short Words Are Words of Might* by Gelett Burgess. Used by permission of Gelett Burgess.

Business Week: the selection from *Business Week*, November 6, 1937. Used by permission of *Business Week*.

H. S. Canby: the selections from *Saturday Papers*, edited by H. S. Canby, and others, and *Designed for Reading* by H. S. Canby, W. R. Benét, and A. Loveman, published by The Macmillan Company. Used by permission of H. S. Canby.

Carlyle House: the selection from *Plotting* by Jack Woodford. Used by permission of Carlyle House.

Chicago Tribune: the graph by R. D. Cahn from the *Chicago Tribune*, October 26, 1938. Used by permission of the *Chicago Tribune*.

The Clarendon Press, Oxford: the selections from *Modern English Usage* by H. W. Fowler, *The Attic Theatre* by A. E. Haigh, *The Rise of the Greek Epic* by Gilbert Murray, and *Modern Prose Style* by Bonamy Dobrée. Used by permission of The Clarendon Press, Oxford.

Country Gentleman: the selection from *Country Gentleman*, January, 1939. Used by permission of *Country Gentleman*.

Covici-Friede, Inc.: the selections from *People Are Fascinating* by Sally Benson and *Redder Than the Rose* by Robert Forsythe. Used by permission of Covici-Friede, Inc.

F. S. Crofts & Co.: the selections from *The Ethics of Journalism* by N. A. Crawford and *The Trend of Economics*, edited by R. G. Tugwell. Used by permission of F. S. Crofts & Co.

Crown Publishers: the selection from *The American Craftsman* by Scott Graham Williamson. Used by permission of Crown Publishers.

Current History: the selection from "The Good and Evil of the New Industrialism" by Stuart Chase from *Current History*, July, 1929. Used by permission of *Current History*.

The John Day Company, Inc.: the selections from *The Myth of Rugged American Individualism* by C. A. Beard and *My Country and My People* by Lin Yutang. Used by permission of The John Day Company, Inc.

The Detroit News: the selection from *The Style Book*. Used by permission of *The Detroit News*.

Dodd, Mead & Company, Inc.: the selections from *Shadow of Doubt* by Arthur Somers Roche, *John Webster and the Elizabethan Drama* by Rupert Brooke, *Siren Land* by Norman Douglas, *Works* by Max Beerbohm, *Behind the Beyond* by Stephen Leacock, and *Modern American Painting* by Peyton Boswell, Jr. Used by permission of the publishers, Dodd, Mead & Company, Inc.

Doubleday, Doran and Company, Inc.: the selections from *Vanity Fair* by P. E. More, copyright 1935, *The Nigger of the Narcissus* by Joseph Conrad, copyright 1897, 1932, *Tales of Unrest* by Joseph Conrad, copyright 1898, 1920, *Youth* by Joseph Conrad, copyright 1903, 1931, *Rebecca* by Daphne du Maurier, copyright 1938, *Trivia* by Logan Pearsall Smith, copyright 1917, *The Almost Perfect State* by Don Marquis, copyright 1927, *Letters from a Chinese Official* by G. Lowes Dickinson, copyright 1903, *Big Money* by P. G. Wodehouse, copyright 1930, 1931, *Casuals of the Sea* by William McFee, copyright 1916, 1934, *Periodical Essays of the Eighteenth Century* by George Carver, copyright 1930, *A Plea for Old Cap Collier* by Irvin S. Cobb, copyright 1921, *Nocturne* by Frank Swinnerton, copyright 1917, and *Northwest Passage* by Kenneth Roberts, copyright 1936, 1937, and *To Step Aside* by Noel Coward, copyright 1939. Reprinted by permission from Doubleday, Doran and Company, Inc.

Duell, Sloan & Pearce, Inc.: the selections from *We Are the Living*, copyright 1935, and *Kneel to the Rising Sun*, copyright 1935, by Erskine Caldwell. Used by permission of Duell, Sloan & Pearce, Inc.

E. P. Dutton & Co., Inc.: the selections from *What I Believe* by Bertrand Russell. Used by permission of E. P. Dutton & Co., Inc., New York.

H. G. Dwight: the selection from *Stamboul Nights* by H. G. Dwight, copyright 1922. Used by permission of H. G. Dwight.

Editor and Publisher: the selection by Arthur Robb from the *Editor and Publisher*, March 7, 1942. Used by permission of *Editor and Publisher*.

The Emporia Gazette: the two selections, one by William Allen White, from *The Emporia Gazette*. Used by permission of *The Emporia Gazette*.

Encyclopaedia Britannica: the selection from the *Encyclopaedia Britannica*. Used by permission of the *Encyclopaedia Britannica*.

The English Journal: the selection from *The English Journal*, June, 1937. Used by permission of *The English Journal*.

Esquire: the selection from *The Bedside Esquire* by Westbrook Pegler which originally appeared in *Esquire*, January, 1934, copyright 1933, by Esquire, Inc., 919 N. Michigan Ave., Chicago, Ill.

Farrar & Rinehart, Inc.: the selections from *Listen for a Lonesome Drum* by Carl Carmer, copyright 1936, and *The Fall of the City* by Archibald MacLeish, copyright 1937, and *The Psychology of Adolescence* by Luella Cole, copyright 1936. Reprinted by permission of Farrar & Rinehart, Inc., Publishers.

John T. Flynn: the selection from *Scribner's Magazine*, July, 1937. Used by permission of John T. Flynn.

Acknowledgments

Fortune: the selections reprinted from *Fortune*, December, 1937, and August, 1938, and the selection from *A Time to Speak* by Archibald MacLeish. Used by permission of *Fortune*.

The Forum: the selection from *The Forum*, December, 1933. Used by permission of *The Forum*.

C. C. Fries: the selection from *What Is Good English?* by C. C. Fries. Used by permission of C. C. Fries.

Funk & Wagnalls Company: the selections from *How Words Get into the Dictionary* by Spencer Armstrong, *Standard Dictionary, New Standard Dictionary,* and *College Standard Dictionary.* Used by permission of Funk & Wagnalls Company.

Gelber, Lilienthal, Inc. (Lantern Press): the selection from *The Modern Writer* by Sherwood Anderson. Used by permission of Gelber, Lilienthal, Inc.

Ginn and Company: the selections from *Studies in English Syntax* by C. Alphonso Smith and *Current English* by Arthur G. Kennedy. Used by permission of Ginn and Company.

Harcourt, Brace and Company, Inc.: the selections from *North to the Orient,* copyright 1935, by Anne Morrow Lindbergh, *Aspects of the Novel,* copyright 1927, by E. M. Forster, *Autobiography* by Lincoln Steffens, *Reperusals and Re-collections* by Logan Pearsall Smith, *The Tyranny of Words* by Stuart Chase, *Abraham Lincoln: The Prairie Years* by Carl Sandburg, *Narrative Technique* by T. H. Uzzell, *Queen Victoria* by Lytton Strachey, *The Development of English Biography* by Harold Nicolson, *Arrowsmith, Main Street,* and *The Man Who Knew Coolidge* by Sinclair Lewis, "Gerontion" and *After Strange Gods* by T. S. Eliot, *Flowering Judas* by Katherine Anne Porter, *You Can't Print That!* by George Seldes, *Reason and Nature* by Morris R. Cohen, *Academic Procession* by James Reid Parker, *Modern American Poetry* by Louis Untermeyer, and *Rough-Hewn* by Dorothy Canfield. Used by permission of Harcourt, Brace and Company, Inc.

Harper & Brothers: the chart by Rudolph Modley from *How to Use Pictorial Statistics* and the selections from *My Life and Hard Times* by James Thurber, "Bubbles" by Wilbur Daniel Steele, *Modern Feature Writing* by H. F. Harrington and E. S. Watson, *Giants in the Earth* by O. E. Rolvaag, *Insurgent America* by Alfred M. Bingham, *The Native's Return* by Louis Adamic, *The Horse and Buggy Doctor* by Arthur E. Hertzler, *Innocents Abroad* by Mark Twain, *The Rise of Liberalism* by Harold J. Laski, *Proper Studies* by Aldous Huxley, and *The American Way* by D. C Coyle and others. Used by permission of Harper & Brothers.

Harper's Magazine: the selections by R. M. Hutchins, October, 1936, and Harold J. Laski, September, 1937, and from "The Two Business Men" by Mary Johnston, September, 1928, and "Washington: Blight on Democracy" by Alden Stevens, December, 1941. Used by permission of *Harper's Magazine*.

Harvard University Press: the selections from *The Founding of Harvard College* and *Harvard College in the Seventeenth Century* by S. E. Morison, *The Use of Poetry and the Use of Criticism* by T. S. Eliot, and *Mankind, Nation and Individual from a Linguistic Point of View* by Otto Jespersen. Used by permission of the President and Fellows of Harvard College.

D. C. Heath and Company: the selections from *Syntax* by G. O. Curme, *How We Think* by John Dewey, and *New Handbook of Composition* by E. C. Woolley. Used by permission of D. C. Heath and Company.

Henry Holt and Company, Inc.: the selections from *Four Ways of Philosophy* by Irwin Edman, *English Prose Style* by Herbert Read, *Fields of Psychology* by G. D. Higginson, and *Proposed Roads to Freedom* by Bertrand Russell (Allen & Unwin, Ltd.), *The Philosophy of Grammar* by Otto Jespersen (Allen & Unwin, Ltd.), *Human Nature and Conduct* by John Dewey, and *A New Plan of English Grammar* by Janet R. Aiken. By permission of Henry Holt and Company, Inc.

Houghton Mifflin Company: the selections from *The Dance of Life* by Havelock Ellis, *O Pioneers!* by Willa Cather, *On Being Creative* by Irving Babbitt, *American Note-Books* by Nathaniel Hawthorne, *Letters* by John Jay Chapman, *Books and Battles* by Irene and Allen Cleaton, *The Pleasures of an Absentee Landlord* by Samuel McChord Crothers, *Patterns of Culture* by Ruth Benedict, and *To College Teachers of English Composition* by L. R. Briggs. Used by permission of, and by arrangement with, Houghton Mifflin Company.

Bruce Humphries, Inc.: the selection from "Dawn," in *Al Que Quiere!* by William Carlos Williams. By permission of Bruce Humphries, Inc.

Alfred A. Knopf, Inc.: the selections from *Life With Father* and *God and My Father* by Clarence Day, *Prejudices: Fifth Series* and *Prejudices: Sixth Series* by H. L. Mencken, "Golden Bough" by Elinor Wylie, *Yet Again* by Max Beerbohm, *Poems* by Rex Warner, *The Garden Party* by Katherine Mansfield, and *The Matriarch* by G. B. Stern. Reprinted by permission of and special arrangement with Alfred A. Knopf, Inc., authorized publishers.

Ladies' Home Journal: the selections from "Who Should Go to College" by John R. Tunis from *Ladies' Home Journal*, September, 1938. Used by permission of *Ladies' Home Journal*.

Linguistic Atlas of the United States and Canada: the earthworm chart. Used by permission of Mr. Hans Kurath, Chairman, *Linguistic Atlas of the United States and Canada*.

Little, Brown & Company: the selections from *Enchanter's Nightshade* by Ann Bridge, *Gone Are the Days* by E. Alexander Powell, *Theodore Parker* by H. S. Commager, *If Winter Comes* by A. S. M. Hutchinson, *On Gilbert Head* by Elizabeth Etnier, and *Unforgotten Years* by Logan Pearsall Smith. Used by permission of Little, Brown & Company.

Liveright Publishing Corporation: the selections from *Virgin Spain* by Waldo Frank, *The Enormous Room* by E. E. Cummings, and *The Conquest of Happiness* by Bertrand Russell. Used bv permission of Liveright Publishing Corporation.

Longmans, Green & Co.: the selection from *Plain Prose* by W. E. Williams. Used by permission of Longmans, Green & Co.

John W. Luce & Company: the selection from *A Dreamer's Tales* by Lord Dunsany. Used by permission of John W. Luce & Company.

The Macmillan Company: the selections from *The Discussion of Human Affairs* by C. A. Beard, *The Everlasting Mercy* and *Gallipoli* by John Masefield, *Words and Their Ways in English Speech* by J. B. Greenough and G. L. Kittredge, *A Preface to Morals* by Walter Lippmann, *The Psychology of Insanity* by Bernard Hart, *Noah Webster* by Harry R. Warfel, *The Universe Around Us* by Sir James Jeans, *The Return to Religion* by Henry C. Link, *The Name and Nature of Poetry* by A. E. Housman (The Macmillan Company and Cambridge University Press), *Silas Crockett* by Mary Ellen Chase, *We or They* by H. F. Armstrong, *Reporting for Beginners* by C. D. MacDougall, *The American Commonwealth* (Vol. II) by James Bryce, *The Middle Classes, Then and Now* by F. C. Palm, *The Nemesis of American Business* by Stuart Chase, *The Timeless Land* by Eleanor Dark (Wm. Collins Sons & Co., Canada, Ltd.), and *The Phantom Public* by Walter Lippmann. Used by permission of The Macmillan Company, publishers.

Macmillan & Co., Ltd.: the selection from *Trio* by Osbert Sitwell. Used by permission of Macmillan & Co., Ltd.

Sir Andrew McFadyean: the selection from "Don't Do It Again" by Sir Andrew McFadyean in the *Atlantic Monthly*, November, 1941. Used by permission of Sir Andrew McFadyean.

McGraw-Hill Book Company, Inc.: the selections from *Propaganda and the News* by Will Irwin and *Biology in Human Affairs*, edited by Edward M. East. By permission of McGraw-Hill Book Company, Inc.

G. & C. Merriam Company: the selection from *Webster's Collegiate Dictionary*, Fifth Edition, reproduced by permission of the publishers of *Webster's Collegiate Dictionary*, Fifth Edition, copyright 1936, by G. & C. Merriam Company, Springfield, Mass.; the selection from *Word Study*, by A. S. Phillips, November, 1937, used by permission of G. & C. Merriam Co., publishers of *Word Study*, copyright 1937.

Modern Age Books, Inc.: the selections from *Kaltenborn Edits the News* by H. V. Kaltenborn, *The Daring Young Man on the Flying Trapeze* by William Saroyan, *Babies Without Tails* by Walter Duranty, and *The Road We Have Covered* by John A. Udmark. Used by permission of Modern Age Books, Inc.

Modern Language Association of America: the selection from "The Spelling Bee" by Allen Walker Read in *PMLA*, June, 1941. Used by permission of the Modern Language Association.

William Morrow & Company: the selections from *Novel on Yellow Paper,* by Stevie Smith, copyright 1937 by Stevie Smith, and *Some Like It Hot,* by Sidney Marshall, copyright 1941 by Sidney Marshall, by permission of William Morrow & Company.

Nation's Business: the selection from *Nation's Business*, December, 1936. Used by permission of *Nation's Business*.

The New Republic: the selections from "We Built the German Air Force" by Melvin M. Fagen, November 23, 1938, "All about Books" by Virginia Woolf, April 15, 1931, "Piano in the Band," November 24, 1937, and "Benny and the Budapests," October 5, 1938, by Otis Ferguson, and the selections by Otis Ferguson, October 16, 1935, and October 21, 1936, Waldo Frank, November 4, 1936, H. N. Brailsford, October 26, 1938, Irving Brant, July 28, 1937, Bennett A. Cerf, April 21, 1937, John Dos Passos, June 3, 1936, and Malcolm Cowley, April 20, 1938; the selection from *The New Republic* of October 26, 1938. Used by permission of *The New Republic*.

New York Herald Tribune: the selection from the *New York Herald Tribune*, November 7, 1937. Used by permission of the *New York Herald Tribune*.

The New York Times: the selections by Charles Poore, November 25, 1938, and March 10, 1939, John Kieran, July 7 and December 30, 1937, Frank S. Nugent, December 3, 1937, Ralph Thompson, February 5, 1937, and Robert F. Kelley ("For a Fierce Game, There's Hockey"), February 27, 1938, and October 14, 1941; the selections on page 519, from the *Book Review* of March 13, 1938, the selection from "War's Impact on the Campus" by Charles Seymour from the *New York Times Magazine*, September 29, 1940, and *The New York Times* of May 20, 1936, November 7, 1937, and May 2, 1942. Used by permission of *The New York Times*.

The New Yorker: the selections from "Independent Cop" by Jack Alexander, October 3, 1936, "The Cliché Expert Takes the Stand," August 31, 1935, and "The Cliché Expert Tells All," June 20, 1936, by Frank Sullivan, "How I Look at Things in General" by Charles G. Shaw, April 25, 1931, "Raconteurs" by Gluyas Williams, October 8, 1938, and "Utopia's Friends," May 25, 1935; the selections by Jack Alexander, August 1, 1936, and October 9, 1937, A. J. Liebling, February 5, 1938, Audax Minor, August 27, 1938, Dorothy Parker, February 5, 1938, Meyer Berger, November 26, 1938, Clifton Fadiman, December 5, 1938, and Howard Brubaker, November 26, 1938, March 18, 1939; the selections from *The New Yorker* of December 30, 1933, June 30 and December 29, 1934, September 19, 1936, January 30, August 14, September 18, October 9 and 30, and December 4, 1937, April 9, September 24, October 27, and November 26, 1938, September 7, 1940, June 7, 1941, January 24, March 7, and April 25, 1942. Used by permission of *The New Yorker*.

W. W. Norton & Company, Inc.: the selections from *Mysticism and Logic* by Bertrand Russell, *Sticks and Stones* by Lewis Mumford, *The Meaning of Culture* by John Cowper Powys, and *Exile's Return* by Malcolm Cowley. Used by permission of W. W. Norton & Company, Inc.

Ohio Wesleyan University: the chart from *Newspaper Organization* by D. J. Hornberger and Douglass W. Miller. Used by permission of Ohio Wesleyan University.

The Oxford University Press (London): the selection from *The Autobiography of Mark Rutherford* by Hale White. Used by permission of The Oxford University Press.

Oxford University Press (New York): the selections from *The Philosophy of Rhetoric* by I. A. Richards and *Manuscript & Proof* by John Benbow. Used by permission of Oxford University Press.

Philadelphia Record: the selections by Cal Tinney from the *Philadelphia Record*, November 17 and December 6, 1938. Used by permission of the *Philadelphia Record*.

James B. Pinker and Son: the selection from *Disenchantment* by C. E. Montague. Used by permission of James B. Pinker and Son.

Robert C. Pooley: the selection from *Grammar and Usage in Textbooks on English* by Robert C. Pooley. Used by permission of Robert C. Pooley.

G. P. Putnam's Sons: the selections from *Individualism Old and New* by John Dewey, *Jungle Days* by William Beebe, *From a College Window* by A. C. Benson, and *An Almanac for Moderns* by D. C. Peattie. Courtesy of G. P. Putnam's Sons.

Rand McNally & Company: the selection from *A Comprehensive Guide to Good English* by G. P. Krapp. Used by permission of Rand McNally & Company.

Random House, Inc.: the selections from *The Little Wife* by William March, *Home Is Where You Hang Your Childhood* by Leane Zugsmith, *Lectures in America* by Gertrude Stein, *The Strange Death of Liberal England* by George Dangerfield, *Now That April's Here* by Morley Callaghan, *Sanctuary* by William Faulkner, *Jurgen* by James Branch Cabell, *The Romance of Leonardo da Vinci* by Dmitri Merejkowski, *Retreat from Reason* by Lancelot Hogben, and *The Last Time I Saw Paris* by Elliot Paul. Used by permission of Random House, Inc.

The Saturday Review of Literature: the selections by Christopher Morley, September 24, 1938, Crane Brinton, December 3, 1938, a portion of an editorial used by permission of *The Saturday Review of Literature*. The selection from "Mister Ben Lilly" by J. Frank Dobie, May 16, 1942, used by permission of *The Saturday Review of Literature* and J. Frank Dobie.

Science and Mechanics: the reproduction from *Science and Mechanics,* February, 1939. Used by permission of *Science and Mechanics.*

Charles Scribner's Sons: selections from *Swan Song, The White Monkey,* and *The Man of Property* by John Galsworthy, *Look Homeward, Angel* and *From Death to Morning* by Thomas Wolfe, *Soliloquies, Soliloquies in England and Later Soliloquies,* and *Reason in Society* by George Santayana, *Green Hills of Africa* and *The Sun Also Rises* by Ernest Hemingway, *English Composition* by Barrett Wendell, *News from Tartary* by Peter Fleming, *The Bookbuyer* by W. C. Abbott, *Enjoyment of Poetry* by Max Eastman, "Spider! Spider!" by Conrad Aiken, *The Greene Murder Case* by S. S. Van Dine, *A Native Argosy* by Morley Callaghan, and *The Yearling* by Marjorie Kinnan Rawlings. Used by permission of Charles Scribner's Sons.

Simon and Schuster, Inc.: the selections from *Time: The Present* by Tess Slesinger, copyrighted 1935, *Hard Lines* by Ogden Nash, copyrighted 1931, *With Malice Toward Some* by Margaret Halsey, copyrighted 1938, *Now in November,* copyrighted 1934, and *Winter Orchard,* copyrighted 1935, by Josephine Johnson, *An American Tragedy* by Theodore Dreiser, copyrighted 1929, *Wake Up and Live!* by Dorothea Brande, copyrighted 1936, *The News and How to Understand It,* copyrighted 1940, by Quincy Howe, "The Net" by Robert M. Coates from *Short Stories from the New Yorker,* copyrighted 1940, and *Reading I've Liked,* copyrighted 1941, by Clifton Fadiman. Used by permission of Simon and Schuster, Inc.

Stackpole Sons: the selections from *Caleb Catlum's America* by Vincent McHugh. Used by permission of Stackpole Sons.

Stanford University Press: the selection from *How to Read Rapidly and Well* by C. Gilbert Wrenn and Luella Cole. Used by permission of Stanford University Press.

Frederick A. Stokes Company: the selection from *The Adventures of Ellery Queen.* Reprinted by permission of the Publishers from *The Adventures of Ellery Queen* by Ellery Queen.

Time: the selections from *Time,* August 10, November 30, and December 21, 1936; September 27, 1937; November 7 and 28, and December 5, 1938; and February 13, 1939.

The University of Chicago Press: the selections from *Linguistic Change* by E. H. Sturtevant and *No Friendly Voice* by Robert Maynard Hutchins; the facsimile of a page from *A Manual of Style.* Used by permission of The University of Chicago Press.

University of London Press Ltd.: the selections from *Thought and Language* by P. B. Ballard. Used by permission of University of London Press Ltd.

The University of North Carolina Press: the selections from *Democracy in Crisis* by Harold J. Laski, and *Institutional Behavior* by Floyd H. Allport. By permission of The University of North Carolina Press.

Acknowledgments

The Vanguard Press: the selections from *Chinese Destinies* by Agnes Smedley and *Representative Opinions of Mr. Justice Holmes*, edited by Alfred Lief. Used by permission of The Vanguard Press.

Variety: the selection from *Variety*, February 11, 1942. Used by permission of *Variety*.

The Viking Press, Inc.: the selections from *On the Shore* by Albert Halper, copyright 1934, *Philosopher's Holiday* by Irwin Edman, copyright 1938, *Winesburg, Ohio* by Sherwood Anderson, copyright 1919, *Sea and Sardinia* by D. H. Lawrence, copyright 1921, *The Long Valley*, copyright 1938, and *The Grapes of Wrath* by John Steinbeck, copyright 1939, *Finnegans Wake* by James Joyce, copyright 1939, *Mr. Weston's Good Wine* by T. F. Powys, copyright 1928, *Sea of Cortez* by John Steinbeck and Edward F. Ricketts, copyright 1941, and *Biography of the Earth* by George Gamow, copyright 1941. Published by The Viking Press, Inc. Used by permission of The Viking Press, Inc., New York.

Warwick & York, Incorporated: the selection from *How Much English Grammar?* by M. J. Stormzand and M. V. O'Shea. Used by permission of Warwick & York, Incorporated.

Waterbury Republican: the selection from *Editor & Publisher*, February 2, 1935. Used by permission of the *Waterbury Republican*.

John Wiley & Sons, Inc.: the selection reprinted by permission from *Shore Processes and Shoreline Development* by Douglas W. Johnson, published by John Wiley & Sons, Inc.

The H. W. Wilson Company: the reproduction from *The Readers' Guide to Periodical Literature*, made with the permission of the publishers, The H. W. Wilson Company.

Yale University Press: the selections from *The Heavenly City of the Eighteenth-Century Philosophers* by Carl L. Becker, *The Realm of the Nebulae* by Edwin Hubble, *The Gentleman from New York: A Life of Roscoe Conkling* by Donald B. Chidsey, and *Sweden—The Middle Way* by Marquis W. Childs. Used by permission of the Yale University Press.

List of Writers

CONCERNING THE TYPE FACES, USED IN THIS BOOK

THE text matter of the *Writer's Guide and Index to English* has been set on the Linotype machine in Electra, an original type face designed by the eminent American artist and illustrator, W. A. Dwiggins. While it falls into the "modern" family of type faces, Electra was drawn to avoid the pronounced thick and thin elements that mark most modern faces. The types used for attention-getting purposes are Metroblack and Metromedium, members of the Linotype Metro family, also designed by W. A. Dwiggins.

TO THE STUDENT

Your papers will be criticized by references to the alphabetical articles in Part Two of this book, and you should revise your papers accordingly:

1. A ring around a word or phrase that you have used means that there is an article on that word or phrase, and that you should look it up.

2. Other references to articles will be written in the margins of your paper. The reference may be the full title of an article (**Comma, Dash, Slang, Trite**), or a slightly shortened form of the title of an article (**Formal**—Formal English, **Tense** —Tenses of verbs, **Run-on**—Run-on sentences).

3. For articles with long words in their titles, the reference may be an abbreviation. The following list shows some references, abbreviations, and a few others which your instructor is likely to use in correcting papers:

Ab **Abbreviations** page 352

Abst **Abstract and concrete words** 355

Adv **Adverbs, types and forms** 364

Agr **Agreement** 369

Amb **Ambiguity** 374

Apos **Apostrophe** 385

Awk **Awkward** 391

Beg **Beginning paragraphs** 395

Big W **Big words** 397

Bus **Business English** 401

C **Carelessness** 410

Cap **Capital letters** 407

Cl **Clearness** 418

Coh **Coherence** 419

Coll **Collective nouns** 420

Colloq **Colloquial and written English** 421

Colon **Colon** 427

Comma **Comma** 430

CF **Comma fault** 441

Comp **Comparison of adjectives and adverbs** 444

Concl **Concluding paragraphs** 451

Concr **Concrete words** 451

Conj **Conjunctions, Use** 453

Const **Constructions** 458

Cont **Contractions** 460

DM **Dangling modifiers** 467

Dead **Deadwood** 472

Det **Details** 475

Dial **Dialects** 479

D **Diction** 479

Div **Division of words** 482

Emph **Emphasis** 496